# Anthropology

*07/08*

*Thirtieth Edition*

D0222141

**EDITOR**

**Elvio Angeloni**

*Pasadena City College*

Elvio Angeloni received his B.A. from UCLA in 1963, his M.A. in anthropology from UCLA in 1965, and his M.A. in communication arts from Loyola Marymount University in 1976. He has produced several films, including *Little Warrior,* winner of the Cinemedia VI Best Bicentennial Theme, and *Broken Bottles*, shown on PBS. He served as an academic adviser on the instructional television series *Faces of Culture*. He received the Pasadena City College Outstanding Teacher Award for 2006. He is the academic editor of *Annual Editions: Anthropology* and *Annual Editions: Physical Anthropology* and co-editor of *Annual Editions: Archaeology*. His primary area of interest has been indigenous peoples of the American Southwest.

 **Contemporary Learning Series**

2460 Kerper Blvd., Dubuque, IA 52001

Visit us on the Internet
*http://www.mhcls.com*

# Credits

1. **Anthropological Perspectives**
   Unit photo—Royalty-Free/CORBIS
2. **Culture and Communication**
   Unit photo—Royalty-Free/CORBIS
3. **The Organization of Society and Culture**
   Unit photo—Photo courtesy of Bigfoto.com
4. **Other Families, Other Ways**
   Unit photo—Kirk Weddle/Getty Images
5. **Gender and Status**
   Unit photo—The Jane Goodall Institute, *www.janegoodall.org*
6. **Religion, Belief, and Ritual**
   Unit photo—D. Normark/PhotoLink/Getty Images
7. **Sociocultural Change: The Impact of the West**
   Unit photo—Courtesy of Bob Buss

# Copyright

Cataloging in Publication Data
Main entry under title: Annual Editions: Anthropology. 2007/2008.
1. Film—Periodicals. I. Angeloni, Elvio, *comp.* II. Title: Anthropology.
ISBN-13: 978–0–07–351627–1      ISBN-10: 0–07–351627–9      658'.05      ISSN 1091–613X

Thirtieth Edition

Cover image: Tim Hall/Getty Images
Printed in the United States of America    1234567890QPDQPD9876    Printed on Recycled Paper

# Editors/Advisory Board

Members of the Advisory Board are instrumental in the final selection of articles for each edition of ANNUAL EDITIONS. Their review of articles for content, level, currentness, and appropriateness provides critical direction to the editor and staff. We think that you will find their careful consideration well reflected in this volume.

# Preface

In publishing ANNUAL EDITIONS we recognize the enormous role played by the magazines, newspapers, and journals of the public press in providing current, first-rate educational information in a broad spectrum of interest areas. Many of these articles are appropriate for students, researchers, and professionals seeking accurate, current material to help bridge the gap between principles and theories and the real world. These articles, however, become more useful for study when those of lasting value are carefully collected, organized, indexed, and reproduced in a low-cost format, which provides easy and permanent access when the material is needed. That is the role played by ANNUAL EDITIONS.

This thirtieth edition of *Annual Editions: Anthropology* contains a variety of articles on contemporary issues in social and cultural anthropology. In contrast to the broad range of topics and minimum depth typical of standard textbooks, this anthology provides an opportunity to read firsthand accounts by anthropologists of their own research. In allowing scholars to speak for themselves about the issues on which they are expert, we are better able to understand the kind of questions anthropologists ask, the ways in which they ask them, and how they go about searching for answers. Indeed, where there is disagreement among anthropologists, this format allows the readers to draw their own conclusions.

Given the very broad scope of anthropology—in time, space, and subject matter—the present collection of highly readable articles has been selected according to certain criteria. The articles have been chosen from both professional and nonprofessional publications for the purpose of supplementing the standard textbook in cultural anthropology that is used in introductory courses. Some of the articles are considered classics in the field, while others have been selected for their timely relevance.

Included in this volume are a number of features designed to make it useful for students, researchers, and professionals in the field of anthropology. While the articles are arranged along the lines of broadly unifying themes, the *topic guide* can be used to establish specific reading assignments tailored to the needs of a particular course of study. Other useful features include the *table of contents* abstracts, which summarize each article and present key concepts in italics, and a comprehensive *index*. In addition, each unit is preceded by an overview, which provides a background for informed reading of the articles, emphasizes critical issues, and presents *key points to consider*.

Finally, there are *internet references* that can be used to further explore the topics.

*Annual Editions: Anthropology 07/08* will continue to be updated annually. Those involved in producing the volume wish to make the next one as useful and effective as possible. Your criticism and advice always are welcome. Please fill out the postage-paid article rating form on the last page of the book and let us know your opinions. Any anthology can be improved. This continues to be—annually.

*Elvio Angeloni*

Elvio Angeloni
*Editor*
*evangeloni@paccd.cc.ca.us*

# Contents

## UNIT 1
## Anthropological Perspectives

The concepts in bold italics are developed in the article. For further expansion, please refer to the Topic Guide and the Index.

# UNIT 2
# Culture and Communication

# UNIT 3
# The Organization of Society and Culture

The concepts in bold italics are developed in the article. For further expansion, please refer to the Topic Guide and the Index.

# UNIT 4
## Other Families, Other Ways

The concepts in bold italics are developed in the article. For further expansion, please refer to the Topic Guide and the Index.

# UNIT 5
## Gender and Status

# UNIT 6
## Religion, Belief, and Ritual

The concepts in bold italics are developed in the article. For further expansion, please refer to the Topic Guide and the Index.

# UNIT 7
# Sociocultural Change: The Impact of the West

The concepts in bold italics are developed in the article. For further expansion, please refer to the Topic Guide and the Index.

The concepts in bold italics are developed in the article. For further expansion, please refer to the Topic Guide and the Index.

# Topic Guide

This topic guide suggests how the selections in this book relate to the subjects covered in your course. You may want to use the topics listed on these pages to search the Web more easily.

On the following pages a number of Web sites have been gathered specifically for this book. They are arranged to reflect the units of this *Annual Edition.* You can link to these sites by going to the student online support site at *http://www.mhcls.com/online/.*

## ALL THE ARTICLES THAT RELATE TO EACH TOPIC ARE LISTED BELOW THE BOLD-FACED TERM.

### Acculturation
2. Lessons from the Field
5. Gardening Tips
7. One Hundred Percent American
20. Who Needs Love! In Japan, Many Couples Don't
24. We Call Ourselves Americans
25. Eyes of the Ngangas: Ethnomedicine and Power in Central African Republic
28. Shamans
34. The Arrow of Disease
36. The Price of Progress
37. A Pacific Haze: Alcohol and Drugs in Oceania
39. What Native Peoples Deserve

### Aggression
34. The Arrow of Disease
35. Burying the White Gods: New Perspectives on the Conquest of Mexico
39. What Native Peoples Deserve

### Altruism
3. Eating Christmas in the Kalahari
14. Ties that Bind
15. Too Many Bananas, Not Enough Pineapples, and No Watermelon at All: Three Object Lessons in Living with Reciprocity

### Child care
17. Death Without Weeping
18. Our Babies, Ourselves
23. Where Fat Is a Mark of Beauty

### Children
17. Death Without Weeping
18. Our Babies, Ourselves
23. Where Fat Is a Mark of Beauty

### Communication
8. Whose Speech is Better?
9. Fighting for Our Lives
10. "I Can't Even Open My Mouth"
11. Shakespeare in the Bush
14. Ties that Bind

### Cooperation
3. Eating Christmas in the Kalahari
15. Too Many Bananas, Not Enough Pineapples, and No Watermelon at All: Three Object Lessons in Living with Reciprocity

### Cross-cultural experience
1. Doing Fieldwork among the Yanomamö
2. Lessons from the Field
3. Eating Christmas in the Kalahari
5. Gardening Tips
7. One Hundred Percent American
8. Whose Speech is Better?
11. Shakespeare in the Bush
12. Understanding Eskimo Science

13. The Inuit Paradox
14. Ties that Bind
15. Too Many Bananas, Not Enough Pineapples, and No Watermelon at All: Three Object Lessons in Living with Reciprocity
17. Death Without Weeping
18. Our Babies, Ourselves
19. Arranging a Marriage in India
24. We Call Ourselves Americans
25. Eyes of the Ngangas: Ethnomedicine and Power in Central African Republic
28. Shamans
39. What Native Peoples Deserve

### Cultural change
7. One Hundred Percent American
13. The Inuit Paradox
18. Our Babies, Ourselves
20. Who Needs Love! In Japan, Many Couples Don't
24. We Call Ourselves Americans
28. Shamans
33. Why Can't People Feed Themselves?
34. The Arrow of Disease
35. Burying the White Gods: New Perspectives on the Conquest of Mexico
36. The Price of Progress
37. A Pacific Haze: Alcohol and Drugs in Oceania
38. From Baffin Island to New Orleans

### Cultural diversity
7. One Hundred Percent American
8. Whose Speech is Better?
14. Ties that Bind
18. Our Babies, Ourselves
19. Arranging a Marriage in India
21. The Berdache Tradition
25. Eyes of the Ngangas: Ethnomedicine and Power in Central African Republic
28. Shamans
29. Drug Culture: Everybody Uses Something

### Cultural identity
2. Lessons from the Field
5. Gardening Tips
7. One Hundred Percent American
8. Whose Speech is Better?
13. The Inuit Paradox
14. Ties that Bind
18. Our Babies, Ourselves
23. Where Fat Is a Mark of Beauty
24. We Call Ourselves Americans
27. The Adaptive Value of Religious Ritual
39. What Native Peoples Deserve

### Cultural relativity
1. Doing Fieldwork among the Yanomamö
2. Lessons from the Field
3. Eating Christmas in the Kalahari
5. Gardening Tips
8. Whose Speech is Better?
13. The Inuit Paradox

# Internet References

The following internet sites have been carefully researched and selected to support the articles found in this reader. The easiest way to access these selected sites is to go to our student online support site at *http://www.mhcls.com/online/.*

# AE: Anthropology 07/08

The following sites were available at the time of publication. Visit our Web site—we update our student online support site regularly to reflect any changes.

## General Sources

### American Anthropologist
*http://www.aaanet.org*

Check out this site—the home page of the American Anthropology Association—for general information about the field of anthropology as well as access to a wide variety of articles.

### Anthropology Links
*http://anthropology.gmu.edu/*

George Mason University's Department of Anthropology Web site provides a number of interesting links.

### Latin American Studies
*http://www.library.arizona.edu/search/subjects/*

Click on Latin American Studies to access an extensive list of resources—links to encyclopedias, journals, indexes, almanacs, and handbooks, and to the Latin American Network Information Center and Internet Resources for Latin American Studies.

### Web Resources for Visual Anthropology
*http://www.usc.edu/dept/elab/urlist/index.html*

This UR-List offers a mouse-click selection of Web resources by cross-indexing 375 anthropological sites according to 22 subject categories.

## UNIT 1: Anthropological Perspectives

### American Indian Sites on the Internet
*http://www.library.arizona.edu/library/teams/sst/anthro/web/indians.html*

This Web page points out a number of Internet sites of interest to different kinds of anthropologists.

### Archaeology and Anthropology Computing and Study Skills
*http://www.bodley.ox.ac.uk/isca/CASShome.html*

Consult this site of the Institute of Social and Cultural Anthropology to learn about ways to use the computer as an aid in conducting fieldwork, methodology, and analysis.

### Introduction to Anthropological Fieldwork and Ethnography
*http://web.mit.edu/dumit/www/syl-anth.html*

This class outline can serve as an invaluable resource for conducting anthropological fieldwork. Addressing such topics as The Interview and Power Relations in the Field, the site identifies many important books and articles for further reading.

### Theory in Anthropology
*http://www.indiana.edu/~wanthro/theory.htm*

These Web pages cover subdisciplines within anthropology, changes in perspectives over time, and prominent theorists, reflecting 30 years of dramatic changes in the field.

## UNIT 2: Culture and Communication

### Exploratorium Magazine: "The Evolution of Languages"
*http://www.exploratorium.edu/exploring/language*

Where did languages come from and how did they evolve? This educational site explains the history and origin of language. You can also investigate words, word stems, and the similarities between different languages.

### Hypertext and Ethnography
*http://www.umanitoba.ca/anthropology/tutor/aaa_presentation.html*

Presented by Brian Schwimmer of the University of Manitoba, this site will be of great value to people who are interested in culture and communication. Schwimmer addresses such topics as multivocality and complex symbolization.

### Language Extinction
*http://www.colorado.edu/iec/alis/articles/langext.htm*

"An often overlooked fact in the ecological race against environmental extinction is that many of the world's languages are disappearing at an alarming rate." This article investigates language extinction and its possible consequences.

### Showcase Anthropology
*http://www.anthropology.wisc.edu/chaysimire/*

Examples of documents that make innovative use of the Web as a tool for "an anthropology of the future"—one consisting of multimedia representations in a nonlinear and interactive form—are provided on this Web site.

## UNIT 3: The Organization of Society and Culture

### Huarochiri, a Peruvian Culture in Time
*http://wiscinfo.doit.wisc.edu/chaysimire/*

Take a tour of this Andean province, visit Tupicocha (a modern village), and learn about the ancient Quechua Book and Khipus, a unique legacy.

### Smithsonian Institution Web Site
*http://www.si.edu*

Looking through this site, which provides access to many of the enormous resources of the Smithsonian, will give a sense of the scope of anthropological inquiry today.

### Sociology Guy's Anthropology Links
*http://www.trinity.edu/~mkearl/anthro.html*

This list of anthropology resources on the Web is suggested by a sociology professor at Trinity University and includes cultures of Asia, Africa, the Middle East; Aztecan, Mayan, and aboriginal cultures; sections on Mythology, Folklore, Legends, and Archaeology; plus much more.

### What Is Culture?
*http://www.wsu.edu:8001/vcwsu/commons/topics/culture/culture-index.html*

Here is a source for everything you might want to know about "culture," starting with a baseline definition.

## UNIT 4: Other Families, Other Ways

### Kinship and Social Organization

*http://www.umanitoba.ca/anthropology/tutor/kinmenu.html*

Kinship, marriage systems, residence rules, incest taboos, and cousin marriages are explored in this kinship tutorial.

## UNIT 5: Gender and Status

### Arranged Marriages

*http://women3rdworld.miningco.com/cs/arrangedmarriage/*

This site, provided by ABOUT, contains a number of papers on arranged marriages. It also has links to other related women's issues, subjects, and forums.

### Bonobo Sex and Society

*http://songweaver.com/info/bonobos.html*

This site includes a *Scientific American* article discussing a primate's behavior that challenges traditional assumptions about male supremacy in human evolution.

### FGM Research

*http://www.amnesty.org/ailib/intcam/femgen/fgm1.htm*

Dedicated to research pertaining to Female Genital Mutilation (FGM), this site presents a variety of perspectives: psychological, cultural, sexual, human rights, and so on.

### OMIM Home Page-Online Mendelian Inheritance in Man

*http://www3.ncbi.nlm.nih.gov/omim/*

This National Center for Biotechnology Information database is a catalog of human genes and genetic disorders. It contains text, pictures, and reference information.

### Reflections on Sinai Bedouin Women

*http://www.sherryart.com/women/bedouin.html*

Social anthropologist Ann Gardner tells something of her culture shock while first living with a Sinai Bedouin family as a teenager. She provides links to sites about organization of society and culture, particularly with regard to women.

## UNIT 6: Religion, Belief, and Ritual

### Anthropology Resources Page

*http://www.usd.edu/anth/*

Many topics can be accessed from this University of South Dakota Web site. Repatriation and reburial are just two.

### Yahoo: Society and Culture: Death

*http://dir.yahoo.com/Society_and_Culture/Death_and_Dying/*

This Yahoo site has an extensive index to diverse issues related to how different people approach death, such as beliefs about euthanasia, reincarnation, and burial.

## UNIT 7: Sociocultural Change: The Impact of the West

### Human Rights and Humanitarian Assistance

*http://www.etown.edu/vl/humrts.html*

Through this site you can conduct research into a number of human rights topics and issues affecting indigenous peoples in the modern era.

### The Indigenous Rights Movement in the Pacific

*http://www.inmotionmagazine.com/pacific.html*

This article addresses issues that pertain to the problems of the Pacific Island peoples as a result of U.S. colonial expansion in the Pacific and Caribbean 100 years ago.

### RomNews Network—Online

*http://www.romnews.com/community/index.php*

This is a Web site dedicated to news and information for and about the Roma (European Gypsies). Visit here to learn more about their culture and the discrimination they constantly face.

### WWW Virtual Library: Indigenous Studies

*http://www.cwis.org/wwwvl/indig-vl.html*

This site presents resources collected by the Center for World Indigenous Studies (CWIS) in Africa, Asia and the Middle East, Central and South America, Europe, and the Pacific.

We highly recommend that you review our Web site for expanded information and our other product lines. We are continually updating and adding links to our Web site in order to offer you the most usable and useful information that will support and expand the value of your Annual Editions. You can reach us at: *http://www.mhcls.com/annualeditions/*.

# UNIT 1

# Anthropological Perspectives

## Unit Selections

1. **Doing Fieldwork among the Yanomamö**, Napoleon A. Chagnon
2. **Lessons from the Field**, George Gmelch
3. **Eating Christmas in the Kalahari**, Richard Borshay Lee
4. **Tricking and Tripping: Fieldwork on Prostitution in the Era of AIDS**, Claire E. Sterk
5. **Gardening Tips**, Lee Cronk
6. **Anthropology and Counterinsurgency: The Strange Story of their Curious Relationship**, Montgomery McFate, J.D., Ph.D.
7. **One Hundred Percent American**, Ralph Linton

## Key Points to Consider

- How can anthropologists who become personally involved with a community through participant observation maintain their objectivity as scientists?

- What kinds of ethical obligations do fieldworkers have toward their informants?

- In what ways do the results of fieldwork depend on the kinds of questions asked?

- In what sense is sharing intrinsic to egalitarianism?

- What lessons can be learned about one's own culture by going into the field?

- To what extent is the concept of "cultural relativity" important to anthropology? Does it necessarily lead to moral relativity?

- What is the "naturalistic fallacy?"

- Why is it meaningless to claim that one is "one hundred percent American?"

## Student Website

www.mhcls.com/online

## Internet References

Further information regarding these websites may be found in this book's preface or online.

**American Indian Sites on the Internet**
*http://www.library.arizona.edu/library/teams/sst/anthro/web/indians.html*

**Archaeology and Anthropology Computing and Study Skills**
*http://www.bodley.ox.ac.uk/isca/CASShome.html*

**Introduction to Anthropological Fieldwork and Ethnography**
*http://web.mit.edu/dumit/www/syl-anth.html*

**Theory in Anthropology**
*http://www.indiana.edu/~wanthro/theory.htm*

For at least a century, the goals of anthropology have been to describe societies and cultures throughout the world and to compare the differences and similarities among them. Anthropologists study in a variety of settings and situations, ranging from small hamlets and villages to neighborhoods and corporate offices of major urban centers throughout the world. They study hunters and gatherers, peasants, farmers, labor leaders, politicians, and bureaucrats. They examine religious life in Latin America as well as revolutionary movements.

Wherever practicable, anthropologists take on the role of "participant observer." Through active involvement in the lifeways of people, they hope to gain an insider's perspective without sacrificing the objectivity of the trained scientist. Sometimes the conditions for achieving such a goal seem to form an almost insurmountable barrier, but anthropologists call on persistence, adaptability, and imagination to overcome the odds against them.

The diversity of focus in anthropology means that it is earmarked less by its particular subject matter than by its perspective. Although the discipline relates to both the biological and social sciences, anthropologists know that the boundaries drawn between disciplines are highly artificial. For example, while in theory it is possible to examine only the social organization of a family unit or the organization of political power in a nation-state, in reality it is impossible to separate the biological from the social, from the economic, from the political. The explanatory perspective of anthropology, as the articles in this unit demonstrate, is to seek out interrelationships among all these factors.

The first four articles in this section illustrate varying degrees of difficulty that an anthropologist may encounter in taking on the role of the participant observer. Napoleon Chagnon's essay, "Doing Fieldwork Among the Yąnomamö," shows the hardships imposed by certain physical conditions and the vast differences in values and attitudes to be bridged by the anthropologist just to get along.

George Gmelch, in "Lessons from the Field," discusses fieldwork as a transformative experience for his students as they embed themselves in a culture so radically different from their own.

Richard Lee, in "Eating Christmas in the Kalahari," apparently had few problems with the physical conditions and the personalities of the people he was studying. He did, however, come to realize that his behavior conveyed a certain attitude incompatible with the values of his hosts. In the process, he learned an impor-

tant lesson about how these hunter-gatherers have been able to survive for so long under conditions which we would consider marginal at best.

Then, of course, there is "Tricking and Tripping: Fieldwork on Prostitution in the Era of AIDS," in which Claire E. Sterk describes the problems, both professional and personal, involved in trying to understand the precarious lives of prostitutes on the urban streets of America.

The final two articles in this unit take a broader view of the human condition. In the classic essay, "One Hundred Percent American," Ralph Linton shows that even modern America, as technologically innovative as it is, will forever owe a great debt to all those inventive cultures that came before it. On the other hand, as Lee Cronk, points out in "Gardening Tips," the furious pace of contemporary social and technological change may be outstripping our ability to cope with it.

Much is at stake in these discussions as we attempt to achieve a more objective understanding of the diversity of peoples' ways. After all, the purpose of anthropology is not only to describe and explain, but also to develop a special vision of the world in which cultural alternatives (past, present, and future) can be measured against one another and used as guides for human action.

# Doing Fieldwork among the Yanomamö [1]

Napoleon A. Chagnon

## Vignette

The Yąnomamö are thinly scattered over a vast and verdant tropical forest, living in small villages that are separated by many miles of unoccupied land. They have no writing, but they have a rich and complex language. Their clothing is more decorative than protective. Well-dressed men sport nothing more than a few cotton strings around their wrists, ankles, and waists. They tie the foreskins of their penises to the waist string. Women dress about the same. Much of their daily life revolves around gardening, hunting, collecting wild foods, collecting firewood, fetching water, visiting with each other, gossiping, and making the few material possessions they own: baskets, hammocks, bows, arrows, and colorful pigments with which they paint their bodies. Life is relatively easy in the sense that they can 'earn a living' with about three hours' work per day. Most of what they eat they cultivate in their gardens, and most of that is plantains—a kind of cooking banana that is usually eaten green, either roasted on the coals or boiled in pots. Their meat comes from a large variety of game animals, hunted daily by the men. It is usually roasted on coals or smoked, and is always well done. Their villages are round and open—and very public. One can hear, see, and smell almost everything that goes on anywhere in the village. Privacy is rare, but sexual discreetness is possible in the garden or at night while others sleep. The villages can be as small as 40 to 50 people or as large as 300 people, but in all cases there are many more children and babies than there are adults. This is true of most primitive populations and of our own demographic past. Life expectancy is short.

The Yąnomamö fall into the category of Tropical Forest Indians called 'foot people.' They avoid large rivers and live in interfluvial plains of the major rivers. They have neighbors to the north, Carib-speaking Ye'kwana, who are true 'river people': They make elegant, large dugout canoes and travel extensively along the major waterways. For the Yąnomamö, a large stream is an obstacle and can be crossed only in the dry season. Thus, they have traditionally avoided larger rivers and, because of this, contact with outsiders who usually come by river.

They enjoy taking trips when the jungle abounds with seasonally ripe wild fruits and vegetables. Then, the large village—the *shabono*—is abandoned for a few weeks and everyone camps out for from one to several days away from the village and garden. On these trips, they make temporary huts from poles, vines, and leaves, each family making a separate hut.

Two major seasons dominate their annual cycle: the wet season, which inundates the low-lying jungle, making travel difficult, and the dry season—the time of visiting other villages to feast, trade, and politic with allies. The dry season is also the time when raiders can travel and strike silently at their unsuspecting enemies. The Yąnomamö are still conducting intervillage warfare, a phenomenon that affects all aspects of their social organization, settlement pattern, and daily routines. It is not simply 'ritualistic' war: At least one-fourth of all adult males die violently in the area I lived in.

Social life is organized around those same principles utilized by all tribesmen: kinship relationships, descent from ancestors, marriage exchanges between kinship/descent groups, and the transient charisma of distinguished headmen who attempt to keep order in the village and whose responsibility it is to determine the village's relationships with those in other villages. Their positions are largely the result of kinship and marriage patterns; they come from the largest kinship groups within the village. They can, by their personal wit, wisdom, and charisma, become autocrats, but most of them are largely 'greaters' among equals. They, too, must clear gardens, plant crops, collect wild foods, and hunt. They are simultaneously peacemakers and valiant warriors. Peacemaking often requires the threat or actual use of force, and most headmen have an acquired reputation for being *waiteri*: fierce.

The social dynamics within villages are involved with giving and receiving marriageable girls. Marriages are arranged by older kin, usually men, who are brothers, uncles, and the father. It is a political process, for girls are promised in marriage while they are young, and the men who do this attempt to create alliances with other men via marriage exchanges. There is a shortage of women due in part to a sex-ratio imbalance in the younger age categories, but also complicated by the fact that some men have multiple wives. Most fighting within the village stems from sexual affairs or failure to deliver a promised woman—or out-and-out seizure of a married woman by some other man. This can lead to internal fighting and conflict of such an intensity that villages split up and fission, each group then becoming a new village and, often, enemies to each other.

But their conflicts are not blind, uncontrolled violence. They have a series of graded forms of violence that ranges from chest-pounding and club-fighting duels to out-and-out shooting to kill. This gives them a good deal of flexibility in settling disputes without immediate resort to lethal violence. In addition, they have developed patterns of alliance and friendship that serve to limit violence—trading and feasting with others in order to become friends. These alliances can, and often do, result in intervillage exchanges of marriageable women, which leads to additional amity between villages. No good thing lasts forever, and most alliances crumble. Old friends become hostile and, occasionally, treacherous. Each village must therefore be keenly aware that its neighbors are fickle and must behave accordingly. The thin line between friendship and animosity must be traversed by the village leaders, whose political acumen and strategies are both admirable and complex.

Each village, then, is a replica of all others in a broad sense. But each village is part of a larger political, demographic, and ecological process, and it is difficult to attempt to understand the village without knowing something of the larger forces that affect it and its particular history with all its neighbors.

## Collecting the Data in the Field

I have now spent over 60 months with Yanomamö, during which time I gradually learned their language and, up to a point, submerged myself in their culture and way of life.[2] As my research progressed, the thing that impressed me most was the importance that aggression played in shaping their culture. I had the opportunity to witness a good many incidents that expressed individual vindictiveness on the one hand and collective bellicosity on the other hand. These ranged in seriousness from the ordinary incidents of wife beating and chest pounding to dueling and organized raids by parties that set out with the intention of ambushing and killing men from enemy villages. One of the villages was raided approximately twenty-five times during my first 15 months of fieldwork—six times by the group among whom I was living. And, the history of every village I investigated, from 1964 to 1991, was intimately bound up in patterns of warfare with neighbors that shaped its politics and determined where it was found at any point in time and how it dealt with its current neighbors.

The fact that the Yanomamö have lived in a chronic state of warfare is reflected in their mythology, ceremonies, settlement pattern, political behavior, and marriage practices. Accordingly, I have organized this case study in such a way that students can appreciate the effects of warfare on Yanomamö culture in general and on their social organization and political relationships in particular.

I collected the data under somewhat trying circumstances, some of which I will describe to give a rough idea of what is generally meant when anthropologists speak of 'culture shock' and 'fieldwork.' It should be borne in mind, however, that each field situation is in many respects unique, so that the problems I encountered do not necessarily exhaust the range of possible problems other anthropologists have confronted in other areas. There are a few problems, however, that seem to be nearly universal among anthropological fieldworkers, particularly those having to do with eating, bathing, sleeping, lack of privacy, loneliness, or discovering that the people you are living with have a lower opinion of you than you have of them or you yourself are not as culturally or emotionally 'flexible' as you assumed.

The Yanomamö can be difficult people to live with at times, but I have spoken to colleagues who have had difficulties living in the communities they studied. These things vary from society to society, and probably from one anthropologist to the next. I have also done limited fieldwork among the Yanomamö's northern neighbors, the Carib-speaking Ye'kwana Indians. By contrast to many experiences I had among the Yanomamö, the Ye'kwana were very pleasant and charming, all of them anxious to help me and honor bound to show any visitor the numerous courtesies of their system of etiquette. In short, they approached the image of 'primitive man' that I had conjured up in my mind before doing fieldwork, a kind of 'Rousseauian' view, and it was sheer pleasure to work with them. Other anthropologists have also noted sharp contrasts in the people they study from one field situation to another. One of the most startling examples of this is in the work of Colin Turnbull, who first studied the Ituri Pygmies (1965, 1983) and found them delightful to live with, but then studied the Ik (1972) of the desolate outcroppings of the Kenya/Uganda/Sudan border region, a people he had difficulty coping with intellectually, emotionally, and physically. While it is possible that the anthropologist's reactions to a particular people are personal and idiosyncratic, it nevertheless remains true that there are enormous differences between whole peoples, differences that affect the anthropologist in often dramatic ways.

Hence, what I say about some of my experiences is probably equally true of the experiences of many other fieldworkers. I describe some of them here for the benefit of future anthropologists—because I think I could have profited by reading about the pitfalls and field problems of my own teachers. At the very least I might have been able to avoid some of my more stupid errors. In this regard there is a growing body of excellent descriptive work on field research. Students who plan to make a career in anthropology should consult these works, which cover a wide range of field situations in the ethnographic present.[3]

## The Longest Day: The First One

My first day in the field illustrated to me what my teachers meant when they spoke of 'culture shock.' I had traveled in a small, aluminum rowboat propelled by a large outboard motor for two and a half days. This took me from the territorial capital, a small town on the Orinoco River, deep into Yanomamö country. On the morning of the third day we reached a small mission settlement, the field 'headquarters' of a group of Americans who were working in two Yanomamö villages. The missionaries had come out of these villages to hold their annual conference on the progress of their mission work and were conducting their meetings when I arrived. We picked up a passenger at the mission station, James P. Barker, the first non-Yanomamö to make a sustained, permanent contact with the tribe (in 1950). He had just returned from a year's furlough in the United States, where I had earlier visited him before leaving for Venezuela. He agreed to accompany me to the village I had selected for my base of operations to introduce me to the Indians. This village was also his own home base, but he had not been there for over a year and did not plan to join me for another three months. Mr. Barker had been living with this particular group about five years.

We arrived at the village, Bisaasi-teri, about 2:00 P.M. and docked the boat along the muddy bank at the terminus of the path used by Yąnomamö to fetch their drinking water. It was hot and muggy, and my clothing was soaked with perspiration. It clung uncomfortably to my body, as it did thereafter for the remainder of the work. The small biting gnats, *bareto*, were out in astronomical numbers, for it was the beginning of the dry season. My face and hands were swollen from the venom of their numerous stings. In just a few moments I was to meet my first Yąnomamö, my first primitive man. What would he be like? I had visions of entering the village and seeing 125 social facts running about altruistically calling each other kinship terms and sharing food, each waiting and anxious to have me collect his genealogy. I would wear them out in turn. Would they like me? This was important to me; I wanted them to be so fond of me that they would adopt me into their kinship system and way of life. I had heard that successful anthropologists always get adopted by their people. I had learned during my seven years of anthropological training at the University of Michigan that kinship was equivalent to society in primitive tribes and that it was a moral way of life, 'moral' being something 'good' and 'desirable.' I was determined to work my way into their moral system of kinship and become a member of their society—to be 'accepted' by them.

## How Did They Accept You?

My heart began to pound as we approached the village and heard the buzz of activity within the circular compound. Mr. Barker commented that he was anxious to see if any changes had taken place while he was away and wondered how many of them had died during his absence. I nervously felt my back pocket to make sure that my notebook was still there and felt personally more secure when I touched it.

The entrance to the village was covered over with brush and dry palm leaves. We pushed them aside to expose the low opening to the village. The excitement of meeting my first Yąomamö was almost unbearable as I duck-waddled through the low passage into the village clearing.

I looked up and gasped when I saw a dozen burly, naked, sweaty, hideous men staring at us down the shafts of their drawn arrows! Immense wads of green tobacco were stuck between their lower teeth and lips making them look even more hideous, and strands of dark-green slime dripped or hung from their nostrils—strands so long that they clung to their pectoral muscles or drizzled down their chins. We arrived at the village while the men were blowing a hallucinogenic drug up their noses. One of the side effects of the drug is a runny nose. The mucus is always saturated with the green powder and they usually let it run freely from their nostrils. My next discovery was that there were a dozen or so vicious, underfed dogs snapping at my legs, circling me as if I were to be their next meal. I just stood there holding my notebook, helpless and pathetic. Then the stench of the decaying vegetation and filth hit me and I almost got sick. I was

horrified. What kind of welcome was this for the person who came here to live with you and learn your way of life, to become friends with you? They put their weapons down when they recognized Barker and returned to their chanting, keeping a nervous eye on the village entrances.

We had arrived just after a serious fight. Seven women had been abducted the day before by a neighboring group, and the local men and their guests had just that morning recovered five of them in a brutal club fight that nearly ended in a shooting war. The abductors, angry because they had lost five of their seven new captives, vowed to raid the Bisaasi-teri. When we arrived and entered the village unexpectedly, the Indians feared that we were the raiders. On several occasions during the next two hours the men in the village jumped to their feet, armed themselves, nocked their arrows and waited nervously for the noise outside the village to be identified. My enthusiasm for collecting ethnographic facts diminished in proportion to the number of times such an alarm was raised. In fact, I was relieved when Barker suggested that we sleep across the river for the evening. It would be safer over there.

As we walked down the path to the boat, I pondered the wisdom of having decided to spend a year and a half with these people before I had even seen what they were like. I am not ashamed to admit that had there been a diplomatic way out, I would have ended my fieldwork then and there. I did not look forward to the next day—and months—when I would be left alone with the Yąnomamö; I did not speak a word of their language, and they were decidedly different from what I had imagined them to be. The whole situation was depressing, and I wondered why I ever decided to switch from physics and engineering in the first place. I had not eaten all day, I was soaking wet from perspiration, the *bareto* were biting me, and I was covered with red pigment, the result of a dozen or so complete examinations I had been given by as many very pushy Yąnomamö men. These examinations capped an otherwise grim day. The men would blow their noses into their hands, flick as much of the mucus off that would separate in a snap of the wrist, wipe the residue into their hair, and then carefully examine my face, arms, legs, hair, and the contents of my pockets. I asked Barker how to say, 'Your hands are dirty'; my comments were met by the Yąnomamö in the following way: They would 'clean' their hands by spitting a quantity of slimy tobacco juice into them, rub them together, grin, and then proceed with the examination.

Mr. Barker and I crossed the river and slung our hammocks. When he pulled his hammock out of a rubber bag, a heavy disagreeable odor of mildewed cotton and stale wood smoke came with it. 'Even the missionaries are filthy,' I thought to myself. Within two weeks, everything I owned smelled the same way, and I lived with that odor for the remainder of the fieldwork. My own habits of personal cleanliness declined to such levels that I didn't even mind being examined by the Yąnomamö, as I was not much cleaner than they were after I had adjusted to the circumstances. It is difficult to blow your nose gracefully when you are stark naked and the invention of handkerchiefs is millennia away.

## Life in the Jungle: Oatmeal, Peanut Butter, and Bugs

It isn't easy to plop down in the Amazon Basin for a year and get immediately into the anthropological swing of things. You have been told about horrible diseases, snakes, jaguars, electric eels, little spiny fish that will swim up your urine into your penis, quicksand, and getting lost. Some of the dangers are real, but your imagination makes them more real and threatening than many of them really are. What my teachers never bothered to advise me about, however, was the mundane, nonexciting, and trivial stuff—like eating, defecating, sleeping, or keeping clean. These turned out to be the bane of my existence during the first several months of field research. I set up my household in Barker's abandoned mud hut, a few yards from the village of Bisaasi-teri, and immediately set to work building my own mud/thatch hut with the help of the Yąnomamö. Meanwhile, I had to eat and try to do my 'field research.' I soon discovered that it was an enormously time-consuming task to maintain my own body in the manner to which it had grown accustomed in the relatively antiseptic environment of the northern United States. Either I could be relatively well fed and relatively comfortable in a fresh change of clothes and do very little fieldwork, or I could do considerably more fieldwork and be less well fed and less comfortable.

It is appalling how complicated it can be to make oatmeal in the jungle. First, I had to make two trips to the river to haul the water. Next, I had to prime my kerosene stove with alcohol to get it burning, a tricky procedure when you are trying to mix powdered milk and fill a coffee pot at the same time. The alcohol prime always burned out before I could turn the kerosene on, and I would have to start all over. Or, I would turn the kerosene on, optimistically hoping that the Coleman element was still hot enough to vaporize the fuel, and start a small fire in my palm-thatched hut as the liquid kerosene squirted all over the table and walls and then ignited. Many amused Yąnomamö onlookers quickly learned the English phrase 'Oh, Shit!' and, once they discovered that the phrase offended and irritated the missionaries, they used it as often as they could in their presence. I usually had to start over with the alcohol. Then I had to boil the oatmeal and pick the bugs out of it. All my supplies, of course, were carefully stored in rat-proof, moisture-proof, and insect-proof containers, not one of which ever served its purpose adequately. Just taking things out of the multiplicity of containers and repacking them afterward was a minor project in itself. By the time I had hauled the water to cook with, unpacked my food, prepared the oatmeal, milk, and coffee, heated water for dishes, washed and dried the dishes, repacked the food in the containers, stored the containers in locked trunks, and cleaned up my mess, the ceremony of preparing breakfast had brought me almost up to lunch time!

Eating three meals a day was simply out of the question. I solved the problem by eating a single meal that could be prepared in a single container, or, at most, in two containers, washed my dishes only when there were no clean ones left, using cold river water, and wore each change of clothing at least a week to cut down on my laundry problem—a courageous undertaking in the tropics. I reeked like a jockstrap that had been left to mildew in the bottom of some dark gym locker. I also became less concerned about sharing my provisions with the rats, insects, Yąnomamö, and the elements, thereby eliminating the need for my complicated storage process. I was able to last most of the day on *café con leche*, heavily sugared espresso coffee diluted about five to one with hot milk. I would prepare this in the evening and store it in a large thermos. Frequently, my single meal was no more complicated than a can of sardines and a package of soggy crackers. But at least two or three times a week I would do something 'special' and sophisticated, like make a batch of oatmeal or boil rice and add a can of tuna fish or tomato paste to it. I even saved time by devising a water system that obviated the trips to the river. I had a few sheets of tin roofing brought in and made a rain water trap; I caught the water on the tin surface, funneled it into an empty gasoline drum, and then ran a plastic hose from the drum to my hut. When the drum was exhausted in the dry season, I would get a few Yąnomamö boys to fill it with buckets of water from the river, 'paying' them with crackers, of which they grew all too fond all too soon.

I ate much less when I traveled with the Yąnomamö to visit other villages. Most of the time my travel diet consisted of roasted or boiled green plantains (cooking bananas) that I obtained from the Yąnomamö, but I always carried a few cans of sardines with me in case I got lost or stayed away longer than I had planned. I found peanut butter and crackers a very nourishing 'trail' meal, and a simple one to prepare. It was nutritious and portable, and only one tool was required to make the meal: a hunting knife that could be cleaned by wiping the blade on a convenient leaf. More importantly, it was one of the few foods the Yąnomamö would let me eat in relative peace. It looked suspiciously like animal feces to them, an impression I encouraged. I referred to the peanut butter as the feces of babies or 'cattle.' They found this disgusting and repugnant. They did not know what 'cattle' were, but were increasingly aware that I ate several canned products of such an animal. Tin cans were thought of as containers made of 'machete skins,' but how the cows got inside was always a mystery to them. I went out of my way to describe my foods in such a way as to make them sound unpalatable to them, for it gave me some peace of mind while I ate: They wouldn't beg for a share of something that was too horrible to contemplate. Fieldworkers develop strange defense mechanisms and strategies, and this was one of my own forms of adaptation to the fieldwork. On another occasion I was eating a can of frankfurters and growing very weary of the demands from one of the onlookers for a share in my meal. When he finally asked what I was eating, I replied: 'Beef.' He then asked: 'Shaki![4] What part of the animal are you eating?' To which I replied, 'Guess.' He muttered a contemptuous epithet, but stopped asking for a share. He got back at me later, as we shall see.

Meals were a problem in a way that had nothing to do with the inconvenience of preparing them. Food sharing is important to the Yąnomamö in the context of displaying friendship. 'I am hungry!' is almost a form of greeting with them. I could not possibly have brought enough food with me to feed the entire village, yet they seemed to overlook this logistic fact as they begged for my food. What became fixed in their minds was the fact that I did not share my food with whomsoever was present—usually a small crowd—at each and every meal. Nor could I easily enter their system of reciprocity with respect to food. Every time one of them 'gave' me something 'freely,' he would dog me for months to 'pay him back,' not necessarily with food but with knives, fishhooks, axes, and so on. Thus, if I accepted a plantain from someone in a different village while I was on a visit, he would most likely visit me in the future and demand a machete as payment for the time that he 'fed' me. I usually reacted to these kinds of demands by giving a banana, the customary reciprocity in their culture—food for food—but this would be a disappointment for the individual who had nursed visions of that single plantain growing into a machete over time. Many years after beginning my fieldwork, I was approached by one of the prominent men who demanded a machete for a piece of meat he claimed he had given me five or six years earlier.

Despite the fact that most of them knew I would not share my food with them at their request, some of them always showed up at my hut during mealtime. I gradually resigned myself to this and learned to ignore their persistent demands while I ate. Some of them would get angry because I failed to give in, but most of them accepted it as just a peculiarity of the subhuman foreigner who had come to live among them. If or when I did accede to a request for a share of my food, my hut quickly filled with Yąnomamö, each demanding their share of the food that I had just given to one of them. Their begging for food was not provoked by hunger, but by a desire to try something new and to attempt to establish a coercive relationship in which I would accede to a demand. If one received something, all others would immediately have to test the system to see if they, too, could coerce me.

A few of them went out of their way to make my meals downright unpleasant—to spite me for not sharing, especially if it was a food that they had tried before and liked, or a food that was part of their own cuisine. For example, I was eating a cracker with peanut butter and honey one day. The Yąnomamö will do almost anything for honey, one of the most prized delicacies in their own diet. One of my cynical onlookers—the fellow who had earlier watched me eating frankfurters—immediately recognized the honey and knew that I would not share the tiny precious bottle. It would be futile to even ask. Instead, he glared at me and queried icily, 'Shaki! What kind of animal semen are you pouring onto your food and eating?' His question had the desired effect and my meal ended.

Finally, there was the problem of being lonely and separated from your own kind, especially your family. I tried to overcome this by seeking personal friendships among the Yąnomamö. This usually complicated the matter because all my 'friends' simply used my confidence to gain privileged access to my hut and my cache of steel tools and trade goods—and looted me when I wasn't looking. I would be bitterly disappointed that my erstwhile friend thought no more of me than to finesse our personal relationship exclusively with the intention of getting at my locked up possessions, and my depression would hit new lows every time I discovered this. The loss of the possessions bothered me much less than the shock that I was, as far as most of them were concerned, nothing more than a source of desirable items. No holds were barred in relieving me of these, since I was considered something subhuman, a non-Yąomamö.

The hardest thing to learn to live with was the incessant, passioned, and often aggressive demands they would make. It would become so unbearable at times that I would have to lock myself in my hut periodically just to escape from it. Privacy is one of our culture's most satisfying achievements, one you never think about until you suddenly have none. It is like not appreciating how good your left thumb feels until someone hits it with a hammer. But I did not want privacy for its own sake; rather, I simply had to get away from the begging. Day and night for almost the entire time I lived with the Yąnomamö, I was plagued by such demands as: 'Give me a knife, I am poor!'; 'If you don't take me with you on your next trip to Widokaiyateri, I'll chop a hole in your canoe!'; 'Take us hunting up the Mavaca River with your shotgun or we won't help you!'; 'Give me some matches so I can trade with the Reyaboböwei-teri, and be quick about it or I'll hit you!'; 'Share your food with me, or I'll burn your hut!'; 'Give me a flashlight so I can hunt at night!'; 'Give me all your medicine, I itch all over!'; 'Give me an ax or I'll break into your hut when you are away and steal all of them!' And so I was bombarded by such demands day after day, month after month, until I could not bear to see a Yąomamö at times.

It was not as difficult to become calloused to the incessant begging as it was to ignore the sense of urgency, the impassioned tone of voice and whining, or the intimidation and aggression with which many of the demands were made. It was likewise difficult to adjust to the fact that the Yąnomamö refused to accept 'No' for an answer until or unless it seethed with passion and intimidation—which it did after a few months. So persistent and characteristic is the begging that the early 'semiofficial' maps made by the Venezuelan Malaria Control Service (*Malarialogía*) designated the site of their first permanent field station, next to the village of Bisaasi-teri, as *Yababuhii*: 'Gimme.' I had to become like the Yąnomamö to be able to get along with them on their terms: somewhat sly, aggressive, intimidating, and pushy.

It became indelibly clear to me shortly after I arrived there that had I failed to adjust in this fashion I would have lost six months of supplies to them in a single day or would have spent most of my time ferrying them around in my canoe or taking them on long hunting trips. As it was, I did spend a considerable amount of time doing these things and did succumb often to their outrageous demands for axes and machetes, at least at first, for things changed as I became more fluent in their language and learned how to defend myself socially as well as verbally. More importantly, had I failed to demonstrate that I could not be pushed around beyond a certain point, I would have been the subject of far more ridicule, theft, and practical jokes than was the actual case. In short, I had to acquire a certain proficiency in their style of interpersonal politics and to learn how to imply subtly that certain potentially undesirable, but unspecified, consequences might follow if they did such and such to me. They do this to each other incessantly in order to establish precisely the point at which they cannot goad or intimidate an individual any further without precipitating some kind of retaliation. As soon as I realized this and gradually acquired the self-confidence to adopt this strategy, it became clear that much of the intimidation was calculated to determine my flash point or my 'last ditch' position—and I got along much better with them. Indeed, I even regained some lost ground. It was sort of like a political, interpersonal game that everyone had to play, but one in which each individual sooner or later had to give evidence that his bluffs and implied threats could be backed up with a sanction. I suspect that the frequency of wife beating is a component in this syndrome, since men can display their *waiteri* (ferocity) and 'show' others that they are capable of great violence. Beating a wife with a club is one way of displaying ferocity, one that does not expose the man to much danger—unless the wife has concerned, aggressive brothers in the village who will come to her aid. Apparently an important thing in wife beating is that the man has displayed his presumed potential for violence and the intended message is that other men ought to treat him with circumspection, caution, and even deference.

After six months, the level of Yanomamö demand was tolerable in Bisaasi-teri, the village I used for my base of operations. We had adjusted somewhat to each other and knew what to expect with regard to demands for food, trade goods, and favors. Had I elected to remain in just one Yanomamö village for the entire duration of my first 15 months of fieldwork, the experience would have been far more enjoyable than it actually was. However, as I began to understand the social and political dynamics of this village, it became patently obvious that I would have to travel to many other villages to determine the demographic bases and political histories that lay behind what I could understand in the village of Bisaasi-teri. I began making regular trips to some dozen neighboring Yanomamö villages as my language fluency improved. I collected local genealogies there, or rechecked and cross-checked those I had collected elsewhere. Hence, the intensity of begging was relatively constant and relatively high for the duration of my fieldwork, for I had to establish my personal position in each village I visited and revisited.

For the most part, my own 'fierceness' took the form of shouting back at the Yanomamö as loudly and as passionately as they shouted at me, especially at first, when I did not know much of the language. As I became more fluent and learned more about their political tactics, I became more sophisticated in the art of bluffing and brinksmanship. For example, I paid one young man a machete (then worth about $2.50) to cut a palm tree and help me make boards from the wood. I used these to fashion a flooring in the bottom of my dugout canoe to keep my possessions out of the water that always seeped into the canoe and sloshed around. That afternoon I was working with one of my informants in the village. The long-awaited mission supply boat arrived and most of the Yanomamö ran out of the village to see the supplies and try to beg items from the crew. I continued to work in the village for another hour or so and then went down to the river to visit with the men on the supply boat. When I reached the river I noticed, with anger and frustration, that the Yanomamö had chopped up all my new floor boards to use as crude paddles to get their own canoes across the river to the supply boat.[5] I knew that if I ignored this abuse I would

have invited the Yanomamö to take even greater liberties with my possessions in the future. I got into my canoe, crossed the river, and docked amidst their flimsy, leaky craft. I shouted loudly to them, attracting their attention. They were somewhat sheepish, but all had mischievous grins on their impish faces. A few of them came down to the canoe, where I proceeded with a spirited lecture that revealed my anger at their audacity and license. I explained that I had just that morning paid one of them a machete for bringing me the palmwood, how hard I had worked to shape each board and place it in the canoe, how carefully and painstakingly I had tied each one in with vines, how much I had perspired, how many *bareto* bites I had suffered, and so on. Then, with exaggerated drama and finality, I withdrew my hunting knife as their grins disappeared and cut each one of their canoes loose and set it into the strong current of the Orinoco River where it was immediately swept up and carried downstream. I left without looking back and huffed over to the other side of the river to resume my work.

They managed to borrow another canoe and, after some effort, recovered their dugouts. Later, the headman of the village told me, with an approving chuckle, that I had done the correct thing. Everyone in the village, except, of course, the culprits, supported and defended my actions—and my status increased as a consequence.

Whenever I defended myself in such ways I got along much better with the Yanomamö and gradually acquired the respect of many of them. A good deal of their demeanor toward me was directed with the forethought of establishing the point at which I would draw the line and react defensively. Many of them, years later, reminisced about the early days of my fieldwork when I was timid and *mohode* ("stupid") and a little afraid of them, those golden days when it was easy to bully me into giving my goods away for almost nothing.

Theft was the most persistent situation that required some sort of defensive action. I simply could not keep everything I owned locked in trunks, and the Yanomamö came into my hut and left at will. I eventually developed a very effective strategy for recovering almost all the stolen items: I would simply ask a child who took the item and then I would confiscate that person's hammock when he was not around, giving a spirited lecture to all who could hear on the antisociality of thievery as I stalked off in a faked rage with the thief's hammock slung over my shoulder. Nobody ever attempted to stop me from doing this, and almost all of them told me that my technique for recovering my possessions was ingenious. By nightfall the thief would appear at my hut with the stolen item or send it over with someone else to make an exchange to recover his hammock. He would be heckled by his covillagers for having got caught and for being embarrassed into returning my item for his hammock. The explanation was usually, 'I just borrowed your ax! I wouldn't think of stealing it!'

## *Collecting Yanomamö Genealogies and Reproductive Histories*

My purpose for living among Yanomamö was to systematically collect certain kinds of information on genealogy, reproduction, marriage practices, kinship, settlement patterns, migrations, and politics. Much of the fundamental data was genealogical—who was the parent of whom, tracing these connections as far back in time as Yąnomamö knowledge and memory permitted. Since 'primitive' society is organized largely by kinship relationships, figuring out the social organization of the Yąnomamö essentially meant collecting extensive data on genealogies, marriage, and reproduction. This turned out to be a staggering and very frustrating problem. I could not have deliberately picked a more difficult people to work with in this regard. They have very stringent name taboos and eschew mentioning the names of prominent living people as well as all deceased friends and relatives. They attempt to name people in such a way that when the person dies and they can no longer use his or her name, the loss of the word in their language is not inconvenient. Hence, they name people for specific and minute parts of things, such as 'toenail of sloth,' 'whisker of howler monkey,' and so on, thereby being able to retain the words 'toenail' or 'whisker' but somewhat handicapped in referring to these anatomical parts of sloths and monkeys respectively. The taboo is maintained even for the living, for one mark of prestige is the courtesy others show you by not using your name publicly. This is particularly true for men, who are much more competitive for status than women in this culture, and it is fascinating to watch boys grow into young men, demanding to be called either by a kinship term in public, or by a teknonymous reference such as 'brother of Himotoma.' The more effective they are at getting others to avoid using their names, the more public acknowledgment there is that they are of high esteem and social standing. Helena Valero, a Brazilian woman who was captured as a child by a Yąnomamö raiding party, was married for many years to a Yąnomamö headman before she discovered what his name was (Biocca, 1970; Valero, 1984). The sanctions behind the taboo are more complex than just this, for they involve a combination of fear, respect, admiration, political deference, and honor.

At first I tried to use kinship terms alone to collect genealogies, but Yąnomamö kinship terms, like the kinship terms in all systems, are ambiguous at some point because they include so many possible relatives (as the term 'uncle' does in our own kinship system). Again, their system of kin classification merges many relatives that we 'separate' by using different terms: They call both their actual father and their father's brother by a single term, whereas we call one 'father' and the other 'uncle.' I was forced, therefore, to resort to personal names to collect unambiguous genealogies or 'pedigrees.' They quickly grasped what I was up to and that I was determined to learn everyone's 'true name,' which amounted to an invasion of their system of prestige and etiquette, if not a flagrant violation of it. They reacted to this in a brilliant but devastating manner: They invented false names for everybody in the village and systematically learned them, freely revealing to me the 'true' identities of everyone. I smugly thought I had cracked the system and enthusiastically constructed elaborate genealogies over a period of some five months. They enjoyed watching me learn their names and kinship relationships. I naively assumed that I would get the 'truth' to each question and the best information by working in public. This set the stage for converting my serious project into an amusing hoax of the grandest proportions. Each 'informant'

would try to outdo his peers by inventing a name even more preposterous or ridiculous than what I had been given by someone earlier, the explanations for discrepancies being 'Well, he has two names and this is the other one.' They even fabricated devilishly improbable genealogical relationships, such as someone being married to his grandmother, or worse yet, to his mother-in-law, a grotesque and horrifying prospect to the Yąnomamö. I would collect the desired names and relationships by having my informant whisper the name of the person softly into my ear, noting that he or she was the parent of such and such or the child of such and such, and so on. Everyone who was observing my work would then insist that I repeat the name aloud, roaring in hysterical laughter as I clumsily pronounced the name, sometimes laughing until tears streamed down their faces. The 'named' person would usually react with annoyance and hiss some untranslatable epithet at me, which served to reassure me that I had the 'true' name. I conscientiously checked and rechecked the names and relationships with multiple informants, pleased to see the inconsistencies disappear as my genealogy sheets filled with those desirable little triangles and circles, thousands of them.

My anthropological bubble was burst when I visited a village about 10 hours' walk to the southwest of Bisaasi-teri some five months after I had begun collecting genealogies on the Bisaasi-teri. I was chatting with the local headman of this village and happened to casually drop the name of the wife of the Bisaasi-teri headman. A stunned silence followed, and then a village-wide roar of uncontrollable laughter, choking, gasping, and howling followed. It seems that I thought the Bisaasi-teri headman was married to a woman named "hairy cunt." It also seems that the Bisaasi-teri headman was called 'long dong' and his brother 'eagle shit.' The Bisaasi-teri headman had a son called "asshole" and a daughter called 'fart breath.' And so on. Blood welled up my temples as I realized that I had nothing but nonsense to show for my five months' of dedicated genealogical effort, and I had to throw away almost all the information I had collected on this the most basic set of data I had come there to get. I understood at that point why the Bisaasi-teri laughed so hard when they made me repeat the names of their covillagers, and why the 'named' person would react with anger and annoyance as I pronounced his 'name' aloud.

I was forced to change research strategy—to make an understatement to describe this serious situation. The first thing I did was to begin working in private with my informants to eliminate the horseplay and distraction that attended public sessions. Once I did this, my informants, who did not know what others were telling me, began to agree with each other and I managed to begin learning the 'real' names, starting first with children and gradually moving to adult women and then, cautiously, adult men, a sequence that reflected the relative degree of intransigence at revealing names of people. As I built up a core of accurate genealogies and relationships—a core that all independent informants had verified repetitiously—I could 'test' any new informant by soliciting his or her opinion and knowledge about these 'core' people whose names and relationships I was confident were accurate. I was, in this fashion, able to immediately weed out the mischievous informants who persisted in trying to deceive me. Still, I had great difficulty getting the names of dead kinsmen, the only accurate way to extend genealogies back in time. Even my best informants continued to falsify names of the deceased, especially closely related deceased. The falsifications at this point were not serious and turned out to be readily corrected as my interviewing methods improved (see below). Most of the deceptions were of the sort where the informant would give me the name of a living man as the father of some child whose actual father was dead, a response that enabled the informant to avoid using the name of a deceased kinsman or friend.

The quality of a genealogy depends in part on the number of generations it embraces, and the name taboo prevented me from making any substantial progress in learning about the deceased ancestors of the present population. Without this information, I could not, for example, document marriage patterns and interfamilial alliances through time. I had to rely on older informants for this information, but these were the most reluctant informants of all for this data. As I became more proficient in the language and more skilled at detecting fabrications, any informants became better at deception. One old man was particularly cunning and persuasive, following a sort of Mark Twain policy that the most effective lie is a sincere lie. He specialized in making a ceremony out of false names for dead ancestors. He would look around nervously to make sure nobody was listening outside my hut, enjoin me never to mention the name again, become very anxious and spooky, and grab me by the head to whisper a secret name into my ear. I was always elated after a session with him, because I managed to add several generations of ancestors for particular members of the village. Others steadfastly refused to give me such information. To show my gratitude, I paid him quadruple the rate that I had been paying the others. When word got around that I had increased the pay for genealogical and demographic information, volunteers began pouring into my hut to 'work' for me, assuring me of their changed ways and keen desire to divest themselves of the 'truth.'

## Enter Rerebawä: Inmarried Tough Guy

I discovered that the old man was lying quite by accident. A club fight broke out in the village one day, the result of a dispute over the possession of a woman. She had been promised to a young man in the village, a man named Rerebawä, who was particularly aggressive. He had married into Bisaasi-teri and was doing his 'bride service'—a period of several years during which he had to provide game for his wife's father and mother, provide them with wild foods he might collect, and help them in certain gardening and other tasks. Rerebawä had already been given one of the daughters in marriage and was promised her younger sister as his second wife. He was enraged when the younger sister, then about 16 years old, began having an affair with another young man in the village, Bäkotawä, making no attempt to conceal it. Rerebawä challenged Bäkotawä to a club fight. He swaggered boisterously out to the duel with his 10-foot-long club, a roof-pole he had cut from the house on the spur of the moment, as is the usual procedure. He hurled insult after insult at both Bäkotawä and his father, trying to goad them into

a fight. His insults were bitter and nasty. They tolerated them for a few moments, but Rerebawä's biting insults provoked them to rage. Finally, they stormed angrily out of their hammocks and ripped out roof-poles, now returning the insults verbally, and rushed to the village clearing. Rerebawä continued to insult them, goading them into striking him on the head with their equally long clubs. Had either of them struck his head—which he held out conspicuously for them to swing at—he would then have the right to take his turn on their heads with his club. His opponents were intimidated by his fury, and simply backed down, refusing to strike him, and the argument ended. He had intimidated them into submission. All three retired pompously to their respective hammocks, exchanging nasty insults as they departed. But Rerebawä had won the showdown and thereafter swaggered around the village, insulting the two men behind their backs at every opportunity. He was genuinely angry with them, to the point of calling the older man by the name of his long-deceased father. I quickly seized on this incident as an opportunity to collect an accurate genealogy and confidentially asked Rerebawä about his adversary's ancestors. Rerebawä had been particularly 'pushy' with me up to this point, but we soon became warm friends and staunch allies: We were both 'outsiders' in Bisaasi-teri and, although he was a Yanomamö, he nevertheless had to put up with some considerable amount of pointed teasing and scorn from the locals, as all inmarried 'sons-in-law' must. He gave me the information I requested of his adversary's deceased ancestors, almost with devilish glee. I asked about dead ancestors of other people in the village and got prompt, unequivocal answers: He was angry with everyone in the village. When I compared his answers to those of the old man, it was obvious that one of them was lying. I then challenged his answers. He explained, in a sort of 'you damned fool, don't you know better?' tone of voice that everyone in the village knew the old man was lying to me and gloating over it when I was out of earshot. The names the old man had given to me were names of dead ancestors of the members of a village so far away that he thought I would never have occasion to check them out authoritatively. As it turned out, Rerebawä knew most of the people in that distant village and recognized the names given by the old man.

I then went over all my Bisaasi-teri genealogies with Rerebawä, genealogies I had presumed to be close to their final form. I had to revise them all because of the numerous lies and falsifications they contained, much of it provided by the sly old man. Once again, after months of work, I had to recheck everything with Rerebawä's aid. Only the living members of the nuclear families turned out to be accurate; the deceased ancestors were mostly fabrications.

Discouraging as it was to have to recheck everything all over again, it was a major turning point in my fieldwork. Thereafter, I began taking advantage of local arguments and animosities in selecting my informants, and used more extensively informants who had married into the village in the recent past. I also began traveling more regularly to other villages at this time to check on genealogies, seeking out villages whose members were on strained terms with the people about whom I wanted information. I would then return to my base in the village of Bisaasi-teri and check with local informants the accuracy of the new information. I had to be careful in this work and scrupulously select my local informants in such a way that I would not be inquiring about *their* closely related kin. Thus, for each of my local informants, I had to make lists of names of certain deceased people that I dared not mention in their presence. But despite this precaution, I would occasionally hit a new name that would put some informants into a rage, or into a surly mood, such as that of a dead 'brother' or 'sister'[6] whose existence had not been indicated to me by other informants. This usually terminated my day's work with that informant, for he or she would be too touchy or upset to continue any further, and I would be reluctant to take a chance on accidentally discovering another dead close kinsman soon after discovering the first.

These were unpleasant experiences, and occasionally dangerous as well, depending on the temperament of my informant. On one occasion I was planning to visit a village that had been raided recently by one of their enemies. A woman, whose name I had on my census list for that village, had been killed by the raiders. Killing women is considered to be bad form in Yąnomamö warfare, but this woman was deliberately killed for revenge. The raiders were unable to bushwhack some man who stepped out of the village at dawn to urinate, so they shot a volley of arrows over the roof into the village and beat a hasty retreat. Unfortunately, one of the arrows struck and killed a woman, an accident. For that reason, her village's raiders *deliberately* sought out and killed a woman in retaliation—whose name was on my list. My reason for going to the village was to update my census data on a name-by-name basis and estimate the ages of all the residents. I knew I had the name of the dead woman in my list, but nobody would dare to utter her name so I could remove it. I knew that I would be in very serious trouble if I got to the village and said her name aloud, and I desperately wanted to remove it from my list. I called on one of my regular and usually cooperative informants and asked him to tell me the woman's name. He refused adamantly, explaining that she was a close relative—and was angry that I even raised the topic with him. I then asked him if he would let me whisper the names of *all* the women of that village in his ear, and he would simply have to nod when I hit the right name. We had been 'friends' for some time, and I thought I was able to predict his reaction, and thought that our friendship was good enough to use this procedure. He agreed to the procedure, and I began whispering the names of the women, one by one. We were alone in my hut so that nobody would know what we were doing and nobody could hear us. I read the names softly, continuing to the next when his response was a negative. When I ultimately hit the dead woman's name, he flew out of his chair, enraged and trembling violently, his arm raised to strike me: 'You son-of-a-bitch!' he screamed. 'If you say her name in my presence again, I'll kill you in an instant!' I sat there, bewildered, shocked, and confused. And frightened, as much because of his reaction, but also because I could imagine what might happen to me should I unknowingly visit a village to check genealogy accuracy without knowing that someone had just died there or had been shot by raiders since my last visit. I reflected on the several articles I had read as a graduate student that explained the 'genealogical method,' but could not recall anything about its being a poten-

tially lethal undertaking. My furious informant left my hut, never again to be invited back to be an informant. I had other similar experiences in different villages, but I was always fortunate in that the dead person had been dead for some time, or was not very closely related to the individual into whose ear I whispered the forbidden name. I was usually cautioned by one of the men to desist from saying any more names lest I get people 'angry.'[7]

## Kaobawä: The Bisaasi-teri Headman Volunteers to Help Me

I had been working on the genealogies for nearly a year when another individual came to my aid. It was Kaobawä, the headman of Upper Bisaasi-teri. The village of Bisaasi-teri was split into two components, each with its own garden and own circular house. Both were in sight of each other. However, the intensity and frequency of internal bickering and argumentation was so high that they decided to split into two separate groups but remain close to each other for protection in case they were raided. One group was downstream from the other; I refer to that group as the 'Lower' Bisaasi-teri and call Kaobawä's group 'Upper' (upstream) Bisaasi-teri, a convenience they themselves adopted after separating from each other. I spent most of my time with the members of Kaobawä's group, some 200 people when I first arrived there. I did not have much contact with Kaobawä during the early months of my work. He was a somewhat retiring, quiet man, and among the Yąnomamö, the outsider has little time to notice the rare quiet ones when most everyone else is in the front row, pushing and demanding attention. He showed up at my hut one day after all the others had left. He had come to volunteer to help me with the genealogies. He was 'poor,' he explained, and needed a machete. He would work only on the condition that I did not ask him about his own parents and other very close kinsmen who had died. He also added that he would not lie to me as the others had done in the past.

This was perhaps the single most important event in my first 15 months of field research, for out of this fortuitous circumstance evolved a very warm friendship, and among the many things following from it was a wealth of accurate information on the political history of Kaobawä's village and related villages, highly detailed genealogical information, sincere and useful advice to me, and hundreds of valuable insights into the Yąnomamö way of life. Kaobawä's familiarity with his group's history and his candidness were remarkable. His knowledge of details was almost encyclopedic, his memory almost photographic. More than that, he was enthusiastic about making sure I learned the truth, and he encouraged me, indeed, *demanded that* I learn all details I might otherwise have ignored. If there were subtle details he could not recite on the spot, he would advise me to wait until he could check things out with someone else in the village. He would often do this clandestinely, giving me a report the next day, telling me who revealed the new information and whether or not he thought they were in a position to know it. With the information provided by Kaobawä and Rerebawä, I made enormous gains in understanding village interrelationships based on common ancestors and political histories and became lifelong friends with both. And both men knew that

I had to learn about his recently deceased kin from the other one. It was one of those quiet understandings we all had but none of us could mention.

Once again I went over the genealogies with Kaobawä to recheck them, a considerable task by this time. They included about two thousand names, representing several generations of individuals from four different villages. Rerebawä's information was very accurate, and Kaobawä's contribution enabled me to trace the genealogies further back in time. Thus, after nearly a year of intensive effort on genealogies, Yanomamö demographic patterns and social organization began to make a good deal of sense to me. Only at this point did the patterns through time begin to emerge in the data, and I could begin to understand how kinship groups took form, exchanged women in marriage over several generations, and only then did the fissioning of larger villages into smaller ones emerge as a chronic and important feature of Yanomamö social, political, demographic, economic, and ecological adaptation. At this point I was able to begin formulating more sophisticated questions, for there was now a pattern to work from and one to flesh out. Without the help of Rerebawä and Kaobawä it would have taken much longer to make sense of the plethora of details I had collected from not only them, but dozens of other informants as well.

I spent a good deal of time with these two men and their families, and got to know them much better than I knew most Yanomamö. They frequently gave their information in a way which related themselves to the topic under discussion. We became warm friends as time passed, and the formal 'informant/anthropologist' relationship faded into the background. Eventually, we simply stopped 'keeping track' of work and pay. They would both spend hours talking with me, leaving without asking for anything. When they wanted something, they would ask for it no matter what the relative balance of reciprocity between us might have been at that point....

For many of the customary things that anthropologists try to communicate about another culture, these two men and their families might be considered to be 'exemplary' or 'typical.' For other things, they are exceptional in many regards, but the reader will, even knowing some of the exceptions, understand Yanomamö culture more intimately by being familiar with a few examples.

Kaobawä was about 40 years old when I first came to his village in 1964. I say "about 40" because the Yanomamö numeration system has only three numbers: one, two, and more-than-two. It is hard to give accurate ages or dates for events when the informants have no means in their language to reveal such detail. Kaobawä is the headman of his village, meaning that he has somewhat more responsibility in political dealings with other Yanomamö groups, and very little control over those who live in his group except when the village is being raided by enemies. We will learn more about political leadership and warfare in a later chapter, but most of the time men like Kaobawä are like the North American Indian 'chief' whose authority was characterized in the following fashion: "One word from the chief, and each man does as he pleases." There are different 'styles' of political leadership among the Yanomamö. Some leaders are

mild, quiet, inconspicuous most of the time, but intensely competent. They act parsimoniously, but when they do, people listen and conform. Other men are more tyrannical, despotic, pushy, flamboyant, and unpleasant to all around them. They shout orders frequently, are prone to beat their wives, or pick on weaker men. Some are very violent. I have met headmen who run the entire spectrum between these polar types, for I have visited some 60 Yanomamö villages. Kaobawä stands at the mild, quietly competent end of the spectrum. He has had six wives thus far—and temporary affairs with as many more, at least one of which resulted in a child that is publicly acknowledged as his child. When I first met him he had just two wives: Bahimi and Koamashima. Bahimi had two living children when I first met her; many others had died. She was the older and enduring wife, as much a friend to him as a mate. Their relationship was as close to what we think of as 'love' in our culture as I have seen among the Yanomamö. His second wife was a girl of about 20 years, Koamashima. She had a new baby boy when I first met her, her first child. There was speculation that Kaobawä was planning to give Koamashima to one of his younger brothers who had no wife; he occasionally allows his younger brother to have sex with Koamashima, but only if he asks in advance. Kaobawä gave another wife to one of his other brothers because she was *beshi* ("horny"). In fact, this earlier wife had been married to two other men, both of whom discarded her because of her infidelity. Kaobawä had one daughter by her. However, the girl is being raised by Kaobawä's brother, though acknowledged to be Kaobawä's child.

Bahimi, his oldest wife, is about five years younger than he. She is his cross-cousin—his mother's brother's daughter. Ideally, all Yanomamö men should marry a cross-cousin.... Bahimi was pregnant when I began my field work, but she destroyed the infant when it was born—a boy in this case—explaining tearfully that she had no choice. The new baby would have competed for milk with Ariwari, her youngest child, who was still nursing. Rather than expose Ariwari to the dangers and uncertainty of an early weaning, she chose to terminate the newborn instead. By Yanomamö standards, this has been a very warm, enduring marriage. Kaobawä claims he beats Bahimi only 'once in a while, and only lightly' and she, for her part, never has affairs with other men.

Kaobawä is a quiet, intense, wise, and unobtrusive man. It came as something of a surprise to me when I learned that he was the headman of his village, for he stayed at the sidelines while others would surround me and press their demands on me. He leads more by example than by coercion. He can afford to be this way at his age, for he established his reputation for being forthright and as fierce as the situation required when he was younger, and the other men respect him. He also has five mature brothers or half-brothers in his village, men he can count on for support. He also has several other mature 'brothers' (parallel cousins, whom he must refer to as 'brothers' in his kinship system) in the village who frequently come to his aid, but not as often as his 'real' brothers do. Kaobawä has also given a number of his sisters to other men in the village and has promised his young (8-year-old) daughter in marriage to a young man who, for that reason, is obliged to help him. In short, his 'natural' or 'kinship' following is large, and partially because of this support, he does not have to display his aggressiveness to remind his peers of his position.

Rerebawä is a very different kind of person. He is much younger—perhaps in his early twenties. He has just one wife, but they have already had three children. He is from a village called Karohi-teri, located about five hours' walk up the Orinoco, slightly inland off to the east of the river itself. Kaobawä's village enjoys amicable relationships with Rerebawä's, and it is for this reason that marriage alliances of the kind represented by Rerebawä's marriage into Kaobawä's village occur between the two groups. Rerebawä told me that he came to Bisaasi-teri because there were no eligible women from him to marry in his own village, a fact that I later was able to document when I did a census of his village and a preliminary analysis of its social organization. Rerebawä is perhaps more typical than Kaobawä in the sense that he is chronically concerned about his personal reputation for aggressiveness and goes out of his way to be noticed, even if he has to act tough. He gave me a hard time during my early months of fieldwork, intimidating, teasing, and insulting me frequently. He is, however, much braver than the other men his age and is quite prepared to back up his threats with immediate action—as in the club fight incident just described above. Moreover, he is fascinated with political relationships and knows the details of inter-village relationships over a large area of the tribe. In this respect he shows all the attributes of being a headman, although he has too many competent brothers in his own village to expect to move easily into the leadership position there.

He does not intend to stay in Kaobawä's group and refuses to make his own garden—a commitment that would reveal something of an intended long-term residence. He feels that he has adequately discharged his obligations to his wife's parents by providing them with fresh game, which he has done for several years. They should let him take his wife and return to his own village with her, but they refuse and try to entice him to remain permanently in Bisaasi-teri to continue to provide them with game when they are old. It is for this reason that they promised to give him their second daughter, their only other child, in marriage. Unfortunately, the girl was opposed to the marriage and ultimately married another man, a rare instance where the woman in the marriage had this much influence on the choice of her husband.

Although Rerebawä has displayed his ferocity in many ways, one incident in particular illustrates what his character can be like. Before he left his own village to take his new wife in Bisaasi-teri, he had an affair with the wife of an older brother. When it was discovered, his brother attacked him with a club. Rerebawä responded furiously: He grabbed an ax and drove his brother out of the village after soundly beating him with the blunt side of the single-bit ax. His brother was so intimidated by the thrashing and promise of more to come that he did not return to the village for several days. I visited this village with Kabawä shortly after this event had taken place; Rerebawä was with me as my guide. He made it a point to introduce me to this man. He approached his hammock, grabbed him by the wrist, and dragged him out on the ground: 'This is the brother whose wife I screwed when he wasn't around!' A deadly insult, one that would usually provoke a bloody club fight among more valiant Yanomamö. The man did nothing. He slunk sheepishly back into his hammock, shamed, but relieved to have Rerebawä release his grip.

Even though Rerebawä is fierce and capable of considerable nastiness, he has a charming, witty side as well. He has a biting sense of humor and can entertain the group for hours with jokes and clever manipulations of language. And, he is one of few Yanomamö that I feel I can trust. I recall indelibly my return to Bisaasi-teri after being away a year—the occasion of my second field trip to the Yanomamö. When I reached Bisaasi-teri, Rerebawä was in his own village visiting his kinsmen. Word reached him that I had returned, and he paddled downstream immediately to see me. He greeted me with an immense bear hug and exclaimed, with tears welling up in his eyes, 'Shaki! Why did you stay away so long? Did you not know that my will was so cold while you were gone that I could not at times eat for want of seeing you again?' I, too, felt the same way about him—then, and now.

Of all the Yanomamö I know, he is the most genuine and the most devoted to his culture's ways and values. I admire him for that, although I cannot say that I subscribe to or endorse some of these values. By contrast, Kaobawä is older and wiser, a polished diplomat. He sees his own culture in a slightly different light and seems even to question aspects of it. Thus, while many of his peers enthusiastically accept the 'explanations' of things given in myths, he occasionally reflects on them—even laughing at some of the most preposterous of them.... Probably more of the Yanomamö are like Rerebawä than like Kaobawä , or at least try to be....

# NOTES

1. The word Yanomamö is nasalized through its entire length, indicated by the diacritical mark ','. When this mark appears on any Yanomamö word, the whole word is nasalized. The vowel 'ö' represents a sound that does not occur in the English language. It is similar to the umlaut 'ö' in the German language or the 'oe' equivalent, as in the poet Goethe's name. Unfortunately, many presses and typesetters simply eliminate diacritical marks, and this has led to multiple spellings of the word Yanomamö—and multiple mispronunciations. Some anthropologists have chosen to introduce a slightly different spelling of the word Yanomamö since I began writing about them, such as Yanomami, leading to additional misspellings as their diacriticals are characteristically eliminated by presses, and to the *incorrect* pronunciation 'Yanomameee.' Vowels indicated as 'ä' are pronounced as the 'uh' sound in the word 'duck'. Thus, the name Kaobawä would be pronounced 'cow-ba-wuh,' but entirely nasalized.

2. I spent a total of 60 months among the Yanomamö between 1964 and 1991. The first edition of this case study was based on the first 15 months I spent among them in Venezuela. I have, at the time of this writing, made 20 field trips to the Yanomamö and this edition reflects the new information and understandings I have acquired over the years. I plan to return regularly to continue what has now turned into a lifelong study.

3. See Spindler (1970) for a general discussion of field research by anthropologists who have worked in other cultures. Nancy How-

ell has recently written a very useful book (1990) on some of the medical, personal, and environmental hazards of doing field research, which includes a selected bibliography on other fieldwork programs.

4. They could not pronounce "Chagnon." It sounded to them like their name for a pesky bee, shaki, and that is what they called me: pesky, noisome bee.

5. The Yąnomamö in this region acquired canoes very recently. The missionaries would purchase them from the Ye'kwana Indians to the north for money, and then trade them to the Yąnomamö in exchange for labor, produce, or 'informant' work in translating. It should be emphasized that those Yąnomamö who lived on navigable portions of the Upper Orinoco River moved there recently from the deep forest in order to have contact with the missionaries and acquire the trade goods the missionaries (and their supply system) brought.

6. Rarely were there actual brothers or sisters. In Yąnomamö kinship classifications, certain kinds of cousins are classified as siblings. See Chapter 4.

7. Over time, as I became more and more 'accepted' by the Yą nomamö, they became less and less concerned about my genealogical inquiries and now, provide me with this information quite willingly because I have been very discrete with it. Now, when I revisit familiar villages I am called aside by someone who whispers to me things like, "Don't ask about so-and-so's father."

# Lessons from the Field

George Gmelch

Sara, Eric, and Kristen heave their backpacks and suitcases—all the gear they'll need for the next ten weeks—into the back of the Institute's battered Toyota pick-up. Sara, a tense grin on her face, gets up front with me, the others climb in the back and try to make themselves comfortable on the luggage.

Leaving Bellairs Research Institute on the west coast of Barbados, we drive north past the island's posh resorts. Their names—Cobblers Cove, Coral Reef Club, Coconut Creek, and Glitter Bay—evoke images of tropical paradise. The scene changes abruptly once we leave the coast and move from tourism to agriculture. Here amid the green and quiet of rolling sugar cane fields, there are no more white faces. Graceful cabbage palms flank a large plantation house, one of the island's former "great houses." On the edge of its cane fields is a tenantry, a cluster of small board houses whose inhabitants are the descendants of the slaves who once worked on the plantation.

Two monkeys emerge from a gully and cross the road. I tell Sara that they came to Barbados aboard slave ships 300 years ago, but she is absorbed in her own thoughts and doesn't seem to hear me. I've taken enough students to the field to have an idea of what's on her mind. What will her village be like—the one we just passed through looked unusually poor. Will the family she is going to live with like her? Will she like them? Will she be up to the challenge? Many people are walking along the road; clusters of men sit outside a rum shop shouting loudly while slamming dominoes on a wobbly plywood table.

Earlier in the day, Eric told me that many of the ten students on the field program thought they had made a mistake coming to Barbados. If they had chosen to go on the term abroad to Greece or England or even Japan, they mused, they would be together on a campus, among friends. They wouldn't have to live in a village. They wouldn't have to go out and meet people and try to make friends with all these strangers. To do it all alone now seemed more of a challenge than many wanted.

We continue driving toward the northeastern corner of the island to the village of Pie Corner, where Sara will live. Several miles out we can see huge swells rolling in off the Atlantic, beating against the cliffs. This is the unsheltered side of the island. The village only has a few hundred people but six churches. Marcus Hinds and his family all come out to the truck to welcome Sara. Mrs. Hinds gives her a big hug, as though she were a returning relative, and daughter Yvette takes her into the yard to show her the pigs and chickens, and then on a tour of the small house. The bedroom is smaller than Sara imagined, barely larger than the bed. She puzzles over where to put all her stuff, while I explain to the Hinds, again, the nature of the program. Sara, I tell them, will be spending most of her time in the village talking to people and participating as much as possible in the life of the community, everything from attending church to cutting sugar cane. My description doesn't fit their conception of what a university education is all about. The everyday lives of people in their community are probably not something they think worthy of a university student's attention.

Back in the truck Eric and Kristen ask me anxiously how their villages compare to Sara's. Kristen begins to bite her nails.

■

For twenty years I have been taking students to the field with my colleague and wife, Sharon Gmelch, and we have acquired a great deal of knowledge about what students have learned from the foreign cultures in which they live. But it wasn't until serving on a committee that was evaluating my college's international study programs, that I ever thought much about what my students learned about their own culture by living in another. The belief that you have to live abroad before you can truly understand your own culture has gained wide acceptance on college campuses today. But what exactly is it students learn?

I questioned other anthropologists who also took students to the field and they too were unclear about its lessons. A search through the literature didn't help. All the research on the educational outcomes of foreign study had been on students who study at universities abroad, not in more immersive, anthropology field schools.

My curiosity aroused, I decided to examine the experiences of our students in Barbados. Through a questionnaire, interviews, and analysis of their field notes and journals, I looked at their adjustment to Bajan village life and what they learned about themselves and their culture by living on a Caribbean island.

## Rural Life

Living in a Barbadian village brings many lessons in the differences between rural and urban. About 90% of our students come from suburbs or cities and have never lived in the countryside before. For them a significant part of their experience in Barbados is living with people who are close to the land. Their host families, like most villagers, grow crops and raise animals. Each morning, before dawn, the students wake to the sounds of animals in the yard. They quickly begin to learn about the behavior of chickens, pigs, sheep, and cows. They witness animals giving birth and being slaughtered. They see the satisfaction families get from consuming food they have produced themselves.

Even inside their village homes the students live close to "nature." They may share their bedrooms with green lizards, mice, cockroaches, and sometimes a whistling frog. They become aware of how different are the sounds of the countryside, and they are struck by the darkness of the sky and the brightness of the stars at night with no city lights to diminish their intensity. A student from Long Island said it was "like living in a planetarium."

The social world of the village is quite unlike the communities they come from. In doing a household survey, they discover that people know virtually everyone in the village. And they often know them in more than one context, not just as neighbors but perhaps also as members of the same church, and as teammates on the village cricket or soccer team. Relationships are not single-stranded as they often are in suburban America.

Most students have never known a place of such intimacy, where relationships are also embedded with so many different meanings and a shared history. In their journals, some students reflect upon and compare the warmth, friendliness, and frequent sharing of food and other resources that occurs in the village with the impersonality, individualism, and detachment of suburban life at home. But they also learn the drawbacks to living in a small community: there is no anonymity. People are nosy and unduly interested in the affairs of their neighbors. The students discover that they too may be the object of local gossip. Several female students learned from village friends that there were stories afoot that they were either mistresses to their host fathers or sleeping with their host brothers. The gossip hurt, for the students, like any anthropologist, had worked hard to gain acceptance and worried about the damage such rumors might do to their reputations.

One of the biggest adjustments students must make to village life is the absence of the diversions and entertainment that they are accustomed to at home. Early in their stay there seems little to do apart from their research. At times they are bored, lonely and desperate to escape the village, but they are not allowed to leave except on designated days. (All students initially hate this restriction, but by the end of the term they understand the rationale behind it.) This isolation forces students to satisfy their needs for recreation and companionship within their communities which they do by hanging out with the villagers, a practice which strengthens friendships and results in a good deal of informal education about Bajan life and culture.

## Pace of Life

Students discover that the pace of life is slower than home. Much slower. As her host mother explained to Sara, "There are only two speeds in Barbados: slow and dead stop." Languor is an accommodation to the hot, tropical climate. But also, compared to Americans, Bajans are in less of a hurry to get things done. At the shop or post office in town customers wait to be served until the clerk finishes chatting with others. Bajans think

little of being late for appointments. Accustomed to the punctuality and hectic pace of North American life, our students are often impatient and frustrated. But as they socialize more with village friends, their compulsive haste begins to dissipate. They sense a different time, one that is unhurried and attuned to the place. They begin to see things they didn't notice before, the bit of earth they're sitting on, the cane fields, the blue sky, and the palm trees. As the term passes, students come to value this unhurried way of life, and by the time they leave the island most are determined to maintain a more tranquil, relaxed lifestyle when they return home.

## Race

In Barbados our students become members of a racial minority for the first time in their lives. During their first few weeks in the field they become acutely aware of their own "race," of their being white while everyone around them is dark. Students are often called "white girl" or "white boy" by people in the village until they get to know one another. Village children have sometimes asked to touch a student's skin, marveling at the blue veins which show through it. They sometimes ask students with freckles if they have a skin disease. Others want to feel straight hair. Characteristically, one student during the second week wrote:

> I have never been in a situation before where I was a minority purely due to the color of my skin, and treated differently because of it. When I approach people I am very conscious of having white skin. Before I never thought of myself as having color.

The students are surprised that Barbadians speak so openly about racial difference, something which is not done at home in the United States. A few students become hypersensitive to race during the early weeks of their stay. When leaving their villages, they travel on a crowded bus on which they are the only whites. Often they are stared at (as the bus heads into the countryside, the passengers may worry that the student has missed his or her stop or has taken the wrong bus). Students notice that as the bus fills up, the seat next to them is often the last to be taken.

Concerns about race, even the very awareness of race, diminish rapidly, however, as the students make friends and become integrated into their villages. In fact, by the end of the term most said they were "rarely" aware of being white. Several students described incidents in which they had become so unaware of skin color that they were shocked when someone made a remark or did something to remind them of their being different. Kristen was startled when, after shaking her hand, an old woman from her village remarked that she had never touched the hand of a white person before. Several students reported being surprised when they walked by a mirror and got a glimpse of their white skin. One student wrote that although she knew she wasn't black, she no longer felt white.

What is the outcome of all this? Do students now have an understanding of what it means to be a minority, and does this translate into their having more empathy at home? I think so. All the students from the previous Barbados programs whom I questioned about the impact of their experiences mentioned a heightened empathy for African-Americans, and some included other minorities as well. Several said that when they first returned home, they wanted to go up to any black person they saw and have a conversation. "But I kept having to remind myself," reported Megan when I saw her on campus later, "that most blacks in America are not West Indians and they wouldn't understand where I am coming from."

## Gender

Female students quickly learn that gender relations are quite different in Barbados. Often, the most difficult adjustment for women students is learning how to deal with the frequent and aggressive advances of Bajan men. At the end of her first week in the field, Jenny described a plight common to the students:

> When I walk through the village, the guys who hang out at the rum shop yell comments. I have never heard men say some of the things they tell me here. My friend Andrew tells me that most of the comments are actually compliments. Yet I still feel weird ... I am merely an object that they would like to conquer. I hate that feeling, so I am trying to get to know these guys. I figure that if they know me as a person and a friend, they will stop with the demeaning comments. Maybe it's a cultural thing they do to all women.

Indeed, many Bajan men feel it is their right as males to accost women in public with hissing, appreciative remarks, and offers of sex. This sexual bantering is tolerated by Bajan women who generally ignore the men's comments. Most women consider it harmless, if annoying; some think it flattering. Students like Jenny, however, are not sure what to make of it. They do not know whether it is being directed at them because local men think white girls are "loose" or whether Bajan men behave in this fashion towards all women. Anxious to be accepted and not wanting to be rude or culturally insensitive, most female students tolerate the remarks the best they can, while searching for a strategy to politely discourage them. Most find that as people get to know them by name, the verbal harassment subsides.

But they still must get accustomed to other sexual behavior. For example, when invited to their first neighborhood parties most are shocked at the sexually explicit dancing, in which movements imitate intercourse. One female student wrote, after having been to several *fetes* or parties:

> I was watching everyone dance when I realized that even the way we dance says a lot about culture. We are so conservative at home. Inhibited. In the U.S. one's body is a personal, private thing, and when it is invaded we get angry. We might give a boyfriend some degree of control over our bodies, but no one else. Bajans aren't nearly as possessive about their bodies. Men and women can freely move from one dance partner to the next without asking, and then grind the other person—it's like having sex with your clothes on.

Students discover that even more than in the U.S., women are regarded by men as both subordinates and sexual objects. Masculinity is largely based on men's sexual conquest of women and on their ability to give them pleasure. Being sexually active, a good sex partner, and becoming a father, all enhance young men's status among their male peers. As time passes, the students see male dominance in other areas of Barbadian life as well: that women earn less than men, are more likely to be unemployed, and are less likely to attain political office, all despite their doing better and going further in school. They conclude that though U.S. society is sexist, Barbados is far more so.

## Materialism and Consumption

Many students arrive at a new awareness of wealth and materialism. One of the strongest initial perceptions the students have of their villages is that the people are poor: most of their houses are tiny, their diets are restricted, and they have few of the amenities and comforts the students are accustomed to. Even little things may remind them of the difference in wealth, as Betsy recounted after her first week in the field:

> At home [Vermont] when I go into a convenience store and buy a soda, I don't think twice about handing the clerk a 20 dollar bill. But here when you hand a man in the rum shop a 20 dollar bill [equals $10 USD], they often ask if you have something smaller. It makes me self conscious of how wealthy I appear, and of how little money the rum shop man makes in a day.

The initial response of the students to the poverty they perceive around them is to feel embarrassed and even guilty that they have and consume so much. However as the students get to know families better, they no longer see poverty. Even the houses no longer seem so small. They discover that most people not only manage quite well on what they have but are also reasonably content. In fact, most students eventually come to believe that the villagers are more satisfied with their lives than are most Americans. Whether or not this is true, it's an important perception for students, whose ideas about happiness have been shaped by an ethos which measures success and satisfaction materially. About his host family, Dan said:

> I ate off the same plate and drank from the same cup every night. We only had an old fridge, an old stove, and an old TV, and a few dishes and pots and pans. But that was plenty. Mrs. H. never felt like she needed any more. And after awhile I never felt like I needed any more either.

Ellen recounted her reactions to a car that her host father had just purchased.

> He was thrilled, talking about how great this car was. When he pulled up in a used Toyota Corolla, I laughed to myself. It was the exact same car that I had just bought at home, the only car that a poor student could afford, and by American standards certainly nothing

flashy. But to my host father it was top of the line, and he was ecstatic. To me it was a reminder that everything is relative…

Many said that when they returned home from Barbados they were surprised at the number of their possessions. Compared to Barbadians, their middle-class parents' lifestyle seemed incredibly extravagant and wasteful. When the students return to campus they don't bring nearly as many things with them as they had before. Some go through their drawers and closets and give the things they don't really need to the Good Will or Salvation Army. Most said they would no longer take luxuries like hot showers for granted. Amy wrote:

> When I came back I saw how out of control the students here are. It's just crazy. They want so much, they talk about how much money they need to make, as if these things are necessities and you'll never be happy without them. Maybe I was like that too, but now I know I don't need those things; sure I'd like a great car, but I don't need it.

When alumni of the program were asked in a survey how they had been changed by their experience in Barbados, most believed they were less materialistic today. For example, Susan said, "I remember bringing some perfume to Barbados because I was used to wearing it every day. But when I got there I only wore it once, it just seemed unnecessary, and I haven't really worn perfume since. Even now, ten years later, I don't mind wearing the same clothes often. I just think Barbados taught me how to find comfort in simple things."

# Social Class

American students, particularly compared to their European counterparts, have little understanding of social class. Even after several weeks in Barbados, most students are fairly oblivious to class and status distinctions in their villages. The U.S. suburbs that most grow up in are fairly homogenous in social composition and housing. Most homes fall in the same general price range. In contrast, the Barbadian villages the students live in exhibit a broad spectrum, ranging from large two-story masonry homes usually built by returning migrants to tiny board houses owned by farmers who eke out a living from a few acres. The students are slow to translate such differences in the material conditions of village households into class differences. Also, Barbadians' well-developed class consciousness, fostered by three centuries of British rule, is foreign to U.S. students steeped in a culture that stresses, at least in its rhetoric, egalitarianism.

Students gradually become aware of status distinctions from the comments that their host families make about other people. But they also learn about class and status by making mistakes, by violating norms concerning relationships between different categories of people. After Kristen walked home through the village carrying a bundle on her head, she learned that there are different standards of behavior for the more affluent families. "Mrs C. told me never to do that again, that only poor people

carry things on their heads, and that my doing it reflected badly on her family."

As in most field situations, the first villagers to offer the student friendship are sometimes marginal members of the community and this creates special problems because the students are usually guests in the homes of respectable and often high-status village families. Host parents become upset when they discover their student has been seeing a disreputable man or woman. Most serious is the occasional female student who goes out with a lower-class local man or "beach boy." She enters into this relationship oblivious to what the local reaction might be, and equally oblivious to how little privacy there is in a village where everyone knows everyone else's business. Amy said she wrongly assumed that people would look favorably upon her going out with a local guy because it would show that she wasn't prejudiced and that she found Blacks just as desirable as whites. Johanna was befriended by some Rastafarians living nearby—orthodox Rastas who wore no clothes, lived off the land, and slept in caves in the hills above her village. When villagers discovered she had been seeing the Rastas, her home stay mother nearly evicted her and others gave her the cold shoulder. Johanna wrote in her field notes, "I have discovered the power of a societal norm: nice girls don't talk to Rastas. When girls who were formerly nice talk to Rastas, they cease to be known as nice. Exceptions none."

# New Perspectives on Being American

In learning about Barbadian society, students inevitably compare Barbadian customs to the way things are done at home in the U.S.. The students are often assisted in such comparisons by villagers who are curious and ask questions. Most villagers already have opinions about the U.S., mostly formed from watching American television and movies, from observing visiting tourists and, for some, from their own travel. The students are surprised at how much Bajans, even the lesser educated, know about the U.S. They discover, however, that the villagers' perspectives are often at odds with their own. Jay put it best: "They have a love/hate attitude towards the U.S. They think of the U.S. as a great place to shop, and that we have good movies and good fashion. But, they also think we are dumb, too talkative, too full of ourselves, too patriotic, and that our government is dangerous." Indeed, most students learn that Bajans like the open friendliness and sunny optimism of individual Americans, and they admire the economic opportunities and freedoms the society affords. But they also think middle class Americans are pampered and overly materialistic. Bajans are puzzled about why such a wealthy nation has so many people living in poverty and in prisons, and why, unlike poor Caribbean islands, there is not good health care for everyone. They also don't think black people get a fair shake in America.

Early in the term, students often find themselves defending the United States from criticism and stereotypes. Jay described in his journal getting very annoyed when a guest at his host family's dinner table railed against the U.S. and talked about the chemical adulteration of American chicken. He knew this to be true, but later he said, "I couldn't take it anymore and fought back. I felt like an idiot afterward, defending American chicken."

Over time the students become less defensive, and more sympathetic to the criticisms, particularly to the notion of Americans as pampered and wastefully materialistic, and that the U.S. government is somewhat of an international bully. What makes our students question their own society after a few months in Barbados? Part of the answer is found in their growing appreciation of Bajan life and local people. They begin to see things from the perspective of their village friends. They begin to understand the degree to which American culture, especially its media, music, entertainment, and consumer goods, overwhelms local cultures. They see that many Bajans, for example, know more about the American President than their own Governor General or Prime Minister, and that they know Tiger Woods and Kobe Bryant better than their own cricket stars. Some students become quite critical of the U.S. government, especially its often unilateral and self-interested policies, as when it refused to sign international treaties on global warming, on land mines, and on a World Criminal Court.

The students' exposure to North Americans vacationing in Barbados also influences their perceptions of themselves as Americans. When they go to the beach or town they often encounter tourists and are reminded of villagers' criticisms. They are sometimes embarrassed by what they see and hear—Americans who are loud, demanding, and even condescending, in their dealings with locals. Some tourists (though not just Americans) enter shops and walk the streets in skimpy beach attire never thinking that it may be offensive to local people. Students are appalled that tourists can come all the way to Barbados to vacation and hardly know anything about the place or its people. They are irritated that many tourists only view Barbados as a playground—a place to lounge on the beach, swim, snorkel, dive, sail, dance, and drink—and have little curiosity about its geography, history of colonization and slavery, or current underdevelopment. They are horrified when they themselves are mistaken for tourists, since they take pride in their knowledge of local culture. One outcome of this, say the alumni of the field programs, is that when they travel today they believe they are more curious and sensitive than other tourists. Some even try to pass themselves off as Canadian.

# Education

Most students return home from Barbados with a more positive attitude towards education. I believe this stems both from their experiences in doing research and from seeing the high value that villagers place on formal education, which is their chief means of upward mobility. Students are accorded respect and adult status largely because they are working toward a university degree. Also, as the weeks pass, most students become deeply involved in their own research. They are surprised at how much satisfaction they get from doing something that they previously regarded as "work." Students from past terms have said they didn't see education as an end in itself, something to be enjoyed, until doing fieldwork in Barbados. Emily wrote about her attitude change after returning from the field:

> I feel isolated from many of my old friends on campus, and I no longer feel guilty missing social events … I appreciate my education more and I do much more work for my own understanding and enjoyment rather than just for the exam or grades. I find myself on a daily basis growing agitated with those who don't appreciate what is being offered to them here. Several of my classmates blow off class and use other peoples' notes. A lot of what I feel is from seeing how important education was to my Bajan friends in Barbados compared to the lax attitude of my friends here.

Students spend much of their time in the field talking to people; a good part of each day is spent in conversations which they must direct onto the topics that they are investigating. To succeed at their studies, they learn to be inquisitive, to probe sensitively into the villager's knowledge of events and culture. They learn to concentrate, to listen to what they are being told, and later to recall it so that they can record it in field notes. They become proficient at maintaining lengthy conversations with adults and at asking pertinent questions. These are interpersonal and communication skills they bring back with them and make use of in many aspects of their own lives, and in their future work.

Clearly, getting to know another culture is to look in the proverbial mirror and get a glimpse of oneself and of what it means to be American. As the world's economies intertwine and its societies move closer to becoming a "global village," it is more imperative than ever that we seek to understand other peoples and cultures. Without understanding there can be neither respect, mutual prosperity, nor lasting peace. "The tragedy about Americans," noted Mexican novelist Carlos Fuentes, "is that they understand others so little." Students who study abroad not only enrich themselves but in countless small ways help bridge the gulf between "them" and "us."

# Eating Christmas in the Kalahari

RICHARD BORSHAY LEE

The !Kung Bushmen's knowledge of Christmas is third-hand. The London Missionary Society brought the holiday to the southern Tswana tribes in the early nineteenth century. Later, native catechists spread the idea far and wide among the Bantu-speaking pastoralists, even in the remotest corners of the Kalahari Desert. The Bushmen's idea of the Christmas story, stripped to its essentials, is "praise the birth of white man's god-chief"; what keeps their interest in the holiday high is the Tswana-Herero custom of slaughtering an ox for his Bushmen neighbors as an annual goodwill gesture. Since the 1930's, part of the Bushmen's annual round of activities has included a December congregation at the cattle posts for trading, marriage brokering, and several days of trance-dance feasting at which the local Tswana headman is host.

As a social anthropologist working with !Kung Bushmen, I found that the Christmas ox custom suited my purposes. I had come to the Kalahari to study the hunting and gathering subsistence economy of the !Kung, and to accomplish this it was essential not to provide them with food, share my own food, or interfere in any way with their food-gathering activities. While liberal handouts of tobacco and medical supplies were appreciated, they were scarcely adequate to erase the glaring disparity in wealth between the anthropologist, who maintained a two-month inventory of canned goods, and the Bushmen, who rarely had a day's supply of food on hand. My approach, while paying off in terms of data, left me open to frequent accusations of stinginess and hard-heartedness. By their lights, I was a miser.

The Christmas ox was to be my way of saying thank you for the cooperation of the past year; and since it was to be our last Christmas in the field, I determined to slaughter the largest, meatiest ox that money could buy, insuring that the feast and trance-dance would be a success.

Through December I kept my eyes open at the wells as the cattle were brought down for watering. Several animals were offered, but none had quite the grossness that I had in mind. Then, ten days before the holiday, a Herero friend led an ox of astonishing size and mass up to our camp. It was solid black, stood five feet high at the shoulder, had a five-foot span of horns, and must have weighed 1,200 pounds on the hoof. Food consumption calculations are my specialty, and I quickly figured that bones and viscera aside, there was enough meat—at least four pounds—for every man, woman, and child of the 150 Bushmen in the vicinity of /ai/ai who were expected at the feast.

Having found the right animal at last, I paid the Herero £20 ($56) and asked him to keep the beast with his herd until Christmas day. The next morning word spread among the people that the big solid black one was the ox chosen by /ontah (my Bushman name; it means, roughly, "whitey") for the Christmas feast. That afternoon I received the first delegation. Ben!a, an outspoken sixty-year-old mother of five, came to the point slowly.

"Where were you planning to eat Christmas?"

"Right here at /ai/ai," I replied.

"Alone or with others?"

"I expect to invite all the people to eat Christmas with me."

"Eat what?"

"I have purchased Yehave's black ox, and I am going to slaughter and cook it."

"That's what we were told at the well but refused to believe it until we heard it from yourself."

"Well, it's the black one," I replied expansively, although wondering what she was driving at.

"Oh, no!" Ben!a groaned, turning to her group. "They were right." Turning back to me she asked, "Do you expect us to eat that bag of bones?"

"Bag of bones! It's the biggest ox at /ai/ai."

"Big, yes, but old. And thin. Everybody knows there's no meat on that old ox. What did you expect us to eat off it, the horns?"

Everybody chuckled at Ben!a's one-liner as they walked away, but all I could manage was a weak grin.

That evening it was the turn of the young men. They came to sit at our evening fire. /gaugo, about my age, spoke to me man-to-man.

"/ontah, you have always been square with us," he lied. "What has happened to change your heart? That sack of guts and bones of Yehave's will hardly feed one camp, let alone all the Bushmen around ai/ai." And he proceeded to enumerate the seven camps in the /ai/ai vicinity, family by family. "Perhaps you have forgotten that we are not few, but many. Or are you too blind to tell the difference between a proper cow and an old wreck? That ox is thin to the point of death."

"Look, you guys," I retorted, "that is a beautiful animal, and I'm sure you will eat it with pleasure at Christmas."

"Of course we will eat it; it's food. But it won't fill us up to the point where we will have enough strength to dance. We will eat and go home to bed with stomachs rumbling."

That night as we turned in, I asked my wife, Nancy: "What did you think of the black ox?"

"It looked enormous to me. Why?"

"Well, about eight different people have told me I got gypped; that the ox is nothing but bones."

"What's the angle?" Nancy asked. "Did they have a better one to sell?"

"No, they just said that it was going to be a grim Christmas because there won't be enough meat to go around. Maybe I'll get an independent judge to look at the beast in the morning."

Bright and early, Halingisi, a Tswana cattle owner, appeared at our camp. But before I could ask him to give me his opinion on Yehave's black ox, he gave me the eye signal that indicated a confidential chat. We left the camp and sat down.

"/ontah, I'm surprised at you: you've lived here for three years and still haven't learned anything about cattle."

"But what else can a person do but choose the biggest, strongest animal one can find?" I retorted.

"Look, just because an animal is big doesn't mean that it has plenty of meat on it. The black one was a beauty when it was younger, but now it is thin to the point of death."

"Well I've already bought it. What can I do at this stage?"

"Bought it already? I thought you were just considering it. Well, you'll have to kill it and serve it, I suppose. But don't expect much of a dance to follow."

My spirits dropped rapidly. I could believe that Ben!a and /gaugo just might be putting me on about the black ox, but Halingisi seemed to be an impartial critic. I went around that day feeling as though I had bought a lemon of a used car.

In the afternoon it was Tomazo's turn. Tomazo is a fine hunter, a top trance performer… and one of my most reliable informants. He approached the subject of the Christmas cow as part of my continuing Bushman education.

"My friend, the way it is with us Bushmen," he began, "is that we love meat. And even more than that, we love fat. When we hunt we always search for the fat ones, the ones dripping with layers of white fat: fat that turns into a clear, thick oil in the cooking pot, fat that slides down your gullet, fills your stomach and gives you a roaring diarrhea," he rhapsodized.

"So, feeling as we do," he continued, "it gives us pain to be served such a scrawny thing as Yehave's black ox. It is big, yes, and no doubt its giant bones are good for soup, but fat is what we really crave and so we will eat Christmas this year with a heavy heart."

The prospect of a gloomy Christmas now had me worried, so I asked Tomazo what I could do about it.

"Look for a fat one, a young one… smaller, but fat. Fat enough to make us //gom ('evacuate the bowels'), then we will be happy."

My suspicions were aroused when Tomazo said that he happened to know of a young, fat, barren cow that the owner was willing to part with. Was Tomazo working on commission, I wondered? But I dispelled this unworthy thought when we approached the Herero owner of the cow in question and found that he had decided not to sell.

The scrawny wreck of a Christmas ox now became the talk of the /ai/ai water hole and was the first news told to the outlying groups as they began to come in from the bush for the feast. What finally convinced me that real trouble might be brewing was the visit from u!au, an old conservative with a reputation for fierceness. His nickname meant spear and referred to an incident thirty years ago in which he had speared a man to death. He had an intense manner; fixing me with his eyes, he said in clipped tones:

"I have only just heard about the black ox today, or else I would have come here earlier. /ontah, do you honestly think you can serve meat like that to people and avoid a fight?" He paused, letting the implications sink in. "I don't mean fight you, /ontah; you are a white man. I mean a fight between Bushmen. There are many fierce ones here, and with such a small quantity of meat to distribute, how can you give everybody a fair share? Someone is sure to accuse another of taking too much or hogging all the choice pieces. Then you will see what happens when some go hungry while others eat."

The possibility of at least a serious argument struck me as all too real. I had witnessed the tension that surrounds the distribution of meat from a kudu or gemsbok kill, and had documented many arguments that sprang up from a real or imagined slight in meat distribution. The owners of a kill may spend up to two hours arranging and rearranging the piles of meat under the gaze of a circle of recipients before handing them out. And I also knew that the Christmas feast at /ai/ai would be bringing together groups that had feuded in the past.

Convinced now of the gravity of the situation, I went in earnest to search for a second cow; but all my inquiries failed to turn one up.

The Christmas feast was evidently going to be a disaster, and the incessant complaints about the meagerness of the ox had already taken the fun out of it for me. Moreover, I was getting bored with the wisecracks, and after losing my temper a few times, I resolved to serve the beast anyway. If the meat fell short, the hell with it. In the Bushmen idiom, I announced to all who would listen:

"I am a poor man and blind. If I have chosen one that is too old and too thin, we will eat it anyway and see if there is enough meat there to quiet the rumbling of our stomachs."

On hearing this speech, Ben!a offered me a rare word of comfort. "It's thin," she said philosophically, "but the bones will make a good soup."

At dawn Christmas morning, instinct told me to turn over the butchering and cooking to a friend and take off with Nancy to spend Christmas alone in the bush. But curiosity kept me from retreating. I wanted to see what such a scrawny ox looked like on butchering and if there *was* going to be a fight, I wanted to catch every word of it. Anthropologists are incurable that way.

The great beast was driven up to our dancing ground, and a shot in the forehead dropped it in its tracks. Then, freshly cut branches were heaped around the fallen carcass to receive the meat. Ten men volunteered to help with the cutting. I asked /gaugo to make the breast bone cut. This cut, which begins the butchering process for most large game, offers easy access for removal of the viscera. But it also allows the hunter to spot-check the amount of fat on the animal. A fat game animal carries a white layer up to an inch thick on the chest, while in a thin one, the knife will quickly cut to bone. All eyes fixed on his hand as /gaugo, dwarfed by the great carcass, knelt to the breast. The first cut opened a pool of solid white in the black skin. The second and third cut widened and deepened the creamy white. Still no bone. It was pure fat; it must have been two inches thick.

"Hey /gau," I burst out, "that ox is loaded with fat. What's this about the ox being too thin to bother eating? Are you out of your mind?"

"Fat?" /gau shot back, "You call that fat? This wreck is thin, sick, dead!" And he broke out laughing. So did everyone else. They rolled on the ground, paralyzed with laughter. Everybody laughed except me; I was thinking.

I ran back to the tent and burst in just as Nancy was getting up. "Hey, the black ox. It's fat as hell! They were kidding about it being too thin to eat. It was a joke or something. A put-on. Everyone is really delighted with it!"

"Some joke," my wife replied. "It was so funny that you were ready to pack up and leave /ai/ai."

If it had indeed been a joke, it had been an extraordinarily convincing one, and tinged, I thought, with more than a touch of malice as many jokes are. Nevertheless, that it was a joke lifted my spirits considerably, and I returned to the butchering site where the shape of the ox was rapidly disappearing under the axes and knives of the butchers. The atmosphere had become festive. Grinning broadly, their arms covered with blood well past the elbow, men packed chunks of meat into the big cast-iron cooking pots, fifty pounds to the load, and muttered and chuckled all the while about the thinness and worthlessness of the animal and /ontah's poor judgment.

We danced and ate that ox two days and two nights; we cooked and distributed fourteen potfuls of meat and no one went home hungry and no fights broke out.

But the "joke" stayed in my mind. I had a growing feeling that something important had happened in my relationship with the Bushmen and that the clue lay in the meaning of the joke. Several days later, when most of the people had dispersed back to the bush camps, I raised the question with Hakekgose, a Tswana man who had grown up among the !Kung, married a !Kung girl, and who probably knew their culture better than any other non-Bushman.

"With us whites," I began, "Christmas is supposed to be the day of friendship and brotherly love. What I can't figure out is why the Bushmen went to such lengths to criticize and belittle the ox I had bought for the feast. The animal was perfectly good and their jokes and wisecracks practically ruined the holiday for me."

"So it really did bother you," said Hakekgose. "Well, that's the way they always talk. When I take my rifle and go hunting with them, if I miss, they laugh at me for the rest of the day. But even if I hit and bring one down, it's no better. To them, the kill is always too small or too old or too thin; and as we sit down on the kill site to cook and eat the liver, they keep grumbling, even with their mouths full of meat. They say things like, 'Oh this is awful! What a worthless animal! Whatever made me think that this Tswana rascal could hunt!'"

"Is this the way outsiders are treated?" I asked.

"No, it is their custom; they talk that way to each other too. Go and ask them."

/gaugo had been one of the most enthusiastic in making me feel bad about the merit of the Christmas ox. I sought him out first.

"Why did you tell me the black ox was worthless, when you could see that it was loaded with fat and meat?"

"It is our way," he said smiling. "We always like to fool people about that. Say there is a Bushman who has been hunting. He must not come home and announce like a braggard, 'I have killed a big one in the bush!' He must first sit down in silence until I or someone else comes up to his fire and asks, 'What did you see today?' He replies quietly, 'Ah, I'm no good for hunting. I saw nothing at all [pause] just a little tiny one.' Then I smile to myself," /gaugo continued, "because I know he has killed something big."

"In the morning we make up a party of four or five people to cut up and carry the meat back to the camp. When we arrive at the kill we examine it and cry out, 'You mean to say you have dragged us all the way out here in order to make us cart home your pile of bones? Oh, if I had known it was this thin I wouldn't have come.' Another one pipes up, 'People, to think I gave up a nice day in the shade for this. At home we may be hungry but at least we have nice cool water to drink.' If the horns are big, someone says, 'Did you think that somehow you were going to boil down the horns for soup?'"

"To all this you must respond in kind. 'I agree,' you say, 'this one is not worth the effort; let's just cook the liver for strength and leave the rest for the hyenas. It is not too late to hunt today and even a duiker or a steenbok would be better than this mess.'"

"Then you set to work nevertheless; butcher the animal, carry the meat back to the camp and everyone eats," /gaugo concluded.

Things were beginning to make sense. Next, I went to Tomazo. He corroborated /gaugo's story of the obligatory insults over a kill and added a few details of his own.

"But," I asked, "why insult a man after he has gone to all that trouble to track and kill an animal and when he is going to share the meat with you so that your children will have something to eat?"

"Arrogance," was his cryptic answer.

"Arrogance?"

"Yes, when a young man kills much meat he comes to think of himself as a chief or a big man, and he thinks of the rest of us as his servants or inferiors. We can't accept this. We refuse one who boasts, for someday his pride will make him kill somebody. So we always speak of his meat as worthless. This way we cool his heart and make him gentle."

"But why didn't you tell me this before?" I asked Tomazo with some heat.

"Because you never asked me," said Tomazo, echoing the refrain that has come to haunt every field ethnographer.

The pieces now fell into place. I had known for a long time that in situations of social conflict with Bushmen I held all the cards. I was the only source of tobacco in a thousand square miles, and I was not incapable of cutting an individual off for non-cooperation. Though my boycott never lasted longer than a few days, it was an indication of my strength. People resented my presence at the water hole, yet simultaneously dreaded my leaving. In short I was a perfect target for the charge of arrogance and for the Bushmen tactic of enforcing humility.

I had been taught an object lesson by the Bushmen; it had come from an unexpected corner and had hurt me in a vulnerable area. For the big black ox was to be the one totally generous, unstinting act of my year at /ai/ai, and I was quite unprepared for the reaction I received.

As I read it, their message was this: There are no totally generous acts. All "acts" have an element of calculation. One black ox slaughtered at Christmas does not wipe out a year of careful manipulation of gifts given to serve your own ends. After all, to kill an animal and share the meat with people is really no more than Bushmen do for each other every day and with far less fanfare.

In the end, I had to admire how the Bushmen had played out the farce—collectively straight-faced to the end. Curiously, the episode reminded me of the *Good Soldier Schweik* and his marvelous encounters with authority. Like Schweik, the Bushmen had retained a thorough-going skepticism of good intentions. Was it this independence of spirit, I wondered, that had kept them culturally viable in the face of generations of contact with more powerful societies, both black and white? The thought that the Bushmen were alive and well in the Kalahari was strangely comforting. Perhaps, armed with that independence and with their superb knowledge of their environment, they might yet survive the future.

**RICHARD BORSHAY LEE** is a full professor of anthropology at the University of Toronto. He has done extensive fieldwork in southern Africa, is coeditor of *Man the Hunter* (1968) and *Kalahari Hunter-Gatherers* (1976), and author of *The !Kung San: Men, Women, and Work in a Foraging Society*.

Reprinted with permission from *Natural History,* December 1969, pp. 14–22, 60–64. © 1969 by Natural History Magazine.

# Tricking and Tripping

## *Fieldwork on Prostitution in the Era of AIDS*

CLAIRE E. STERK

Students often think of anthropological fieldwork as requiring travel to exotic tropical locations, but that is not necessarily the case. This reading is based on fieldwork in the United States—on the streets in New York City as well as Atlanta. Claire Sterk is an anthropologist who works in a school of public health and is primarily interested in issues of women's health, particularly as it relates to sexual behavior. In this selection, an introduction to a recent book by the same title, she describes the basic fieldwork methods she used to study these women and their communities. Like most cultural anthropologists, Sterk's primary goal was to describe "the life" of prostitution from the women's own point of view. To do this, she had to be patient, brave, sympathetic, trustworthy, curious, and nonjudgmental. You will notice these characteristics in this selection; for example, Sterk begins her book with a poem written by one of her informants. Fieldwork is a slow process, because it takes time to win people's confidence and to learn their language and way of seeing the world. In this regard, there are probably few differences between the work of a qualitative sociologist and that of a cultural anthropologist (although anthropologists would not use the term "deviant" to describe another society or a segment of their own society).

Throughout the world, HIV/AIDS is fast becoming a disease found particularly in poor women. Sex workers or prostitutes have often been blamed for AIDS, and they have been further stigmatized because of their profession. In reality, however, entry into prostitution is not a career choice; rather, these women and girls are themselves most often victims of circumstances such as violence and poverty. Public health officials want to know why sex workers do not always protect their health by making men wear condoms. To answer such questions, we must know more about the daily life of these women. The way to do that, the cultural anthropologist would say, is to ask and to listen.

*As you read this selection, ask yourself the following questions:*

- What happens when Sterk says, "I'm sorry for you" to one of her informants? Why?
- Why do you think fieldwork might be a difficult job?
- Do you think that the fact that Sterk grew up in Amsterdam, where prostitution is legal, affected her research?

- Which of the six themes of this work, described at the end of the article, do you think is most important?

*The following terms discussed in this selection are included in the Glossary at the back of the book:*

demography      sample
fieldwork        stroll
key respondent

One night in March of 1987 business was slow. I was hanging out on a stroll with a group of street prostitutes. After a few hours in a nearby diner/coffee shop, we were kicked out. The waitress felt bad, but she needed our table for some new customers. Four of us decided to sit in my car until the rain stopped. While three of us chatted about life, Piper wrote this poem. As soon as she read it to us, the conversation shifted to more serious topics—pimps, customers, cops, the many hassles of being a prostitute, to name a few. We decided that if I ever finished a book about prostitution, the book would start with her poem.

This book is about the women who work in the lower echelons of the prostitution world. They worked in the streets and other public settings as well as crack houses. Some of these women viewed themselves primarily as prostitutes, and a number of them used drugs to cope with the pressures of the life. Others identified themselves more as drug users, and their main reason for having sex for money or other goods was to support their own drug use and often the habit of their male partner. A small group of women interviewed for this book had left prostitution, and most of them were still struggling to integrate their past experiences as prostitutes in their current lives.

The stories told by the women who participated in this project revealed how pimps, customers, and others such as police officers and social and health service providers treated them as "fallen" women. However, their accounts also showed their strengths and the many strategies they developed to challenge these others. Circumstances, including their drug use, often forced them to sell sex, but they all resisted the notion that they might be selling themselves. Because they engaged in an illegal profession, these women had little status: their working conditions were poor, and their work was physically and mentally exhausting. Nevertheless, many women described the ways in which they gained a sense of control over their lives. For instance, they learned how to manipulate pimps, how to control the types of services and length of time bought by their customers, and how to select customers. While none of these schemes explicitly enhanced their working conditions, they did make the women feel stronger and better about themselves.

In this book, I present prostitution from the point of view of the women themselves. To understand their current lives, it was necessary to learn how they got started in the life, the various processes involved in their continued prostitution careers, the link between prostitution and drug use, the women's interactions with their pimps and customers, and the impact of the AIDS epidemic and increasing violence on their experiences. I also examined the implications for women. Although my goal was to present the women's thoughts, feelings, and actions in their own words, the final text is a sociological monograph compiled by me as the researcher. Some women are quoted more than others because I developed a closer relationship with them, because they were more able to verbalize and capture their circumstances, or simply because they were more outspoken.

## The Sample

The data for this book are qualitative. The research was conducted during the last ten years in the New York City and Atlanta metropolitan areas. One main data source was participant observation on streets, in hotels and other settings known for prostitution activity, and in drug-use settings, especially those that allowed sex-for-drug exchanges. Another data source was in-depth, life-history interviews with 180 women ranging in age from 18 to 59 years, with an average age of 34. One in two women was African-American and one in three white; the remaining women were Latina. Three in four had completed high school, and among them almost two-thirds had one or more years of additional educational training. Thirty women had graduated from college.

Forty women worked as street prostitutes and did not use drugs. On average, they had been prostitutes for 11 years. Forty women began using drugs an average of three years after they began working as prostitutes, and the average time they had worked as prostitutes was nine years. Forty women used drugs an average of five years before they became prostitutes, and on the average they had worked as prostitutes for eight years. Another forty women began smoking crack and exchanging sex for crack almost simultaneously, with an average of four years in the life. Twenty women who were interviewed were ex-prostitutes.

## Comments On Methodology

When I tell people about my research, the most frequent question I am asked is how I gained access to the women rather than what I learned from the research. For many, prostitution is an unusual topic of conversation, and many people have expressed surprise that I, as a woman, conducted the research. During my research some customers indeed thought I was a working woman, a fact that almost always amuses those who hear about my work. However, few people want to hear stories about the women's struggles and sadness. Sometimes they ask questions about the reasons why women become prostitutes. Most of the time, they are surprised when I tell them that the prostitutes as well as their customers represent all layers of society. Before presenting the findings, it seems important to discuss the research process, including gaining access to the women, developing relationships, interviewing, and then leaving the field.[2]

## Locating Prostitutes and Gaining Entree

One of the first challenges I faced was to identify locations where street prostitution took place. Many of these women worked on strolls, streets where prostitution activity is concentrated, or in hotels known for prostitution activity. Others, such as the crack prostitutes, worked in less public settings such as a crack house that might be someone's apartment.

I often learned of well-known public places from professional experts, such as law enforcement officials and health care providers at emergency rooms and sexually transmitted disease clinics. I gained other insights from lay experts, including taxi drivers, bartenders, and community representatives such as members of neighborhood associations. The contacts universally mentioned some strolls as the places where many women worked, where the local police focused attention, or where residents had organized protests against prostitution in their neighborhoods.

As I began visiting various locales, I continued to learn about new settings. In one sense, I was developing ethnographic maps of street prostitution. After several visits to a specific area, I also was able to expand these maps by adding information about the general atmosphere on the stroll, general characteristics of the various people present, the ways in which the women and customers connected, and the overall flow of action. In addition, my visits allowed the regular actors to notice me.

I soon learned that being an unknown woman in an area known for prostitution may cause many people to notice you, even stare at you, but it fails to yield many verbal interactions. Most of the time when I tried to make eye contact with one of the women, she quickly averted her eyes. Pimps, on the other hand, would stare at me straight on and I ended up being the one to look away. Customers would stop, blow their horn, or wave me over, frequently yelling obscenities when I ignored them. I realized that gaining entree into the prostitution world was not going to be as easy as I imagined it. Although I lacked such training in any of my qualitative methods classes, I decided to move slowly and not force any interaction. The most I said during the initial weeks in a new area was limited to "how are you" or "hi." This strategy paid off during my first visits to one of the strolls in Brooklyn, New York. After several appearances, one of the women walked up to me and sarcastically asked if I was looking for something. She caught me off guard, and all the answers I had practiced did not seem to make sense. I mumbled something about just wanting to walk around. She did not like my answer, but she did like my accent. We ended up talking about the latter and she was especially excited when I told her I came from Amsterdam. One of her friends had gone to Europe with her boyfriend, who was in the military. She understood from her that prostitution and drugs were legal in the Netherlands. While explaining to her that some of her friend's impressions were incorrect, I was able to show off some of my knowledge about prostitution. I mentioned that I was interested in prostitution and wanted to write a book about it.

Despite the fascination with my background and intentions, the prostitute immediately put me through a Streetwalker 101 test, and apparently I passed. She told me to make sure to come back. By the time I left, I not only had my first conversation but also my first connection to the scene. Variations of this entry process occurred on the other strolls. The main lesson I learned in these early efforts was the importance of having some knowledge of the lives of the people I wanted to study, while at the same time refraining from presenting myself as an expert.

Qualitative researchers often refer to their initial connections as gatekeepers and key respondents. Throughout my fieldwork I learned that some key respondents are important in providing initial access, but they become less central as the research evolves. For example, one of the women who introduced me to her lover, who was also her pimp, was arrested and disappeared for months. Another entered drug treatment soon after she facilitated my access. Other key respondents provided access to only a segment of the players on a scene. For example, if a woman worked for a pimp, [she] was unlikely … to introduce me to women working for another pimp. On one stroll my initial contact was with a pimp whom nobody liked. By associating with him, I almost lost the opportunity to meet other pimps. Some key respondents were less connected than promised—for example, some of the women who worked the street to support their drug habit. Often their connections were more frequently with drug users and less so with prostitutes.

Key respondents tend to be individuals central to the local scene, such as, in this case, pimps and the more senior prostitutes. Their function as gatekeepers often is to protect the scene and to screen outsiders. Many times I had to prove that I was not an undercover police officer or a woman with ambitions to become a streetwalker. While I thought I had gained entree, I quickly learned that many insiders subsequently wondered about my motives and approached me with suspicion and distrust.

Another lesson involved the need to proceed cautiously with self-nominated key respondents. For example, one of the women presented herself as knowing everyone on the stroll. While she did know everyone, she was not a central figure. On the contrary, the other prostitutes viewed her as a failed streetwalker whose drug use caused her to act unprofessionally. By associating with me, she hoped to regain some of her status. For me, however, it meant limited access to the other women because I affiliated myself with a woman who was marginal to the scene. On another occasion, my main key respondent was a man who claimed to own three crack houses in the neighborhood. However, he had a negative reputation, and people accused him of cheating on others. My initial alliance with him delayed, and almost blocked, my access to others in the neighborhood. He in-

tentionally tried to keep me from others on the scene, not because he would gain something from that transaction but because it made him feel powerful. When I told him I was going to hang out with some of the other people, he threatened me until one of the other dealers stepped in and told him to stay away. The two of them argued back and forth, and finally I was free to go. Fortunately, the dealer who had spoken up for me was much more central and positively associated with the local scene. Finally, I am unsure if I would have had success in gaining entrance to the scene had I not been a woman.

## Developing Relationships and Trust

The processes involved in developing relationships in research situations amplify those involved in developing relationships in general. Both parties need to get to know each other, become aware and accepting of each other's roles, and engage in a reciprocal relationship. Being supportive and providing practical assistance were the most visible and direct ways for me as the researcher to develop a relationship. Throughout the years, I have given countless rides, provided child care on numerous occasions, bought groceries, and listened for hours to stories that were unrelated to my initial research questions. Gradually, my role allowed me to become part of these women's lives and to build rapport with many of them.

Over time, many women also realized that I was uninterested in being a prostitute and that I genuinely was interested in learning as much as possible about their lives. Many felt flattered that someone wanted to learn from them and that they had knowledge to offer. Allowing women to tell their stories and engaging in a dialogue with them probably were the single most important techniques that allowed me to develop relationships with them. Had I only wanted to focus on the questions I had in mind, developing such relationships might have been more difficult.

At times, I was able to get to know a woman only after her pimp endorsed our contact. One of my scariest experiences occurred before I knew to work through the pimps, and one such man had some of his friends follow me on my way home one night. I will never know what plans they had in mind for me because I fortunately was able to escape with only a few bruises. Over a year later, the woman acknowledged that her pimp had gotten upset and told her he was going to teach me a lesson.

On other occasions, I first needed to be screened by owners and managers of crack houses before the research could continue. Interestingly, screenings always were done by a man even if the person who vouched for me was a man himself. While the women also were cautious, the ways in which they checked me out tended to be much more subtle. For example, one of them would tell me a story, indicating that it was a secret about another person on the stroll. Although I failed to realize this at the time, my field notes revealed that frequently after such a conversation, others would ask me questions about related topics. One woman later acknowledged that putting out such stories was a test to see if I would keep information confidential.

Learning more about the women and gaining a better understanding of their lives also raised many ethical questions. No textbook told me how to handle situations in which a pimp abused a woman, a customer forced a woman to engage in unwanted sex acts, a customer requested unprotected sex from a woman who knew she was HIV infected, or a boyfriend had realistic expectations regarding a woman's earnings to support his drug habit. I failed to know the proper response when asked to engage in illegal activities such as holding drugs or money a woman had stolen from a customer. In general, my response was to explain that I was there as a researcher. During those occasions when pressures became too severe, I decided to leave a scene. For example, I never returned to certain crack houses because pimps there continued to ask me to consider working for them.

Over time, I was fortunate to develop relationships with people who "watched my back." One pimp in particular intervened if he perceived other pimps, customers, or passersby harassing me. He also was the one who gave me my street name: Whitie (indicating my racial background) or Ms. Whitie for those who disrespected me. While this was my first street name, I subsequently had others. Being given a street name was a symbolic gesture of acceptance. Gradually, I developed an identity that allowed me to be both an insider and an outsider. While hanging out on the strolls and other gathering places, including crack houses, I had to deal with some of the same uncomfortable conditions as the prostitutes, such as cold or warm weather, lack of access to a rest room, refusals from owners for me to patronize a restaurant, and of course, harassment by customers and the police.

I participated in many informal conversations. Unless pushed to do so, I seldom divulged my opinions. I was more open with my feelings about situations and showed empathy. I learned quickly that providing an opinion can backfire. I agreed that one of the women was struggling a lot and stated that I felt sorry for her. While I meant to indicate my "genuine concern for her, she heard that I felt sorry for her because she was a failure. When she finally, after several weeks, talked with me again, I was able to explain to "her that I was not judging her, but rather felt concerned for her. She remained cynical and many times asked me for favors to make up for my mistake. It took me months before I felt comfortable telling her that I felt I had done enough and that it was time to let go. However, if she was not ready, she needed to know that I would no longer go along. This was one of many occasions when I learned that although I wanted to facilitate my work as a researcher, that I wanted people to like and trust me, I also needed to set boundaries.

Rainy and slow nights often provided good opportunities for me to participate in conversations with groups of women. Popular topics included how to work safely, what to do about condom use, how to make more money. I often served as a health educator and a supplier of condoms, gels, vaginal douches, and other feminine products. Many women were very worried about the AIDS epidemic. However, they also were worried about how to use a condom when a customer refused to do so. They worried particularly about condom use when they needed money badly and, consequently, did not want to propose that the customer use one for fear of rejection. While some women became experts at "making" their customers use a condom—for

example, "by hiding it in their mouth prior to beginning oral sex—others would carry condoms to please me but never pull one out. If a woman was HIV positive and I knew she failed to use a condom, I faced the ethical dilemma of challenging her or staying out of it.

Developing trusting relationships with crack prostitutes was more difficult. Crack houses were not the right environment for informal conversations. Typically, the atmosphere was tense and everyone was suspicious of each other. The best times to talk with these women were when we bought groceries together, when I helped them clean their homes, or when we shared a meal. Often the women were very different when they were not high than they were when they were high or craving crack. In my conversations with them, I learned that while I might have observed their actions the night before, they themselves might not remember them. Once I realized this, I would be very careful to omit any detail unless I knew that the woman herself did remember the event.

## In-Depth Interviews

All interviews were conducted in a private setting, including women's residences, my car or my office, a restaurant of the women's choice, or any other setting the women selected. I did not begin conducting official interviews until I developed relationships with the women. Acquiring written informed consent prior to the interview was problematic. It made me feel awkward. Here I was asking the women to sign a form after they had begun to trust me. However, often I felt more upset about this technicality than the women themselves. As soon as they realized that the form was something the university required, they seemed to understand. Often they laughed about the official statements, and some asked if I was sure the form was to protect them and not the school.[3] None of the women refused to sign the consent form, although some refused to sign it right away and asked to be interviewed later.

In some instances the consent procedures caused the women to expect a formal interview. Some of them were disappointed when they saw I only had a few structured questions about demographic characteristics, followed by a long list of open-ended questions. When this disappointment occurred, I reminded the women that I wanted to learn from them and that the best way to do so was by engaging in a dialogue rather than interrogating them. Only by letting the women identify their salient issues and the topics they wanted to address was I able to gain an insider's perspective. By being a careful listener and probing for additional information and explanation, I as the interviewer, together with the women, was able to uncover the complexities of their lives. In addition, the nature of the interview allowed me to ask questions about contradictions in a woman's story. For example, sometimes a woman would say that she always used a condom. However, later on in the conversation she would indicate that if she needed drugs she would never use one. By asking her to elaborate on this, I was able to begin developing insights into condom use by type of partner, type of sex acts, and social context.

The interviewer becomes much more a part of the interview when the conversations are in-depth than when a structured questionnaire is used. Because I was so integral to the process, the way the women viewed me may have biased their answers. On the one hand, this bias might be reduced because of the extent to which both parties already knew each other; on the other, a woman might fail to give her true opinion and reveal her actions if she knew that these went against the interviewer's opinion. I suspected that some women played down the ways in which their pimps manipulated them once they knew that I was not too fond of these men. However, some might have taken more time to explain the relationship with their pimp in order to "correct" my image.

My background, so different from that of these women, most likely affected the nature of the interviews. I occupied a higher socioeconomic status. I had a place to live and a job. In contrast to the nonwhite women, I came from a different racial background. While I don't know to what extent these differences played a role, I acknowledge that they must have had some effect on this research.

## Leaving the Field

Leaving the field was not something that occurred after completion of the fieldwork, but an event that took place daily. Although I sometimes stayed on the strolls all night or hung out for several days, I always had a home to return to. I had a house with electricity, a warm shower, a comfortable bed, and a kitchen. My house sat on a street where I had no fear of being shot on my way there and where I did not find condoms or syringes on my doorstep.

During several stages of the study, I had access to a car, which I used to give the women rides or to run errands together. However, I will never forget the cold night when everyone on the street was freezing, and I left to go home. I turned up the heat in my car, and tears streamed down my cheeks. I appreciated the heat, but I felt more guilty about that luxury than ever before. I truly felt like an outsider, or maybe even more appropriate, a betrayer.

Throughout the years of fieldwork, there were a number of times when I left the scene temporarily. For example, when so many people were dying from AIDS, I was unable to ignore the devastating impact of this disease. I needed an emotional break.

Physically removing myself from the scene was common when I experienced difficulty remaining objective. Once I became too involved in a woman's life and almost adopted her and her family. Another time I felt a true hatred for a crack house owner and was unable to adhere to the rules of courteous interactions. Still another time, I got angry with a woman whose steady partner was HIV positive when she failed to ask him to use a condom when they had sex.

I also took temporary breaks from a particular scene by shifting settings and neighborhoods. For example, I would invest most of my time in women from a particular crack house for several weeks. Then I would shift to spending more time on one of the strolls, while making shorter and less frequent visits to the crack house. By shifting scenes, I was able to tell people why I was leaving and to remind all of us of my researcher role.

While I focused on leaving the field, I became interested in women who had left the life. It seemed important to have an understanding of their past and current circumstances. I knew some of them from the days when they were working, but identifying others was a challenge. There was no gathering place for ex-prostitutes. Informal networking, advertisements in local newspapers; and local clinics and community settings allowed me to reach twenty of these women. Conducting interviews with them later in the data collection process prepared me to ask specific questions. I realized that I had learned enough about the life to know what to ask. Interviewing ex-prostitutes also prepared me for moving from the fieldwork to writing.

It is hard to determine exactly when I left the field. It seems like a process that never ends. Although I was more physically removed from the scene, I continued to be involved while analyzing the data and writing this book. I also created opportunities to go back, for example, by asking women to give me feedback on parts of the manuscript or at times when I experienced writer's block and my car seemed to automatically steer itself to one of the strolls. I also have developed other research projects in some of the same communities. For example, both a project on intergenerational drug use and a gender-specific intervention project to help women remain HIV negative have brought me back to the same population. Some of the women have become key respondents in these new projects, while others now are members of a research team. For example, Beth, one of the women who has left prostitution, works as an outreach worker on another project.

## Six Themes in the Ethnography of Prostitution

The main intention of my work is to provide the reader with a perspective on street prostitution from the point of view of the women themselves. There are six fundamental aspects of the women's lives as prostitutes that must be considered. The first concerns the women's own explanations for their involvement in prostitution and their descriptions of the various circumstances that led them to become prostitutes. Their stories include justifications such as traumatic past experiences, especially sexual abuse, the lack of love they experienced as children, pressures by friends and pimps, the need for drugs, and most prominently, the economic forces that pushed them into the life. A number of women describe these justifications as excuses, as reflective explanations they have developed after becoming a prostitute.

The women describe the nature of their initial experiences, which often involved alienation from those outside the life. They also show the differences in the processes between women who work as prostitutes and use drugs and women who do not use drugs.

Although all these women work either on the street or in drug-use settings, their lives do differ. My second theme is a typology that captures these differences, looking at the women's prostitution versus drug-use identities. The typology distinguishes among (a) streetwalkers, women who work strolls and who do not use drugs; (b) hooked prostitutes, women who identify themselves mainly as prostitutes but who upon their entrance into the life also began using drugs; (c) prostituting addicts, women who view themselves mainly as drug users and who became prostitutes to support their drug habit; and (d) crack prostitutes, women who trade sex for crack.

This typology explains the differences in the women's strategies for soliciting customers, their screening of customers, pricing of sex acts, and bargaining for services. For example, the streetwalkers have the most bargaining power, while such power appears to be lacking among the crack prostitutes.

Few prostitutes work in a vacuum. The third theme is the role of pimps, a label that most women dislike and for which they prefer to substitute "old man" or "boyfriend." Among the pimps, one finds entrepreneur lovers, men who mainly employ streetwalkers and hooked prostitutes and sometimes prostituting addicts. Entrepreneur lovers engage in the life for business reasons. They treat the women as their employees or their property and view them primarily as an economic commodity. The more successful a woman is in earning them money, the more difficult it is for that woman to leave her entrepreneur pimp.

Most prostituting addicts and some hooked prostitutes work for a lover pimp, a man who is their steady partner but who also lives off their earnings. Typically, such pimps employ only one woman. The dynamics in the relationship between a prostitute and her lover pimp become more complex when both partners use drugs. Drugs often become the glue of the relationship.

For many crack prostitutes, their crack addiction serves as a pimp. Few plan to exchange sex for crack when they first begin using; often several weeks or months pass before a woman who barters sex for crack realizes that she is a prostitute.

Historically, society has blamed prostitutes for introducing sexually transmitted diseases into the general population. Similarly, it makes them scapegoats for the spread of HIV/AIDS. Yet their pimps and customers are not held accountable. The fourth theme in the anthropological study of prostitution is the impact of the AIDS epidemic on the women's lives. Although most are knowledgeable about HIV risk behaviors and the ways to reduce their risk, many misconceptions exist. The women describe the complexities of condom use, especially with steady partners but also with paying customers. Many women have mixed feelings about HIV testing, wondering how to cope with a positive test result while no cure is available. A few of the women already knew their HIV-infected status, and the discussion touches on their dilemmas as well.

The fifth theme is the violence and abuse that make common appearances in the women's lives. An ethnography of prostitution must allow the women to describe violence in their neighborhoods as well as violence in prostitution and drug-use settings. The most common violence they encounter is from customers. These men often assume that because they pay for sex they buy a woman. Apparently, casual customers pose more of a danger than those who are regulars. The types of abuse the women encounter are emotional, physical, and sexual. In addition to customers, pimps and boyfriends abuse the women. Finally, the women discuss harassment by law enforcement officers.

When I talked with the women, it often seemed that there were no opportunities to escape from the life. Yet the sixth and final theme must be the escape from prostitution. Women who have left prostitution can describe the process of their exit from prostitution. As ex-prostitutes they struggle with the stigma of their past, the challenges of developing a new identity, and the impact of their past on current intimate relationships. Those who were also drug users often view themselves as ex-prostitutes and recovering addicts, a perspective that seems to create a role conflict. Overall, most ex-prostitutes find that their past follows them like a bad hangover.

# Notes

1. The names of the women who were interviewed for this study, as well as those of their pimps and customers, have been replaced by pseudonyms to protect their privacy. The use of pseudonyms is suggested by guidelines to protect the privacy of study participants (American Anthropological Association; American Sociological Association).

2. For more information about qualitative research methods, see, for example, Patricia Adler and Peter Adler, *Membership Roles in Field Research* (Newbury Park: Sage, 1987); Michael Agar, *The Professional Stranger* (New York: Academic Press, 1980) and *Speaking of Ethnography* (Beverly Hills: Sage, 1986); Howard Becker and Blanche Geer, "Participant Observation and Interviewing: A Comparison," *Human Organization* 16 (1957): 28–32; Norman Denzin, *Sociological Methods: A Sourcebook* (Chicago: Aldine, 1970); Barney Glaser and Anselm Strauss, *The Discovery of Grounded Theory: Strategies for Qualitative Research* (Chicago: Aldine, 1967); Y. Lincoln and E. Guba, *Naturalistic Inquiry* (Beverly Hills: Sage, 1985); John Lofland, "Analytic Ethnography: Features, Failings, and Futures," *Journal of Contemporary Ethnography* 24 (1996): 30–67; and James Spradley, *The Ethnographic Interview* (New York: Holt, Rinehart and Winston, 1979) and *Participant Observation* (New York: Holt, Rinehart and Winston, 1980).

3. For a more extensive discussion of informed consent procedures and related ethical issues, see Bruce L. Berg, *Qualitative Research Methods for the Social Sciences*, 3rd edition, Chapter 3: "Ethical Issues" (Boston: Allyn and Bacon, 1998).

# Gardening Tips

LEE CRONK

In the spring of 1996, two stories made American headlines. The first concerned a young woman named Fauziya Kassindja from the West African country of Togo. She had fled her country a year and a half earlier to avoid genital mutilation and an arranged marriage, only to spend her time in the United States subjected to dehumanizing treatment in a series of detention centers and prisons while she waited for a hearing on her request for asylum. The other concerned the FBI's capture of Theodore Kaczynski, age 53, a loner from the Montana backwoods, on suspicion of being the "Unabomber," a mysterious figure who had spent seventeen years terrorizing the nation by sending carefully crafted letter bombs to academics and others involved with the development of industrial technology.

It would be hard to find two people any more different than Kassindja and Kaczynski or any two more unrelated news stories. Perhaps the only characteristic that their stories do share is that they hold lessons for the subject of this chapter: What might be the practical benefits of seeking insights into human behavior by looking at the dance between culture and our shared, evolved human nature? In short, what good will this approach do us as social engineers? The experiences of Kassindja and other women like her provide an example of how the abuse of the culture concept can result in the rights of culture being elevated above the rights of people, while Kaczynski is a symptom of just how much modern society and culture have diverged from those that fostered the evolution of our shared human nature.

"Social engineering" is an ugly and frightening phrase to many people, but, like so many of the ideas, it is only a metaphor. "Social gardening" would be every bit as apt a way to describe the efforts of people to alter, in big and little ways, their behavior, the behavior of others, and the institutional frameworks in which they all live. Even those of us who prefer the decentralized, naturalistic, bottoms-up approach of an English-style social garden to the rigid lines and neatly trimmed hedges of the French style are still advocating a type of gardening, at a minimum, a set of policies favoring some sorts of behaviors and social arrangements over others. Although as a scientist I am a strong advocate of knowledge for its own sake, I also recognize that for many people this is not enough. For them, science must justify itself not just in terms of the intellectual satisfaction it provides scientists, but by the practical benefits it provides everyone else.

## Tolerating the Intolerable

Let's begin by looking at the practical benefits provided by one alternative: cultural determinism. What practical good has the average person received from the doctrine that culture is the only significant influence on human behavior? It can be argued, with some justification, that when the culturalist approach was new it was a key element in the argument against racism in particular and against the broader idea that biology is destiny. In the intellectual milieu of the early twentieth century, it was a major step forward. Nativist and racist doctrines of the inherent superiority of Whites in general, and of northern Europeans in particular, were rampant and were fueled in the United States by alarm over growing rates of immigration mainly from Eastern and Southern Europe. In response to arguments that such immigrants were watering down America's good Anglo-Saxon stock, Franz Boas, the founder of academic anthropology in the United States, conducted a key piece of research, showing that although immigrants' physical forms, particularly the shapes of their heads, may have varied from the American average on arrival, their children's bodies and head shapes showed a definite shift toward the American pattern. Not only was biology not destiny as far as behavior was concerned, in this case it was not even destiny for the development of the human body!

Research such as this, along with ethnographies that revealed the wisdom and logic behind the customs of culturally different peoples, set the stage for the tremendous advances in race relations, such as the desegregation of schools and armed forces, that followed World War II, as well as for the widespread interest in cultural diversity that has bloomed in the late twentieth century. As an anthropologist and as a citizen of the world, I consider these accomplishments to be enormous and, I hope, pivotal in human history. Before the development of the culture concept, only two explanations were given for the behavior of people different from oneself: ignorance or stupidity. The first left open the possibility that these others could be taught the "correct" way to behave; the second did not. It is a privilege to be part of the discipline that made such explanations unacceptable.

Perhaps because the doctrine of cultural relativism has had such an admirable history in terms of its influence on our social lives, there has been a tendency in recent years to take it a bit too far, to allow an idea that began simply as the scientist's disinterested detachment from his subject to slide into moral relativism. College students in particular tend to be relativistic and tolerant to a fault. When I have raised the issue of cultural relativism in my own classes, some students—students with otherwise mainstream political and moral opinions—have earnestly used the idea of "culture" to exonerate the efforts of the Nazis to exterminate European Jewry. "It's *their* culture, so who are *we* to judge it?" is the reasoning offered, implicitly putting the Holocaust on the same moral level as eating bratwurst.

The same sort of radical relativism has stymied the efforts of Fauziya Kassindja and other African women who have sought asylum in the United States because of the threat and promise of female circumcision in their homelands. Although the practice of female circumcision is becoming more widely known in the West, most people in our society are not clear on what it entails. The name is really a euphemism. To call it "circumcision" is to call what Lorena Bobbit did to her husband John "circumcision." While the male operation involves only the removal of the foreskin, the female operation is usually much more drastic. While in some societies it involves only a ceremonial knick of the hood covering the clitoris, in most cases it involves anything ranging from removal of the clitoris to removal of the clitoris and some or all of the labia minora, to removal of the clitoris and labia minora and sewing up the opening, leaving only a small passage for menstrual blood and urine. In some societies it is performed on babies and young girls, while others, including the Mukogodo and other Maasai-speakers, wait until a girl has had her first menses. It is a common practice in some parts of Africa and the Middle East, though even in the West removal of the clitoris was used by a few physicians in the nineteenth century to control women thought to have an excessive interest in sex. My wife, Beth Leech, is one of the few Westerners to have seen a female circumcision. Here are her field notes, reproduced here with only minor editing to preserve the privacy of those mentioned, from the first of two circumcisions she witnessed in 1986, one that involved a girl from an ethnic group neighboring the Mukogodo who was preparing to marry a man from yet another neighboring group:

*Arrived at the settlement just before 6:00 A.M. Still dark out. Stood at gate and a girl saw me, greeted me, and asked me why I was there. I told her for the circumcision, so she said, "Let's go" and led me through the settlement to her mother's house. Outside the house, dressed in a white cloak, was Natito, her head freshly shaved. With her was a girl about her age dressed in a school uniform. Natito asked if I had brought a knife. I didn't understand except literally, so said quizzically, "You want a knife? No, I don't have one." Later I heard her ask others the same question and figured out that it was rhetorical and meant to show that she wasn't afraid. By about 6:10 several girls had gathered and Natito's aunt came up and told us, "Sing now." So the girls, including Natito and I, stood up by the side of the house and began to sing. Natito's older sister and Natito were among the song leaders. After we'd sung for a while, the leaders stopped. During a several-minute silence, tears filled the eyes of Natito's older sister, and Natito and several others seemed to be trying to force tears to their eyes. Some young brides and young mothers came up and we began to sing again, sometimes with one of them leading. Mostly just the girls sang, although a young married woman would occasionally lead a verse.*

*About 6:30 Natito's aunt said, "Now." The girls and young women joined the old women a few steps away outside the door of the house. A hide was brought out of the house and arranged in the doorway. The men now all were outside the settlement. Another lady brought a pot of water. The pot looked like it hadn't been washed—like there was cooked-on porridge around the edges. The lady took a spearhead out of the water and put it on top of the house. Natito was led onto the hide. She removed her white cape and stood naked on the hide, her body shielded from the view of men outside by a semicircle of women and girls. Cold water from the pot was poured over Natito's head. She shivered. More water was splashed on her body, and the pot was set down on the edge of the hide. Natito kicked it angrily (part of the ceremony) all over me (not part of the ceremony). Natito then sat on the hide, facing me, arms akimbo, legs bent and spread. Her aunt holds one of her shoulders; three other women hold the other shoulder and her two legs. The circumcision lady unwrapped her razorblade and the operation began. All I can see is the woman's butt and the squinched-up face of Natito. She does not cry or cry out, just squinches her face tighter and tighter. Her aunt kept saying the equivalent of "Come on, that's right, chin up, you're almost done, brave girl, you can do it, come on." The lady's butt moved aside and I could see her fingering the bloody area, moving the lips aside. It was as if the clitoris was a plant: she had cut the stem and now must dig out the root. The women and girls crowded closer, watching every movement. Within two minutes it was over. The mother brought a gourd of milk from the house. A woman poured milk in the lid, allowing the milk to splatter onto the ground and onto what was left of Natito's genitals. Sheep fat was then smeared, globbed over the wound. Natito was then picked up under the arms and by the legs and carried into the house. On the hide I could see about a pint of Natito's blood, mixed with milk. She still had not cried out, but as they carried her in, her eyes were wet and her breath came in high wheezes. As Natito was carried in, another woman carried in the hide, folding it in half and lifting up the ends to keep in the blood and milk. An old woman picked up a broom of branches and swept the doorway clean. Natito was married the next day.*

A strict application of the logic of cultural relativism would lead us to tolerate and even support this practice, despite how reluctant we might be to have it performed on ourselves, our daughters, our sisters, or our wives. This is the position taken by John E Gossart, Jr., an immigration judge in Baltimore. In refusing the asylum claim of a woman from Sierra Leone in 1995, Judge Gossart described female circumcision as "an important ritual" that "binds the tribe," noting that "while some cultures view FGM [female genital mutilation] as abhorrent and/or even barbaric, others do not." The woman from Sierra Leone, he said, "cannot change that she is a female, but she can change her mind with regards to her position toward the FGM practices. It is not beyond [her] control to acquiesce to the tribal position on FGM." Not all immigration judges take similar positions. Judge Paul Nejelsky of Arlington, Virginia, ruled in favor of the asylum claim of another woman from Sierra Leone, arguing that "forced female genital mutilation clearly merits being recognized as a form of persecution."

# Absolutist Alternatives

Explaining behavior and justifying behavior are two very different things. Although culture is overused as an explanation for behavior, it is still a perfectly good and legitimate explanation in many, many cases. Yet, to move from using culture as an explanation of behavior to using it as a moral justification for behavior in the style of radical relativists like Judge Gossart is to slide from an "is" statement to an "ought" statement, a violation of a principle laid down convincingly by the Scottish philosopher David Hume more than two centuries ago. Ironically, many of those who are quick to justify and defend others' behaviors on cultural grounds also denounce biological approaches to behavior because they imagine that biological explanations might be used to justify unsavory, antisocial behaviors. To do so is to commit what is often called the "naturalistic fallacy," the idea that if something is "natural" it must therefore be "good." This sort of logic may work for granola, but it does not work for behavior. There may be biological reasons for jealousy, rape, xenophobia, and murder, but no biological explanation of those behaviors can be used to justify them in a moral sense. To use the culture concept to give a moral defense of any behavior is to commit the naturalistic fallacy in a new guise—call it the "culturatistic fallacy." No explanation of a behavior, whether it is based on biology, culture, or the phases of the moon, can ever be used to justify a behavior in moral terms.

If culture cannot be used to justify behavior, then perhaps we should get rid of cultural relativism entirely and replace it with something else, some approach to human affairs based on an absolute and universalistic moral code. For example, perhaps rather than just marveling at human diversity we should be social activists engaged in a moralistic quest to identify oppressors and oppressed, exploiters and exploited. This is what is advocated by, for example, Nancy Scheper-Hughes, an anthropologist at the University of California at Berkeley. Scheper-Hughes has shown how the poor of northeastern Brazil are kept poor and their children are kept sick and undernourished by a system involving physicians and the folk medical notion of a condition called "*nervos*." People who suffer from *nervos* may show a variety of symptoms including weakness, sleeplessness, headaches, and fainting. Scheper-Hughes argues that it is far from coincidental that these symptoms are the same one would expect from anyone who is chronically hungry. The solution offered by the Brazilian medical establishment is not food but tranquilizers, which make it doubly difficult for the people to do anything about their condition. Other cultural practices around the world as troubling as the notion of *nervos* are not difficult to find. One that sometimes shocks Americans even more than female circumcision is the practice of hacking off little girls' fingers among the Dani of Irian Jaya, the western part of the island of New Guinea. The practice is part of a particular Dani mourning ritual, and as a result of it some adult Dani women end up with only the thumb and two adjacent fingers of one hand remaining. People all over the political spectrum are bothered by the doctrine of cultural relativism in light of human rights abuses around the world. Recently Donald Hodel, a former Reagan administration official and now president of the Christian

Coalition, a conservative, religious lobbying organization, argued in favor of a bill in Congress that would tie American foreign policy to religious freedom overseas. At a press conference where he lent the bill his group's support, Hodel argued that "this is an atrocity that's going on out there, and for people to suggest for a moment that well maybe we shouldn't be too concerned about somebody being hung upside down and beaten nearly to death and boiling oil poured over his feet ... because maybe that's a cultural problem, I think is an abdication of our responsibility as free citizens of what ought to be a religiously safe world." Scheper-Hughes gets the moral code she applies to other societies from leftist political doctrines; Hodel gets his from the Judeo-Christian tradition and ideas about human rights developed during the Enlightenment. Still others propose a biological route around the problem of cultural relativism and toward a universal ethical system. Edward O. Wilson, for example, has recently argued that the naturalistic fallacy is no fallacy at all, and that, rather than rejecting evolutionary biology as a source of moral and ethical insights, we should be using it as the basis of a new and potentially universal ethical code. Ethical precepts, he writes, are not "ethereal messages outside humanity awaiting revelation" but rather "physical products of the brain and culture." Wilson argues that individuals are "predisposed biologically to make certain choices" about what is right and what is wrong that are then elevated through a process of cultural evolution to general principles. For example, here is the development he sees behind rules against adultery:

1. "Let's not go further; it doesn't feel right, it would lead to trouble."
2. "Adultery not only causes feelings of guilt, it is generally disapproved of by society, so these are other reasons to avoid it."
3. "Adultery isn't just disapproved of, it's against the law."
4. "God commands that we avoid this mortal sin."

Does Wilson's "empirical" approach to ethics really let us escape from the problem of cultural relativism? What if someone with a somewhat different cultural background (say, a Mukogodo man) were faced with a similar concern with adultery? His ethical code might develop in quite a different way, such as this:

1. "Adultery is a problem. It destroys families and causes conflict in our society."
2. "One of the main reasons for adultery is women in pursuit of sexual pleasure."
3. "The clitoris is the main organ of sexual pleasure for most women."
4. "Therefore we should remove the clitorides of our women."
5. "Failure to remove the clitoris is shameful and dirty. No man should marry such an unclean woman."
6. "God wants us to perform clitoridectomies on all our women."

Although I certainly agree with Wilson that biology has much to teach us about the choices people make in life and also that evolutionary biology has an important role to play in the empirical study of moral sentiments and systems , it is not clear that it is a sound basis on which to develop a system of ethics or that it truly offers us any way around the problem of cultural relativism.

# Finding a Middle Ground

The very fact that, despite their common Western, Euro-American, Judeo-Christian cultural backgrounds, Scheper-Hughes, Hodel, and Wilson all come up with different sorts of absolutist moral codes suggests that there may be some life left in the old doctrine of cultural relativism after all. In defense of relativism, it is helpful to remember that our own behaviors are often just as disturbing to people with other cultural backgrounds as, say, female genital mutilation and the removal of little girls' fingers among the Dani are to us. This was brought home to me while I was among the Mukogodo. A teenage boy had heard from someone else that white people do not circumcise their girls and asked me whether it was true. When I told him that it was and then confirmed his logical conclusion that my own wife must not be circumcised, he came close to vomiting. To him, an uncircumcised woman is unclean, and certainly not to be married. Capital punishment is another custom that disturbs many people from other societies. Although it is popular among the American voting public, it is opposed as a human rights abuse by international human rights organizations and the governments of many other Western democracies. Clearly, some approach must be found that allows us to reap the benefits of cultural relativism while avoiding its pitfalls—to make moral judgments without assuming that ours is always the only "right" way of doing things.

I can offer three simple suggestions for how to reconcile our species' cultural diversity with our desire for a common, universal moral code. First, we need to stop thinking of cultures as coherent, integrated, bounded wholes and replace this with the idea that they are amorphous, unbounded bundles of ideas, knowledge, and beliefs that are continually being contested and renegotiated. Something close to this position has already become more or less the consensus among most cultural anthropologists, and it is in keeping with the approach to defining and using the culture concept described earlier. This allows us to better understand the diversity that exists within cultures as well as between them; it also allows us to be less hesitant in judging the effects of culture traits. I can, for example, feel free to deplore the practice of female circumcision as a specific Mukogodo culture trait while simultaneously having deep respect for the rest of Mukogodo culture. I can love and respect my own American culture while opposing the death penalty. And so on.

Second, we need to keep in mind that culture traits are not and cannot be rights-bearing entities. The only things capable of having rights are people. This is one place where the viral analogy is particularly useful. If culture traits are essentially like viruses, then clearly it makes no more sense to extend the protections of human rights to them than it would to extend them to, say, the smallpox virus. Students who defend the Holocaust and the judges who deny asylum to women avoiding circumcision on the grounds that such things are simply someone else's culture are, in effect, elevating the rights of culture traits above those of real, living people. The realization that culture is often a tool used by some people to manipulate others also helps

us to see through the cloak that extreme relativism draws around it. If some cultural idea amounts to an attempt by some people to manipulate others, whether it is the concept of *nervos*, the doctrine of the divine right of kings, or the idea that those people who are different from us are somehow our enemies, then it is easy to see how protecting such a notion under the protective banner of cultural relativism can serve to perpetuate oppression and exploitation.

There is another, more defensible and legitimate argument for the preservation of cultural traits, but acting on it does not require violating anyone's rights. We may wish to preserve the many cultural traits that are rapidly disappearing from the world's societies for their potential usefulness in the future. Just as genetic diversity may be worth preserving because it may help the world deal with future biological crises, so we might be wise to keep a storehouse of the world's cultural knowledge in case it, too, can help us through hard times ahead. We are already beginning to recognize, for example, that we can learn a thing or two from traditional medical practices around the world, and it is likely that we would benefit from preserving and learning to appreciate many other sorts of folk knowledge and skills. Indeed, helping to preserve the world's cultural diversity, just as it is so rapidly disappearing, is one of the main ways in which anthropology can make itself useful. Fortunately for all concerned, doing so does not involve the violation of anyone's rights or forcing anyone to conform to traditional cultural traits that they no longer wish to follow.

Third, we need to foster the development of connections between the social sciences and the rest of the sciences. To reject all attempts to separate facts from values puts anthropologists and all other social scientists who deal with cultural difference on no firmer ground than religious missionaries, zealots with a passion not for understanding but for righting the wrongs of the world as they see them. As Roy D'Andrade of the University of California at San Diego has pointed out, we are more likely to have positive effects on the world if we first attempt to understand other societies before attempting to change them. Understanding behavior across cultural gaps requires a sort of limited relativism that is no different from the usual detachment scientists show toward their subjects. Medical science is a good example of the power of this sort of attitude. Physicians, whose job it is to apply biological knowledge, have clear ideas about good and bad. Things that make people suffer, like viruses, are bad. Relieving people of problems caused by viruses and other pathogens is good. To achieve their goals, physicians must make use of knowledge gained by scientists about things like viruses. But it does not do any good for virologists to think of viruses as "bad" in some moralistic sense. They are simply fascinating and worthy of study in their own right. Similarly, it does the social scientist no good to make value judgments about the people, cultures, and societies he studies if his goal is simply to understand them. Such judgments may simply cloud his mind and make his primary tasks of explanation and understanding all the more difficult. Connecting the study of human affairs with the rest of the scientific project will help to foster an appropriate attitude of scientific detachment.

# Sperm Banks and Shotgun Pellets

If a limited form of cultural relativism is worth salvaging from the wreckage of cultural determinism, another of its artifacts deserves to be jettisoned altogether: the treatment of culture as a political football. Culture itself has become a hot political issue for the left and the right. These "culture wars" are based, fundamentally, on the idea that culture is such an overwhelmingly and uniquely powerful force in human affairs that it is worth waging a political struggle over it. If culture, though important, is by no means the only thing influencing human behavior, then we might do better as a society to try to appreciate and to concentrate on what we all share despite our various cultural exteriors and to focus our attention on more important sources of social problems.

It is not that William Bennett and others who would politicize culture don't have a point. Indeed, at the root of their discontent is something that I have also felt, something that has been increasingly felt by more and more people around the world. For most, it is simply a general malaise, a sense of unconnectedness, of not fitting in, a sense that we were not quite made for *this* world. And, of course, we weren't. We were made for a world that has mostly disappeared, a world in which we almost never dealt with strangers, in which an individual might see, let alone meet, just hundreds or at most thousands of other individuals in an entire lifetime, a world in which all activities were enmeshed in webs of kinship and friendship, a world in which things rarely changed much over the course of a lifetime. In contrast, when I stroll across the campus of my university during the few minutes between classes, I can see thousands of people, none of whom are my relatives, almost all of whom are complete strangers to me, all at an institution that, just in the time since I was born, has gone from a 2,000-student, virtually all white, all male, military school of agriculture and engineering to a well-rounded, coed, multiracial and multicultural university with 43,000 students. In many ways, it would be hard even for science fiction authors to dream up a world any more alien to the world in which humans evolved than the fast-changing, stranger-filled one in which we currently live. It is as if the dance between biology and culture has suddenly taken a nasty turn, with culture dancing to a fast, new tempo while biology continues its own steady waltz. Consider, for instance, the following "help wanted" ad:

> Help wanted: Healthy males wanted as semen donors. Help infertile couples. Confidentiality ensured. Ages 18 to 35, excellent compensation.

Here, one would think, is a perfect opportunity for young men to reproduce their genes. By the basic logic of natural selection, they should be flocking to sperm banks like the one that placed the advertisement, paying large sums of money and trying to look their best to be worthy of the chance to make a donation. But, of course, that is not how it works. Men are hardly knocking down sperm banks' doors for a chance to make a donation, despite the reproductive opportunity and good money that a frequent donor can make from literally a few minutes' work a week.

Observing people's glaring failure to take advantage of such an obvious opportunity for reproduction, a very naive student of natural selection might drop the whole theory like a hot potato. But a more sophisticated one would realize that evolution occurs to organisms in specific environments, and we can expect their adaptations to fit only those environments. If we take an organism out of the environment in which it evolved, or if its environment changes rapidly for some other reason, we have no reason to expect it to be able to cope adaptively with the new situation. British psychologist John Bowlby, in his seminal work *Attachment and Loss*, summed up this problem with the phrase "the environment of evolutionary adaptedness." In an organism's environment of evolutionary adaptedness, we should be able to use the theory of natural selection to predict how it develops and behaves. Outside that environment, all bets are off. The psychology of human sexual attraction evolved in a world in which males' reproductive opportunities came in the form of human females, not petri dishes.

We humans are not the only ones who lately have found themselves in an unfamiliar world. Just as the growth of human populations, cities, and industrialism has altered our environment, so has it altered the environments of many animal species. Drivers in Texas are reminded of this almost daily by the carnage of armadillo carcasses on the state's highways. The armadillo's natural defense mechanism is to spring vertically into the air two or three feet. This must work well if the threat is a coyote, but it is not so good a defense against pick-up trucks. Many other animals have similar problems with highways and cars. Rabbits, for example, sometimes dart back and forth in the paths of oncoming cars, attempting to confuse what in their evolutionary past would have been a predator bearing down on them at high speed. Many other animals, like the feral hog I once killed with my Mazda, are notoriously bad at judging vehicles' speeds.

Toads have a different problem that stems from how they eat. A good amount of a normal toad lifetime is spent sitting around, eating small things that fly or crawl past its field of vision. In the environment of toad evolution, the only small things that flew or crawled were insects, so toads needed to make no more complex a judgment about what to eat than "is it small, and is it moving?" But bored American GIs in Korea found that they could kill time by rolling pellet after pellet past toads, watching them fill up like little amphibious beanbags. Toads were presented with another, similar problem when they were introduced to the Hawaiian islands in 1932. Some trees in those islands produce blossoms that are loaded with strychnine poison as a protection against insects, blossoms which blow off the trees and across the ground, where unsuspecting toads snatch them up. Shotgun pellets and poisonous flower blossoms acting like insects did not exist in the environment of toad evolution, and they had no reason to evolve any way to discriminate against them.

We can begin to see the price we pay for living in our alien world with a look at modern health problems. It turns out that many of them, from various types of cancer to obesity to tooth decay to repetitive motion disorders, are the result of the mismatch between the way our ancestors lived and the way we do now. Obesity is an excellent example. How do we know what our palate has evolved to find tasty? All we can learn from the diets of the world's few remaining hunter-gatherer groups is what they find palatable given a restricted range of choices. To find out what people really like to eat, what they have evolved to like to eat, we need look no further than the local McDonald's, where the key ingredients are fat, salt, and sugar. In the environment of human evolution, these were relatively difficult things to get. Natural foods tend to be quite lean, not very sweet, and not very salty. In large amounts, all three are potential killers, but in small amounts they are excellent sources of calories and other nutrients, which, in naturally available foods, usually come packaged with a variety of nutrients in the form of animals, fruits, nuts, and vegetables. Even honey, which is little more than sugar and water, is traditionally eaten by the Mukogodo of Kenya and many other people together with the bee brood, a rich source of vitamin A. It made sense, then, for evolution to equip us with a strong yearning for these three basic things, because they were hard to get and worth spending some extra effort to find. In the modern environment, though, fat, sugar, and salt are easy to find, and as a result many people have a terrible time keeping weight off, keeping their blood pressure, cholesterol, and triglyceride levels down, and fighting a daily battle against tooth decay. One person who can testify first hand to the problems of a modern diet and the benefits of an ancient one is Vaughn M. Bryant, Jr., head of my department at Texas A&M University. Bryant has spent much of his career using pollen, desiccated feces called coprolites, and other plant and animal remains to reconstruct the diets of people who lived thousands of years ago in the caves of Texas' Rio Grande valley. What he and his coworkers have found is that, in what must have been a difficult desert environment, the ancient Texans ate pretty much anything they could get their hands on, from small rodents swallowed whole to cactus pads, a diet rich in fiber and indigestible roughage and low in fat, sugar, and salt. Faced with health problems, Bryant designed his own high-fiber, low-fat, caveman diet, munching peanuts whole, including their shells, and gobbling up fruit, including cores, peels, seeds, and stems. Such a regime would not appeal to most people, but it is essentially what doctors recommend we all eat: less fat, sugar, and salt and more fiber and other roughage. In other words, we should be eating more of what our ancestors ate and less of what our tastebuds would like us to eat.

We also should not be doing so much of what I am doing now (i.e., sitting at a computer, tapping at the keyboard and clicking a mouse for hour after hour). As so many office workers now know, this is a sure way to produce carpal tunnel syndrome and other potentially crippling repetitive motion disorders. Not very long ago, such repetitive activities were a rarity, partly because the division of labor was so much more simple. In a traditional farming community, for example, virtually everyone must do a wide variety of things just to make a living, from plowing and weeding to milking and cleaning stables. As the division of labor becomes more and more fine-grained, people find themselves doing more and more specialized tasks, often the same one for hour after hour, whether deboning chicken or soldering transistors onto circuit boards all day. In carpal tunnel syndrome, such repetitive actions inflame the tissues of the wrist and hand so that they

press on the nerves that run through the carpal tunnel, causing pain, numbness, and weakness. Although assembly line workers have suffered from such ailments for years, the proliferation of computers has made the syndrome widespread. In some circles carpal tunnel syndrome is known as "computeritis" or "journalist's disease." In the words of Linda H. Morse, medical director of the Repetitive Motion Institute in San Jose, California, "the electronic revolution has outstripped our human muscular and skeletal evolution."

Most modern humans also suffer from far too little physical activity. My fingers may be busy as I write this, but using a keyboard is hardly an aerobic exercise. Many of us know that sedentism is a health problem and spend large amounts of money on exercise equipment and little-used memberships to health clubs. Our ancestors faced the opposite problem. Just making a living demanded plenty of exercise, and they did not need to take morning jogs on the savannah or steppe to stay in shape. Among the Mukogodo, most people are kept fit by herding and hauling water and firewood through the hills. The prevalence of cancer in modern populations may also be a result of how different our environment is from that of our ancestors. Cancer is mostly a disease that strikes older people, and one reason why it seems to be much more common these days is simply because more people are living long enough—that is, *not* dying of the things that probably would have killed them in ages past—to die of cancer. In addition, some specific cancers—particularly breast cancer and cancers of the female reproductive system—seem to be made more common than they otherwise would be by certain aspects of our modern lives. A modern American woman typically has her first menses as early as age twelve, does not reproduce until she is at least in her twenties, and sometimes in her thirties or early forties, breastfeeds not at all or for only a short period, and experiences menopause in, say, her late 40s. Tampon manufacturers thrive because women who follow this pattern are rarely pregnant and rarely experience the suppression of the menstrual cycle that comes with steady breastfeeding, and thus experience a lot of cycles. This is not at all what women just a few generations ago experienced in Western society or what women experience in existing societies resembling those in which our ancestors lived. In those societies, menarche comes relatively late, usually after age 15, menopause comes relatively early, and for most of the time in between women are usually either pregnant or nursing, and thus not menstruating. This is true even of some women in our own society. While explaining why the Yanomamö pattern of squatting on the ground during a menstrual period is not such an inconvenience for women who rarely menstruate, Napoleon Chagnon recalls a time when his mother turned to him on a city bus and whispered, "My menstrual period is starting. This is the first one I've had in ten years." Though she lived in Michigan, Mrs. Chagnon followed a traditional reproductive pattern, bearing twelve children and breastfeeding each of them until they were about two years old.

Such a way of life does have its health benefits. Studies have shown that breast cancer and cancers of the female reproductive system are reduced significantly if women get pregnant early, have several children, and breast-feed them for long periods.

Breastfeeding's power to reduce the incidence of breast cancer can be most dramatically seen in a study among the Tanka, a fishing people in Hong Kong. Many Tanka women nurse their children with only the right breast, which is more convenient because their clothes open on the right. While breast cancer rates among older Tanka women in the right breast are quite low, in the other, unused breast they are equal to those found among modern American women. In one study conducted on American women by Peter M. Layde and his colleagues at the Centers for Disease Control, those who breast-fed for more than twenty-five months were 33 percent less likely to develop breast cancer than women who had children but had never breast-fed. Having more children helps, too, although it may require a large number of children for the effect to be measurable. Layde's study found that women with only one child had more than twice the cancer risk of women with seven or more children. A woman's reproductive history has similar effects on her chances of developing ovarian cancer and other cancers of the reproductive tract. At every age, there is a correlation between a woman's risk of developing a cancer of her reproductive tissues and the number of menstrual cycles she has experienced. Breastfeeding might also reduce the incidence of postpartum depression. Nursing stimulates a mother's production of a hormone called oxytocin, which has been shown to produce a warm, fuzzy feeling in humans and to encourage a variety of maternal behaviors in nonhuman mammals. Kelly Peyton, a recent product of my department's graduate program, has proposed that women who do not breast-feed may experience more postpartum depression than those who do because of their lack of oxytocin. Until very recently no mammalian mother, human or otherwise, would not breast-feed following a successful pregnancy, so the body of a woman who does not nurse her newborn is essentially receiving a signal of a failed pregnancy at precisely the same time that she is saddled with the responsibility of caring for a helpless, crying baby.

Changes in what we eat, how we work, and how we reproduce are intimately connected to broader changes in our social lives, and it is those changes that may be at the root of the general malaise and sense of despair that plagues so many people in modern society. Sad to say, Theodore Kaczynski, the "Unabomber," may turn out to have been the defining figure of fin-de-siecle America. Kaczynski is at once one of the most glaring symptoms of the late twentieth century blues—an antisocial, alienated loner whose only way of interacting with the rest of society is to send death anonymously through the mail—and a surprisingly keen observer of the problem at hand. The "Unabomber's Manifesto," published in 1995 by the *Washington Post* and purportedly written by Kaczynski, describes the Industrial Revolution as "a disaster for the human race." Technology, he writes, has "made life unfulfilling" and has "led to widespread psychological suffering." Furthermore, he claims, the overwhelming demands of our society's moral code "can lead to low self-esteem, a sense of powerlessness, defeatism, guilt, etc." Because in "modern industrial society only minimal effort is necessary to satisfy one's physical needs" and all one needs to survive are "a moderate amount of intelligence, and, most of all, simple OBEDIENCE," people "become acutely bored and demoralized." What they need to be happy is a satisfying sequence of setting goals, striving for them, and attaining them, coupled with a sense of autonomy. Although "not all was sweetness and light in primitive societies," "primitive man suffered from less stress and frustration and was better satisfied with his way of life than modern man is."

The Unabomber's account is not very different from what is coming to be known as "mismatch theory," the idea that many of our social and psychological problems arise from a mismatch between our ancestral and modern environments. David P. Barash, a professor of psychology and zoology at the University of Washington in Seattle, has argued that social pathologies such as drug use and crimes against strangers may reflect this mismatch. Although most traditional societies had a variety of drugs, they typically were not highly refined and required a lot of time and patience to acquire and prepare, so they rarely became the center of a person's life. Crime is less of a problem in such societies, or even in small towns in our society, because it is difficult to accomplish anonymously. "A small-town resident doesn't rob the corner grocery; everyone knows nice old Mr. McPherson," writes Barash. "But if McPherson is a nameless, familyless, disembodied, and anonymous spirit in a big city, he can be attacked with relative ease." John Papworth, an Anglican priest, recently suggested that this sort of moral flexibility is understandable and even acceptable, remarking that "Jesus said, 'Love your neighbor,' he didn't say, 'Love Marks and Spencers.'" The Reverend Papworth continued, "If people wander in and wander out without paying for the stuff I think it is a perfectly comprehensible action."

Tim Miller, a psychologist and author of a self-help book titled *How to Want What You Have: Discovering the Magic and Grandeur of Ordinary Existence* that incorporates some of the lessons of evolutionary psychology, argues that human nature equips us with desires for things that would have enhanced our ancestors' reproductive success, mainly wealth, status, and love. We strive to get them for the same reason we try to obtain fat, sugar, and salt: We are the descendants of those who were good at obtaining them in past environments. And, just as the modern environment allows us to overindulge our desires for fatty, sweet, and salty foods that turn out to be unhealthy and unsatisfying, so does it allow us to indulge our quest for wealth, status, and love, with an endless stream of new products, nearly limitless access to credit (and thus debt), and an ethic that, for many people, puts career advancement above practically all other goals. But an increasing number of people seem to be finding themselves on a treadmill, real happiness always just slightly out of reach.

Although the first step to alleviating these sorts of problems of the modern condition is to understand them, none of the solutions will be easy or obvious. Breast cancer rates might be greatly reduced by a return to Paleolithic reproductive patterns, but to most people such a cure would be worse than the disease, in terms of how it would limit women's hard-won autonomy and in the population growth that would ensue. Once we have a better understanding of the details of the links between reproductive patterns and female cancers, a more probable solution would be to develop hormonal treatments that mimic the effects of our ancestors' reproductive habits of early and multiple pregnancies with long periods of breastfeeding in between. It may seem premature to consider such a drastic hormonal intervention into women's reproductive systems, but the recent changes in reproductive patterns have intervened in a way that is no less drastic, with no planning and no regard to possible side effects.

Solving the problem of the mismatch between the social environment of our ancestors and our own will undoubtedly be the most difficult of all these problems. Of course, the Unabomber has made one clear and simple suggestion, that we have a revolution to overthrow technology altogether, but the suffering caused by the modern condition would seem tiny in comparison with that produced by such a change. As problematic as technology, a complex division of labor, and the rest of the modern industrial system may be, there is no avoiding that in many ways they make happiness easier rather than more difficult for many people to achieve. We can, after all, be confident that our children will survive to adulthood, and we can choose our mates and our occupations and even how to spend our spare time, luxuries unavailable to most of our ancestors. Whatever solutions are offered must not come at the expense of our health or our newfound freedoms.

# When Things Were Really Rotten

As problematic as modern society may be for organisms like us who evolved to deal with a different environment, it could be worse. Indeed, not long ago it *was* worse for quite a lot of the world's population. This is because, in many ways, the societies that are most unlike those in which we evolved are not modern, industrialized ones but, rather, the sort of rigid, hierarchical, and politically oppressive ones that sprung up after the development of agriculture like mushrooms after a rain. I am thinking in particular of the more elaborate chiefdoms and early state societies that first developed in places like Mesopotamia and the Nile Valley but that are better documented in places where they developed more recently such as the Americas, parts of Africa, and Polynesia. Admittedly, most available accounts of these sorts of societies were written by opinionated and often unfriendly folks with their own religious, political, and economic agendas, and so need to be taken with a grain of salt or two. However, the picture they paint is a consistently and painfully bleak one. These complex chiefdoms and early states appear to be have been remarkably nasty places, rife with torture, arbitrary killing, and religious doctrines that were designed to maintain the positions of the elites, sometimes even requiring human sacrifices. Rigid caste systems and onerously heavy taxation were routine. Typically, the status of women also dropped as the patriarchal state became a new tool for their oppression.

The extreme nastiness of such societies probably had a lot to do with their own novelty. Everything about them was new, including not only the differentiation of people into different social classes with different rights, privileges, and amounts of wealth but even the idea of the "state" and its central monopoly on the use of force. In earlier societies, as in contemporary band and tribal societies, everyone had the right to use force as they saw fit. No one had the right to push anyone else around. But states involve the centralization of the right to use force, and making that concentration of force seem legitimate and right—or at least unchangeable—to the bulk of the population seems to have been a major worry of early state rulers. Ideology played its part in crowd control, with notions such as the divinity of the king being invented independently in several different times and places, but the basic tools of elite domination were often much more simple: violence and the threat of violence. Consider, for instance, the kingdom of Buganda in what is now Uganda. Buganda was a centralized, bureaucratic state ruled by an autocratic king known as the kabaka. It was similar to a series of other kingdoms around East Africa's great lakes, including Bunyoro, Ankole, Rwanda, and Burundi. Buganda's kabakas had an enormous amount of arbitrary power over the life and death of their subjects and, before the arrival of Islamic and Christian missionaries in the nineteenth century, their word was absolute law. If the kabaka decided, on the advice of a fortune teller, that everyone in the kingdom with cataracts should be put to death, it was done. When the kabaka Mwanga's rule was threatened in the late nineteenth century by conversions to Christianity, his response was swift and simple: the murders of two hundred Protestant and Catholic converts. Similar stories are told of despots from many similar societies. Tanoa, a nineteenth-century king of Fiji, for example, is said to have killed and cannibalized slaves and maybe other subjects with no provocation.

In comparison to such terror-filled, hierarchical, oppressive societies, our society bears some surprising similarities to those in which we evolved. As the power of despots has declined and the power of average citizens has risen, we have managed, mostly without planning, to recreate some of the practices and social patterns that are typical of simple, hunting and gathering band societies. For instance, while there is no arguing that our society is divided into social classes, it is much more egalitarian in ideology and in reality than were the rigid hierarchical societies of the not too distant past. This relative egalitarianism has many aspects. Economically, there is a great deal more movement among socioeconomic classes in our society than in most historically recorded ones. Politically, the expansion of suffrage over the past couple of centuries has done much to open the government to participation by many groups who were previously excluded, including the landless, religious and racial minorities, and women. Socially, modern societies take seriously the idea that we all should be maritally equal. In contrast to many historical societies, where men in the upper classes, especially rulers, typically had more wives and concubines than average men, in our society the rule of one spouse per person at a time is taken seriously. Sexually, although we still have a long way to go in creating a society without gender biases, it is safe to say that a person's gender has much less to do with his or her occupation or status in society than it has in almost all previous human societies. In terms of religion and ideology, we are a long way from the mandatory adherence to official dogma that characterized earlier state societies. Rather, we are free to believe and worship as we wish. Increasingly, phenomena such as the New Age movement have opened the door to personal spiritual experimentation, with each individual being encouraged to find his or her own mix of beliefs and practices with few worries about any form of orthodoxy.

These patterns are not that different from those found in band societies. In bands, there is no measurable "wealth," there are no social classes or heritable differences in status or prestige, and everyone has an equal voice in group activities. Typically in band societies, although men and women may have different economic roles, their status is roughly equal. Although polygyny and polyandry are usually permitted and occasionally found in band societies, monogamy is the norm for almost everyone. And the sort of individualized religion that is becoming so popular in our society bears some resemblance to the freedom people in band societies have been observed to have concerning precisely what to believe and how to worship.

In other ways, modern society actually makes good, constructive use of our evolved human nature. Adoption of the babies of strangers, for instance, is virtually unheard of in most traditional societies. In large part, this is simply because people in such societies almost never interact with strangers. Adoption does occur in traditional societies, but it almost always involves nieces, nephews, and other relatives. Our mass society, on the other hand, allows us to take advantage of the desire so many people have to nurture and care for babies and children by connecting them with children whose own parents are not in a position to provide such care. Perhaps this sort of creative coupling of our evolved psychological propensities with cultural innovations that are possible only in a mass society such as ours will provide a way to build a new society that retains the best features of our ancestors' worlds and our own.

## Lonesome No More?

It may be possible to try to mimic, in small ways at least, aspects of the environment of human evolutionary adaptedness that might help make this world seem less alien and more familiar. Our ancestors lived their entire lives in the nexus of kinship, with families, kindreds, and lineages providing economic aid, child care, help in finding mates, emotional support, and a variety of other types of assistance. In his novel *Slapstick*, Kurt Vonnegut noted the alienation of modern society and offered a suggestion for how to solve it. The subtitle of the book, *Lonesome No More!*, refers to the campaign slogan of Wilbur Daffodil-11 Swain, the last president of the United States. His sole issue is the loneliness of his compatriots, and his solution is to use the computers of the federal government to recreate kinship networks like those of our ancestors. In this fantasy, everyone gets a new middle name corresponding to something in nature—Chipmunk, Hollyhock,

Raspberry, Uranium—and a number. By name and number everyone is instantly related to 10,000 brothers and sisters and 190,000 cousins, all obligated to help fellow clan members. That is a lot of kin, but, as Swain observes, "We need all the help we can get in a country as big and clumsy as ours."

Closer to reality, my institution, Texas A&M University, has done an admirable job of keeping a small-scale feel at the same time that it has exploded in enrollment. This was accomplished through a deliberate policy of indoctrinating students into what it means to be an Aggie, as A&M students are called. The socialization process begins during the summer before the freshmen (or "fish," as they are called here) arrive at "Fish Camp," where upper classmen teach the new students the university's folklore and its many traditions. This creates a strong feeling of shared identity and common purpose, and helps to make an institution with 43,000 students feel a great deal smaller and more personal than most big state universities while still tolerant and open to diversity (drawing the line, perhaps, at incursions from the rival University of Texas at Austin). One of the Aggie traditions is simply saying the word "howdy" to virtually anyone one might pass on campus. It may sound contrived, but receiving greetings from strangers just walking across campus creates a real sense of friendliness and openness that I honestly miss when I visit other universities and large cities, where eye contact with strangers is avoided at almost all costs. I see no reason why a variety of institutions, not just universities but corporations and other bureaucracies, could not adopt similar policies of encouraging behaviors that make friendliness and sociability routine and give people a feeling of belonging to an inclusive, supportive social network.

In the long run, perhaps we will evolve to fit our new environment. We may feel less need for supportive networks of kin and friends, our bodies may come to cope with the abundance of fat in our environment, and, as sperm banks account for more and more babies, men may even evolve a propensity to find test tubes downright arousing. Men like Cecil B. Jacobson, a Fairfax, Virginia infertility specialist who, unbeknownst to the women involved, used his own sperm to sire perhaps as many as seventy children, may be the fathers of the future (he certainly is leaving many more copies of his genes behind than most of us). But, surely, it will be a long time before laboratory supply catalogs are sold from behind the counter at convenience stores, and before armadillos stop littering Texas highways. In the meantime, we must strive for ways to live peacefully and happily with one another, products of the Stone Age living in an all too modern world.

# Anthropology and Counterinsurgency: The Strange Story of their Curious Relationship

Montgomery McFate

SOMETHING MYSTERIOUS is going on inside the U.S. Department of Defense (DOD). Over the past 2 years, senior leaders have been calling for something unusual and unexpected—cultural knowledge of the adversary. In July 2004, retired Major General Robert H. Scales, Jr., wrote an article for the Naval War College's Proceedings magazine that opposed the commonly held view within the U.S. military that success in war is best achieved by overwhelming technological advantage. Scales argues that the type of conflict we are now witnessing in Iraq requires "an exceptional ability to understand people, their culture, and their motivation."[1] In October 2004, Arthur Cebrowski, Director of the Office of Force Transformation, concluded that "knowledge of one's enemy and his culture and society may be more important than knowledge of his order of battle."[2] In November 2004, the Office of Naval Research and the Defense Advanced Research Projects Agency (DARPA) sponsored the Adversary Cultural Knowledge and National Security Conference, the first major DOD conference on the social sciences since 1962.

Why has cultural knowledge suddenly become such an imperative? Primarily because traditional methods of warfighting have proven inadequate in Iraq and Afghanistan. U.S. technology, training, and doctrine designed to counter the Soviet threat are not designed for low-intensity counterinsurgency operations where civilians mingle freely with combatants in complex urban terrain.

The major combat operations that toppled Saddam Hussein's regime were relatively simple because they required the U.S. military to do what it does best—conduct maneuver warfare in flat terrain using overwhelming firepower with air support. However, since the end of the "hot" phase of the war, coalition forces have been fighting a complex war against an enemy they do not understand. The insurgents' organizational structure is not military, but tribal. Their tactics are not conventional, but asymmetrical. Their weapons are not tanks and fighter planes, but improvised explosive devices (IEDs). They do not abide by the Geneva Conventions, nor do they appear to have any informal rules of engagement.

Countering the insurgency in Iraq requires cultural and social knowledge of the adversary. Yet, none of the elements of U.S. national power—diplomatic, military, intelligence, or economic—explicitly take adversary culture into account in the formation or execution of policy. This cultural knowledge gap has a simple cause—the almost total absence of anthropology within the national-security establishment.

Once called "the handmaiden of colonialism," anthropology has had a long, fruitful relationship with various elements of national power, which ended suddenly following the Vietnam War. The strange story of anthropology's birth as a warfighting discipline, and its sudden plunge into the abyss of postmodernism, is intertwined with the U.S. failure in Vietnam. The curious and conspicuous lack of anthropology in the national-security arena since the Vietnam War has had grave consequences for countering the insurgency in Iraq, particularly because political policy and military operations based on partial and incomplete cultural knowledge are often worse than none at all.

## A Lack of Cultural Awareness

In a conflict between symmetric adversaries, where both are evenly matched and using similar technology, understanding the adversary's culture is largely irrelevant. The Cold War, for all its complexity, pitted two powers of European heritage against each other. In a counterinsurgency operation against a non-Western adversary, however, culture matters. U.S. Department of the Army Field Manual (FM) (interim) 3-07.22, Counterinsurgency Operations, defines insurgency as an "organized movement aimed at the overthrow of a constituted government through use of subversion and armed conflict. It is a protracted politico-military struggle designed to weaken government control and legitimacy while increasing insurgent control. Political power is the central issue in an insurgency [emphasis added]." Political considerations must therefore circumscribe military action as a fundamental matter of strategy. As British Field Marshall Gerald Templar explained in 1953, "The answer lies not in pouring more troops into the jungle, but rests in the hearts and minds of the ... people." Winning hearts and minds requires understanding the local culture.[3]

Aside from Special Forces, most U.S. soldiers are not trained to understand or operate in foreign cultures and societies. One U.S. Army captain in Iraq said, "I was never given classes on how to sit down with a sheik…. He is giving me the traditional dishdasha and the entire outfit of a sheik because he claims that I am a new sheik in town so I must be dressed as one. I don't know if he is trying to gain favor with me because he wants something [or if it is] something good or something bad." In fact, as soon as coalition forces toppled Saddam Hussein, they became de facto players in the Iraqi social system. The young captain had indeed become the new sheik in town and was being properly honored by his Iraqi host.[4]

As this example indicates, U.S. forces frequently do not know who their friends are, and just as often they do not know who their enemies are. A returning commander from the 3d Infantry Division observed: "I had perfect situational awareness. What I lacked was cultural awareness. I knew where every enemy tank was dug in on the outskirts of Tallil. Only problem was, my soldiers had to fight fanatics charging on foot or in pickups and firing AK-47s and RPGs [rocket-propelled grenades]. Great technical intelligence. Wrong enemy."[5]

While the consequences of a lack of cultural knowledge might be most apparent (or perhaps most deadly) in a counterinsurgency, a failure to understand foreign cultures has been a major contributing factor in multiple national-security and intelligence failures. In her 1962 study, Pearl Harbor: Warning and Decision, Roberta Wohlstetter demonstrated that although the U.S. Government picked up Japanese signals (including conversations, decoded cables, and ship movements), it failed to distinguish signals from noise—to understand which signals were meaningful—because it was unimaginable that the Japanese might do something as "irrational" as attacking the headquarters of the U.S. Pacific fleet.[6]

Such ethnocentrism (the inability to put aside one's own cultural attitudes and imagine the world from the perspective of a different group) is especially dangerous in a national-security context because it can distort strategic thinking and result in assumptions that the adversary will behave exactly as one might behave. India's nuclear tests on 11 and 13 May 1998 came as a complete surprise because of this type of "mirror-imaging" among CIA analysts. According to the internal investigation conducted by former Vice Chairman of the Joint Chiefs of Staff David Jeremiah, the real problem was an assumption by intelligence analysts and policymakers that the Indians would not test their nuclear weapons because Americans would not test nuclear weapons in similar circumstances. According to Jeremiah, "The intelligence and the policy communities had an underlying mind-set going into these tests that the B.J.R [Bharatiya Janata Party] would behave as we [would] behave."[7]

The United States suffers from a lack of cultural knowledge in its national-security establishment for two primary, interrelated reasons. First, anthropology is largely and conspicuously absent as a discipline within our national-security enterprise, especially within the intelligence community and DOD. Anthropology is a social science discipline whose primary object of study has traditionally been non-Western, tribal societies. The methodologies of anthropology include participant observation, fieldwork, and historical research. One of the central epistemological tenets of anthropology is cultural relativism—understanding other societies from within their own framework.

The primary task of anthropology has historically been translating knowledge gained in the "field" back to the West. While it might seem self-evident that such a perspective would be beneficial to the national-security establishment, only one of the national defense universities (which provide master's degree-level education to military personnel) currently has an anthropologist on its faculty. At West Point, which traditionally places a heavy emphasis on engineering, anthropology is disparagingly referred to by cadets as "nuts and huts." And, although political science is well represented as a discipline in senior policymaking circles, there has never been an anthropologist on the National Security Council.

The second and related reason for the current lack of cultural knowledge is the failure of the U.S. military to achieve anything resembling victory in Vietnam. Following the Vietnam War, the Joint Chiefs of Staff collectively put their heads in the sand and determined they would never fight an unconventional war again. From a purely military perspective, it was easier for them to focus on the threat of Soviet tanks rolling through the Fulda Gap, prompting a major European land war—a war they could easily fight using existing doctrine and technology and that would have a clear, unequivocal winner.[8]

The preference for the use of overwhelming force and clear campaign objectives was formalized in what has become known as the Weinberger doctrine. In a 1984 speech, Secretary of Defense Caspar Weinberger articulated six principles designed to ensure the Nation would never become involved in another Vietnam. By the mid-1980s, there was cause for concern: deployment of troops to El Salvador seemed likely and the involvement in Lebanon had proved disastrous following the bombing of the U.S. Marine barracks in Beirut. Responding to these events, Weinberger believed troops should be committed only if U.S. national interests were at stake; only in support of clearly defined political and military objectives; and only "with the clear intention of winning."[9]

In 1994, Chairman of the Joint Chiefs of Staff Colin Powell (formerly a military assistant to Weinberger) rearticulated the Weinberger doctrine's fundamental elements, placing a strong emphasis on the idea that force, when used, should be overwhelming and disproportionate to the force used by the enemy. The Powell-Weinberger doctrine institutionalized a preference for "major combat operations"—big wars—as a matter of national preference. Although the Powell-Weinberger doctrine was eroded during the Clinton years; during operations other than war in Haiti, Somali, and Bosnia; and during the second Bush Administration's pre-emptive strikes in Afghanistan and Iraq, no alternative doctrine has emerged to take its place.[10]

We have no doctrine for "nationbuilding," which the military eschews as a responsibility because it is not covered by Title 10 of the U.S. Code, which outlines the responsibilities of the military as an element of national power. Field Manual 3-07, Stability Operations and Support Operations, was not finalized until February 2003, despite the fact the U.S. military was already deeply engaged in such operations in Iraq. Field Manual

3-07.22—meant to be a temporary document—is still primarily geared toward fighting an enemy engaged in Maoist revolutionary warfare, a type of insurgency that has little application to the situation in Iraq where multiple organizations are competing for multiple, confusing objectives.[11]

Since 1923, the core tenet of U.S. warfighting strategy has been that overwhelming force deployed against an equally powerful state will result in military victory. Yet in a counterinsurgency situation such as the one the United States currently faces in Iraq, "winning" through overwhelming force is often inapplicable as a concept, if not problematic as a goal. While negotiating in Hanoi a few days before Saigon fell, U.S. Army Colonel Harry Summers, Jr., said to a North Vietnamese colonel, "You know, you never defeated us on the battlefield." The Vietnamese colonel replied, "That may be so, but it is also irrelevant."[12] The same could be said of the conflict in Iraq.

Winning on the battlefield is irrelevant against an insurgent adversary because the struggle for power and legitimacy among competing factions has no purely military solution. Often, the application of overwhelming force has the negative, unintended effect of strengthening the insurgency by creating martyrs, increasing recruitment, and demonstrating the "brutality" of state forces.

The alternative approach to fighting insurgency, such as the British eventually adopted through trial and error in Northern Ireland, involves the following: A comprehensive plan to alleviate the political conditions behind the insurgency; civil-military cooperation; the application of minimum force; deep intelligence; and an acceptance of the protracted nature of the conflict. Deep cultural knowledge of the adversary is inherent to the British approach.[13]

Although cultural knowledge of the adversary matters in counterinsurgency, it has little importance in major combat operations. Because the Powell-Weinberger doctrine meant conventional, large-scale war was the only acceptable type of conflict, no discernable present or future need existed to develop doctrine and expertise in unconventional war, including counterinsurgency. Thus, there was no need to incorporate cultural knowledge into doctrine, training, or warfighting. Until now, that is.

On 21 October 2003, the House Armed Services Committee held a hearing to examine lessons learned from Operation Iraqi Freedom. Scales' testimony at the hearing prompted U.S. Representative "Ike" Skelton to write a letter to Secretary of Defense Donald Rumsfeld in which he said: "In simple terms, if we had better understood the Iraqi culture and mindset, our war plans would have been even better than they were, the plan for the postwar period and all of its challenges would have been far better, and we [would have been] better prepared for the 'long slog' … to win the peace in Iraq."[14]

Even such DOD luminaries as Andrew Marshall, the mysterious director of the Pentagon's Office of Net Assessment, are now calling for "anthropology-level knowledge of a wide range of cultures" because such knowledge will prove essential to conducting future operations. Although senior U.S. Government officials such as Skelton are calling for "personnel in our civilian ranks who have cultural knowledge and understanding to inform the policy process," there are few anthropologists either available or willing to play in the same sandbox with the military.[15]

# …The Perils of Incomplete Knowledge

DOD yearns for cultural knowledge, but anthropologists en masse, bound by their own ethical code and sunk in a mire of postmodernism, are unlikely to contribute much of value to reshaping national-security policy or practice. Yet, if anthropologists remain disengaged, who will provide the relevant subject matter expertise? As Anna Simons, an anthropologist who teaches at the Naval Postgraduate School, points out: "If anthropologists want to put their heads in the sand and not assist, then who will the military, the CIA, and other agencies turn to for information? They'll turn to people who will give them the kind of information that should make anthropologists want to rip their hair out because the information won't be nearly as directly connected to what's going on on the local landscape."[60]

Regardless of whether anthropologists decide to enter the national-security arena, cultural information will inevitably be used as the basis of military operations and public policy. And, if anthropologists refuse to contribute, how reliable will that information be? The result of using incomplete "bad" anthropology is, invariably, failed operations and failed policy. In a May 2004 New Yorker article, "The Gray Zone: How a Secret Pentagon Program Came to Abu Ghraib," Seymour Hersh notes that Raphael Patai's 1973 study of Arab culture and psychology, The Arab Mind, was the basis of the military's understanding of the psychological vulnerabilities of Arabs, particularly to sexual shame and humiliation.[61]

Patai says: "The segregation of the sexes, the veiling of the women …, and all the other minute rules that govern and restrict contact between men and women, have the effect of making sex a prime mental preoccupation in the Arab world." Apparently, the goal of photographing the sexual humiliation was to blackmail Iraqi victims into becoming informants against the insurgency. To prevent the dissemination of photos to family and friends, it was believed Iraqi men would do almost anything.[62]

As Bernard Brodie said of the French Army in 1914, "This was neither the first nor the last time that bad anthropology contributed to bad strategy." Using sexual humiliation to blackmail Iraqi men into becoming informants could never have worked as a strategy since it only destroys honor, and for Iraqis, lost honor requires its restoration through the appeasement of blood. This concept is well developed in Iraqi culture, and there is even a specific Arabic word for it: al-sharaf, upholding one's manly honor. The alleged use of Patai's book as the basis of the psychological torment at Abu Ghraib, devoid of any understanding of the broader context of Iraqi culture, demonstrates the folly of using decontextualized culture as the basis of policy.[63]

Successful counterinsurgency depends on attaining a holistic, total understanding of local culture. This cultural understanding must be thorough and deep if it is to have any practical benefit at all. This fact is not lost on the Army. In the language of interim FM 3-07.22: "The center of gravity in counterinsurgency operations is the population. Therefore, understanding the local society and gaining its support is critical to success. For U.S. forces to operate effectively among a local population and gain and maintain their support, it is important to develop a thorough understanding of the society and its culture, including its history, tribal/family/social structure, values, religions, customs, and needs."[64]

To defeat the insurgency in Iraq, U.S. and coalition forces must recognize and exploit the underlying tribal structure of the country; the power wielded by traditional authority figures; the use of Islam as a political ideology; the competing interests of the Shia, the Sunni, and the Kurds; the psychological effects of totalitarianism; and the divide between urban and rural, among other things.

Interim FM 3-07.22 continues: "Understanding and working within the social fabric of a local area is initially the most influential factor in the conduct of counterinsurgency operations. Unfortunately, this is often the factor most neglected by U.S. forces."[65]

And, unfortunately, anthropologists, whose assistance is urgently needed in time of war, entirely neglect U.S. forces. Despite the fact that military applications of cultural knowledge might be distasteful to ethically inclined anthropologists, their assistance is necessary.

# Notes

1. MG Robert H. Scales, Jr., "Culture-Centric Warfare," Proceedings (October 2004).

2. Megan Scully, "'Social Intel' New Tool For U.S. Military," Defense News, 26 April 2004, 21.

3. U.S. Department of the Army Field Manual (FM) (Interim) 3-07.22, Counterinsurgency Operations (Washington, DC: U.S. Government Printing Office [GPO], 1 October 2004), sec. 1-1; David Charters, "From Palestine to Northern Ireland: British Adaptation to Low-Intensity Operations," in Armies in Low-Intensity Conflict." A Comparative Analysis, eds., D. Charters and M. Tugwell (London: Brassey's Defence Publishers, 1989), 195.

4. Leonard Wong, "Developing Adaptive Leaders: The Crucible Experience of Operation Iraqi Freedom," Strategic Studies Institute, U.S. Army War College, Carlisle Barracks, Pennsylvania, July 2004, 14.

5. Scales, "Army Transformation: Implications for the Future," testimony before the House Armed Services Committee, Washington, D.C., 15 July 2004.

6. Roberta Wohlstetter, Pearl Harbor: Warning and Decision (California: Stanford University Press, 1962).

7. Jeffrey Goldberg, "The Unknown: The C.I.A. and the Pentagon take another look at Al Qaeda and Iraq," The New Yorker, 10 February 2003.

8. See Max Boot, The Savage Wars of Peace: Small Wars and the Rise of American Power (New York: Basic Books, 2003).

9. Casper W. Weinberger, "The Uses of Military Power," speech at the National Press Club, Washington, D.C., 28 November 1984.

10. Jeffrey Record, "Weinberger-Powell Doctrine Doesn't Cut It," Proceedings (October 2000) The Powell doctrine also "translates into a powerful reluctance to engage in decisive combat, or to even risk combat, and an inordinate emphasis at every level of command on force protection." Stan Goff, "Full-Spectrum Entropy: Special Operations in a Special Period," Freedom Road Magazine, on-line at <www.freedom.read.org/fr/03/ english/07_entropy.html>, accessed 18 February 2005.

11. U.S. Code, Title 10, "Armed Forces," on-line at <www.access.gpo.gov/uscode/ title10/title10.html>, accessed 18 February 2005; FM 3-07, Stability Operations and Support Operations (Washington, DC: GPO, February, 2003); FM 3-07.22, Interim.

12. The 1923 Field Service Regulations postulate that the ultimate objective of all military operations is the destruction of the enemy's armed forces and that decisive results are obtained only by the offensive. The Regulations state that the Army must prepare to fight against an "opponent organized for war on modern principles and equipped with all the means of modern warfare ...." The preference for use of offensive force is found continuously in U.S. military thought, most recently in FM 3-0, Operations (Washington, DC: GPO, 2001), which says: "The doctrine holds warfighting as the Army's primary focus and recognizes that the ability of Army forces to dominate land warfare also provide the ability to dominate any situation in military operations other than war"; Richard Darilek and David Johnson, "Occupation of Hostile Territory: History, Theory, Doctrine; Past and Future Practice, "conference presentation, Future Warfare Seminar V. Carlisle, Pennsylvania, 18 January 2005; Peter Grier, "Should US Fight War in Bosnia? Question Opens an Old Debate," Christian Science Monitor, 14 September 1992, 9.

13. For a full discussion of British principles of counterinsurgency, see Thomas Mockaitis, British Counterinsurgency, 1919-1960 (New York: St. Martin's Press, 1990); Ian Beckett and John Pimlott, eds., Armed Forces and modern Counter-Insurgency (London: Croom Helm, 1985)

14. Office of Congressman Ike Skelton, "Skelton Urges Rumsfeld To Improve Cultural Awareness Training," press release, 23 October 2003, on-line at <www.house.gov/skelton/ pr031023.html>, accessed 18 February 2005.

15. Jeremy Feller, "Marshall US. Needs To Sustain Long-Distance Power Projection," Inside The Pentagon, 4 March 2004, 15.

60. Renee Montagne, "Interview: Anna Simons and Catherine Lutz on the involvement of anthropologists in war," National Public Radio's Morning Edition, 14 August 2002.

61. Raphael Patai in Seymour M. Hersh, "The Gray Zone How a secret Pentagon program came to Abu Ghraib," The New Yorker, 24 May 2004; Patai, The Arab Mind (Now York: Scribner's 1973).

62. Patai.

63. Bernard Brodie, Strategy in the Missile Age (New Jersey: Princeton University Press, 1959), 52.

64. Amatzia Baram, "Victory in Iraq, One Tribe at a Time," New York Times, 28 October 2003; FM (Interim) 3-07.22, sec 4-11.

65. FM (Interim) 3-07.22, sec. 4-13.

**MONTGOMERY MCFATE, J.D., Ph.D.,** is an American Association for the Advancement of Science Defense Policy Fellow at the Office of Naval Research, Arlington, Virginia. She received a B.A. from the University of California at Berkeley, an M.A., M. Phil., and a Ph.D. from Yale University, and a J.D. from Harvard Law School. She was formerly at RAND's Intelligence Policy Center.

From *Military Review*, March/April 2005. Published in 2005 by Military Review, a publication of the U.S. Army. Reprinted by permission.

# One Hundred Percent American[1]

R. LINTON[2]

There can be no question about the average American's Americanism or his desire to preserve this precious heritage at all costs. Nevertheless, some insidious foreign ideas have already wormed their way into his civilization without his realizing what was going on. Thus dawn finds the unsuspecting patriot garbed in pajamas, a garment of East Indian origin; and lying in a bed built on a pattern which originated in either Persia or Asia Minor.[3] He is muffled to the ears in un-American materials: cotton, first domesticated in India; linen, domesticated in the Near East; wool from an animal native to Asia Minor; or silk whose uses were first discovered by the Chinese. All these substances have been transformed into cloth by methods invented in Southwestern Asia. If the weather is cold enough he may even be sleeping under an eiderdown quilt invented in Scandinavia.

On awakening he glances at the clock, a medieval European invention, uses one potent Latin word in abbreviated form, rises in haste, and goes to the bathroom. Here, if he stops to think about it, he must feel himself in the presence of a great American institution; he will have heard stories of both the quality and frequency of foreign plumbing and will know that in no other country does the average man perform his ablutions in the midst of such splendor. But the insidious foreign influence pursues him even here. Glass was invented by the ancient Egyptians, the use of glazed tiles for floors and walls in the Near East, porcelain in China, and the art of enameling on metal by Mediterranean artisans of the Bronze Age. Even his bathtub and toilet are but slightly modified copies of Roman originals. The only purely American contribution to the ensemble is the steam radiator, against which our patriot very briefly and unintentionally places his posterior.

In this bathroom the American washes with soap invented by the ancient Gauls. Next he cleans his teeth, a subversive European practice which did not invade America until the latter part of the eighteenth century. He then shaves, a masochistic rite first developed by the heathen priests of ancient Egypt and Sumer. The process is made less of a penance by the fact that his razor is of steel, an iron-carbon alloy discovered in either India or Turkestan. Lastly, he dries himself on a Turkish towel.

Returning to the bedroom, the unconscious victim of un-American practices removes his clothes from a chair, invented in the Near East, and proceeds to dress. He puts on close-fitting tailored garments whose form derives from the skin clothing of the ancient nomads of the Asiatic steppes and fastens them with buttons whose prototypes appeared in Europe at the close of the Stone Age. This costume is appropriate enough for outdoor exercise in a cold climate, but is quite unsuited to American summers, steam-heated houses, and Pullmans.[4] Nevertheless, foreign ideas and habits hold the unfortunate man in thrall even when common sense tells him that the authentically American costume of gee string and moccasins would be far more comfortable. He puts on his feet stiff coverings made from hide prepared by a process invented in ancient Egypt and cut to a pattern which can be traced back to ancient Greece, and makes sure that they are properly polished, also a Greek idea. Lastly, he ties about his neck a strip of bright-colored cloth which is a vestigial survival of the shoulder shawls worn by seventeenth century Greeks. He gives himself a final appraisal in the mirror, an old Mediterranean invention, and goes downstairs to breakfast.

Here a whole new series of foreign things confronts him. His food and drink are placed before him in pottery vessels, the proper name of which–china–is sufficient evidence of their origin. His fork is a medieval Italian invention and his spoon a copy of a Roman original. He will usually begin the meal with coffee, an Abyssinian[5] plant first discovered by the Arabs. The American is quite likely to need it to dispel the morning-after effects of overindulgence in fermented drinks, invented in the Near East; or distilled ones, invented by the alchemists of medieval Europe.[6] Whereas the Arabs took their coffee straight, he will probably sweeten it with sugar, discovered in India; and dilute it with cream, both the domestication of cattle and the technique of milking having originated in Asia Minor.

If our patriot is old-fashioned enough to adhere to the so-called American breakfast, his coffee will be accompanied by an orange, domesticated in the Mediterranean region, a cantaloupe domesticated in Persia, or grapes domesticated in Asia Minor. He will follow this with a bowl of cereal made from grain domesticated in the Near East and prepared by methods also invented there. From this he will go on to waffles, a Scandinavian invention with plenty of butter, originally a Near Eastern cosmetic. As a side dish he may have the egg of a bird domesticated in Southeastern Asia or strips of the flesh of an animal domesticated in the same region, which has been salted and smoked by a process invented in Northern Europe.

Breakfast over, he places upon his head a molded piece of felt, invented by the nomads of Eastern Asia, and, if it looks like rain, puts on outer shoes of rubber, discovered by the ancient Mexicans, and takes an umbrella, invented in India. He then sprints for his train–the train, not sprinting, being an English invention. At the station he pauses for a moment to buy a newspaper, paying for it with coins invented in ancient Lydia.[7] Once on board he settles back to inhale the fumes of a cigarette invented in Mexico, or a cigar invented in Brazil.[8] Meanwhile, he reads the news of the day, imprinted in characters invented by the ancient Semites by a process invented in Germany upon a material invented in China. As he scans the latest editorial pointing out the dire results to our institutions of accepting foreign ideas, he will not fail to thank a Hebrew God in an Indo-European language that he is a one hundred percent (decimal system invented by the Greeks) American (from Americus Vespucci, Italian geographer).

# Notes

1. With additional comments added by Parman.

2. American anthropologist. The article was published in *The American Mercury* in 1937 (40:427–429), a time of unrest just before WWII.

3. A peninsula in West Asia between the Black and Mediterranean seas, including most of Asiatic Turkey. (Part of Turkey is in Europe.)

4. Railroad sleeping car or parlor invented by the 19th-century American inventor and railroad car designer, George Mortimer.

5. Ethiopian.

6. According to the *Oxford English Dictionary*, the word "alcohol" derives from a process of sublimation (a Latin word that means to purify, as through distillation) invented by the Arabs by which powders were produced (Arab *al-koh'l*, collyrium, the fine powder used to stain the eyelids). The word "alcohol" itself appears in English in the 16th century, from medieval Latin, referring to the process of distillation of fluids (an extension of the concept of distillation or purification of powder).

7. An ancient kingdom in West Asia Minor; under Croesus, a wealthy empire including most of Asia Minor. See footnote 3.

8. Tobacco is indigenous to the New World, just as the "Irish potato" is indigenous to the New World.

From *The Study of Man*, by Ralph Linton, published by the Appleton–Century Company, 1936.

# UNIT 2
# Culture and Communication

## Unit Selections

## Key Points to Consider

- In what sense are all languages "equal"?

- How can language restrict our thought processes?

- In what ways is communication difficult in a cross-cultural situation?

- How has the "argument culture" affected the way we conduct ourselves vis-à-vis others?

- Does body art express individuality, conformity, or both?

- How has this section enhanced your ability to communicate more effectively?

## Student Website
www.mhcls.com/online

## Internet References
Further information regarding these websites may be found in this book's preface or online.

**Exploratorium Magazine: "The Evolution of Languages"**
*http://www.exploratorium.edu/exploring/language*
**Hypertext and Ethnography**
*http://www.umanitoba.ca/anthropology/tutor/aaa_presentation.html*
**Language Extinction**
*http://www.colorado.edu/iec/alis/articles/langext.htm*
**Showcase Anthropology**
*http://www.anthropology.wisc.edu/chaysimire/*

Anthropologists are interested in all aspects of human behavior and how they interrelate with each other. Language is a form of such behavior (albeit primarily verbal behavior) and, therefore, worthy of study. Although it changes over time, language is patterned and passed down from one generation to the next through learning, not instinct. In keeping with the idea that language is integral to human social interaction, it has long been recognized that human communication through language is by its nature different from the kind of communication found among other animals. Central to this difference is the fact that humans communicate abstractly, with symbols that have meaning independent of the immediate sensory experiences of either the sender or the receiver of messages. For instance humans are able to refer to the future and the past instead of just the here and now.

Recent experiments have shown that anthropoid apes can be taught a small portion of Ameslan or American Sign Language. It must be remembered, however, that their very rudimentary ability has to be tapped by painstaking human effort, and that the degree of difference between apes and humans serves only to emphasize the peculiarly human need for and development of language.

Just as the abstract quality of symbols lifts our thoughts beyond immediate sense perception, it also inhibits our ability to think about and convey the full meaning of our personal experience. No categorical term can do justice to its referents— the variety of forms to which the term refers. The degree to which this is an obstacle to clarity of thought and communication relates to the degree of abstraction in the symbols involved. The word "chair," for instance, would not present much difficulty, since it has objective referents. However, consider the trouble we have in thinking and communicating with words whose referents are not tied to immediate sense perception—words such as "freedom," "democracy," and "justice." Deborah Tannen's discussion of the "argument culture" (in "Fighting for our Lives") is a prime example of this. At best, the likely result is symbolic confusion: an inability to think or communicate in objectively definable symbols. At worst, language may be used to purposefully obfuscate.

A related issue has to do with the fact that languages differ as to what is relatively easy to express within the restrictions of their particular vocabularies. Thus, although a given language may not have enough words to cope with a new situation or a new field of activity, the typical solution is to invent words or to borrow them. In this way, it may be said that any language can be used to teach anything. This point is illustrated by Laura Bohannan's attempt to convey the "true" meaning of Shakespeare's *Hamlet*

to the West African Tiv (see "Shakespeare in the Bush"). Much of her task was devoted to finding the most appropriate words in the Tiv language to convey her Western thoughts. At least part of her failure was due to the fact that some of the words are just not there, and her inventions were unacceptable to the Tiv.

In a somewhat different manner, both Donna Jo Napoli in "Whose Speech is Better?" and Deborah Tannen, in "I Can't Even Open My Mouth," point out that there are subtleties to language that cannot be found in a dictionary and whose meaning can only be interpreted in the context of the social situation.

Taken collectively, the articles in this unit show how symbolic confusion may occur between individuals or groups. In addition, they demonstrate the tremendous potential of recent research to enhance effective communication among all of us.

# Whose Speech Is Better?

Donna Jo Napoli

Not all speakers of a given language speak the same way. You've noticed speech variations on television. Maybe you've seen the movie *My Fair Lady*, in which Henry Higgins believes that the Queen's English is the superior language of England (and, perhaps, of the world). So the question arises, whose speech is better? And this question is subsumed under the larger question of whether any language is intrinsically superior to another.

Before facing this issue, though, we need to face another matter. Consider these utterances:

Would you mind if I borrowed that cushion for a few moments?

Could I have that pillow for a sec?

Give me that, would you?

All of these utterances could be used to request a pillow.

Which one(s) would you use in addressing a stranger? If you use the first one, perhaps you sense that the stranger is quite different from you (such as a much older person or a person with more stature or authority). Perhaps you're trying to show that you're polite or refined or not a threat. Pay attention to the use of the word "cushion" instead of "pillow." Pillows often belong behind our heads, typically in bed. If you wanted to avoid any hint of intimacy, you might choose to use the word "cushion" for what is clearly a pillow.

Consider the third sentence. It's harder for some people to imagine using this one with a stranger. When I help to renovate urban housing for the poor with a group called Chester Community Improvement Project and I am pounding in nails next to some guy and sweat is dripping off both our brows, I have no hesitation in using this style sentence. With the informality of such a sentence, I'm implying, or perhaps trying to bring about, a sense of comradery.

Of course, it's easy to imagine a scene in which you could use the second sentence with a stranger.

Which one(s) would you use in addressing someone you know well? Again, it could be all three. But now if you use the first one, you might be insulting the addressee. It's not hard to think of a scenario in which this sentence carries a nasty tone rather than a polite one. And you can describe scenarios for the second and third sentences easily.

The point is that we command different registers of language. We can use talk that is fancy or ordinary or extremely informal, and we can choose which register to use in which situations to get the desired effect. So we have lots of variation in our own speech in the ways we phrase things (syntax) and the words we use (lexicon vocabulary).

Other variation in an individual's speech involves sound rules (phonology). Say the third sentence aloud several times, playing with different ways of saying it. Contrast "give me" to "gimme" and "would you" to "wudja." When we say words in a sequence, sometimes we contract them, but even a single word can be said in multiple ways. Say the word "interesting" in several sentences, imagining scenarios that differ in formality. Probably your normal (or least marked) pronunciation has three syllables: "in-tres-ting." But maybe it has four, and if it does, they are probably "in-er-es-ting."

The pronunciation that is closest to the spelling ("in-ter-es-ting") is more formal and, as a result, is sometimes used for humor (as in "very in-ter-es-ting," with a noticeably foreign flair to the pronunciation of "very" or with a drawn-out "e" in "very").

So you have plenty of variation in your own speech, no matter who you are, and the more different speech communities you belong to, the more variation you will have. With my mother's relatives, I will say, for example, "I hate lobsters anymore," whereas with other people I'm more likely to say, "I hate lobsters these days." This particular use of "anymore" is common to people from certain geographical areas (the North and South Midland, meaning the area from Philadelphia westward through southern Pennsylvania, northern West Virginia, Ohio, Indiana, and Illinois to the Mississippi River) but not to people from other places, who may not even understand what I mean. With my sister, I used to say, "Ain't nobody gonna tell me what to do," but I'd never say that to my mother or to other people unless I was trying to make a sociolinguistic point. This kind of talk signaled for us a comradery outside of the socioeconomic group my mother aspired to. In a speech to a convention of librarians recently, I said, "That had to change, for I, like you, do not lead a charmed life," but I'd probably never say that in conversation to anyone—it's speech talk. Also, think about the language you use in e-mail and contrast it to your job-related writings, for example.

Although we cannot explicitly state the rules of our language, we do choose to use different rules in different contexts. We happily exploit variation, which we encounter in a wide range, from simple differences in pronunciation and vocabulary to more marked differences that involve phrasing and sentence structure. When the differences are greater and more numerous, we tend to talk of dialects rather than just variations. Thus the languages of upper class and lower class Bostonians would probably be called variations of American English, whereas the languages of upper class and lower class Londoners (Queen's English versus Cockney) would probably be called dialects of British English. When the dialects are so different as to be mutually incomprehensible and/or when they gain a cultural or political status, we tend to talk of separate languages (such as French versus Spanish).

There's one more point I want to make before we return to our original question. I often ask classes to play the game of telephone in the following way. We line up twenty-one chairs, and volunteers sit on them. Then I whisper in the middle person's ear, perhaps something very simple, such as "Come with me to the store." The middle person then whispers the phrase into the ears of people on both sides, and the whisper chain goes on to each end of the line. Finally, the first and twenty-first persons say aloud what they heard.

Next we do the same experiment but this time with a sentence that's a little more tricky, perhaps something such as "Why choose white shoes for winter sports?" Then we do the experiment with a sentence in a language that the first whisperer (who is often not me at this point) speaks reasonably well and might be familiar to some of the twenty-one people in the chairs—perhaps something such as *La lune, c'est magnifique* (which in French means "the moon is wonderful"). Finally, we do the experiment with a sentence whispered initially by a native speaker of a language that none of the twenty-one people speak.

Typically, the first and twenty-first persons do not come up with the same results. Furthermore, the distance between them seems greater with each successive experiment.

Part of the problem is in the listening. We don't all hear things the same way. When we haven't heard something clearly, we ask people to repeat what they said. But sometimes we don't realize we haven't heard something clearly, until our inappropriate response is corrected. At times the other person doesn't correct us and the miscommunication remains, leading to various other difficulties.

Part of the problem in the experiment is in the repeating. You may say, "My economics class is a bore," and you begin the second word with the syllable "eek." I might repeat the sentence but use my pronunciation of the second word, which would begin with "ek." If you speak French well, you might say "magnifique" quite differently from me. In high school or college language classes, the teacher drilled the pronunciation of certain words over and over—but some people never mimicked to her satisfaction. A linguist told me a story about a little girl who introduced herself as "Litha." The man she was introducing herself to said, "Litha?" The child said, "No, Litha." The man said, "Litha?" The child said, "No, no. Litha. Li-tha." The man said, "Lisa?" The child smiled and said, "Right." Repetitions are not exact and lead to change.

Imperfections in hearing and repeating are two of the reasons that language must change over time. When the Romans marched into Gaul and into the Iberian peninsula and northeast-

ward into what is now Romania, they brought large populations who stayed and spoke a form of street Latin. But over time, the street Latin in Gaul developed into French; that in the Iberian Peninsula developed into Portuguese along the west and Spanish along the east and central portions; that in Romania developed into Romanian. Moreover, the street Latin spoken in the original community on the Italian peninsula changed as well, developing into Italian.

Other factors (besides our imperfections in hearing and in repeating sounds) can influence the speed with which language changes and the ways in which it changes—but the fact is that living languages necessarily change. They always have and they always will.

Many political groups have tried to control language change. During the French Revolution, a controlling faction decided that a standard language would pave the way for unity. Parish priests, who were ordered to survey spoken language, found that many dialects were spoken in different geographic areas, and many of them were quite distinct from the dialect of Paris. Primary schools in every region of France were established with teachers proficient in the Parisian dialect. The effect of this educational reform was not significant until 1881, when state education became free and mandatory, and the standard dialect (that is, Parisian) took hold more firmly. Still, the geographic dialects continued, though weakened, and most important, the standard kept changing. Standard French today is different from the Parisian dialect of 1790. In addition, new varieties of French have formed, as new subcultures have appeared. Social dialects persist and/or arise even when geographic dialects are squelched. Change is the rule in language, so variation will always be with us.

Now we can ask whose speech is better. This is a serious question because our attitudes about language affect how we treat speakers in personal, as well as in business and professional, situations. In what follows I will use the term "standard American English" (a term riddled with problems, which will become more and more apparent as you read)—the variety that we hear in news reports on television and radio. It doesn't seem to be strongly associated with any particular area of the country, although those who aren't from the Midwest often call it midwestern. This variety is also more frequently associated with the middle class than with the lower class, and it is more frequently associated with whites than with other races.

A few years ago a white student from Atlanta, Georgia, recorded herself reading a passage of James Joyce both in standard American English pronunciation and in her Atlanta pronunciation. She then asked strangers (adults of varying ages who lived in the town of Swarthmore, Pennsylvania) to listen to the two readings and answer a set of questions she had prepared. She did not tell the strangers that the recordings were made by a single person (nor that they were made by her). Without exception, the strangers judged the person who read the passage with standard English pronunciation as smarter and better educated, and most of them judged the person who read the passage with Atlanta pronunciation as nicer and more laid-back. This was just a small, informal study, but its findings are consistent with those of larger studies.

Studies have shown that prejudice against certain varieties of speech can lead to discriminatory practices. For example, Professor John Baugh of Stanford University directed a study of housing in which he used different English pronunciations when telephoning people who had advertised apartments for rent. In one call he would use standard American pronunciation; in another, African-American; in another, Latino. (He is African American, but he grew up in the middle class in Los Angeles with many Latino friends. He can sound white, African American, or Latino, at will.) He said exactly the same words in every call, and he controlled for the order in which he made the calls (i.e., sometimes the Latino pronunciation would be used first, sometimes the African-American, and sometimes the standard). He asked if the apartments were still available. More were available when he used the standard pronunciation. Thus it is essential that we examine carefully the question of "better" with regard to language variety.

When I knock on a door and my friend inside says, "Who's there?" I'm likely to answer, "It's me," but I don't say, "It's I" (or, even more unlikely for me, "It is I"). Do you? If you do, do you say that naturally, that is, not self-consciously? Or do you say it because you've been taught that that's the correct thing to say? If you do it naturally, your speech contains an archaism—a little fossil from the past. We all have little fossils. I say, "I'm different from you." Most people today would say, "I'm different than you." My use of "from" after "different" was typical in earlier generations, but it's not typical today. Some of us hold onto archaisms longer than others, and even the most linguistically innovative of us probably have some. So don't be embarrassed by your fossils: They're a fact of language.

But if you say "It's I" self-consciously because you've been taught that that's correct, what does "correct" mean in this situation? If that's what most people used to say but is not what most people say today, you're saying it's correct either because you revere the past (which many of us do) or because you believe that there's a rule of language that's being obeyed by "It's I" and being broken by "It's me."

I'm going to push the analysis of just this one contrast—"It's I" versus "It's me"—quite a distance because I believe that many relevant issues about how people view language will come out of the discussion. Consider the former reason for preferring "It's I," that of revering the past. Many people have this reason for using archaic speech patterns and for preferring that others use them. For some reason, language is treated in a unique way here. We certainly don't hold up the past as superior in other areas, for example, mathematics or physics. So why do some of us feel that changes in language are evidence of decay?

If it were true that the older way of saying something were better simply because it's older, your grandparents spoke better than your parents and your great-grandparents spoke better than your grandparents and so on. Did Chaucer speak a form of English superior to that spoken by Shakespeare? Shall we go further back than Chaucer for our model? There is no natural stopping point. We can go all the way to prehistoric times if we use "older" as the only standard for "better."

The latter reason—believing that "It's I" obeys a rule that "It's me" breaks—is more defensible, if it is indeed true. De-

fenders of the "It's I" school of speech point out that with the verb "be" the elements on both sides of it are grammatically equivalent—so they should naturally have the same case.

I've used a linguistic term here: "case." To understand it (or review it), look at these Hungarian sentences:

Megnézhetem a szobát?
Van rádió a szobában?
Hol a szoba?

May I see the room?
Is there a radio in the room?
Where's the room?

I have translated the sentences in a natural way rather than word by word. Can you pick out the word in each sentence that means "room"? I hope you chose *szobát, szobában,* and *szoba.* These three forms can be thought of as variants of the same word. The difference in form is called case marking. Textbooks on Hungarian typically claim that a form like *szoba* is used when the word is the subject of the sentence, a form like *szobát* when the word is the direct object, and a form like *szobában* when the word conveys a certain kind of location (comparable to the object of the preposition "in" in English). So a word can have various forms—various cases—based on how it is used in the sentence.

English does not have different case forms for nouns (with the exception of genitive nouns, such as "boy's" in "the boy's book"). So in the English translations of the Hungarian sentences above, the word "room" was invariable. However, English does have different case forms for pronouns:

I like tennis.
That tennis racket is mine.
Everyone likes me.

These three forms indicate the first-person singular: "I," "mine," and "me." They distinguish subjects ("I") from genitives ("mine") from everything else ("me").

Now let's return to "It's I." Must elements on either side of "be" be equivalent? In the following three sentences, different syntactic categories are on either side of "be" (here "NP" stands for "noun phrase"):

Bill is tall
Bill is off his rocker.
Bill is to die for.

NP "be" AP
NP "be" PP
NP "be" VP

"Tall" is an adjective (here, an adjective phrase, AP). "Off" is a preposition, and it's part of the prepositional phrase (PP) "off his rocker." "To die for" is a verb phrase (VP). Thus the two elements that flank "be" do not have to be equivalent in category.

Still, in the sentence "It's I," the elements that flank "be" are both pronouns ("It" and "I"), so maybe these elements are equivalent in this sentence. Let's test that claim by looking at agreement. Verbs agree with their subject in English, whether that subject precedes or follows them:

John's nice.
Is John nice?

But "be" in our focus sentence agrees with the NP to its left, not to its right:

It's I.
*It am I.

No one would say "It am I." Therefore, the NP to the right of "be" is not the subject of the sentence, which means that the NPs flanking "be" are not equivalent—"It" is the subject, but "I" is not.

Perhaps you think that the equivalency that matters here has to do with meaning, not with syntax. Let's pursue that: Do "It" and "I" have equivalent meaning in "It's I"? Notice that you can also say:

"It's you."

In fact, the slot after "It's" can be filled by several different pronouns. "It" in these sentences is not meaningful; it is simply a place holder, just as in sentences about time and weather:

It's four o'clock.
It's hailing.

But "I" is meaningful because it refers to a person (the speaker). Therefore, "It" and "I" are not equivalent in meaning in the sentence "It's I."

In sum, it's not clear that the elements on either side of "be" in the sentence "It's I" are equivalent in any linguistic way. We can conclude something even stronger. We noted that "It" in these sentences is the subject and that the pronoun following a form of "be" is not the subject. But the pronoun following "be" is also not a genitive. Given the pronoun case system of English discussed above, we expect the pronoun to take the third form (the "elsewhere" form), which is "me," not "I." In other words, our case system would lead us to claim that "It's me" is the grammatical sentence.

I am not saying "It's I" is ungrammatical. I want to show that the issue may not be as clean-cut as you might have thought. Indeed, the conclusion I come to is that more than one case system is at play here. Those who say "It's me" are employing regular case rules. But those who say "It's I" have a special case rule for certain sentences that contain "be." The important point is that both sets of speakers have rules that determine what they say. Their speech is systematic; they are not speaking randomly.

That is the key issue of this whole chapter. When we consider variation in language, we must give up the idea of errors and accept the idea of patterns. Some people produce one pattern because they are following one set of rules; other people produce a different pattern because they are following a different set of rules. (For several different types of language variations in English, visit the websites of the West Virginia Dialect Project: http://www.as.wvu.edu/dialect.) From a linguistic perspective, asking whose speech is better would amount to asking whose system is better. But what standards do we have for evaluating systems? What standards do you, as a speaker of the language, employ when you judge between varieties of speech? To answer that question, consider variation in your own speech. Do you consider some varieties better than others? And which ones? If you're like most people, you consider formal or polite speech to be better. But that standard concerns behavior in society—behavior that may reveal or perhaps even determine one's position. We tend to think that the speech of those who hold cultural, economic, or other social power is better, but this has little to do with linguistic structure. Now ask yourself what standards you are using to judge the speech of others.

Such questions often boil down to your politics (who do you esteem?) or to your experience (what are you familiar with?) but not to your grammatical rules. Consider the common claim that some varieties of speech are lazy. Try to find a recording of English speech that you consider lazy. Now mimic it. Some people are good at mimicking the speech of others, but accurately mimicking the speech of anyone else (anyone at all) takes a good ear, good control over the parts of your body that produce speech, and mostly a grasp of the sound rules that are being used. So the speech you thought was lazy wasn't lazy at all. Rather, different rules are being employed in different varieties of speech. What makes each variety distinct from others is its inventory of rules.

Consider learning a foreign language. People who feel confident about their ability to speak and to understand a foreign language in a classroom often visit a place where that language is spoken, only to find that no one is speaking the classroom variety. One of the big differences is usually speed: Ordinary speech can be quite rapid. Again, some claim that fast speech is sloppy, but fast speech is notoriously hard to mimic. It is typically packed with sound rules, so it takes more experience with the language to master all the rules and to be able to produce fast speech.

Among American speakers a common misconception is that British speech is superior to American speech. Part of this belief follows from reverence of the past, already discussed. Part of it follows from the misperception that American upper class speech is closer to British speech—so British speech is associated with high society and with politeness. In fact, the speech of the British changed over time, just as the speech of the American colonialists changed over time. Therefore, modern British speech is not, in general, closer to older forms of English than American speech is. Pockets of conservative varieties of English occur both in the British Isles and in the United States, but most varieties on either side of the Atlantic Ocean have changed considerably. Also, British society is stratified, just as American society is, and not all British speech is either upper class or polite.

Linguists claim that all varieties of a language—all dialects and all languages, for that matter—are equal linguistic citizens. Linguists have recognized that all languages are systematic, obeying certain universal principles regarding the organization and interaction of sounds, the ways we build words and phrases and sentences, and how we code meaning. However, this doesn't mean that all language is esthetically equal. I can recognize a beautiful line in a poem or a story, as I'm sure you can (though we might not agree). But that beautiful line might be in archaic English, formal contemporary English, ordinary contemporary English, very informal contemporary English, African-American Atlanta English, Italian-American Yonkers English, Philadelphia gay English, Chinese-American Seattle English, or so many others. Within our different varieties of speech, we can speak in ways that affect people's hearts or resonate in their minds, or we can speak in ways that are unremarkable. These are personal (esthetic or political) choices.

Some possible effects of the goal of the English only movement (EOM) of minimizing certain language variations in the United States [exist]. But even if English were declared the official language of the United States, variation would not be wiped out. What would be threatened is the richness of the range of variation most speakers are exposed to. Once that exposure is lost, Americans might start thinking that English is a superior language simply because they would no longer hear other languages being spoken by people they know personally and respect. They might become severely provincial in their linguistic attitudes, and given the necessity of global respect these days, such provincialism could be dangerous.

The fact that variation in language is both unavoidable and sometimes the result of esthetic and political choices does not mean that educational institutions should not insist that children master whatever variety of language has been deemed the standard—just for purely practical reasons. There's little doubt that linguistic prejudice is a reality. The adult who cannot speak and write the standard variety may encounter a range of difficulties, from finding suitable employment to achieving social advancement.

At the same time, all of us—and educational institutions, in particular—should respect all varieties of language and show that respect in relevant ways. Look at one notorious controversy: In 1996 the school board in Oakland, California, declared Ebonics to be the official language of the district's African-American students. Given funding regulations for bilingual education in that time and place, this decision had the effect of allowing the school district to use funds set aside for bilingual education to teach their African-American children in Ebonics, as well as in the standard language.

The debate was particularly hot, I believe, because of the sociological issues involved. Many people thought that Ebonics should be kept out of the classroom purely because the dialect was associated with race. Some of these people were African Americans who did not want their children to be disadvantaged by linguistic prejudice; they were afraid that teaching in Ebonics would exaggerate racial linguistic prejudice rather than redress it. Many good books written about the Ebonics controversy for the general public look at the issue from a variety of perspectives (see the suggested readings). But from a linguistic perspective, the issue is more a question of bilingual (or bi-dialectal) education than anything else.

In sum, variation in language is something we all participate in, and, as a linguist and a writer, I believe it's something we should revel in. Language is not a monolith, nor can it be, nor should it be, given the complexity of culture and the fact that language is the fabric of culture. Some of us are more eloquent than others, and all of us have moments of greater or lesser eloquence. But that range in eloquence is found in every language, every dialect, and every variety of speech.

# Further Reading on Variation

Andersson, L. G., and P. Trudgill. 1990. *Bad language*. Cambridge: Blackwell.

Baron, D. 1994. *Guide to home language repair*. Champaign, Ill.: National Council of Teachers of English.

Baugh, J. 1999. *Out of the mouths of slaves*. Austin: University of Texas Press.

Biber, D., and E. Finegan. 1997. *Sociolinguistic perspectives on register*. Oxford: Oxford University Press.

Cameron, D. 1995. *Verbal hygiene*. London: Routledge.

Carver, C. 1989. *American regional dialects: A word geography*. Ann Arbor: University of Michigan Press.

Coulmas, F. 1998. *Handbook of sociolinguistics*. Cambridge: Blackwell.

Fasold, R. 1984. *The sociolinguistics of society*. New York: Blackwell.

Finegan, E. 1980. *Attitudes toward language usage*. New York: Teachers College Press.

Fishman, J. 1968. *Readings in the sociology of language*. Paris: Mouton.

Herman, L. H., and M. S. Herman. 1947. *Manual of American dialects for radio, stage, screen, and television*. New York: Ziff Davis.

Hock, H., and B. Joseph. 1996. *An introduction to historical and comparative linguistics*. Berlin: Mouton de Gruyter.

Labov, W. 1972. *The logic of nonstandard English in language and social context: Selected readings*. Compiled by Pier Paolo Giglioli. Baltimore Md.: Penguin.

Labov, W. 1972. *Sociolinguistic patterns*. Philadelphia: University of Pennsylvania Press.

LeClerc, F., Schmitt, B. H., and Dube, L. 1994, May. Foreign branding and its effects on product perceptions and attitudes. *Journal of Marketing Research*, 31: 263–270.

Lippi-Green, R. 1997. *English with an accent*. New York: Routledge.

McCrum, R., W. Cran, and R. MacNeil. 1986. *The story of English*. New York: Viking Penguin.

Millward, C. M. 1989. *A biography of the English language*. Orlando, Fla.: Holt, Rinehart and Winston.

Milroy, J., and L. Milroy. 1991. *Authority in language*, 2nd ed. London: Routledge.

Moss, B., and K. Walters. 1993. Rethinking diversity: Axes of difference in the writing classroom. In L. Odell, ed., *Theory and practice in the teaching of writing: Rethinking the discipline*. Carbondale: Southern Illinois University Press.

Peyton, J., S. McGinnis, and D. Ranard, eds. 2001. *Heritage languages in America: Preserving a national resource* (from Delta Systems, phone 800–323–8270), Arlington, Va.

Romaine, S. 1994. *Language in society: An introduction to sociolinguistics*. Oxford: Oxford University Press.

Scherer, K., and H. Giles, eds. 1979. *Social markers in speech*. New York: Cambridge University Press.

Seligman, C. R., G. R. Tucker, and W. Lambert. 1972. The effects of speech style and other attributes on teachers' attitudes toward pupils. *Language and Society*, 1: 131–42.

Trask, R. L. 1994. *Language change*. London: Routledge.

Weinreich, U. [1953] 1968. *Languages in contact*. The Hague: Mouton.

Wolfram, W. 1991. *Dialects and American English*. Englewood Cliffs, N.J.: Prentice Hall.

Wolfram, W., and N. Schilling-Estes. 1998. *American English—dialects and variation*. Oxford: Blackwell.

# Web Sites

Center for Applied Linguistics—Sources on Dialects. http://www.cal.org/topics/dialres.htm

Hazen, K. (ongoing—accessed April 2001). Variety is the spice of life. http://www.as.wvu.edu/~khazen/WVDP.HTML

Labov, W. How I got into linguistics, and what I got out of it. http://www.ling.upenn.edu/~labov/Papers/HowIgot.html

Thomason, S. Language variation and change. http://www.lsadc.org/web2/variation.html

University of Oregon—Explore linguistics and sociolinguistics. http://logos.uoregon.edu/explore/socioling/

University of Pennsylvania—Can reading failure be reversed? http://www.ling.upenn.edu/phono_atlas/RFR.html

University of Pennsylvania—Phonological atlas of North America. http://www.ling.upenn.edu/phono_atlas/home.html

# Further Reading on Ebonics

Adger, C. 1994. Enhancing the delivery of services to black special education students from non-standard English backgrounds. Final Report. University of Maryland, Institute for the Study of Exceptional Children and Youth. (Available through ERIC Document Reproduction Service. Document No. ED 370 377.)

Adger, C., D. Christian, and O. Taylor. 1999. *Making the connection: Language and academic achievement among African American students*. Washington, D.C. and McHenry, Ill.: Center for Applied Linguistics and Delta Systems.

Adger, C., W. Wolfram, and J. Detwyler. 1993. Language differences: A new approach for special educators. *Teaching Exceptional Children*, 26, no. (1): 44–47.

Adger, C., W. Wolfram, J. Detwyler, and B. Harry. 1993. Confronting dialect minority issues in special education: Reactive and proactive perspectives. In *Proceedings of the Third National Research Symposium on Limited English Proficient Student Issues: Focus on Middle and High School Issues*, 2: 737–62. U.S. Department of Education, Office of Bilingual Education and Minority Languages Affairs. (Available through ERIC Document Reproduction Service. Document No. ED 356 673.)

Baratz, J. C., and R. W. Shuy, eds. 1969. Teaching black children to read. Available as reprints from the University of Michigan, Ann Arbor (313–761–4700).

Baugh, J. 2000. *Beyond Ebonics*. New York: Oxford University Press.

Christian, D. 1997. Vernacular dialects and standard American English in the classroom. ERIC Minibib. Washington, D.C.: ERIC Clearinghouse on Languages and Linguistics. (This minibibliography cites seven journal articles and eight documents related to dialect usage in the classroom. The documents can be accessed on microfiche at any institution with the ERIC collection, or they can be ordered directly from EDRS.)

Dillard, J. L. 1972. *Black English: Its history and use in the U.S.* New York: Random House.

Fasold, R. W. 1972. Tense marking in black English: A linguistic and social analysis. Available as reprints from the University of Michigan, Ann Arbor (313–761–4700).

Fasold, R. W., and R. W. Shuy, eds. 1970. *Teaching standard English in the inner city*. Washington, D.C.: Center for Applied Linguistics.

Wiley, T. G. 1996. The case of African American language. In *Literacy and language diversity in the United States*, pp. 125–32. Washington, D. C.: Center for Applied Linguistics and Delta Systems.

Wolfram, W. 1969. A sociolinguistic description of Detroit Negro speech. Available as reprints from the University of Michigan, Ann Arbor (313–761–4700).

Wolfram, W. 1990, February. Incorporating dialect study into the language arts class. *ERIC Digest*. Available from the ERIC Clearinghouse on Languages and Linguistics, Center for Applied Linguistics, 4646 40th Street NW, Washington, D.C. 20016-1859, (202–362–0700).

Wolfram, W. 1994. Bidialectal literacy in the United States. In D.Spencer, ed., *Adult biliteracy in the United States*, pp. 71–88. Washington, D.C.: Center for Applied Linguistics and Delta Systems.

Wolfram, W., and C. Adger. 1993. *Handbook on language differences and speech and language pathology: Baltimore City public schools*. Washington, D.C.: Center for Applied Linguistics.

Wolfram, W., C. Adger, and D. Christian. 1999. Dialects in schools and communities. Mahwah, N.J.: Erlbaum.

Wolfram, W., and N. Clarke, eds. 1971. *Black-white speech relationships*. Washington, D.C.: Center for Applied Linguistics.

Chapter 7 from *Language Matters: A Guide to Everyday Questions About Language*, Oxford University Press, 2003, pp. 99–120. Copyright © 2003 by Oxford University Press, Ltd. Reprinted by permission.

# Fighting for Our Lives

Deborah Tannen, Ph.D.

This is not another book about civility. "Civility" suggests a superficial, pinky-in-the-air veneer of politeness spread thin over human relations like a layer of marmalade over toast. This book is about a pervasive warlike atmosphere that makes us approach public dialogue, and just about anything we need to accomplish, as if it were a fight. It is a tendency in Western culture in general, and in the United States in particular, that has a long history and a deep, thick, and far-ranging root system. It has served us well in many ways but in recent years has become so exaggerated that it is getting in the way of solving our problems. Our spirits are corroded by living in an atmosphere of unrelenting contention—an argument culture.

The argument culture urges us to approach the world—and the people in it—in an adversarial frame of mind. It rests on the assumption that opposition is the best way to get anything done: The best way to discuss an idea is to set up a debate; the best way to cover news is to find spokespeople who express the most extreme, polarized views and present them as "both sides"; the best way to settle disputes is litigation that pits one party against the other; the best way to begin an essay is to attack someone; and the best way to show you're really thinking is to criticize.

Our public interactions have become more and more like having an argument with a spouse. Conflict can't be avoided in our public lives any more than we can avoid conflict with people we love. One of the great strengths of our society is that we can express these conflicts openly. But just as spouses have to learn ways of settling their differences without inflicting real damage on each other, so we, as a society, have to find constructive ways of resolving disputes and differences. Public discourse requires *making* an argument for a point of view, not *having* an argument—as in having a fight.

The war on drugs, the war on cancer, the battle of the sexes, politicians' turf battles—in the argument culture, war metaphors pervade our talk and shape our thinking. Nearly everything is framed as a battle or game in which winning or losing is the main concern. These all have their uses and their place, but they are not the only way—and often not the best way—to understand and approach our world. Conflict and opposition are as necessary as cooperation and agreement, but the scale is off balance, with conflict and opposition overweighted. In this book, I show how deeply entrenched the argument culture is, the forms it takes, and how it affects us every day—sometimes in useful ways, but often creating more problems than it solves,

causing rather than avoiding damage. As a sociolinguist, a social scientist, I am trained to observe and explain language and its role in human relations, and that is my biggest job here. But I will also point toward other ways for us to talk to each other and get things done in our public lives.

## The Battle of the Sexes

My interest in the topic of opposition in public discourse intensified in the years following the publication of *You Just Don't Understand,* my book about communication between women and men. In the first year I appeared on many television and radio shows and was interviewed for many print articles in newspapers and magazines. For the most part, that coverage was extremely fair, and I was—and remain—indebted to the many journalists who found my ideas interesting enough to make them known to viewers, listeners, and readers. But from time to time—more often than I expected—I encountered producers who insisted on setting up a television show as a fight (either between the host and me or between another guest and me) and print journalists who made multiple phone calls to my colleagues, trying to find someone who would criticize my work. This got me thinking about what kind of information comes across on shows and in articles that take this approach, compared to those that approach topics in other ways.

At the same time, my experience of the academic world that had long been my intellectual home began to change. For the most part, other scholars, like most journalists, were welcoming and respectful in their responses to my work, even if they disagreed on specific points or had alternative views to suggest. But about a year after *You Just Don't Understand* became a best-seller—the wheels of academia grind more slowly than those of the popular press—I began reading attacks on my work that completely misrepresented it. I had been in academia for over fifteen years by then, and had valued my interaction with other researchers as one of the greatest rewards of academic life. Why, I wondered, would someone represent me as having said things I had never said or as having failed to say things I had said?

The answer crystallized when I put the question to a writer who I felt had misrepresented my work: "Why do you need to make others wrong for you to be right?" Her response: "It's an argument!" Aha, I thought, that explains it. When you're having an argument with someone, your goal is not to listen and understand. Instead, you use every tactic you can think of—including distorting what your opponent just said—in order to win the argument.

Not only the level of attention *You Just Don't Understand* received but, even more, the subject of women and men, triggered the tendency to polarize. This tendency to stage a fight on television or in print was posited on the conviction that opposition leads to truth. Sometimes it does. But the trouble is, sometimes it doesn't. I was asked at the start of more than one talk show or print interview, "What is the most controversial thing about your book?" Opposition does not lead to truth when the most controversial thing is not the most important.

The conviction that opposition leads to truth can tempt not only members of the press but just about anyone seeking to attract an audience to frame discussions as a fight between irreconcilable opposites. Even the Smithsonian Institution, to celebrate its 150th anniversary, sponsored a series of talks billed as debates. They invited me to take part in one titled "The Battle of the Sexes." The organizer preempted my objection: "I know you won't be happy with this title, but we want to get people interested." This is one of many assumptions I question in this book: Is it necessary to frame an interchange as a battle to get people interested? And even if doing so succeeds in capturing attention, does it risk dampening interest in the long run, as audiences weary of the din and begin to hunger for more substance?

## Thought-Provoking or Just Provocative?

In the spring of 1995, Horizons Theatre in Arlington, Virginia, produced two one-act plays I had written about family relationships. The director, wanting to contribute to the reconciliation between Blacks and Jews, mounted my plays in repertory with two one-act plays by an African American playwright, Caleen Sinnette Jennings. We had both written plays about three sisters that explored the ethnic identities of our families (Jewish for me, African-American for her) and the relationship between those identities and the American context in which we grew up. To stir interest in the plays and to explore the parallels between her work and mine, the theater planned a public dialogue between Jennings and me, to be held before the plays opened.

As production got under way, I attended the audition of actors for my plays. After the auditions ended, just before everyone headed home, the theater's public relations volunteer distributed copies of the flyer announcing the public dialogue that she had readied for distribution. I was horrified. The flyer announced that Caleen and I would discuss "how past traumas create understanding and conflict between Blacks and Jews today." The flyer was trying to grab by the throat the issue that we wished to address indirectly. Yes, we were concerned with conflicts between Blacks and Jews, but neither of us is an authority on that conflict, and we had no intention of expounding on it. We hoped to do our part to ameliorate the conflict by focusing on commonalities. Our plays had many resonances between them. We wanted to talk about our work and let the resonances speak for themselves.

Fortunately, we were able to stop the flyers before they were distributed and devise new ones that promised something we could deliver: "a discussion of heritage, identity, and complex family relationships in African-American and Jewish-American culture as represented in their plays." Jennings noticed that the original flyer said the evening would be "provocative" and changed it to "thought-provoking." What a world of difference is implied in that small change: how much better to make people think, rather than simply to "provoke" them—as often as not, to anger.

It is easy to understand why conflict is so often highlighted: Writers of headlines or promotional copy want to catch attention and attract an audience. They are usually under time pressure, which lures them to established, conventionalized ways of expressing ideas in the absence of leisure to think up entirely new ones. The promise of controversy seems an easy and natural way to rouse interest. But serious consequences are often unintended: Stirring up animosities to get a rise out of people, though easy and "provocative," can open old wounds or create new ones that are hard to heal. This is one of many dangers inherent in the argument culture.

## For the Sake of Argument

In the argument culture, criticism, attack, or opposition are the predominant if not the the only ways of responding to people or ideas. I use the phrase "culture of critique" to capture this aspect. "Critique" in this sense is not a general term for analysis or interpretation but rather a synonym for criticism.

It is the *automatic* nature of this response that I am calling attention to—and calling into question. Sometimes passionate opposition, strong verbal attack, are appropriate and called for. No one knows this better than those who have lived under repressive regimes that forbid public opposition. The Yugoslavian-born poet Charles Simic is one. "There are moments in life," he writes, "when true invective is called for, when it becomes an absolute necessity, out of a deep sense of justice, to denounce, mock, vituperate, lash out, in the strongest possible language." I applaud and endorse this view. There are times when it is necessary and right to fight—to defend your country or yourself, to argue for right against wrong or against offensive or dangerous ideas or actions.

What I question is the ubiquity, the knee-jerk nature, of approaching almost any issue, problem, or public person in an adversarial way. One of the dangers of the habitual use of adversarial rhetoric is a kind of verbal inflation—a rhetorical boy who cried wolf: The legitimate, necessary denunciation is muted, even lost, in the general cacophony of oppositional shouting. What I question is using opposition to accomplish *every* goal, even those that do not require fighting but might also (or better) be accomplished by other means, such as exploring, expanding, discussing, investigating, and the exchanging of ideas suggested by the word "dialogue." I am questioning the assumption that *everything* is a matter of polarized opposites, the proverbial "two sides to every question" that we think embodies open-mindedness and expansive thinking.

In a word, the type of opposition I am questioning is what I call "agonism." I use this term, which derives from the Greek word for "contest," *agonia,* to mean an automatic warlike stance—not the literal opposition of fighting against an attacker or the unavoidable opposition that arises organically in response to conflicting ideas or actions. An agonistic response, to me, is a kind of programmed contentiousness—a prepatterned, unthinking use of fighting to accomplish goals that do not necessarily require it.

## How Useful are Fights?

Noticing that public discourse so often takes the form of heated arguments—of having a fight—made me ask how useful it is in our personal lives to settle differences by arguing. Given what I know about having arguments in private life, I had to conclude that it is, in many cases, not very useful.

In close relationships it is possible to find ways of arguing that result in better understanding and solving problems. But with most arguments, little is resolved, worked out, or achieved when two people get angrier and less rational by the minute. When you're having an argument with someone, you're usually not trying to understand what the other person is saying, or what in their experience leads them to say it. Instead, you're readying your response: listening for weaknesses in logic to leap on, points you can distort to make the other person look bad and yourself look good. Sometimes you know, on some back burner of your mind, that you're doing this—that there's a kernel of truth in what your adversary is saying and a bit of unfair twisting in what you're saying. Sometimes you do this because you're angry, but sometimes it's just the temptation to take aim at a point made along the way because it's an easy target.

Here's an example of how this happened in an argument between a couple who had been married for over fifty years. The husband wanted to join an HMO by signing over their Medicare benefits to save money. The wife objected because it would mean she could no longer see the doctor she knew and trusted. In arguing her point of view, she said, "I like Dr. B. He knows me, he's interested in me. He calls me by my first name." The husband parried the last point: "I don't like that. He's much younger than we are. He shouldn't be calling us by first name." But the form of address Dr. B. uses was irrelevant. The wife was trying to communicate that she felt comfortable with the doctor she knew, that she had a relationship with him. His calling her by first name was just one of a list of details she was marshaling to explain her comfort with him. Picking on this one detail did not change her view—and did not address her concern. It was just a way to win the argument.

We all are guilty, at times, of seizing on irrelevant details, distorting someone else's position the better to oppose it, when we're arguing with those we're closest to. But we are rarely dependent on these fights as sources of information. The same tactics are common when public discourse is carried out on the model of personal fights. And the results are dangerous when listeners are looking to these interchanges to get needed information or practical results.

Fights have winners and losers. If you're fighting to win, the temptation is great to deny facts that support your opponent's views and to filter what you know, saying only what supports your side. In the extreme form, it encourages people to misrepresent or even to lie. We accept this risk because we believe we can tell when someone is lying. The problem is, we can't.

Paul Ekman, a psychologist at the University of California, San Francisco, studies lying. He set up experiments in which individuals were videotaped talking about their emotions, actions, or beliefs—some truthfully, some not. He has shown these videotapes to thousands of people, asking them to identify the liars and also to say how sure they were about their judgments. His findings are chilling: Most people performed not much better than chance, and those who did the worst had just as much confidence in their judgments as the few who were really able to detect lies. Intrigued by the implications of this research in various walks of life, Dr. Ekman repeated this experiment with groups of people whose jobs require them to sniff out lies: judges, lawyers, police, psychotherapists, and employees of the CIA, FBI, and ATF (Bureau of Alcohol, Tobacco, and Firearms). They were no better at detecting who was telling the truth than the rest of us. The only group that did significantly better were members of the U.S. Secret Service. This finding gives some comfort when it comes to the Secret Service but not much when it comes to every other facet of public life.

## Two Sides to Every Question

Our determination to pursue truth by setting up a fight between two sides leads us to believe that every issue has two sides—no more, no less: If both sides are given a forum to confront each other, all the relevant information will emerge, and the best case will be made for each side. But opposition does not lead to truth when an issue is not composed of two opposing sides but is a crystal of many sides. Often the truth is in the complex middle, not the oversimplified extremes.

We love using the word "debate" as a way of representing issues: the abortion debate, the health care debate, the affirmative action debate—even "the great backpacking vs. car camping debate." The ubiquity of this word in itself shows our tendency to conceptualize issues in a way that predisposes public discussion to be polarized, framed as two opposing sides that give each other no ground. There are many problems with this approach. If you begin with the assumption that there *must* be an "other side," you may end up scouring the margins of science or the fringes of lunacy to find it. As a result, proven facts, such as what we know about how the earth and its inhabitants evolved, are set on a par with claims that are known to have no basis in fact, such as creationism.

The conviction that there are two sides to every story can prompt writers or producers to dig up an "other side," so kooks who state outright falsehoods are given a platform in public discourse. This accounts, in part, for the bizarre phenomenon of Holocaust denial. Deniers, as Emory University professor Deborah Lipstadt shows, have been successful in gaining television airtime and campus newspaper coverage by masquerading as "the other side" in a "debate."

Appearance in print or on television has a way of lending legitimacy, so baseless claims take on a mantle of possibility. Lipstadt shows how Holocaust deniers dispute established facts of history, and then reasonable spokespersons use their having been disputed as a basis for questioning known facts. The actor Robert Mitchum, for example, interviewed in *Esquire*, expressed doubt about the Holocaust. When the interviewer asked about the slaughter of six million Jews, Mitchum replied, "I don't know. People dispute that." Continual reference to "the other side" results in a pervasive conviction that everything has another side—with the result that people begin to doubt the existence of any facts at all.

## The Expense of Time and Spirit

Lipstadt's book meticulously exposes the methods used by deniers to falsify the overwhelming historic evidence that the Holocaust occurred. That a scholar had to invest years of her professional life writing a book unraveling efforts to deny something that was about as well known and well documented as any historical fact has ever been—while those who personally experienced and witnessed it are still alive—is testament to another way that the argument culture limits our knowledge rather than expanding it. Talent and effort was wasted when individuals who have been unfairly attacked must spend years of their creative lives defending themselves rather than advancing their work. The entire society loses their creative efforts. This is what happened with scientist Robert Gallo.

Dr. Gallo is the American virologist who codiscovered the AIDS virus. He is also the one who developed the technique for studying T-cells, which made that discovery possible. And Gallo's work was seminal in developing the test to detect the AIDS virus in blood, the first and for a long time the only means known of stemming the tide of death from AIDS. But in 1989, Gallo became the object of a four-year investigation into allegations that he had stolen the AIDS virus from Luc Montagnier of the Pasteur Institute in Paris, who had independently identified the AIDS virus. Simultaneous investigations by the National Institutes of Health, the office of Michigan Congressman John Dingell, and the National Academy of Sciences barreled ahead long after Gallo and Montagnier settled the dispute to their mutual satisfaction. In 1993 the investigations concluded that Gallo had done nothing wrong. Nothing. But this exoneration cannot be considered a happy ending. Never mind the personal suffering of Gallo, who was reviled when he should have been heralded as a hero. Never mind that, in his words, "These were the most painful years and horrible years of my life." The dreadful, unconscionable result of the fruitless investigations is that Gallo had to spend four years fighting the accusations instead of fighting AIDS.

The investigations, according to journalist Nicholas Wade, were sparked by an article about Gallo written in the currently popular spirit of demonography: not to praise the person it features but to bury him—to show his weaknesses, his villainous side. The implication that Gallo has stolen the AIDS virus was created to fill a requirement of the discourse: In demonography, writers must find negative sides of their subjects to display for readers who enjoy seeing heroes transformed into villains. The suspicion led to investigations, and the investigations became a juggernaut that acquired a life of its own, fed by the enthusiasm for attack on public figures that is the culture of critique.

## Metaphors: We Are What We Speak

Perhaps one reason suspicions of Robert Gallo were so zealously investigated is that the scenario of an ambitious scientist ready to do anything to defeat a rival appeals to our sense of story; it is the kind of narrative we are ready to believe. Culture, in a sense, is an environment of narratives that we hear repeatedly until they seem to make self-evident sense in explaining human behavior. Thinking of human interactions as battles is a metaphorical frame through which we learn to regard the world and the people in it.

All language uses metaphors to express ideas; some metaphoric words and expressions are novel, made up for the occasion, but more are calcified in the language. They are simply the way we think it is natural to express ideas. We don't think of them as metaphors. Someone who says, "Be careful: You aren't a cat, you don't have nine lives," is explicitly comparing you to a cat, because the cat is named in words. But what if someone says, "Don't pussyfoot around; get to the point"? There is no explicit comparison to a cat, but the comparison is there nonetheless, implied in the word "pussyfoot." This expression probably developed as a reference to the movement of a cat cautiously circling a suspicious object. I doubt that individuals using the word "pussyfoot" think consciously of cats. More often than not, we use expressions without thinking about their metaphoric implications. But that doesn't mean those implications are not influencing us.

At a meeting, a general discussion became so animated that a participant who wanted to comment prefaced his remark by saying, "I'd like to leap into the fray." Another participant called out, "Or share your thoughts." Everyone laughed. By suggesting a different phrasing, she called attention to what would probably have otherwise gone unnoticed: "Leap into the fray" characterized the lively discussion as a metaphorical battle.

Americans talk about almost everything as if it were a war. A book about the history of linguistics is called *The Linguistics Wars*. A magazine article about claims that science is not completely objective is titled "The Science Wars." One about breast cancer detection is "The Mammogram War"; about competition among caterers, "Party Wars"—and on and on in a potentially endless list. Politics, of course, is a prime candidate. One of innumerable possible examples, the headline of a story reporting that the Democratic National Convention nominated Bill Clinton to run for a second term declares, "DEMOCRATS SEND CLINTON INTO BATTLE FOR A 2D TERM." But medicine is as frequent a candidate, as we talk about battling and conquering disease.

Headlines are intentionally devised to attract attention, but we all use military or attack imagery in everyday expressions without thinking about it: "Take a shot at it," "I don't want to be shot down," "He went off half cocked," "That's half the battle." Why does it matter that our public discourse is filled with military metaphors? Aren't they just words? Why not talk about something that matters—like actions?

Because words matter. When we think we are using language, language is using us. As linguist Dwight Bolinger put it (employing a military metaphor), language is like a loaded gun:

It can be fired intentionally, but it can wound or kill just as surely when fired accidentally. The terms in which we talk about something shape the way we think about it—and even what we see.

The power of words to shape perception has been proven by researchers in controlled experiments. Psychologist Elizabeth Loftus and John Palmer, for example, found that the terms in which people are asked to recall something affect what they recall. The researchers showed subjects a film of two cars colliding, then asked how fast the cars were going; one week later, they asked whether there had been any broken glass. Some subjects were asked, "About how fast were the cars going when they smashed into each other?" Those who read the question with the verb "smashed" estimated that the cars were going faster. They were also more likely to "remember" having seen broken glass. (There wasn't any.)

This is how language works. It invisibly molds our way of thinking about people, actions, and the world around us. Military metaphors train us to think about—and see—everything in terms of fighting, conflict, and war. This perspective then limits our imaginations when we consider what we can do about situations we would like to understand or change.

Even in science, common metaphors that are taken for granted influence how researchers think about natural phenomena. Evelyn Fox Keller describes a case in which acceptance of a metaphor led scientists to see something that was not there. A mathematical biologist, Keller outlines the fascinating behavior of cellular slime mold. This unique mold can take two completely different forms: It can exist as single-cell organisms, or the separate cells can come together to form multicellular aggregates. The puzzle facing scientists was: What triggers aggregation? In other words, what makes the single cells join together? Scientist focused their investigations by asking what entity issued the order to start aggregating. They first called this bosslike entity a "founder cell," and later a "pacemaker cell," even though no one had seen any evidence for the existence of such a cell. Proceeding nonetheless from the assumption that such a cell must exist, they ignored evidence to the contrary: For example, when the center of the aggregate is removed, other centers form.

Scientists studying slime mold did not examine the interrelationship between the cells and their environment, nor the interrelationship between the functional systems within each cell, because they were busy looking for the pacemaker cell, which, as eventually became evident, did not exist. Instead, under conditions of nutritional deprivation, each individual cell begins to feel the urge to merge with others to form the conglomerate. It is a reaction of the cells to their environment, not to the orders of a boss. Keller recounts this tale to illustrate her insight that we tend to view nature through our understanding of human relations as hierarchical. In her words, "We risk imposing on nature the very stories we like to hear." In other words, the conceptual metaphor of hierarchical governance made scientists "see" something—a pacemaker cell—that wasn't there.

Among the stories many Americans most like to hear are war stories. According to historian Michael Sherry, the American war movie developed during World War II and has been with us

ever since. He shows that movies not explicitly about war were also war movies at heart, such as westerns with their good guy–bad guy battles settled with guns. *High Noon,* for example, which became a model for later westerns, was an allegory of the Second World War: The happy ending hinges on the pacifist taking up arms. We can also see this story line in contemporary adventure films: Think of *Star Wars,* with its stirring finale in which Han Solo, having professed no interest in or taste for battle, returns at the last moment to destroy the enemy and save the day. And precisely the same theme is found in a contemporary low-budget independent film, *Sling Blade,* in which a peace-loving retarded man becomes a hero at the end by murdering the man who has been tormenting the family he has come to love.

## Put Up Your Dukes

If war provides the metaphors through which we view the world and each other, we come to view others—and ourselves—as warriors in battle. Almost any human encounter can be framed as a fight between two opponents. Looking at it this way brings particular aspects of the event into focus and obscures others.

Framing interactions as fights affects not only the participants but also the viewers. At a performance, the audience, as well as the performers, can be transformed. This effect was noted by a reviewer in *The New York Times,* commenting on a musical event:

> **Showdown at Lincoln Center.** Jazz's ideological war of the last several years led to a pitched battle in August between John Lincoln Collier, the writer, and Wynton Marsalis, the trumpeter, in a debate at Lincoln Center. Mr. Marsalis demolished Mr. Collier, point after point after point, but what made the debate unpleasant was the crowd's blood lust; humiliation, not elucidation, was the desired end.

Military imagery pervades this account: the difference of opinions between Collier and Marsalis was an "ideological war," and the "debate" was a "pitched battle" in which Marsalis "demolished" Collier (not his arguments, but him). What the commentator regrets, however, is that the audience got swept up in the mood instigated by the way the debate was carried out: "the crowd's blood lust" for Collier's defeat.

This is one of the most dangerous aspects of regarding intellectual interchange as a fight. It contributes to an atmosphere of animosity that spreads like a fever. In a society that includes people who express their anger by shooting, the result of demonizing those with whom we disagree can be truly tragic.

But do audiences necessarily harbor within themselves a "blood lust," or is it stirred in them by the performances they are offered? Another arts event was set up as a debate between a playwright and a theater director. In this case, the metaphor through which the debate was viewed was not war but boxing—a sport that is in itself, like a debate, a metaphorical battle that pitches one side against the other in an all-out effort to win. A headline describing the event set the frame: "AND IN THIS CORNER…," followed by the subhead "A Black Playwright and White Critic Duke It Out." The story then reports:

the face-off between August Wilson, the most successful black playwright in the American theater, and Robert Brustein, longtime drama critic for The New Republic and artistic director of the American Repertory Theatre in Cambridge, Mass. These two heavyweights had been battling in print since last June....

Entering from opposite sides of the stage, the two men shook hands and came out fighting—or at least sparring.

Wilson, the article explains, had given a speech in which he opposed Black performers taking "white" roles in color-blind casting; Brustein had written a column disagreeing; and both followed up with further responses to each other.

According to the article, "The drama of the Wilson-Brustein confrontation lies in their mutual intransigence." No one would question that audiences crave drama. But is intransigence the most appealing source of drama? I happened to hear this debate broadcast on the radio. The line that triggered the loudest cheers from the audience was the final question put to the two men by the moderator, Anna Deavere Smith: "What did you each learn from the other in this debate?" The loud applause was evidence that the audience did not crave intransigence. They wanted to see another kind of drama: the drama of change—change that comes from genuinely listening to someone with a different point of view, not the transitory drama of two intransigent positions in stalemate.

To encourage the staging of more dramas of change and fewer of intransigence, we need new metaphors to supplement and complement the pervasive war and boxing match metaphors through which we take it for granted issues and events are best talked about and viewed.

## Mud Splatters

Our fondness for the fight scenario leads us to frame many complex human interactions as a battle between two sides. This then shapes the way we understand what happened and how we regard the participants. One unfortunate result is that fights make a mess in which everyone is muddied. The person attacked is often deemed just as guilty as the attacker.

The injustice of this is clear if you think back to childhood. Many of us still harbor anger as we recall a time (or many times) a sibling or playmate started a fight—but both of us got blamed. Actions occur in a stream, each a response to what came before. Where you punctuate them can change their meaning just as you can change the meaning of a sentence by punctuating it in one place or another.

Like a parent despairing of trying to sort out which child started a fight, people often respond to those involved in a public dispute as if both were equally guilty. When champion figure skater Nancy Kerrigan was struck on the knee shortly before the 1994 Olympics in Norway and the then-husband of another champion skater, Tonya Harding, implicated his wife in planning the attack, the event was characterized as a fight between two skaters that obscured their differing roles. As both skaters headed for the Olympic competition, their potential meeting was described as a "long-anticipated figure-skating shootout." Two years later, the event was referred to not as "the attack on Nancy Kerrigan" but as "the rivalry surrounding Tonya Harding and Nancy Kerrigan."

By a similar process, the Senate Judiciary Committee hearings to consider the nomination of Clarence Thomas for Supreme Court justice at which Anita Hill was called to testify are regularly referred to as the "Hill-Thomas hearings," obscuring the very different roles played by Hill and Thomas. Although testimony by Anita Hill was the occasion for reopening the hearings, they were still the Clarence Thomas confirmation hearings: Their purpose was to evaluate Thomas's candidacy. Framing these hearings as a two-sides dispute between Hill and Thomas allowed the senators to focus their investigation on cross-examining Hill rather than seeking other sorts of evidence, for example by consulting experts on sexual harassment to ascertain whether Hill's account seemed plausible.

## Slash-and-Burn Thinking

Approaching situations like warriors in battle leads to the assumption that intellectual inquiry, too, is a game of attack, counterattack, and self-defense. In this spirit, critical thinking is synonymous with criticizing. In many classrooms, students are encouraged to read someone's life work, then rip it to shreds. Though criticism is one form of critical thinking—and an essential one—so are integrating ideas from disparate fields and examining the context out of which ideas grew. Opposition does not lead to the whole truth when we ask only "What's wrong with this?" and never "What can we use from this in building a new theory, a new understanding?"

There are many ways that unrelenting criticism is destructive in itself. In innumerable small dramas mirroring what happened to Robert Gallo (but on a much more modest scale), our most creative thinkers can waste time and effort responding to critics motivated less by a genuine concern about weaknesses in their work than by a desire to find something to attack. All of society loses when creative people are discouraged from their pursuits by unfair criticism. (This is particularly likely to happen since, as Kay Redfield Jamison shows in her book Touched with Fire, many of those who are unusually creative are also unusually sensitive; their sensitivity often drives their creativity.)

If the criticism is unwarranted, many will say, you are free to argue against it, to defend yourself. But there are problems with this, too. Not only does self-defense take time and draw off energy that would better be spent on new creative work, but any move to defend yourself makes you appear, well, defensive. For example, when an author wrote a letter to the editor protesting a review he considered unfair, the reviewer (who is typically given the last word) turned the very fact that the author defended himself into a weapon with which to attack again. The reviewer's response began, "I haven't much time to waste on the kind of writer who squanders his talent drafting angry letters to reviewers."

The argument culture limits the information we get rather than broadening it in another way. When a certain kind of interaction is the norm, those who feel comfortable with that type of interaction are drawn to participate, and those who do not feel comfortable with it recoil and go elsewhere. If public discourse included a broad range of types, we would be making room for individuals with different temperaments to take part and contribute their perspectives and insights. But when debate, opposition, and fights overwhelmingly predominate, those who enjoy verbal sparring are likely to take part—by calling in to talk shows, writing letters to the editor or articles, becoming journalists—and those who cannot comfortably take part in oppositional discourse, or do not wish to, are likely to opt out.

This winnowing process is easy to see in apprenticeship programs such as acting school, law school, and graduate school. A woman who was identified in her university drama program as showing exceptional promise was encouraged to go to New York to study acting. Full of enthusiasm, she was accepted by a famous acting school where the teaching method entailed the teacher screaming at students, goading and insulting them as a way to bring out the best in them. This worked well with many of the students but not with her. Rather than rising to the occasion when attacked, she cringed, becoming less able to draw on her talent, not more. After a year, she dropped out. It could be that she simply didn't have what it took—but this will never be known, because the adversarial style of teaching did not allow her to show what talent she had.

## Polarizing Complexity: Nature or Nurture?

Few issues come with two neat, and neatly opposed, sides. Again, I have seen this in the domain of gender. One common polarization is an opposition between two sources of differences between women and men: "culture," or "nurture," on one hand and "biology," or "nature," on the other.

Shortly after the publication of *You Just Don't Understand,* I was asked by a journalist what question I most often encountered about women's and men's conversational styles. I told her, "Whether the differences I describe are biological or cultural." The journalist laughed. Puzzled, I asked why this made her laugh. She explained that she had always been so certain that any significant differences are cultural rather than biological in origin that the question struck her as absurd. So I should not have been surprised when I read, in the article she wrote, that the two questions I am most frequently asked are "Why do women nag?" and "Why won't men ask for directions?" Her ideological certainty that the question I am most frequently asked was absurd led her to ignore my answer and get a fact wrong in her report of my experience.

Some people are convinced that any significant differences between men and women are entirely or overwhelmingly due to cultural influences—the way we treat girls and boys, and men's dominance of women in society. Others are convinced that any significant differences are entirely or overwhelmingly due to biology: the physical facts of female and male bodies, hormones, and reproductive functions. Many problems are caused by framing the question as a dichotomy: Are behaviors that pattern by sex biological or cultural? This polarization encourages those on one

side to demonize those who take the other view, which leads in turn to misrepresenting the work of those who are assigned to the opposing camp. Finally, and most devastatingly, it prevents us from exploring the interaction of biological and cultural factors—factors that must, and can only, be understood together. By posing the question as either/or, we reinforce a false assumption that biological and cultural factors are separable and preclude the investigations that would help us understand their interrelationship. When a problem is posed in a way that polarizes, the solution is often obscured before the search is under way.

## Who's Up? Who's Down?

Related to polarization is another aspect of the argument culture: our obsession with ratings and rankings. Magazines offer the 10, 50, or 100 best of everything: restaurants, mutual funds, hospitals, even judges. Newsmagazines tell us Who's up, Who's down, as in *Newsweek*'s "Conventional Wisdom Watch" and *Time*'s "Winners and Losers." Rankings and ratings pit restaurants, products, schools, and people against each other on a single scale, obscuring the myriad differences among them. Maybe a small Thai restaurant in one neighborhood can't really be compared to a pricey French one in another, any more than judges with a vast range of abilities and beliefs can be compared on a single scale. And timing can skew results: Ohio State University protested to *Time* magazine when its football team was ranked at the bottom of a scale because only 29 percent of the team graduated. The year before it would have ranked among the top six with 72 percent.

After a political debate, analysts comment not on what the candidates said but on the question "Who won?" After the president delivers an important speech, such as the State of the Union Address, expert commentators are asked to give it a grade. Like ranking, grading establishes a competition. The biggest problem with asking what grade the president's speech deserves, or who won and who lost a campaign debate, is what is not asked and is therefore not answered: What was said, and what is the significance of this for the country?

## An Ethic of Aggression

In an argument culture aggressive tactics are valued for their own sake. For example, a woman called in to a talk show on which I was a guest to say, "When I'm in a place where a man is smoking, and three's a no-smoking sign, instead of saying to him 'You aren't allowed to smoke in here. Put that out,' I say, 'I'm awfully sorry, but I have asthma, so your smoking makes it hard for me to breathe. Would you mind terribly not smoking?' Whenever I say this, the man is extremely polite and solicitous, and he puts his cigarette out, and I say, 'Oh, thank you, thank you!' as if he's done a wonderful thing for me. Why do I do that?"

I think this woman expected me to say that she needs assertiveness training to learn to confront smokers in a more aggressive manner. Instead, I told her that there was nothing wrong with her style of getting the man to stop smoking. She gave him a face-saving way of doing what she asked, one that allowed him to feel chivalrous rather than chastised. This is kind to him, but it is also kind to herself, since it is more likely to lead to the result she desires. If she tried to alter his behavior by reminding him of the rules, he might well rebel: "Who made you the enforcer? Mind your own business!" Indeed, who gives any of us the authority to set others straight when we think they're breaking rules?

Another caller disagreed with me, saying the first caller's style was "self-abasing" and there was no reason for her to use it. But I persisted: There is nothing necessarily destructive about conventional self-effacement. Human relations depend on the agreement to use such verbal conventions. I believe the mistake this caller was making—a mistake many of us make—was to confuse *ritual* self-effacement with the literal kind. All human relations require us to find ways to get what we want from others without seeming to dominate them. Allowing others to feel they are doing what you want for a reason less humiliating to them fulfills this need.

Thinking of yourself as the wronged party who is victimized by a lawbreaking boor makes it harder to see the value of this method. But suppose you are the person addicted to smoking who lights up (knowingly or not) in a no-smoking zone. Would you like strangers to yell at you to stop smoking, or would you rather be allowed to save face by being asked politely to stop in order to help them out? Or imagine yourself having broken a rule inadvertently (which is not to imply rules are broken only by mistake; it is only to say that sometimes they are). Would you like some stranger to swoop down on you and begin berating you, or would you rather be asked politely to comply?

As this example shows, conflicts can sometimes be resolved without confrontational tactics, but current conventional wisdom often devalues less confrontational tactics even if they work well, favoring more aggressive strategies even if they get less favorable results. It's as if we value a fight for its own sake, not for its effectiveness in resolving disputes.

This ethic shows up in many contexts. In a review of a contentious book, for example, a reviewer wrote, "Always provocative, sometimes infuriating, this collection reminds us that the purpose of art is not to confirm and coddle but to provoke and confront." This false dichotomy encapsulates the belief that if you are not provoking and confronting, then you are conforming and coddling—as if there weren't myriad other ways to question and learn. What about exploring, exposing, delving, analyzing, understanding, moving, connecting, integrating, illuminating… or any of innumerable verbs that capture other aspects of what art can do?

## The Broader Picture

The increasingly adversarial spirit of our contemporary lives is fundamentally related to a phenomenon that has been much remarked upon in recent years: the breakdown of a sense of community. In this spirit, distinguished journalist and author Orville Schell points out that in his day journalists routinely based their writing on a sense of connection to their subjects—and that this sense of connection is missing from much that is written by journalists today. Quite the contrary, a spirit of demonography

often prevails that has just the opposite effect: Far from encouraging us to feel connected to the subjects, it encourages us to feel critical, superior—and, as a result, distanced. The cumulative effect is that citizens feel more and more cut off from the people in public life they read about.

The argument culture dovetails with a general disconnection and breakdown of community in another way as well. Community norms and pressures exercise a restraint on the expression of hostility and destruction. Many cultures have rituals to channel and contain aggressive impulses, especially those of adolescent males. In just this spirit, at the 1996 Republican National Convention, both Colin Powell and Bob Dole talked about growing up in small communities where everyone knew who they were. This meant that many people would look out for them, but also that if they did something wrong, it would get back to their parents. Many Americans grew up in ethnic neighborhoods that worked the same way. If a young man stole something, committed vandalism, or broke a rule or law, it would be reported to his relatives, who would punish him or tell him how his actions were shaming the family. American culture today often lacks these brakes.

Community is a blend of connections and authority, and we are losing both. As Robert Bly shows in his book by that title, we now have a *Sibling Society:* Citizens are like squabbling siblings with no authority figures who can command enough respect to contain and channel their aggressive impulses. It is as if every day is a day with a substitute teacher who cannot control the class and maintain order.

The argument culture is both a product of and a contributor to this alienation, separating people, disconnecting them from each other and from those who are or might have been their leaders.

## What Other Way Is There?

Philosopher John Dewey said, on his ninetieth birthday, "Democracy begins in conversation." I fear that it gets derailed in polarized debate.

In conversation we form the interpersonal ties that bind individuals together in personal relationships; in public discourse, we form similar ties on a larger scale, binding individuals into a community. In conversation, we exchange the many types of information we need to live our lives as members of a community. In public discourse, we exchange the information that citizens in a democracy need in order to decide how to vote. If public discourse provides entertainment first and foremost—and if entertainment is first and foremost watching fights—then citizens do not get the information they need to make meaningful use of their right to vote.

Of course it is the responsibility of intellectuals to explore potential weaknesses in others' arguments, and of journalists to represent serious opposition when it exists. But when opposition becomes the overwhelming avenue of inquiry—a formula that *requires* another side to be found or a criticism to be voiced; when the lust for opposition privileges extreme views and obscures complexity; when our eagerness to find weaknesses blinds us to strengths; when the atmosphere of animosity precludes respect and poisons our relations with one another; then the argument culture is doing more damage than good.

I offer this book not as a formal assault in the argument culture. That would be in the spirit of attack that I am questioning. It is an attempt to examine the argument culture—our use of attack, opposition, and debate in public discourse—to ask, What are its limits as well as its strengths? How has it served us well, but also how has it failed us? How is it related to culture and gender? What other options do we have?

I do not believe we should put aside the argument model of public discourse entirely, but we need to rethink whether this is the *only* way, or *always* the best way, to carry out our affairs. A step toward broadening our repertoires would be to pioneer reform by experimenting with metaphors other than sports and war, and with formats other than debate for framing the exchange of ideas. The change might be as simple as introducing a plural form. Instead of asking "What's the other side?" we might ask instead, "What are the other sides?" Instead of insisting on hearing "both sides," we might insist on hearing "all sides."

Another option is to expand our notion of "debate" to include more dialogue. This does not mean there can be no negativity, criticism, or disagreement. It simply means we can be more creative in our ways of managing all of these, which are inevitable and useful. In dialogue, each statement that one person makes is qualified by a statement made by someone else, until the series of statements and qualifications moves everyone closer to a fuller truth. Dialogue does not preclude negativity. Even saying "I agree" makes sense only against the background assumption that you might disagree. In dialogue, there is opposition, yes, but no head-on collision. Smashing heads does not open minds.

There are times when we need to disagree, criticize, oppose, and attack—to hold debates and view issues as polarized battles. Even cooperation, after all, is not the absence of conflict but a means of managing conflict. My goal is not a make-nice false veneer of agreement or a dangerous ignoring of true opposition. I'm questioning the *automatic* use of adversarial formats—the assumption that it's *always* best to address problems and issues by fighting over them. I'm hoping for a broader repertoire of ways to talk to each other and address issues vital to us.

# Notes

*Note:* Sources referred to by short form are cited in full in the References.

[Numbers indicate page numbers of original document. Ed]

7. *"culture of critique"*: I first introduced this term in an op-ed essay, "The Triumph of the Yell," *The New York Times,* Jan. 14, 1994, p. A29.

7. *"There are moments"*: Charles Simic, "In Praise of Invective," *Harper's,* Aug. 1997, pp. 24, 26–27; the quote is from p. 26. The article is excerpted from *Orphan Factory* (Ann Arbor: University of Michigan Press, 1997). I am grateful to Amitai Etizioni for calling this article to my attention.

8. Both the term "agonism" and the phrase "programmed contentiousness" come from Walter Ong, *Fighting for Life.*

10. *"the great backpacking vs. car camping debate"*: Steven Hendrix, "Hatchback vs. Backpack," *The Washington Post Weekend,* Mar. 1, 1996, p. 6.

11. *creationism*: See, for example, Jessica Mathews, "Creationism Makes a Comeback," *The Washington Post,* Apr. 8, 1996, p. A21.

11. *"People dispute that"*: Lipstadt, *Denying the Holocaust,* p. 15. Lipstadt cites *Esquire,* Feb. 1983, for the interview with Mitchum.

12. *Gallo had to spend*: See Nicholas Wade, "Method and Madness: The Vindication of Robert Gallo," *The New York Times Magazine,* Dec. 26, 1993, p. 12, and Elaine Richman, "The Once and Future King," *The Sciences,* Nov.–Dec. 1996, pp. 12–15. The investigations of Gallo were among a series of overly zealous investigations of suspected scientific misconduct—all of which ended in the exoneration of the accused, but not before they had caused immense personal anguish and professional setbacks. Others similarly victimized were Gallo's colleague Mike Popovic, immunologist Thereza Imanishi-Kari, and her coauthor (not accused of wrongdoing but harmed as a result of his defense of her), Nobel Prize winner David Baltimore. On Popovic, see Malcolm Gladwell, "Science Friction," *The Washington Post Magazine,* Dec. 6, 1992, pp. 18–21, 49–51. On Imanishi-Kari and Baltimore, see *The New Yorker,* May 27, 1996, pp. 94–98ff.

14. *potentially endless list:* Randy Allen Harris, *The Linguistics Wars* (New York: Oxford University Press, 1993); "The Science Wars," *Newsweek,* Apr. 21, 1997, p. 54; "The Mammogram War," *Newsweek,* Feb. 24, 1997, p. 54; "Party Wars," *New York,* June 2, 1997, cover. The subhead of the latter reads, "In the battle to feed New York's elite, the top caterers are taking off their white gloves and sharpening their knives."

14. "DEMOCRATS SEND CLINTON": *The New York Times,* Aug. 29, 1996, p. A1.

15. *"We risk imposing"*: Keller, *Reflections on Gender and Science,* p. 157. Another such case is explained by paleontologist Stephen Jay Gould in his book *Wonderful Life* about the Burgess shale—a spectacular deposit of 530-million-year-old fossils. In 1909, the first scientist to study these fossils missed the significance of the find, because he "shoehorned every last Burgess animal into a modern group, viewing the fauna collectively as a set of primitive or ancestral versions of later, improved forms" (p. 24). Years later, observers looked at the Burgess shale fossils with a fresh eye and saw a very different reality: a panoply of life forms, far more diverse and numerous than what exists today. The early scientists missed what was right before their eyes because, Gould shows, they proceeded from a metaphoric understanding of evolution as a linear march of progress from the ancient and primitive to the modern and complex, with humans the inevitable, most complex apex. Accepting the metaphor of "the cone of increasing diversity" prevented the early scientists from seeing what was really there.

16. *"Showdown at Lincoln Center"*: Peter Watrous, "The Year in the Arts: Pop & Jazz/1994," *The New York Times,* Dec. 25, 1994, sec. 2, p. 36.

17. *"the face-off between"*: Jack Kroll, "And in This Corner...," *Newsweek,* Feb. 10, 1997, p. 65.

18. *a fight between two skaters:* Though Harding was demonized somewhat more as an unfeminine, boorish "Wicked Witch of the West" (George Vecsey, "Let's Begin the Legal Olympics," *The New York Times,* Feb. 13, 1994, sec. 8, p. 1.), Kerrigan was also demonized as cold and aloof, an "ice princess."

18. *"long-anticipated figure-skating shootout"*: Jere Longman, "Kerrigan Glides Through Compulsory Interviews," *The New York Times,* Feb. 13, 1994, sec. 8, p. 9.

18. *"the rivalry surrounding"*: Paul Farhi, "For NBC, Games Not Just for Guys; Network Tailors Its Coverage to Entice Women to Watch," *The Washington Post,* July 26, 1996, p. A1.

20. *"I haven't time"*: *The Washington Post Book World,* June 16, 1996, p. 14.

21. *even judges: Washingtonian,* June 1996, ranked judges.

22. *Ohio State University protested:* Letter to the editor by Malcolm S. Baroway, Executive Director, University Communications, *Time,* Oct. 3, 1994, p. 14.

22. Overlaid on the talk show example is the gender issue: The woman who called wished she had the courage to stand up to a man and saw her habitual way of speaking as evidence of her insecurity. This interpretation is suggested by our assumptions about women and men. Many people, researchers included, start from the assumption that women are insecure, so ways they speak are scrutinized for evidence of insecurity. The result is often a failure to understand or appreciate women's styles on their own terms, so women are misinterpreted as defective men.

23. *"Always provocative, sometimes infuriating"*: Jill Nelson, "Fighting Words," review of Ishmael Reed, *Airing Dirty Laundry, The New York Times Book Review,* Feb. 13, 1994, p. 28.

24. *In this spirit:* John Krich, "To Teach Is Glorious: A Conversation with the New Dean of Cal's Journalism School," Orville Schell, *Express,* Aug. 23, 1996, pp. 1, 14–16, 18, 20–22. The remark is from p. 15.

24. *Many cultures have rituals:* See Schlegel and Barry, *Adolescence.*

25. *"Democracy begins in conversation"*: *Dialogue on John Dewey,* Corliss Lamont, ed. (New York: Horizon Press, 1959), p. 88. Thanks to Pete Becker for this reference.

26. *In dialogue, there is:* This insight comes from Walter Ong, who writes, "There is opposition here but no head-on collision, which stops dialogue. (Of course, sometimes dialogue has to be stopped, but that is another story.)" (*Fighting for Life,* p. 32).

# References

Gould, Stephen Jay. *Wonderful Life: The Burgess Shale and the Nature of History* (New York: W. W. Norton, 1989).

Keller, Evelyn Fox. *Reflections on Gender and Science* (New Haven: Yale University Press, 1985).

Krich, John. "To Teach Is Glorious: A Conversation with the New Dean of Cal's Journalism School, Orville Schell." *Express,* Aug. 23, 1996, pp. 1, 14–16, 18, 20–22.

Lipstadt, Deborah. *Denying the Holocaust: The Growing Assault on Truth and Memory* (New York: Free Press, 1993).

Ong, Walter J. *Fighting for Life: Contest, Sexuality, and Consciousness* (Ithaca, N.Y.: Cornell University Press, 1981).

Schlegel, Alice, and Herbert Barry III. *Adolescence: An Anthropological Inquiry* (New York: Free Press, 1991).

**DEBORAH TANNEN** is best known as the author of *You Just Don't Understand: Women and Men in Conversation,* which was on *The New York Times* bestseller list for nearly four years, including eight months as number one, and has been translated into twenty-four languages. Her book, *Talking from 9 to 5: Women and Men in the Workplace: Language, Sex, and Power,* was a *New York Times* Business bestseller. She has written for and been featured in *The New York Times, Newsweek, Time, USA Today, People,* and *The Washington Post.* Her many national television and radio appearances include *20/20, 48 Hours,* CBS *News,* ABC *World News Tonight,* and *Good Morning America.* She is one of only three University Professors at Georgetown University in Washington, D.C., where she is on the Linguistics Department faculty. *The Argument Culture* is her sixteenth book.

Deborah Tannen has also published short stories, essays, and poems. Her first play, *An Act of Devotion,* is included in *Best Short Plays 1993–1994.* It was produced, together with her play *Sisters,* by Horizons Theatre in Arlington, VA.

# "I Can't Even Open My Mouth"

## *Separating Messages from Metamessages in Family Talk*

DEBORAH TANNEN

**"D**O YOU REALLY need another piece of cake?" Donna asks George.

"You bet I do," he replies, with that edge to his voice that implies, "If I wasn't sure I needed it before, I am darned sure now."

Donna feels hamstrung. She knows that George is going to say later that he wished he hadn't had that second piece of cake.

"Why are you always watching what I eat?" George asks.

"I was just watching out for you," Donna replies. "I only say it because I love you."

Elizabeth, in her late twenties, is happy to be making Thanksgiving dinner for her extended family in her own home. Her mother, who is visiting, is helping out in the kitchen. As Elizabeth prepares the stuffing for the turkey, her mother remarks, "Oh, you put onions in the stuffing?"

Feeling suddenly as if she were sixteen years old again, Elizabeth turns on her mother and says, "*I'm* making the stuffing, Mom. Why do you have to criticize everything I do?"

"I didn't criticize," her mother replies. "I just asked a question. What's got into you? I can't even open my mouth."

The allure of family—which is, at heart, the allure of love—is to have someone who knows you so well that you don't have to explain yourself. It is the promise of someone who cares enough about you to protect you against the world of strangers who do not wish you well. Yet, by an odd and cruel twist, it is the family itself that often causes pain. Those we love are looking at us so close-up that they see all our blemishes—see them as if through a magnifying glass. Family members have innumerable opportunities to witness our faults and feel they have a right to point them out. Often their intention is to help us improve. They feel, as Donna did, "I only say it because I love you."

Family members also have a long shared history, so everything we say in a conversation today echoes with meanings from the past. If you have a tendency to be late, your parent, sibling, or spouse may say, "We have to leave at eight"—and then add, "It's really important. Don't be late. Please start your shower at seven, not seven-thirty!" These extra injunctions are demeaning and interfering, but they are based on experience. At the same time, having experienced negative judgments in the past, we develop a sixth sense to sniff out criticism in almost anything a loved one says—even an innocent question about ingredients in the stuffing. That's why Elizabeth's mother ends up feeling as if she can't even open her mouth—and Elizabeth ends up feeling criticized.

When we are children our family constitutes the world. When we grow up, family members—not only our spouses but also our grown-up children and adult sisters and brothers—keep this larger-than-life aura. We overreact to their judgments because it feels as if they were handed down by the Supreme Court and are unassailable assessments of our value as human beings. We bristle because these judgments seem unjust; or because we sense a kernel of truth we would rather not face; or because we fear that if someone who knows us so well judges us harshly we must really be guilty, so we risk losing not only that person's love but everyone else's, too. Along with this heavy load of implications comes a dark resentment that a loved one is judging us at all—and has such power to wound.

"I still fight with my father," a man who had reached a high position in journalism said to me. "He's been dead twenty-one years." I asked for an example. "He'd tell me that I had to comb my hair and dress better, that I'd learn when I grew up that appearance is important." When he said this I noticed that his hair was uncombed, and the tails of his faded shirt were creeping out from the waist of his pants. He went on, "I told him I'd ignore that. And now sometimes when I'm going somewhere important, I'll look in the mirror and think—I'll say to him in my mind, 'See? I *am* a success and it didn't matter.'"

This man's "fights" with his father are about approval. No matter what age we've reached, no matter whether our parents are alive or dead, whether we were close to them or not, there are times when theirs are the eyes through which we view ourselves, theirs the standards against which we measure ourselves when we wonder whether we have measured up. The criticism of parents carries extra weight, even when children are adults.

## I Care, Therefore I Criticize

Some family members feel they have not only a right but an obligation to tell you when they think you're doing something wrong. A woman from Thailand recalls that when she was in her late teens and early twenties, her mother frequently had talks with her in which she tried to set her daughter straight. "At the end of each lecture," the woman says, "my mother would always tell me, 'I have to complain about you because I am your mother and I love you. Nobody else will talk to you the way I do because they don't care.'"

It sometimes seems that family members operate under the tenet "I care, therefore I criticize." To the one who is being told to do things differently, what comes through loudest and clearest is the criticism. But the one offering suggestions and judgments is usually focused on the caring. A mother, for example, was expressing concern about her daughter's boyfriend: He didn't have a serious job, he didn't seem to want one, and she didn't think he was a good prospect for marriage. The daughter protested that her mother disapproved of everyone she dated. Her mother responded indignantly, "Would you rather I didn't care?"

As family members we wonder why our parents, children, siblings, and spouses are so critical of us. But as family members we also feel frustrated because comments we make in the spirit of caring are taken as criticizing.

Both sentiments are explained by the double meaning of giving advice: a loving sign of caring, a hurtful sign of criticizing. It's impossible to say which is right; both meanings are there. Sorting out the ambiguous meanings of caring and criticizing is difficult because language works on two levels: the message and the metamessage. Separating these levels—and being aware of both—is crucial to improving communication in the family.

# The Intimate Critic: When Metamessages Hurt

Because those closest to us have front-row seats to view our faults, we quickly react—sometimes overreact—to any hint of criticism. The result can be downright comic, as in Phyllis Richman's novel *Who's Afraid of Virginia Ham?* One scene, a conversation between the narrator and her adult daughter, Lily, shows how criticism can be the metronome providing the beat for the family theme song. The dialogue goes like this:

*LILY:* Am I too critical of people?

*MOTHER:* What people? Me?

*LILY:* Mamma, don't be so self-centered.

*MOTHER:* Lily, don't be so critical.

*LILY:* I knew it. You do think I'm critical. Mamma, why do you always have to find something wrong with me?

The mother then protests that it was Lily who asked if she was too critical, and now she's criticizing her mother for answering. Lily responds, "I can't follow this. Sometimes you're impossibly hard to talk to."

It turns out that Lily is upset because her boyfriend, Brian, told her she is too critical of him. She made a great effort to stop criticizing, but now she's having a hard time keeping her resolve. He gave her a sexy outfit for her birthday—it's expensive and beautiful—but the generous gift made her angry because she took it as criticism of the way she usually dresses.

In this brief exchange Richman captures the layers of meaning that can make the most well-intentioned comment or action

a source of conflict and hurt among family members. Key to understanding why Lily finds the conversation so hard to follow—and her mother so hard to talk to—is separating messages from metamessages. The *message* is the meaning of the words and sentences spoken, what anyone with a dictionary and a grammar book could figure out. Two people in a conversation usually agree on what the message is. The *metamessage* is meaning that is not said—at least not in so many words—but that we glean from every aspect of context: the way something is said, who is saying it, or the fact that it is said at all.

Because they do not reside in the words themselves, metamessages are hard to deal with. Yet they are often the source of both comfort and hurt. The message (as I've said) is the word meaning while the metamessage is the heart meaning—the meaning that we react to most strongly, that triggers emotion.

When Lily asked her mother if she was too critical of people, the message was a question about Lily's own personality. But her mother responded to what she perceived as the metamessage: that Lily was feeling critical of *her*. This was probably based on experience: Her daughter had been critical of her in the past. If Lily had responded to the message alone, she would have answered, "No, not you. I was thinking of Brian." But she, too, is reacting to a metamessage—that her mother had made herself the point of a comment that was not about her mother at all. Perhaps Lily's resentment was also triggered because her mother still looms so large in her life.

The mixing up of message and metamessage also explains Lily's confused response to the gift of sexy clothing from her boyfriend. The message is the gift. But what made Lily angry was what she thought the gift implied: that Brian finds the way she usually dresses not sexy enough—and unattractive. This implication is the metamessage, and it is what made Lily critical of the gift, of Brian, and of herself. Metamessages speak louder than messages, so this is what Lily reacted to most strongly.

It's impossible to know whether Brian intended this metamessage. It's possible that he wishes Lily would dress differently; it's also possible that he likes the way she dresses just fine but simply thought this particular outfit would look good on her. That's what makes metamessages so difficult to pinpoint and talk about: They're implicit, not explicit.

When we talk about messages, we are talking about the meanings of words. But when we talk about metamessages, we are talking about relationships. And when family members react to each other's comments, it's metamessages they are usually responding to. Richman's dialogue is funny because it shows how we all get confused between messages and metamessages when we talk to those we are close to. But when it happens in the context of a relationship we care about, our reactions often lead to hurt rather than to humor.

In all the conversations that follow, both in this chapter and throughout the book, a key to improving relationships within the family is distinguishing the message from the metamessage, and being clear about which one you are reacting to. One way you can do this is *metacommunicating*—talking about communication.

# "What's Wrong with French Bread?" Try Metacommunicating

The movie *Divorce American Style* begins with Debbie Reynolds and Dick Van Dyke preparing for dinner guests—and arguing. She lodges a complaint: that all he does is criticize. He protests that he doesn't. She says she can't discuss it right then because she has to take the French bread out of the oven. He asks, "French bread?"

A simple question, right? Not even a question, just an observation. But on hearing it Debbie Reynolds turns on him, hands on hips, ready for battle: "What's wrong with French bread?" she asks, her voice full of challenge.

"Nothing," he says, all innocence. "It's just that I really like those little dinner rolls you usually make." This is like the bell that sets in motion a boxing match, which is stopped by another bell—the one at the front door announcing their guests have arrived.

Did he criticize or didn't he? On the message level, no. He simply asked a question to confirm what type of bread she was preparing. But on the metamessage level, yes. If he were satisfied with her choice of bread, he would not comment, except perhaps to compliment. Still, you might ask, So what? So what if he prefers the dinner rolls she usually makes to French bread? Why is it such a big deal? The big deal is explained by her original complaint: She feels that he is *always* criticizing—always telling her to do things differently than she chose to do them.

The big deal, in a larger sense, is a paradox of family: We depend on those closest to us to see our best side, and often they do. But because they are so close, they also see our worst side. You want the one you love to be an intimate ally who reassures you that you're doing things right, but sometimes you find instead an intimate critic who implies, time and again, that you're doing things wrong. It's the cumulative effect of minor, innocent suggestions that creates major problems. You will never work things out if you continue to talk about the message—about French bread versus dinner rolls—rather than the metamessage—the implication that your partner is dissatisfied with everything you do. (*Divorce American Style* was made in 1967; that it still rings true today is evidence of how common—and how recalcitrant—such conversational quagmires are.)

One way to approach a dilemma like this is to *metacommunicate*—to talk about ways of talking. He might *say* that he feels he can't open his mouth to make a suggestion or comment because she takes everything as criticism. She might *say* that she feels he's always dissatisfied with what she does, rather than turn on him in a challenging way. Once they both understand this dynamic, they will come up with their own ideas about how to address it. For example, he might decide to preface his question with a disclaimer: "I'm not criticizing the French bread." Or maybe he *does* want to make a request—a direct one—that she please make dinner rolls because he likes them. They might also set a limit on how many actions of hers he can question in a day. The important thing is to talk about the metamessage she is reacting to: that having too many of her actions questioned makes her feel that her partner in life has changed into an in-house inspection agent, on the lookout for wrong moves.

# Living with the Recycling Police

"This is recyclable," Helen exclaims, brandishing a small gray cylinder that was once at the center of a roll of toilet paper. There she stops, as if the damning evidence is sufficient to rest her case.

"I know it's recyclable," says Samuel. "You don't have to tell me." He approves of recycling and generally practices it, if not quite as enthusiastically (he would say obsessively) as Helen. But this time he slipped: In a moment of haste he tossed the cardboard toilet paper tube into the wastebasket. Now Helen has found it and wants to know why it was there. "You can't go through the garbage looking for things I threw away," Samuel protests. "Our relationship is more important than a toilet paper carcass."

"I'm not talking about our relationship," Helen protests. "I'm talking about recycling."

Helen was right: She *was* talking about recycling. But Samuel was right, too. If you feel like you're living with the recycling police—or the diet police, or the neatness police—someone who assumes the role of judge of your actions and repeatedly finds you guilty—it takes the joy out of living together. Sometimes it even makes you wish, for a fleeting moment, that you lived alone, in peace. In that sense, Samuel was talking about the relationship.

Helen was focusing on the message: the benefits of recycling. Samuel was focusing on the metamessage: the implication he perceives that Helen is enforcing rules and telling him he broke one. Perhaps, too, he is reacting to the metamessage of moral superiority in Helen's being the more fervent recycler. Because messages lie in words, Helen's position is more obviously defensible. But it's metamessages that have clout, because they stir emotions, and emotions are the currency of relationships.

In understanding Samuel's reaction, it's also crucial to bear in mind that the meaning of Helen's remark resides not just in the conversation of the moment but in the resonance of all the conversations on the subject they've had in their years together—as well as the conversations Samuel had before that, especially while growing up in his own family. Furthermore, it's her *repeatedly* remarking on what he does or does not recycle that gives Samuel the impression that living with Helen is like living with the recycling police.

# Give Me Connection, Give Me Control

There is another dimension to this argument—another aspect of communication that complicates everything we say to each other but that is especially powerful in families. That is our simultaneous but conflicting desires for connection and for control.

In her view Helen is simply calling her husband's attention to a small oversight in their mutual pursuit of a moral good—an expression of their connection. Their shared policy on recycling reflects their shared life: his trash is her trash. But Samuel feels that by installing herself as the judge of his actions, she is placing herself one-up. In protest he accuses, "You're trying to control me."

Both connection and control are at the heart of family. There is no relationship as close—and none as deeply hierarchical—as the relationship between parent and child, or between older and younger sibling. To understand what goes on when family members talk to each other, you have to understand how the forces of connection and control reflect both closeness and hierarchy in a family.

"He's like family," my mother says of someone she likes. Underlying this remark is the assumption that *family* connotes closeness, being connected to each other. We all seek connection: It makes us feel safe; it makes us feel loved. But being close means you care about what those you are close to think. Whatever you do has an impact on them, so you have to take their needs and preferences into account. This gives them power to control your actions, limiting your independence and making you feel hemmed in.

Parents and older siblings have power over children and younger siblings as a result of their age and their roles in the family. At the same time, *ways of talking create power*. Younger siblings or children can make life wonderful or miserable for older siblings or parents by what they say—or refuse to say. Some family members increase their chances of getting their way by frequently speaking up, or by speaking more loudly and more forcefully. Some increase their influence by holding their tongues, so others become more and more concerned about winning them over.

"Don't tell me what to do. Don't try to control me" are frequent protests within families. It is automatic for many of us to think in terms of power relations and to see others' incursions on our freedom as control maneuvers. We are less likely to think of them as connection maneuvers, but they often are that, too. At every moment we're struggling not only for control but also for love, approval, and involvement. What's tough is that the *same* actions and comments can be either control maneuvers or connection maneuvers—or, as in most cases, both at once.

## Control Maneuver Or Connection Maneuver?

"Don't start eating yet," Louis says to Claudia as he walks out of the kitchen. "I'll be right there."

Famished, Claudia eyes the pizza before her. The aroma of tomato sauce and melted cheese is so sweet, her mouth thinks she has taken a bite. But Louis, always slow-moving, does not return, and the pizza is cooling. Claudia feels a bit like their dog Muffin when she was being trained: "Wait!" the instructor told Muffin, as the hungry dog poised pitifully beside her bowl of food. After pausing long enough to be convinced Muffin would wait forever, the trainer would say, "Okay!" Only then would Muffin fall into the food.

Was Louis intentionally taking his time in order to prove he could make Claudia wait no matter how hungry she was? Or was he just eager for them to sit down to dinner together? In other words, when he said, "Don't start eating yet," was it a con-

trol maneuver, to make her adjust to his pace and timing, or a connection maneuver, to preserve their evening ritual of sharing food? The answer is, it was both. Eating together is one of the most evocative rituals that bond individuals as a family. At the same time, the requirement that they sit down to dinner together gave Louis the power to make Claudia wait. So the need for connection entailed control, and controlling each other is in itself a kind of connection.

Control and connection are intertwined, often conflicting forces that thread through everything said in a family. These dual forces explain the double meaning of caring and criticizing. Giving advice, suggesting changes, and making observations are signs of caring when looked at through the lens of connection. But looked at through the lens of control, they are put-downs, interfering with our desire to manage our own lives and actions, telling us to do things differently than we choose to do them. That's why caring and criticizing are tied up like a knot.

The drives toward connection and toward control are the forces that underlie our reactions to metamessages. So the second step in improving communication in the family—after distinguishing between message and metamessage—is understanding the double meaning of control and connection. Once these multiple layers are sorted out and brought into focus, talking about ways of talking—metacommunicating—can help solve family problems rather than making them worse.

## Small Spark, Big Explosion

Given the intricacies of messages and metamessages, and of connection and control, the tiniest suggestion or correction can spark an explosion fueled by the stored energy of a history of criticism. One day, for example, Vivian was washing dishes. She tried to fix the drain cup in an open position so it would catch debris and still allow water to drain, but it kept falling into the closed position. With a mental shrug of her shoulders, she decided to leave it, since she didn't have many dishes to wash and the amount of water that would fill the sink wouldn't be that great. But a moment later her husband, Mel, happened by and glanced at the sink. "You should keep the drain open," he said, "so the water can drain."

This sounds innocent enough in the telling. Vivian could have said, "I tried, but it kept slipping in, so I figured it didn't matter that much." Or she could have said, "It's irritating to feel that you're looking over my shoulder all the time, telling me to do things differently from the way I'm doing them." This was, in fact, what she was feeling—and why she experienced, in reaction to Mel's suggestion, a small eruption of anger that she had to expend effort to suppress.

Vivian was surprised at what she did say. She made up a reason and implied she had acted on purpose: "I figured it would be easier to clean the strainer if I let it drain all at once." This thought *had* occurred to her when she decided not to struggle any longer to balance the drain cup in an open position, though it wasn't true that she did it on purpose for that reason. But by justifying her actions, Vivian gave Mel the opening to argue for his method, which he did.

"The whole sink gets dirty if you let it fill up with water," Mel said. Vivian decided to let it drop and remained silent. Had she spoken up, the result would probably have been an argument.

Throughout this interchange Vivian and Mel focused on the message: When you wash the dishes, should the drain cup be open or closed? Just laying out the dilemma in these terms shows how ridiculous it is to argue about. Wars are being fought; people are dying; accident or illness could throw this family into turmoil at any moment. The position of the drain cup in the sink is not a major factor in their lives. But the conversation wasn't really about the message—the drain cup—at least not for Vivian.

Mel probably thought he was just making a suggestion about the drain cup, and in the immediate context he was. But messages always bring metamessages in tow: In the context of the history of their relationship, Mel's comment was not so much about a drain cup as it was about Vivian's ability to do things right and Mel's role as judge of her actions.

This was clear to Vivian, which is why she bristled at his comment, but it was less clear to Mel. Our field of vision is different depending on whether we're criticizing or being criticized. The critic tends to focus on the message: "I just made a suggestion. Why are you so touchy?" The one who feels criticized, however, is responding to the metamessage, which is harder to explain. If Vivian had complained, "You're always telling me how to do things," Mel would surely have felt, and might well have said, "I can't even open my mouth."

At the same time, connection and control are in play. Mel's assumption that he and Vivian are on the same team makes him feel comfortable giving her pointers. Furthermore, if a problem develops with the sink's drainage, he's the one who will have to fix it. Their lives are intertwined; that's where the connection lies. But if Vivian feels she can't even wash dishes without Mel telling her to do it differently, then it seems to her that he is trying to control her. It's as if she has a boss to answer to in her own kitchen.

Vivian might explain her reaction in terms of metamessages. Understanding and respecting her perspective, Mel might decide to limit his suggestions and corrections. Or Vivian might decide that she is overinterpreting the metamessage and make an effort to focus more on the message, taking some of Mel's suggestions and ignoring others. Once they both understand the metamessages as well as the messages they are communicating and reacting to, they can metacommunicate: talk about each other's ways of talking and how they might talk differently to avoid hurt and recriminations.

## "Wouldn't You Rather Have Salmon?"

Irene and David are looking over their menus in a restaurant. David says he will order a steak. Irene says, "Did you notice they also have salmon?"

This question exasperates David; he protests, "Will you please stop criticizing what I eat?"

Irene feels unfairly accused: "I didn't criticize. I just pointed out something on the menu I thought you might like."

The question "Did you notice they also have salmon?" is not, on the message level, a criticism. It could easily be friendly and helpful, calling attention to a menu item her husband might have missed. But, again, conversations between spouses—or between any two people who have a history—are always part of an ongoing relationship. David knows that Irene thinks he eats too much red meat, too much dessert, and, generally speaking, too much.

Against the background of this aspect of their relationship, any indication that Irene is noticing what he is eating is a reminder to David that she disapproves of his eating habits. That's why the question "Do you really want to have dessert?" will be heard as "You shouldn't have dessert," and the observation "That's a big piece of cake" will communicate "That piece of cake is too big," regardless of how they're intended. The impression of disapproval comes not from the message—the words spoken—but from the metamessage, which grows out of their shared history.

It's possible that Irene really was not feeling disapproval when she pointed out the salmon on the menu, but it's also possible that she was and preferred not to admit it. Asking a question is a handy way of expressing disapproval without seeming to. But to the extent that the disapproval comes through, such indirect means of communicating can make for more arguments, and more hurt feelings on both sides. Irene sees David overreacting to an innocent, even helpful, remark, and he sees her hounding him about what he eats and then denying having done so. Suppose he had announced he was going to order salmon. Would she have said, "Did you notice they also have steak?" Not likely. It is reasonable, in this context, to interpret any alternative suggestion to an announced decision as dissatisfaction with that decision.

Though Irene and David's argument has much in common with the previous examples, the salmon versus steak decision is weightier than French bread versus dinner rolls, recycling, or drain cups. Irene feels that David's health—maybe even his life—is at stake. He has high cholesterol, and his father died young of a heart attack. Irene has good reason to want David to eat less red meat. She loves him, and his health and life are irrevocably intertwined with hers. Here is another paradox of family: A blessing of being close is knowing that someone cares about you: cares what you do and what happens to you. But caring also means interference and disapproval.

In other words, here again is the paradox of connection and control. From the perspective of control, Irene is judging and interfering; from the perspective of connection, she is simply recognizing that her life and David's are intertwined. This potent brew is family: Just knowing that someone has the closeness to care and the right to pass judgment—and that you care so much about that judgment—creates resentment that can turn into anger.

## Crying Literal Meaning: How Not to Resolve Arguments

When Irene protested, "I didn't criticize," she was crying literal meaning: taking refuge in the message level of talk, ducking the metamessage. All of us do that when we want to avoid a fight but still get our point across. In many cases this defense is sincere, though it does not justify ignoring or denying the metamessage someone else may have perceived. If the person we're talking to believes it wasn't "just a suggestion," keeping the conversation focused on the message can result in interchanges that sound like a tape loop playing over and over. Let's look more closely at an actual conversation in which this happened—one that was taped by the people who had it.

Sitting at the dining room table, Evelyn is filling out an application. Because Joel is the one who has access to a copy machine at work, the last step of the process will rest on his shoulders. Evelyn explains, "Okay, so you'll have to attach the voided check here, after you make the Xerox copy. Okay?" Joel takes the papers, but Evelyn goes on: "Okay just—Please get that out tomorrow. I'm counting on you, hon. I'm counting on you, love."

Joel reacts with annoyance: "Oh, for Pete's sake."

Evelyn is miffed in turn: "What do you mean by that?"

Joel turns her words back on her: "What do *you* mean by that?"

The question "What do you mean by that?" is a challenge. When communication runs smoothly, the meanings of words are self-evident, or at least we assume they are. (We may discover later that we misinterpreted them.) Although "What do you mean?" might be an innocent request for clarification, adding "by that" usually signals not so much that you didn't understand what the other person meant but that you understood—all too well—the *implication* of the words, and you didn't like it.

Evelyn cries literal meaning. She sticks to the message: "Oh, honey, I just mean I'm *counting* on you."

Joel calls attention to the metamessage: "Yes, but you say it in a way that suggests I can't be counted on."

Evelyn protests, accurately, "I never said that."

But Joel points to evidence of the metamessage: "I'm talking about your *tone*."

I suspect Joel was using *tone* as a catchall way of describing the metamessage level of talk. Moreover, it probably wasn't only the way Evelyn spoke—her tone—that he was reacting to but the fact that Evelyn said it at all. If she really felt she could count on him, she would just hand over the task. "I'm counting on you" is what people say to reinforce the importance of doing something when they believe extra reinforcement is needed. Here, the shared history of the relationship adds meaning to the metamessage as well. Joel has reason to believe that Evelyn feels she can't count on him.

Later in the same conversation, Joel takes a turn crying literal meaning. He unplugs the radio from the wall in the kitchen and brings it into the dining room so they can listen to the news. He sets it on the table and turns it on.

"Why aren't you using the plug?" Evelyn asks. "Why waste the batteries?" This sparks a heated discussion about the relative importance of saving batteries. Evelyn then suggests, "Well, we could plug it in right here," and offers Joel the wire.

Joel shoots her a look.

Evelyn protests, "Why are you giving me a dirty look?"

And Joel cries literal meaning: "I'm not!" After all, you can't prove a facial expression; it's not in the message.

"You are!" Evelyn insists, reacting to the metamessage: "Just because I'm handing this to you to plug in."

I have no doubt that Joel did look at Evelyn with annoyance or worse, but not because she handed him a plug—that would be literal meaning, too. He was surely reacting to the metamessage of being corrected, of her judging his actions. For her part, Evelyn probably felt Joel was irrationally refusing to plug in the radio when an electrical outlet was staring them in the face.

How to sort through this jumble of messages and metamessages? The message level is a draw. Some people prefer the convenience of letting the radio run on batteries when it's moved from its normal perch to a temporary one. Others find it obviously reasonable to plug the radio in when there's an outlet handy, to save batteries. Convenience or frugality, take your pick. We all do. But when you live with someone else—caution! It may seem natural to suggest that others do things the way you would do them, but that is taking account only of the message. Giving the metamessage its due, the expense in spirit and goodwill is more costly than batteries. Being corrected all the time is wearying. And it's even more frustrating when you try to talk about what you believe they implied and they cry literal meaning—denying having "said" what you know they communicated.

Consider, too, the role of connection and control. Telling someone what to do is a control maneuver. But it is also a connection maneuver: Your lives are intertwined, and anything one person does has an impact on the other. In the earlier example, when Evelyn said, "I'm counting on you," I suspect some readers sympathized with Joel and others with Evelyn, depending on their own experience with people they've lived with. Does it affect your reaction to learn that Joel forgot to mail the application? Evelyn had good reason, based on years of living with Joel, to have doubts about whether he would remember to do what he said he would do.

Given this shared history, it might have been more constructive for Evelyn to admit that she did not feel she could completely count on Joel, rather than cry literal meaning and deny the metamessage of her words. Taking into account Joel's forgetfulness—or maybe his being overburdened at work—they could devise a plan: Joel might write himself a reminder and place it strategically in his briefcase. Or Evelyn might consider mailing the form herself, even though that would mean a trip to make copies. Whatever they decide, they stand a better chance of avoiding arguments—and getting the application mailed on time—if they acknowledge their metamessages and the reasons motivating them.

## Who Burned the Popcorn?

Living together means coordinating so many tasks, it's inevitable that family members will have different ideas of how to perform those tasks. In addition, everyone makes mistakes; sometimes the dish breaks, you forget to mail the application, the drain cup falls into the closed position. At work, lines of responsibility and authority are clear (at least in principle). But in a family—especially when adults are trying to share responsibilities and authority—there are fewer and fewer domains that belong solely to one person. As couples share responsibility for more and more tasks, they also develop unique and firm opinions about how those tasks should be done—and a belief in their right to express their opinions.

Even the most mundane activity, such as making popcorn (unless you buy the microwave type or an electric popper), can spark conflict. First, it takes a little going, and people have their own ideas of how to do it best. Second, popcorn is often made in the evening, when everyone's tired. Add to that the paradox of connection and control—wanting the person you love to approve of what you do, yet having someone right there to witness and judge mistakes—and you have a potful of kernels sizzling in oil, ready to pop right out of the pot.

More than one couple have told me of arguments about how to make popcorn. One such argument broke out between another couple who were taping their conversations. Since their words were recorded, we have a rare opportunity to listen in on a conversation very much like innumerable ones that vanish into air in homes all around the country. And we have the chance to think about how it could have been handled differently.

The seed of trouble is planted when Molly is in the kitchen and Kevin is watching their four-year-old son, Benny. Kevin calls out, "Molly! Mol! Let's switch. You take care of him. I'll do whatever you're doing."

"I'm making popcorn," Molly calls back. "You always burn it."

Molly's reply is, first and foremost, a sign of resistance. She doesn't want to switch jobs with Kevin. Maybe she's had enough of a four-year-old's company and is looking forward to being on her own in the kitchen. Maybe she is enjoying making popcorn. And maybe her reason is truly the one she gives: She doesn't want Kevin to make the popcorn because he always burns it. Whatever her motivation, Molly resists the switch Kevin proposes by impugning his ability to make popcorn. And this comes across as a call to arms.

Kevin protests, "No I don't! I never burn it. I make it perfect." He joins Molly in the kitchen and peers over her shoulder. "You making popcorn? In the big pot?" (Remember this line; it will become important later.)

"Yes," Molly says, "but you're going to ruin it."

"No I won't," Kevin says. "I'll get it just right." With that they make the switch. Kevin becomes the popcorn chef, Molly the caretaker. But she is not a happy caretaker.

Seeing a way she can be both caretaker and popcorn chef, Molly asks Benny, "You want to help Mommy make popcorn? Let's not let Daddy do it. Come on."

Hearing this, Kevin insists, "I know how to make popcorn!" Then he ups the ante: "I can make popcorn better than you can!" After that the argument heats up faster than the popcorn. "I cook every kernel!" Kevin says.

"No you won't," says Molly.

"I will too! It's never burned!" Kevin defends himself. And he adds, "It always burns when you do it!"

"Don't make excuses!"

"There's a trick to it," he says.

And she says, "I know the trick!"

"No you don't," he retorts, "'cause you always burn it."

"*I do not!*" she says. "What are you, crazy?"

It is possible that Kevin is right—that Molly, not he, is the one who always burns the popcorn. It is also possible that Molly is right—that he always burns the popcorn, that she doesn't, and that he has turned the accusation back onto her as a self-defense strategy. Move 1: I am not guilty. Move 2: You are guilty.

In any case, Kevin continues as popcorn chef. After a while Molly returns to the kitchen. "Just heat it!" she tells Kevin. "Heat it! No, I don't want you—"

"It's going, it's going," Kevin assures her. "Hear it?"

Molly is not reassured, because she does not like what she hears. "It's too slow," she says. "It's all soaking in. You hear that little—"

"It's not soaking in," Kevin insists. "It's fine."

"It's just a few kernels," Molly disagrees.

But Kevin is adamant: "All the popcorn is being popped!"

Acting on her mounting unease about the sounds coming from the popping corn, Molly makes another suggestion. She reminds Kevin, "You gotta take the trash outside."

But Kevin isn't buying. "I can't," he says. "I'm doing the popcorn." And he declines Molly's offer to watch it while he takes out the trash.

In the end Molly gets to say, "See, what'd I tell you?" But Kevin doesn't see the burned popcorn as a reason to admit fault. Remember his earlier question, "In the big pot?" Now he protests, "Well, I never *use* this pot, I use the other pot."

Molly comes back, "It's not the pot! It's you!"

"It's the pot," Kevin persists. "It doesn't heat up properly. If it did, then it would get hot." But pots can't really be at fault; those who choose pots can. So Kevin accuses, "You should have let me do it from the start."

"You *did* it from the start!" Molly says.

"No, I didn't," says Kevin. "You chose this pan. I would've chosen a different pan." So it's the pot's fault, and Molly's fault for choosing the pot.

This interchange is almost funny, especially for those of us—most of us, I'd bet—who have found ourselves in similar clashes.

How could Kevin and Molly have avoided this argument? Things might have turned out better if they had talked about their motivations: Is either one of them eager to get a brief respite from caring for Benny? If so, is there another way they can accomplish that goal? (Perhaps they could set Benny up with a task he enjoys on his own.) With this motivation out in the open, Molly might have declined to switch places when Kevin proposed it, saying something like, "I'm making popcorn. I'm enjoying making it. I'd rather not switch." The justification Molly used, "You always burn it," may have seemed to her a better tactic because it claims her right to keep making popcorn on the basis of the family good rather than her own preference. But the metamessage of incompetence can come across as provocative, in addition to being hurtful.

It's understandable that Kevin would be offended to have his popcorn-making skills impugned, but he would have done better to avoid the temptation to counterattack by insisting he does it better, that it's Molly who burns it. He could have prevented the argument rather than escalate it if he had metacommunicated: "You can make the popcorn if you want," he might have said, "but you don't have to say I can't do it." For both Molly and Kevin—as for any two people negotiating who's going to do what—metacommunicating is a way to avoid the flying metamessages of incompetence.

## "I Know a Thing or Two"

One of the most hurtful metamessages, and one of the most frequent, that family talk entails is the implication of incompetence—even (if not especially) when children grow up. Now that we're adults we feel we should be entitled to make our own decisions, lead our own lives, imperfect though they may be. But we still want to feel that our parents are proud of us, that they believe in our competence. That's the metamessage we yearn for. Indeed, it's because we want their approval so much that we find the opposite metamessage—that they don't trust our competence—so distressing.

Martin and Gail knew that Gail's mother tended to be critical of whatever they did, so they put off letting her see their new home until the purchase was final. Once the deal was sealed they showed her, with pride, the home they had chosen while the previous owner's furniture was still in it. They were sure she would be impressed by the house they were now able to afford, as well as its spotless condition. But she managed to find something to criticize—even if it was invisible: "They may've told you it's in move-in condition," she said with authority, "but I know a thing or two, and when they take those pictures off the wall, there will be holes!" Even though they were familiar with her tendency to find fault, Gail and Martin were flummoxed.

The aspect of the house Gail's mother found to criticize was profoundly insignificant: Every home has pictures on the wall, every picture taken down leaves holes, and holes are easily spackled in and painted over. It seems that Gail's mother was really reaching to find *something* about their new home to criticize. From the perspective of control, it would be easy to conclude that Gail's mother was trying to take the role of expert in order to put them down, or even to spoil the joy of their momentous purchase. But consider the perspective of connection. Pointing out a problem that her children might not have noticed shows that she can still be of use, even though they are grown and have found this wonderful house without her help. She was being protective, watching out for them, making sure no one pulled the wool over their eyes.

Because control and connection are inextricably intertwined, protection implies incompetence. If Gail and Martin need her mother's guidance, they are incapable of taking care of themselves. Though Gail's mother may well have been reacting to—and trying to overcome—the metamessage that they don't need her anymore, the metamessage they heard is that she can't approve wholeheartedly of anything they do.

## "She Knew What Was Right"

In addition to concern about their children's choice of home, parents often have strong opinions about adult children's partners, jobs, and—especially—how they treat their own children.

Raising children is something at which parents self-evidently have more experience, but metamessages of criticism in this area, though particularly common, are also particularly hurtful, because young parents want so much to be good parents.

A woman of seventy still recalls the pain she felt when her children were small and her mother-in-law regarded her as an incompetent parent. It started in the first week of her first child's life. Her mother-in-law had come to help—and didn't want to go home. Finally, her father-in-law told his wife it was time to leave the young couple on their own. Unconvinced, she said outright—in front of her son and his wife—"I can't trust them with the baby."

Usually signs of distrust are more subtle. For example, during a dinner conversation among three sisters and their mother, the sisters were discussing what the toddlers like to eat. When one said that her two-year-old liked fish, their mother cautioned, "Watch the bones." How easy it would be to take offense (though there was no indication this woman did): "You think I'm such an incompetent mother that I'm going to let my child swallow fish bones?" Yet the grandmother's comment was her way of making a contribution to the conversation—one that exercises her lifelong responsibility of protecting children.

It is easy to scoff at the mother-in-law who did not want to leave her son and his wife alone with their own baby. But consider the predicament of parents who become grandparents and see (or believe they see) their beloved grandchildren treated in ways they feel are hurtful. One woman told me that she loves being a grandmother—but the hardest part is having to bite her tongue when her daughter-in-law treats her child in a way the grandmother feels is misguided, unfair, or even harmful. "You see your children doing things you think aren't right," she commented, "but at least they're adults; they'll suffer the consequences. But a child is so defenseless."

In some cases grandparents really do know best. My parents recall with lingering guilt a time they refused to take a grandparent's advice—and later wished they had. When their first child, my sister Naomi, was born, my parents, like many of their generation, relied on expert advice for guidance in what was best for their child. At the time, the experts counseled that, once bedtime comes, a child who cries should not be picked up. After all, the reasoning went, that would simply encourage the baby to cry rather than go to sleep.

One night when she was about a year old, Naomi was crying after being put to sleep in her crib. My mother's mother, who lived with my parents, wanted to go in and pick her up, but my parents wouldn't let her. "It tore us apart to hear her cry," my father recalls, "but we wanted to do what was best for her." It later turned out that Naomi was crying because she was sick. My parents cringe when they tell this story. "My mother pleaded with us to pick her up," my mother says. "She knew what was right."

## I'm Grown Up Now

Often a parent's criticism is hurtful—or makes us angry—even when we know it is right, maybe especially if we sense it is right. That comes clear in the following example.

Two couples were having dinner together. One husband, Barry, was telling about how he had finally—at the age of forty-five—learned to ignore his mother's criticism. His mother, he said, had commented that he is too invested in wanting the latest computer gizmo, the most up-to-date laptop, regardless of whether he needs it. At that point his wife interrupted. "It's true, you are," she said—and laughed. He laughed, too: "I know it's true." Then he went back to his story and continued, unfazed, about how in the past he would have been hurt by his mother's comment and would have tried to justify himself to her, but this time he just let it pass. How easily Barry acknowledged the validity of his mother's criticism—when it was his wife making it. Yet acknowledging that the criticism was valid didn't change his view of his mother's comment one whit: He still thought she was wrong to criticize him.

When we grow up we feel we should be free from our parents' judgment (even though we still want their approval). Ironically, there is often extra urgency in parents' tendency to judge children's behavior when children are adults, because parents have a lot riding on how their children turn out. If the results are good, everything they did as parents gets a seal of approval. My father, for example, recalls that as a young married man he visited an older cousin, a woman he did not know well. After a short time the cousin remarked, "Your mother did a good job." Apparently, my father had favorably impressed her, but instead of complimenting him, she credited his mother.

By the same token, if their adult children have problems—if they seem irresponsible or make wrong decisions—parents feel their life's work of child rearing has been a failure, and those around them feel that way, too. This gives extra intensity to parents' desire to set their children straight. But it also can blind them to the impact of their corrections and suggestions, just as those in power often underestimate the power they wield.

When adult children move into their own homes, the lid is lifted off the pressure cooker of family interaction, though the pot may still be simmering on the range. If they move far away—as more and more do—visits turn into intense interactions during which the pressure cooker lid is clicked back in place and the steam builds up once again. Many adult children feel like they're kids again when they stay with their parents. And parents often feel the same way: that their adult children are acting like kids. Visits become immersion courses in return-to-family.

Parents with children living at home have the ultimate power—asking their children to move out. But visiting adult children have a new power of their own: They can threaten not to return, or to stay somewhere else. Margaret was thrilled that her daughter Amanda, who lives in Oregon, would be coming home for a visit to the family farm in Minnesota. It had been nearly a year since Margaret had seen her grandchildren, and she was eager to get reacquainted with them. But near the end of the visit, there was a flare-up. Margaret questioned whether Amanda's children should be allowed to run outside barefoot. Margaret thought it was dangerous; Amanda thought it was harmless. And Amanda unsheathed her sword: "This isn't working," she said. "Next time I won't stay at the farm. I'll find somewhere else to stay." Because Margaret wants connection—time with her daughter and grandchildren—the ability to dole out that connection gives her daughter power that used to be in Margaret's hands.

# The Paradox Of Family

When I was a child I walked to elementary school along Coney Island Avenue in Brooklyn, praying that if a war came I'd be home with my family when it happened. During my childhood in the 1950s my teachers periodically surprised the class by calling out, "Take cover!" At that cry we all ducked under our desks and curled up in the way we had been taught: elbows and knees tucked in, heads down, hands clasped over our necks. With the possibility of a nuclear attack made vivid by these exercises, I walked to school in dread—not of war but of the possibility that it might strike when I was away from my family.

But there is another side to family, the one I have been exploring in this chapter. My nephew Joshua Marx, at thirteen, pointed out this paradox: "If you live with someone for too long, you notice things about them," he said. "That's the reason you don't like your parents, your brother. There's a kid I know who said about his friend, 'Wouldn't it be cool if we were brothers?' and I said, 'Then you'd hate him.'"

We look to communication as a way through the minefield of this paradox. And often talking helps. But communication itself is a minefield because of the complex workings of message and metamessage. Distinguishing messages from metamessages, and taking into account the underlying needs for connection and control, provides a basis for metacommunicating. With these insights as foundation, we can delve further into the intricacies of family talk. Given our shared and individual histories of talk in relationships, and the enormous promise of love, understanding, and listening that family holds out, it's worth the struggle to continue juggling—and talking.

From *I Only Say This Because I Love You*, by Deborah Tannen, pp. 3-28 © 2001, by Deborah Tannen. Used by permission of Random House, Inc.

# Shakespeare in the Bush

LAURA BOHANNAN

Just before I left Oxford for the Tiv in West Africa, conversation turned to the season at Stratford. "You Americans," said a friend, "often have difficulty with Shakespeare. He was, after all, a very English poet, and one can easily misinterpret the universal by misunderstanding the particular."

I protested that human nature is pretty much the same the whole world over; at least the general plot and motivation of the greater tragedies would always be clear—everywhere—although some details of custom might have to be explained and difficulties of translation might produce other slight changes. To end an argument we could not conclude, my friend gave me a copy of *Hamlet* to study in the African bush: it would, he hoped, lift my mind above its primitive surroundings, and possibly I might, by prolonged meditation, achieve the grace of correct interpretation.

It was my second field trip to that African tribe, and I thought myself ready to live in one of its remote sections—an area difficult to cross even on foot. I eventually settled on the hillock of a very knowledgeable old man, the head of a homestead of some hundred and forty people, all of whom were either his close relatives or their wives and children. Like the other elders of the vicinity, the old man spent most of his time performing ceremonies seldom seen these days in the more accessible parts of the tribe. I was delighted. Soon there would be three months of enforced isolation and leisure, between the harvest that takes place just before the rising of the swamps and the clearing of new farms when the water goes down. Then, I thought, they would have even more time to perform ceremonies and explain them to me.

I was quite mistaken. Most of the ceremonies demanded the presence of elders from several homesteads. As the swamps rose, the old men found it too difficult to walk from one homestead to the next, and the ceremonies gradually ceased. As the swamps rose even higher, all activities but one came to an end. The women brewed beer from maize and millet. Men, women, and children sat on their hillocks and drank it.

People began to drink at dawn. By midmorning the whole homestead was singing, dancing, and drumming. When it rained, people had to sit inside their huts: there they drank and sang or they drank and told stories. In any case, by noon or before, I either had to join the party or retire to my own hut and my books. "One does not discuss serious matters when there is beer. Come, drink with us." Since I lacked their capacity for the thick native beer, I spent more and more time with *Hamlet*. Before the end of the second month, grace descended on me. I was quite sure that *Hamlet* had only one possible interpretation, and that one universally obvious.

Early every morning, in the hope of having some serious talk before the beer party, I used to call on the old man at his reception hut—a circle of posts supporting a thatched roof above a low mud wall to keep out wind and rain. One day I crawled through the low doorway and found most of the men of the homestead sitting huddled in their ragged cloths on stools, low plank beds, and reclining chairs, warming themselves against the chill of the rain around a smoky fire. In the center were three pots of beer. The party had started.

The old man greeted me cordially. "Sit down and drink." I accepted a large calabash full of beer, poured some into a small drinking gourd, and tossed it down. Then I poured some more into the same gourd for the man second in seniority to my host before I handed my calabash over to a young man for further distribution. Important people shouldn't ladle beer themselves.

"It is better like this," the old man said, looking at me approvingly and plucking at the thatch that had caught in my hair. "You should sit and drink with us more often. Your servants tell me that when you are not with us, you sit inside your hut looking at a paper."

The old man was acquainted with four kinds of "papers": tax receipts, bride price receipts, court fee receipts, and letters. The messenger who brought him letters from the chief used them mainly as a badge of office, for he always knew what was in them and told the old man. Personal letters for the few who had relatives in the government or mission stations were kept until someone went to a large market where there was a letter writer and reader. Since my arrival, letters were brought to me to be read. A few men also brought me bride price receipts, privately, with requests to change the figures to a higher sum. I found moral arguments were of no avail, since in-laws are fair game, and the technical hazards of forgery difficult to explain to an illiterate people. I did not wish them to think me silly enough to look at any such papers for days on end, and I hastily explained that my "paper" was one of the "things of long ago" of my country.

"Ah," said the old man. "Tell us."

I protested that I was not a storyteller. Story telling is a skilled art among them; their standards are high, and the audiences critical—and vocal in their criticism. I protested in vain. This morning they wanted to hear a story while they drank. They threatened to tell me no more stories until I told them one of mine. Finally, the old man promised that no one would criticize my style "for we know you are struggling with our language." "But," put in one of the elders, "you must explain what we do not understand, as we do when we tell you our stories." Realizing that here was my chance to prove *Hamlet* universally intelligible, I agreed.

The old man handed me some more beer to help me on with my storytelling. Men filled their long wooden pipes and knocked coals from the fire to place in the pipe bowls; then, puffing contentedly, they sat back to listen. I began in the proper style, "Not yesterday, not yesterday, but long ago, a thing occurred. One night three men were keeping watch outside the homestead of the great chief, when suddenly they saw the former chief approach them."

"Why was he no longer their chief?"

"He was dead," I explained. "That is why they were troubled and afraid when they saw him."

"Impossible," began one of the elders, handing his pipe on to his neighbor, who interrupted, "Of course it wasn't the dead chief. It was an omen sent by a witch. Go on."

Slightly shaken, I continued. "One of these three was a man who knew things"—the closest translation for scholar, but unfortunately it also meant witch. The second elder looked triumphantly at the first. "So he spoke to the dead chief saying, 'Tell us what we must do so you may rest in your grave,' but the dead chief did not answer. He vanished, and they could see him no more. Then the man who knew things—his name was Horatio—said this event was the affair of the dead chief's son, Hamlet."

There was a general shaking of heads round the circle. "Had the dead chief no living brothers? Or was this son the chief?"

"No," I replied. "That is, he had one living brother who became the chief when the elder brother died."

The old men muttered: such omens were matters for chiefs and elders, not for youngsters; no good could come of going behind a chief's back; clearly Horatio was not a man who knew things.

"Yes, he was," I insisted, shooing a chicken away from my beer. "In our country the son is next to the father. The dead chief's younger brother had become the great chief. He had also married his elder brother's widow only about a month after the funeral."

"He did well," the old man beamed and announced to the others, "I told you that if we knew more about Europeans, we would find they really were very like us. In our country also," he added to me, "the younger brother marries the elder brother's widow and becomes the father of his children. Now, if your uncle, who married your widowed mother, is your father's full brother, then he will be a real father to you. Did Hamlet's father and uncle have one mother?"

His question barely penetrated my mind; I was too upset and thrown too far off balance by having one of the most important elements of *Hamlet* knocked straight out of the picture. Rather uncertainly I said that I thought they had the same mother, but I wasn't sure—the story didn't say. The old man told me severely that these genealogical details made all the difference and that when I got home I must ask the elders about it. He shouted out the door to one of his younger wives to bring his goatskin bag.

Determined to save what I could of the mother motif, I took a deep breath and began again. "The son Hamlet was very sad because his mother had married again so quickly. There was no need for her to do so, and it is our custom for a widow not to go to her next husband until she has mourned for two years."

"Two years is too long," objected the wife, who had appeared with the old man's battered goatskin bag. "Who will hoe your farms for you while you have no husband?"

"Hamlet," I retorted without thinking, "was old enough to hoe his mother's farms himself. There was no need for her to remarry." No one looked convinced. I gave up. "His mother and the great chief told Hamlet not to be sad, for the great chief himself would be a father to Hamlet. Furthermore, Hamlet would be the next chief: therefore he must stay to learn the things of a chief. Hamlet agreed to remain, and all the rest went off to drink beer."

While I paused, perplexed at how to render Hamlet's disgusted soliloquy to an audience convinced that Claudius and Gertrude had behaved in the best possible manner, one of the younger men asked me who had married the other wives of the dead chief.

"He had no other wives," I told him.

"But a chief must have many wives! How else can he brew beer and prepare food for all his guests?"

I said firmly that in our country even chiefs had only one wife, that they had servants to do their work, and that they paid them from tax money.

It was better, they returned, for a chief to have many wives and sons who would help him hoe his farms and feed his people; then everyone loved the chief who gave much and took nothing—taxes were a bad thing.

I agreed with the last comment, but for the rest fell back on their favorite way of fobbing off my questions: "That is the way it is done, so that is how we do it."

I decided to skip the soliloquy. Even if Claudius was here thought quite right to marry his brother's widow, there remained the poison motif, and I knew they would disapprove of fratricide. More hopefully I resumed, "That night Hamlet kept watch with the three who had seen his dead father. The dead chief again appeared, and although the others were afraid, Hamlet followed his dead father off to one side. When they were alone, Hamlet's dead father spoke."

"Omens can't talk!" The old man was emphatic.

"Hamlet's dead father wasn't an omen. Seeing him might have been an omen, but he was not." My audience looked as confused as I sounded. "It *was* Hamlet's dead father. It was a thing we call a 'ghost.'" I had to use the English word, for unlike many of the neighboring tribes, these people didn't believe in the survival after death of any individuating part of the personality.

"What is a 'ghost?' An omen?"

"No, a 'ghost' is someone who is dead but who walks around and can talk, and people can hear him and see him but not touch him."

They objected. "One can touch zombis."

"No, no! It was not a dead body the witches had animated to sacrifice and eat. No one else made Hamlet's dead father walk. He did it himself."

"Dead men can't walk," protested my audience as one man.

I was quite willing to compromise. "A 'ghost' is the dead man's shadow."

But again they objected. "Dead men cast no shadows."

"They do in my country," I snapped.

The old man quelled the babble of disbelief that arose immediately and told me with that insincere, but courteous, agreement one extends to the fancies of the young, ignorant, and superstitious, "No doubt in your country the dead can also walk without being zombis." From the depths of his bag he produced a withered fragment of kola nut, bit off one end to show it wasn't poisoned, and handed me the rest as a peace offering.

"Anyhow," I resumed, "Hamlet's dead father said that his own brother, the one who became chief, had poisoned him. He wanted Hamlet to avenge him. Hamlet believed this in his heart, for he did not like his father's brother." I took another swallow of beer. "In the country of the great chief, living in the same homestead, for it was a very large one, was an important elder who was often with the chief to advise and help him. His name was Polonius. Hamlet was courting his daughter, but her father and her brother… [I cast hastily about for some tribal analogy] warned her not to let Hamlet visit her when she was alone on her farm, for he would be a great chief and so could not marry her."

"Why not?" asked the wife, who had settled down on the edge of the old man's chair. He frowned at her for asking stupid questions and growled, "They lived in the same homestead."

"That was not the reason," I informed them. "Polonius was a stranger who lived in the homestead because he helped the chief, not because he was a relative."

"Then why couldn't Hamlet marry her?"

"He could have," I explained, "but Polonius didn't think he would. After all, Hamlet was a man of great importance who ought to marry a chief's daughter, for in his country a man could have only one wife. Polonius was afraid that if Hamlet made love to his daughter, then no one else would give a high price for her."

"That might be true," remarked one of the shrewder elders, "but a chief's son would give his mistress's father enough presents and patronage to more than make up the difference. Polonius sounds like a fool to me."

"Many people think he was," I agreed. "Meanwhile Polonius sent his son Laertes off to Paris to learn the things of that country, for it was the homestead of a very great chief indeed. Because he was afraid that Laertes might waste a lot of money on beer and women and gambling, or get into trouble by fighting, he sent one of his servants to Paris secretly, to spy out what Laertes was doing. One day Hamlet came upon Polonius's daughter Ophelia. He behaved so oddly he frightened her. Indeed"—I was fumbling for words to express the dubious quality of Hamlet's madness—"the chief and many others had also noticed that when Hamlet talked one could understand the words but not what they meant. Many people thought that he had become mad." My audience suddenly became much more attentive. "The great chief wanted to know what was wrong with Hamlet, so he sent for two of Hamlet's age mates [school friends would have taken long explanation] to talk to Hamlet and find out what troubled his heart. Hamlet, seeing that they had been bribed by the chief to betray him, told them nothing.

Polonius, however, insisted that Hamlet was mad because he had been forbidden to see Ophelia, whom he loved."

"Why," inquired a bewildered voice, "should anyone bewitch Hamlet on that account?"

"Bewitch him?"

"Yes, only witchcraft can make anyone mad, unless, of course, one sees the beings that lurk in the forest."

I stopped being a storyteller, took out my notebook and demanded to be told more about these two causes of madness. Even while they spoke and I jotted notes, I tried to calculate the effect of this new factor on the plot. Hamlet had not been exposed to the beings that lurk in the forests. Only his relatives in the male line could bewitch him. Barring relatives not mentioned by Shakespeare, it had to be Claudius who was attempting to harm him. And, of course, it was.

For the moment I staved off questions by saying that the great chief also refused to believe that Hamlet was mad for the love of Ophelia and nothing else. "He was sure that something much more important was troubling Hamlet's heart."

"Now Hamlet's age mates," I continued, "had brought with them a famous storyteller. Hamlet decided to have this man tell the chief and all his homestead a story about a man who had poisoned his brother because he desired his brother's wife and wished to be chief himself. Hamlet was sure the great chief could not hear the story without making a sign if he was indeed guilty, and then he would discover whether his dead father had told him the truth."

The old man interrupted, with deep cunning, "Why should a father lie to his son?" he asked.

I hedged: "Hamlet wasn't sure that it really was his dead father." It was impossible to say anything, in that language, about devil-inspired visions.

"You mean," he said, "it actually was an omen, and he knew witches sometimes send false ones. Hamlet was a fool not to go to one skilled in reading omens and divining the truth in the first place. A man-who-sees-the-truth could have told him how his father died, if he really had been poisoned, and if there was witchcraft in it; then Hamlet could have called the elders to settle the matter."

The shrewd elder ventured to disagree. "Because his father's brother was a great chief, one-who-sees-the-truth might therefore have been afraid to tell it. I think it was for that reason that a friend of Hamlet's father—a witch and an elder—sent an omen so his friend's son would know. Was the omen true?"

"Yes," I said, abandoning ghosts and the devil; a witch-sent omen it would have to be. "It was true, for when the storyteller was telling his tale before all the homestead, the great chief rose in fear. Afraid that Hamlet knew his secret he planned to have him killed."

The stage set of the next bit presented some difficulties of translation. I began cautiously. "The great chief told Hamlet's mother to find out from her son what he knew. But because a woman's children are always first in her heart, he had the important elder Polonius hide behind a cloth that hung against the wall of Hamlet's mother's sleeping hut. Hamlet started to scold his mother for what she had done."

There was a shocked murmur from everyone. A man should never scold his mother.

"She called out in fear, and Polonius moved behind the cloth. Shouting, 'A rat!' Hamlet took his machete and slashed through the cloth." I paused for dramatic effect. "He had killed Polonius!"

The old men looked at each other in supreme disgust. "That Polonius truly was a fool and a man who knew nothing! What child would not know enough to shout, 'It's me!'" With a pang, I remembered that these people are ardent hunters, always armed with bow, arrow, and machete; at the first rustle in the grass an arrow is aimed and ready, and the hunter shouts "Game!" If no human voice answers immediately, the arrow speeds on its way. Like a good hunter Hamlet had shouted, "A rat!"

I rushed in to save Polonius's reputation. "Polonius did speak. Hamlet heard him. But he thought it was the chief and wished to kill him earlier that evening...." I broke down, unable to describe to these pagans, who had no belief in individual afterlife, the difference between dying at one's prayers and dying "unhousell'd, disappointed, unaneled."

This time I had shocked my audience seriously. "For a man to raise his hand against his father's brother and the one who has become his father—that is a terrible thing. The elders ought to let such a man be bewitched."

I nibbled at my kola nut in some perplexity, then pointed out that after all the man had killed Hamlet's father.

"No," pronounced the old man, speaking less to me than to the young men sitting behind the elders. "If your father's brother has killed your father, you must appeal to your father's age mates; *they* may avenge him. No man may use violence against his senior relatives." Another thought struck him. "But if his father's brother had indeed been wicked enough to bewitch Hamlet and make him mad that would be a good story indeed, for it would be his fault that Hamlet, being mad, no longer had any sense and thus was ready to kill his father's brother."

There was a murmur of applause. *Hamlet* was again a good story to them, but it no longer seemed quite the same story to me. As I thought over the coming complications of plot and motive, I lost courage and decided to skim over dangerous ground quickly.

"The great chief," I went on, "was not sorry that Hamlet had killed Polonius. It gave him a reason to send Hamlet away, with his two treacherous mates, with letters to a chief of a far country, saying that Hamlet should be killed. But Hamlet changed the writing on their papers, so that the chief killed his age mates instead." I encountered a reproachful glare from one of the men whom I had told undetectable forgery was not merely immoral but beyond human skill. I looked the other way.

"Before Hamlet could return, Laertes came back for his father's funeral. The great chief told him Hamlet had killed Polonius. Laertes swore to kill Hamlet because of this, and because his sister Ophelia, hearing her father had been killed by the man she loved, went mad and drowned in the river."

"Have you already forgotten what we told you?" The old man was reproachful. "One cannot take vengeance on a madman; Hamlet killed Polonius in his madness. As for the girl, she not only went mad, she was drowned. Only witches can make

people drown. Water itself can't hurt anything. It is merely something one drinks and bathes in."

I began to get cross. "If you don't like the story, I'll stop."

The old man made soothing noises and himself poured me some more beer. "You tell the story well, and we are listening. But it is clear that the elders of your country have never told you what the story really means. No, don't interrupt! We believe you when you say your marriage customs are different, or your clothes and weapons. But people are the same everywhere; therefore, there are always witches and it is we, the elders, who know how witches work. We told you it was the great chief who wished to kill Hamlet, and now your own words have proved us right. Who were Ophelia's male relatives?"

"There were only her father and her brother." *Hamlet* was clearly out of my hands.

"There must have been many more; this also you must ask of your elders when you get back to your country. From what you tell us, since Polonius was dead, it must have been Laertes who killed Ophelia, although I do not see the reason for it."

We had emptied one pot of beer, and the old men argued the point with slightly tipsy interest. Finally one of them demanded of me, "What did the servant of Polonius say on his return?"

With difficulty I recollected Reynaldo and his mission. "I don't think he did return before Polonius was killed."

"Listen," said the elder, "and I will tell you how it was and how your story will go, then you may tell me if I am right. Polonius knew his son would get into trouble, and so he did. He had many fines to pay for fighting, and debts from gambling. But he had only two ways of getting money quickly. One was to marry off his sister at once, but it is difficult to find a man who will marry a woman desired by the son of a chief. For if the chief's heir commits adultery with your wife, what can you do? Only a fool calls a case against a man who will someday be his judge. Therefore Laertes had to take the second way: he killed his sister by witchcraft, drowning her so he could secretly sell her body to the witches."

I raised an objection. "They found her body and buried it. Indeed Laertes jumped into the grave to see his sister once more—so, you see, the body was truly there. Hamlet, who had just come back, jumped in after him."

"What did I tell you?" The elder appealed to the others. "Laertes was up to no good with his sister's body. Hamlet prevented him, because the chief's heir, like a chief, does not wish any other man to grow rich and powerful. Laertes would be angry, because he would have killed his sister without benefit to himself. In our country he would try to kill Hamlet for that reason. Is this not what happened?"

"More or less," I admitted. "When the great chief found Hamlet was still alive, he encouraged Laertes to try to kill Hamlet and arranged a fight with machetes between them. In the fight both the young men were wounded to death. Hamlet's mother drank the poisoned beer that the chief meant for Hamlet in case he won the fight. When he saw his mother die of poison, Hamlet, dying, managed to kill his father's brother with his machete."

"You see, I was right!" exclaimed the elder.

"That was a very good story," added the old man, "and you told it with very few mistakes. There was just one more error, at the very end. The poison Hamlet's mother drank was obviously meant for the survivor of the fight, whichever it was. If Laertes had won, the great chief would have poisoned him, for no one would know that he arranged Hamlet's death. Then, too, he need not fear Laertes' witchcraft; it takes a strong heart to kill one's only sister by witchcraft.

"Sometime," concluded the old man, gathering his ragged toga about him, "you must tell us some more stories of your country. We, who are elders, will instruct you in their true meaning, so that when you return to your own land your elders will see that you have not been sitting in the bush, but among those who know things and who have taught you wisdom."

**LAURA BOHANNAN** is a former professor of anthropology at the University of Illinois, at Chicago.

# UNIT 3
# The Organization of Society and Culture

## Unit Selections

12. **Understanding Eskimo Science**, Richard Nelson
13. **The Inuit Paradox**, Patricia Gadsby
14. **Ties that Bind**, Peter M. Whiteley
15. **Too Many Bananas, Not Enough Pineapples, and No Watermelon at All: Three Object Lessons in Living with Reciprocity**, David Counts

## Key Points to Consider

- What traditional Inuit (Eskimo) practices do you find contrary to values professed in your society but important to Eskimo survival under certain circumstances?

- What can contemporary hunter-collector societies tell us about the quality of life in the prehistoric past?

- What is the "Inuit paradox" and what can we learn from it regarding modern-day eating practices?

- What are the rules of reciprocity?

- What is the significance of "the gift" in traditional Hopi society?

## Student Website

www.mhcls.com/online

## Internet References

Further information regarding these websites may be found in this book's preface or online.

**Huarochiri, a Peruvian Culture in Time**
*http://wiscinfo.doit.wisc.edu/chaysimire/*

**Smithsonian Institution Web Site**
*http://www.si.edu*

**Sociology Guy's Anthropology Links**
*http://www.trinity.edu/~mkearl/anthro.html*

**What Is Culture?**
*http://www.wsu.edu:8001/vcwsu/commons/topics/culture/culture-index.html*

www.bigfoto.com

**H**uman beings do not interact with one another or think about their world in random fashion. Instead, they engage in both structured and recurrent physical and mental activities. In this section, such patterns of behavior and thought—referred to here as the organization of society and culture—may be seen in a number of different contexts, from the hunting tactics of the Inupiaq Eskimos of the Arctic (see "Understanding Eskimo Science") to the experiences of the Japanese Brazilians as they shockingly discover that they are foreigners in the country of their ancestors (as described in "No Place to Call Home").

Of special importance are the ways in which people make a living—in other words, the production, distribution, and consumption of goods and services. It is only by knowing the basic subsistence systems that we can hope to gain insight into the other levels of social and cultural phenomena, for, as anthropologists have found, they are all inextricably bound together.

Noting the various aspects of a sociocultural system in harmonious balance, however, does not imply an anthropological seal of approval. To understand infanticide (killing of the newborn) in the manner that it is practiced among some peoples is

neither to condone nor condemn it. The adaptive patterns that have been in existence for a great length of time, such as many of the patterns of hunters and gatherers, probably owe their existence to their contributions to long-term human survival (see "The Inuit Paradox"). Anthropologists, however, are not content with the data derived from individual experience. On the contrary, personal descriptions must become the basis for sound anthropological theory. Otherwise, they remain meaningless, isolated relics of culture in the manner of museum pieces. Thus, in "Too Many Bananas, Not Enough Pineapples, and No Watermelon at All: Three Object Lessons in Living With Reciprocity," David Counts provides us with ground rules for reciprocity that were derived from his own particular field of experience and yet are cross-culturally applicable.

While the articles in this unit are to some extent descriptive, they also serve to challenge both academic and common-sense notions about why people behave and think as they do. They remind us that assumptions are never really safe. Anytime anthropologists can be kept on their toes, their field as a whole is the better for it.

# Understanding Eskimo Science

**Traditional hunters' insights into the natural world are worth rediscovering.**

RICHARD NELSON

J ust below the Arctic Circle in the boreal forest of interior Alaska; an amber afternoon in mid-November; the temperature -20°; the air adrift with frost crystals, presaging the onset of deeper cold.

Five men—Koyukon Indians—lean over the carcass of an exceptionally large black bear. For two days they've traversed the Koyukuk River valley, searching for bears that have recently entered hibernation dens. The animals are in prime condition at this season but extremely hard to find. Den entrances, hidden beneath 18 inches of powdery snow, are betrayed only by the subtlest of clues—patches where no grass protrudes from the surface because it's been clawed away for insulation, faint concavities hinting of footprint depressions in the moss below.

Earlier this morning the hunters took a yearling bear. In accordance with Koyukon tradition, they followed elaborate rules for the proper treatment of killed animals. For example, the bear's feet were removed first, to keep its spirit from wandering. Also, certain parts were to be eaten away from the village, at a kind of funeral feast. All the rest would be eaten either at home or at community events, as people here have done for countless generations.

Koyukon hunters know that an animal's life ebbs slowly, that it remains aware and sensitive to how people treat its body. This is especially true for the potent and demanding spirit of the bear.

The leader of the hunting group is Moses Sam, a man in his 60s who has trapped in this territory since childhood. He is known for his detailed knowledge of the land and for his extraordinary success as a bear hunter. "No one else has that kind of luck with bears," I've been told. "Some people are born with it. He always takes good care of his animals—respects them. That's how he keeps his luck."

Moses pulls a small knife from his pocket, kneels beside the bear's head, and carefully slits the clear domes of its eyes. "Now," he explains softly, "the bear won't see if one of us makes a mistake or does something wrong."

C ontemporary Americans are likely to find this story exotic, but over the course of time episodes like this have been utterly commonplace, the essence of people's relationship to the natural world. After all, for 99 percent of human history we lived exclusively as hunter-gatherers; by comparison, agriculture has existed only for a moment and urban societies scarcely more than a blink.

From this perspective, much of human experience over the past several million years lies beyond our grasp. Probably no society has been so deeply alienated as ours from the community of nature, has viewed the natural world from a greater distance of mind, has lapsed into a murkier comprehension of its connections with the sustaining environment. Because of this, we have great difficulty understanding our rootedness to earth, our affinities with nonhuman life.

I believe it's essential that we learn from traditional societies, especially those whose livelihood depends on the harvest of a wild environment—hunters, fishers, trappers, and gatherers. These people have accumulated bodies of knowledge much like our own sciences. And they can give us vital insights about responsible membership in the community of life, insights founded on a wisdom we'd long forgotten and now are beginning to rediscover.

Since the mid-1960s I have worked as an ethnographer in Alaska, living intermittently in remote northern communities and recording native traditions centered around the natural world. I spent about two years in Koyukon Indian villages and just over a year with Inupiaq Eskimos on the Arctic coast—traveling by dog team and snowmobile, recording traditional knowledge, and learning the hunter's way.

Eskimos have long inhabited some of the harshest environments on earth, and they are among the most exquisitely adapted of all human groups. Because plant life is so scarce in their northern terrain, Eskimos depend more than any other people on hunting.

Eskimos are famous for the cleverness of their technology—kayaks, harpoons, skin clothing, snow houses, dog teams. But I believe their greatest genius, and the basis of their success, lies in the less tangible realm of the intellect—the nexus of mind and nature. For what repeatedly struck me above all else was their profound knowledge of the environment.

Several times, when my Inupiaq hunting companion did something especially clever, he'd point to his head and declare: "You see—Eskimo scientist!" At first I took it as hyperbole, but as time went by I realized he was speaking the truth. Scientists had often come to his village, and he saw in them a familiar commitment to the empirical method.

Traditional Inupiaq hunters spend a lifetime acquiring knowledge—from others in the community and from their own observations. If they are to survive, they must have absolutely reliable information. When I first went to live with Inupiaq people, I doubted many things they told me. But the longer I stayed, the more I trusted their teachings.

For example, hunters say that ringed seals surfacing in open leads—wide cracks in the sea ice—can reliably forecast the weather. Because an unexpected gale might set people adrift on the pack ice, accurate prediction is a matter of life and death. When seals rise chest-high in the water, snout pointed skyward, not going anywhere in particular, it indicates stable weather, the Inupiaq say. But if they surface briefly, head low, snout parallel to the water, and show themselves only once or twice, watch for a sudden storm. And take special heed if you've also noticed the sled dogs howling incessantly, stars twinkling erratically, or the current running strong from the south. As time passed, my own experiences with seals and winter storms affirmed what the Eskimos said.

Like a young Inupiaq in training, I gradually grew less skeptical and started to apply what I was told. For example, had I ever been rushed by a polar bear, I would have jumped away to the animal's *right* side. Inupiaq elders say polar bears are left-handed, so you have a slightly better chance to avoid their right paw, which is slower and less accurate. I'm pleased to say I never had the chance for a field test. But in judging assertions like this, remember that Eskimos have had close contact with polar bears for several thousand years.

## The Inupiaq hunter possesses as much knowledge as a highly trained scientist in our own society

During winter, ringed and bearded seals maintain tunnel-like breathing holes in ice that is many feet thick. These holes are often capped with an igloo-shaped dome created by water sloshing onto the surface when the animal enters from below. Inupiaq elders told me that polar bears are clever enough to excavate around the base of this dome, leaving it perfectly intact but weak enough that a hard swat will shatter the ice and smash the seal's skull. I couldn't help wondering if this were really true; but then a younger man told me he'd recently followed the tracks of a bear that had excavated one seal hole after another, exactly as the elders had described.

In the village where I lived, the most respected hunter was Igruk, a man in his 70s. He had an extraordinary sense of animals—a gift for understanding and predicting their behavior. Although he was no longer quick and strong, he joined a crew hunting bowhead whales during the spring migration, his main role being that of adviser. Each time Igruk spotted a whale coming from the south, he counted the number of blows, timed how long it stayed down, and noted the distance it traveled along the open lead, until it vanished toward the north. This way he learned to predict, with uncanny accuracy, where hunters could expect the whale to resurface.

I believe the expert Inupiaq hunter possesses as much knowledge as a highly trained scientist in our own society, although the information may be of a different sort. Volumes could be written on the behavior, ecology, and utilization of Arctic animals—polar bear, walrus, bowhead whale, beluga, bearded seal, ringed seal, caribou, musk ox, and others—based entirely on Eskimo knowledge.

Comparable bodies of knowledge existed in every Native American culture before the time of Columbus. Since then, even in the far north, Western education and cultural change have steadily eroded these traditions. Reflecting on a time before Europeans arrived, we can imagine the whole array of North American animal species—deer, elk, black bear, wolf, mountain lion, beaver, coyote, Canada goose, ruffed grouse, passenger pigeon, northern pike—each known in hundreds of different ways by tribal communities; the entire continent, sheathed in intricate webs of knowledge. Taken as a whole, this composed a vast intellectual legacy, born of intimacy with the natural world. Sadly, not more than a hint of it has ever been recorded.

Like other Native Americans, the Inupiaq acquired their knowledge through gradual accretion of naturalistic observations—year after year, lifetime after lifetime, generation after generation, century after century. Modern science often relies on other techniques—specialized full-time observation, controlled experiments, captive-animal studies, technological devices like radio collars—which can provide similar information much more quickly.

Yet Eskimo people have learned not only *about* animals but also *from* them. Polar bears hunt seals not only by waiting at their winter breathing holes, but also by stalking seals that crawl up on the ice to bask in the spring warmth. Both methods depend on being silent, staying downwind, keeping out of sight, and moving only when the seal is asleep or distracted. According to the elders, a stalking bear will even use one paw to cover its conspicuous black nose.

Inupiaq methods for hunting seals, both at breathing holes and atop the spring ice, are nearly identical to those of the polar bear. Is this a case of independent invention? Or did ancestral Eskimos learn the techniques by watching polar bears, who had perfected an adaptation to the sea-ice-environment long before humans arrived in the Arctic?

The hunter's genius centers on knowing an animal's behavior so well he can turn it to his advantage. For instance, Igruk once saw a polar bear far off across flat ice, where he couldn't stalk it without being seen. But he knew an old technique of mimicking a seal. He lay down in plain sight, conspicuous in his dark parka and pants, then lifted and dropped his head like a seal, scratched the ice, and imitated flippers with his hands. The bear mistook his pursuer for prey. Each time Igruk lifted his head the animal kept still; whenever Igruk "slept" the bear crept closer. When it came near enough, a gunshot pierced the snowy silence. That night, polar bear meat was shared among the villagers.

A traditional hunter like Igruk plumbs the depths of his intellect—his capacity to manipulate complex knowledge. But he also delves into his animal nature, drawing from intuitions of sense and body and heart: feeling the wind's touch, listening for the tick of moving ice, peering from crannies, hiding as if he himself were the hunted. He moves in a world of eyes, where everything watches—the bear, the seal, the wind, the moon and stars, the drifting ice, the silent waters below. He is beholden to powers we have long forgotten or ignored.

In Western society we rest comfortably on our own accepted truths about the nature of nature. We treat the environment as if it were numb to our presence and blind to our behavior. Yet despite our certainty on this matter, accounts of traditional people throughout the world reveal that most of humankind has concluded otherwise. Perhaps our scientific method really does follow the path to a single, absolute truth. But there may be wisdom in accepting other possibilities and opening ourselves to different views of the world.

I remember asking a Koyukon man about the behavior and temperament of the Canada goose. He described it as a gentle and good-natured animal, then added: "Even if [a goose] had the power to knock you over, I don't think it would do it."

For me, his words carried a deep metaphorical wisdom. They exemplified the Koyukon people's own restraint toward the world around them. And they offered a contrast to our culture, in which possessing the power to overwhelm the environment has long been sufficient justification for its use.

## "Each animal knows way more than you do," a Koyukon Indian elder was fond of telling me.

We often think of this continent as having been a pristine wilderness when the first Europeans arrived. Yet for at least 12,000 years, and possibly twice that long, Native American people had inhabited and intensively utilized the land; had gathered, hunted, fished, settled, and cultivated; had learned the terrain in all its details, infusing it with meaning and memory; and had shaped every aspect of their life around it. That humans could sustain membership in a natural community for such an enormous span of time without profoundly degrading it fairly staggers the imagination. And it gives strong testimony to the adaptation of mind—the braiding together of knowledge and ideology—that linked North America's indigenous people with their environment.

A Koyukon elder, who took it upon himself to be my teacher, was fond of telling me: "Each animal knows way more than you do." He spoke as if it summarized all that he understood and believed.

This statement epitomizes relationships to the natural world among many Native American people. And it goes far in explaining the diversity and fecundity of life on our continent when the first sailing ship approached these shores.

There's been much discussion in recent years about what biologist E. O. Wilson has termed "biophilia"—a deep, pervasive, ubiquitous, all-embracing affinity for nonhuman life. Evidence for this "instinct" may be elusive in Western cultures, but not among traditional societies. People like the Koyukon manifest biophilia in virtually all dimensions of their existence. Connectedness with nonhuman life infuses the whole spectrum of their thought, behavior, and belief.

It's often said that a fish might have no concept of water, never having left it. In the same way, traditional peoples might never stand far enough outside themselves to imagine a generalized concept of biophilia. Perhaps it would be impossible for people to intimately bound with the natural world, people who recognize that all nature is our own embracing community. Perhaps, to bring a word like *biophilia* into their language, they would first need to separate themselves from nature.

In April 1971 I was in a whaling camp several miles off the Arctic coast with a group of Inupiaq hunters, including Igruk, who understood animals so well he almost seemed to enter their minds.

Onshore winds had closed the lead that migrating whales usually follow, but one large opening remained, and here the Inupiaq men placed their camp. For a couple of days there had been no whales, so everyone stayed inside the warm tent, talking and relaxing. The old man rested on a soft bed of caribou skins with his eyes closed. Then, suddenly, he interrupted the conversation: "I think a whale is coming, and perhaps it will surface very close…."

To my amazement everyone jumped into action, although none had seen or heard anything except Igruk's words. Only he stayed behind, while the others rushed for the water's edge. I was last to leave the tent. Seconds after I stepped outside, a broad, shining back cleaved the still water near the opposite side of the opening, accompanied by the burst of a whale's blow.

Later, when I asked how he'd known, Igruk said, "There was a ringing inside my ears." I have no explanation other than his; I can only report what I saw. None of the Inupiaq crew members even commented afterward, as if nothing out of the ordinary had happened.

This article originally appeared in *Audubon* magazine, September/October 1993, pp. 102–109. Adapted from *Biophilia* by Richard Nelson, 1993. Published by Island Press. © 1993 by Richard Nelson. Reprinted by permission of Susan Bergholz Literary Services, New York. All rights reserved.

# The Inuit Paradox

**How can people who gorge on fat and rarely see a vegetable be healthier than we are?**

Patricia Gadsby

PATRICIA COCHRAN, AN INUPIAT FROM NORTHWESTERN Alaska, is talking about the native foods of her childhood: "We pretty much had a subsistence way of life. Our food supply was right outside our front door. We did our hunting and foraging on the Seward Peninsula and along the Bering Sea."

"Our meat was seal and walrus, marine mammals that live in cold water and have lots of fat. We used seal oil for our cooking and as a dipping sauce for food. We had moose, caribou, and reindeer. We hunted ducks, geese, and little land birds like quail, called ptarmigan. We caught crab and lots of fish—salmon, whitefish, tomcod, pike, and char. Our fish were cooked, dried, smoked, or frozen. We ate frozen raw whitefish, sliced thin. The elders liked stinkfish, fish buried in seal bags or cans in the tundra and left to ferment. And fermented seal flipper, they liked that too."

Cochran's family also received shipments of whale meat from kin living farther north, near Barrow. Beluga was one she liked; raw muktuk, which is whale skin with its underlying blubber, she definitely did not. "To me it has a chew-on-a-tire consistency," she says, "but to many people it's a mainstay." In the short subarctic summers, the family searched for roots and greens and, best of all from a child's point of view, wild blueberries, crowberries, or salmonberries, which her aunts would mix with whipped fat to make a special treat called *akutuq*—in colloquial English, Eskimo ice cream.

Now Cochran directs the Alaska Native Science Commission, which promotes research on native cultures and the health and environmental issues that affect them. She sits at her keyboard in Anchorage, a bustling city offering fare from Taco Bell to French cuisine. But at home Cochran keeps a freezer filled with fish, seal, walrus, reindeer, and whale meat, sent by her family up north, and she and her husband fish and go berry picking—"sometimes a challenge in Anchorage," she adds, laughing. "I eat fifty-fifty," she explains, half traditional, half regular American.

No one, not even residents of the northernmost villages on Earth, eats an entirely traditional northern diet anymore. Even the groups we came to know as Eskimo—which include the Inupiat and the Yupiks of Alaska, the Canadian Inuit and Inuvialuit, Inuit Greenlanders, and the Siberian Yupiks—have probably seen more changes in their diet in a lifetime than their ancestors did over thousands of years. The closer people live to towns and the more access they have to stores and cash-paying jobs, the more likely they are to have westernized their eating. And with westernization, at least on the North American continent, comes processed foods and cheap carbohydrates—Crisco, Tang, soda, cookies, chips, pizza, fries. "The young and urbanized," says Harriet Kuhnlein, director of the Centre for Indigenous Peoples' Nutrition and Environment at McGill University in Montreal, "are increasingly into fast food." So much so that type 2 diabetes, obesity, and other diseases of Western civilization are becoming causes for concern there too.

Today, when diet books top the best-seller list and nobody seems sure of what to eat to stay healthy, it's surprising to learn how well the Eskimo did on a high-protein, high-fat diet. Shaped by glacial temperatures, stark landscapes, and protracted winters, the traditional Eskimo diet had little in the way of plant food, no agricultural or dairy products, and was unusually low in carbohydrates. Mostly people subsisted on what they hunted and fished. Inland dwellers took advantage of caribou feeding on tundra mosses, lichens, and plants too tough for humans to stomach (though predigested vegetation in the animals' paunches became dinner as well). Coastal people exploited the sea. The main nutritional challenge was avoiding starvation in late winter if primary meat sources became too scarce or lean.

These foods hardly make up the "balanced" diet most of us grew up with, and they look nothing like the mix of grains, fruits, vegetables, meat, eggs, and dairy we're accustomed to seeing in conventional food pyramid diagrams. How could such a diet possibly be adequate? How did people get along on little else but fat and animal protein?

## 'The diet of the Far North shows that there are no essential foods—only essential nutrients'

What the diet of the Far North illustrates, says Harold Draper, a biochemist and expert in Eskimo nutrition, is that there are no essential foods—only essential nutrients. And humans can get those nutrients from diverse and eye-opening sources.

One might, for instance, imagine gross vitamin deficiencies arising from a diet with scarcely any fruits and vegetables. What furnishes vitamin A, vital for eyes and bones? We derive much of ours from colorful plant foods, constructing it from pigmented plant precursors called carotenoids (as in carrots). But vitamin A, which is oil soluble, is also plentiful in the oils of cold-water fishes and sea mammals, as well as in the animals' livers, where fat is processed. These dietary staples also provide vitamin D, another oil-soluble vitamin needed for bones. Those of us living in temperate and tropical climates, on the other hand, usually make vitamin D indirectly by exposing skin to strong sun—hardly an option in the Arctic winter—and by consuming fortified cow's milk, to which the indigenous northern groups had little access until recent decades and often don't tolerate all that well.

As for vitamin C, the source in the Eskimo diet was long a mystery. Most animals can synthesize their own vitamin C, or ascorbic acid, in their livers, but humans are among the exceptions, along with other primates and oddballs like guinea pigs and bats. If we don't ingest enough of it, we fall apart from scurvy, a gruesome connective-tissue disease. In the United States today we can get ample supplies from orange juice, citrus fruits, and fresh vegetables. But vitamin C oxidizes with time; getting enough from a ship's provisions was tricky for early 18th- and 19th-century voyagers to the polar regions. Scurvy—joint pain, rotting gums, leaky blood vessels, physical and mental degeneration—plagued European and U.S. expeditions even in the 20th century. However, Arctic peoples living on fresh fish and meat were free of the disease.

Impressed, the explorer Vilhjalmur Stefansson adopted an Eskimo-style diet for five years during the two Arctic expeditions he led between 1908 and 1918. "The thing to do is to find your antiscorbutics where you are," he wrote. "Pick them up as you go." In 1928, to convince skeptics, he and a young colleague spent a year on an Americanized version of the diet under medical supervision at Bellevue Hospital in New York City. The pair ate steaks, chops, organ meats like brain and liver, poultry, fish, and fat with gusto. "If you have some fresh meat in your diet every day and don't overcook it," Stefansson declared triumphantly, "there will be enough C from that source alone to prevent scurvy."

In fact, all it takes to ward off scurvy is a daily dose of 10 milligrams, says Karen Fediuk, a consulting dietitian and former graduate student of Harriet Kuhnlein's who did her master's thesis on vitamin C. (That's far less than the U.S. recommended daily allowance of 75 to 90 milligrams—75 for women, 90 for men.) Native foods easily supply those 10 milligrams of scurvy prevention, especially when organ meats—preferably raw—are on the menu. For a study published with Kuhnlein in 2002, Fediuk compared the vitamin C content of 100-gram (3.55-ounce) samples of foods eaten by Inuit women living in the Canadian Arctic: Raw caribou liver supplied almost 24 milligrams, seal brain close to 15 milligrams, and raw kelp more than 28 milligrams. Still higher levels were found in whale skin and muktuk.

As you might guess from its antiscorbutic role, vitamin C is crucial for the synthesis of connective tissue, including the matrix of skin. "Wherever collagen's made, you can expect vitamin C," says Kuhnlein. Thick skinned, chewy, and collagen rich, raw muktuk can serve up an impressive 36 milligrams in a 100-gram piece, according to Fediuk's analyses. "Weight for weight, it's as good as orange juice," she says. Traditional Inuit practices like freezing meat and fish and frequently eating them raw, she notes, conserve vitamin C, which is easily cooked off and lost in food processing.

Hunter-gatherer diets like those eaten by these northern groups and other traditional diets based on nomadic herding or subsistence farming are among the older approaches to human eating. Some of these eating plans might seem strange to us—diets centered around milk, meat, and blood among the East African pastoralists, enthusiastic tuber eating by the Quechua living in the High Andes, the staple use of the mongongo nut in the southern African !Kung—but all proved resourceful adaptations to particular eco-niches. No people, though, may have been forced to push the nutritional envelope further than those living at Earth's frozen extremes. The unusual makeup of the far-northern diet led Loren Cordain, a professor of evolutionary nutrition at Colorado State University at Fort Collins, to make an intriguing observation.

FOUR YEARS AGO, CORDAIN REVIEWED THE MACRONUTRIENT content (protein, carbohydrates, fat) in the diets of 229 hunter-gatherer groups listed in a series of journal articles collectively known as the Ethnographic Atlas. These are some of the oldest surviving human diets. In general, hunter-gatherers tend to eat more animal protein than we do in our standard Western diet, with its reliance on agriculture and carbohydrates derived from grains and starchy plants. Lowest of all in carbohydrate, and highest in combined fat and protein, are the diets of peoples living in the Far North, where they make up for fewer plant foods with extra fish. What's equally striking, though, says Cordain, is that these meat-and-fish diets also exhibit a natural "protein ceiling." Protein accounts for no more than 35 to 40 percent of their total calories, which suggests to him that's all the protein humans can comfortably handle.

## 'Wild-animal fats are different from other fats. Farm animals typically have lots of highly saturated fat'

This ceiling, Cordain thinks, could be imposed by the way we process protein for energy. The simplest, fastest way to make energy is to convert carbohydrates into glucose, our body's primary fuel. But if the body is out of carbs, it can burn fat, or if necessary, break down protein. The name given to the convoluted business of making glucose from protein is gluconeogenesis. It takes place in the liver, uses a dizzying slew of enzymes, and creates nitrogen waste that has to be converted into urea and disposed of through the kidneys. On a truly traditional diet, says Draper, recalling his studies in the 1970s, Arctic people had plenty of protein but little carbohydrate, so they often relied on gluconeogenesis. Not only did they have bigger livers to handle the additional work but their urine volumes were also typically larger to get rid of the extra urea. Nonetheless, there appears to be a limit on how much protein the human liver can safely cope with: Too much overwhelms the liver's waste-disposal system, leading to protein poisoning—nausea, diarrhea, wasting, and death.

Whatever the metabolic reason for this syndrome, says John Speth, an archaeologist at the University of Michigan's Museum of Anthropology, plenty of evidence shows that hunters through the ages avoided protein excesses, discarding fat-depleted animals even when food was scarce. Early pioneers and trappers in North America encountered what looks like a similar affliction, sometimes referred to as rabbit starvation because rabbit meat is notoriously lean. Forced to subsist on fat-deficient meat, the men would gorge themselves, yet wither away. Protein can't be the sole source of energy for humans, concludes Cordain. Anyone eating a meaty diet that is low in carbohydrates must have fat as well.

Stefansson had arrived at this conclusion, too, while living among the Copper Eskimo. He recalled how he and his Eskimo companions had become quite ill after weeks of eating "caribou so skinny that there was no appreciable fat behind the eyes or in the marrow." Later he agreed to repeat the miserable experience at Bellevue Hospital, for science's sake, and for a while ate nothing but defatted meat. "The symptoms brought on at Bellevue by an incomplete meat diet [lean without fat] were exactly the same as in the Arctic … diarrhea and a feeling of general baffling discomfort," he wrote. He was restored with a fat fix but "had lost considerable weight." For the remainder of his year on meat, Stefansson tucked into his rations of chops and steaks with fat intact. "A normal meat diet is not a high-protein diet," he pronounced. "We were really getting three-quarters of our calories from fat." (Fat is more than twice as calorie dense as protein or carbohydrate, but even so, that's a lot of lard. A typical U.S diet provides about 35 percent of its calories from fat.)

Stefansson dropped 10 pounds on his meat-and-fat regimen and remarked on its "slenderizing" aspect, so perhaps it's no surprise he's been co-opted as a posthumous poster boy for Atkins-type diets. No discussion about diet these days can avoid Atkins. Even some researchers interviewed for this article couldn't resist referring to the Inuit way of eating as the "original Atkins." "Superficially, at a macronutrient level, the two diets certainly look similar," allows Samuel Klein, a nutrition researcher at Washington University in St. Louis, who's attempting to study how Atkins stacks up against conventional weight-loss diets. Like the Inuit diet, Atkins is low in carbohydrates and very high in fat. But numerous researchers, including Klein, point out that there are profound differences between the two diets, beginning with the type of meat and fat eaten.

Fats have been demonized in the United States, says Eric Dewailly, a professor of preventive medicine at Laval University in Quebec. But all fats are not created equal. This lies at the heart of a paradox—the Inuit paradox, if you

will. In the Nunavik villages in northern Quebec, adults over 40 get almost half their calories from native foods, says Dewailly, and they don't die of heart attacks at nearly the same rates as other Canadians or Americans. Their cardiac death rate is about half of ours, he says. As someone who looks for links between diet and cardiovascular health, he's intrigued by that reduced risk. Because the traditional Inuit diet is "so restricted," he says, it's easier to study than the famously heart-healthy Mediterranean diet, with its cornucopia of vegetables, fruits, grains, herbs, spices, olive oil, and red wine.

A key difference in the typical Nunavik Inuit's diet is that more than 50 percent of the calories in Inuit native foods come from fats. Much more important, the fats come from wild animals.

Wild-animal fats are different from both farm-animal fats and processed fats, says Dewailly. Farm animals, cooped up and stuffed with agricultural grains (carbohydrates) typically have lots of solid, highly saturated fat. Much of our processed food is also riddled with solid fats, or so-called trans fats, such as the re-engineered vegetable oils and shortenings cached in baked goods and snacks. "A lot of the packaged food on supermarket shelves contains them. So do commercial french fries," Dewailly adds.

Trans fats are polyunsaturated vegetable oils tricked up to make them more solid at room temperature. Manufacturers do this by hydrogenating the oils—adding extra hydrogen atoms to their molecular structures—which "twists" their shapes. Dewailly makes twisting sound less like a chemical transformation than a perversion, an act of public-health sabotage: "These man-made fats are dangerous, even worse for the heart than saturated fats." They not only lower high-density lipoprotein cholesterol (HDL, the "good" cholesterol) but they also raise low-density lipoprotein cholesterol (LDL, the "bad" cholesterol) and triglycerides, he says. In the process, trans fats set the stage for heart attacks because they lead to the increase of fatty buildup in artery walls.

Wild animals that range freely and eat what nature intended, says Dewailly, have fat that is far more healthful. Less of their fat is saturated, and more of it is in the monounsaturated form (like olive oil). What's more, cold-water fishes and sea mammals are particularly rich in polyunsaturated fats called n-3 fatty acids or omega-3 fatty acids. These fats appear to benefit the heart and vascular system. But the polyunsaturated fats in most Americans' diets are the omega-6 fatty acids supplied by vegetable oils. By contrast, whale blubber consists of 70 percent monounsaturated fat and close to 30 percent omega-3s, says Dewailly.

## 'Dieting is the price we pay for too little exercise and too much mass-produced food'

Omega-3s evidently help raise HDL cholesterol, lower triglycerides, and are known for anticlotting effects. (Ethnographers have remarked on an Eskimo propensity for nosebleeds.) These fatty acids are believed to protect the heart from life-threatening arrhythmias that can lead to sudden cardiac death. And like a "natural aspirin," adds Dewailly, omega-3 polyunsaturated fats help put a damper on runaway inflammatory processes, which play a part in atherosclerosis, arthritis, diabetes, and other so-called diseases of civilization.

You can be sure, however, that Atkins devotees aren't routinely eating seal and whale blubber. Besides the acquired taste problem, their commerce is extremely restricted in the United States by the Marine Mammal Protection Act, says Bruce Holub, a nutritional biochemist in the department of human biology and nutritional sciences at the University of Guelph in Ontario.

"In heartland America it's probable they're not eating in an Eskimo-like way," says Gary Foster, clinical director of the Weight and Eating Disorders Program at the Pennsylvania School of Medicine. Foster, who describes himself as open-minded about Atkins, says he'd nonetheless worry if people saw the diet as a green light to eat all the butter and bacon—saturated fats—they want. Just before rumors surfaced that Robert Atkins had heart and weight problems when he died, Atkins officials themselves were stressing saturated fat should account for no more than 20 percent of dieters' calories. This seems to be a clear retreat from the diet's original don't-count-the-calories approach to bacon and butter and its happy exhortations to "plow into those prime ribs." Furthermore, 20 percent of calories from saturated fats is *double* what most nutritionists advise. Before plowing into those prime ribs, readers of a recent edition of the *Dr. Atkins' New Diet Revolution* are urged to take omega-3 pills to help protect their hearts. "If you watch carefully," says Holub wryly, "you'll see many popular U.S. diets have quietly added omega-3 pills, in the form of fish oil or flaxseed capsules, as supplements."

Needless to say, the subsistence diets of the Far North are not "dieting." Dieting is the price we pay for too little exercise and too much mass-produced food. Northern diets were a way of life in places too cold for agriculture, where food, whether hunted, fished, or foraged, could not be taken for granted. They were about keeping weight on.

This is not to say that people in the Far North were fat: Subsistence living requires exercise—hard physical work. Indeed, among the good reasons for native people to maintain their old way of eating, as far as it's possible today, is that it provides a hedge against obesity, type 2 diabetes, and heart disease. Unfortunately, no place on Earth is immune to the spreading taint of growth and development. The very well-being of the northern food chain is coming under threat from global warming, land

development, and industrial pollutants in the marine environment. "I'm a pragmatist," says Cochran, whose organization is involved in pollution monitoring and disseminating food-safety information to native villages. "Global warming we don't have control over. But we can, for example, do cleanups of military sites in Alaska or of communication cables leaching lead into fish-spawning areas. We can help communities make informed food choices. A young woman of childbearing age may choose not to eat certain organ meats that concentrate contaminants. As individuals, we do have options. And eating our salmon and our seal is still a heck of a better option than pulling something processed that's full of additives off a store shelf."

NOT OFTEN IN OUR INDUSTRIAL SOCIETY DO WE HEAR someone speak so familiarly about "our" food animals. We don't talk of "our pig" and "our beef." We've lost that creature feeling, that sense of kinship with food sources. "You're taught to think in boxes," says Cochran. "In our culture the connectivity between humans, animals, plants, the land they live on, and the air they share is ingrained in us from birth.

"You truthfully can't separate the way we get our food from the way we live," she says. "How we get our food is intrinsic to our culture. It's how we pass on our values and knowledge to the young. When you go out with your aunts and uncles to hunt or to gather, you learn to smell the air, watch the wind, understand the way the ice moves, know the land. You get to know where to pick which plant and what animal to take."

"It's part, too, of your development as a person. You share food with your community. You show respect to your elders by offering them the first catch. You give thanks to the animal that gave up its life for your sustenance. So you get all the physical activity of harvesting your own food, all the social activity of sharing and preparing it, and all the spiritual aspects as well," says Cochran. "You certainly don't get all that, do you, when you buy prepackaged food from a store."

"That's why some of us here in Anchorage are working to protect what's ours, so that others can continue to live back home in the villages," she adds. "Because if we don't take care of our food, it won't be there for us in the future. And if we lose our foods, we lose who we are." The word Inupiat means "the real people." "That's who we are," says Cochran.

From *Discover* magazine, August 2002, pp. 12-14. Copyright © 2002 by Patricia Gadsby. Reprinted by permission of the author.

# Ties That Bind

## Hopi gift culture and its first encounter with the United States

PETER M. WHITELEY

In 1852, shortly after the United States had nominally annexed Hopi country, in northern Arizona, the Hopi people arranged for a diplomatic packet to reach President Millard Fillmore at the White House. Part message and part magical gift, the packet was delivered by a delegation of five prominent men from another Pueblo tribe, the Tewas of Tesuque Pueblo in New Mexico, who wanted to gain legal protection from Anglo and Hispanic settlers who were encroaching on their lands. The delegation traveled for nearly three months, on horseback, steamboat, and train, from Santa Fe to Washington, D.C., more than 2,600 miles away. The five men spoke fluent Spanish, the dominant European language of the region at the time—which made them ideally suited to convey the gift packet and its message to the president.

At the time, no U.S. government official had visited the Hopi (and few would do so before the 1890s). Their "unique diplomatic pacquet," in the words of the nineteenth-century ethnologist Henry Rowe Schoolcraft, offered "friendship and intercommunication ... opening, symbolically, a road from the Moqui [Hopi] country to Washington." The packet was in two parts. The first part comprised two *pahos*, or prayer-sticks, at either end of a long cotton cord, dyed for part of its length. Separating the dyed from the undyed part of the cord were six varicolored feathers, knotted into a bunch. The *pahos* "represent the Moqui [Hopi] people and the President [respectively]," Schoolcraft wrote; "the cord is the road which separates them; the [bunch of feathers] tied to the cord is the meeting point."

As well as encoding a message, the *pahos* were an offering of a kind that Hopi deities such as Taawa, the Sun god, traditionally like to receive. By giving the president *pahos* worthy of the Sun, the Hopi signaled their expectation that he would reciprocate. Just as the Sun, on receiving the appropriate offerings, would send rain clouds for sustaining life and growth, so, too, the president would send protection for Hopi lives and lands—in this instance, protection from assaults by neighboring tribes such as the Navajo.

The second part of the packet comprised a cornstalk cigarette filled with tobacco ("to be smoked by the president") and a small cornhusk package that en closed honey-soaked cornmeal. According to the Tesuque delegation, the honey-meal package was "a charm to call down rain from heaven." When the president smoked the cigarette, he would exhale clouds of smoke, which would sympathetically attract the clouds of the sky. Then, when he chewed the cornmeal and spat the wild honey on ground that needed rain, the Tesuque statement concluded, "the Moquis assure him that it [the rain] will come."

In sum, the packet was three things at once: message, offering, and gift of magical power. In conveying those elements, the Hopi sought to open diplomatic relations with the U.S.

But their intent appears to have been lost on their recipient. As so often happens when two cultures make contact, deep misunderstandings can arise: What does a gift mean? What, if anything, does the gift giver expect in return? Do the giver and the recipient both assign the same value to the gift? In twenty-five years of ethnographic fieldwork with the Hopi, it has been my goal to learn something of their history and culture. Recently I turned my attention to certain important events, such as the Millard Fillmore episode, that might shed light on how Hopi society changed as the U.S. developed. In that context Hopi gift giving and the ways it functions as a pillar of Hopi social organization have been central to my studies. One lesson of my work shines through: When nations exchange gifts, all the parties would do best to keep in mind the old adage, "It's the thought that counts."

Given the differences between Hopi and Western traditions and culture, perhaps it is not surprising that the Hopi idea of "gift" is only loosely equivalent to the Western one. In 1852 the Hopi people were still little affected by outside populations, and Hopi land use spread across much of northern Arizona and even into southern Utah. At that time, the Hopi lifestyle was traditional, based on farming, foraging, and some pastoralism. Even today, important elements of the subsistence economy persist, though wage labor and small business provide supplemental income.

The Hopi typically divide their work according to gender. Work done by men (such as farming and harvesting of crops) is perceived as a gift to the women; work done by women (such as gardening, gathering of piñon nuts, grasses, wild fruits, berries, and the like) is perceived as a gift to the men. Women also own and manage the distribution of their household's goods and crops. In fact, Hopi women control most of the material economic life, whereas Hopi men largely control the ritual and spiritual aspects.

The Hopi take part in an elaborate cycle of religious ceremonies, to which a range of specialized offices and privileges is attached. But individuals gain those distinctive social positions not through material wealth but rather through gender and kinship relations, which are ordered in a matrilineal manner. In fact, clan heads and chiefs of religious societies are typically worse off materially than the average member of the clan. Hopi leaders are supposed to be materially poor, and a wealthy individual is often criticized as *qahopi*, un-Hopi, for failing to share. Wealth and status among the Hopi is thus phrased in ritual terms: a poor person is one without ceremonial prerogatives, not one without money. So averse are the Hopi to material accumulation that in May 2004, for the second time, they voted against casino gambling, despite substantial poverty on the reservation.

Does such a primacy of value placed on ceremonial roles explain the evanescent nature of the gift given to President Fillmore? In what world of meaning did the packet represent great value? Indeed, what's in a gift?

Anthropologists have been making hay of that last question ever since 1925, when the French anthropologist Marcel Mauss published his groundbreaking *Essai sur le Don* (translated into English as "The Gift"). Mauss convincingly argued that in small-scale societies (10,000 or fewer persons) gifts are "total social facts." What he meant is that, in gift- or barter-based social systems, divisions of social life into discrete domains—such as economy, politics, law, or religion—are meaningless; each sphere interpenetrates and overlaps the others.

As in strict barter, an exchange in Hopi culture that begins by making a gift to someone does not involve money, but it does require reciprocity. Thus goods, services, or knowledge "given" to an individual or a group are answered with something of equivalent value. "Gifts" develop an interconnectedness between Hopi individuals in a way that outright purchases cannot. Furthermore, the Hopi offer girls in a much broader range of circumstances than people in Western cultures do, and the value of those gifts extends to the religious realm, tying individuals and groups to each other and to the realm of the spirits.

Probably the key to understanding a gift-based system such as that of the Hopi is to recognize that such systems are built on kinship. "Kinship"—the godzilla that has driven multitudes of college students screaming from anthropology 101—is, in this regard at least, straightforward. It means simply that the great majority of human social activity is framed in terms of reciprocal family ties. Where all personal relationships are cast within the "kinship idiom" there are no members of the society who are not kin to me, nor I to them.

Kinship terms encode behavioral expectations as well as familial role. As anthropologists never tire of saying, such terms are primarily social, not biological: obviously if I call fifteen women "mother," as the average Hopi can do, I do not assume that each woman physically gave birth to me. But my "mothers" all have rights and duties in relation to me. And, reciprocally, I

have duties and rights with respect to them: in fact, their duties are my rights, and my duties are their rights in the relationship. That is what reciprocity is all about. You give me food, I plant your cornfield, to give a crude example. But, in a kinship society, such a basic structure of mutual expectations forms the foundation for an entire apparatus of courtesy and manners, deference and respect, familiarity or distance. Those expectations are concretely expressed by gifts—spontaneous and planned, routine and special, trivial and grand. Gifts are thus communications in a language of social belonging.

## So averse are the Hopi to material accumulation that in May 2004 they voted against casino gambling.

So-called gift economies entail a certain kind of sociality, or sense of what it means to belong to a community. In such an economy, one gives a gift to mark social relations built on kinship and altruism, but without the expectation of direct repayment. According to some arguments, gifts are also given to foster a sense of community, as well as sustainable interrelations with the local environment. In fact, in some respects the giver still "owns" some part of the gift, and it is the intangible connection between the two parties, mediated by the gift, that forms the basis of interpersonal relationships.

In contrast, in exchange economies, commodities dominate social interchange. Competitive markets, governed by the profit motive, connect buyer and seller, and social relations are characterized by individualism. A gift, once given, belongs entirely to the recipient; only when the item given has sentimental value does it keep the bond between giver and recipient alive.

That is not to say the Hopi did not engage in the more impersonal, "Western" forms of material exchange. In the Hopi language, as in English, several words describe how an item is transferred from one person to another: *maqa* ("to give"); *hùuya* ("to barter or trade"); and *tu'i* ("to buy"). Those words all antedate the arrival of Europeans—and anthropological classifications. Barter and purchase, as well as gifts, have all long been present in Hopi life. Furthermore, gift exchange in the West can also function as it does among the Hopi, as part of kinship obligations or ordinary social life.

What is distinctive about Hopi custom is the fact that the gift economy is responsible for the great majority of exchanges. Furthermore, there is no such thing as a free gift. The strong interpersonal bonds created by a gift make giving almost de rigueur at ceremonial events. Gifts, particularly gifts of food or utensils, are transmitted during ceremonies of personal milestones (at a birth or a marriage), as well as at public gatherings.

For example, at the annual so-called basket dances, girls and women distribute a variety of objects they have collected for the occasion. The dances illustrate the Hopi lack of acquisitiveness. The women form a semicircle and dance and sing; after each song two girls fling gifts into the crowd of men assembled outside the circle. Among the gifts are valuable baskets and buckskins, though inexpensive utensils and manufactured items are also popular. Each man zealously grabs for the flying objects, and if two men happen to catch the same item, both wrestle with the object, often until it has been totally destroyed.

Although gift giving has been a pillar of Hopi society, trade has also flourished in Hopi towns since prehistory, with a network that extended from the Great Plains to the Pacific Coast, and from the Great Basin, centered on present-day Nevada and Utah, to the Valley of Mexico. Manufactured goods, raw materials, and gems drove the trade, supplemented by exotic items such as parrots. The Hopis were producers as well, manufacturing large quantities of cotton cloth and ceramics for the trade. To this day, interhousehold trade and barter, especially for items of traditional manufacture for ceremonial use (such as basketry, bows, cloth, moccasins, pottery, and rattles), remain vigorous.

For hundreds of years, at least, the Hopi traded with the Rio Grande Pueblos to acquire turquoise, *heishi* (shell necklaces), and buckskins; one long string of *heishi*, for instance, was worth two Hopi woven cotton mantas. Similarly, songs, dances, and other ritual elements were often exchanged for an agreed-upon equivalent.

The high value the Hopi placed on the items they acquired by trade correlate, in many respects, with the value Europeans placed on them. Silver, for instance, had high value among both Westerners and Native Americans as money and as jewelry. *Siiva*, the Hopi word both for "money" and for "silver jewelry" was borrowed directly from the English word "silver" Paper money itself was often treated the way traditional resources were: older Hopi men bundled it and stored it in trunks, stacked by denomination.

It was not until the 1890s, however, that silver jewelry began to be produced by the Hopi. A man named Sikyatala learned silversmithing from a Zuni man, and his craftsmanship quickly made silver jewelry into treasured adornments. Those among the Hopi who cared for it too much, though, were criticized for vanity; one nickname, Siisiva ("[wearing] a lot of silver"), characterized a fop.

Some jewels, such as turquoise, traditionally had a sacred value, beyond adornment. Even today, flakes of turquoise are occasionally offered to the spirits in religious ceremonies. Turquoise and shell necklaces appear in many ritual settings, frequently adorning the costumes of *katsinas* (ceremonial figures) and performers in the social dances.

How much the Hopi value turquoise becomes apparent toward the close of a ritual enactment known as the Clown Ceremony. The "clowns"—more than mere entertainers—represent unbridled human impulses. Warrior *katsinas* arrive to punish the clowns for licentious behavior and teach them good Hopi behavior: modest and quiet in conduct, careful and decorous in speech, abstemious and sharing about food, and unselfish about other things. The clowns fail miserably (and hilariously) at their lessons. Eventually the warrior chief presents an ultimatum: stop flaunting chaos or die. The clown chief then offers him a turquoise necklace as a "mortgage" on the clowns' lives. The warrior chief accepts, the downs receive a lesser punishment, and community life goes on—not with perfection, but with a human mixture of the virtuous and the flawed.

In Hopi tradition, the first clan among the Hopi, and the one that supplied the *kikmongwi*, or village chief, was Bear. When other clans arrived, their leaders approached the *kikmongwi* to request entry into the village. He asked what they had to contribute, such as a beneficial ceremony. So challenged, each clan performed its ceremony, and if successful, say, in producing rain, its members were invited to live in the village, assigned an area for housing, and granted agricultural lands to work in the valley below. In return, the clan agreed to perform its ceremony, as part of a cycle of ceremonies throughout the year, and to intermarry with the other clans of the community, a practice called exogamous marriage. In that way, the Snake clan brought the Snake Dance, the Badger clan introduced principal katsina ceremonies, and the Fire clan brought the Warriors' society to the Hopi village. The villages thus came to be made up of mutually interdependent clans.

One of the essential principles expressed here, and the very cornerstone of Hopi society and sociality, is the exchange of mutually beneficial gifts—ceremonies for land, people in exogamous marriage—and the relationships reconfigured by those exchanges. And the same model is extended to the supernatural world: the gods must be propitiated with offerings of ritual gifts, and thus reminded of their dependence upon and obligations to mortal people.

The items sent to President Fillmore conform to the archetypal Hopi offering. Seeking to incorporate the president into the Hopi world, the appropriate strategy was to give him valuable presents that sought something in return, and to make sure he understood what that meant. Addressing him with prayersticks the way they might address the Sun father, the delegation sought to engage him within the gifting and kinship idiom. The instructions delivered with the packet—even across a succession of translations—spoke clearly of the Hopi intent. As with the turquoise mortgage of the *katsina* clowns, the idea of reciprocity is central. If the president wants more of, say, rainmagic, he must give back: he must receive the gift and its political proposal, and provide something in return.

Alas, the magico-religious sensibility of the Hopi worldview and the offer of serial reciprocity clashed with Manifest Destiny and the assimilationist ideology of Fillmore's presidency. Historical records make it clear that he did not smoke the cigarette, nor chew nor spit the honey-meal, and, so far as we know, he sent no formal reply. None of the objects has survived.

What the five men of the Tesuque delegation received no doubt perplexed them as much as the packet they delivered perplexed the president: Each man was given a Millard Fillmore peace medal, a Western-style business suit, and a daguerreotype portrait (all now lost, as well). They also got a tour of standard destinations in Washington, including the Patent Office and the Smithsonian Institution, where they were introduced to the "wonders of electricity," according to a contemporary newspaper account in the *Daily National Intelligencer*. In their meeting with Fillmore they heard the president say he "hoped the Great Spirit would bless and sustain them till they again returned to the bosom of their families."

Certainly Fillmore expressed the goodwill of the U.S. toward the Pueblos in general and to the Tesuque party in particular—who, in all probability, conveyed that sentiment to the Hopi. But the dissonance between gift and exchange economies helps explain why the Hopis did not achieve their goals. (The U.S. did not protect the Hopi from intrusions by the Navajo or by anyone else.)

The Hopi sought to embrace the president in their own sphere of sociality and mutuality—to extend kinship to him. But in a social system like the president's, where gifts are not total social facts, the political belongs in a separate domain from the religious or the economic, and kinship is secondary. The gift of a jeweled sword, for instance, might have impressed Fillmore more, but for the Hopi, its strictly symbolic value—as an item for display, but with no political, religious, or social value—would not have ensured a return, a social connection built on mutual exchange. More, by Hopi standards, presenting such a gift might have seemed inhospitable and materialistic, indeed, undiplomatic and even selfish. Thus does understanding fail between nations.

# Too Many Bananas, Not Enough Pineapples, and No Watermelon at All

## Three Object Lessons in Living with Reciprocity

DAVID COUNTS

## No Watermelon at All

The woman came all the way through the village, walking between the two rows of houses facing each other between the beach and the bush, to the very last house standing on a little spit of land at the mouth of the Kaini River. She was carrying a watermelon on her head, and the house she came to was the government "rest house," maintained by the villagers for the occasional use of visiting officials. Though my wife and I were graduate students, not officials, and had asked for permission to stay in the village for the coming year, we were living in the rest house while the debate went on about where a house would be built for us. When the woman offered to sell us the watermelon for two shillings, we happily agreed, and the kids were delighted at the prospect of watermelon after yet another meal of rice and bully beef. The money changed hands and the seller left to return to her village, a couple of miles along the coast to the east.

It seemed only seconds later that the woman was back, reluctantly accompanying Kolia, the man who had already made it clear to us that he was the leader of the village. Kolia had no English, and at that time, three or four days into our first stay in Kandoka Village on the island of New Britain in Papua New Guinea, we had very little Tok Pisin. Language difficulties notwithstanding, Kolia managed to make his message clear: The woman had been outrageously wrong to sell us the watermelon for two shillings and we were to return it to her and reclaim our money immediately. When we tried to explain that we thought the price to be fair and were happy with the bargain, Kolia explained again and finally made it clear that we had missed the point. The problem wasn't that we had paid too much; it was that we had paid at all. Here he was, a leader, responsible for us while we were living in his village, and we had shamed him. How would it look if he let guests in his village *buy* food? If we wanted watermelons, or bananas, or anything else, all that was necessary was to let him know. He told us that it would be all right for us to give little gifts to people who brought food to us (and they surely would), but *no one* was to sell food to us. If anyone were to try—like this woman from Lauvore—then we

should refuse. There would be plenty of watermelons without us buying them.

The woman left with her watermelon, disgruntled, and we were left with our two shillings. But we had learned the first lesson of many about living in Kandoka. We didn't pay money for food again that whole year, and we did get lots of food brought to us... but we never got another watermelon. That one was the last of the season.

> LESSON 1: *In a society where food is shared or gifted as part of social life, you may not buy it with money.*

## Too Many Bananas

In the couple of months that followed the watermelon incident, we managed to become at least marginally competent in Tok Pisin, to negotiate the construction of a house on what we hoped was neutral ground, and to settle into the routine of our fieldwork. As our village leader had predicted, plenty of food was brought to us. Indeed, seldom did a day pass without something coming in—some sweet potatoes, a few taro, a papaya, the occasional pineapple, or some bananas—lots of bananas.

We had learned our lesson about the money, though, so we never even offered to buy the things that were brought, but instead made gifts, usually of tobacco to the adults or chewing gum to the children. Nor were we so gauche as to haggle with a giver over how much of a return gift was appropriate, though the two of us sometimes conferred as to whether what had been brought was a "two-stick" or a "three-stick" stalk, bundle, or whatever. A "stick" of tobacco was a single large leaf, soaked in rum and then twisted into a ropelike form. This, wrapped in half a sheet of newsprint (torn for use as cigarette paper), sold in the local trade stores for a shilling. Nearly all of the adults in the village smoked a great deal, and they seldom had much cash, so our stocks of twist tobacco and stacks of the Sydney *Morning Herald* (all, unfortunately, the same day's issue) were seen as a real boon to those who preferred "stick" to the locally grown product.

We had established a pattern with respect to the gifts of food. When a donor appeared at our veranda we would offer our thanks and talk with them for a few minutes (usually about our children, who seemed to hold a real fascination for the villagers and for whom most of the gifts were intended) and then we would inquire whether they could use some tobacco. It was almost never refused, though occasionally a small bottle of kerosene, a box of matches, some laundry soap, a cup of rice, or a tin of meat would be requested instead of (or even in addition to) the tobacco. Everyone, even Kolia, seemed to think this arrangement had worked out well.

Now, what must be kept in mind is that while we were following their rules—or seemed to be—we were *really still buying food*. In fact we kept a running account of what came in and what we "paid" for it. Tobacco as currency got a little complicated, but since the exchange rate was one stick to one shilling, it was not too much trouble as long as everyone was happy, and meanwhile we could account for the expenditure of "informant fees" and "household expenses." Another thing to keep in mind is that not only did we continue to think in terms of our buying the food that was brought, we thought of them as *selling it*. While it was true they never quoted us a price, they also never asked us if we needed or wanted whatever they had brought. It seemed clear to us that when an adult needed a stick of tobacco, or a child wanted some chewing gum (we had enormous quantities of small packets of Wrigley's for just such eventualities) they would find something surplus to their own needs and bring it along to our "store" and get what they wanted.

By late November 1966, just before the rainy season set in, the bananas were coming into flush, and whereas earlier we had received banana gifts by the "hand" (six or eight bananas in a cluster cut from the stalk), donors now began to bring bananas, "for the children," by the *stalk!* The Kaliai among whom we were living are not exactly specialists in banana cultivation—they only recognize about thirty varieties, while some of their neighbors have more than twice that many—but the kinds they produce differ considerably from each other in size, shape, and taste, so we were not dismayed when we had more than one stalk hanging on our veranda. The stalks ripen a bit at the time, and having some variety was nice. Still, by the time our accumulation had reached *four* complete stalks, the delights of variety had begun to pale a bit. The fruits were ripening progressively and it was clear that even if we and the kids ate nothing but bananas for the next week, some would still fall from the stalk onto the floor in a state of gross overripeness. This was the situation as, late one afternoon, a woman came bringing yet another stalk of bananas up the steps of the house.

Several factors determined our reaction to her approach: one was that there was literally no way we could possibly use the bananas. We hadn't quite reached the point of being crowded off our veranda by the stalks of fruit, but it was close. Another factor was that we were tired of playing the gift game. We had acquiesced in playing it—no one was permitted to sell us anything, and in turn we only gave things away, refusing under any circumstances to sell tobacco (or anything else) for money. But there had to be a limit. From our perspective what was at issue was that the woman wanted something and she had come

to trade for it. Further, what she had brought to trade was something we neither wanted nor could use, and it should have been obvious to her. So we decided to bite the bullet.

The woman, Rogi, climbed the stairs to the veranda, took the stalk from where it was balanced on top of her head, and laid it on the floor with the words, "Here are some bananas for the children." Dorothy and I sat near her on the floor and thanked her for her thought but explained, "You know, we really have too many bananas—we can't use these; maybe you ought to give them to someone else...." The woman looked mystified, then brightened and explained that she didn't want anything for them, she wasn't short of tobacco or anything. They were just a gift for the kids. Then she just sat there, and we sat there, and the bananas sat there, and we tried again. "Look," I said, pointing up to them and counting, "we've got four stalks already hanging here on the veranda—there are too many for us to eat now. Some are rotting already. Even if we eat only bananas, we can't keep up with what's here!"

Rogi's only response was to insist that these were a gift, and that she didn't want anything for them, so we tried yet another tack: "Don't *your* children like bananas?" When she admitted that they did, and that she had none at her house, we suggested that she should take them there. Finally, still puzzled, but convinced we weren't going to keep the bananas, she replaced them on her head, went down the stairs, and made her way back through the village toward her house.

As before, it seemed only moments before Kolia was making his way up the stairs, but this time he hadn't brought the woman in tow. "What was wrong with those bananas? Were they no good?" he demanded. We explained that there was nothing wrong with the bananas at all, but that we simply couldn't use them and it seemed foolish to take them when we had so many and Rogi's own children had none. We obviously didn't make ourselves clear because Kolia then took up the same refrain that Rogi had—he insisted that we shouldn't be worried about taking the bananas, because they were a gift for the children and Rogi hadn't wanted anything for them. There was no reason, he added, to send her away with them—she would be ashamed. I'm afraid we must have seemed as if we were hard of hearing or thought he was, for our only response was to repeat our reasons. We went through it again—there they hung, one, two, three, *four* stalks of bananas, rapidly ripening and already far beyond our capacity to eat—we just weren't ready to accept any more and let them rot (and, we added to ourselves, pay for them with tobacco, to boot).

Kolia finally realized that we were neither hard of hearing nor intentionally offensive, but merely ignorant. He stared at us for a few minutes, thinking, and then asked: "Don't you frequently have visitors during the day and evening?" We nodded. Then he asked, "Don't you usually offer them cigarettes and coffee or milo?" Again, we nodded. "Did it ever occur to you to suppose," he said, "that your visitors might be hungry?" It was at this point in the conversation, as we recall, that we began to see the depth of the pit we had dug for ourselves. We nodded, hesitantly. His last words to us before he went down the stairs and stalked away were just what we were by that time afraid they might be. "When your guests are hungry, *feed them bananas!*"

LESSON 2: *Never refuse a gift, and never fail to return a gift. If you cannot use it, you can always give it away to someone else—there is no such thing as too much—there are never too many bananas.*

# Not Enough Pineapples

During the fifteen years between that first visit in 1966 and our residence there in 1981 we had returned to live in Kandoka village twice during the 1970s, and though there were a great many changes in the village, and indeed for all of Papua New Guinea during that time, we continued to live according to the lessons of reciprocity learned during those first months in the field. We bought no food for money and refused no gifts, but shared our surplus. As our family grew, we continued to be accompanied by our younger children. Our place in the village came to be something like that of educated Kaliai who worked far away in New Guinea. Our friends expected us to come "home" when we had leave, but knew that our work kept us away for long periods of time. They also credited us with knowing much more about the rules of their way of life than was our due. And we sometimes shared the delusion that we understood life in the village, but even fifteen years was not long enough to relieve the need for lessons in learning to live within the rules of gift exchange.

In the last paragraph I used the word *friends* to describe the villagers intentionally, but of course they were not all our friends. Over the years some really had become friends, others were acquaintances, others remained consultants or informants to whom we turned when we needed information. Still others, unfortunately, we did not like at all. We tried never to make an issue of these distinctions, of course, and to be evenhanded and generous to all, as they were to us. Although we almost never actually refused requests that were made of us, over the long term our reciprocity in the village was balanced. More was given to those who helped us the most, while we gave assistance or donations of small items even to those who were not close or helpful.

One elderly woman in particular was a trial for us. Sara was the eldest of a group of siblings and her younger brother and sister were both generous, informative, and delightful persons. Her younger sister, Makila, was a particularly close friend and consultant, and in deference to that friendship we felt awkward in dealing with the elder sister.

Sara was neither a friend nor an informant, but she had been, since she returned to live in the village at the time of our second trip in 1971, a constant (if minor) drain on our resources. She never asked for much at a time. A bar of soap, a box of matches, a bottle of kerosene, a cup of rice, some onions, a stick or two of tobacco, or some other small item was usually all that was at issue, but whenever she came around it was always to ask for something—or to let us know that when we left, we should give her some of the furnishings from the house. Too, unlike almost everyone else in the village, when she came, she was always empty-handed. We ate no taro from her gardens, and the kids chewed none of her sugarcane. In short, she was, as far as we could tell, a really grasping, selfish old woman—and we were not the only victims of her greed.

Having long before learned the lesson of the bananas, one day we had a stalk that was ripening so fast we couldn't keep up with it, so I pulled a few for our own use (we only had one stalk at the time) and walked down through the village to Ben's house, where his five children were playing. I sat down on his steps to talk, telling him that I intended to give the fruit to his kids. They never got them. Sara saw us from across the open plaza of the village and came rushing over, shouting, "My bananas!" Then she grabbed the stalk and went off gorging herself with them. Ben and I just looked at each other.

Finally it got to the point where it seemed to us that we had to do something. Ten years of being used was long enough. So there came the afternoon when Sara showed up to get some tobacco—again. But this time, when we gave her the two sticks she had demanded, we confronted her.

First, we noted the many times she had come to get things. We didn't mind sharing things, we explained. After all, we had plenty of tobacco and soap and rice and such, and most of it was there so that we could help our friends as they helped us, with folktales, information, or even gifts of food. The problem was that she kept coming to get things, but never came to talk, or to tell stories, or to bring some little something that the kids might like. Sara didn't argue—she agreed. "Look," we suggested, "it doesn't have to be much, and we don't mind giving you things—but you can help us. The kids like pineapples, and we don't have any—the next time you need something, bring something—like maybe a pineapple." Obviously somewhat embarrassed, she took her tobacco and left, saying that she would bring something soon. We were really pleased with ourselves. It had been a very difficult thing to do, but it was done, and we were convinced that either she would start bringing things or not come. It was as if a burden had lifted from our shoulders.

It worked. Only a couple of days passed before Sara was back, bringing her bottle to get it filled with kerosene. But this time, she came carrying the biggest, most beautiful pineapple we had seen the entire time we had been there. We had a friendly talk, filled her kerosene container, and hung the pineapple up on the veranda to ripen just a little further. A few days later we cut and ate it, and whether the satisfaction it gave came from the fruit or from its source would be hard to say, but it was delicious. That, we assumed, was the end of that irritant.

We were wrong, of course. The next afternoon, Mary, one of our best friends for years (and no relation to Sara), dropped by for a visit. As we talked, her eyes scanned the veranda. Finally she asked whether we hadn't had a pineapple there yesterday. We said we had, but that we had already eaten it. She commented that it had been a really nice-looking one, and we told her that it had been the best we had eaten in months. Then, after a pause, she asked, "Who brought it to you?" We smiled as we said, "Sara!" because Mary would appreciate our coup—she had commented many times in the past on the fact that Sara only *got* from us and never gave. She was silent for a moment, and then she said, "Well, I'm glad you enjoyed it—my father was waiting until it was fully ripe to harvest it for you, but when it went missing I thought maybe it was the one you had here. I'm glad to see you got it. I thought maybe a thief had eaten it in the bush."

LESSON 3: *Where reciprocity is the rule and gifts are the idiom, you cannot demand a gift, just as you cannot refuse a request.*

It says a great deal about the kindness and patience of the Kaliai people that they have been willing to be our hosts for all these years despite our blunders and lack of good manners. They have taught us a lot, and these three lessons are certainly not the least important things we learned.

From *The Humbled Anthropologist: Tales from the Pacific* by David Counts, 1990, pp. 18–24. Published by Wadsworth Publishing Company. © 1990 by David Counts. Reprinted by permission of the author.

# UNIT 4
# Other Families, Other Ways

## Unit Selections

## Key Points to Consider

- If the incest taboo has to do with biology, then why is it culturally variable?

- Why do you think "fraternal polyandry" is socially acceptable in Tibet but not in our society?

- How have dietary changes affected birth rates and women's health?

- Why do child care practices vary from culture to culture?

- What are the pros and cons of arranged marriages versus freedom of choice?

- Does the stability of Japanese marriages necessarily imply compatibility and contentment?

## Student Website

www.mhcls.com/online

## Internet References

Further information regarding these websites may be found in this book's preface or online.

**Kinship and Social Organization**
*http://www.umanitoba.ca/anthropology/tutor/kinmenu.html*

Since most people in small-scale societies of the past spent their whole lives within a local area, it is understandable that their primary interactions—economic, religious, and otherwise—were with their relatives. It also makes sense that through marriage customs, they strengthened those kinship relationships that clearly defined their mutual rights and obligations. Indeed, the resulting family structure may be surprisingly flexible and adaptive, as witnessed in the essays "When Brothers Share a Wife" by Melvyn Goldstein, and "Arranging a Marriage in India" by Serena Nanda.

For these reasons, anthropologists have looked upon family and kinship as the key mechanisms for transmitting culture from one generation to the next. (See "Our Babies, Ourselves" by Meredith Small.) Social changes may have been slow to take place throughout the world, but as social horizons have widened, family relationships and community alliances are increasingly based upon new principles. Even as birth rates have increased, kinship networks have diminished in size and strength. As people have increasingly become involved with others as coworkers in a market economy, our associations depend more and more upon factors such as personal aptitudes, educa-

tional backgrounds, and job opportunities. Yet the family is still there. Except for some rather unusual exceptions, the family is smaller, but still functions in its age-old nurturing and protective role, even under conditions where there is little affection (see "Who Needs Love! In Japan, Many Couples Don't" by Nicholas Kristof) or under conditions of extreme poverty and a high infant mortality rate (see "Death Without Weeping" by Nancy Scheper-Hughes). Beyond the immediate family, the situation is in a state of flux. Certain ethnic groups, especially those in poverty, still have a need for the broader network and in some ways seem to be reformulating those ties.

We do not know where the changes described in this section will lead us and which ones will ultimately prevail. One thing is certain: anthropologists will be there to document the trends, for the discipline of anthropology has had to change as well. One important feature of the essays in this section is the growing interest of anthropologists in the study of complex societies where old theoretical perspectives are increasingly inadequate.

Current trends, however, do not necessarily mean the eclipse of the kinship unit. The large family network is still the best guarantee of individual survival and well-being in an urban setting.

# When Brothers Share a Wife

## Among Tibetans, the good life relegates many women to spinsterhood

MELVYN C. GOLDSTEIN

Eager to reach home, Dorje drives his yaks hard over the 17,000-foot mountain pass, stopping only once to rest. He and his two older brothers, Pema and Sonam, are jointly marrying a woman from the next village in a few weeks, and he has to help with the preparations.

Dorje, Pema, and Sonam are Tibetans living in Limi, a 200-square-mile area in the northwest corner of Nepal, across the border from Tibet. The form of marriage they are about to enter—fraternal polyandry in anthropological parlance—is one of the world's rarest forms of marriage but is not uncommon in Tibetan society, where it has been practiced from time immemorial. For many Tibetan social strata, it traditionally represented the ideal form of marriage and family.

The mechanics of fraternal polyandry are simple. Two, three, four, or more brothers jointly take a wife, who leaves her home to come and live with them. Traditionally, marriage was arranged by parents, with children, particularly females, having little or no say. This is changing somewhat nowadays, but it is still unusual for children to marry without their parents' consent. Marriage ceremonies vary by income and region and range from all the brothers sitting together as grooms to only the eldest one formally doing so. The age of the brothers plays an important role in determining this: very young brothers almost never participate in actual marriage ceremonies, although they typically join the marriage when they reach their midteens.

The eldest brother is normally dominant in terms of authority, that is, in managing the household, but all the brothers share the work and participate as sexual partners. Tibetan males and females do not find the sexual aspect of sharing a spouse the least bit unusual, repulsive, or scandalous, and the norm is for the wife to treat all the brothers the same.

Offspring are treated similarly. There is no attempt to link children biologically to particular brothers, and a brother shows no favoritism toward his child even if he knows he is the real father because, for example, his other brothers were away at the time the wife became pregnant. The children, in turn, consider all of the brothers as their fathers and treat them equally, even if they also know who is their real father. In some regions children use the term "father" for the eldest brother and "father's brother" for the others, while in other areas they call all the brothers by one term, modifying this by the use of "elder" and "younger."

Unlike our own society, where monogamy is the only form of marriage permitted, Tibetan society allows a variety of marriage types, including monogamy, fraternal polyandry, and polygyny. Fraternal polyandry and monogamy are the most common forms of marriage, while polygyny typically occurs in cases where the first wife is barren. The widespread practice of fraternal polyandry, therefore, is not the outcome of a law requiring brothers to marry jointly. There is choice, and in fact, divorce traditionally was relatively simple in Tibetan society. If a brother in a polyandrous marriage became dissatisfied and wanted to separate, he simply left the main house and set up his own household. In such cases, all the children stayed in the main household with the remaining brother(s), even if the departing brother was known to be the real father of one or more of the children.

The Tibetans' own explanation for choosing fraternal polyandry is materialistic. For example, when I asked Dorje why he decided to marry with his two brothers rather than take his own wife, he thought for a moment, then said it prevented the division of his family's farm (and animals) and thus facilitated all of them achieving a higher standard of living. And when I later asked Dorje's bride whether it wasn't difficult for her to cope with three brothers as husbands, she laughed and echoed the rationale of avoiding fragmentation of the family and land, adding that she expected to be better off economically, since she would have three husbands working for her and her children.

Exotic as it may seem to Westerners, Tibetan fraternal polyandry is thus in many ways analogous to the way primogeniture functioned in nineteenth-century England. Primogeniture dictated that the eldest son inherited the family estate, while younger sons had to leave home and seek their own employment—for example, in the military or the clergy. Primogeniture maintained family estates intact over generations by permitting only one heir per generation. Fraternal polyandry also accomplishes this but does so by keeping all the brothers together with just one wife so that there is only one *set* of heirs per generation.

While Tibetans believe that in this way fraternal polyandry reduces the risk of family fission, monogamous marriages among brothers need not necessarily precipitate the division of the family estate: brothers could continue to live together, and the family land could continue to be worked jointly. When I asked Tibetans about this, however, they invariably responded that such joint families are unstable because each wife is primarily oriented to her own children and interested in their success and well-being over that of the children of the other wives. For example, if the youngest brother's wife had three sons while the eldest brother's wife had only one daughter, the wife of the youngest brother might begin to demand more resources for her children since, as males, they represent the future of the family. Thus, the children from different wives in the same generation are competing sets of heirs, and this makes such families inherently unstable. Tibetans perceive that conflict will spread from the wives to their husbands and consider this likely to cause family fission. Consequently, it is almost never done.

Although Tibetans see an economic advantage to fraternal polyandry, they do not value the sharing of a wife as an end in itself. On the contrary, they articulate a number of problems inherent in the practice. For example, because authority is customarily exercised by the eldest brother, his younger male siblings have to subordinate themselves with little hope of changing their status within the family. When these younger brothers are aggressive and individualistic, tensions and difficulties often occur despite there being only one set of heirs.

In addition, tension and conflict may arise in polyandrous families because of sexual favoritism. The bride normally sleeps with the eldest brother, and the two have the responsibility to see to it that the other males have opportunities for sexual access. Since the Tibetan subsistence economy requires males to travel a lot, the temporary absence of one or more brothers facilitates this, but there are also other rotation practices. The cultural ideal unambiguously calls for the wife to show equal affection and sexuality to each of the brothers (and vice versa), but deviations from this ideal occur, especially when there is a sizable difference in age between the partners in the marriage.

Dorje's family represents just such a potential situation. He is fifteen years old and his two older brothers are twenty-five and twenty-two years old. The new bride is twenty-three years old, eight years Dorje's senior. Sometimes such a bride finds the youngest husband immature and adolescent and does not treat him with equal affection; alternatively, she may find his youth attractive and lavish special attention on him. Apart from that consideration, when a younger male like Dorje grows up, he may consider his wife "ancient" and prefer the company of a woman his own age or younger. Consequently, although men and women do not find the idea of sharing a bride or bridegroom repulsive, individual likes and dislikes can cause familial discord.

Two reasons have commonly been offered for the perpetuation of fraternal polyandry in Tibet: that Tibetans practice female infanticide and therefore have to marry polyandrously, owing to a shortage of females; and that Tibet, lying at extremely high altitudes, is so barren and bleak that Tibetans would starve without resort to this mechanism. A Jesuit who lived in Tibet during the eighteenth century articulated this second view: "One reason for this most odious custom is the sterility of the soil, and the small amount of land that can be cultivated owing to the lack of water. The crops may suffice if the brothers all live together, but if they form separate families they would be reduced to beggary."

Both explanations are wrong, however. Not only has there never been institutionalized female infanticide in Tibet, but Tibetan society gives females considerable rights, including inheriting the family estate in the absence of brothers. In such cases, the woman takes a bridegroom who comes to live in her family and adopts her family's name and identity. Moreover, there is no demographic evidence of a shortage of females. In Limi, for example, there were (in 1974) sixty females and fifty-three males in the fifteen- to thirty-five-year age category, and many adult females were unmarried.

The second reason is also incorrect. The climate in Tibet is extremely harsh, and ecological factors do play a major role perpetuating polyandry, but polyandry is not a means of preventing starvation. It is characteristic, not of the poorest segments of the society, but rather of the peasant landowning families.

In the old society, the landless poor could not realistically aspire to prosperity, but they did not fear starvation. There was a persistent labor shortage throughout Tibet, and very poor families with little or no land and few animals could subsist through agricultural labor, tenant farming, craft occupations such as carpentry, or by working as servants. Although the per person family income could increase somewhat if brothers married polyandrously and pooled their wages, in the absence of inheritable land, the advantage of fraternal polyandry was not generally sufficient to prevent them from setting up their own households. A more skilled or energetic younger brother could do as well or better alone, since he would completely control his income and would not have to share it with his siblings. Consequently, while there was and is some polyandry among the poor, it is much less frequent and more prone to result in divorce and family fission.

An alternative reason for the persistence of fraternal polyandry is that it reduces population growth (and thereby reduces the pressure on resources) by relegating some females to lifetime spinsterhood. Fraternal polyandrous marriages in Limi (in 1974) averaged 2.35 men per woman, and not surprisingly, 31 percent of the females of child-bearing age (twenty to forty-nine) were unmarried. These spinsters either continued to live at home, set up their own households, or worked as servants for other families. They could also become Buddhist nuns. Being unmarried is not synonymous with exclusion from the reproductive pool. Discreet extramarital relationships are tolerated, and actually half of the adult unmarried women in Limi had one or more children. They raised these children as single mothers, working for wages or weaving cloth and blankets for sale. As a group, however, the unmarried woman had far fewer offspring than the married women, averaging only 0.7 children per woman, compared with 3.3 for married women, whether polyandrous, monogamous, or polygynous. While polyandry helps regulate population, this function of polyandry is not consciously perceived by Tibetans and is not the reason they consistently choose it.

If neither a shortage of females nor the fear of starvation perpetuates fraternal polyandry, what motivates brothers, particularly younger brothers, to opt for this system of marriage? From the perspective of the younger brother in a landholding family, the main incentive is the attainment or maintenance of the good life. With polyandry, he can expect a more secure and higher standard of living, with access not only to this family's land and animals but also to its inherited collection of clothes, jewelry, rugs, saddles, and horses. In addition, he will experience less work pressure and much greater security because all responsibility does not fall on one "father." For Tibetan brothers, the question is whether to trade off the greater personal freedom inherent in monogamy for the real or potential economic security, affluence, and social prestige associated with life in a larger, labor-rich polyandrous family.

A brother thinking of separating from his polyandrous marriage and taking his own wife would face various disadvantages. Although in the majority of Tibetan regions all brothers theoretically have rights to their family's estate, in reality Tibetans are reluctant to divide their land into small fragments. Generally, a younger brother who insists on leaving the family will receive only a small plot of land, if that. Because of its power and wealth, the rest of the family usually can block any attempt of the younger brother to increase his share of land through litigation. Moreover, a younger brother may not even get a house and cannot expect to receive much above the minimum in terms of movable possessions, such as furniture, pots, and pans. Thus, a brother contemplating going it on his own must plan on achieving economic security and the good life not through inheritance but through his own work.

The obvious solution for younger brothers—creating new fields from virgin land—is generally not a feasible option. Most Tibetan populations live at high altitudes (above 12,000 feet), where arable land is extremely scarce. For example, in Dorje's village, agriculture ranges only from about 12,900 feet, the lowest point in the area, to 13,300 feet. Above that altitude, early frost and snow destroy the staple barley crop. Furthermore, because of the low rainfall caused by the Himalayan rain shadow, many areas in Tibet and northern Nepal that are within the appropriate altitude range for agriculture have no reliable sources of irrigation. In the end, although there is plenty of unused land in such areas, most of it is either too high or too arid.

Even where unused land capable of being farmed exists, clearing the land and building the substantial terraces necessary for irrigation constitute a great undertaking. Each plot has to be completely dug out to a depth of two to two and half feet so that the large rocks and boulders can be removed. At best, a man might be able to bring a few new fields under cultivation in the first years after separating from his brothers, but he could not expect to acquire substantial amounts of arable land this way.

In addition, because of the limited farmland, the Tibetan subsistence economy characteristically includes a strong emphasis on animal husbandry. Tibetan farmers regularly maintain cattle, yaks, goats, and sheep, grazing them in the areas too high for agriculture. These herds produce wool, milk, cheese, butter, meat, and skins. To obtain these resources, however, shepherds must accompany the animals on a daily basis. When first setting up a monogamous household, a younger brother like Dorje would find it difficult to both farm and manage animals.

In traditional Tibetan society, there was an even more critical factor that operated to perpetuate fraternal polyandry—a form of hereditary servitude somewhat analogous to serfdom in Europe. Peasants were tied to large estates held by aristocrats, monasteries, and the Lhasa government. They were allowed the use of some farmland to produce their own subsistence but were required to provide taxes in kind and corvée (free labor) to their lords. The corvée was a substantial hardship, since a peasant household was in many cases required to furnish the lord with one laborer daily for most of the year and more on specific occasions such as the harvest. This enforced labor, along with the lack of new land and ecological pressure to pursue both agriculture and animal husbandry, made polyandrous families particularly beneficial. The polyandrous family allowed an internal division of adult labor, maximizing economic advantage. For example, while the wife worked the family fields, one brother could perform the lord's corvée, another could look after the animals, and a third could engage in trade.

Although social scientists often discount other people's explanations of why they do things, in the case of Tibetan fraternal polyandry, such explanations are very close to the truth. The custom, however, is very sensitive to changes in its political and economic milieu and, not surprisingly, is in decline in most Tibetan areas. Made less important by the elimination of the traditional serf-based economy, it is disparaged by the dominant non-Tibetan leaders of India, China, and Nepal. New opportunities for economic and social mobility in these countries, such as the tourist trade and government employment, are also eroding the rationale for polyandry, and so it may vanish within the next generation.

---

**MELVYN C. GOLDSTEIN,** now a professor of anthropology at Case Western Reserve University in Cleveland, has been interested in the Tibetan practice of fraternal polyandry (several brothers marrying one wife) since he was a graduate student in the 1960s.

Reprinted with permission from *Natural History,* March 1987, pp. 39–48. © 1987 by Natural History Magazine.

# Death Without Weeping

## Has poverty ravaged mother love in the shantytowns of Brazil?

NANCY SCHEPER-HUGHES

*I have seen death without weeping,*
*The destiny of the Northeast is death,*
*Cattle they kill,*
*To the people they do*
*something worse*
*—Anonymous Brazilian singer (1965)*

"WHY DO THE CHURCH BELLS RING SO often?" I asked Nailza de Arruda soon after I moved into a corner of her tiny mud-walled hut near the top of the shantytown called the Alto do Cruzeiro (Crucifix Hill). I was then a Peace Corps volunteer and community development/health worker. It was the dry and blazing hot summer of 1965, the months following the military coup in Brazil, and save for the rusty, clanging bells of N. S. das Dores Church, an eerie quiet had settled over the market town that I call Bom Jesus da Mata. Beneath the quiet, however, there was chaos and panic. "It's nothing," replied Nailza, "just another little angel gone to heaven."

Nailza had sent more than her share of little angels to heaven, and sometimes at night I could hear her engaged in a muffled but passionate discourse with one of them, two-year-old Joana. Joana's photograph, taken as she lay propped up in her tiny cardboard coffin, her eyes open, hung on a wall next to one of Nailza and Ze Antonio taken on the day they eloped.

Nailza could barely remember the other infants and babies who came and went in close succession. Most had died unnamed and were hastily baptized in their coffins. Few lived more than a month or two. Only Joana, properly baptized in church at the close of her first year and placed under the protection of a powerful saint, Joan of Arc, had been expected to live. And Nailza had dangerously allowed herself to love the little girl.

In addressing the dead child, Nailza's voice would range from tearful imploring to angry recrimination: "Why did you leave me? Was your patron saint so greedy that she could not allow me one child on this earth?" Ze Antonio advised me to ignore Nailza's odd behavior, which he understood as a kind of madness that, like the birth and death of children, came and went. Indeed, the premature birth of a stillborn son some months later "cured" Nailza of her "inappropriate" grief, and the day came when she removed Joana's photo and carefully packed it away.

More than fifteen years elapsed before I returned to the Alto do Cruzeiro, and it was anthropology that provided the vehicle of my return. Since 1982 I have returned several times in order to pursue a problem that first attracted my attention in the 1960s. My involvement with the people of the Alto do Cruzeiro now spans a quarter of a century and three generations of parenting in a community where mothers and daughters are often simultaneously pregnant.

The Alto do Cruzeiro is one of three shantytowns surrounding the large market town of Bom Jesus in the sugar plantation zone of Pernambuco in Northeast Brazil, one of the many zones of neglect that have emerged in the shadow of the now tarnished economic miracle of Brazil. For the women and children of the Alto do Cruzeiro the only miracle is that some of them have managed to stay alive at all.

The Northeast is a region of vast proportions (approximately twice the size of Texas) and of equally vast social and developmental problems. The nine states that make up the region are the poorest in the country and are representative of the Third World within a dynamic and rapidly industrializing nation. Despite waves of migrations from the interior to the teeming shantytowns of coastal cities, the majority still live in rural areas on farms and ranches, sugar plantations and mills.

Life expectancy in the Northeast is only forty years, largely because of the appallingly high rate of infant and child mortality. Approximately one million children in Brazil under the age of five die each year. The children of the Northeast, especially those born in shantytowns on the periphery of urban life, are at a very high risk of death. In these areas, children are born without the traditional protection of breast-feeding, subsistence gardens, stable marriages, and multiple adult caretakers that exists in the interior. In the hillside shantytowns that spring up around cities or, in this case, interior market towns, marriages are brittle, single parenting is the norm, and women are frequently forced into the shadow economy of domestic work in the homes of the rich or into unprotected and oftentimes "scab" wage labor on the surrounding sugar plantations, where they clear land for planting and weed for a pittance, sometimes less than a dollar a day. The women of the Alto may not bring their babies with them into the homes of the wealthy, where the often-sick infants are considered sources of contamination, and they cannot carry the little ones to the riverbanks where they wash clothes because the river is heavily infested with schistosomes and other deadly parasites. Nor can they carry their young children to the plantations, which are often several miles away. At wages of a dollar a day, the women of the Alto cannot hire baby sitters. Older children who are not in school will sometimes serve as somewhat indifferent caretakers. But any child not in school is also expected to find wage work. In most cases, babies are simply left at home alone, the door securely fastened. And so many also die alone and unattended.

Bom Jesus da Mata, centrally located in the plantation zone of Pernambuco, is within commuting distance of several sugar plantations and mills. Consequently, Bom Jesus has been a magnet for rural workers forced off their small subsistence plots by large landowners wanting to use every available piece of land for sugar cultivation. Initially, the rural migrants to Bom Jesus were squatters who were given tacit approval by the mayor to put up temporary straw huts on each of the three hills overlooking the town. The Alto do Cruzeiro is the oldest, the largest, and the poorest of the shantytowns. Over the past three decades many of the original migrants have become permanent residents, and the primitive and temporary straw huts have been replaced by small homes (usually of two rooms) made of wattle and daub, sometimes covered with plaster. The more affluent residents use bricks and tiles. In most Alto homes, dangerous kerosene lamps have been replaced by light bulbs. The once tattered rural garb, often fashioned from used sugar sacking, has likewise been replaced by store-brought clothes, often castoffs from a wealthy *patrão* (boss). The trappings are modern, but the hunger, sickness, and death that they conceal are traditional, deeply rooted in a history of feudalism, exploitation, and institutionalized dependency.

My research agenda never wavered. The questions I addressed first crystalized during a veritable "die-off" of Alto babies during a severe drought in 1965. The food and water shortages and the political and economic chaos occasioned by the military coup were reflected in the handwritten entries of births and deaths in the dusty, yellowed pages of the ledger books kept at the public registry office in Bom Jesus. More than 350 babies died in the Alto during 1965 alone—this from a shantytown population of little more than 5,000. But that wasn't what surprised me. There were reasons enough for the deaths in the miserable conditions of shantytown life. What puzzled me was the seeming indifference of Alto women to the death of their infants, and their willingness to attribute to their own tiny offspring an aversion to life that made their death seem wholly natural, indeed all but anticipated.

Although I found that it was possible, and hardly difficult, to rescue infants and toddlers from death by diarrhea and dehydration with a simple sugar, salt, and water solution (even bottled Coca-Cola worked fine), it was more difficult to enlist a mother herself in the rescue of a child she perceived as ill-fated for life or better off dead, or to convince her to take back into her threatened and besieged home a baby she had already come to think of as an angel rather than as a son or daughter.

I learned that the high expectancy of death, and the ability to face child death with stoicism and equanimity, produced patterns of nurturing that differentiated between those infants thought of as thrivers and survivors and those thought of as born already "wanting to die." The survivors were nurtured, while stigmatized, doomed infants were left to die, as mothers say, *a mingua*, "of neglect." Mothers stepped back and allowed nature to take its course. This pattern, which I call mortal selective neglect, is called passive infanticide by anthropologist Marvin Harris. The Alto situation, although culturally specific in the form that it takes, is not unique to Third World shantytown communities and may have its correlates in our own impoverished urban communities in some cases of "failure to thrive" infants.

I use as an example the story of Zezinho, the thirteen-month-old toddler of one of my neighbors, Lourdes. I became involved with Zezinho when I was called in to help Lourdes in the delivery of another child, this one a fair and robust little tyke with a lusty cry. I noted that while Lourdes showed great interest in the newborn, she totally ignored Zezinho who, wasted and severely malnourished, was curled up in a fetal position on a piece of urine- and feces-soaked cardboard placed under his mother's hammock. Eyes open and vacant, mouth slack, the little boy seemed doomed.

When I carried Zezinho up to the community day-care center at the top of the hill, the Alto women who took turns caring for one another's children (in order to free themselves for part-time work in the cane fields or washing clothes) laughed at my efforts to save Ze, agreeing with Lourdes that here was a baby without a ghost of a chance. Leave him alone, they cautioned. It makes no sense to fight with death. But I did do battle with Ze, and after several weeks of force-feeding (malnourished babies lose their interest in food), Ze began to succumb to my ministrations. He acquired some flesh across his taut chest bones, learned to sit up, and even tried to smile. When he seemed well enough, I returned him to Lourdes in her miserable scrap-material lean-to, but not without guilt about what I had done. I wondered whether returning Ze was at all fair to Lourdes and to his little brother. But I was busy and washed my hands of the matter. And Lourdes did seem more interested in Ze now that he was looking more human.

When I returned in 1982, there was Lourdes among the women who formed my sample of Alto mothers—still struggling to put together some semblance of life for a now grown Ze and her five other surviving children. Much was made of my reunion with Ze in 1982, and everyone enjoyed retelling the story of Ze's rescue and of how his mother had given him up for dead. Ze would laugh the loudest when told how I had had to force-feed him like a fiesta turkey. There was no hint of guilt on the part of Lourdes and no resentment on the part of Ze. In fact, when questioned in private as to who was the best friend he ever had in life, Ze took a long drag on his cigarette and answered without a trace of irony, "Why my mother, of course." "But of course," I replied.

Part of learning how to mother in the Alto do Cruzeiro is learning when to let go of a child who shows that it "wants" to die or that it has no "knack" or no "taste" for life. Another part is learning when it is safe to let oneself love a child. Frequent child death remains a powerful shaper of maternal thinking and practice. In the absence of firm expectation that a child will survive, mother love as we conceptualize it (whether in popular terms or in the psychobiological notion of maternal bonding) is attenuated and delayed with consequences for infant survival. In an environment already precarious to young life, the emotional detachment of mothers toward some of their babies contributes even further to the spiral of high mortality—high fertility in a kind of macabre lock-step dance of death.

The average woman of the Alto experiences 9.5 pregnancies, 3.5 child deaths, and 1.5 stillbirths. Seventy percent of all child deaths in the Alto occur in the first six months of life, and 82 percent by the end of the first year. Of all deaths in the community each year, about 45 percent are of children under the age of five.

Women of the Alto distinguish between child deaths understood as natural (caused by diarrhea and communicable diseases) and those resulting from sorcery, the evil eye, or other magical or supernatural afflictions. They also recognize a large category of infant deaths seen as fated and inevitable. These hopeless cases are classified by mothers under the folk terminology "child sickness" or "child attack." Women say that there are at least fourteen different types of hopeless child sickness, but most can be subsumed under two categories—chronic and acute. The chronic cases refer to infants who are born small and wasted. They are deathly pale, mothers say, as well as weak and passive. They demonstrate no vital force, no liveliness. They do not suck vigorously; they hardly cry. Such babies can be this way at birth or they can be born sound but soon show no resistance, no "fight" against the common crises of infancy: diarrhea, respiratory infections, tropical fevers.

The acute cases are those doomed infants who die suddenly and violently. They are taken by stealth overnight, often following convulsions that bring on head banging, shaking, grimacing, and shrieking. Women say it is horrible to look at such a baby. If the infant begins to foam at the mouth or gnash its teeth or go rigid with its eyes turned back inside its head, there is absolutely no hope. The infant is "put aside"—left alone—often on the floor in a back room, and allowed to die. These symptoms (which accompany high fevers, dehydration, third-stage malnutrition, and encephalitis) are equated by Alto women with madness, epilepsy, and worst of all, rabies, which is greatly feared and highly stigmatized.

Most of the infants presented to me as suffering from chronic child sickness were tiny, wasted famine victims, while those labeled as victims of acute child attack seemed to be infants suffering from the deliriums of high fever or the convulsions that can accompany electrolyte imbalance in dehydrated babies.

Local midwives and traditional healers, praying women, as they are called, advise Alto women on when to allow a baby to die. One midwife explained: "If I can see that a baby was born unfortuitously, I tell the mother that she need not wash the infant or give it a cleansing tea. I tell her just to dust the infant with baby powder and wait for it to die." Allowing nature to take its course is not seen as sinful by these often very devout Catholic women. Rather, it is understood as cooperating with God's plan.

Often I have been asked how consciously women of the Alto behave in this regard. I would have to say that consciousness is always shifting between allowed and disallowed levels of awareness. For example, I was awakened early one morning in 1987 by two neighborhood children who had been sent to fetch me to a hastily organized wake for a two-month-old infant whose mother I had unsuccessfully urged to breast-feed. The infant was being sustained on sugar water, which the mother referred to as *soro* (serum), using a medical term for the infant's starvation regime in light of his chronic diarrhea. I had cautioned the mother that an infant could not live on *soro* forever.

The two girls urged me to console the young mother by telling her that it was "too bad" that her infant was so weak that Jesus had to take him. They were coaching me in proper Alto etiquette. I agreed, of course, but asked, "And what do *you* think?" Xoxa, the eleven-year-old, looked down at her dusty flip-flops and blurted out, "Oh, Dona Nanci, that baby never got enough to eat, but you must never say that!" And so the death of hungry babies remains one of the best kept secrets of life in Bom Jesus da Mata.

Most victims are waked quickly and with a minimum of ceremony. No tears are shed, and the neighborhood children form a tiny procession, carrying the baby to the town graveyard where it will join a multitude of others. Although a few fresh flowers may be scattered over the tiny grave, no stone or wooden cross will mark the place, and the same spot will be reused within a few months' time. The mother will never visit the grave, which soon becomes an anonymous one.

What, then, can be said of these women? What emotions, what sentiments motivate them? How are they able to do what, in fact, must be done? What does mother love mean in this inhospitable context? Are grief, mourning, and melancholia present, although deeply repressed? If so, where shall we look for them? And if not, how are we to understand the moral visions and moral sensibilities that guide their actions?

I have been criticized more than once for presenting an unflattering portrait of poor Brazilian women, women who are, after all, themselves the victims of severe social and institutional neglect. I have described these women as allowing some of their children to die, as if this were an unnatural and inhuman act rather than, as I would assert, the way any one of us might act, reasonably and rationally, under similarly desperate conditions. Perhaps I have not emphasized enough the real pathogens in this environment of high risk: poverty, deprivation, sexism, chronic hunger, and economic exploitation. If mother love is, as many psychologists and some feminists believe, a seemingly natural and universal maternal script, what does it mean to women for whom scarcity, loss, sickness, and deprivation have made that love frantic and robbed them of their grief, seeming to turn their hearts to stone?

Throughout much of human history—as in a great deal of the impoverished Third World today—women have had to give birth and to nurture children under ecological conditions and social arrangements hostile to child survival, as well as to their own well-being. Under circumstances of high childhood mortality, patterns of selective neglect and passive infanticide may be seen as active survival strategies.

They also seem to be fairly common practices historically and across cultures. In societies characterized by high childhood mortality and by a correspondingly high (replacement) fertility, cultural practices of infant and child care tend to be organized primarily around survival goals. But what this means is a pragmatic recognition that not all of one's children can be expected to live. The nervousness about child survival in areas of northeast Brazil, northern India, or Bangladesh, where a 30 percent or 40 percent mortality rate in the first years of life is common, can lead to forms of delayed attachment and a casual or benign neglect that serves to weed out the worst bets so as to enhance the life chances of healthier siblings, including those yet to be born. Practices similar to those that I am describing have been recorded for parts of Africa, India, and Central America.

Life in the Alto do Cruzeiro resembles nothing so much as a battlefield or an emergency room in an overcrowded inner-city public hospital. Consequently, mortality is guided by a kind of "life-boat ethics," the morality of triage. The seemingly studied indifference toward the suffering of some of their infants, conveyed in such sayings as "little critters have no feelings," is understandable in light of these women's obligation to carry on with their reproductive and nurturing lives.

In their slowness to anthropomorphize and personalize their infants, everything is mobilized so as to prevent maternal over-attachment and, therefore, grief at death. The bereaved mother is told not to cry, that her tears will dampen the wings of her little angel so that she cannot fly up to her heavenly home. Grief at the death of an angel is not only inappropriate, it is a symptom of madness and of a profound lack of faith.

Infant death becomes routine in an environment in which death is anticipated and bets are hedged. While the routinization of death in the context of shantytown life is not hard to understand, and quite possible to empathize with, its routinization in the formal institutions of public life in Bom Jesus is not as easy to accept uncritically. Here the social production of indifference takes on a different, even a malevolent, cast.

In a society where triplicates of every form are required for the most banal events (registering a car, for example), the registration of infant and child death is informal, incomplete, and rapid. It requires no documentation, takes less than five minutes, and demands no witnesses other than office clerks. No questions are asked concerning the circumstances of the death, and the cause of death is left blank, unquestioned and unexamined. A neighbor, grandmother, older sibling, or common-law husband may register the death. Since most infants die at home, there is no question of a medical record.

From the registry office, the parent proceeds to the town hall, where the mayor will give him or her a voucher for a free baby coffin. The full-time municipal coffinmaker cannot tell you exactly how many baby coffins are dispatched each week. It varies, he says, with the seasons. There are more needed during the drought months and during the big festivals of Carnaval and Christmas and São Joao's Day because people are too busy, he supposes, to take their babies to the clinic. Record keeping is sloppy.

Similarly, there is a failure on the part of city-employed doctors working at two free clinics to recognize the malnutrition of babies who are weighed, measured, and immunized without comment and as if they were not, in fact, anemic, stunted, fussy, and irritated starvation babies. At best the mothers are told to pick up free vitamins or a health "tonic" at the municipal chambers. At worst, clinic personnel will give tranquilizers and sleeping pills to quiet the hungry cries of "sick-to-death" Alto babies.

The church, too, contributes to the routinization of, and indifference toward, child death. Traditionally, the local Catholic church taught patience and resignation to domestic tragedies that were said to reveal the imponderable workings of God's will. If an infant died suddenly, it was because a particular saint had claimed the child. The infant would be an angel in the service of his or her heavenly patron. It would be wrong, a sign of a lack of faith, to weep for a child with such good fortune. The infant funeral was, in the past, an event celebrated with joy. Today, however, under the new regime of "liberation theology," the bells of N. S. das Dores parish church no longer peal for the death of Alto babies, and no priest accompanies the procession of angels to the cemetery where their bodies are disposed of casually and without ceremony. Children bury children in Bom Jesus da Mata. In this most Catholic of communities, the coffin is handed to the disabled and irritable municipal gravedigger, who often chides the children for one reason or another. It may be that the coffin is larger than expected and the gravedigger can find no appropriate space. The children do not wait for the gravedigger to complete his task. No prayers are recited and no sign of the cross made as the tiny coffin goes into its shallow grave.

When I asked the local priest, Padre Marcos, about the lack of church ceremony surrounding infant and childhood death today in Bom Jesus, he replied; "In the old days, child death was richly celebrated. But those were the baroque customs of a conservative church that wallowed in death and misery. The new church is a church of hope and joy. We no longer celebrate the death of child angels. We try to tell mothers that Jesus doesn't want all the dead babies they send him." Similarly, the new church has changed its baptismal customs, now often refusing to baptize dying babies brought to the back door of a church or rectory. The mothers are scolded by the church attendants and told to go home and take care of their sick babies. Baptism, they are told, is for the living; it is not to be confused with the sacrament of extreme unction, which is the anointing of the dying. And so it appears to the women of the Alto that even the church has turned away from them, denying the traditional comfort of folk Catholicism.

The contemporary Catholic church is caught in the clutches of a double bind. The new theology of liberation imagines a kingdom of God on earth based on justice and equality, a world without hunger, sickness, or childhood mortality. At the same time, the church has not changed its official position on sexuality and reproduction, including its sanctions against birth control, abortion, and sterilization. The padre of Bom Jesus da Mata recognizes this contradiction intuitively, although he shies away from discussions on the topic, saying that he prefers to leave questions of family planning to the discretion and the "good consciences" of his impoverished parishioners. But this, of course, sidesteps the extent to which those good consciences have been shaped by traditional church teachings in Bom Jesus, especially by his recent predecessors. Hence, we can begin to see that the seeming indifference of Alto mothers toward the death of some of their infants is but a pale reflection of the official indifference of church and state to the plight of poor women and children.

Nonetheless, the women of Bom Jesus are survivors. One woman, Biu, told me her life history, returning again and again to the themes of child death, her first husband's suicide, abandonment by her father and later by her second husband, and all the other losses and disappointments she had suffered in her long forty-five years. She concluded with great force, reflecting on the days of Carnaval '88 that were fast approaching:

> No, Dona Nanci, I won't cry, and I won't waste my life thinking about it from morning to night.... Can I argue with God for the state that I'm in? No! And so I'll dance and I'll jump and I'll play Carnaval! And yes, I'll laugh and people will wonder at a *pobre* like me who can have such a good time.

And no one did blame Biu for dancing in the streets during the four days of Carnaval—not even on Ash Wednesday, the day following Carnaval '88 when we all assembled hurriedly to assist in the burial of Mercea, Biu's beloved *casula*, her last-born daughter who had died at home of pneumonia during the festivities. The rest of the family barely had time to change out of their costumes. Severino, the child's uncle and godfather, sprinkled holy water over the little angel while he prayed: "Mercea, I don't know whether you were called, taken, or thrown out of this world. But look down at us from your heavenly home with tenderness, with pity, and with mercy." So be it.

---

**NANCY SCHEPER-HUGHES** is a professor in the Department of Anthropology at the University of California, Berkeley. She has written *Death Without Weeping: Violence of Everyday Life in Brazil* (1992).

# Our Babies, Ourselves

MEREDITH F. SMALL

During one of his many trips to Gusiiland in southwestern Kenya, anthropologist Robert LeVine tried an experiment: he showed a group of Gusii mothers a videotape of middle-class American women tending their babies. The Gusii mothers were appalled. Why does that mother ignore the cries of her unhappy baby during a simple diaper change? And how come that grandmother does nothing to soothe the screaming baby in her lap? These American women, the Gusii concluded, are clearly incompetent mothers. In response, the same charge might be leveled at the Gusii by American mothers. What mother hands over her tiny infant to a six-year-old sister and expects the older child to provide adequate care? And why don't those Gusii women spend more time talking to their babies, so that they will grow up smart?

Both culture—the traditional way of doing things in a particular society—and individual experience guide parents in their tasks. When a father chooses to pick up his newborn and not let it cry, when a mother decides to bottle-feed on a schedule rather than breast-feed on demand, when a couple bring the newborn into their bed at night, they are prompted by what they believe to be the best methods of caregiving.

For decades, anthropologists have been recording how children are raised in different societies. At first, the major goals were to describe parental roles and understand how child-rearing practices and rituals helped to generate adult personality. In the 1950s, for example, John and Beatrice Whiting, and their colleagues at Harvard, Yale, and Cornell Universities, launched a major comparative study of childhood, looking at six varied communities in different regions: Okinawa, the Philippines, northern India, Kenya, Mexico, and New England. They showed that communal expectations play a major role in setting parenting styles, which in turn play a part in shaping children to become accepted adults.

More recent work by anthropologists and child-development researchers has shown that parents readily accept their society's prevailing ideology on how babies should be treated,

---

## Gusii Survival Skills

## By Robert A. LeVine

Farming peoples of sub-Saharan Africa have long faced the grim reality that many babies fail to survive, often succumbing to gastrointestinal diseases, malaria, or other infections. In the 1970s, when I lived among the Gusii in a small town in southwestern Kenya, infant mortality in that nation was on the decline but was still high—about eighty deaths per thousand live births during the first years, compared with about ten in the United States at that time and six to eight in Western Europe.

The Gusii grew corn, millet, and cash crops such as coffee and tea. Women handled the more routine tasks of cultivation, food processing, and trading, while men were supervisors or entrepreneurs. Many men worked at jobs outside the village, in urban centers or on plantations. The society was polygamous, with perhaps 10 percent of the men having two or more wives. A woman was expected to give birth every two years, from marriage to menopause, and the average married women bore about ten live children—one of the highest fertility rates in the world.

Nursing mothers slept alone with a new infant for fifteen months to insure its health. For the first three to six months, the Gusii mothers were especially vigilant for signs of ill health or slow growth, and they were quick to nurture unusually small or sick infants by feeding and holding them more often. Mothers whose newborns were deemed particularly at risk—including twins and those born prematurely—entered a ritual seclusion for several weeks, staying with their infants in a hut with a constant fire.

Mothers kept infants from crying in the early months by holding them constantly and being quick to comfort them. After three to six months—if the baby was growing normally—mothers began to entrust the baby to the care of other children (usually six to twelve years old) in order to pursue tasks that helped support the family. Fathers did not take care of infants, for this was not a traditional male activity.

Because they were so worried about their children's survival, Gusii parents did not explicitly strive to foster cognitive, social, and emotional development. These needs were not neglected, however, because from birth Gusii babies entered an active and responsive interpersonal environment, first with their mothers and young care-givers, and later as part of a group of children.

# An Infant's Three Rs

## By Sara Harkness and Charles M. Super

You are an American visitor spending a morning in a pleasant middle-class Dutch home to observe the normal routine of a mother and her six-month-old baby. The mother made sure you got there by 8:30 to witness the morning bath, an opportunity for playful interaction with the baby. The baby was then dressed in cozy warm clothes, her hair brushed and styled with a tiny curlicue atop her head. The mother gave her the midmorning bottle, then sang to her and played patty-cake for a few minutes before placing her in the playpen to entertain herself with a mobile while the mother attended to other things nearby. Now, about half an hour later, the baby is beginning to get fussy.

The mother watches for a minute, then offers a toy and turns away. The baby again begins to fuss. "Seems bored and in need of attention," you think. But the mother looks at the baby sympathetically and in a soothing voice says, "Oh, are you tired?" Without further ado she picks up the baby, carries her upstairs, tucks her into her crib, and pulls down the shades. To your surprise, the baby fusses for only a few more moments, then is quiet. The mother returns looking serene. "She needs plenty of sleep in order to grow," she explains. "When she doesn't have her nap or go to bed on time, we can always tell the difference—she's not so happy and playful."

Different patterns in infant sleep can be found in Western societies that seem quite similar to those of the United States. We discovered the "three R's" of Dutch child rearing—*rust* (rest), *regelmaat* (regularity) and *reinheid* (cleanliness)—while doing research on a sample of sixty families with infants or young children in a middle-class community near Leiden and Amsterdam, the sort of community typical of Dutch life styles in all but the big cities nowadays. At six months, the Dutch babies were sleeping more than a comparison group of American babies—a total of fifteen hours per day compared with thirteen hours for the Americans. While awake at home, the Dutch babies were more often left to play quietly in their playpens or infant seats. A daily ride in the baby carriage provided time for the baby to look around at the passing scene or to doze peacefully. If the mother needed to go out for a while without the baby, she could leave it alone in bed for a short period or time her outing with the baby's nap time and ask a neighbor to monitor with a "baby phone."

To understand how Dutch families manage to establish such a restful routine by the time their babies are six months old, we made a second research visit to the same community. We found that by two weeks of age, the Dutch babies were already sleeping more than same-age American babies. In fact, a dilemma for some Dutch parents was whether to wake the baby after eight hours, as instructed by the local health care providers, or let them sleep longer. The main method for establishing and maintaining this pattern was to create a calm, regular, and restful environment for the infant throughout the day.

Far from worrying about providing "adequate stimulation," these mothers were conscientious about avoiding overstimulation in the form of late family outings, disruptions in the regularity of eating and sleeping, or too many things to look at or listen to. Few parents were troubled by their babies' nighttime sleep routines. Babies's feeding schedules were structured following the guidelines of the local baby clinic (a national service). If a baby continued to wake up at night when feeding was no longer considered necessary, the mother (or father) would most commonly give it a pacifier and a little back rub to help it get back to sleep. Only in rare instances did parents find themselves forced to choose between letting the baby scream and allowing too much night waking.

Many aspects of Dutch society support the three Rs throughout infancy and childhood—for example, shopping is close to home, and families usually have neighbors and relatives nearby who are available to help out with child care. The small scale of neighborhoods and a network of bicycle paths provide local play sites and a safe way for children to get around easily on their own (no "soccer moms" are needed for daily transportation!). Work sites for both fathers and mothers are also generally close to home, and there are many flexible or part-time job arrangements.

National policies for health and other social benefits insure universal coverage regardless of one's employment status, and the principle of the "family wage" has prevailed in labor relations so that mothers of infants and young children rarely work more than part-time, if at all. In many ways, the three Rs of Dutch child rearing are just one aspect of a calm and unhurried life style for the whole family.

usually because it makes sense in their environmental or social circumstances. In the United States, for example, where individualism is valued, parents do not hold babies as much as in other cultures, and they place them in rooms of their own to sleep. Pediatricians and parents alike often say this fosters independence and self-reliance. Japanese parents, in contrast, believe that individuals should be well integrated into society, and so they "indulge" their babies: Japanese infants are held more often, not left to cry, and sleep with their parents. Efe parents in Congo believe even more in a communal life, and their infants are regularly nursed, held, and comforted by any number of group members, not just parents. Whether

such practices help form the anticipated adult personality traits remains to be shown, however.

Recently, a group of anthropologists, child-development experts, and pediatricians have taken the cross-cultural approach in a new direction by investigating how differing parenting styles affect infant health and growth. Instead of emphasizing the development of adult personality, these researchers, who call themselves ethnopediatricians, focus on the child as an organism. Ethnopediatricians see the human infant as a product of evolution, geared to enter a particular environment of care. What an infant actually gets is a compromise, as parents are pulled by their offspring's needs and pushed by social and personal expectations.

# Doctor's Orders

## By Edward Z. Tronick

In Boston, a pediatric resident is experiencing a vague sense of disquiet as she interviews a Puerto Rican mother who has brought her baby in for a checkup. When she is at work, the mother explains, the two older children, ages six and nine, take care of the two younger ones, a two-year-old and the three-month-old baby. Warning bells go off for the resident: young children cannot possibly be sensitive to the needs of babies and toddlers. And yet the baby is thriving; he is well over the ninetieth percentile in weight and height and is full of smiles.

The resident questions the mother in detail: How is the baby fed? Is the apartment safe for a two-year-old? The responses are all reassuring, but the resident nonetheless launches into a lecture on the importance of the mother to normal infant development. The mother falls silent, and the resident is now convinced that something is seriously wrong. And something is— the resident's model of child care.

The resident subscribes to what I call the "continuous care and contact" model of parenting, which demands a high level of contact, frequent feeding, and constant supervision, with almost all care provided by the mother. According to this model, a mother should also enhance cognitive development with play and verbal engagement. The pediatric resident is comfortable with this formula—she is not even conscious of it—because she was raised this way and treats her own child in the same manner. But at the Child Development Unit of Children's Hospital in Boston, which I direct, I want residents to abandon the idea that there is only one way to raise a child. Not to do so may interfere with patient care.

Many models of parenting are valid. Among Efe foragers of Congo's Ituri Forest, for example, a newborn is routinely cared for by several people. Babies are even nursed by many women. But few individuals ever play with the infant; as far as the Efe are concerned, the baby's job is to sleep.

In Peru, the Quechua swaddle their infants in a pouch of blankets that the mother, or a child caretaker, carries on her back. Inside the pouch, the infant cannot move, and its eyes are covered. Quechua babies are nursed in a perfunctory fashion, with three or four hours between feedings.

As I explain to novice pediatricians, such practices do not fit the continuous care and contact model; yet these babies grow up just fine. But my residents see these cultures as exotic, not relevant to the industrialized world. And so I follow up with examples closer to home: Dutch parents who leave an infant alone in order to go shopping, sometimes pinning the child's shirt to the bed to keep the baby on its back; or Japanese mothers who periodically wake a sleeping infant to teach the child who is in charge. The questions soon follow. "How could a mother leave her infant alone?" "Why would a parent ever want to wake up a sleeping baby?"

The data from cross-cultural studies indicate that child-care practices vary, and that these styles aim to make the child into a culturally appropriate adult. The Efe make future Efe. The resident makes future residents. A doctor who has a vague sense that something is wrong with how someone cares for a baby may first need to explore his or her own assumptions, the hidden "shoulds" that are based solely on tradition. Of course, pediatric residents must make sure children are cared for responsibly. I know I have helped residents broaden their views when their lectures on good mothering are replaced by such comments as "What a gorgeous baby! I can't imagine how you manage both work and three others at home!"

---

Compared with offspring of many other mammals, primate infants are dependent and vulnerable. Baby monkeys and apes stay close to the mother's body, clinging to her stomach or riding on her back, and nursing at will. They are protected in this way for many months, until they develop enough motor and cognitive skills to move about. Human infants are at the extreme: virtually helpless as newborns, they need twelve months just to learn to walk and years of social learning before they can function on their own.

Dependence during infancy is the price we pay for being hominids, members of the group of upright-walking primates that includes humans and their extinct relatives. Four million years ago, when our ancestors became bipedal, the hominid pelvis underwent a necessary renovation. At first, this new pelvic architecture presented no problem during birth because the early hominids, known as australopithecines, still had rather small brains, one-third the present size. But starting about 1.5 million years ago, human brain size ballooned. Hominid babies now had to twist and bend to pass through the birth canal, and more important, birth had to be triggered before the skull grew too big.

As a result, the human infant is born neurologically unfinished and unable to coordinate muscle movement. Natural selection has compensated for this by favoring a close adult-infant tie that lasts years and goes beyond meeting the needs of food and shelter. In a sense, the human baby is not isolated but is part of a physiologically and emotionally entwined dyad of infant and caregiver. The adult might be male or female, a birth or adoptive parent, as long as at least one person is attuned to the infant's needs.

The signs of this interrelationship are many. Through conditioning, a mother's breast milk often begins to flow at the sound of her own infant's cries, even before the nipple is stimulated. New mothers also easily recognize the cries (and smells) of their infants over those of other babies. For their part, newborns recognize their own mother's voice and prefer it over others. One experiment showed that a baby's heart rate quickly synchronizes with Mom's or Dad's, but not with that of a friendly stranger. Babies are also predisposed to be socially engaged with caregivers. From birth, infants move their bodies in synchrony with adult speech and the general nature of language. Babies quickly

# The Crying Game

## By Ronald G. Barr

All normal human infants cry, although they vary a great deal in how much. A mysterious and still unexplained phenomenon is that crying tends to increase in the first few weeks of life, peaks in the second or third month, and then decreases. Some babies in the United States cry so much during the peak period—often in excess of three hours a day—and seem so difficult to soothe that parents come to doubt their nurturing skills or begin to fear that their offspring is suffering from a painful disease. Some mothers discontinue nursing and switch to bottle-feeding because they believe their breast milk is insufficiently nutritious and that their infants are always hungry. In extreme cases, the crying may provoke physical abuse, sometimes even precipitating the infant's death.

A look at another culture, the !Kung San hunter-gatherers of southern Africa, provides us with an opportunity to see whether caregiving strategies have any effect on infant crying. Both the !Kung San and Western infants escalate their crying during the early weeks of life, with a similar peak at two or three months. A comparison of Dutch, American, and !Kung San infants shows that the number of individual crying episodes are virtually identical. What differs is their length: !Kung San infants cry about half as long as Western babies. This implies that caregiving can influence only some aspects of crying, such as duration.

What is particularly striking about child-rearing among the !Kung San is that infants are in constant contact with a caregiver; they are carried or held most of the time, are usually in an upright position, and are breast-fed about four times an hour for one to two minutes at a time. Furthermore, the mother almost always responds to the smallest cry or fret within ten seconds.

I believe that crying was adaptive for our ancestors. As seen in the contemporary !Kung San, crying probably elicited a quick response, and thus consisted of frequent but relatively short episodes. This pattern helped keep an adult close by to provide adequate nutrition as well as protection from predators. I have also argued that crying helped an infant forge a strong attachment with the mother and—because new pregnancies are delayed by the prolongation of frequent nursing—secure more of her caregiving resources.

In the United States, where the threat of predation has receded and adequate nutrition is usually available even without breast-feeding, crying may be less adaptive. In any case, caregiving in the United States may be viewed as a cultural experiment in which the infant is relatively more separated—and separable—from the mother, both in terms of frequency of contact and actual distance.

The Western strategy is advantageous when the mother's employment outside of the home and away from the baby is necessary to sustain family resources. But the trade-off seems to be an increase in the length of crying bouts.

recognize the arrangement of a human face—two eyes, a nose, and a mouth in the right place—over other more Picasso-like rearrangements. And mothers and infants will position themselves face-to-facewhen they lie down to sleep.

Babies and mothers seem to follow a typical pattern of play, a coordinated waltz that moves from attention to inattention and back again. This innate social connection was tested experimentally by Jeffrey Cohn and Edward Tronick in a series of three-minute laboratory experiments at the University of Massachusetts, in which they asked mothers to act depressed and not respond to baby's cues. When faced with a suddenly unresponsive mother, a baby repeatedly reaches out and flaps around, trying to catch her eye. When this tactic does not work, the baby gives up, turning away and going limp. And when the mother begins to respond again, it takes thirty seconds for the baby to reengage.

Given that human infants arrive in a state of dependency, ethnopediatricians have sought to define the care required to meet their physical, cognitive, and emotional needs. They assume there must be ways to treat babies that have proved adaptive over time and are therefore likely to be most appropriate. Surveys of parenting in different societies reveal broad patterns. In almost all cultures, infants sleep with their parents in the same room and most often in the same bed. At all other times, infants are usually carried. Caregivers also usually respond quickly to infant cries; mothers most often by offering the breast. Since most hunter-gatherer groups also follow this over-

all style, this is probably the ancestral pattern. If there is an exception to these generalizations, it is the industrialized West.

Nuances of caretaking, however, do vary with particular social situations. !Kung San mothers of Botswana usually carry their infants on gathering expeditions, while the forest-living Ache of Paraguay, also hunters and gatherers, usually leave infants in camp while they gather. Gusii mothers working in garden plots leave their babies in the care of older children, while working mothers in the West may turn to unrelated adults. Such choices have physiological or behavioral consequences for the infant. As parents navigate between infant needs and the constraints of making a life, they may face a series of trade-offs that set the caregiver-infant dyad at odds. The areas of greatest controversy are breast-feeding, crying, and sleep—the major preoccupations of babies and their parents.

Strapped to their mothers' sides or backs in traditional fashion, human infants have quick access to the breast. Easy access makes sense because of the nature of human milk. Compared with that of other mammals, primate milk is relatively low in fat and protein but high in carbohydrates. Such milk is biologically suitable if the infant can nurse on a frequent basis. Most Western babies are fed in a somewhat different way. At least half are bottle-fed from birth, while others are weaned from breast to bottle after only a few months. And most—whether nursed or bottle-fed—are fed at scheduled times, waiting hours between feedings. Long intervals in nursing disrupt the manufacture of

# When to Wean

## By Katherine A. Dettwyler

Breast-feeding in humans is a biological process grounded in our mammalian ancestry. It is also an activity modified by social and cultural constraints, including a mother's everyday work schedule and a variety of beliefs about personal autonomy, the proper relationship between mother and child (or between mother and father), and infant health and nutrition. The same may be said of the termination of breast-feeding, or weaning.

In the United States, children are commonly bottle-fed from birth or weaned within a few months. But in some societies, children as old as four or five years may still be nursed. The American Academy of Pediatrics currently advises breast-feeding for a minimum of one year (this may be revised upward), and the World Health Organization recommends two years or more. Amid conflicting advice, many wonder how long breast-feeding should last to provide an infant with optimal nutrition and health.

Nonhuman primates and other mammals give us some clues as to what the "natural" age of weaning would be if humans were less bound by cultural norms. Compared with most other orders of placental mammals, primates (including humans) have longer life spans and spend more time at each life stage, such as gestation, infant dependency, and puberty. Within the primate order itself, the trend in longevity increases from smaller-bodied, smaller-brained, often solitary prosimians through the larger-bodied, larger-brained, and usually social apes and humans. Gestation, for instance, is eighteen weeks in lemurs, twenty-four weeks in macaques, thirty-three weeks in chimpanzees, and thirty-eight weeks in humans.

Studies of nonhuman primates offer a number of different means of estimating the natural time for human weaning. First, large-bodied primates wean their offspring some months after the young have quadrupled their birth weight. In modern humans, this weight milestone is passed at about two and a half to three years of age. Second, like many other mammals, primate offspring tend to be weaned when they have attained about one third of their adult weight; humans reach this level between four and seven years of age. Third, in all species studied so far, primates also wean their offspring at the time the first permanent molars erupt; this occurs at five and a half to six years in modern humans. Fourth, in chimpanzees and gorillas, breast-feeding usually lasts about six times the duration of gestation. On this basis, a human breast-feeding would be projected to continue for four and a half years.

Taken together, these and other projections suggest that somewhat more than two and a half years is the natural minimum age of weaning for humans and seven years the maximum age, well into childhood. The high end of this range, six to seven years, closely matches both the completion of human brain growth and the maturation of the child's immune system.

In many non-Western cultures, children are routinely nursed for three to five years. Incidentally, this practice inhibits ovulation in the mother, providing a natural mechanism of family planning. Even in the United States, a significant number of children are breast-fed beyond three years of age. While not all women are able or willing to nurse each of their children for many years, those who do should be encouraged and supported. Health care professionals, family, friends, and nosy neighbors should be reassured that "extended" breast-feeding, for as long as seven years, appears physiologically normal and natural.

Substantial evidence is already available to suggest that curtailing the duration of breast-feeding far below two and a half years—when the human child has evolved to expect more—can be deleterious. Every study that includes the duration of breast-feeding as a variable shows that, on average, the longer a baby is nursed, the better its health and cognitive development. For example, breast-fed children have fewer allergies, fewer ear infections, and less diarrhea, and their risk for sudden infant death syndrome (a rare but devastating occurrence) is lower. Breast-fed children also have higher cognitive test scores and lower incidence of attention deficit hyperactivity disorder.

In many cases, specific biochemical constituents of breast milk have been identified that either protect directly against disease or help the child's body develop its own defense system. For example, in the case of many viral diseases, the baby brings the virus to the mother, and her gut-wall cells manufacture specific antibodies against the virus, which then travel to the mammary glands and go back to the baby. The docosahesanoic acid in breast milk may be responsible for improved cognitive and attention functions. And the infant's exposure to the hormones and cholesterol in the milk appears to condition the body, reducing the risk of heart disease and breast cancer in later years. These and other discoveries show that breast-feeding serves functions for which no simple substitute is available.

breast milk, making it still lower in fat and thus less satisfying the next time the nipple is offered. And so crying over food and even the struggles of weaning result from the infant's unfulfilled expectations.

Sleep is also a major issue for new parents. In the West, babies are encouraged to sleep all through the night as soon as possible. And when infants do not do so, they merit the label "sleep problem" from both parents and pediatricians. But infants seem predisposed to sleep rather lightly, waking many times during the night. And while sleeping close to an adult allows infants to nurse more often and may have other beneficial effects, Westerners usually expect babies to sleep alone. This practice has roots in ecclesiastical laws enacted to protect against the smothering of infants by "lying over"—often a thinly disguised cover for infanticide—which was a concern in Europe beginning in the Middle Ages. Solitary sleep is reinforced by the rather recent notion of parental privacy. Western parents are also often convinced that solitary sleep will mold strong character.

# Bedtime Story

## By James J. McKenna

For as far back as you care to go, mothers have followed the protective and convenient practice of sleeping with their infants. Even now, for the vast majority of people across the globe, "co-sleeping" and nighttime breast-feeding remain inseparable practices. Only in the past 200 years, and mostly in Western industrialized societies, have parents considered it normal and biologically appropriate for a mother and infant to sleep apart.

In the sleep laboratory at the University of California's Irvine School of Medicine, my colleagues and I observed mother-infant pairs as they slept both apart and together over three consecutive nights. Using a polygraph, we recorded the mother's and infant's heart rates, brain waves (EEGs), breathing, body temperature, and episodes of nursing. Infrared video photography simultaneously monitored their behavior.

We found that bed-sharing infants face their mothers for most of the night and that both mother and infants are highly responsive to each other's movements, wake more frequently, and spend more time in lighter stages of sleep than they do while sleeping alone. Bed-sharing infants nurse almost twice as often, and three times as long per bout, than they do when sleeping alone. But they rarely cry. Mothers who routinely sleep with their infants get at least as much sleep as mothers who sleep without them.

In addition to providing more nighttime nourishment and greater protection, sleeping with the mother supplies the infant with a steady stream of sensations of the mother's presence, including touch, smell, movement, and warmth. These stimuli can perhaps even compensate for the human infant's extreme neurological immaturity at birth.

Cosleeping might also turn out to give some babies protection from sudden infant death syndrome (SIDS), a heartbreaking and enigmatic killer. Co-sleeping infants nurse more often, sleep more lightly, and have practice responding to maternal arousals. Arousal deficiencies are suspected in some SIDS deaths, and long periods in deep sleep may exacerbate this problem. Perhaps the physiological changes induced by cosleeping, especially when combined with nighttime breast-feeding, can benefit some infants by helping them sleep more lightly. At the same time, cosleeping makes it easier for a mother to detect and respond to an infant in crisis. Rethinking another sleeping practice has already shown a dramatic effect: In the United States, SIDS rates fell at least 30 percent after 1992, when the American Academy of Pediatrics recommended placing sleeping babies on their backs, rather than face down.

The effect of cosleeping on SIDS remains to be proved, so it would be premature to recommend it as the best arrangement for all families. The possible hazards of cosleeping must also be assessed. Is the environment otherwise safe, with appropriate bedding materials? Do the parents smoke? Do they use drugs or alcohol? (These appear to be the main factors in those rare cases in which a mother inadvertently smothers her child.) Since cosleeping was the ancestral condition, the future for our infants may well entail a borrowing back from ancient ways.

---

Infants' care is shaped by tradition, fads, science, and folk wisdom. Cross-cultural and evolutionary studies provide a useful perspective for parents and pediatricians as they sift through the alternatives. Where these insights fail to guide us, however, important clues are provided by the floppy but interactive babies themselves. Grinning when we talk to them, crying in distress when left alone, sleeping best when close at heart, they teach us that growth is a cooperative venture.

# Recommended Reading

Parents' Cultural Belief Systems: Their Origins, Expressions, and Consequences, by Sara Harkness and Charles M. Super (Guilford Press, 1996)

Child Care and Culture: Lessons from Africa, by Robert A. LeVine et al. (Cambridge University Press, 1994)

Our Babies, Ourselves, by Meredith F. Small (Anchor Books/ Doubleday, 1998)

Breastfeeding: Biocultural Perspectives, edited by Patricia Stuart-Macadam and Katherine A. Dettwyler (Aldine de Gruyler, 1995)

The Family Bed: An Age Old Concept in Childrearing, by Tine Thevenin (Avery Publishing Group, 1987)

Human Birth: An Evolutionary Perspective, by Wenda R. Trevathan (Aldine de Gruyter, 1987)

Six Cultures: Studies of Child Rearing, edited by Beatrice B. Whiting (John Wiley, 1963)

A professor of anthropology at Cornell University, **MEREDITH F. SMALL** became interested in "ethnopediatrics" in 1995, after interviewing anthropologist James J. McKenna on the subject of infant sleep. Trained as a primate behaviorist, Small has observed female mating behavior in three species of macaque monkeys. She now writes about science for a general audience; her book *Our Babies, Ourselves* is published by Anchor Books/Doubleday (1998). Her previous contributions to *Natural History* include "These Animals Think, Therefore..." (August 1996) and "Read in the Bone" (June 1997).

# Arranging a Marriage in India

SERENA NANDA

Sister and doctor brother-in-law invite correspondence from North Indian professionals only, for a beautiful, talented, sophisticated, intelligent sister, 5'3", slim, M.A. in textile design, father a senior civil officer. Would prefer immigrant doctors, between 26–29 years. Reply with full details and returnable photo. A well-settled uncle invites matrimonial correspondence from slim, fair, educated South Indian girl, for his nephew, 25 years, smart, M.B.A., green card holder, 5'6". Full particulars with returnable photo appreciated.

*Matrimonial Advertisements*,
India Abroad

IN INDIA, ALMOST ALL MARRIAGES ARE arranged. Even among the educated middle classes in modern, urban India, marriage is as much a concern of the families as it is of the individuals. So customary is the practice of arranged marriage that there is a special name for a marriage which is not arranged: It is called a "love match."

On my first field trip to India, I met many young men and women whose parents were in the process of "getting them married." In many cases, the bride and groom would not meet each other before the marriage. At most they might meet for a brief conversation, and this meeting would take place only after their parents had decided that the match was suitable. Parents do not compel their children to marry a person who either marriage partner finds objectionable. But only after one match is refused will another be sought.

## Young men and women do not date and have very little social life involving members of the opposite sex.

As a young American woman in India for the first time, I found this custom of arranged marriage oppressive. How could any intelligent young person agree to such a marriage without great reluctance? It was contrary to everything I believed about the importance of romantic love as the only basis of a happy marriage. It also clashed with my strongly held notions that the choice of such an intimate and permanent relationship could be made only by the individuals involved. Had anyone tried to arrange my marriage, I would have been defiant and rebellious!

At the first opportunity, I began, with more curiosity than tact, to question the young people I met on how they felt about this practice. Sita, one of my young informants, was a college graduate with a degree in political science. She had been waiting for over a year while her parents were arranging a match for her. I found it difficult to accept the docile manner in which this well-educated young woman awaited the outcome of a process that would result in her spending the rest of her life with a man she hardly knew, a virtual stranger, picked out by her parents.

"How can you go along with this?" I asked her, in frustration and distress. "Don't you care who you marry?"

"Of course I care," she answered." This is why I must let my parents choose a boy for me. My marriage is too important to be arranged by such an inexperienced person as myself. In such matters, it is better to have my parents' guidance."

I had learned that young men and women in India do not date and have very little social life involving members of the opposite sex. Although I could not disagree with Sita's reasoning, I continued to pursue the subject.

"But how can you marry the first man you have ever met? Not only have you missed the fun of meeting a lot of different people, but you have not given yourself the chance to know who is the right man for you."

"Meeting with a lot of different people doesn't sound like any fun at all," Sita answered. "One hears that in America the girls are spending all their time worrying about whether they will meet a man and get married. Here we have the chance to enjoy our life and let our parents do this work and worrying for us."

She had me there. The high anxiety of the competition to "be popular" with the opposite sex certainly was the most prominent feature of life as an American teenager in the late fifties. The endless worrying about the rules that governed our behavior and about our popularity ratings sapped both our self-esteem and our enjoyment of adolescence. I reflected that absence of this competition in India most certainly may have contributed to the self-confidence and natural charm of so many of the young women I met.

And yet, the idea of marrying a perfect stranger, whom one did not know and did not "love," so offended my American ideas of individualism and romanticism, that I persisted with my objections.

"I still can't imagine it," I said. "How can you agree to marry a man you hardly know?"

"But of course he will be known. My parents would never arrange a marriage for me without knowing all about the boy's family background. Naturally we will not rely only on what the family tells us. We will check the particulars out ourselves. No one will want their daughter to marry into a family that is not good. All these things we will know beforehand."

Impatiently, I responded, "Sita, I don't mean know the family, I mean, know the man. How can you marry someone you don't know personally and don't love? How can you think of spending your life with someone you may not even like?"

"If he is a good man, why should I not like him?" she said. "With you people, you know the boy so well before you marry, where will be the fun to get married? There will be no mystery and no romance. Here we have the whole of our married life to get to know and love our husband. "This way is better, is it not?"

Her response made further sense, and I began to have second thoughts on the matter. Indeed, during months of meeting many intelligent young Indian people, both male and female, who had the same ideas as Sita, I saw arranged marriages in a different light. I also saw the importance of the family in Indian life and realized that a couple who took their marriage into their own hands was taking a big risk, particularly if their families were irreconcilably opposed to the match. In a country where every important resource in life—a job, a house, a social circle—is gained through family connections, it seemed foolhardy to cut oneself off from a supportive social network and depend solely on one person for happiness and success.

Six years later I returned to India to again do fieldwork, this time among the middle class in Bombay, a modern, sophisticated city. From the experience of my earlier visit, I decided to include a study of arranged marriages in my project. By this time I had met many Indian couples whose marriages had been arranged and who seemed very happy. Particularly in contrast to the fate of many of my married friends in the United States who were already in the process of divorce, the positive aspects of arranged marriages appeared to me to outweigh the negatives. In fact, I thought I might even participate in arranging a marriage myself. I had been fairly successful in the United States in "fixing up" many of my friends, and I was confident that my matchmaking skills could be easily applied to this new situation, once I learned the basic rules. "After all," I thought, "how complicated can it be? People want pretty much the same things in a marriage whether it is in India or America."

An opportunity presented itself almost immediately. A friend from my previous Indian trip was in the process of arranging for the marriage of her eldest son. In India there is a perceived shortage of "good boys," and since my friend's family was eminently respectable and the boy himself personable, well educated, and nice looking, I was sure that by the end of my year's fieldwork, we would have found a match.

The basic rule seems to be that a family's reputation is most important. It is understood that matches would be arranged only within the same caste and general social class, although some crossing of subcastes is permissible if the class positions of the bride's and groom's families are similar. Although dowry is now prohibited by law in India, extensive gift exchanges took place with every marriage. Even when the boy's family do not "make demands," every girl's family nevertheless feels the obligation to give the traditional gifts, to the girl, to the boy, and to the boy's family. Particularly when the couple would be living in the joint family—that is, with the boy's parents and his married brothers and their families, as well as with unmarried siblings—which is still very common even among the urban, upper-middle class in India, the girls' parents are anxious to establish smooth relations between their family and that of the boy. Offering the proper gifts, even when not called "dowry," is often an important factor in influencing the relationship between the bride's and groom's families and perhaps, also, the treatment of the bride in her new home.

---

**In a society where divorce is still a scandal and where, in fact, the divorce rate is exceedingly low, an arranged marriage is the beginning of a lifetime relationship not just between the bride and groom but between their families as well.**

---

In a society where divorce is still a scandal and where, in fact, the divorce rate is exceedingly low, an arranged marriage is the beginning of a lifetime relationship not just between the bride and groom but between their families as well. Thus, while a girl's looks are important, her character is even more so, for she is being judged as a prospective daughter-in-law as much as a prospective bride. Where she would be living in a joint family, as was the case with my friend, the girls's ability to get along harmoniously in a family is perhaps the single most important quality in assessing her suitability.

My friend is a highly esteemed wife, mother, and daughter-in-law. She is religious, soft-spoken, modest, and deferential. She rarely gossips and never quarrels, two qualities highly desirable in a woman. A family that has the reputation for gossip and conflict among its womenfolk will not find it easy to get good wives for their sons. Parents will not want to send their daughter to a house in which there is conflict.

My friend's family were originally from North India. They had lived in Bombay, where her husband owned a business, for forty years. The family had delayed in seeking a match for their eldest son because he had been an Air Force pilot for several years, stationed in such remote places that it had seemed fruitless to try to find a girl who would be willing to accompany him. In their social class, a military career, despite its economic security, has little prestige and is considered a drawback in finding a suitable bride. Many families would not allow their daughters to marry a man in an occupation so potentially dangerous and which requires so much moving around.

The son had recently left the military and joined his father's business. Since he was a college graduate, modern, and well traveled, from such a good family, and, I thought, quite handsome, it seemed to me that he, or rather his family, was in a position to pick and choose. I said as much to my friend.

While she agreed that there were many advantages on their side, she also said, "We must keep in mind that my son is both short and dark; these are drawbacks in finding the right match." While the boy's height had not escaped my notice, "dark" seemed to me inaccurate; I would have called him "wheat" colored perhaps, and in any case, I did not realize that color would be a consideration. I discovered, however, that while a boy's skin color is a less important consideration than a girl's, it is still a factor.

An important source of contacts in trying to arrange her son's marriage was my friend's social club in Bombay. Many of the women had daughters of the right age, and some had already expressed an interest in my friend's son. I was most enthusiastic about the possibilities of one particular family who had five daughters, all of whom were pretty, demure, and well educated. Their mother had told my friend, "You can have your pick for your son, whichever one of my daughters appeals to you most."

I saw a match in sight. "Surely," I said to my friend, "we will find one there. Let's go visit and make our choice." But my friend held back; she did not seem to share my enthusiasm, for reasons I could not then fathom.

When I kept pressing for an explanation of her reluctance, she admitted, "See, Serena, here is the problem. The family has so many daughters, how will they be able to provide nicely for any of them? We are not making any demands, but still, with so many daughters to marry off, one wonders whether she will even be able to make a proper wedding. Since this is our eldest son, it's best if we marry him to a girl who is the only daughter, then the wedding will truly be a gala affair." I argued that surely the quality of the girls themselves made up for any deficiency in the elaborateness of the wedding. My friend admitted this point but still seemed reluctant to proceed.

"Is there something else," I asked her, "some factor I have missed?" "Well," she finally said, "there is one other thing. They have one daughter already married and living in Bombay. The mother is always complaining to me that the girl's in-laws don't let her visit her own family often enough. So it makes me wonder, will she be that kind of mother who always wants her daughter at her own home? This will prevent the girl from adjusting to our house. It is not a good thing." And so, this family of five daughters was dropped as a possibility.

Somewhat disappointed, I nevertheless respected my friend's reasoning and geared up for the next prospect. This was also the daughter of a woman in my friend's social club. There was clear interest in this family and I could see why. The family's reputation was excellent; in fact, they came from a sub-caste slightly higher than my friend's own. The girl, who was an only daughter, was pretty and well educated and had a brother studying in the United States. Yet, after expressing an interest to me in this family, all talk of them suddenly died down and the search began elsewhere.

"What happened to that girl as a prospect?" I asked one day. "You never mention her any more. She is so pretty and so educated, what did you find wrong?"

"She is too educated. We've decided against it. My husband's father saw the girl on the bus the other day and thought

her forward. A girl who 'roams about' the city by herself is not the girl for our family." My disappointment this time was even greater, as I thought the son would have liked the girl very much. But then I thought, my friend is right, a girl who is going to live in a joint family cannot be too independent or she will make life miserable for everyone. I also learned that if the family of the girl has even a slightly higher social status than the family of the boy, the bride may think herself too good for them, and this too will cause problems. Later my friend admitted to me that this had been an important factor in her decision not to pursue the match.

The next candidate was the daughter of a client of my friend's husband. When the client learned that the family was looking for a match for their son, he said, "Look no further, we have a daughter." This man then invited my friends to dinner to see the girl. He had already seen their son at the office and decided that "he liked the boy." We all went together for tea, rather than dinner—it was less of a commitment—and while we were there, the girl's mother showed us around the house. The girl was studying for her exams and was briefly introduced to us.

After we left, I was anxious to hear my friend's opinion. While her husband liked the family very much and was impressed with his client's business accomplishments and reputation, the wife didn't like the girl's looks. "She is short, no doubt, which is an important plus point, but she is also fat and wears glasses." My friend obviously thought she could do better for her son and asked her husband to make his excuses to his client by saying that they had decided to postpone the boy's marriage indefinitely.

---

## "If a mistake is made we have not only ruined the life of our son or daughter, but we have spoiled the reputation of our family as well."

---

By this time almost six months had passed and I was becoming impatient. What I had thought would be an easy matter to arrange was turning out to be quite complicated. I began to believe that between my friend's desire for a girl who was modest enough to fit into her joint family, yet attractive and educated enough to be an acceptable partner for her son, she would not find anyone suitable. My friend laughed at my impatience: "Don't be so much in a hurry," she said. "You Americans want everything done so quickly. You get married quickly and then just as quickly get divorced. Here we take marriage more seriously. We must take all the factors into account. It is not enough for us to learn by our mistakes. This is too serious a business. If a mistake is made we have not only ruined the life of our son or daughter, but we have spoiled the reputation of our family as well. And that will make it much harder for their brothers and sisters to get married. So we must be very careful."

What she said was true and I promised myself to be more patient, though it was not easy. I had really hoped and expected that the match would be made before my year in India was up. But it was not to be. When I left India my friend seemed no fur-

## Appendix

# Further Reflections on Arranged Marriage...

This essay was written from the point of view of a family seeking a daughter-in-law. Arranged marriage looks somewhat different from the point of view of the bride and her family. Arranged marriage continues to be preferred, even among the more educated, Westernized sections of the Indian population. Many young women from these families still go along, more or less willingly, with the practice, and also with the specific choices of their families. Young women do get excited about the prospects of their marriage, but there is also ambivalence and increasing uncertainty, as the bride contemplates leaving the comfort and familiarity of her own home, where as a "temporary guest" she had often been indulged, to live among strangers. Even in the best situation she will now come under the close scrutiny of her husband's family. How she dresses, how she behaves, how she gets along with others, where she goes, how she spends her time, her domestic abilities—all of this and much more—will be observed and commented on by a whole new set of relations. Her interaction with her family of birth will be monitored and curtailed considerably. Not only will she leave their home, but with increasing geographic mobility, she may also live very far from them, perhaps even on another continent. Too much expression of her fondness for her own family, or her desire to visit them, may be interpreted as an inability to adjust to her new family, and may become a source of conflict. In an arranged marriage the burden of adjustment is clearly heavier for a woman than for a man. And that is in the best of situations.

In less happy circumstances, the bride may be a target of resentment and hostility from her husband's family, particularly her mother-in-law or her husband's unmarried sisters, for whom she is now a source of competition for the affection, loyalty, and economic resources of their son or brother. If she is psychologically, or even physically abused, her options are limited, as returning to her parents' home, or divorce, are still very stigmatized. For most Indians, marriage and motherhood are still considered the only suitable roles for a woman, even for those who have careers, and few women can comfortably contemplate remaining unmarried. Most families still consider "marrying off" their daughters as a compelling religious duty and social necessity. This increases a bride's sense of obligation to make the marriage a success, at whatever cost to her own personal happiness.

The vulnerability of a new bride may also be intensified by the issue of dowry, which although illegal, has become a more pressing issue in the consumer conscious society of contemporary urban India. In many cases, where a groom's family is not satisfied with the amount of dowry a bride brings to her marriage, the young bride will be constantly harassed to get her parents to give more. In extreme cases, the bride may even be murdered, and the murder disguised as an accident or suicide. This also offers the husband's family an opportunity to arrange another match for him, thus bringing in another dowry. This phenomena, called dowry death, calls attention not just to the "evils of dowry" but also to larger issues of the powerlessness of women as well.

*Serena Nanda*
March 1998

ther along in finding a suitable match for her son than when I had arrived.

Two years later, I returned to India and still my friend had not found a girl for her son. By this time, he was close to thirty, and I think she was a little worried. Since she knew I had friends all over India, and I was going to be there for a year, she asked me to "help her in this work" and keep an eye out for someone suitable. I was flattered that my judgment was respected, but knowing now how complicated the process was, I had lost my earlier confidence as a matchmaker. Nevertheless, I promised that I would try.

It was almost at the end of my year's stay in India that I met a family with a marriageable daughter whom I felt might be a good possibility for my friend's son. The girl's father was related to a good friend of mine and by coincidence came from the same village as my friend's husband. This new family had a successful business in a medium-sized city in central India and were from the same subcaste as my friend. The daughter was pretty and chic; in fact, she had studied fashion design in college. Her parents would not allow her to go off by herself to any of the major cities in India where she could make a career, but they had compromised with her wish to work by allowing her to

run a small dress-making boutique from their home. In spite of her desire to have a career, the daughter was both modest and home-loving and had had a traditional, sheltered upbringing. She had only one other sister, already married, and a brother who was in his father's business.

I mentioned the possibility of a match with my friend's son. The girl's parents were most interested. Although their daughter was not eager to marry just yet, the idea of living in Bombay—a sophisticated, extremely fashion-conscious city where she could continue her education in clothing design—was a great inducement. I gave the girl's father my friend's address and suggested that when they went to Bombay on some business or whatever, they look up the boy's family.

Returning to Bombay on my way to New York, I told my friend of this newly discovered possibility. She seemed to feel there was potential but, in spite of my urging, would not make any moves herself. She rather preferred to wait for the girl's family to call upon them. I hoped something would come of this introduction, though by now I had learned to rein in my optimism.

A year later I received a letter from my friend. The family had indeed come to visit Bombay, and their daughter and my friend's daughter, who were near in age, had become very good friends. During that year, the two girls had frequently visited each other. I thought things looked promising.

Last week I received an invitation to a wedding: My friend's son and the girl were getting married. Since I had found the match, my presence was particularly requested at the wedding.

I was thrilled. Success at last! As I prepared to leave for India, I began thinking, "Now, my friend's younger son, who do I know who has a nice girl for him… ?"

Edited by Philip R. DeVita.

From *Stumbling Toward Truth: Anthropologists at Work,* edited by Philip R. DeVita, 2000, pp. 196–204. Published by Waveland Press. © 2000 by Serena Nanda. Reprinted by permission of the author.

# Who Needs Love!
# In Japan, Many Couples Don't

Nicholas D. Kristof

OMIYA, Japan—Yuri Uemura sat on the straw tatami mat of her living room and chatted cheerfully about her 40-year marriage to a man whom, she mused, she never particularly liked.

"There was never any love between me and my husband," she said blithely, recalling how he used to beat her. "But, well, we survived."

A 72-year-old midwife, her face as weathered as an old baseball and etched with a thousand seams, Mrs. Uemura said that her husband had never told her that he liked her, never complimented her on a meal, never told her "thank you," never held her hand, never given her a present, never shown her affection in any way. He never calls her by her name, but summons her with the equivalent of a grunt or a "Hey, you."

"Even with animals, the males cooperate to bring the females some food," Mrs. Uemura said sadly, noting the contrast to her own marriage. "When I see that, it brings tears to my eyes."

In short, the Uemuras have a marriage that is as durable as it is unhappy, one couple's tribute to the Japanese sanctity of family.

The divorce rate in Japan is at a record high but still less than half that of the United States, and Japan arguably has one of the strongest family structures in the industrialized world. As the United States and Europe fret about the disintegration of the traditional family, most Japanese families remain as solid as the small red table on which Mrs. Uemura rested her tea.

**It does not seem that Japanese families survive because husbands and wives love each other more than American couples, but rather because they perhaps love each other less**

A study published last year by the Population Council, an international nonprofit group based in New York, suggested that the traditional two-parent household is on the wane not only in America but throughout most of the world. There was one prominent exception: Japan.

In Japan, for example, only 1.1 percent of births are to unwed mothers—virtually unchanged from 25 years ago. In the United States, the figure is 30.1 percent and rising rapidly.

Yet if one comes to a little Japanese town like Omiya to learn the secrets of the Japanese family, the people are not as happy as the statistics.

"I haven't lived for myself," Mrs. Uemura said, with a touch of melancholy, "but for my kids, and for my family, and for society."

Mrs. Uemura's marriage does not seem exceptional in Japan, whether in the big cities or here in Omiya. The people of Omiya, a community of 5,700 nestled in the rain-drenched hills of the Kii Peninsula in Mie Prefecture, nearly 200 miles southwest of Tokyo, have spoken periodically to a reporter about various aspects of their daily lives. On this visit they talked about their families.

## SURVIVAL SECRETS
## Often, the Couples Expect Little

Osamums Torida furrowed his brow and looked perplexed when he was asked if he loved his wife of 33 years.

"Yeah, so-so, I guess," said Mr. Torida, a cattle farmer. "She's like air or water. You couldn't live without it, but most of the time, you're not conscious of its existence."

The secret to the survival of the marriage, Mr. Torida acknowledged, was not mutual passion.

"Sure, we had fights about our work," he explained as he stood beside his barn. "But we were preoccupied by work and our debts, so we had no time to fool around."

That is a common theme in Omiya. It does not seem that Japanese families survive because husbands and wives love each other more than American couples, but rather because they perhaps love each other less.

"I think love marriages are more fragile than arranged marriages," said Tomika Kusukawa, 49, who married her high-school sweetheart and now runs a car repair shop with him. "In love marriages, when something happens or if the couple falls out of love, they split up."

If there is a secret to the strength of the Japanese family it consists of three ingredients: low expectations, patience, and shame.

The advantage of marriages based on low expectations is that they have built in shock absorbers. If the couple discover that they have nothing in common, that they do not even like

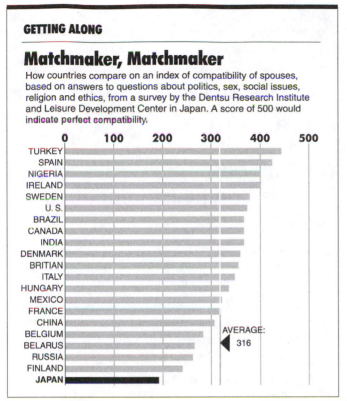

**GETTING ALONG**

## Matchmaker, Matchmaker

How countries compare on an index of compatibility of spouses, based on answers to questions about politics, sex, social issues, religion and ethics, from a survey by the Dentsu Research Institute and Leisure Development Center in Japan. A score of 500 would indicate perfect compatibility.

TURKEY
SPAIN
NIGERIA
IRELAND
SWEDEN
U.S.
BRAZIL
CANADA
INDIA
DENMARK
BRITIAN
ITALY
HUNGARY
MEXICO
FRANCE
CHINA
BELGIUM
BELARUS
RUSSIA
FINLAND
JAPAN

AVERAGE: 316

NEW YORK TIMES

was patient. And then she got pregnant and had a kid, and now they're close again."

The word that Mrs. Fukuyama used for patience is "gaman," a term that comes up whenever marriage is discussed in Japan. It means toughing it out, enduring hardship, and many Japanese regard gaman with pride as a national trait.

Many people complain that younger folks divorce because they do not have enough gaman, and the frequency with which the term is used suggests a rather bleak understanding of marriage.

"I didn't know my husband very well when we married, and afterward we used to get into bitter fights," said Yoshiko Hirowaki, 56, a store owner. "But then we had children, and I got very busy with the kids and with this shop. Time passed."

Now Mrs. Hirowaki has been married 34 years, and she complains about young people who do not stick to their vows.

"In the old days, wives had more gaman," she said. "Now kids just don't have enough gaman."

The durability of the Japanese family is particularly wondrous because couples are, by international standards, exceptionally incompatible.

One survey asked married men and their wives in 37 countries how they felt about politics, sex, religion, ethics and social issues. Japanese couples ranked dead last in compatibility of views, by a huge margin. Indeed, another survey found that if they were doing it over again, only about one-third of Japanese would marry the same person.

each other, then that is not so much a reason for divorce as it is par for the course.

Even the discovery that one's spouse is having an affair is often not as traumatic in a Japanese marriage as it is in the West. A little sexual infidelity on the part of a man (though not on the part of his wife) was traditionally tolerated, so long as he did not become so besotted as to pay his mistress more than he could afford.

Tsuzuya Fukuyama, who runs a convenience store and will mark her 50th wedding anniversary this year, toasted her hands on an electric heater in the front of the store and declared that a woman would be wrong to get angry if her husband had an affair.

## The durability of the Japanese family is particularly wondrous because couples are, by international standards, exceptionally incompatible

"It's never just one side that's at fault," Mrs. Fukuyama said sternly. "Maybe the husband had an affair because his wife wasn't so hot herself. So she should look at her own faults."

Mrs. Fukuyama's daughter came to her a few years ago, suspecting that her husband was having an affair and asking what to do.

"I told her, 'Once you left this house, you can only come back if you divorce; if you're not prepared to get a divorce, then you'd better be patient,'" Mrs. Fukuyama recalled. "And so she

## A national survey found that 30 percent of fathers spend less than 15 minutes a day on weekends talking with or playing with their children

Incompatibility might not matter so much, however, because Japanese husbands and wives spend very little time talking to each other.

"I kind of feel there's nothing new to say to her," said Masayuki Ogita, an egg farmer, explaining his reticence.

In a small town like Omiya, couples usually have dinner together, but in Japanese cities there are many "7-11 husbands," so called because they leave at 7 A.M. and return after 11 P.M.

Masahiko Kondo now lives in Omiya, working in the chamber of commerce, but he used to be a salesman in several big cities. He would leave work each morning at 7, and about four nights a week would go out for after-work drinking or mahjongg sessions with buddies.

"I only saw my baby on Saturdays or Sundays," said Mr. Kondo, a lanky good-natured man of 37. "But in fact, I really enjoyed that life. It didn't bother me that I never spent time with my kid on weekdays."

Mr. Kondo's wife, Keiko, had her own life, spent with her child and the wives of other workaholic husbands.

"We had birthday parties, but they were with the kids and the mothers," she remembers. "No fathers ever came."

A national survey found that 30 percent of fathers spend less than 15 minutes a day on weekdays talking with or playing with their children. Among eighth graders, 51 percent reported that they never spoke with their fathers on weekdays.

---

**Traditionally, many companies were reluctant to promote employees who had divorced or who had major problems at home**

---

As a result, the figures in Japan for single-parent households can be deceptive. The father is often more a theoretical presence than a homework-helping reality.

Still, younger people sometimes want to see the spouses in daylight, and a result is a gradual change in focus of lives from work to family. Two decades ago, nearly half of young people said in surveys that they wanted their fathers to put priority on work rather than family. Now only one-quarter say that.

## SOCIAL PRESSURES
## Shame Is Keeping Bonds In Place

For those who find themselves desperately unhappy, one source of pressure to keep plugging is shame.

"If you divorce, you lose face in society," said Tatsumi Kinoshita, a tea farmer. "People say, 'His wife escaped.' So folks remain married because they hate to be gossiped about."

Shame is a powerful social sanction in Japan, and it is not just a matter of gossip. Traditionally, many companies were reluctant to promote employees who had divorced or who had major problems at home.

"If you divorce, it weakens your position at work," said Akihiko Kanda, 27, who works in a local government office. "Your bosses won't give you such good ratings, and it'll always be a negative factor."

The idea, Mr. Kanda noted, is that if an employee cannot manage his own life properly, he should not be entrusted with important corporate matters.

Financial sanctions are also a major disincentive for divorce. The mother gets the children in three-quarters of divorces, but most mothers in Japan do not have careers and have few financial resources. Fathers pay child support in only 15 percent of all divorces with children, partly because women often hesitate to go to court to demand payments and partly because men often fail to pay even when the court orders it.

"The main reason for lack of divorce is that women can't support themselves," said Mizuko Kanda, a 51-year-old housewife. "My friends complain about their husbands and say that they'd divorce if they could, but they can't afford to."

The result of these social and economic pressures is clear.

Even in Japan, there are about 24 divorces for every 100 marriages, but that compares with 32 in France, and 42 in England, and 55 in the United States.

## THE OUTLOOK
## Change Creeps In, Imperiling Family

But society is changing in Japan, and it is an open question whether these changes will undermine the traditional family as they have elsewhere around the globe.

The nuclear family has already largely replaced the extended family in Japan, and shame is eroding as a sanction. Haruko Okumura, for example, runs a kindergarten and speaks openly about her divorce.

"My Mom was uneasy about it, but I never had an inferiority complex about being divorced," said Mrs. Okumura, as dozens of children played in the next room. "And people accepted me easily."

Mrs. Okumura sees evidence of the changes in family patterns every day: fathers are playing more of a role in the kindergarten. At Christmas parties and sports contests, fathers have started to show up along with mothers. And Mrs. Okumura believes that divorce is on the upswing.

"If there's a weakening of the economic and social pressures to stay married," she said, "surely divorce rates will soar."

Already divorce rates are rising, approximately doubling over the last 25 years. But couples are very reluctant to divorce when they have children, and so single-parent households account for exactly the same proportion today as in 1965.

Shinsuke Kawaguchi, a young tea farmer, is one of the men for whom life is changing. Americans are not likely to be impressed by Mr. Kawaguchi's open-mindedness, but he is.

"I take good care of my wife," he said. "I may not say 'I love you,' but I do hold her hand. And I might say, after she makes dinner, 'This tastes good.'"

"Of course," Mr. Kawaguchi quickly added, "I wouldn't say that unless I'd just done something really bad."

Even Mrs. Uemura, the elderly woman whose husband used to beat her, said that her husband was treating her better.

"The other day, he tried to pour me a cup of tea," Mrs. Uemura recalled excitedly. "It was a big change. I told all my friends."

---

# UNIT 5
# Gender and Status

## Unit Selections

## Key Points to Consider

- What is a "berdache" and how does it highlight the ways in which different societies accommodate atypical individuals?

- Why do many cultures the world over treat menstruating women as taboo?

- How and why do perceptions of feminine beauty vary from culture to culture?

- Why is it just as wrong to stereotype White Anglo-Saxon Protestants as it is to stereotype other ethnic groups in America?

## Student Website
www.mhcls.com/online

## Internet References
Further information regarding these websites may be found in this book's preface or online.

**Arranged Marriages**
  *http://women3rdworld.miningco.com/cs/arrangedmarriage/*
**Bonobo Sex and Society**
  *http://songweaver.com/info/bonobos.html*
**FGM Research**
  *http://www.amnesty.org/ailib/intcam/femgen/fgm1.htm*
**OMIM Home Page-Online Mendelian Inheritance in Man**
  *http://www3.ncbi.nlm.nih.gov/omim/*
**Reflections on Sinai Bedouin Women**
  *http://www.sherryart.com/women/bedouin.html*

The feminist movement in the United States has had a significant impact upon the development of anthropology. Feminists have rightly charged that anthropologists have tended to gloss over the lives of women in studies of society and culture. In part this is because, until recent times, most anthropologists have been men. The result has been an undue emphasis upon male activities as well as male perspectives in descriptions of particular societies.

These charges, however, have proven to be a firm corrective. In the last few years, anthropologists have begun to study women and, more particularly, the sexual division of labor and its relation to biology as well as to social and political status. In addition, these changes in emphasis have been accompanied by an increase in the number of women in the field. (See "A Woman's Curse?" by Meredith Small.)

Feminist anthropologists have begun to attack critically many of the established anthropological beliefs. They have shown, for example, that field studies of nonhuman primates, which were often used to demonstrate the evolutionary basis of male dominance, distorted the actual evolutionary record by focusing primarily on baboons. (Male baboons are especially dominant and aggressive.) Other, less-quoted primate studies show how dominance and aggression are highly situational phenomena, sensitive to ecological variation. Feminist anthropologists have also shown that the subsistence contribution of women has likewise been ignored by anthropologists. A classic case is that of the !Kung, a hunting and gathering people in southern Africa, where women provide the bulk of the foodstuffs, including most of the available protein, and who, not coincidentally, enjoy a more egalitarian relationship than usual with men. Thus, since political control is a matter of cultural variation, male authority is not biologically predetermined. In fact, there are many cultures in which some men may play a more feminine or, at least, asexual role, as described in "The Berdache Tradition" and, as we see in and "Where Fat Is a Mark of Beauty," gender relationships are deeply embedded in social experience.

Finally, as Laura Zimmer-Tamakosh tells us, in the context of her personal biography ("We Call Ourselves 'Americans'"), the struggle for equality in the modern world has more to do with power and privilege than it has to do with gender.

# The Berdache Tradition

WALTER L. WILLIAMS

**B**ecause it is such a powerful force in the world today, the Western Judeo-Christian tradition is often accepted as the arbiter of "natural" behavior of humans. If Europeans and their descendant nations of North America accept something as normal, then anything different is seen as abnormal. Such a view ignores the great diversity of human existence.

This is the case of the study of gender. How many genders are there? To a modern Anglo-American, nothing might seem more definite than the answer that there are two: men and women. But not all societies around the world agree with Western culture's view that all humans are either women or men. The commonly accepted notion of "the opposite sex," based on anatomy, is itself an artifact of our society's rigid sex roles.

Among many cultures, there have existed different alternatives to "man" or "woman." An alternative role in many American Indian societies is referred to by anthropologists as *berdache*.... The role varied from one Native American culture to another, which is a reflection of the vast diversity of aboriginal New World societies. Small bands of hunter-gatherers existed in some areas, with advanced civilizations of farming peoples in other areas. With hundreds of different languages, economies, religions, and social patterns existing in North America alone, every generalization about a cultural tradition must acknowledge many exceptions.

This diversity is true for the berdache tradition as well, and must be kept in mind. My statements should be read as being specific to a particular culture, with generalizations being treated as loose patterns that might not apply to peoples even in nearby areas.

Briefly, a berdache can be defined as a morphological male who does not fill a society's standard man's role, who has a nonmasculine character. This type of person is often stereotyped as effeminate, but a more accurate characterization is androgyny. Such a person has a clearly recognized and accepted social status, often based on a secure place in the tribal mythology. Berdaches have special ceremonial roles in many Native American religions, and important economic roles in their families. They will do at least some women's work, and mix together much of the behavior, dress, and social roles of women and men. Berdaches gain social prestige by their spiritual, intellectual, or craftwork/artistic contributions, and by their reputation for hard work and generosity. They serve a mediating function between women and men, precisely because their character is seen as distinct from either sex. They are not seen as men, yet they are not seen as women either. They occupy an alternative gender role that is a mixture of diverse elements.

In their erotic behavior berdaches also generally (but not always) take a nonmasculine role, either being asexual or becoming the passive partner in sex with men. In some cultures the berdache might become a wife to a man. This male-male sexual behavior became the focus of an attack on berdaches as "sodomites" by the Europeans who, early on, came into contact with them. From the first Spanish conquistadors to the Western frontiersmen and the Christian missionaries and government officials, Western culture has had a considerable impact on the berdache tradition. In the last two decades, the most recent impact on the tradition is the adaptation of a modern Western gay identity.

To Western eyes berdachism is a complex and puzzling phenomenon, mixing and redefining the very concepts of what is considered male and female. In a culture with only two recognized genders, such individuals are gender nonconformist, abnormal, deviant. But to American Indians, the institution of another gender role means that berdaches are not deviant—indeed, they do conform to the requirements of a custom in which their culture tells them they fit. Berdachism is a way for society to recognize and assimilate some atypical individuals without imposing a change on them or stigmatizing them as deviant. This cultural institution confirms their legitimacy for what they are.

Societies often bestow power upon that which does not neatly fit into the usual. Since no cultural system can explain everything, a common way that many cultures deal with these inconsistencies is to imbue them with negative power, as taboo, pollution, witchcraft, or sin. That which is not understood is seen as a threat. But an alternative method of dealing with such things, or people, is to take them out of the realm of threat and to sanctify them.[1] The berdaches' role as mediator is thus not just between women and men, but also between the physical and the spiritual. American Indian cultures have taken what Western culture calls negative, and made it a positive; they have successfully utilized the different skills and insights of a class of people that Western culture has stigmatized and whose spiritual powers have been wasted.

Many Native Americans also understood that gender roles have to do with more than just biological sex. The standard Western view that one's sex is always a certainty, and that one's gender identity and sex role always conform to one's morphological sex is a view that dies hard. Western thought is typified by such dichotomies of groups perceived to be mutually exclusive: male and female, black and white, right and wrong, good and evil. Clearly, the world is not so simple; such clear divisions are not always realistic. Most American Indian worldviews generally are much more accepting of the ambiguities of life. Acceptance of gender variation in the berdache tradition is typical of many native cultures' approach to life in general.

Overall, these are generalizations based on those Native American societies that had an accepted role for berdaches. Not all cultures recognized such a respected status. Berdachism in aboriginal North America was most established among tribes in four areas: first, the Prairie and western Great Lakes, the northern and central Great Plains, and the lower Mississippi Valley; second, Florida and the Caribbean; third, the Southwest, the Great Basin, and California; and fourth, scattered areas of the Northwest, western Canada, and Alaska. For some reason it is not noticeable in eastern North America, with the exception of its southern rim....

## American Indian Religions

Native American religions offered an explanation for human diversity by their creation stories. In some tribal religions, the Great Spiritual Being is conceived as neither male nor female but as a combination of both. Among the Kamia of the Southwest, for example, the bearer of plant seeds and the introducer of Kamia culture was a man-woman spirit named Warharmi.[2] A key episode of the Zuni creation story involves a battle between the kachina spirits of the agricultural Zunis and the enemy hunter spirits. Every four years an elaborate ceremony commemorates this myth. In the story a kachina spirit called *ko'lhamana* was captured by the enemy spirits and transformed in the process. This transformed spirit became a mediator between the two sides, using his peacemaking skills to merge the differing lifestyles of hunters and farmers. In the ceremony, a dramatic reenactment of the myth, the part of the transformed *ko'lhamana* spirit, is performed by a berdache.[3] The Zuni word for berdache is *lhamana*, denoting its closeness to the spiritual mediator who brought hunting and farming together.[4] The moral of this story is that the berdache was created by the deities for a special purpose, and that this creation led to the improvement of society. The continual reenactment of this story provides a justification for the Zuni berdache in each generation.

In contrast to this, the lack of spiritual justification in a creation myth could denote a lack of tolerance for gender variation. The Pimas, unlike most of their Southwestern neighbors, did not respect a berdache status. *Wi-kovat*, their derogatory word, means "like a girl," but it does not signify a recognized social role. Pima mythology reflects this lack of acceptance, in a folk tale that explains male androgyny as due to Papago witchcraft. Knowing that the Papagos respected berdaches, the Pimas blamed such an occurrence on an alien influence.[5] While the Pimas' condemnatory attitude is unusual, it does point out the importance of spiritual explanations for the acceptance of gender variance in a culture.

Other Native American creation stories stand in sharp contrast to the Pima explanation. A good example is the account of the Navajos, which presents women and men as equals. The Na-vajo origin tale is told as a story of five worlds. The first people were First Man and First Woman, who were created equally and at the same time. The first two worlds that they lived in were bleak and unhappy, so they escaped to the third world. In the third world lived two twins, Turquoise Boy and White Shell Girl, who were the first berdaches. In the Navajo language the world for berdache is *nadle*, which means "changing one" or "one who is transformed." It is applied to hermaphrodites—those who are born with the genitals of both male and female—and also to "those who pretend to be *nadle*," who take on a social role that is distinct from either men or women.[6]

In the third world, First Man and First Woman began farming, with the help of the changing twins. One of the twins noticed some clay and, holding it in the palm of his/her hand, shaped it into the first pottery bowl. Then he/she formed a plate, a water dipper, and a pipe. The second twin observed some reeds and began to weave them, making the first basket. Together they shaped axes and grinding stones from rocks, and hoes from bone. All these new inventions made the people very happy.[7]

The message of this story is that humans are dependent for many good things on the inventiveness of *nadle*. Such individuals were present from the earliest eras of human existence, and their presence was never questioned. They were part of the natural order of the universe, with a special contribution to make.

Later on in the Navajo creation story, White Shell Girl entered the moon and became the Moon Bearer. Turquoise Boy, however, remained with the people. When First Man realized that Turquoise Boy could do all manner of women's work as well as women, all the men left the women and crossed a big river. The men hunted and planted crops. Turquoise Boy ground the corn, cooked the food, and weaved cloth for the men. Four years passed with the women and men separated, and the men were happy with the *nadle*. Later, however the women wanted to learn how to grind corn from the *nadle*, and both the men and women had decided that it was not good to continue living separately. So the women crossed the river and the people were reunited.[8]

They continued living happily in the third world, until one day a great flood began. The people ran to the highest mountaintop, but the water kept rising and they all feared they would be drowned. But just in time, the ever-inventive Turquoise Boy found a large reed. They climbed upward inside the tall hollow reed, and came out at the top into the fourth world. From there, White Shell Girl brought another reed, and the climbed again to the fifth world, which is the present world of the Navajos.[9]

These stories suggest that the very survival of humanity is dependent on the inventiveness of berdaches. With such a mythological belief system, it is no wonder that the Navajos held *nadle* in high regard. The concept of the *nadle* is well formulated in the creation story. As children were educated by these stories, and all Navajos believed in them, the high status accorded to gender variation was passed down from generation to generation. Such stories also provided instruction for *nadle* themselves to live by. A spiritual explanation guaranteed a special place for a person who was considered different but not deviant.

For American Indians, the important explanations of the world are spiritual ones. In their view, there is a deeper reality than the here-and-now. The real essence or wisdom occurs when one finally gives up trying to explain events in terms of "logic" and "reality." Many confusing aspects of existence can better be explained by actions of a multiplicity of spirits. Instead of a concept of a single god, there is an awareness of "that which we do not understand." In Lakota religion, for example, the term *Wakan Tanka* is often translated as "god." But a more proper translation, according to the medicine people who taught me, is "The Great Mystery."[10]

While rationality can explain much, there are limits to human capabilities of understanding. The English language is structured to account for cause and effect. For example, English speakers say, "It is raining," with the implication that there is a cause "it" that leads to rain. Many Indian languages, on the other hand, merely note what is most accurately translated as "raining" as an observable fact. Such an approach brings a freedom to stop worrying about causes of things, and merely to relax and accept that our human insights can go only so far. By not taking ourselves too seriously, or overinflating human importance, we can get beyond the logical world.

The emphasis of American Indian religions, then, is on the spiritual nature of all things. To understand the physical world, one must appreciate the underlying spiritual essence. Then one can begin to see that the physical is only a faint shadow, a partial reflection, of a supernatural and extrarational world. By the Indian view, everything that exists is spiritual. Every object—plants, rocks, water, air, the moon, animals, humans, the earth itself—has a spirit. The spirit of one thing (including a human) is not superior to the spirit of any other. Such a view promotes a sophisticated ecological awareness of the place that humans have in the larger environment. The function of religion is not to try to condemn or to change what exists, but to accept the realities of the world and to appreciate their contributions to life. Everything that exists has a purpose.[11]

One of the basic tenets of American Indian religion is the notion that everything in the universe is related. Nevertheless, things that exist are often seen as having a counterpart: sky and earth, plant and animal, water and fire. In all of these polarities, there exist mediators. The role of the mediator is to hold the polarities together, to keep the world from disintegrating. Polarities exist within human society also. The most important category within Indian society is gender. The notions of Woman and Man underlie much of social interaction and are comparable to the other major polarities. Women, with their nurtural qualities, are associated with the earth, while men are associated with the sky. Women gatherers and farmers deal with plants (of the earth), while men hunters deal with animals.

The mediator between the polarities of woman and man, in the American Indian religious explanation, is a being that combines the elements of both genders. This might be a combination in a physical sense, as in the case of hermaphrodites. Many Native American religions accept this phenomenon in the same way that they accept other variations from the norm. But more important is their acceptance of the idea that gender can be combined in ways other than physical hermaphroditism. The physical aspects of a thing or a person, after all, are not nearly as important as its spirit. American Indians use the concept of a person's *spirit* in the way that other Americans use the concept

of a person's *character*. Consequently, physical hermaphroditism is not necessary for the idea of gender mixing. A person's character, their spiritual essence, is the crucial thing.

## The Berdache's Spirit

Individuals who are physically normal might have the spirit of the other sex, might range somewhere between the two sexes, or might have a spirit that is distinct from either women or men. Whatever category they fall into, they are seen as being different from men. They are accepted spiritually as "Not Man." Whichever option is chosen, Indian religions offer spiritual explanations. Among the Arapahos of the Plains, berdaches are called *haxu'xan* and are seen to be that way as a result of a supernatural gift from birds or animals. Arapaho mythology recounts the story of Nih'a'ca, the first *haxu'xan*. He pretended to be a woman and married the mountain lion, a symbol for masculinity. The myth, as recorded by ethnographer Alfred Kroeber about 1900, recounted that "These people had the natural desire to become women, and as they grew up gradually became women. They gave up the desires of men. They were married to men. They had miraculous power and could do supernatural things. For instance, it was one of them that first made an intoxicant from rainwater."[12] Besides the theme of inventiveness, similar to the Navajo creation story, the berdache role is seen as a product of a "natural desire." Berdaches "gradually became women," which underscores the notion of woman as a social category rather than as a fixed biological entity. Physical biological sex is less important in gender classification than a person's desire—one's spirit.

They myths contain no prescriptions for trying to change berdaches who are acting out their desires of the heart. Like many other cultures' myths, the Zuni origin myths simply sanction the idea that gender can be transformed independently of biological sex.[13] Indeed, myths warn of dire consequences when interference with such a transformation is attempted. Prince Alexander Maximilian of the German state of Wied, traveling in the northern Plains in the 1830s, heard a myth about a warrior who once tried to force a berdache to avoid women's clothing. The berdache resisted, and the warrior shot him with an arrow. Immediately the berdache disappeared, and the warrior saw only a pile of stones with his arrow in them. Since then, the story concluded, no intelligent person would try to coerce a berdache.[14] Making the point even more directly, a Mandan myth told of an Indian who tried to force *mihdake* (berdaches) to give up their distinctive dress and status, which led the spirits to punish many people with death. After that, no Mandans interfered with berdaches.[15]

With this kind of attitude, reinforced by myth and history, the aboriginal view accepts human diversity. The creation story of the Mohave of the Colorado River Valley speaks of a time when people were not sexually differentiated. From this perspective, it is easy to accept that certain individuals might combine elements of masculinity and femininity.[16] A respected Mohave elder, speaking in the 1930s, stated this viewpoint simply: "From the very beginning of the world it was meant that there should be [berdaches], just as it was instituted that there should be shamans. They were intended for that purpose."[17]

This elder also explained that a child's tendencies to become a berdache are apparent early, by about age nine to twelve, before the child reaches puberty: "That is the time when young persons become initiated into the functions of their sex.... None but young people will become berdaches as a rule."[18] Many tribes have a public ceremony that acknowledges the acceptance of berdache status. A Mohave shaman related the ceremony for his tribe: "When the child was about ten years old his relatives would begin discussing his strange ways. Some of them disliked it, but the more intelligent began envisaging an initiation ceremony." The relatives prepare for the ceremony without letting the boy know if it. It is meant to take him by surprise, to be both an initiation and a test of his true inclinations. People from various settlements are invited to attend. The family wants the community to see it and become accustomed to accepting the boy as an *alyha*.

On the day of the ceremony, the shaman explained, the boy is led into a circle: "If the boy showed a willingness to remain standing in the circle, exposed to the public eye, it was almost certain that he would go through with the ceremony. The singer, hidden behind the crowd, began singing the songs. As soon as the sound reached the boy he began to dance as women do." If the boy is unwilling to assume *alyha* status, he would refuse to dance. But if his character—his spirit—is *alyha*, "the song goes right to his heart and he will dance with much intensity. He cannot help it. After the fourth song he is proclaimed." After the ceremony, the boy is carefully bathed and receives a woman's skirt. He is then led back to the dance ground, dressed as an *alyha*, and announces his new feminine name to the crowd. After that he would resent being called by his old male name.[19]

Among the Yuman tribes of the Southwest, the transformation is marked by a social gathering, in which the berdache prepares a meal for the friends of the family.[20] Ethnographer Ruth Underhill, doing fieldwork among the Papago Indians in the early 1930s, wrote that berdaches were common among the Papago Indians, and were usually publicly acknowledged in childhood. She recounted that a boy's parents would test him if they noticed that he preferred female pursuits. The regular pattern, mentioned by many of Underhill's Papago informants, was to build a small brush enclosure. Inside the enclosure they placed a man's bow and arrows, and also a woman's basket. At the appointed time the boy was brought to the enclosure as the adults watched from outside. The boy was told to go inside the circle of brush. Once he was inside, the adults "set fire to the enclosure. They watched what he took with him as he ran out and if it was the basketry materials, they reconciled themselves to his being a berdache."[21]

What is important to recognize in all of these practices is that the assumption of a berdache role was not forced on the boy by others. While adults might have their suspicions, it was only when the child made the proper move that he was considered a berdache. By doing woman's dancing, preparing a meal, or taking the woman's basket he was making an important symbolic gesture. Indian children were not stupid, and they knew the implications of these ceremonies beforehand. A boy in the enclosure could have left without taking anything, or could have taken both the man's and the woman's tools. With the community standing by watching, he was well aware that his choice would mark his assumption of berdache status. Rather than being seen as an involuntary test of his reflexes, this ceremony may be interpreted as a definite statement by the child to take on the berdache role.

Indians do not see the assumption of berdache status, however, as a free will choice on the part of the boy. People felt that the boy was acting out his basic character. The Lakota shaman Lame Deer explained:

> They were not like other men, but the Great Spirit made them *winktes* and we accepted them as such.... We think that if a woman has two little ones growing inside her, if she is going to have twins, sometimes instead of giving birth to two babies they have formed up in her womb into just one, into a half-man/half-woman kind of being.... To us a man is what nature, or his dreams, make him. We accept him for what he wants to be. That's up to him.[22]

While most of the sources indicate that once a person becomes a berdache it is a lifelong status, directions from the spirits determine everything. In at least one documented case, concerning a nineteenth-century Klamath berdache named Lele'ks, he later had a supernatural experience that led him to leave the berdache role. At that time Lele'ks began dressing and acting like a man, then married women, and eventually became one of the most famous Klamath chiefs.[23] What is important is that both in assuming berdache status and in leaving it, supernatural dictate is the determining factor.

# Dreams and Visions

Many tribes see the berdache role as signifying an individual's proclivities as a dreamer and a visionary....

Among the northern Plains and related Great Lakes tribes, the idea of supernatural dictate through dreaming—the vision quest—had its highest development. The goal of the vision quest is to try to get beyond the rational world by sensory deprivation and fasting. By depriving one's body of nourishment, the brain could escape from logical thought and connect with the higher reality of the supernatural. The person doing the quest simply sits and waits for a vision. But a vision might not come easily; the person might have to wait for days.

The best way that I can describe the process is to refer to my own vision quest, which I experienced when I was living on a Lakota reservation in 1982. After a long series of prayers and blessings, the shaman who had prepared me for the ceremony took me out to an isolated area where a sweat lodge had been set up for my quest. As I walked to the spot, I worried that I might not be able to stand it. Would I be overcome by hunger? Could I tolerate the thirst? What would I do if I had to go to the toilet? The shaman told me not to worry, that a whole group of holy people would be praying and singing for me while I was on my quest.

He had me remove my clothes, symbolizing my disconnection from the material would, and crawl into the sweat lodge. Before he left me I asked him, "What do I think about?" He said, "Do not think. Just pray for spiritual guidance." After a prayer he closed the flap tightly and I was left in total darkness. I still do not understand what happened to me during my vision quest, but during the day and a half that I was out there, I never once felt hungry or thirsty or the need to go to the toilet. What happened was an intensely personal experience that I cannot and do not wish to explain, a process of being that cannot be described in rational terms.

When the shaman came to get me at the end of my time, I actually resented having to end it. He did not need to ask if my vision quest were successful. He knew that it was even before seeing me, he explained, because he saw an eagle circling over me while I underwent the quest. He helped interpret the signs I had seen, then after more prayers and singing he led me back to the others. I felt relieved, cleansed, joyful, and serene. I had been through an experience that will be a part of my memories always.

If a vision quest could have such an effect on a person not even raised in Indian society, imagine its impact on a boy who from his earliest years had been waiting for the day when he could seek his vision. Gaining his spiritual power from his first vision, it would tell him what role to take in adult life. The vision might instruct him that he is going to be a great hunter, a craftsman, a warrior, or a shaman. Or it might tell him that he will be a berdache. Among the Lakotas, or Sioux, there are several symbols for various types of visions. A person becomes *wakan* (a sacred person) if she or he dreams of a bear, a wolf, thunder, a buffalo, a white buffalo calf, or Double Woman. Each dream results in a different gift, whether it is the power to cure illness or wounds, a promise of good hunting, or the exalted role of a *heyoka* (doing things backward).

A white buffalo calf is believed to be a berdache. If a person has a dream of the sacred Double Woman, this means that she or he will have the power to seduce men. Males who have a vision of Double Woman are presented with female tools. Taking such tools means that the male will become a berdache. The Lakota word *winkte* is composed of *win*, "woman," and *kte*, "would become."[24] A contemporary Lakota berdache explains, "To become a *winkte*, you have a medicine man put you up on the hill, to search for your vision. "You can become a *winkte* if you truly are by nature. You see a vision of the White Buffalo Calf Pipe. Sometimes it varies. A vision is like a scene in a movie."[25] Another way to become a *winkte* is to have a vision given by a *winkte* from the past.[26]…

By interpreting the result of the vision as being the work of a spirit, the vision quest frees the person from feeling responsible for his transformation. The person might even claim that the change was done against his will and without his control. Such a claim does not suggest a negative attitude about berdache status, because it is common for people to claim reluctance to fulfill their spiritual duty no matter what vision appears to them. Becoming any kind of sacred person involves taking on various social responsibilities and burdens.[27]…

A story was told among the Lakotas in the 1880s of a boy who tried to resist following his vision from Double Woman. But according to Lakota informants "few men succeed in this effort after having taken the strap in the dream." Having rebelled against the instructions given him by the Moon Being, he committed suicide.[28] The moral of that story is that one should

not resist spiritual guidance, because it will lead only to grief. In another case, an Omaha young man told of being addressed by a spirit as "daughter," whereupon he discovered that he was unconsciously using feminine styles of speech. He tried to use male speech patterns, but could not. As a result of this vision, when he returned to his people he resolved himself to dress as a woman.[29] Such stories function to justify personal peculiarities as due to a fate over which the individual has no control.

Despite the usual pattern in Indian societies of using ridicule to enforce conformity, receiving instructions from a vision inhibits others from trying to change the berdache. Ritual explanation provides a way out. It also excuses the community from worrying about the cause of that person's difference, or the feeling that it is society's duty to try to change him.[30] Native American religions, above all else, encourage a basic respect for nature. If nature makes a person different, many Indians conclude, a mere human should not undertake to counter this spiritual dictate. Someone who is "unusual" can be accommodated without being stigmatized as "abnormal." Berdachism is thus not alien or threatening; it is a reflection of spirituality.

# Notes

1. Mary Douglas, *Purity and Danger* (Baltimore: Penguin, 1966), p. 52. I am grateful to Theda Perdue for convincing me that Douglas's ideas apply to berdachism. For an application of Douglas's thesis to berdaches, see James Thayer, "The Berdache of the Northern Plains: A Socioreligious Perspective," *Journal of Anthropological Research 36* (1980): 292–93.

2. E. W. Gifford, "The Kamia of Imperial Valley," *Bureau of American Ethnology Bulletin 97* (1931): 12.

3. By using present tense verbs in this text, I am not implying that such activities are necessarily continuing today. I sometimes use the present tense in the "ethnographic present," unless I use the past tense when I am referring to something that has not continued. Past tense implies that all such practices have disappeared. In the absence of fieldwork to prove such disappearance, I am not prepared to make that assumption, on the historic changes in the berdache tradition.

4. Elsie Clews Parsons, "The Zuni La' Mana," *American Anthropologist 18* (1916): 521; Matilda Coxe Stevenson, "Zuni Indians," *Bureau of American Ethnology Annual Report 23* (1903): 37; Franklin Cushing, "Zuni Creation Myths," *Bureau of American Ethnology Annual Report 13* (1894): 401–3. Will Roscoe clarified this origin story for me.

5. W. W. Hill, "Note on the Pima Berdache," *American Anthropologist 40* (1938): 339.

6. Aileen O'Bryan, "The Dine': Origin Myths of the Navaho Indians," *Bureau of American Ethnology Bulletin 163* (1956): 5; W. W. Hill, "The Status of the Hermaphrodite and Transvestite in Navaho Culture," *American Anthropologist 37* (1935): 273.

7. Martha S. Link, *The Pollen Path: A Collection of Navajo Myths* (Stanford: Stanford University Press, 1956).

8. O'Bryan, "Dine'," pp. 5, 7, 9–10.

9. Ibid.

10. Lakota informants, July 1982. See also William Powers, *Oglala Religion* (Lincoln: University of Nebraska Press, 1977).

11. For this admittedly generalized overview of American Indian religious values, I am indebted to traditionalist informants of many tribes, but especially those of the Lakotas. For a discussion of na-

tive religions see Dennis Tedlock, *Finding the Center* (New York: Dial Press, 1972); Ruth Underhill, *Red Man's Religion* (Chicago: University of Chicago Press, 1965); and Elsi Clews Parsons, *Pueblo Indian Religion* (Chicago: University of Chicago Press, 1939).

12. Alfred Kroeber, "The Arapaho," *Bulletin of the American Museum of Natural History 18* (1902–7): 19.

13. Parsons, "Zuni La' Mana," p. 525.

14. Alexander Maximilian, *Travels in the interior of North America, 1832–1834*, vol. 22 of *Early Western Travels,* ed. Reuben Gold Thwaites, 32 vols. (Cleveland: A. H. Clark, 1906), pp. 283–84, 354. Maximilian was quoted in German in the early homosexual rights book by Ferdinand Karsch-Haack, *Das Gleichgeschlechtliche Leben der Naturvölker* (The same-sex life of nature peoples) (Munich: Verlag von Ernst Reinhardt, 1911; reprinted New York: Arno Press, 1975), pp. 314, 564.

15. Oscar Koch, *Der Indianishe Eros* (Berlin: Verlag Continent, 1925), p. 61.

16. George Devereux, "Institutionalized Homosexuality of the Mohave Indians," *Human Biology 9* (1937): 509.

17. Ibid., p. 501

18. Ibid.

19. Ibid., pp. 508–9.

20. C. Daryll Forde, "Ethnography of the Yuma Indians," *University of California Publications in American Archaeology and Ethnology 28* (1931): 157.

21. Ruth Underhill, *Social Organization of the Papago Indians* (New York: Columbia University Press, 1938), p. 186. This story is also mentioned in Ruth Underhill, ed., *The Autobiography of a Papago Woman* (Menasha, Wisc.: American Anthropological Association, 1936), p. 39.

22. John Fire and Richard Erdoes, *Lame Deer, Seeker of Visions* (New York: Simon and Schuster, 1972), pp. 117, 149.

23. Theodore Stern, *The Klamath Tribe: A People and Their Reservation* (Seattle: University of Washington Press, 1965), pp. 20, 24; Theodore Stern, "Some Sources of Variability in Klamath Mythology," *Journal of American Folklore 69* (1956): 242ff; Leshe Spier, *Klamath Ethnography* (Berkeley: University of California Press, 1930), p. 52.

24. Clark Wissler, "Societies and Ceremonial Associations in the Oglala Division of the Teton Dakota," *Anthoropological Papers of the american Museum of Natural History 11*, pt. 1 (1916): 92; Powers, *Oglala Religion*, pp. 57–59.

25. Ronnie Loud Hawk, Lakota informant 4, July 1982.

26. Terry Calling Eagle, Lakota informant 5, July 1982.

27. James S. Thayer, "The Berdache of the Northern Plains: A Socioreligious Perspective," *Journal of Anthropological Research 36* (1980): 289.

28. Fletcher, "Elk Mystery," p. 281.

29. Alice Fletcher and Francis La Flesche, "The Omaha Tribe," *Bureau of American Ethnology Annual Report 27* (1905–6): 132.

30. Harriet Whitehead offers a valuable discussion of this element of the vision quest in "The Bow and the Burden Strap: A New Look at Institutionalized Homosexuality in Native North America," in *Sexual Meanings,* ed. Sherry Ortner and Harriet Whitehead (Cambridge: Cambridge University Press, 1981), pp. 99–102. See also Erikson, "Childhood," p. 329.

# A Woman's Curse?

**Why do cultures the world over treat menstruating women as taboo? An anthropologist offers a new answer—and a challenge to Western ideas about contraception**

MEREDITH F. SMALL

THE PASSAGE FROM GIRLHOOD TO womanhood is marked by a flow of blood from the uterus. Without elaborate ceremony, often without discussion, girls know that when they begin to menstruate, their world is changed forever. For the next thirty years or so, they will spend much energy having babies, or trying not to, reminded at each menstruation that either way, the biology of reproduction has a major impact on their lives.

Anthropologists have underscored the universal importance of menstruation by documenting how the event is interwoven into the ideology as well as the daily activities of cultures around the world. The customs attached to menstruation take peculiarly negative forms: the so-called menstrual taboos. Those taboos may prohibit a woman from having sex with her husband or from cooking for him. They may bar her from visiting sacred places or taking part in sacred activities. They may forbid her to touch certain items used by men, such as hunting gear or weapons, or to eat certain foods or to wash at certain times. They may also require that a woman paint her face red or wear a red hip cord, or that she segregate herself in a special hut while she is menstruating. In short, the taboos set menstruating women apart from the rest of their society, marking them as impure and polluting.

Anthropologists have studied menstrual taboos for decades, focusing on the negative symbolism of the rituals as a cultural phenomenon. Perhaps, suggested one investigator, taking a Freudian perspective, such taboos reflect the anxiety that men feel about castration, an anxiety that would be prompted by women's genital bleeding. Others have suggested that the taboos serve to prevent menstrual odor from interfering with hunting, or that they protect men from microorganisms that might otherwise be transferred during sexual intercourse with a menstruating woman. Until recently, few investigators had considered the possibility that the taboos—and the very fact of menstruation—might instead exist because they conferred an evolutionary advantage.

In the mid-1980s the anthropologist Beverly I. Strassmann of the University of Michigan in Ann Arbor began to study the ways men and women have evolved to accomplish (and regulate) reproduction. Unlike traditional anthropologists, who focus on how culture affects human behavior, Strassmann was convinced that the important role played by biology was being neglected. Menstruation, she suspected, would be a key for observing and understanding the interplay of biology and culture in human reproductive behavior.

To address the issue, Strassmann decided to seek a culture in which making babies was an ongoing part of adult life. For that she had to get away from industrialized countries, with their bias toward contraception and low birthrates. In a "natural-fertility population," she reasoned, she could more clearly see the connection between the physiology of women and the strategies men and women use to exploit that physiology for their own reproductive ends.

Strassmann ended up in a remote corner of West Africa, living in close quarters with the Dogon, a traditional society whose indigenous religion of ancestor worship requires that menstruating women spend their nights at a small hut. For more than two years Strassmann kept track of the women staying at the hut, and she confirmed the menstruations by testing urine samples for the appropriate hormonal changes. In so doing, she amassed the first long-term data describing how a traditional society appropriates a physiological event—menstruation—and refracts that event through a prism of behaviors and beliefs.

What she found explicitly challenges the conclusions of earlier investigators about the cultural function of menstrual taboos. For the Dogon men, she discovered, enforcing visits to the menstrual hut serves to channel parental resources into the upbringing of their own children. But more, Strassmann, who also had training as a reproductive physiologist, proposed a new theory of why menstruation itself evolved as it did—and again, the answer is essentially a story of conserving resources. Finally, her observations pose provocative questions about women's health in industrialized societies, raising serious doubts about the tactics favored by Western medicine for developing contraceptive technology.

MENSTRUATION IS THE VISIBLE stage of the ovarian cycle, orchestrated primarily by hormones secreted by the ovaries: progesterone and a family of hormones called estrogens. At the beginning of each cycle (by convention, the first day of a woman's period) the levels of the estrogens begin to rise. After about five days, as their concentrations increase, they cause the blood- and nutrient-rich inner lining of the uterus, called the endometrium, to thicken and acquire a densely branching network of blood vessels. At about the middle of the cycle, ovulation takes place, and an egg makes its way from one of the two ovaries down one of the paired fallopian tubes to the uterus. The follicle from which the egg was released in the ovary now begins to secrete progesterone as well as estrogens, and the progesterone causes the endometrium to swell and become even richer with blood vessels—in short, fully ready for a pregnancy, should conception take place and the fertilized egg become implanted.

If conception does take place, the levels of estrogens and progesterone continue to rise throughout the pregnancy. That keeps the endometrium thick enough to support the quickening life inside the uterus. When the baby is born and the new mother begins nursing, the estrogens and progesterone fall to their initial levels, and lactation hormones keep them suppressed. The uterus thus lies quiescent until frequent lactation ends, which triggers the return to ovulation.

If conception does not take place after ovulation, all the ovarian hormones also drop to their initial levels, and menstruation—the shedding of part of the uterine lining—begins. The lining is divided into three layers: a basal layer that is constantly maintained, and two superficial layers, which shed and regrow with each menstrual cycle. All mammals undergo cyclical changes in the state of the endometrium. In most mammals the sloughed-off layers are resorbed into the body if fertilization does not take place. But in some higher primates, including humans, some of the shed endometrium is not resorbed. The shed lining, along with some blood, flows from the body through the vaginal opening, a process that in humans typically lasts from three to five days.

OF COURSE, PHYSIOLOGICAL FACTS alone do not explain why so many human groups have infused a bodily function with symbolic meaning. And so in 1986 Strassmann found herself driving through the Sahel region of West Africa at the peak of the hot season, heading for a sandstone cliff called the Bandiagara Escarpment, in Mali. There, permanent Dogon villages of mud or stone houses dotted the rocky plateau. The menstrual huts were obvious: round, low-roofed buildings set apart from the rectangular dwellings of the rest of the village.

The Dogon are a society of millet and onion farmers who endorse polygyny, and they maintain their traditional culture despite the occasional visits of outsiders. In a few Dogon villages, in fact, tourists are fairly common, and ethnographers had frequently studied the Dogon language, religion and social structure before Strassmann's arrival. But her visit was the first time

someone from the outside wanted to delve into an intimate issue in such detail.

It took Strassmann a series of hikes among villages, and long talks with male elders under the thatched-roof shelters where they typically gather, to find the appropriate sites for her research. She gained permission for her study in fourteen villages, eventually choosing two. That exceptional welcome, she thinks, emphasized the universality of her interests. "I'm working on all the things that really matter to [the Dogon]—fertility, economics—so they never questioned my motives or wondered why I would be interested in these things," she says. "It seemed obvious to them." She set up shop for the next two and a half years in a stone house in the village, with no running water or electricity. Eating the daily fare of the Dogon, millet porridge, she and a research assistant began to integrate themselves into village life, learning the language, getting to know people and tracking visits to the menstrual huts.

Following the movements of menstruating women was surprisingly easy. The menstrual huts are situated outside the walled compounds of the village, but in full view of the men's thatched-roof shelters. As the men relax under their shelters, they can readily see who leaves the huts in the morning and returns to them in the evening. And as nonmenstruating women pass the huts on their way to and from the fields or to other compounds, they too can see who is spending the night there. Strassmann found that when she left her house in the evening to take data, any of the villagers could accurately predict whom she would find in the menstrual huts.

THE HUTS THEMSELVES ARE CRAMPED, dark buildings—hardly places where a woman might go to escape the drudgery of work or to avoid an argument with her husband or a co-wife. The huts sometimes become so crowded that some occupants are forced outside—making the women even more conspicuous. Although babies and toddlers can go with their mothers to the huts, the women consigned there are not allowed to spend time with the rest of their families. They must cook with special pots, not their usual household possessions. Yet they are still expected to do their usual jobs, such as working in the fields.

Why, Strassmann wondered, would anyone put up with such conditions?

The answer, for the Dogon, is that a menstruating woman is a threat to the sanctity of religious altars, where men pray and make sacrifices for the protection of their fields, their families and their village. If menstruating women come near the altars, which are situated both indoors and outdoors, the Dogon believe that their aura of pollution will ruin the altars and bring calamities upon the village. The belief is so ingrained that the women themselves have internalized it, feeling its burden of responsibility and potential guilt. Thus violations of the taboo are rare, because a menstruating woman who breaks the rules knows that she is personally responsible if calamities occur.

NEVERTHELESS, STRASSMANN STILL thought a more functional explanation for menstrual taboos might also exist, one closely related to reproduction. As she was well aware, even before her studies among the Dogon, people around the world have a fairly sophisticated view of how reproduction works. In general, people everywhere know full well that menstruation signals the absence of a pregnancy and the possibility of another one. More precisely, Strassmann could frame her hypothesis by reasoning as follows: Across cultures, men and women recognize that a lack of menstrual cycling in a woman implies she is either pregnant, lactating or menopausal. Moreover, at least among natural-fertility cultures that do not practice birth control, continual cycles during peak reproductive years imply to people in those cultures that a woman is sterile. Thus, even though people might not be able to pinpoint ovulation, they can easily identify whether a woman will soon be ready to conceive on the basis of whether she is menstruating. And that leads straight to Strassmann's insightful hypothesis about the role of menstrual taboos: information about menstruation can be a means of tracking paternity.

"There are two important pieces of information for assessing paternity," Strassmann notes: timing of intercourse and timing of menstruation. "By forcing women to signal menstruation, men are trying to gain equal access to one part of that critical information." Such information, she explains, is crucial to Dogon men, because they invest so many resources in their own offspring. Descent is marked through the male line; land and the food that comes from the land is passed down from fathers to sons. Information about paternity is thus crucial to a man's entire lineage. And because each man has as many as four wives, he cannot possibly track them all. So forcing women to signal their menstrual periods, or lack thereof, helps men avoid cuckoldry.

TO TEST HER HYPOTHESIS, STRASSMANN tracked residence in the menstrual huts for 736 consecutive days, collecting data on 477 complete cycles. She noted who was at each hut and how long each woman stayed. She also collected urine from ninety-three women over a ten-week period, to check the correlation between residence in the menstrual hut and the fact of menstruation.

The combination of ethnographic records and urinalyses showed that the Dogon women mostly play by the rules. In 86 percent of the hormonally detected menstruations, women went to the hut. Moreover, none of the tested women went to the hut when they were not menstruating. In the remaining 14 percent of the tested menstruations, women stayed home from the hut, in violation of the taboo, but some were near menopause and so not at high risk for pregnancy. More important, none of the women who violated the taboo did it twice in a row. Even they were largely willing to comply.

Thus, Strassmann concluded, the huts do indeed convey a fairly reliable signal, to men and to everyone else, about the status of a woman's fertility. When she leaves the hut, she is considered ready to conceive. When she stops going to the hut, she is evidently pregnant or menopausal. And women of prime reproductive age who visit the hut on a regular basis are clearly infertile.

It also became clear to Strassmann that the Dogon do indeed use that information to make paternity decisions. In several cases a man was forced to marry a pregnant woman, simply because everyone knew that the man had been the woman's first sexual partner after her last visit to the menstrual hut. Strassmann followed one case in which a child was being brought up by a man because he was the mother's first sexual partner after a hut visit, even though the woman soon married a different man. (The woman already knew she was pregnant by the first man at the time of her marriage, and she did not visit the menstrual hut before she married. Thus the truth was obvious to everyone, and the real father took the child.)

In general, women are cooperative players in the game because without a man, a woman has no way to support herself or her children. But women follow the taboo reluctantly. They complain about going to the hut. And if their husbands convert from the traditional religion of the Dogon to a religion that does not impose menstrual taboos, such as Islam or Christianity, the women quickly cease visiting the hut. Not that such a religious conversion quells a man's interest in his wife's fidelity: far from it. But the rules change. Perhaps the sanctions of the new religion against infidelity help keep women faithful, so the men can relax their guard. Or perhaps the men are willing to trade the reproductive advantages of the menstrual taboo for the economic benefits gained by converting to the new religion. Whatever the case, Strassmann found an almost perfect correlation between a husband's religion and his wives' attendance at the hut. In sum, the taboo is established by men, backed by supernatural forces, and internalized and accepted by women until the men release them from the belief.

BUT BEYOND THE CULTURAL MACHINATIONS of men and women that Strassmann expected to find, her data show something even more fundamental—and surprising—about female biology. On average, she calculates, a woman in a natural-fertility population such as the Dogon has only about 110 menstrual periods in her lifetime. The rest of the time she will be prepubescent, pregnant, lactating or menopausal. Women in industrialized cultures, by contrast, have more than three times as many cycles: 350 to 400, on average, in a lifetime. They reach menarche (their first menstruation) earlier—at age twelve and a half, compared with the onset age of sixteen in natural-fertility cultures. They have fewer babies, and they lactate hardly at all. All those factors lead women in the industrialized world to a lifetime of nearly continuous menstrual cycling.

The big contrast in cycling profiles during the reproductive years can be traced specifically to lactation. Women in more traditional societies spend most of their reproductive years in lactation amenorrhea, the state in which the hormonal changes required for nursing suppress ovulation and inhibit menstruation. And it is not just that the Dogon bear more children (eight to nine on average); they also nurse each child on demand rather than in scheduled bouts, all through the night as well as the day, and intensely enough that ovulation simply stops for about twenty months per child. Women in industrialized societies typically do not breast-feed as intensely (or at all), and rarely breast-feed each child for as long as the Dogon women do. (The average for American women is four months.)

The Dogon experience with menstruation may be far more typical of the human condition over most of evolutionary history than is the standard menstrual experience in industrialized nations. If so, Strassmann's findings alter some of the most closely held beliefs about female biology. Contrary to what the Western medical establishment might think, it is not particularly "normal" to menstruate each month. The female body, according to Strassmann, is biologically designed to spend much more time in lactation amenorrhea than in menstrual cycling. That in itself suggests that oral contraceptives, which alter hormone levels to suppress ovulation and produce a bleeding, could be forcing a continual state of cycling for which the body is ill-prepared. Women might be better protected against reproductive cancers if their contraceptives mimicked lactation amenorrhea and depressed the female reproductive hormones, rather than forcing the continual ebb and flow of menstrual cycles.

Strassmann's data also call into question a recently popularized idea about menstruation: that regular menstrual cycles might be immunologically beneficial for women. In 1993 the controversial writer Margie Profet, whose ideas about evolutionary and reproductive biology have received vast media attention, proposed in *The Quarterly Review of Biology* that menstruation could have such an adaptive value. She noted that viruses and bacteria regularly enter the female body on the backs of sperm, and she hypothesized that the best way to get them out is to flush them out. Here, then, was a positive, adaptive role for something unpleasant, an evolutionary reason for suffering cramps each month. Menstruation, according to Profet, had evolved to rid the body of pathogens. The "anti-pathogen" theory was an exciting hypothesis, and it helped win Profet a MacArthur Foundation award. But Strassmann's work soon showed that Profet's ideas could not be supported because of one simple fact: under less-industrialized conditions, women menstruate relatively rarely.

Instead, Strassmann notes, if there is an adaptive value to menstruation, it is ultimately a strategy to conserve the body's resources. She estimates that maintaining the endometrial lining during the second half of the ovarian cycle takes substantial metabolic energy. Once the endometrium is built up and ready to receive a fertilized egg, the tissue requires a sevenfold metabolic increase to remain rich in blood and ready to support a pregnancy. Hence, if no pregnancy is forthcoming, it makes a lot of sense for the body to let part of the endometrium slough off and then regenerate itself, instead of maintaining that rather costly but unneeded tissue. Such energy conservation is common among vertebrates: male rhesus monkeys have shrunken testes during their nonbreeding season, Burmese pythons shrink

their guts when they are not digesting, and hibernating animals put their metabolisms on hold.

Strassmann also suggests that periodically ridding oneself of the endometrium could make a difference to a woman's long-term survival. Because female reproductive hormones affect the brain and other tissues, the metabolism of the entire body is involved during cycling. Strassmann estimates that by keeping hormonal low through half the cycle, a woman can save about six days' worth of energy for every four nonconceptive cycles. Such caloric conservation might have proved useful to early hominids who lived by hunting and gathering, and even today it might be helpful for women living in less affluent circumstances than the ones common in the industrialized West.

B UT PERHAPS THE MOST PROVOCATIVE implications of Strassmann's work have to do with women's health. In 1994 a group of physicians and anthropologists published a paper, also in *The Quarterly Review of Biology*, suggesting that the reproductive histories and lifestyles of women in industrialized cultures are at odds with women's naturally evolved biology, and that the differences lead to greater risks of reproductive cancers. For example, the investigators estimated that women in affluent cultures may have a hundredfold greater risk of breast cancer than do women who subsist by hunting and gathering. The increased risk is probably caused not only by low levels of exercise and a high-fat diet, but also by a relatively high number of menstrual cycles over a lifetime. Repeated exposure to the hormones of the ovarian cycle—because of early menarche, late menopause, lack of pregnancy and little or no breast-feeding—is implicated in other reproductive cancers as well.

Those of us in industrialized cultures have been running an experiment on ourselves. The body evolved over millions of years to move across the landscape looking for food, to live in small kin-based groups, to make babies at intervals of four years or so and to invest heavily in each child by nursing intensely for years. How many women now follow those traditional patterns? We move little, we rely on others to get our food, and we rarely reproduce or lactate. Those culturally initiated shifts in lifestyles may pose biological risks.

Our task is not to overcome that biology, but to work with it. Now that we have a better idea of how the female body was designed, it may be time to rework our lifestyles and change some of our expectations. It may be time to borrow from our distant past or from our contemporaries in distant cultures, and treat our bodies more as nature intended.

**MEREDITH F. SMALL** is a professor of anthropology at Cornell University in Ithaca, New York. Her latest book, *Our Babies, Ourselves: How Biology And Culture Shape The Way We Parent*, was published in May 1998 [see Laurence A. Marschall's review in Books in Brief, November/December 1998].

Reprinted by permission of *The Sciences*, January/February 1999, pp. 24–29. © 1999 by the New York Academy of Science. For subscriptions e-mail: publications@nyas.org.

# Where Fat Is a Mark of Beauty

**In a rite of passage, some Nigerian girls spend months gaining weight and learning customs in a special room. "To be called a 'slim princess' is an abuse," says a defender of the practice.**

ANN M. SIMMONS

AKPABUYO, Nigeria—Margaret Bassey Ene currently has one mission in life: gaining weight.

The Nigerian teenager has spent every day since early June in a "fattening room" specially set aside in her father's mud-and-thatch house. Most of her waking hours are spent eating bowl after bowl of rice, yams, plantains, beans and *gari*, a porridge-like mixture of dried cassava and water.

After three more months of starchy diet and forced inactivity, Margaret will be ready to reenter society bearing the traditional mark of female beauty among her Efik people: fat.

In contrast to many Western cultures where thin is in, many culture-conscious people in the Efik and other communities in Nigeria's southeastern Cross River state hail a woman's rotundity as a sign of good health, prosperity and allure.

The fattening room is at the center of a centuries-old rite of passage from maidenhood to womanhood. The months spent in pursuit of poundage are supplemented by daily visits from elderly matrons who impart tips on how to be a successful wife and mother. Nowadays, though, girls who are not yet marriage-bound do a tour in the rooms purely as a coming-of-age ceremony. And sometimes, nursing mothers return to the rooms to put on more weight.

"The fattening room is like a kind of school where the girl is taught about motherhood," said Sylvester Odey, director of the Cultural Center Board in Calabar, capital of Cross River state. "Your daily routine is to sleep, eat and grow fat."

Like many traditional African customs, the fattening room is facing relentless pressure from Western influences. Health campaigns linking excess fat to heart disease and other illnesses are changing the eating habits of many Nigerians, and urban dwellers are opting out of the time-consuming process.

Effiong Okon Etim, an Efik village chief in the district of Akpabuyo, said some families cannot afford to constantly feed a daughter for more than a few months. That compares with a stay of up to two years, as was common earlier this century, he said.

But the practice continues partly because "people might laugh at you because you didn't have money to allow your child to pass through the rite of passage," Etim said. What's more, many believe an unfattened girl will be sickly or unable to bear children.

Etim, 65, put his two daughters in a fattening room together when they were 12 and 15 years old, but some girls undergo the process as early as age 7, after undergoing the controversial practice of genital excision.

## Bigger is Better, According to Custom

As for how fat is fat enough, there is no set standard. But the unwritten rule is the bigger the better, said Mkoyo Edet, Etim's sister.

"Beauty is in the weight," said Edet, a woman in her 50s who spent three months in a fattening room when she was 7. "To be called a 'slim princess' is an abuse. The girl is fed constantly whether she likes it or not."

In Margaret's family, there was never any question that she would enter the fattening room.

"We inherited it from our forefathers; it is one of the heritages we must continue," said Edet Essien Okon, 25, Margaret's stepfather and a language and linguistics graduate of the University of Calabar. "It's a good thing to do; it's an initiation rite."

His wife, Nkoyo Effiong, 27, agreed: "As a woman, I feel it is proper for me to put my daughter in there, so she can be educated."

Effiong, a mother of five, spent four months in a fattening room at the age of 10.

Margaret, an attractive girl with a cheerful smile and hair plaited in fluffy bumps, needs only six months in the fattening room because she was already naturally plump, her stepfather said.

During the process, she is treated as a goddess, but the days are monotonous. To amuse herself, Margaret has only an instrument made out of a soda bottle with a hole in it, which she taps on her hand to play traditional tunes.

Still, the 16-year-old says she is enjoying the highly ritualized fattening practice.

"I'm very happy about this," she said, her belly already distended over the waist of her loincloth. "I enjoy the food, except for *gari*."

Day in, day out, Margaret must sit cross-legged on a special stool inside the secluded fattening room. When it is time to eat, she sits on the floor on a large, dried plantain leaf, which also serves as her bed. She washes down the mounds of food with huge pots of water and takes traditional medicine made from leaves and herbs to ensure proper digestion.

As part of the rite, Margaret's face is decorated with a white, claylike chalk.

"You have to prepare the child so that if a man sees her, she will be attractive," Chief Etim said.

Tufts of palm leaf fiber, braided and dyed red, are hung around Margaret's neck and tied like bangles around her wrists and ankles. They are adjusted as she grows.

Typically, Margaret would receive body massages using the white chalk powder mixed with heavy red palm oil. But the teen said her parents believe the skin-softening, blood-stimulating massages might cause her to expand further than necessary.

Margaret is barred from doing her usual chores or any other strenuous physical activities. And she is forbidden to receive visitors, save for the half a dozen matrons who school Margaret in the etiquette of the Efik clan.

They teach her such basics as how to sit, walk and talk in front of her husband. And they impart wisdom about cleaning, sewing, child care and cooking—Efik women are known throughout Nigeria for their chicken pepper soup, pounded yams and other culinary creations.

"They advise me to keep calm and quiet, to eat the *gari*, and not to have many boyfriends so that I avoid unwanted pregnancy," Margaret said of her matron teachers. "They say that unless you have passed through this, you will not be a full-grown woman."

What little exercise Margaret gets comes in dance lessons. The matrons teach her the traditional *ekombi*, which she will be expected to perform before an audience on the day she emerges from seclusion—usually on the girl's wedding day, Etim said.

But Okon said his aim is to prepare his stepdaughter for the future, not to marry her off immediately. Efik girls receive more education than girls in most parts of Nigeria, and Okon hopes Margaret will return to school and embark on a career as a seamstress before getting married.

# Weddings Also Steeped in Tradition

Once she does wed, Margaret will probably honor southeastern Nigeria's rich marriage tradition. It begins with a letter from the family of the groom to the family of the bride, explaining that "our son has seen a flower, a jewel, or something beautiful in your family, that we are interested in," said Josephine Effah-Chukwuma, program officer for women and children at the Constitutional Rights Project, a law-oriented nongovernmental organization based in the Nigerian commercial capital of Lagos.

If the girl and her family consent, a meeting is arranged. The groom and his relatives arrive with alcoholic beverages, soft drinks and native brews, and the bride's parents provide the food. The would-be bride's name is never uttered, and the couple are not allowed to speak, but if all goes well, a date is set for handing over the dowry. On that occasion, the bride's parents receive about $30 as a token of appreciation for their care of the young woman. "If you make the groom pay too much, it is like selling your daughter," Effah-Chukwuma said. Then, more drinks are served, and the engagement is official.

On the day of the wedding, the bride sits on a specially built wooden throne, covered by an extravagantly decorated canopy. Maidens surround her as relatives bestow gifts such as pots, pans, brooms, plates, glasses, table covers—everything she will need to start her new home. During the festivities, the bride changes clothes three times.

The high point is the performance of the *ekombi*, in which the bride twists and twirls, shielded by maidens and resisting the advances of her husband. It is his task to break through the ring and claim his bride.

Traditionalists are glad that some wedding customs are thriving despite the onslaught of modernity.

Traditional weddings are much more prevalent in southeastern Nigeria than so-called white weddings, introduced by colonialists and conducted in a church or registry office.

"In order to be considered married, you have to be married in the traditional way," said Maureen Okon, a woman of the Qua ethnic group who wed seven years ago but skipped the fattening room because she did not want to sacrifice the time. "Tradition identifies a people. It is important to keep up a culture. There is quite a bit of beauty in Efik and Qua marriages."

# We Call Ourselves "Americans"

LAURA ZIMMER-TAMAKOSHI

## Wasps by Any Other Name?

The first time I was called a "WASP" to my face was at the University of Pennsylvania, in an undergraduate class on American Ethnicity. At the time, I was a thirty-two-year-old, part-time "nontraditional" student in anthropology. Nontraditional referred to my being a mother and housewife, while commuting to Philadelphia two or three times a week from the suburbs. Hurt by my accuser's evident hostility, I was further stunned by the realization that I was indeed the closest thing to a WASP in the class of twenty-five or so students. My defense that I am an American mongrel (part English, Scots Irish, German, and Cherokee) and that I came from a less privileged background than any of the other students was swept aside. I was a member of an "oppressive ethnic group" and as such was on the giving (versus the receiving) end of WASP snubs and prejudices. Because of my "privileged ethnicity" I was seen as more likely to succeed and to enter the ranks of America's elite society.

Over the years I have pondered my classmates' assessment of my ethnicity and future life chances. Certainly WASP was not my chosen identity, nor was it a fair reflection of my experiential reality. To lump together millions of white, AngloSaxonish type peoples is to ignore distinctive varieties of white ethnic experience in this country. One need think only of the Shakers or Mormons to realize the distortions involved in assuming a homogeneity among white Anglo-Saxon Protestants (Kephart 1982). Moreover, it is as wrong to assume that all WASPs occupy the same level in society as it would be to assume that the men hanging out on Talley's Corner in Liebow's classic (1967) are representative of all black men in this country, or that the youthful gang members from the Italian slum described in Whyte *Streetcorner Society* (1955) are typical of all Italian-Americans. Recently, there has been a chipping away of such monolithic categories as "WASP" and "white power structure," more among the academic community, however, than among the general populace. In a book of essays on the multicultural experience in America (Aguero 1993) several apparently white, Anglo-Saxon Protestant contributors deny having—as women, formerly working class white males, and gay men—any part in the "white power structure" in this country. While "power structure" implies an elite aspect to the term WASP, the essays suggest that most white middle-class males are also "in the soup" as it were.

Interestingly, while many Americans are struggling with their identities, elite WASPs who are part of America's real power elite have no such crisis to deal with. While they may or may not like the term, they are a self-conscious and proud elite, well bred, well educated, well connected, and capable of protecting their economic and social privileges against persons of the "wrong" class, religion, ethnicity, or race (Mills 1956:64). For example, while America's elite occasionally welcome "new money" into their families through the marriage of a son or a daughter, money is only one requirement for acceptance. The other requirement is that the newcomer be white, Anglo-Saxon Protestant. In *The Proper Bostonians,* Cleveland Amory (1947:12–13), himself a proper Bostonian, noted that out of a city of some 2,350,000 people in the mid-1940s, only 8,000 were listed in the Boston Social Register. Out of these 8,000, there was only one Jewish man and less than a dozen Catholic families. Excluded were some one million Irish Bostonians, as well as hundreds of thousands Bostonians of Italian, Jewish, Polish, German, and other backgrounds, including several hundred thousand persons whose backgrounds were Anglo-Saxon and Protestant. No blacks or Asians were included in the Register.

A member of the Philadelphia elite, Digby Baltzell (1964), criticized this ethnic and racial exclusiveness and class snobbery as detrimental, keeping out many clever and bright people from America's leadership class. Elizabeth Ameisen, a "main line WASP" and anthropology student, took a different approach to the subject of WASP racism, arguing that it perpetuates WASP position and privilege by making clear the boundaries of this particular social group. Ameisen recounts how she and a group of friends were once refused admittance to the Premier Club, to which her family belonged, because one of the girls had a "Jewish-sounding name" (1990:54). Ameisen gives plentiful examples from her interviews with main-line WASPs of open and ingrained racism. This racism came in the form of jokes and other behaviors. Asking her younger informants if they ever would consider marrying a black person or person of the Jewish faith, one young girl said she was dating a Jewish boy but that her father would likely disinherit her if she married him. Another said, "I could never marry anybody black, my father would kill me" (1990:73). In a recent case where the son of a respected Philadelphia family did marry a black woman, "They have been virtually ignored by his family and Philadelphia society in general" (1990:73).

By contrast, my identity and that of many other white Americans is based less on "good breeding" and wealth than on a sense of being a fundamental part of America's history. Most people, including white Anglo-Saxon Protestants, simply call themselves "Americans." In the case of my own family, although our ancestors helped wrestle this land from its original heirs, they have been here for centuries, in many cases before the American Revolution. Our English or German heritage is no longer salient to our self-identities, and no stories are passed down in my family about "life in the old country." Rather, it is clear that my ancestors came here to make a better life for themselves. The stories that have come down to me, the product of a Pennsylvanian and a Floridian, are part of an American history text. I have, for example, forbearers who fought on both sides of the American Revolution and Civil War, who farmed and homesteaded in Pennsylvania, in the mountains of North Carolina and Florida Keys. Daniel Boone was a relative who pushed forward the American frontier into Kentucky and Missouri. Two of my ancestors, Frankie and Johnny Silvers, had a folksong written about them. Frankie was the first woman to be hanged in North Carolina for killing Johnny, and then chopping up his body and burning it in the wood stove in their log cabin.

While elite WASPs left the old country for many of the same reasons as non-elite WASPS (e.g., religious freedom, economic opportunity, and adventure), they generally came to this land already wealthy, in charge of the new religions and settlements, and conscious of themselves as America's power elite. Elite WASPs did not start from scratch like other settlers, and they felt no affinity with the "American Rabble." In his account of the Boston Brahmins and Philadelphia Gentlemen, Baltzell (1979:248) demonstrates how many of the founding families of Puritan Boston (e.g., Adamses and Cabots) and Quaker Philadelphia (e.g., Biddles) have enjoyed an unbroken tradition to the present of upper-class affiliations and leadership in church, state, and business. These privileges were maintained in part through private education. Baltzell points out that of the 207 institutions of higher learning in America founded before the Civil War (Harvard was founded in 1636), all but 27 were founded by religious groups, most of which were "heirs of rational and hierarchical Calvinism" stirring the "passions of the successful to use their privileges to take the lead in many areas of American Life" (1979: 38–39). C. Wright Mills noted how many of the nation's command posts were occupied by the elite in 1942. He points out that, "of the thirty-two ambassadors and the top ministers of 1942, almost half were graduates of private preparatory schools frequented by children of the Metropolitan 400; and of the top one hundred and eighteen officers in the Foreign Service, fifty-one were Harvard, Princeton, or Yale" (Mills 1956:207). While many of our nation's presidents and congressmen have come from elite WASP families, just as significantly, the majority of their advisors and White House staff have come from the same backgrounds, including attendance at Ivy League colleges (Mills 1956:234).

While the power WASPs snub the *nouveau riche*, money is an important element of their power, and, unlike most Americans, they started out with it and have continued making a lot of it. While my own ancestors were working small farms, wealthy Americans were cooking up schemes that resulted in land speculation and higher land taxes (e.g., Flagler's Railroad to Key West, Florida). The resulting higher taxes drove most of my

grandparents' generation off their farms and into towns and cities where they worked as nurses aides, clerks, or in unskilled jobs for meager wages. During the Great Depression of the 1930s, they and their children suffered considerable hardships. Being too proud to accept charity, they deepened their work ethic and desire never to be poor again. Later, with the help of working wives, night classes, and, in some cases, the G.I. Bill, some of my uncles became small-town insurance agents, realtors, and bankers. In contrast, most elite families made it through the Depression with few difficulties, being connected to one another and economically well advised against total ruin. Mills argued that middle-class competitiveness and mistrust is lacking among America's power elite (1956:66). He points out that the chief executives of America's financial institutions, many well-known lawyers and politicians, and the very rich are not distinct and segregated groups (1956:119). Rather, they are friends, relatives, partners, and members of the same clubs, churches, and schools. They are "insiders" who share information and tips with one another. Their pride is in their class and extended families, not the individual or nuclear family that is the obsession of most Americans. While the middle class grew rapidly following World War II, and came to include members of many different ethnic and racial groups, the upper class remained content to keep their wealth and power within their white, largely Anglo-Saxon Protestant ranks. One need only look at the back of today's stock reports to see that the top executives and board members are almost to a man white and upper class. Multicultural and egalitarian gender images are more hype than corporate reality.

For my generation of "baby-boomers," being female, white, and middle class looms larger in my self- or ascribed identity than my WASP ancestry. For my kind of "American," America stands for freedom, high aspirations, and the possibility of success, unless you are a woman and then there are limitations on your choices, aspirations, and the degree of success you are likely to achieve. Many middle-class and working-class women of all ethnic and racial groups have been fighting to improve their working and living conditions and to achieve parity with men. Not so among women of the upper class. According to Elizabeth Ameisen, WASP women are satisfied to take second place to their husbands, busying themselves with their families, friends, homes, charities, and clubs. In the mid-1980s, when a few younger women wanted to challenge the Premier Club's all-male member policy, some women were shocked and agreed with the harsh words of one matron that, "We don't need a woman on the Board of Governors. Women are putting themselves in places they don't belong today. The men have the last say. It's a men's club and it should stay that way" (Ameisen 1990:53). Lest we think elite women are more passive than other women, it should be remembered that many are educated at places like Bryn Mawr and Vassar, where they are taught to reject organized feminism as "unnecessary" and "unseemly," but where they also are encouraged to become self-confident and competent women. In a chapter on "The Boston Woman," Amory describes the "female of the Proper Bostonian species" as possessing an incredible vitality and determination to fill their lives with activity. During World War II, one First Family woman, "in the neighborhood of seventy," spent her Mondays and Fridays running ward errands for four hours a day in the Massachusetts General Hospital, her Tuesdays traveling all over town for Boston's Family Welfare Society, and her Thursdays at the Red Cross" (1947: 95–97). Amory goes on to recount that she liked to keep her Wednesdays and Saturdays open for gardening and other compulsory pursuits of Proper Boston women: lectures, concerts, indignation meetings, etc. Further, while such women deferred to the men in the family, they did not do so, however, to men of lower classes (1947:110).

In much of the world, the term "American" has become a negative or dirty word as Americans and members of other core countries are blamed (justifiably or unjustifiably) for the destruction of the environment and exploitation of indigenous peoples. White Americans especially are blamed for destroying the planet with their heavy consumption patterns. There are various degrees, however, of guilt and differences in white Americans' powers and ethics. Moreover, it would be fairer to say that all Americans out-consume the rest of the world. To be sure, the major decision-makers and owners of the multinational companies live far from the consequences of their actions, and it is the middle and lower classes who must face the consequences of the misjudgments and the misdeeds of the higher-ups. An example of the intertwining and direction of consequences from elite policy-making is the case of "red-lining." In the 1950s and 1960s, America became a nation of suburbs with white ethnics fleeing the discomforts of city life. Poor rural blacks left the South to seek work in the northern cities and took their places. Watching the trends, big-city bankers and realtors bought up urban neighborhoods. Rather than make low-cost home improvement loans and mortgages available to the new arrivals, they circled large residential areas in red ink on their maps as "undesirable" for such loans and better slated for future business development.

They then rented the rundown properties at exorbitant cost to the millions of blacks seeking a "better life" in northern cities (Polenberg 1980). Old neighborhoods were turned into soul-destroying places and the center of the race riots of the 1960s and 1970s. Predictably, the persons hurt were not the elite whites, but lower-class blacks and whites.

## The Things We Do (or Don't Do)

According to Polenberg (1980), during World War II there was a sense of equality among the different ethnic, racial, and religious groups in America. This sense was captured in cartoonist Ernie Pyle's soldiers portrayed as individualistic, democratic, optimistic, and united with their comrades. This same image was fostered by the nation's leaders with such notions as "the battlefield does produce a brotherhood" and "America is the international country" (Polenberg 1980:46–54). That the "new brotherhood" was temporary and more ideology than anything became apparent soon after the war ended. In the expanding suburbs of "four thousand identical houses," and as the nation and civil rights movement began the push for racial integration, suburban dwellers were choosing to live in segregated neighborhoods where they would have minimal or no interactions with persons of different race, ethnicity, and class (Polenberg 1980:127–137).

The small-town neighborhood I grew up in, however, *was* integrated and provided me with an opportunity to observe ethnic differences and prejudices close up. On my block there were Irish and Italian Catholics living alongside white Protestants, Jews, and an old Black woman who took in boarders, (including Puerto Rican labor migrants). Closer to the center of town and the Catholic Church, there was more segregation with a block of blacks, a block of Irish, and a block of Italians, each with its own small family-run corner grocery store. Closer to the country club were the "rich folk," genuine WASPs with large estates and homes. My mother was friendly with all the neighbors, learning the art of making "real Italian" spaghetti sauce, being best friends with the kids of the only Chinese family in town, joining the Episcopal Church, and participating in an acting group with some of the equally less conservative "rich people" from the north end of town. There were, however, pressures to conform to particular standards of behavior, to not get "too close" to the neighbors. My uncles (on my mother's side) were the primary "culture police" in this regard, teasing my sister and I as we grew up about our use of makeup and instructing us that we were never to marry Catholics, Jews, Negroes, or "Spicks." They forgot to warn us against marrying a "Japanese" man, for, at the time, there were no Japanese anywhere near where we lived and the possibility that any one in the family would know much less marry one of the "perpetrators of Pearl Harbor" was unthinkable.

The process of making "others" seem more peculiar than mysterious, and less desirable, and of teaching us "who we are" and "what we stand for" took place in many ways. We learned the reasoning behind our uncles' prejudices by listening in on their conversations during family visits, in school, at the movies, on television, and in the books we read. We made our own limited observations of the differences between the things we were being taught and what we did in church and the religious practices and beliefs of our neighbors. As a child I was morbidly fascinated by one uncle's assertion that because Catholics believe a child is less sinful than its mother, Catholic doctors will sacrifice a mother's life in favor of her newborn child if it is a question of one or the other. This uncle truly feared for my life when I had a Catholic doctor in attendance for the births of my three children. Another stereotype was that Catholic women are little more than baby-makers. "Proof" of this was the young woman I baby-sat for who bore her husband one child a year (several were stillborn) until after seven pregnancies she looked like a bedraggled woman in her forties instead of her late twenties. Catholics and blacks alike were accused of "living for the moment" and deserving of their poverty due to their lack of thrift and family planning. The fact that most of our Irish and Italian neighbors were more prosperous than we were at the time, and had only two or three children, was conveniently overlooked!

While we played with the neighborhood kids on weekends and in the summer, the rest of the time we went to separate schools and belonged to separate clubs and organizations. Even scout troops were segregated, a process begun in the mid-1930s when the Catholic Church accepted scouting as part of the church's program for its young people on the condition that the troops it sponsored would be primarily for Catholic boys and girls (Gordon 1964:223). When I was a girl scout in the 1950s, scouting groups were sponsored by Protestant and Catholic Churches and Jewish Synagogues as well as by the YMCA and other sectarian groups. Our parents also led segregated lives belonging to different churches (there were both white and black Episcopal Churches in our small town) and clubs, like the Italian Social Club and the Star Social Club where only Italians or blacks went to dance on weekends. Because of this social and religious segregation, we had only vague notions of what the neighbors said and did in their schools and organizations. Today, with two of my children married to Catholics, the nuns seem less bizarre to me. Back in the 1950s and 1960s, however, in their black habits and extreme sanctimony, they were more than a little scary.

What we learned, on the other hand, was that we are not bizarre. Rather, we were the central characters in the school books we and every other kid in America read—the Dicks and Janes versus the Silvios and Eileens. We learned that America was a strong and powerful country, largely—it was asserted—because of people like our parents, who worked hard, saved their money, bought second-hand cars rather than buy on credit, invested in their children's education, went to church on Sunday, stayed home on the weekends to teach "junior" how to play ball and "sis" how to sew rather than hang out in "pubs" and "saloons," were patriotic, supporting no foreign prince or Pope, and practiced simple (e.g., Protestant) Christian virtues. The biases and assumptions about other races and religions in this self-portrait are blatantly obvious! Back then, however, the "all-American" image of white Anglo-Saxon Protestants was everywhere: on the cover of *Life* magazine and the *Saturday Evening Post* (e.g., Norman Rockwell paintings), on television, and at the movies. Our favorite pulp fiction provided WASP models for adolescent success. For girls there was Nancy Drew (Montague 1976), for boys the Hardy brothers (Wasylyshyn 1982). As a teenager I read every Nancy Drew mystery ever written, and from her I learned that a girl could be and do anything she wants as long, that is, as she knows when and for whom to take a back seat. Nancy had the best of both worlds (the male and the female) by being a successful sleuth and demure girlfriend, the latter made possible by her Ivy Leaguer boyfriend Ned conveniently being away and engrossed in his studies most of the time, and her widowed father treating her like the son he never had (Montague 1976:114).

Mixed messages were common in our upbringing, with both boys and girls encouraged to attend college but, in the case of girls, more as a back-up policy for what to do if your husband died or lost his (presumably more important) job. The women in my family worked in addition to being primary caretakers of their children, but, like Nancy Drew, they "knew their place". At Thanksgiving the women did the shopping, preparing, cooking, setting the table, and cleaning up after. The men's sole Thanksgiving duties were to carve the turkey and to watch football—the quintessential American sport. (It amuses me now to realize that women, who used all kinds of knives in their food preparation,

were not allowed to touch the "men's carving knife" or that they were seen as incapable of carving a turkey!)

One thing that was taught less at school or Girl Scouts but was ingrained in us at home was the fear of what "they" thought. Along with learning table manners and "proper" morals (do unto others as you would have them do onto you), we learned to fear public censure ("What will people think?!"). In addition to learning who we should or should not marry then, we also learned never to show weakness in public ("They'll never let you live it down."), never to seek psychiatric care ("They'll think you're crazy."), never to get arrested ("They'll think we're a family of criminals."), and never, ever, to carry tales outside of the family ("They don't need to know."). The sum of these prescriptions and proscriptions is a tremendous insecurity *and* work ethic that often places family pride and business often taking priority over family life and pleasure.

## Camelot and Its Aftermath

In the 1960s and 1970s, however, my generation chucked our inhibitions and the contradictions that had ruled our lives. John F. Kennedy proved to non-Catholics that a Catholic could uphold the principle of the Separation of Church and State. He and his wife and family were attractive and sophisticated models for a younger generation hungry for a less constrained life-style. And, tapping into the social forces emerging against white privilege (especially upper-class privilege) and poor working conditions, Kennedy ended up receiving more votes from Protestants than from the Catholics and Jews combined (Polenberg 1980:169). For Catholics, Kennedy's election as president of the United States produced a greater sense of identification with "America" (Polenberg 1980:172).

Ecumenism was the order of the day, and young people everywhere gave themselves up to the romantic, idealistic "Age of Aquarius." As their hard-headed elders shook their heads in shock and dismay, young Protestants, Jews, and Catholics worked together against racial injustice and in Lyndon Johnson's "War on Poverty". Assimilation *and* the coming together of the American people as one nation, united in purpose and marriage, seemed ever more possible and desirable. Intermarriage between white ethnics (but especially white Protestants and Irish Catholics) took place in unprecedented numbers. And in a rainbow of friendships and relationships white Protestant youth discovered the lies and half-truths of their parents' teachings. Blacks, Catholics, and Jews were *not* simply more superstitious or self-indulgent than we were, they were just as committed to life in America, and they were as bright, friendly, sensitive, hard-working, and young.

In actuality, however, I and most young Americans of all backgrounds were not immersed in the 1960s and 1970s "youth culture." As a very young mother and housewife, I taught Sunday School and Girl Scouts, bowled with and attended meetings of the Junior New Century Club (a middle- to upper-middle-class social club for women in the 20-40 age bracket), and when I wasn't taking the kids to the park or pre-kindergarten I read a lot of romantic mysteries (the grown-up versions of Nancy Drew). Even when I returned to school and was exposed to college activists, I did not march on Washington or Selma. I did not smoke dope or go to Woodstock. And only rarely did I dress like a hippie or wear flowers in my hair. I did, however, participate in some of the liberation of mind and spirit. I went back to college after reading Betty Friedan *The Feminine Mystique* (which was mystifying to many of my Junior Club associates who advised me to "have another baby" instead!). And while some of the men then in charge of American colleges and universities radicalized me with their put-downs of married women returning to school, I gained support from other students and my mother *and* aunts—older and more experienced than the Junior Club women—who assured me that they, too, would do what I was doing if they had been born in my generation.

Like many in my generation, I socialized my children far differently than I had been. There were no lectures from either me or their father on whom they should or should not marry. And although they heard racist remarks from time to time from their German grandfather and other relatives, they did not take effect. The environment my children grew up in was very different from the one I was nurtured in. This was reflected in the liberal attitudes portrayed on television (e.g., the biracial and sexually egalitarian "Mod Squad") and at the movies (e.g., the interracial and icon-busting Jesus Christ Superstar and other, sexually liberal and explicit movies). Above all, there was less worry about what "they would think" and more emphasis on personal and individual development. Some children, like my own, attended alternative schooling, and there was more concern about developing children's self-esteem. Dr. Spock was the expert on child-rearing, and there was little of the old "children should be seen and not heard" pedagogy. Trouble was on its way, however, and hopes for a more just world were about to be shattered, or at least severely tempered. Those of us who lived through them will never forget the television images of the assassinations of JFK, Martin Luther King, Robert Kennedy, and so many others. In elementary school, we had been taught to look down on Latin American countries with their dictators and weekly political assassinations. Now we felt shame. We also shall never forget the shock and horror of Vietnam, race riots, and the burning down of America's cities. We Northerners, who had felt superior to "dumb prejudiced Southerners," were now humbled that so much ugliness and hate had been smoldering in our own society. It was even more shocking when a small group of radicals from Philadelphia came to our hometown to stir up the local "Negroes" and a few office and store windows had bricks thrown through them. Suddenly, we (meaning we supposedly "upstanding white people") did not feel safe and in charge of America anymore, much less the universe.

It was a harsh but overdue comeuppance. It was obvious that America's "melting pot" was not working and that the structural assimilation of blacks and other oppressed minorities had not taken place (Gordon 1964:114). On a more positive note, at least from the perspective of everyone but die-hard WASPs and white supremacists, after the riots there followed a flowering of ethnic consciousness, a realization on the part of many ethnics that they could pull together and bring about their own economic improvement and pride (Gordon 1964:244–247). While some of us looked on with more than a touch of envy and a

sense that we were no longer at the center of American history, blacks and other ethnics openly touted their rediscovered (or newly created) cultural heritage and values, moved into the political mainstream, and snubbed and mocked us as often as they could (or so some of us felt).

## Late Capitalism and Radical Americans

Snubs and nasty shocks were not the worst of it for the majority of white Americans, however. Not only were Americans getting older, but the 1980s and early 1990s ushered in a period of late capitalism and devastating economic uncertainty that struck the middle class almost as hard as the lower classes of American society. As Baby Boomers and Flower Children turned middle-aged and their parents enjoyed their "Golden Years" and the support of social security and Medicare, the Vietnam war, more liberal immigration laws, and changes in industry were loosing floods of "exotic" new immigrants (Haitians, Vietnamese, Thai, etc.) into the country, and mainstream Americans felt as if their jobs and homes were being plucked right from under them. My Florida relatives are now mostly out of Miami. But they were there during the time of the first boatloads of Cubans fleeing Castro's oppression, the Haitian inundations, and all of the other legal and illegal immigrations that have turned Miami, once a sleepy lower-middle- and middleclass area with a fringe of tourism, into what has been variously called by white Americans "Little Havana," a "third-world country," and "Hell." More humiliating and almost as bothersome as the drugs and crime (which are bad) and the loss of jobs to hungry, hustling immigrants, has been the Cubans' success at turning Miami into a Hispanic economic and social success story. For people who were born in Miami and whose parents settled the area, people who went through the Depression and World War II to preserve the "American Way," and now face an unknown and financially insecure future, seeing Spanish street signs and advertisements and hearing Spanish take over as the primary language in their hometown is a bitter pill. The same restructuring of the American economic and social scene is taking place all over, with Mexicans and Thai workers moving to the Heartland to work in the meat-processing plants that have moved there from Chicago and other Midwestern cities, and Koreans and other Asians moving into and revitalizing crumbling neighborhoods in Philadelphia and other Rustbelt cities (Lamphere et al. 1994).

Sensibly, local leadership, following national guidelines and policies, coped with the major influx of immigrants and the social pressures they brought to bear on American cities with affirmative action, bilingual education, "political-correctness" education, an ethos of multiculturalism, and other liberal policies. While this has not always worked out well, there are large numbers of new immigrants who are successfully adapting into the American way of life in both economic and social terms. Displaced blacks and whites, on the other hand, feel (and in some cases justifiably so) extremely threatened. In such a climate, a large segment of the white European population, from lower to middle class, feels let down by their leaders and especially big business. While some may say that they deserve a taste of injustice, human nature is such that the newly down-and-out will not agree and will try to find someone else to blame. With television announcers reminding us daily of yet a newer form of "victimization," the dastardliness of our leaders, crooked doctors, lawyers, and welfare recipients, and all sorts of other depredations on the average American citizen, it is no wonder (whether justifiable or not) that many white Americans are beginning to see themselves as victims, too.

Accordingly, more and more white Americans are participating in and joining the ranks of radical fringe and majority fundamentalists groups, seeking a return to more "natural" or older ways of life (from the flaccid New Age fascination with the various Native American life-styles in places like Boulder, Colorado, to even more dangerous flirtations with pioneer and survivalist ethics that mark some of the new anti-government militia groups) and seeing demons and destroyers in every corner of society (the New Agers fearing the fundamentalists, the fundamentalists the New Agers and liberal government). In many American families, it is no longer possible to hold a conversation with the born-again Christians in the family who have added to their demons pro-choice advocates, women's libbers, homosexuals, affirmative action, the National Wildlife Federation, testing on animals, and a host of liberal causes. New Republican member of the House of Representatives, Helen Chenoweth from Idaho, speaks for millions of disgruntled Americans when she equates many right-wing movements (anti-environmentalists, the religious right, advocates of states' rights, citizens militias, gun owners, and "country sovereignty" anarchists) with "real Americans" fight for our freedoms and our liberties, and our way of life. We're fighting for our culture" (Blumenthal 1995:27). It does not need to be said that most of the people in those right-wing groups are white European Americans (although not all by a long shot). Similar sentiments are echoed by Montana Militiamen Bob Fletcher and John Trochmann. Their targeted conspiracy is the New World Order, an alleged mega-conspiracy that is seeking to destroy the United States (meaning "real Americans" like themselves). Just how paranoid such people are is their belief that a map on the back of a 1993 Kix cereal box, showing the country divided into eleven regions, is a "representation of the New World Order plan for dividing the United States into regional departments after the invaders emerge to take over the country, which is scheduled to happen any day now" (Kelly 1995:61). Kelly drolly adds, "Why the conspirators have chosen to publicize their intentions on the back of a cereal box is not clear."

## Conclusion: The Politics of Ethnicity and Class

With the emergence of militancy among white European Americans and their increased sense of themselves as an oppressed group, one might assume that white Anglo-Saxon Protestants and other white European Americans are becoming America's new underclass and that WASPs are no longer in control of America. It is true that there are many poor white Americans (there always has been more white Americans living below the "poverty line" than any other category of Americans). It is also true that Caroline Kennedy married a Jew and that former president George Bush has grandchildren who are half-Hispanic. None of which necessarily means, as Christopher (1989) has argued, that WASP defenses have been irrevocably breached by increased intermarriage with outsiders or that a majority of white Americans still cannot achieve the American Dream. What is most interesting and useful to understand about the changes going on in white society is not ethnic mixing and lost privilege so much as a perceived and possibly real moral break between upper- and lower-class whites. Upper-class persons of all ethnic backgrounds are reaping the rewards of a more "multicultural" society (especially cheap labor of many of the new immigrants) and promoting liberal ideologies of pluralistic harmony and national economic growth. At the same time, lower-class persons and all those who are not part of cyberspace (as the students at the University of Pennsylvania are, according to Meyer (1995) and cannot afford BMWs or to live in very expensive, postmodern communities where street names like Hunters Run and Hummingbird Lane evoke the very world they have destroyed (MacCannell 1992) and for who ethnicity is a survival strategy and not a trivial "what kind of ethnic shall we do tonight?" are very angry that their lives, their beliefs, and their aspirations are being mocked, ignored, and no longer are part of the American Agenda. No longer, that is, until the Republicans focused on the negative feelings running through large portions of white society and have tried to channel it into a new agenda or "contract," as Newt Gingrich likes to call it. Neither Gingrich, however, who believes America can be a better place if all the "victims" and "poor ethnics" stop "whining" (1995:26) nor Adler, who worries about whether or not our country can survive all the diversity (1995:16) have it right about the direction some white ethnics want this country to take. For many, if the ones I know are any indication, what they are engaged in is more of a religious war than an ethnic or class battle. America is not just a land of freedoms to them. It is a religion. One they died for in World War II. One they are willing to share with most other immigrants (as long as they continue to act "American"). One that contradictorily they see as based on diversity and freedom of choice versus special privilege and the watering down of cherished morals.

Note: References omitted.

# UNIT 6
# Religion, Belief, and Ritual

## Unit Selections

## Key Points to Consider

• How can modern medicine be combined with traditional healing to take advantage of the best aspects of both? In what respects do perceptions of disease affect treatment and recovery?

• Why should scarce research funds be used to assess indigenous peoples' knowledge and approaches to health?

• How do beliefs about the supernatural contribute to a sense of personal security, individual responsibility, and social harmony?

• In what sense have ritual, ceremony, and social relations been important to traditional drug use? Why does the debilitating, recreational and excessive use of drugs become characteristic of modern society?

• How has voodoo become such an important form of social control in rural Haiti?

• In what ways are magic rituals practical and rational?

• How do rituals and taboos get established in the first place?

• How important are ritual and taboo in our modern industrial society?

## Student Website
www.mhcls.com/online

## Internet References
Further information regarding these websites may be found in this book's preface or online.

**Anthropology Resources Page**
  http://www.usd.edu/anth/
**Yahoo: Society and Culture: Death**
  http://dir.yahoo.com/Society_and_Culture/Death_and_Dying/

The anthropological interest in religion, belief, and ritual is not concerned with the scientific validity of such phenomena but rather with the way in which people relate various concepts of the supernatural to their everyday lives. From this practical perspective, some anthropologists have found that traditional spiritual healing is just as helpful in the treatment of illness as is modern medicine (see "Shamans," "Ancient Teachings, Modern Lessons" and "Drug Culture: Everybody Uses Something"), that voodoo is a form of social control (as in "The Secrets of Haiti's Living Dead"), and that the ritual and spiritual preparation for playing the game of baseball can be just as important as spring training (see "Baseball Magic").

Every society is composed of feeling, thinking, and acting human beings who at one time or another are either conforming to or altering the social order into which they were born. As described in "The Adaptive Value of Religious Ritual," religion is an ideological framework that gives special legitimacy and validity to human experience within any given sociocultural system. In this way, monogamy as a marriage form, or monarchy as a political form, ceases to be simply one of many alternative ways in which a society can be organized, but becomes, for the believer, the only legitimate way. Religion considers certain human values and activities as sacred and inviolable. It is this mythic function that helps to explain the strong ideological attachments that some people have regardless of the scientific merits of their points of view.

While under some conditions religion may in fact be "the opiate of the masses," under other conditions such a belief system

may be a rallying point for social and economic protest. A contemporary example of the former might be the "Moonies" (members of the Unification Church founded by Sun Myung Moon), while a good example of the latter is the role of the black church in the American civil rights movement, along with the prominence of such religious figures as Martin Luther King Jr. and Jesse Jackson. A word of caution must be set forth concerning attempts to understand belief systems of other cultures. At times the prevailing attitude seems to be, "What I believe in is religion, and what you believe in is superstition." While anthropologists generally do not subscribe to this view, some tend to explain behavior that seems, on the surface, to be incomprehensible and impractical as some form of religious ritual. The articles in this unit should serve as a strong warning concerning the pitfalls of that approach.

"Eyes of the Ngangas" shows how important a person's traditional belief systems, combined with community involvement, can be to the physical and psychological well-being of the individual. This perspective is so important that the treatment of illness is hindered without it. Thus, beliefs about the supernatural may be subtle, informal, and yet absolutely necessary for social harmony and stability.

Mystical beliefs and ritual are not absent from the modern world. "Body Ritual Among the Nacirema" reveals that our daily routines have mystic overtones and "Baseball Magic" examines the need for ritual and taboo in the "great American pastime."

In summary, the writings in this unit show religion, belief, and ritual in relationship to practical human affairs.

# Eyes of the *Ngangas*: Ethnomedicine and Power in Central African Republic

People of the Third World have a variety of therapies available for combating diseases, but because of cost, availability, and cultural bias, most rely on ethnomedical traditional treatment rather than "biomedical" or Western therapies. Dr. Lehmann's field research focuses on the importance of *ngangas* (traditional healers) as a source of primary health care for both the Aka Pygmy hunters and their horticultural neighbors, the Ngando of Central African Republic. Tracing the basis and locus of the *ngangas'* mystical diagnostic and healing powers, he shows that they are particularly effective with treatments for mental illness and, to an unknown extent, with herbal treatment of physical illnesses as well. The powers of the Aka *ngangas*, however, are also used to reduce the tensions between themselves and their patrons and to punish those Ngando who have caused the hunters harm. Lehmann points out the necessity of recognizing and treating the social as well as the biological aspects of illness and appeals to health care planners to establish counterpart systems that mobilize popular and biomedical specialists to improve primary health care in the Third World.

ARTHUR C. LEHMANN

*E*THNOMEDICINE (ALSO REFERRED TO AS FOLK, TRADITIONAL, or popular medicine) is the term used to describe the primary health care system of indigenous people whose medical expertise lies outside "biomedicine" the "modem" medicine of Western societies. Biomedicine does exist in the Third World, but it is unavailable to the masses of inhabitants for a number of reasons. Conversely, although popular medicine has largely been supplanted by biomedicine in the Western World, it still exists and is revived from time to time by waves of dissatisfaction with modem medicine and with the high cost of health care, by the health food movement, and by a variety of other reasons. The point is, all countries have pluralistic systems of health care, but for many members of society the combat against the diseases that have plagued mankind is restricted to the arena of popular medicine.

This is particularly true in the developing nations, such as those of the sub-Saharan regions of Africa, where over 80 percent of the population live in rural areas with a dearth of modem medical help (Bichmann 1979; Green 1980). Between 1984 and the present, I have made six field trips to one such rural area (the most recent in 1994), to study the primary health care practices of Aka Pygmy hunter-gatherers and their horticultural neighbors, the Ngando of Central African Republic (C.A.R.).

## The Aka and the Ngando

Several groups of the Pygmies live in a broad strip of forested territory stretching east and west across the center of Equatorial Africa. The two largest societies are the Mbuti of the Inturi Forest of Zaire and the Aka, who live in the Southern Rainforest that extends from the Lobaye River in Central African Republic into the People's Republic of the Congo and into Cameroun (Cavalli-Sforza 1971). Like the Mbuti, the Aka are long-time residents of their region. It is on the edge of the Southern Rainforest in and near the village of Bagandu that the Aka Pygmies and the Ngando come into most frequent contact. The proximity, particularly during the dry season from December to April, allows for comparisons of health care systems that would be difficult otherwise, for the Aka move deep into the forest and are relatively inaccessible for a good portion of the year.

Since Turnbull described the symbiotic relationship between Mbuti Pygmies and villagers in Zaire (1965), questions remain as to why Pygmy hunters continue their association with their sedentary neighbors. Bahuchet's work shows that the relationship between the Aka and the Ngando of C.A.R. is one of voluntary mutual dependence in which both groups benefit; indeed, the Aka consider the villagers responsible for their well-being (1985: 549). Aka provide the Ngando with labor, meat, and forest materials while the Ngando pay the Aka with plantation foods, clothes, salt, cigarettes, axes and knives, alcohol, and infrequently, money.

This mutual dependence extends to the health care practices of both societies. Ngando patrons take seriously ill Aka to the dispensary for treatment; Aka consider this service a form of payment that may be withheld by the villagers as a type of punishment. On the other hand, Aka *ngangas* (traditional healers) are called upon to diagnose and treat Ngando illnesses. The powers believed to be held by the *ngangas* are impressive, and few, particularly rural residents, question these powers or the roles they play in everyday life in Central African Republic.

# Eyes of the *Ngangas*

The people believe that the *ngangas* intervene on their behalf with the supernatural world to combat malevolent forces and also use herbal expertise to protect them from the myriad of tropical diseases. Elisabeth Motte (1980) has recorded an extensive list of medicines extracted by the *ngangas* from the environment to counter both natural and supernatural illnesses; 80 percent are derived from plants and the remaining 20 percent from animals and minerals.

Both Aka and Ngando *ngangas* acquire their power to diagnose and cure through an extensive apprenticeship ordinarily served under the direction of their fathers, who are practicing healers themselves. This system of inheritance is based on primogeniture, although other than first sons may be chosen to become *ngangas*. Although Ngando *ngangas* may be either male or female, the vast majority are males; all Aka *ngangas* are males. In the absence of the father or if a younger son has the calling to become a healer, he may study under an *nganga* outside the immediate family.

During my six trips to the field, *ngangas* permitted me to question them on their training and initiation into the craft; it became apparent that important consistencies existed. First, almost all male *ngangas* are first sons. Second, fathers expect first sons to become *ngangas*; as they said, "It is natural." Third, the apprenticeship continues from boyhood until the son is himself a *nganga*, at which time he trains his own son. Fourth, every *nganga* expresses firm belief in the powers of his teacher to cure and, it follows, in his own as well. As is the case with healers around the world, despite the trickery sometimes deemed necessary to convince clients of the effectiveness of the cure, the *ngangas* are convinced that their healing techniques will work unless interrupted by stronger powers. Fifth, every *nganga* interviewed maintained strongly that other *ngangas* who were either envious or have a destructive spirit can destroy or weaken the power of a healer, causing him to fail. Sixth, and last, the origin and locus of the *ngangas'* power is believed to be in their eyes.

Over and over I was told that during the final stages of initiation, the master *nganga* had vaccinated the initiate's eyes and placed "medicine" in the wound, thus giving the new *nganga* power to divine and effectively treat illnesses. At first I interpreted the term *vaccination* to mean simply the placement of "medicine" in the eyes, but I was wrong. Using a double-edged razor blade and sometimes a needle, the master *nganga* may cut his apprentice's lower eyelids, the exterior corners of the eyes, or below the eyes (although making marks below the eyes is now considered "antique" I was told); he concludes the ceremony by placing magical medicine in the cuts. At this moment, the student is no longer an apprentice; he has achieved the status of an *nganga* and the ability to diagnose illnesses with the newly acquired power of his eyes.

Not until my last field trip in 1994 did I witness a master *nganga* actually cut the whites of his apprentice's eyes. At the end of an hour-long interview with an *nganga*, which focused on my eliciting his concept of disease etiology in treatment of illness, I casually posed the question I had asked other *ngangas* many times before: "Do you vaccinate your apprentice's eyes?" The *nganga* beckoned his apprentice seated nearby, and, to my amazement, the apprentice immediately placed his head on the master's lap. I quickly retrieved my camcorder which I had just put away! The master removed a razor blade from a match box, spread the student's eyelids apart, deftly made five cuts on the whites of each eye, and squeezed the juice of a leaf (the "medicine") into the wounds. This astounding procedure performed on perhaps the most sensitive of all human parts took less than a total of three minutes and did not appear to cause the apprentice any degree of pain, albeit his eyes were red and his tears profuse.

During the career of an *nganga*, his eyes will be vaccinated many times, thus, it is believed, rejuvenating the power of the eyes to correctly diagnose illness and ensure proper therapy. It is clear that the multiple powers of *ngangas* to cure and to protect members of their band from both physical and mental illnesses as well as from a variety of types of supernatural attacks reside in their eyes.

It follows that the actual divinatory act involves a variety of techniques, particular to each *nganga*, that allows him to use his powers to "see" the cause or the illness and determine its treatment. Some bum a dear, rocklike amber resin called *paka* found deep in the rain forest, staring into the flames to learn the mystery of illness and the appropriate therapy. Some stare into the rays of the sun during diagnosis or gaze into small mirrors to unlock the secret powers of the ancestors in curing. Others concentrate on plates filled with water or large, brilliant chunks of glass. The most common but certainly the most incongruous method of acquiring a vision by both Aka and Ngando *ngangas* today is staring into a light bulb. These are simply stuck into the ground in front of the *nganga* or, as is the case among many village healers, the light bulb is floated in a glass of water during consultation. The appearance of a light bulb surfacing from an Aka *nganga's* healing paraphernalia in the middle of a rain forest is, to say the least, unique. Western methods of divining—of knowing the unknown—were not, and to some degree are not now, significantly different from the techniques of the *ngangas*. Our ways of "seeing," involving gazing at and "reading" tea leaves, crystal balls, cards, palms, and stars, are still considered appropriate techniques by many.

# Therapy Choices and Therapy Managers

A wide variety of therapies coexist in contemporary Africa, and the situation in the village of Bagandu is no exception. The major sources of treatment are Aka *ngangas,* Ngando *ngangas*, kinship therapy (family councils called to resolve illness-causing conflicts between kin), home remedies, Islamic healers (marabouts), and the local nurse at the government dispensary, who is called "doctor" by villagers and hunters alike. In addition, faith healers, herbalists, and local specialists (referred to as "fetishers") all attempt, in varying degrees, to treat mental or physical illness in Bagundu. Intennittently Westerners, such as missionaries, personnel from the U.S. Agency for International Development, and anthropologists, also treat physical ailments. Bagandu is a large village of approximately 3,400 inhabitants, however; most communities are much smaller and have little access to modem treatment. And, as Cavalli-Sforza has noted,

> If the chances of receiving Western medical help for Africans living in remote villages are very limited, those of Pygmies are practically nonexistent. They are even further removed from hospitals. African health agents usually do not treat Pygmies. Medical help comes exceptionally and almost always from rare visiting foreigners. (Cavalli-Sforza 1986: 421)

Residents of Bagandu are fortunate in having both a government dispensary and a pharmacy run by the Catholic church, but prescriptions are extremely costly relative to income, and ready cash is scarce. A more pressing problem is the availability of drugs. Frequently the "doctor" has only enough to treat the simplest ailments such as headaches and small cuts; he must refer thirty to forty patients daily to the Catholic pharmacy, which has more drugs than the dispensary but still is often unable to fill prescriptions for the most frequently prescribed drugs such as penicillin, medicine to counteract parasites, and antibiotic salves. Although the doctor does the best he can under these conditions, patients must often resort only to popular medical treatment—in spite of the fact that family members, the therapy managers, have assessed the illness as one best treated by biomedicine. In spite, too, of the regular unavailability of medicine, the doctor's diagnosis and advice is still sought out— "although many people will consent to go to the dispensary only after having exhausted the resources of traditional medicine" (Motte 1980: 311).

Popular, ethnomedical treatment is administered by kin, *ngangas* (among both the Aka and Ngando villagers), other specialists noted for treatment of specific maladies, and Islamic marabouts, who are recent immigrants from Chad. According to both Aka and Ngando informants, the heaviest burden for health care falls to these ethnomedical systems. Ngando commonly utilize home, kin remedies for minor illnesses, but almost 100 percent indicated that for more serious illnesses they consulted either the doctor or *ngangas* (Aka, Ngando, or both); to a lesser extent they visited specialists. The choice of treatment, made by the family therapy managers, rests not only on the cause and severity of the illness, but also on the availability of therapists expert in the disease or problem, their: cost, and their proximity to the patient. Rarely do the residents of Bagandu seek the aid of the marabouts, for example, in part because of the relatively high cost of consultation. Clearly, both popular and biomedical explanations for illness play important roles in the maintenance of health among Bagandu villagers, although popular medicine is the most important therapy resource available. Popular medicine is especially vital for the Aka hunters, whose relative isolation and inferior status (in the eyes of the Ngando) have resulted in less opportunity for biomedical treatment. Yet even they seek out modem medicine for illnesses.

Whatever the system of treatment chosen, it is important to understand that "the management of illness and therapy by a set of close kin is a central aspect of the medical scene in central Africa.... The therapy managing group ... exercises a brokerage function between the sufferer and the specialist" (Janzen 1978: 4). It is the kingroup that determines which therapy is to be used.

# Explanations of Illness

The choice of therapy in Bagandu is determined by etiology and severity, as in the West. Unlike Western medicine, however, African ethnomedicine is not restricted to an etiology of only natural causation. Both the Aka and the Ngando spend a great deal of time, energy, and money (or other forms of payments) treating illnesses perceived as being the result of social and cultural imbalances, often described in supernatural terms. Aka and Ngando nosology has accommodated biomedicine without difficulty, but traditional etiology has not become less important to the members of these societies. Frequent supernatural explanations of illness by Aka and Ngando informants inevitably led me to the investigation of witchcraft, curses, spells, or the intervention of ancestors and nameless spirits, all of which were viewed as being responsible for poor health and misfortune. The Aka maintain, for example, that the fourth leading cause of death in Bagandu is witchcraft (diarrhea is the principal cause; measles, second, and convulsions, third [Hewlett 1986: 56]). During my research, it became apparent that a dual model of disease explanation exists among the Aka and Ngando: first, a naturalistic model that fits its Western biomedical counterpart well, and second, a supernaturalistic explanation.

Interviews with village and Pygmy *ngangas* indicated that their medical systems are not significantly different. Indeed, both groups agree that their respective categories of illness etiology are identical. Further, the categories are not mutually exclusive: an illness may be viewed as being natural, but it may be exacerbated by supernatural forces such as witchcraft and spells. Likewise, this phenomenon can be reversed: an illness episode may be caused by supernatural agents but progress into a form that is treatable through biomedical techniques. For example, my relatively educated and ambitious young field assistant, a villager, was cut on the lower leg by a piece of stone while working on a new addition to his house. The wound, eventually becoming infected, caused swelling throughout the leg and groin. As was the case in some of his children's illnesses, the explanation for the wound was witchcraft. It was clear to him that the witch was a neighbor who envied his possessions and his employment by a foreigner. Although the original cut was caused by a supernatural agent, the resulting infection fitted the biomedical model. Treatment by a single injection of penicillin quickly brought the infection under control, although my assistant believed that had the witch been stronger the medicine would not have worked. Here is a case in which, "in addition to the patient's physical signs and social relationships," the passage of time is also crucial to "the unfolding of therapeutic action" (Feierman 1985: 77). As the character of an illness changes with time as the illness runs its course, the therapy manager's decisions may change, because the perceived etiology can shift as a result of a variety of signs, such as a slow-healing wound or open conflict in the patient's social group (Janzen 1978: 9)

Studies on disease etiologies among select African societies (Bibeau 1979; Janzen 1978; Warren 1974) reported that most illnesses had natural causes, and this finding holds for the Ngando villagers as well. At first glance, these data would seem to reduce the importance of *nganga*s and of popular medicine generally, but it is necessary to recognize that *nganga*s treat both natural and supernatural illnesses utilizing both medical and mystical techniques. The question posed by Feierman, "Is popular medicine effective?" (1985: 5), is vital to the evaluation of *nganga*s as healers. Surely some traditional medicines used by these cures must in many cases work, and work regularly enough to earn the sustained support of the general public.

## Illnesses of God and Illnesses of Man

Both the Ngando and Aka explanations for natural illnesses lack clarity. Some *nganga*s refer to them as "illnesses of God"; others simply identify them as "natural"; and still others frequently use both classifications, regularly assigning each label to specific ailments. Hewlett maintains that the Aka sometimes labelled unknown maladies as illnesses of God (1986: personal communication). On the other hand, the Bakongo of neighboring Zaire defined illnesses of God as those "generally, mild conditions which respond readily to therapy when no particular disturbance exists in the immediate social relationships of the sufferer.... The notion of 'god' does not imply divine intervention or retribution but simply that the cause is an affliction in the order of things unrelated to human intentions" (Janzen 1978: 9).

Both Janzen's and Hewlett's data are accurate, but my field data show as well as that the explanations of natural illnesses among the Ngando and Aka not only refer to normal mild diseases and sometimes unknown ones but also to specific illnesses named by the *nganga*s and the residents of Bagandu. The confusion surrounding these mixed explanations of disease causation is an important topic for future ethnosemantic or other techniques of emic inquiry by ethnographers.

Residents of Bagandu and both Aka and Ngando *nganga*s categorized sickness caused by witchcraft, magic, curses, spells, and spirits as "illnesses of man." This is the second major disease category. Witchcraft, for example, while not the main cause of death, is the most frequently named cause of illness in Bagandu. Informants in Bagandu cite the frequency of witchcraft accusations as proof of their viewpoint. Antisocial or troublesome neighbors are frequently accused of being witches and are jailed if the charge is proven. Maladies of all sorts, such as sterility among females, are also commonly attributed to the innate and malevolent power of witches. These types of explanations are not unusual in rural Africa. What is surprising are reports of new illnesses in the village caused by witches.

All Ngando informants claimed, furthermore, that the problem of witchcraft has not diminished over time; on the contrary, it has increased. The thinking is logical: because witchcraft is believed to be inherited, any increase in population is seen also as an inevitable increase in the number of witches in the village. Population figures in the region of the Southern Rainforest have increased somewhat in the past few decades despite epidemics such as measles; accordingly, the incidence of maladies attrib-

uted to witches has increased. One informant from Bagandu strongly insisted that witches are not only more numerous but also much more powerful today than before. Offiong (1983) reported a marked increase of witchcraft in Nigeria and adjacent states in West Africa, caused not by inflation of population but by the social strain precipitated by the frustration accompanying lack of achievement after the departure of colonial powers.

Insanity is not a major problem among the Ngando. When it does occur, it is believed to be caused by witchcraft, clan or social problems, evil spirits, and breaking taboos. Faith healers, marabouts, and *nganga*s are seen as effective in the treatment of mental illness due to witchcraft or other causes. The role of faith healers is particularly important in the lives of members of the Prophetical Christian Church in Bagandu. They have strong faith in the healing sessions and maintain that the therapy successfully treats the victims of spirits' attacks. Informants also claim the therapy lasts a long time.

The curse is a common method of venting anger in Bagandu, used by both male and female witches. Informants stated that women use curses more than men and that the subjects of their attacks are often males. The curses of witches are counted as being extremely dangerous in the intended victim. One villager accused the elderly of using the curse as a weapon most frequently. Spell-casting is also common in the area, and males often use spells as a method of seduction.

Most, if not all, residents of Bagandu use charms, portable "fetishes," and various types of magical objects placed in and around their houses for protection. Some of these objects are counter-magical: they simultaneously protect the intended victim and turn the danger away from the victim to the attackers. Counter-magic is not always immediate; results may take years to appear. Charms, fetishes, and other forms of protection are purchased from *nganga*s, marabouts, and other specialists such as herbalists. For example, the Aka and Ngando alike believe that wearing a mole's tooth on a bracelet is the most powerful protection from attacks by witches.

To a lesser extent, spirits are also believed to cause illness. It is problematic whether or not this source of illness deserves a separate category of disease causation. Bahuchet thinks not; rather, he holds that spirit-caused illnesses should be labeled illnesses of God (1986: personal communication). It is interesting to note that in addition to charms and other items put to use in Bagandu, residents supplicate ancestors for aid in times of difficulty. If the ancestors do not respond, and if the victim of the misfortune practices Christianity, he or she will seek the aid of God. Non-Christians and Christians alike commonly ask diviners the cause of their problem, after which they seek the aid of the proper specialist. Revenge for real or imagined attacks on oneself or on loved ones is common. One method is to point a claw of a mole at the wrongdoer. Ngando informants maintain the victim dies soon after. Simple possession of a claw, if discovered, means jail for the owner.

My initial survey of Aka and Ngando *nganga*s in 1984 brought out other origins of illness. Two *nganga*s in Bagandu specifically cited the devil, rather than unnamed evil spirits, as a cause for disease. The higher exposure of villagers to Christianity may account for this attribution: seven denominations are currently represented in the churches of Bagandu. Urban *ngangas* questioned in Bangui, the capital, stressed the use of poison as a cause of illness and death. Although poisonings do not figure prominently as a cause of death among the Aka and Ngando, it is common belief that *ngangas* and others do use poison.

Finally, while not a cause for illness, informants maintained that envious *ngangas* have the power to retard or halt the progress of a cure administered by another. All *ngangas* interviewed in 1984 and 1985 confirmed not only that they have the power to interrupt the healing process of a patient but also that they frequently invoke it. Interestingly, *ngangas* share this awesome power with witches, who are also believed by members of both societies to be able to spoil the "medicine" of healers. This kind of perception of the *ngangas*' power accounts, in part, for their dual character: primarily beneficial to the public, they can also be dangerous.

While the numerical differences in the frequency of physiologically and psychologically rooted illnesses in Bagandu are unknown, Ngando respondents in a small sample were able to list a number of supernaturally caused illnesses that are treatable by *ngangas*, but only a few naturally caused ones. Among the naturalistic illnesses were illnesses of the spleen; *laltungba*, deformation of the back; and *Kongo*, "illness of the rainbow." According to Hewlett (1986: 53), *Kongo* causes paralysis of the legs (and sometimes of the arms) and death after the victim steps on a dangerous mushroom growing on a damp spot in the forest where a rainbow-colored snake has rested. Had the Ngando sample been more exhaustive, it is probable that the list of natural diseases would have been greater, although perhaps not as high as the twenty natural illnesses the *ngangas* said they could treat successfully. That impressive list includes malaria, hernia, diarrhea, stomach illness, pregnancy problems, dysentery, influenza, abscesses, general fatigue, traumas (snake bite, miscellaneous wounds, and poisoning), and general and specific bodily pain (spleen, liver, ribs, head, and uterus).

## Powers of the *Ngangas*

The powers of the *ngangas* are not limited to controlling and defeating supernatural or natural diseases alone. In the village of Bagandu and in the adjacent Southern Rainforest where the Ngando and Aka hunters come into frequent contact, tensions exist due to the patron-client relationship, which by its very economic nature is negative. These tensions are magnified by ethnic animosity. Without the Akas' mystical power, their economic and social inferiority would result in an even more difficult relationship with the Ngando. Here the powers of the Pygmy *ngangas* play an important part in leveling, to bearable limits, the overshadowing dominance of the Ngando, and it is here that the *ngangas* demonstrate their leadership outside the realm of health care. Each Aka has some form of supernatural protection provided by the *nganga* of his camp to use while in the village. Still, the need exists for the extraordinary powers of the *nganga* himself for those moments of high tension when Aka are confronted by what they consider the most menacing segments of the village population: the police, the mayor, and

adolescent males, all of whom, as perceived by the Aka, are dangerous to their personal safety while in the village.

In the summer of 1986, I began to study the attitudes of village patrons toward their Aka clients and, conversely, the attitudes of the so-called wayward servants (Turnbull's term for the Mbuti Pygmy of Zaire, 1965) toward the villagers. Participant observation and selective interviews of patrons, on the one hand, and of hunters, on the other, disclosed other important tangents of power of the Aka in general and of their *ngangas* in particular. First, the Aka often have visible sources of power such as scarification, cords worn on the wrist and neck, and bracelets strung with powerful charms for protection against village witches. These protective devices are provided the Aka by their *ngangas*. Second, and more powerful still, are the hidden powers of the Aka in general, bolstered by the specific powers of the *ngangas*. Although the villagers believe the hunters' power is strongest in the forest, and therefore weaker in the village setting, Aka power commands the respect of the farmers. Third, the villagers acknowledge the Aka expertise in the art of producing a variety of deadly poisons, such as *sepi*, which may be used to punish farmers capable of the most serious crimes against the Pygmies. The obvious functions of these means of protection and retribution, taken from the standpoint of the Aka, are positive. Clearly these powers reduce the tension of the Aka while in the village, but they also control behavior of villagers toward the hunters to some undefinable degree.

Villagers interpret the variety of punishments which the Aka are capable of meting out to wrongdoers as originating in their control of mystical or magical. powers. Interestingly, even poisonings are viewed in this way by villagers because of the difficulty of proving that poison rather than mystical power caused illness or death. Although the use of poison is rare, it is used and the threat remains. Georges Guille-Escuret, a French ethnohistorian working in Bagandu in 1985, reported to me that prior to my arrival in the field that year three members of the same household had died on the same day. The head of the family had been accused of repeated thefts of game from the traps and from the camp of an Aka hunter. When confronted with the evidence—a shirt the villager had left at the scene of the thefts—the family rejected the demands of the hunter for compensation for the stolen meat. Soon thereafter, the thief, his wife, and his mother died on the same day. Villagers, who knew of the accusations of theft, interpreted the deaths as the result of poisoning or the mystical powers of the hunter.

Stories of Aka revenge are not uncommon, nor are the Akas' accusations of wrongdoing leveled against the villagers. To the Ngando farmers, the powers of the Aka *ngangas* include the ability to cause death through the use of fetishes, to cause illness to the culprit's eyes, and to direct lightning to strike the perpetrator. These and other impressive powers to punish are seen as real threats to villagers—but the power of the *ngangas* to cure is even more impressive.

Attempts in my research to delineate the strengths and weaknesses of the *ngangas* and other health care specialists discovered a number of qualities/ characteristics widely held to be associated with each. First, each specialist is known for specific medical abilities; that is, Aka and Ngando *ngangas* recognize the therapeutic expertise of others in a variety of cures. A *nganga* from Bangui maintained that Aka *ngangas* were generally superior to the village healers in curing. This view is shared by a number of villagers interviewed, who maintained that the power of Aka *ngangas* is greater than that of their own specialists.

The Aka strongly agree with this view, and in a sense the Aka are more propertied in the realm of curing than are the villagers. There is no question that the Aka are better hunters. Despite the Ngandos' greater political and economic power in the area and the social superiority inherent in their patron status, the Ngando need the Aka. All these elements help balance the relationship between the two societies, although the supernatural and curative powers of Aka *ngangas* have not previously been considered to be ingredients in the so-called symbiotic relationship between Pygmy hunters and their horticultural neighbors.

Second, *ngangas* noted for their ability to cure particular illnesses are often called upon for treatment by other *ngangas* who have contracted the disease. Third, with one exception, all the *ngangas* interviewed agree that European drugs, particularly those contained in hypodermic syringes and in pills, are effective in the treatment of natural diseases. One dissenting informant from the capital disdained biomedicine altogether because, as he said, "White men don't believe in us." Fourth, of the fourteen Aka and Ngando *ngangas* interviewed in 1985, only five felt that it was possible for a *nganga* to work successfully with the local doctor (male nurse) who directed the dispensary in Bagandu. All five of these *ngangas* said that if such cooperation did come about, their special contribution would be the treatment of patients having illnesses of man, including mental illness resulting from witchcraft, from magical and spiritual attacks, and from breaking taboos. None of the *ngangas* interviewed had been summoned to work in concert with the doctor. Fifth, as a group of the *ngangas* held that biomedical practitioners are unable to successfully treat mental illnesses and other illnesses resulting from attacks of supernatural agents. In this the general population of the village agree. This is a vitally important reason for the sustained confidence in popular therapy in the region—a confidence that is further strengthened by the belief that the *ngangas* can treat natural illnesses as well. Sixth, the village doctor recognized that the *ngangas* and marabouts do have more success in the treatment of mental illnesses than he does. Although the doctor confided that he has called in a village *nganga* for consultation in a case of witchcraft, he also disclosed that upon frequent occasions he had to remedy the treatment administered by popular specialists for natural diseases. It is important to recognize that unlike biomedical specialists in the capital, the local doctor does appreciate the talents of traditional therapists who successfully practice ethnopsychiatry.

All respondents to this survey recognized the value of biomedicine in the community, and little variation in the types of cures the doctor could effect was brought out. No doubts were raised regarding the necessity of both biomedicine and popular therapy to the proper maintenance of public health. The spheres of influence and expertise of both types of practitioners, while generally agreed upon by participants of the Ngando survey, did show some variation, but these were no more serious than our own estimates of the abilities of our physicians in the West. In short, all informants utilized both systems of therapy when necessary and if possible.

The continuation of supernatural explanations of illness by both the Ngando and the Aka results in part from tradition, in combination with their lack of knowledge of scientific disease etiology, and in part because of the hidden positive functions of such explanations. Accusations of witchcraft and the use of curses and malevolent magic function to express the anxiety, frustrations, and social disruptions in these societies. These are traditional explanations of disease, with more than a single focus, for they focus on both the physical illness and its sociological cause. "Witchcraft (and by extension other supernatural explanations for illness and disaster) provides an indispensable component in many philosophies of misfortune. It is the friend rather than the foe of mortality" (Lewis 1986: 16). Beyond this rationale, reliance upon practitioners of popular medicine assures the patient that medicine is available for treatment in the absence of Western drugs.

## The Role of Ethnomedicine

Among the Aka and Ngando and elsewhere, systems of popular medicine have sustained African societies for centuries. The evolution of popular medicine has guaranteed its good fit to the cultures that have produced it; even as disruptive an element of the system as witchcraft can claim manifest and latent functions that contribute to social control and the promotion of proper behavior.

Unlike Western drug therapies, no quantifiable measure exists for the effectiveness of popular medicine. Good evidence from World Health Organization studies can be brought forth, however, to illustrate the relatively high percentage of success of psychotherapeutic treatment through ethnomedicine in the Third World compared to that achieved in the West. The results of my research in Bagandu also demonstrate the strong preference of villagers for popular medicine in cases involving mental illness and supernaturally caused mental problems. At the same time, the doctor is the preferred source of therapy for the many types of natural disease, while *ngangas* and other specialists still have the confidence of the public in treating other maladies; referred to as illnesses of man and some illnesses of God. Whatever the perceived etiology by kingroup therapy managers, both popular and biomedical therapists treat natural illnesses. It is in this realm of treatment that it is most important to ask, "What parts of popular medicine work?" rather than, "Does popular medicine work?" Because evidence has shown that psychotherapy is more successful in the hands of traditional curers, it is therefore most important to question the effectiveness of popular therapy in handling natural illnesses. Currently, the effectiveness of traditional drugs used for natural diseases is unknown; however, the continued support of popular therapists by both rural and urban Africans indicates a strength in the system. The effectiveness of the *ngangas* may be both psychological and pharmaceutical, and if the ecological niche does provide drugs that do cure natural illnesses, it is vital that these be determined and manufactured commercially in their countries of origin. If we can assume that some traditional drugs are effective, governments must utilize the expertise of healers in identifying these.

It is unrealistic to attempt to train popular therapists in all aspects of biomedicine, just as it is unrealistic to train biomedical specialists in the supernatural treatments applied by popular practitioners. However, neither type of therapist, nor the public, will benefit from the expertise of the other if they remain apart. The task is to make both more effective by incorporating the best of each into a counterpart system that focuses on a basic training of healers in biomedicine. This combination must certainly be a more logical and economic choice than attempting to supply biomedical specialists to every community in Central African Republic, a task too formidable for any country north or south of the Sahara. The significance of this proposal is magnified by the massive numbers for whom biomedicine is unavailable, those who must rely only upon ethnomedicine.

Even if available to all, biomedicine alone is not the final answer to disease control in the Third World. Hepburn succinctly presents strong arguments against total reliance upon the biomedical approach:

> Biomedicine is widely believed to be effective in the cure of sickness. A corollary of this is the belief that if adequate facilities could be provided in the Third World and "native" irrationalities and cultural obstacles could be overcome, the health problems of the people would largely be eliminated. However, this belief is not true, because the effectiveness of biomedicine is limited in three ways. First, many conditions within the accepted defining properties of biomedicine (i.e., physical diseases) cannot be treated effectively. Second, by concentrating on the purely physical, biomedicine simply cannot treat the social aspects of sickness (i.e., illness). Third, cures can only be achieved under favorable environmental and political conditions: if these are not present, biomedicine will be ineffective (1988: 68).

The problems facing societies in Africa are not new. These same issues faced Westerners in the past, and our partial solutions, under unbelievably better conditions, took immense time and effort to achieve. If primary health care in the non-Western world is to improve, the evolutionary process must be quickened by the utilization of existing popular medical systems as a counterpart of biomedicine, by the expansion of biomedical systems, and by the cooperation of international funding agencies with African policymakers, who themselves must erase their antagonism toward ethnomedicine.

# Ancient Teachings, Modern Lessons

DAVID A. TAYLOR

In recent years, researchers have looked for areas where indigenous knowledge, also called local or traditional knowledge, can meet modern science for better environmental health. A 1999 conference titled "Science for the 21st Century—A New Commitment" that was cosponsored by the United Nations Educational, Scientific and Cultural Organization (UNESCO) produced a declaration recognizing that "traditional and local knowledge systems, as dynamic expressions of perceiving and understanding the world, can make and historically have made a valuable contribution to science and technology."

The declaration suggested that as a fund of cultural heritage and empirical information, indigenous knowledge should be preserved and researched. The conference called on the International Council for Science—a Paris-based nongovernmental organization composed of 98 multidisciplinary national scientific research councils and 26 international single-discipline scientific unions—to study how traditional knowledge might best relate with science. (One tool for doing this is ethnography, the study and systematic recording of human cultures.) More recently, researchers shared results at the Seventh International Congress of Ethnobiology, held at the University of Georgia in Athens in October 2000.

These efforts have sparked warnings from those who view them merely as gestures of political correctness—gestures that, while validating minority cultures, threaten to compromise the rigor of the scientific method. Perhaps more importantly, critics say that unmerited trust in tradition can endanger human health. A month before the UNESCO conference, the 17 May 1999 issue of *Forensic Science International* published an analysis of forensic data from Johannesburg, South Africa, where traditional remedies containing toxic substances were cited as causes for over 200 deaths in a five-year period. And a 14 October 1999 *Nature* editorial responding to the UNESCO conference declaration acknowledged that traditional knowledge deserves more respect from modern science than it has received, but noted that "such acceptance also requires due caution and a rigorous assessment of more and less deserving forms of traditional knowledge." The editorial further warned that integrating different forms of knowledge would not be easy.

For one thing, indigenous knowledge rarely comes in the form of scientific data. Often it involves complex narratives. Yet as viewers of detective dramas know, even a tangential discussion can sometimes yield important clues. In her 1997 book *The Spirit Catches You and You Fall Down* about the health care received by a young Hmong girl in California with epilepsy, Anne Fadiman wrote, "The Hmong have a phrase, *hais cuaj txub kaum txub*, which means 'to speak of all kinds of things.' It is often used at the beginning of an oral narrative as a way of reminding the listeners that the world is full of things that may not seem to be connected but actually are; that no event occurs in isolation; that you can miss a lot by sticking to the point; and that the storyteller is likely to be rather long-winded."

Fadiman proceeds to show how the girl's immigrant family and cultural origins in Southeast Asia—and her American doctors' approach to them—seriously influenced the treatment she received. The girl's family interpreted her doctors' behavior as uncaring and regarded the medical treatment with suspicion; thus, they decided to forgo the recommended treatment. It is a story of contrasting ways of understanding health, and it's a situation that is likely to occur more and more often as populations spread across the globe.

## Drug Discovery: The Greatest Interest?

Perhaps the greatest interest in indigenous knowledge comes from its potential for discovering new drugs and new uses for indigenous medicines. The ethnobotanical approach to drug discovery has experienced a resurgence in recent decades [see *EHP* 105:1186–1191 (1997)] and has yielded many new medicines, including several that the National Cancer Institute considers promising for the treatment of AIDS, cancer, and other serious illnesses.

Joshua Rosenthal, a program officer for the NIH International Cooperative Biodiversity Groups (ICBG), notes that traditionally used compounds have yielded new antimalarial drugs (for example, artemisinin is derived from the herb *Artemisia annua*, also known as sweet Annie or qing hao and long used in Chinese medicine to combat fevers), painkillers (a potent alkaloid from the skin of the frog *Epipedobates tricolor*—used to make poison darts for immobilizing small animals—is being tested at Abbot Laboratories), and antidiarrheal medicines (such as Normal Stool Formula from Shaman Pharmaceuticals, which uses the sap of the Amazonian rain forest tree *Croton lechleri*).

In addition to the drugs themselves, says Rosenthal, indigenous knowledge can help to identify mechanisms of action for therapeutic agents. "In starting from the knowledge that something works when tested in broad-based functional assays," he says, "we have the opportunity to discover new molecular targets that we might not have identified using approaches that begin with our current understanding of a disease."

The ICBG program, begun in 1992, aims to integrate drug discovery, biodiversity conservation, and sustainable economic benefits for populations where new drugs are found. Starting from the broad outline of the United Nations Convention on Biological Diversity—a 1992 global agreement that recognized the need for drug discovery to provide fair returns to the places where drugs orginate and support in the form of financial, political, and other incentives for communities to conserve the natural sources of new medicines—the ICBG developed regional research groups in Latin America, Africa, and Southeast Asia.

The program is a partnership in which traditional knowledge can guide the search for new medicines and support decisions for research follow-up. In turn, modern medicine channels research findings back to traditional healers and communities. Under the program, scientists propose studies and approach traditional healers for insights on how they use plants, which may lead to broader medical application of natural compounds. The pairing of scientists and traditional healers varies depending on the program and the study proposed.

Achieving a feasible, equitable solution hasn't been easy. The convention provided an important framework and recognition of the relationships between drug discovery, ecosystems, and traditional knowledge. However, its implementation has often mired in national politics, according to Rosenthal. Constructing agreements among international companies, universities, national governments, and local communities that return benefits to source communities without obstructing the research process is very difficult. "Very few countries have been able to do it yet," he notes. In one instance, well-intentioned researchers encountered a politically charged atmosphere in Chiapas, Mexico, where minority indigenous groups, stung by previous injustices and a lack of respect for their customs, moved to block sharing of their traditional knowledge with Western medicine.

Efforts to compare the effectiveness of scientific and traditional systems have had limited success. In Suriname, one study aimed to compare the rate of drug discovery of an ethnobotanically led process with that of a conventional approach of random biologic assays. It found a slightly higher success rate for the traditional approach, but the study encountered two main difficulties. First, the biologic assays skewed the basis for comparison toward the modern drug discovery model because those assays screen mainly for illnesses faced by temperate-zone populations, and not for health problems such as malaria or tuberculosis that are far more common in the tropics where the plants grow. Second, the fast turnover in the types of bioassays used by pharmaceutical companies—sometimes a complete change in a matter of months—meant that there was no consistent bioassay benchmark for compounds studied even a year apart. "It's difficult to get a comparison of all the samples hitting the same screens," Rosenthal says.

What the ICBG has found are promising areas of interchange between traditional systems and modern medicine, not only in the drug discovery process but also in creating channels for information exchange between very different knowledge systems. In Central and West Africa, researchers have worked with traditional healers' unions, providing opportunities for the healers to learn about Western medical research and exploring the potential of traditional medicine for treating HIV/AIDS and malaria. A network of medical professionals from both systems has emerged, with leadership from Maurice Iwu, a Nigerian-born ethnopharmacologist. Iwu is working on a treatment for infection with the Ebola virus using a traditional West African chewstick (a tooth cleaning instrument) made from the *Garcinia kola* tree.

Shaman Pharmaceuticals, a small company based in South San Francisco, California, notes its debt to indigenous knowledge from the start. "[Indigenous] knowledge greatly reduces the number of plants that we screen intensively and increases our potential for success," observes Steven King, the company's senior vice president for ethnobotany and conservation. Shaman takes pains to create new paths for sharing the benefits of the discovery process and provides direct reciprocal payments to the communities it works with. But because money alone isn't always the best way to share profits with a remote community with no bank, Shaman also uses other means including public health projects that provide potable water. Such projects are managed by the company's nonprofit foundation, The Healing Forest Conservancy.

"Historically, ethnobotany and forest conservation projects have not been conducted with public health and medical projects," King and coauthors noted in the 1996 book *Valuing Local Knowledge: Indigenous People and Intellectual Property Rights*. But when modern industries such as mining, oil extraction, and logging damage ecosystems where promising plants are found, there can be grave environmental health effects, including contamination of streams and drinking water with toxic runoff from mines.

Public health projects can address these impacts, for example by providing clean water and preventive medicine. The Healing Forest Conservancy has provided clean water for Quechua villages in Ecuador and Dayak villages in Indonesia. According to King, such projects, when integrated thoughtfully, can complement indigenous medical systems. For example, projects can involve local people in project planning and implementation, and can address health priorities that they identify.

Still, the narrowly focused discovery process used by most pharmaceutical companies is poorly suited for gauging other values of indigenous knowledge. For a more systematic look, Rosenthal points to a new NIH grants program through the National Center for Complementary and Alternative Medicine, called Traditional, Indigenous Systems of Medicine. Begun in 2000, the program is intended to fund examinations of systems of traditional knowledge such as the Indian system of Ayurveda, American Indian medicine, traditional Chinese medicine, and Latin American folk medicine with the goal of increasing the quality of clinical research evaluating the efficacy of such traditional, indigenous systems of medicine. Such studies must, according to the program's announcement, study the system in the cultural context of its origin and as adopted and adapted in other cultures.

# Nutrition and Ecosystem Knowledge from the Past

While the path from ethnomedicine to new drugs is fairly direct, other sciences are also using ethnographic methods to assess indigenous knowledge for health benefits. Nutrition and agriculture may also benefit by exploring farmers' crop-breeding choices and local nutritional strategies. At the ethnobiology conference in Georgia, plant breeder Mary Eubanks, president of Sun Dance Genetics in Durham, North Carolina, and adjunct professor of plant genetics at Duke University, proposed that archaeobotanical investigations into the cultivation history of maize can yield safer, more robust varieties free of the potential health risks of genetically engineered varieties.

Traditional cultivation practices use naturally occurring genetic variation and a wider genetic base, making the varieties they yield less vulnerable to diseases and pests. By contrast, a genetically engineered crop has a narrower genetic base and therefore less variability to defend the crop from devastation by pests and disease that could cause food shortages and thus nutritional deficiencies. In the March 2000 issue of *Latin American Antiquity*, Eubanks and her coauthor observed that "the evolution of maize is intricately interwoven with culture history and environmental change." They emphasized that "the more we know about important crop plants, their relationships to their wild relatives … and how and under what conditions humans exploited and altered them … the greater our chances will be for identifying beneficial genes from wild plants"—and possibly recovering beneficial traits lost over time.

Elsewhere, anthropologists have found lessons for modern agriculture in traditional landscape management systems. In Indonesia, Bali's volcanic slopes and deep ravines make it difficult to irrigate rice fields. Traditionally the Balinese have diverted water through tunnels—some longer than a kilometer—to networks of canals and aqueducts. These networks are coordinated by rituals at community "water temples" across the island. Besides formalizing who takes care of each stretch of canal, the rituals bring together the people who maintain the system. While at a temple for a ritual, canal managers might discuss the sequence of opening locks, fields to be inundated, water volume, and other group decisions to be made. The hierarchy of water temples starts upstream at the volcanic Lake Batur and extends down to the smallest group of water users, about the size of a neighborhood.

With the introduction of modern farming practices in the 1970s and 1980s, however, agricultural scientists advised farmers to plant modern rice varieties, which can produce higher yields but which also require more fertilizers and pesticides. They also advised farmers to plant their fields independently, without waiting for communal workdays or synchronizing with others who use the canals.

In the mid-1980s Steven Lansing, an ecological anthropologist doing field research in Bali, heard farmers complain of rising pest damage to rice crops. Pest outbreaks were hurting rice yields despite the introduction of the modern varieties and cropping patterns. By 1987 rodent infestations were more serious than they had ever been before. Continued crop losses were threatening the area's nutritional status and introducing other risks of disease from the rats that infested the crop fields.

To assess the effects of various influences on the situation, Lansing and a computer expert developed a computer model of two river systems in southern Bali based on hydrology, rice growth, pest dynamics, and social/behavioral factors, including the community water temple rituals. Using the model, Lansing found that the water temple network managed water resources more effectively and kept pest damage low. By clustering planting and harvesting of nearby fields, the network created a sort of artificial ecosystem that kept pest populations in check. The computer model showed that the rice system reached a stable level of high productivity after several seasons of such management. Under the fragmented, random planting schedule of the introduced method, pest problems increased both in the model and in the rice fields. These results helped convince officials that the communal water temple network had important benefits.

Stuart Plattner, a program director at the National Science Foundation, which supported the work, observed that Lansing's research started from a traditional ethnographic perspective and followed connections that emerged between religion and irrigation, undeterred by officials who insisted that the two were unrelated. "Things that we think are separate are not at all separate," Plattner wrote in a 6 April 1997 article in the *Earth Times*. "Steve Lansing has been tremendously successful in making that point." Balinese scientists have since presented the experience of combining new and traditional agricultural technologies at international workshops.

Studies in which indigenous knowledge and modern science meaningfully complement each other remain few, but other promising examples come from Canada's far north. Researchers there have documented environmental health from both indigenous and scientific perspectives. Studies funded by the West Kitikmeot/Slave Study Society, a nonprofit partnership of government, industry, aboriginal, and environmental organizations, have monitored the effects of mining and other development on the environment and people in the area between the Great Slave Lake in the Northwest Territories and Bathurst Inlet to the north in Nunavut. In that area, indigenous peoples such as the Dogrib, Dene, and Inuit predominate. Outside influences have heavily impacted the health and social conditions of these groups and have prompted many of them to look within their traditional systems for solutions.

One pair of studies in the late 1990s examined caribou migration patterns using satellite collars placed on each herd's leader in one and traditional oral narrative accounts from Dogrib elders in the other. Dogrib elders advised wildlife scientist Anne Gunn in developing the satellite-collar study, and information from the Dogrib traditional knowledge study of caribou was placed in a geographic information system database for further analysis.

Caribou provided a natural starting point for collaboration: elders and scientists shared concerns over declining caribou population and habitat, and indigenous groups in the region have long relied on caribou for nutrition, cultural health, and identity. The groups' diet and materials for clothing and shelter comes from caribou (some use the animal's skins for tipis, for example). Perhaps more importantly, the groups interpret the health of their society through their relationship with the caribou and take pride in their ability to hunt and track. In that way, caribou give them a sense of belonging and order. (When placed in new surroundings without bearings on where to find caribou, for example, some groups lose a sense of purpose; alcoholism rates are often higher among these groups.)

The two studies correlated closely on migration patterns and showed that traditional Dogrib methods for diverting caribou from mine sites—where they risk exposure to toxic residues— were effective. Other studies have tracked the health effects of mining with community observations about contaminated plant, wildlife, and water resources and adverse symptoms experienced by mine workers. A *State of Knowledge* report posted on the society's Web site at http://www.wkss.nt.ca/ synthesizes these studies.

The West Kitikmeot/Slave Society even studied how Dogrib place-names convey information about biologic features of the people's natural surroundings. A 1998 report by the Dogrib Renewable Resources Committee titled *Habitat of Dogrib Traditional Territory: Place Names as Indicators of Bio-Geographical Knowledge* documents indigenous knowledge of the area as a baseline for tracking changes in ecosystems. In documenting over 2,100 sites, the study found that Dogrib place names such as "gooseberry lake" and "red-throated loons on big fish lake" signaled facets of habitat and local biodiversity that have since been incorporated in habitat maps based on satellite images.

## Where Language, Health, and the Environment Overlap

For Luisa Maffi, an anthropological linguist, the place-name study confirms that language is a vital key to indigenous peoples' community health. "The obvious fact is that much of knowledge, if not all, is encoded in language," says Maffi, who is also president of Terralingua, a nonprofit research group that conducts studies on ecosystems and cultural diversity in order to support maintenance of that diversity. Their studies involve ethnographic interviews and local participation in ecosystem inventories.

Maffi says that the number of languages in an area can be a good indicator of cultural range, which in turn is linked to the store of knowledge of a given ecosystem and its biological diversity. "If you look at a map of the world's biodiversity hot spots and overlay on that a map of linguistic diversity, you see a striking overlap," she says. That suggests a correlation between the number of discrete cultures in an area and biological diversity.

Terralingua has explored that correlation globally in a project with the World Wide Fund For Nature International that mapped biocultural diversity as a step toward sustaining ecosystems. On a smaller scale, the group's Sierra Tarahumara Diversity Project aims to understand those interrelationships in a part of northern Mexico where mining and logging have degraded the environment and undermined local cultures by discouraging the use of native language on the job and presenting Western consumer goods that may entice young workers away

from Tarahumara customs. Indigenous societies in the Sierra Tarahumara depend on both subsistence agriculture and a wide array of local plant and animal species for their survival. Project researchers have met with Tarahumara communities to assess priorities, document the linkages among biologic, cultural, and linguistic resources, assess local impacts of commercial activities (including tourism), and suggest various alternatives. The project aims to advance basic scientific research as well as conservation planning.

Besides expressing how people understand their environment, Maffi finds that people's words express how they perceive symptoms of illness. When a minority language is marginalized, that can affect the quality of health care the speakers receive. In the Chiapas region of Mexico, Maffi found that the Tzeltal Maya had a sophisticated range of terms for describing symptoms in their language (distinguishing a wheezing cough from a hacking cough, for example). Yet when a field medic would visit the village and ask the townspeople about their illnesses in Spanish, she said, "People would be completely unable to talk about it, to convey the subtleties that they could in their own language." That chasm, she says, together with the medic's impatience with local customs, seriously affected the quality of health care they received.

## Community Health

A community's environmental health therefore depends not just on integrating local knowledge with scientific understanding, but on recognizing the differences in power and access enjoyed by different cultures. Many indigenous cultures exist at the margins of mainstream society, tend to be poor, and often lack political clout in managing natural resources or influencing the allocation of funds for their public health care, education, and other needs. In a November 1999 speech, Gro Harlem Brundtland, director-general of the World Health Organization, said, "Indigenous peoples continue to be subject to systematic denial of their fundamental human rights—to cultural identity, to land, to liberty, to health, and to life itself."

This disparity supports society's mandate for cultural competence among health professionals today, according to Richard Levinson, associate executive director of programs and policy at the American Public Health Association (APHA), a nonprofit professional organization. "Cultural competence means that health professionals need to understand the cultural characteristics of the groups from which their patients come," says Levinson. Physicians treating the Hmong family of Anne Fadiman's book, for example, needed a basic familiarity with the Hmong community's approach to health and illness in order to understand how to treat them. Levinson says that in the United States that concept has extended beyond immigrant groups to include long-naturalized populations such as Latino and African-American communities, which may trust their local experience more than outside health professionals.

Dwight Conquergood, an associate professor of performance studies at Northwestern University in Evanston, Illinois, who in 1985 was a young ethnographer at a refugee camp in Thailand, demonstrated this principle at a community level by engaging Hmong values and customs in a campaign to eradicate rabies.

Efforts by the camp's medical staff to get pets inoculated produced no results. Fadiman's book relates that Conquergood organized a "rabies parade," with Hmong participants and characters from Hmong folktales explaining the etiology of rabies. The day after the procession, wrote Fadiman, "The vaccination stations were so besieged by dogs—dogs carried in their owners' arms, dogs dragged on rope leashes, dogs rolled in on two-wheeled pushcarts—that the health workers could hardly inoculate them fast enough."

Anthropology has also supplied methods for applying community-based knowledge to environmental health research. Elizabeth Guillette, an anthropologist with the Center for Bioenvironmental Research at Tulane and Xavier Universities in New Orleans, Louisiana, has applied those methods to gain valuable information related to long-term pesticide exposure. In some cases, ethnographic interviews helped to guide the direction of research. For example, mothers in a Mexican pesticide exposure study begun in 1995 repeatedly noted that their children engaged in less play than the parents recalled from their own childhoods. That led Guillette to investigate the children's abilities through directed activities. She found that pesticide-exposed children indeed did have less endurance and coordination than lesser-exposed children [see *EHP* 106:347–353 (1998); *EHP* 108 (suppl 3):389–393 (2000)].

Again, channeling study findings back to the community is an important but often neglected part of the research process. "It does not have to take a lot of time," Guillette says, and it can yield further benefits. She presented her results on pesticide exposure to the study groups in the Mexican cohort and has since noticed a decline in home use of pesticides.

Community-based initiatives to monitor environmental health foster collaboration between Western science and indigenous knowledge. In Canada, the Dogrib and neighboring Dene have launched ambitious efforts that include technical training, counsel by elders in documenting local knowledge, and developing indicators of nutritional status, economic development, and mining conditions. Residents have helped to identify hazardous waste sites for cleanup and mapped their locations for others to view on the Nunavut Planning Commission's Web site, located online at http://npc.nunavut.ca/. Similar efforts are under way among the Mohawk Nation in Akwesasne, New York [see *EHP* 106(suppl 3):833–840 (1998)].

# Considering the Merits of Two Systems

Still, questions remain: Why should efforts by small groups, many with problems rarely found in industrialized societies, concern the broader medical community? These would not seem to be promising sources of health wisdom as indigenous communities tend to have shorter life expectancies than the mainstream population and are more likely to suffer from problems such as emerging infectious diseases that are less common in the rest of the population. And why should scarce research funds be used to assess nonscientific approaches to health?

Levinson responds that indigenous peoples are not just marginal groups with remote illnesses. A continuing rise in travel and immigration brings new people—along with their beliefs about the medical conditions they face—to industrialized countries. According to the American Medical Student Association, a national student-run organization, generalist physicians can soon expect more than 40% of their patients to be from minority cultures. The association offers training material on cross-cultural competency in a downloadable document titled *Module on Cross-Cultural Issues in Health*, located online at http://www.amsa.org/programs/ccimain.cfm.

"[The United States has] always been a nation of immigrants," says Levinson, inextricably tying it to the health concerns of groups around the world; health concerns that appear distant now will eventually be ours, he maintains. "In terms of health, we really have one world," he says, adding that an international flow of emerging infectious diseases means that insular attitudes about these illnesses must change.

As for why to consider indigenous knowledge, Levinson reiterates the importance of health professionals understanding where their patients come from so they will be alert not only to possible dangers but also to possible benefits as well. Many traditional customs, such as practicing yoga and taking herbal remedies, have a healthy effect. "The problem," says Levinson, "is when the practices are harmful, for example native drugs that contain toxic substances or rituals that may prevent appropriate diagnosis or treatment. Either way, good treatment requires awareness of these factors."

Experiences from ethnomedicine, ecosystem management, and community health all suggest that health professionals in the twenty-first century may gain new tools by innovatively combining the best of science with the best of the old ways. These lessons are not lost on the medical professionals in California who dealt with Lia Lee, the Hmong girl with epilepsy. In a response to a review of Fadiman's book in the March-April 1998 issue of *Pediatric Nursing*, June L. Harney Boffman, who worked in the Merced County Medical Center during the period covered by the book, urged that nurses, doctors, and social workers recognize the power of belief. "Knowing is in the context of one's world," Boffman wrote. "This should never be overlooked in the future."

From *Environmental Health Perspectives*, Vol. 109, no. 5, 2001. Published by National Institute of Environmental Health Sciences. www.ehponline.org

**150**

# The Adaptive Value of Religious Ritual

**Rituals promote group cohesion by requiring members to engage in behavior that is too costly to fake**

RICHARD SOSIS

I was 15 years old the first time I went to Jerusalem's Old City and visited the 2,000-year-old remains of the Second Temple, known as the Western Wall. It may have foreshadowed my future life as an anthropologist, but on my first glimpse of the ancient stones I was more taken by the people standing at the foot of the structure than by the wall itself. Women stood in the open sun, facing the Wall in solemn worship, wearing long-sleeved shirts, head coverings and heavy skirts that scraped the ground. Men in their thick beards, long black coats and fur hats also seemed oblivious to the summer heat as they swayed fervently and sang praises to God. I turned to a friend, "Why would anyone in their right mind dress for a New England winter only to spend the afternoon praying in the desert heat?" At the time I thought there was no rational explanation and decided that my fellow religious brethren might well be mad.

Of course, "strange" behavior is not unique to ultraorthodox Jews. Many religious acts appear peculiar to the outsider. Pious adherents the world over physically differentiate themselves from others: Moonies shave their heads, Jain monks of India wear contraptions on their heads and feet to avoid killing insects, and clergy almost everywhere dress in outfits that distinguish them from the rest of society. Many peoples also engage in some form of surgical alteration. Australian aborigines perform a ritual operation on adolescent boys in which a bone or a stone is inserted into the penis through an incision in the urethra. Jews and Muslims submit their sons to circumcision, and in some Muslim societies daughters are also subject to circumcision or other forms of genital mutilation. Groups as diverse as the Nuer of Sudan and the Iatmul of New Guinea force their adolescents to undergo ritual scarification. Initiation ceremonies, otherwise known as rites of passage, are often brutal. Among Native Americans, Apache boys were forced to bathe in icy water, Luiseno initiates were required to lie motionless while being bitten by hordes of ants, and Tukuna girls had their hair plucked out.

How can we begin to understand such behavior? If human beings are rational creatures, then why do we spend so much time, energy and resources on acts that can be so painful or, at the very least, uncomfortable? Archaeologists tell us that our species has engaged in ritual behavior for at least 100,000 years, and every known culture practices some form of religion. It even survives covertly in those cultures where governments have attempted to eliminate spiritual practices. And, despite the unparalleled triumph of scientific rationalism in the 20th century, religion continued to flourish. In the United States a steady 40 percent of the population attended church regularly throughout the century. A belief in God (about 96 percent), the afterlife (about 72 percent), heaven (about 72 percent) and hell (about 58 percent) remained substantial and remarkably constant. Why do religious beliefs, practices and institutions continue to be an essential component of human social life?

Such questions have intrigued me for years. Initially my training in anthropology did not provide an answer. Indeed, my studies only increased my bewilderment. I received my training in a subfield known as human behavioral ecology, which studies the adaptive design of behavior with attention to its ecological setting. Behavioral ecologists assume that natural selection has shaped the human nervous system to respond successfully to varying ecological circumstances. All organisms must balance trade-offs: Time spent doing one thing prevents them from pursuing other activities that can enhance their survival or reproductive success. Animals that maximize the rate at which they acquire resources, such as food and mates, can maximize the number of descendants, which is exactly what the game of natural selection is all about.

Behavioral ecologists assume that natural selection has designed our decision-making mechanisms to optimize the rate at which human beings accrue resources under diverse ecological conditions—a basic prediction of *optimal foraging theory*. Optimality models offer predictions of the "perfectly adapted" behavioral response, given a set of environmental constraints. Of course, a perfect fit with the environment is almost never achieved because organisms rarely have perfect information and because environments are always changing. Nevertheless, this assumption has provided a powerful framework to analyze a variety of decisions, and most research (largely conducted among foraging populations) has shown that our species broadly conforms to these expectations.

If our species is designed to optimize the rate at which we extract energy from the environment, why would we engage in religious behavior that seems so counterproductive? Indeed, some religious practices, such as ritual sacrifices, are a conspicuous display of wasted resources. Anthropologists can explain why foragers regularly share their food with others in the group, but why would anyone share their food with a dead ancestor by burning it to ashes on an altar? A common response to this question is that people believe in the efficacy of the rituals and the tenets of the faith that give meaning to the ceremonies. But this response merely begs the question. We must really ask why natural selection has favored a psychology that believes in the supernatural and engages in the costly manifestations of those beliefs.

# Ritual Sacrifice

Behavioral ecologists have only recently begun to consider the curiosities of religious activities, so at first I had to search other disciplines to understand these practices. The scholarly literature suggested that I wasn't the only one who believed that intense religious behavior was a sign of madness. Some of the greatest minds of the past two centuries, such as Marx and Freud, supported my thesis. And the early anthropological theorists also held that spiritual beliefs were indicative of a primitive and simple mind. In the 19th century, Edward B. Tylor, often noted as one of the founding fathers of anthropology, maintained that religion arose out of a misunderstanding among "primitives" that dreams are real. He argued that dreams about deceased ancestors might have led the primitives to believe that spirits can survive death.

Eventually the discipline of anthropology matured, and its practitioners moved beyond the equation that "primitive equals irrational." Instead, they began to seek functional explanations of religion. Most prominent among these early 20th-century theorists was the Polish-born anthropologist Bronislaw Malinowski. He argued that religion arose out of "the real tragedies of human life, out of the conflict between human plans and realities." Although religion may serve to allay our fears of death, and provide comfort from our incessant search for answers, Malinowski's thesis did not seem to explain the origin of rituals. Standing in the midday desert sun in several layers of black clothing seems more like a recipe for increasing anxiety than treating it. The classical anthropologists didn't have the right answers to my questions. I needed to look elsewhere.

Fortunately, a new generation of anthropologists has begun to provide some explanations. It turns out that the strangeness of religious practices and their inherent costs are actually the critical features that contribute to the success of religion as a universal cultural strategy and why natural selection has favored such behavior in the human lineage. To understand this unexpected benefit we need to recognize the adaptive problem that ritual behavior solves. William Irons, a behavioral ecologist at Northwestern University, has suggested that the universal dilemma is the promotion of cooperation within a community. Irons argues that the primary adaptive benefit of religion is its ability to facilitate cooperation within a group—while hunting, sharing food, defending against attacks and waging war—all critical activities in our evolutionary history. But,

as Irons points out, although everyone is better off if everybody cooperates, this ideal is often very difficult to coordinate and achieve. The problem is that an individual is even better off if everyone else does the cooperating, while he or she remains at home enjoying an afternoon siesta. Cooperation requires social mechanisms that prevent individuals from free riding on the efforts of others. Irons argues that religion is such a mechanism.

The key is that religious rituals are a form of communication, which anthropologists have long maintained. They borrowed this insight from ethologists who observed that many species engage in patterned behavior, which they referred to as "ritual." Ethologists recognized that ritualistic behaviors served as a form of communication between members of the same species, and often between members of different species. For example, the males of many avian species engage in courtship rituals—such as bowing, head wagging, wing waving and hopping (among many other gestures)—to signal their amorous intents before a prospective mate. And, of course, the vibration of a rattlesnake's tail is a powerful threat display to other species that enter its personal space.

Irons's insight is that religious activities signal commitment to other members of the group. By engaging in the ritual, the member effectively says, "I identify with the group and I believe in what the group stands for." Through its ability to signal commitment, religious behavior can overcome the problem of free riders and promote cooperation within the group. It does so because trust lies at the heart of the problem: A member must assure everyone that he or she will participate in acquiring food or in defending the group. Of course, hunters and warriors may make promises—"you have my word, I'll show up tomorrow"—but unless the trust is already established such statements are not believable.

It turns out that there is a robust way to secure trust. Israeli biologist Amotz Zahavi observes that it is often in the best interest of an animal to send a dishonest signal—perhaps to fake its size, speed, strength, health or beauty. The only signal that can be believed is one that is too costly to fake, which he referred to as a "handicap." Zahavi argues that natural selection has favored the evolution of handicaps. For example, when a springbok antelope spots a predator it often *stots*—it jumps up and down. This extraordinary behavior puzzled biologists for years: Why would an antelope waste precious energy that could be used to escape the predator? And why would the animal make itself more visible to something that wants to eat it? The reason is that the springbok is displaying its quality to the predator—its ability to escape, effectively saying, "Don't bother chasing me. Look how strong my legs are, you won't be able to catch me." The only reason a predator believes the springbok is because the signal is too costly to fake. An antelope that is not quick enough to escape cannot imitate the signal because it is not strong enough to repeatedly jump to a certain height. Thus, a display can provide honest information if the signals are so costly to perform that lower quality organisms cannot benefit by imitating the signal.

In much the same way, religious behavior is also a costly signal. By donning several layers of clothing and standing out in the midday sun, ultraorthodox Jewish men are signaling to others: "Hey! Look, I'm a *haredi* Jew. If you are also a member of

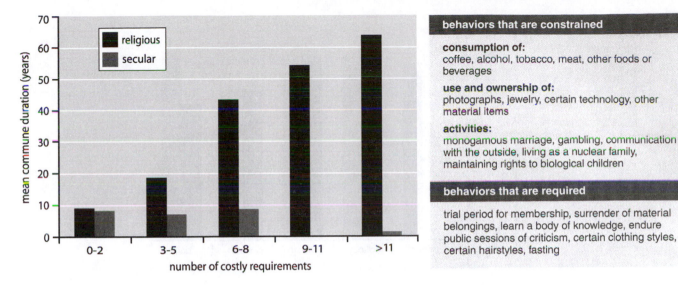

behaviors that are constrained

**consumption of:**
coffee, alcohol, tobacco, meat, other foods or beverages

**use and ownership of:**
photographs, jewelry, certain technology, other material items

**activities:**
monogamous marriage, gambling, communication with the outside, living as a nuclear family, maintaining rights to biological children

behaviors that are required

trial period for membership, surrender of material belongings, learn a body of knowledge, endure public sessions of criticism, certain clothing styles, certain hairstyles, fasting

this group you can trust me because why else would I be dressed like this? No one would do this *unless* they believed in the teachings of ultraorthodox Judaism and were fully committed to its ideals and goals." The quality that these men are signaling is their level of commitment to a specific religious group.

Adherence to a set of religious beliefs entails a host of ritual obligations and expected behaviors. Although there may be physical or psychological benefits associated with some ritual practices, the significant time, energy and financial costs involved serve as effective deterrents for anyone who does not believe in the teachings of a particular religion. There is no incentive for nonbelievers to join or remain in a religious group, because the costs of maintaining membership—such as praying three times a day, eating only kosher food, donating a certain part of your income to charity and so on—are simply too high.

Those who engage in the suite of ritual requirements imposed by a religious group can be trusted to believe sincerely in the doctrines of their respective religious communities. As a result of increased levels of trust and commitment among group members, religious groups minimize costly monitoring mechanisms that are otherwise necessary to overcome free-rider problems that typically plague communal pursuits. Hence, the adaptive benefit of ritual behavior is its ability to promote and maintain cooperation, a challenge that our ancestors presumably faced throughout our evolutionary history.

## Benefits of Membership

One prediction of the "costly signaling theory of ritual" is that groups that impose the greatest demands on their members will elicit the highest levels of devotion and commitment. Only committed members will be willing to dress and behave in ways that differ from the rest of society. Groups that maintain more-committed members can also offer more because it's easier for them to attain their collective goals than groups whose members are less committed. This may explain a paradox in the religious marketplace: Churches that require the most of their adherents are experiencing rapid rates of growth. For example, the Church of Jesus Christ of Latter-day Saints (Mormons), Seventh-day

Adventists and Jehovah's Witnesses, who respectively abstain from caffeine, meat and blood transfusions (among other things), have been growing at exceptional rates. In contrast, liberal Protestant denominations such as the Episcopalians, Methodists and Presbyterians have been steadily losing members.

Economist Lawrence Iannaccone, of George Mason University, has also noted that the most demanding groups also have the greatest number of committed members. He found that the more distinct a religious group was—how much the group's lifestyle differed from mainstream America—the higher its attendance rates at services. Sociologists Roger Finke and Rodney Stark, of Penn State and the University of Washington, respectively, have argued that when the Second Vatican Council in 1962 repealed many of the Catholic Church's prohibitions and reduced the level of strictness in the church, it initiated a decline in church attendance among American Catholics and reduced the enrollments in seminaries. Indeed, in the late 1950s almost 75 percent of American Catholics were attending Mass weekly, but since the Vatican's actions there has been a steady decline to the current rate of about 45 percent.

The costly signaling theory of ritual also predicts that greater commitment will translate into greater cooperation within groups. My colleague Eric Bressler, a graduate student at McMaster University, and I addressed this question by looking at data from the records of 19th-century communes. All communes face an inherent problem of promoting and sustaining cooperation because individuals can free ride on the efforts of others. Because cooperation is key to a commune's survival, we employed commune longevity as a measure of cooperation. Compared to their secular counterparts, the religious communes did indeed demand more of their members, including such behavior as celibacy, the surrender of all material possessions and vegetarianism. Communes that demanded more of their members survived longer, overcoming the fundamental challenges of cooperation. By placing greater demands on their members, they were presumably able to elicit greater belief in and commitment toward the community's common ideology and goals.

I also wanted to evaluate the costly signaling theory of ritual within modern communal societies. The kibbutzim I had visited

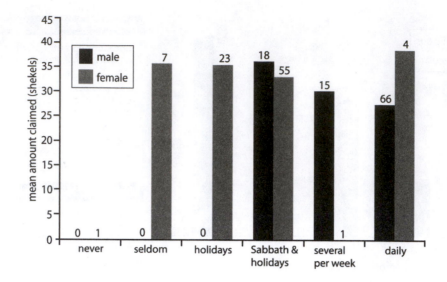

in Israel as a teenager provided an ideal opportunity to examine these hypotheses. For most of their 100-year history, these communal societies have lived by the dictum, "From each according to his abilities, to each according to his needs." The majority of the more than 270 kibbutzim are secular (and often ideologically antireligious); fewer than 20 are religiously oriented. Because of a massive economic failure—a collective debt of more than $4 billion—the kibbutzim are now moving in the direction of increased privatization and reduced communality. When news of the extraordinary debt surfaced in the late 1980s, it went largely unnoticed that the religious kibbutzim were financially stable. In the words of the Religious Kibbutz Movement Federation, "the economic position of the religious kibbutzim is sound, and they remain uninvolved in the economic crisis."

The success of the religious kibbutzim is especially remarkable given that many of their rituals inhibit economic productivity. For example, Jewish law does not permit Jews to milk cows on the Sabbath. Although rabbinic rulings now permit milking by kibbutz members to prevent the cows from suffering, in the early years none of this milk was used commercially. There are also significant constraints imposed by Jewish law on agricultural productivity. Fruits are not allowed to be eaten for the first few years of the tree's life, agricultural fields must lie fallow every seven years, and the corners of fields can never be harvested—they must be left for society's poor. Although these constraints appear detrimental to productivity, the costly signaling theory of ritual suggests that they may actually be the key to the economic success of the religious kibbutzim.

I decided to study this issue with economist Bradley Ruffle of Israel's Ben Gurion University. We developed a game to determine whether there were differences in how the members of secular and religious kibbutzim cooperated with each other. The game involves two members from the same kibbutz who remain anonymous to each other. Each member is told there are 100 shekels in an envelope to which both members have access. Each participant decides how many shekels to withdraw and keep. If the sum of both requests exceeds 100 shekels, both members receive no money and the game is over. However, if the requests are less than or equal to 100 shekels, the money re-

maining in the envelope is increased by 50 percent and divided evenly among the participants. Each member also keeps the original amount he or she requested. The game is an example of a common-pool resource dilemma in which publicly accessible goods are no longer available once they are consumed. Since the goods are available to more than one person, the maintenance of the resources requires individual self-restraint; in other words, cooperation.

After we controlled for a number of variables, including the age and size of the kibbutz and the amount of privatization, we found not only that religious kibbutzniks were more cooperative with each other than secular kibbutzniks, but that male religious kibbutz members were also significantly more cooperative than female members. Among secular kibbutzniks we found no sex differences at all. This result is understandable if we appreciate the types of rituals and demands imposed on religious Jews. Although there are a variety of requirements that are imposed equally on males and females, such as keeping kosher and refraining from work on the Sabbath, male rituals are largely performed in public, whereas female rituals are generally pursued privately. Indeed, none of the three major requirements imposed exclusively on women—attending a ritual bath, separating a portion of dough when baking bread and lighting Shabbat and holiday candles—are publicly performed. They are not rituals that signal commitment to a wider group; instead they appear to signal commitment to the family. Men, however, engage in highly visible rituals, most notably public prayer, which they are expected to perform three times a day. Among male religious kibbutz members, synagogue attendance is positively correlated with cooperative behavior. There is no similar correlation among females. This is not surprising given that women are not required to attend services, and so their presence does not signal commitment to the group. Here the costly signaling theory of ritual provides a unique explanation of these findings. We expect that further work will provide even more insight into the ability of ritual to promote trust, commitment and cooperation.

We know that many other species engage in ritual behaviors that appear to enhance trust and cooperation. For example, anthropologists John Watanabe of Dartmouth University and Bar-

bara Smuts at the University of Michigan have shown that greetings between male olive baboons serve to signal trust and commitment between former rivals. So why are human rituals often cloaked in mystery and the supernatural? Cognitive anthropologists Scott Atran of the University of Michigan and Pascal Boyer at Washington University in St. Louis have pointed out that the counterintuitive nature of supernatural concepts are more easily remembered than mundane ideas, which facilitates their cultural transmission. Belief in supernatural agents such as gods, spirits and ghosts also appears to be critical to religion's ability to promote long-term cooperation. In our study of 19th-century communes, Eric Bressler and I found that the strong positive relationship between the number of costly requirements imposed on members and commune longevity only held for religious communes, not secular ones. We were surprised by this result because secular groups such as militaries and fraternities appear to successfully employ costly rituals to maintain cooperation. Cultural ecologist Roy Rappaport explained, however, that although religious and secular rituals can both promote cooperation, religious rituals ironically generate greater belief and commitment because they sanctify unfalsifiable statements that are beyond the possibility of examination. Since statements containing supernatural elements, such as "Jesus is the son of God," cannot be proved or disproved, believers verify them "emotionally." In contrast to religious propositions, the kibbutz's guiding dictum, taken from Karl Marx, is not beyond question; it can be evaluated by living according to its directives by distributing labor and resources appropriately. Indeed, as the economic situation on the kibbutzim has worsened, this fundamental proposition of kibbutz life has been challenged and is now disregarded by many who are pushing their communities to accept differential pay scales. The ability of religious rituals to evoke emotional experiences that can be associated with enduring supernatural concepts and symbols differentiates them from both animal and secular rituals and lies at the heart of their efficiency in promoting and maintaining long-term group cooperation and commitment.

Evolutionary research on religious behavior is in its infancy, and many questions remain to be addressed. The costly signaling theory of ritual appears to provide some answers, and, of course, it has given me a better understanding of the questions I asked as a teenager. The real value of the costly signaling theory of ritual will be determined by its ability to explain religious phenomena across societies. Most of us, including ultraorthodox Jews, are not living in communes. Nevertheless, contemporary religious congregations that demand much of their members are able to achieve a close-knit social community—an impressive accomplishment in today's individualistic world.

Religion has probably always served to enhance the union of its practitioners; unfortunately, there is also a dark side to this unity. If the intragroup solidarity that religion promotes is one of its significant adaptive benefits, then from its beginning religion has probably always played a role in intergroup conflicts. In other words, one of the benefits for individuals of intragroup solidarity is the ability of unified groups to defend and compete against other groups. This seems to be as true today as it ever was, and is nowhere more apparent than in the region I visited as a 15-year-old boy—which is where I am as I write these words. As I conduct my fieldwork in the center of this war zone, I hope that by appreciating the depth of the religious need in the human psyche, and by understanding this powerful adaptation, we can learn how to promote cooperation rather than conflict.

# Bibliography

Atran, S. 2002. *In Gods We Trust.* New York: Oxford University Press.

Iannaccone, L. 1992. Sacrifice and stigma: Reducing free-riding in cults, communes, and other collectives. *Journal of Political Economy* 100:271-291.

Iannaccone, L. 1994. Why strict churches are strong. *American Journal of Sociology* 99:1180-1211.

Irons, W. 2001. Religion as a hard-to-fake sign of commitment. In *Evolution and the Capacity for Commitment,* ed. R. Nesse, pp. 292-309. New York: Russell Sage Foundation.

Rappaport, R. 1999. *Ritual and Religion in the Making of Humanity.* Cambridge: Cambridge University Press.

Sosis, R. 2003. Why aren't we all Hutterites? Costly signaling theory and religious behavior. *Human Nature* 14:91-127.

Sosis, R., and C. Alcorta. 2003. Signaling, solidarity, and the sacred: The evolution of religious behavior. *Evolutionary Anthropology* 12:264-274.

Sosis, R., and E. Bressler. 2003. Cooperation and commune longevity: A test of the costly signaling theory of religion. *Cross-Cultural Research* 37:211-239.

Sosis, R., and B. Ruffle. 2003. Religious ritual and cooperation: Testing for a relationship on Israeli religious and secular kibbutzim. *Current Anthropology* 44:713-722.

Zahavi, A., and A. Zahavi. 1997. *The Handicap Principle.* New York: Oxford University Press.

**RICHARD SOSIS** is an assistant professor of anthropology at the University of Connecticut. His research interests include the evolution of cooperation, utopian societies and the behavioral ecology of religion. Address: Department of Anthropology, U-2176, University of Connecticut, Storrs, CT 06269-2176. Internet: richard.sosis@uconn.edu

From *American Scientist,* March-April 2004, pp. 166–172. Copyright © 2004 by American Scientist, magazine of Sigma Xi, The Scientific Research Society. Reprinted by permission.

# Shamans

MARK J. PLOTKIN

*Contrary to popular belief, the medicine man, or shaman (usually an accomplished botanist), represents the most ancient profession in the evolution of human culture.*

—Dr. Richard Evans Schultes, 1963

He didn't look like a medicine man to me when I first met him.

Having been raised on a steady diet of Tarzan films, I first entered the rain forest expecting to find the medicine man (or "witch doctor") outfitted in full forest regalia: grass skirts, carnivore tooth necklaces, feather headdress. And indeed I did eventually work with shamans wearing even more fantastic costumes (or almost nothing, in some instances) when I entered the jungles of the northeast Amazon in the late 1970s. But as ever-encroaching Western civilization began making its appearance throughout the most remote corners of Amazonia, the young indigenous people lost interest in the old ways. Living in a world where the cultural global icons were people like Bruce Lee, Madonna, and Michael Jordan, the young Indians showed little or no interest in their own traditional cultures. The world of the shamans, with their belief in magic spirit worlds and astral travel, seemed less useful and effective than antibiotics. And if the missionaries or government-sponsored nurses insisted that shamanism was a sham, why pay any attention to a great-grandfather who said otherwise? So I would enter villages to find ancient wizards and plant masters wearing traditional breechcloths and jaguar-tooth necklaces but their descendants dressed in National Basketball Association T-shirts and high-top tennis shoes. In fifteen years of field experience, I had met few shamans who were not at least twice as old (and, more often, thrice as old) as I was.

But this fellow was different.

It was the first day of August, 1995, and I was seated in a cotton hammock under a thatched roof in the western Amazon of Colombia. To get there, I had to fly south from the Andean city of Bogota to the burgeoning frontier town of Florencia, the capital city of the state of Caquetá; then an all-day bus ride past the military checkpoints and through the depressingly deforested landscape. In the 1960s, the national government, with the best of intentions, had encouraged landless peasants to settle on the "fertile" soils of the "uninhabited" Amazon region. The peasants' in-ability to manage the (admittedly challenging) tropical landscape resulted in forest destruction of staggering proportions. When my mentor Richard Schultes carried out ethnobotanical research here in the 1940s and 1950s, he marveled at "the seemingly limitless forest that stretched unbroken to the far horizon." Schultes returned to the area only a decade later, and writer William Burroughs was there to record the scientist's reaction: "My God, what have they done to the forest.... It's all gone!"

I had traveled to the area at the invitation of a Colombian colleague to participate in an ayahuasca ritual, the vision-vine ceremony conducted by Amazonian shamans for purposes of curing and divination. In South and North America, ayahuasca had attained an enormous and devoted following among certain New Age groups, though none of the practitioners whom I met were Native American shamans. The invitation to the Colombian Amazon seemed to represent the opportunity to participate in a truly traditional ceremony.

On that torrid afternoon, sweat poured off me and a few mosquitoes buzzed hungrily around my ears as I conversed with a fellow who stood leaning against the wooden post from which one end of my hammock was strung. He stood about five-foot-two, the typical height of a forest Indian, though the local campesinos (peasants) were not much taller. He had jet black hair and spoke excellent Spanish, again making it difficult for me to ascertain whether he was a Native American or not (knowing that such a question can be considered extremely rude by both cultures, I would not ask him outright). He took a last, long draught of his warm beer, and asked me if I'd ever been to the jungle before. I replied that I had worked in several South American countries searching for healing plants. A brief smile flickered across his face. "Have you ever participated in a *toma*, an ayahuasca session?" he asked.

"Once," I replied, "in Peru. But I know I have much to learn about the use of the vision vine for curing purposes." A fleeting, Mona Lisa smile played across his face as he stubbed out his cigarette on the dirt floor and said, "Then I'll see you at the ceremony tonight." And with that, he wandered off.

The session was held at a small tribal meetinghouse constructed at the edge of the village. I was crestfallen—the poured concrete floor, cinderblock walls, and corrugated aluminum roof seemed the very antithesis of rain forest culture. Where was the traditional *maloca*, the fantastic elongated conical roundhouse that was supposed to be the characteristic indigenous dwelling of the northwest Amazon? I asked a local Ingano fellow who wandered past. "The ayahuasca journey only begins there," he said, pointing with his chin at the structure. "But you will depart very quickly and travel very far away." He smiled and walked on.

The light of the moon on that clear evening was strong enough to illuminate enormous sandstone boulders that marked the edge of a small river running a few hundred meters to the west of the meetinghouse. On the other side of the water began the Andean foothills, home to the only pristine forest in the area. Surrounding the other sides of the meeting hall was nothing but depleted cattle pastures that had harbored magnificent rain forest until a few decades before.

There was an audible murmur from the other Indians as the shaman entered the hut. I marveled at the traditional *cushma*, the sky blue cotton tunic that covered him from shoulders to waist. Wrapped tightly around his thick biceps were dense strings of *shoroshoro* seeds that produced a hissing rattle as he walked. And around his neck was a magnificent necklace of jaguar teeth, the symbol of the shaman in many Amazonian tribes. It was only after admiring the medicine man's finery that I was startled to recognize him as the fellow with whom I had been chatting earlier that afternoon. In his ceremonial garb he looked every inch the great shaman, and I wondered how I could have ever thought otherwise.

The shaman took his seat on a low bench at one end of the hut while the rest of us sat in a circle on the dirt floor at his feet. A chilly breeze blew in from the Andean slopes and I shivered as much from anticipation as from the cold. The night was alive with jungle sounds: crickets buzzed and chirped, frogs croaked and trilled, night jars cooed and whooped. Howler monkeys hooted briefly, indicating that rain would fall the next day.

The shaman dipped a calabash into an earthen pot between his feet. Holding it high over his head with both hands, he mumbled a few incantations before drinking the ayahuasca in a single draught. Wiping his mouth clean with the back of his hand, he refilled the container from the pot, repeated the incantation, and passed it to me.

I looked down at the cup and saw it filled to the brim with a thick reddish brown liquid. I tried to knock it back in one swallow as I had seen the shaman do. The dreadful bitterness of the potion, however, caught me by surprise and I struggled to keep from retching. The Indian seated on the other side of the shaman noted my distress and passed me a cup of *aguardiente*, a fiery sugar cane brandy whose sweet anise aftertaste erased the disagreeable brackishness of the ayahuasca. I sat and watched the shaman slowly repeat the procedure with everyone in the circle.

All seemed quiet and peaceful until the shaman picked up a handful of *wai-rah sacha* leaves and began to shake them in a fanning motion. The leaves produced a whistling sound not unlike a high wind rushing through the rain forest canopy before a heavy thunderstorm: *shhhhhh-shhhhhh*. He shook it in a slow, rhythmic pattern that proved hypnotic, and I felt as if my brain waves were being organized in a fixed laser like pattern under his control. My body began to relax, and I lay back onto a blanket I had brought to ward off the cold. Glancing around, I noticed that everyone else had also reclined, as if the shaman had willed us to do so. Only the medicine man remained seated up-

right, and he began a mesmerizing chant: *Hey-yah-hey! Hey-yah-hey!*

What seems simple in retrospect was emotionally enrapturing at the time. And the shaking of the leaves added a layer of complexity and fascination that reverberated through my brain from the right front lobe to the rear left lobe to the rear right lobe to the front left lobe, and back again. By now the shaman seemed master of time, space, and my entire being.

I drifted off into a gentle trance. I felt myself lying in a tucum palm fiber hammock as comfortable as a giant feather bed. I was floating as in a dream. Looking up, I could see a beautiful blue tropical sky with only a few wisps of clouds above me. The hammock was slung between two towering columnar *epena* trees with a dark Amazonian lake below me. At the far edge of the lake I could make out the tiny figure of the shaman in this blue tunic continuing his chant. By the peaceful look on his face that I could just make out at this distance, I could tell that he was deep into his own ayahuasca visions. As I floated there with my hands propped comfortably behind my head, I peacefully reviewed scenes from my life that reenacted themselves for my analysis. Aside from a few mild waves of nausea, all seemed peaceful and calm; I was at one with the cosmos.

Soon the shaman ceased his chant, and I opened my eyes to find myself seated at his feet once more. He refilled the calabash, prayed over it, and drank it down. Repeating the first two steps, he then passed the container to me. I drained it but it didn't sit right in my stomach. I tried to ignore the volcanic nausea welling up inside. I promised myself that I would lie back down as soon as everyone had had their turn and began to feel a bit better by focusing all my attention on the shaman. I knew that he was able to feel my gaze, and he turned to me. As he did so, the beaded bracelets on his biceps produced the sound of rushing water and turned into tiny glowing diamonds that all but obscured my field of vision. As the diamonds dissipated, I could see that the shaman was staring at me with a look that combined equal parts power, disdain, humor, and kindness. I stared at his black pupils growing larger and larger, finally combining into one giant black vortex into which I was sucked. I was underwater now in waters as pitch-black as the Rio Negro. Huge black caimans and anacondas swarmed in the river, menacing me with their size and demeanor, though not attacking me directly. Running out of air, and afraid of the creatures that surrounded me in this aquatic realm, I swam desperately.

I broke the surface and crawled on all fours onto a white sandy beach along the riverbank. Having been underwater too long, I became sick, vomiting and vomiting. I was unable to stop; the life began ebbing from my body. I could not regain my feet and sank face down into the sand, rising up enough only to retch over to the side. I began weeping and begging for help as I continued to fade. Pain racked my body and my head felt as if it had exploded. I tried fighting for my life but no longer had the strength. I had managed to crawl up the riverbank toward the jungle but only made it far enough to pass out in the grass at the edge of the forest. I lay face down. I died.

I don't know how long I lay in the grass, inert, comatose, inanimate. But I could hear something in the back of my head. The shaman continued to chant, deep in the forest in front of me.

With a Herculean effort, I managed to raise myself on all fours. I began weeping again because I did not have the strength to go to him. As I sat mired in this predicament, I was frightened by a deep guttural grunt in the jungle in front of me. A jaguar! Now I was weak *and* terrified. But a most extraordinary thing happened: the great cat's roar caused a wave of nausea to well up inside me and I puked as I never had before. Horrible things poured out of me: purple frogs and bloodred snakes and phosphorescent orange scorpions. I thought I was dying a second death, yet when it stopped I felt a bit stronger. So close was the jaguar that I could smell him, yet I was no longer afraid. I stumbled a bit as I followed him into the jungle; I knew that he was leading me toward the shaman. Tripping over roots, I tried to keep pace with the great cat. I momentarily worried about snakes until I realized that nothing could be worse than what I was enduring.

Falling to my knees, I looked up to see the shaman standing over me. He began a peculiar chant that made my head hurt even more until he pressed his palms against my temples and started to squeeze. As he twisted my neck to the right I felt my vertebrae pop; the pain began to abate, ever so slightly. He seated me on a tree trunk and began to dance around me. Taking a swig of an herbal tea, he circled me, spitting the aromatic liquid at me in a cold spray at each of the four cardinal points of the compass. The pain and confusion that racked my body began to subside as he massaged my arms and neck. The sun had started to rise in the east. He sang and rubbed my upper body with leaves, pausing every now and again to cast off some invisible film he seemed to be scraping off me. I managed to croak out a question: "Why did you do this to me?"

He gave a cryptic, Cheshire cat smile and replied: "You have had a glimpse of our world. You have been purged, cleaned, healed. You will never again fear death as you have now died and been reborn."

In a classic treatise on ayahuasca (1979), R. E. Schultes wrote:

> There is a magic intoxicant in northwesternmost South America which the Indians believe can free the soul from corporeal confinement, allowing it to wander free and return to the body at will. The soul, thus untrammeled, liberates its owner from the everyday life and introduces him to wondrous realms of what he considers reality and permits him to communicate with his ancestors. The Kechua term for this inebriating drink—ayahuasca ("vine of the soul")—refers to this freeing of the spirit. The plants involved are truly plants of the gods, for their powers are laid to supernatural forces residing in their tissues, and they were the divine gifts to the earliest Indians on earth. The drink employed for prophecy, divination, sorcery, and medical purposes, is so deeply rooted in native mythology and philosophy that there can be no doubt of its great age as part of aboriginal life.

In the northwest Amazon, ayahuasca represents an essential component of most—if not all—shamanic healing ceremonies. Yet there are aspects of these shamanic practices that are used by other cultures around the world, only some of which employ psychotropic plants in their healing rituals. According to Dr. Piers Vitebsky, an authority on Eurasian shamanism, the word "shaman" comes from the language of the Evenk peoples, reindeer herders in Siberia. To the Evenk, a shaman is a person who can "will his or her spirit to leave the body and journey to upper or lower world." Common elements unite the shamanic tradition found on every continent except Antarctica.

Curing disease, preventing famine, controlling the weather, entering trances, fighting evil spirits sent by malevolent shamans of other tribes, traveling up to the spirit world, or conveying souls to the underworld are common denominators among most practitioners of what we consider shamanism. In most groups, the shaman serves as the only tribal member who fully comprehends both the "real" world and the "spirit" world and is therefore responsible for maintaining the balance between the two.

Within the context of the source culture, shamanism is often considered a profoundly holy profession. Unlike in much of the industrialized world, in which healing is essentially divorced from spirituality, the shaman also functions as the priest-rabbi, which greatly augments his or her ability to heal. As Western science finally begins to study and appreciate the therapeutic benefits of spirituality, the practice and effectiveness of shamanism becomes not only more comprehensible but also more appreciated.

An integral component of shamanistic healing is what has been called "the placebo effect." Many leaders of the Western medical establishment came of age during the antibiotic revolution, the single greatest therapeutic advance of the mid-twentieth century. However, the development of these drugs also led several generations of physicians to equate (to a large degree) chemistry and healing. Spirituality (its nature and its role in healing) was part of few (if any) medical school curricula. The placebo effect, in which patients recovered because they believed they would, was not in and of itself shunned, but more often noted with bemusement rather than harnessed and put to work.

Shamans, on the other hand, are masters of the placebo effect. Much has been made of the shamanic practice of sucking the "evil darts" (or other foreign substances) out of the patient's body by the healer. References in the literature often refer to it as trickery or sleight of hand, usually in a condescending way. Two aspects, however, are overlooked. First, it often provides the patient some relief, convincing them that they are on the road to recovery and creating a mind-set that facilitates healing. Second, therapeutic compounds, usually in the form of plants, are also employed because the shaman is customarily a master botanist. The shaman's genius as a healer stems from his (or her) ability to combine the spiritual (sucking out evil darts, communing with the forces of nature, etc.) with the chemical (the plants, insects, etc.)

Chief Pierce of Flat Iron, an Oglala Sioux, explained the inextricable link between the holy and the botanical almost a century ago: "From Wakan-Tanka, the Great Mystery, comes all power.... Man knows that all healing plants are given by Wakan-Tanka: therefore they are holy.... The Great Mystery gave to men all things for their food, their clothing, their welfare. And to man he gave also the knowledge how to use these gifts ... how to find the holy healing plants."

The sophisticated botanical knowledge of these "uneducated" shamans astonishes Western researchers. In the rain forest, these healers can sometimes identify almost every single species of tree merely by the smell, appearance, or feel of the bark, a feat no university-trained botanist can accomplish. And their knowledge of the ecology of these plants—when they fruit, when they flower, what pollinates them, what disperses the seeds, what preys on them, what type of soil they prefer—is no less impressive. As nature continues to provide us with a cornucopia of new medicines, these shamans (in the rain forest and elsewhere) will prove to be the ultimate sources of knowledge about which species offer therapeutic promise and how they might best be employed.

Almost every plant species that has been put to use by Western medicine was originally discovered and utilized by indigenous cultures. Despite the fact that a single shaman may know and employ over a hundred species for medicinal purposes, or that a single tribe (which may have several shamans) may know and utilize several hundred species for medical purposes, few of the world's remaining tribal peoples have been the subject of comprehensive ethnobotanical/ethnomedical studies. Yet the more we study, the more we learn how little we know about how much they know.

Ayahuasca, the vision vine, represents a classic example. The early accounts of ayahuasca focused on a single species of vine (*Banisteriopsis caapi*). Subsequent research has revealed that other plants added to the mixture determine the actual type, intensity, and duration of the hallucinations—proving the sophistication of these shamans as both botanists and chemists. For example, leaves of a species of the *Psychotria* shrub of the coffee family are often added to the ayahuasca mixture. These leaves contain chemicals called tryptamines that induce hallucinations. The compounds, however, are inactive when taken orally unless activated by the presence of another type of chemical known as monoamine oxidase inhibitors. The psychotropic compounds in the ayahuasca vine not only induce hallucinations but also function as monoamine oxidase inhibitors. The result: a brew much more potent than one prepared from either species.

Furthermore, the shamans often have the remarkable ability to distinguish between, describe, and make use of distinct healing and/or chemical properties of different parts of the same plant. A shaman, for example, will note that bark from the upper stem of the ayahuasca vine may cause visions of jaguars, while the root bark results in scenes of anacondas. Schultes wrote:

> Among the Tukano of the Colombian Vaupes, for example, six "kinds" of Ayahuasca or Kahi are recognized.... *Kahi riama*, the strongest, produces auditory hallucinations and announces future events. It is said to cause death if improperly employed. The second strongest, *Mene-kahi-ma*, reputedly causes visions of green snakes.... These two "kinds" may not belong to Banisteriopsis or even to the family Malpighiaceae. The third in strength is called *Suana-kahi-ma* ("Kahi of the red jaguar"), producing visions in red. *Kahi-vai Bucura-rijoma* ("Kahi of the monkey head") causes monkeys to hallucinate and howl.... All of these "kinds" are referable probably to *Banisteriopsis caapi* [e.g., what to Western botanists is all the same species].

Hallucinogens, while an integral part of shamanic healing practices in the western Amazon, still represent only a very small portion of plants employed for therapeutic purposes. As we have seen before, natural products employed for a particular purpose in one culture may offer promise of a different use in our own culture. In the case of ayahuasca, for example, Western-trained physicians in both Brazil and Peru are using the vine as an experimental treatment for chronic alcoholism and crack addiction, with promising results.

An example of using one therapeutic plant for different purposes in a different culture comes to us from the tropical forests of American Samoa in the South Pacific, where the herbal healers—the *taulasea*—are primarily women. These herbalists know 200 species of plants and recognize 180 types of diseases. Ethnobotanist Dr. Paul Cox of the National Tropical Botanical Garden had been working with this culture for over a decade when, in 1984, a *taulasea* named Epenesa Mauigoa showed him an herbal treatment for acute hepatitis prepared from the inner bark of a local species of rubber tree. Cox was particularly intrigued when she insisted that only one "variety" of the tree could be employed when, in Western botanical terms, both varieties were the same species. Investigation of the plant in the laboratories of the National Cancer Institute outside Washington, D.C., yielded a new molecule that the scientists named prostratin. This compound belongs to a class of chemicals known as phorbols, many of which cause tumors in the human body. Intriguingly, however, prostratin not only inhibited the formation of tumors but, in the test tube, prevented cells from becoming infected by the HIV-1 virus and extended the life of infected cells! Of course, it is a long way from the jungle to the laboratory and, in some ways, an even longer trail from the test tube to the pharmacy. Nonetheless, research on prostratin continues. And it is precisely these finds that validate indigenous wisdom in Western eyes, leading to pharmaceutical companies' increased interest in shamanic wisdom.

Scientists continue to be astonished at the breadth and depth of indigenous wisdom. Ethnobotanists at the New York Botanical Garden recently conducted a classic comparative study of indigenous ethnobotanical sagacity in the Amazon Basin. Working with the Chacobo tribe in Bolivia, Dr. Brian Boom found they used 95 percent of the local tree species. His colleague Dr. Bill Balee learned that the Tembe peoples of Brazil employed 61.3 percent of local trees while the Ka'apor tribe used 76.8 percent.

The effectiveness of this wisdom is being validated in the laboratory. Dr. Bernard Ortiz de Montellano of Wayne State University sifted through accounts of the ethnomedicine of the Aztec peoples of ancient Mexico and was able to identify 118 plants that they employed as medicines. When he subjected them to laboratory examination, he found that almost 85 percent were at least somewhat efficacious, strikingly similar to data gathered by Paul Cox and his colleagues in Polynesia. The joint Swedish-American research team tested the Samoan medicinal plants in the laboratory. The results: 86 percent demonstrated significant pharmacological activity.

Of course, new mechanisms must be developed to protect the intellectual property rights of these local peoples and local governments: fortunately, the colonial/neocolonial model of "Let's take what we need of local plants and wisdom and cart it off to the marketplace" is completely unacceptable as we enter the twenty-first century. New economic models and legal frameworks are being devised and put in place to share benefits from these new discoveries and avoid the "rape and run" approach to commercializing natural resources that characterized much of human history.

Nonetheless, an enormous body of shamanic knowledge remains untested (or untestable) in the laboratory because we cannot (or have not yet been able to) understand it outside of the context of indigenous culture. The Tirio Indians of the northeast Amazon, for example, employ a series of plants to treat ailments that (they claim) are caused by the breaking of hunting taboos. One ancient medicine man showed me a plant that he explained was "boiled into a tea and given to an infant who was crying at night because he couldn't sleep because his father had killed a giant anteater." Another species was used for the same purpose, except that the child suffered insomnia because the father had killed a tapir. Most Westerners would regard these ailments as imaginary. A much more effective utilitarian approach, instead of dismissing this seemingly incomprehensible claim, would be to investigate whether the plant potion contained compounds that might serve as the basis for a safe, effective, nonaddictive sleeping pill—a potion that Western medicine has been unable to devise.

In our culture, we have been taught that our system of medicine (and other things!) is the most advanced, the most successful, the most sophisticated, and so on—a valid statement, in many regards. This "lesson," however, often results in a cultural arrogance that underestimates or even denigrates other systems, either because they seem "primitive" and/or because we don't understand what they are trying to tell or teach us. In his brilliant book *Witchdoctors and Psychiatrists*, Dr. E. Fuller Torrey wrote: "A psychiatrist who tells an illiterate African that his phobia is related to fear of failure and a witch doctor who tells an American tourist that his phobia is related to possession by an ancestral spirit will be met by equally blank stares."

Our culture teaches us to "cut to the chase," to get that one plant or (better yet) one molecule that is responsible for the shaman's cure—and you can spare us the magic rattle and the sacred smoke, thank you very much. Some of these cures only work within their cultural context, be it a treatment for possession by an ancestral spirit, a cure that involves ceremony, ritual, and healing plants, or a mundane remedy that simply requires rubbing a few crushed leaves on the afflicted area. Clearly, some of these treatments harness powerful chemicals that can be used effectively far from their site of origin and within a Western (or other) clinical context.

The Western tendency to adopt a reductionist approach is not just an interest in getting to the basic chemistry (preferably a single molecule that is responsible for the therapeutic effect) or merely a question of being in a hurry—it is also a question of safety and economics. It has proven difficult, if not impossible, to patent a complex plant extract that may contain a multitude of chemicals, even if proven safe and effective. Still, our cultural propensity to reduce everything to the simplest common denominator can cause us to underestimate or even deny the shaman's healing wisdom. A recent example: two ethnobotanists were intrigued by a West African medicine man who appeared to have an extremely potent potion for reducing blood-sugar levels in diabetic patients. They asked whether he might be willing to provide them with the plants he used so they could take them back to the United States for testing. The shaman readily agreed and gave the scientists three different plants. In the lab, they tested species A, which had no effect; they tried species B, which had no effect. They tested species C, still with no positive results. Finally, they boiled them all together and analyzed the resulting potion. Nothing! A year later, back in Africa, they returned to the medicine man. "Your potion doesn't seem to work," said one of the ethnobotanists to the witch doctor.

"What do you mean?" he replied. "You saw me give it to my patients, and measured their blood-sugar levels with your instruments. You yourself told me that the blood-sugar level went down. How could you now claim it doesn't work?"

The ethnobotanists then asked the medicine man if he would be willing to prepare a batch of the potion they could then take with them. He agreed. The shaman boiled water in a big aluminum pot over a wood fire. He added the first plant species, then the second, then the third. Just as he was preparing to take the pot off the fire, he reached into a wet muslin sack, extracted a crab, and dropped it in the pot.

"What is that?" asked one of the ethnobotanists.

"What does it look like?" replied the shaman. "It is a crab!"

"Yeah, I know," responded the scientist. "But why did you add it to the pot? You didn't tell us that was part of the recipe."

The shaman smiled. "Look," he said, "you asked me if I would give you the plants used to make the potion. I did!"

The scientists took the potion back to the United States, found it to be effective at lowering blood sugar, and it is currently being investigated in the lab.

Of course, a shaman's healing wizardry does not necessarily entail the use of nature's chemistry. Dr. Charles Limbach, an American physician with extensive experience in Latin America, recently related an intriguing encounter. A friend of his, also a physician, had returned from a sojourn in the Oriente, the Amazonian territory of eastern Ecuador:

> My friend was visiting a missionary acquaintance who was working with the Shuar people, also called the Jivaro, who were once renowned for their then common practice of removing and then shrinking the heads of their enemies. He was sitting on the porch of the missionary's house and chatting with his fellow American and an elderly Shuar who had a reputation as a powerful shaman. While they were conversing, another Shuar arrived and asked the missionary for help with a botfly larva (through a complicated process, botfly eggs enter the human body and hatch into larvae which feed on human flesh. The standard western treatment

is to cut them out with a scalpel). The missionary, who had received some medical training, ducked into the house and came back out with alcohol, cotton swabs, a bandage, and a scalpel. The Shuar shaman asked what he planned to do with all that equipment. The American replied that he would cut out the larva. The shaman smiled, and said he would handle it. He sat the patient in a hammock, leaned over the arm with the botfly and began to sing. Within minutes, the botfly larva emerged from the man's arm, fell onto the floor of the porch, and the shaman crushed it beneath his bare foot.

Neither Limbach nor his colleague was able to explain the incident. Had the shaman sung at a particular frequency maddening to the insect, as opera singers are able to hit a note that can shatter glass? Or did the shaman surreptitiously exhale tobacco smoke into the larva's breathing hole, causing it to crawl out in search of air? In some ways, this situation is analogous to the use of aspirin for most of the past century: even though we didn't fully understand how it functioned in the human body until relatively recently, we nonetheless used the drug because it was safe, effective, and painless.

The extraordinary antiquity of shamanistic practices is well documented. Southern France has long been famous for a series of caves, the walls of which are covered with the oldest known art of human origin. Several years ago, the most ancient of all was discovered not far from other subterranean caverns that had been known and studied for over a century. This cave, christened Chauvet, contained art that was noticeably similar to that found in the earlier discoveries, with portrayals of large mammals like the cave bear and woolly rhinoceros that flourished in Europe at that time. On a hanging rock near the entrance, however, is a striking portrait of a composite creature, the bottom half of which is a human, the upper half a bison. Here, in the earliest known example of human art ever discovered, we see the portrait of the shaman.

Chauvet Cave has been dated at well over thirty thousand years old, which means that this art was created twenty-five thousand years before the more familiar paintings and sculpture of "ancient" Egypt. Similar half-man half-beast motifs are found in many caverns painted and carved in the distant past. The best known and most thoroughly studied of the caves is at Lascaux; a man in a bird mask lies next to a staff with a bird on the end of it. The bird that—unlike most humans—can soar over the forest and through the heavens represents the symbol of the shaman in many cultures. Joseph Campbell suggested that this particular figure lies "rapt in a shamanistic trance" and that "in that remote period of our species the arts of the wizard, shaman, or magician were already well developed."

The Trois Frères sanctuary dates from fourteen thousand years ago and harbors what is probably the most famous prehistoric painting of a shaman: the Dancing Sorcerer. The magnificent portrait features a male creature composed of the parts of many different animals. It has antlers on its head, yet dances on its hind legs in a clearly human manner. Adding further credence that this is a human rather than an animal is the headdress of caribou antlers worn in sacred dances by shamans of Arctic

and subarctic tribes, much as Indian medicine men on the Great Plains wore headdresses of buffalo horns.

The antiquity of healing-plant knowledge is assumed to be equally great. A Neanderthal grave at Shanidar in Iraq, near the Iran border, held seven species of plants carefully buried around the corpse. People living in the region today use five of those seven species for medicinal purposes. At Monte Verde in southern Chile, recently concluded to be the site of the earliest known habitation in South America, researchers found what had been gardens of medicinal plants. A ubiquitous species was an evergreen shrub known locally as *boldo*, and widely used as a diuretic, a laxative, and a treatment for liver problems. Laboratory research has proven that this plant is an effective diuretic; investigations in Germany have led to its official approval for the treatment of stomach and intestinal cramps as well as dyspepsia.

The question then arises as to the source of ethnomedical wisdom: simply stated, how did the shamans learn which plants had healing properties? Trial and error undoubtedly played a central role. But in it place like the Amazon, with eighty thousand species of flowering plants (not to mention tens of millions of other organisms), how would the healers know not only which plant to employ but which part of the plant to use? And at what dosage? How did the shaman learn at which phase of the moon these plants should be collected? Even more curious is how they devised such clever recipes that sometimes consist of over twenty components. In the instance of the diabetes case history presented in the introduction, the shaman made the potion from four plants. What would be the odds of recreating that potion using the correct dosage, species, and particular plant parts from a forest of eighty thousand species if we tried to do it based on random collections, which has been the major approach used by most pharmaceutical companies up to the present date?

One key as to how the shamans and others have found and utilized species with therapeutic compounds is the taste test. The concept of "bitter" exists in most cultures, and bitterness often indicates the presence of alkaloids, which represent the single most important chemical components of modern medicine. Quinine and ayahuasca are some of the bitterest substances known.

Yet another clue for the shamans also serves as a lead for Western scientists like David Newman or William Fenical, who look for new medicines from marine organisms: color equals chemistry. If a plant (particularly a tree sap) has a peculiar color, it may well contain interesting chemicals. The clear red sap of the *Virola* tree led shamans of the Yanomami people of Venezuela to develop it into a powerful hallucinogenic snuff, just as the brilliant orange sap of the *Vismia* bush of Suriname led the Tirio shamans to use it as an effective treatment for fungal infections of the skin. The milky red sap of the *Croton* tree led Shuar shamans to employ it as a safe and effective agent for healing wounds.

Another key is the so-called doctrine of signatures. Simply stated, if a plant (or plant part) looks like something, it is somehow good for that something. In other words, because a walnut looks like a brain, it must be good for diseases afflicting the brain (a common belief in medieval Europe). As ludicrous as it sounds, the doctrine has yielded at least one medicinal compound in wide use until recently. The Vedas of ancient India were written about four thousand years ago and included a remedy for snakebite from the snakeroot plant, so named because the twisted roots resembled squirming serpents. Tested in the laboratory in the 1950s, it was found ineffective for countering the toxic effects of the snake venom. One of the problems associated with snakebite, however, is that the trauma of being bitten causes the heart to beat faster, thus pumping the poison throughout the system. What the alkaloid in snakeroot does do is slow down the heartbeat and, because of this, was developed into one of the first effective tranquilizers used by Western medicine.

Once again, this demonstrates why we should not reject ideas, gleaned from other medical systems without first investigating them. The Aztecs valued a Mexican species of magnolia with a heart-shaped fruit as a treatment for cardiac problems. Recent investigations in the lab have found that this fruit contains compounds with a digitalis-like activity.

The most intriguing source of ideas for which plants can be utilized medicinally is perhaps the most difficult concept for Westerners to accept: a shaman's dreams. After a ten-year hiatus, in 1995 I returned to the village of Tepoe in Suriname while searching for diabetes treatments and sought out the great shaman Mahshewah. The old healer, though he appeared pleased at my return, said that he was unable to help me. "I'm sorry," he said, "but I don't recall ever seeing that disease so I can't tell you what plant might be useful for treating it."

Six days later, Mahshewah summoned me to his hut, where he related a most interesting occurrence: "This afternoon I was sleeping in my hammock and I had a dream. And in this dream I saw a tree, and the bark of this tree may help to treat this disease that you said is killing your people. If you canoe down the river for about an hour and a half, you will find a trail on the west bank. If you walk up this trail for about an hour, you will find an enormous tree with yellowish peeling bark. That is the species whose bark may help your people."

I followed his directions down the river and found the trail. I followed his directions up the trail and found the tree. Mahshewah's legs have been paralyzed since he was born. When I asked the other Indians if the old medicine man had ever been up that trail, they told me unequivocally that he had not. How does one explain this through the prism of Western science? I gathered a few scrapings of the bark because my guide said it was a rare and sacred tree that could not be collected in bulk. We still do not know if it might prove efficacious in treating the disease.

The question as to whether something useful can be "discovered" through dreams is one that many people in our society would be inclined to answer negatively. Yet how many remember the discovery of the structure of benzene? Friedrich August Kekulé von Stradowitz, one of the greatest chemists of nineteenth-century Europe, simply could not figure out the structure of the molecule of this enormously important industrial solvent. Quitting in frustration, he decided to turn in for the night and tackle the problem again in the morning. Soon he was dreaming and in his dream he saw several snakes. One of the reptiles be-

gan chasing another and then the others joined in, forming a circle. Kekule woke up with the solution to the problem: benzene is a ring! When British scientists dream the answer to perplexing problems, they may become famous, rich, well-respected, and sometimes offered a knighthood. But when Amazonian shamans do it, we dismiss it as "unscientific."

Mother Nature herself is a great teacher. In the words of the gifted natural history writer Sy Montgomery: "In other, older cultures than our own, in which people live closer to the earth, humans do not look down on animals from an imaginary pinnacle. Life is not divided between animals and people, nonhuman and human: life is a continuum, interactive, interdependent. Humans and animals are considered companions and cop layers in the drama of life. Animals' lives, their motives and thoughts and feelings, deserve human attention and respect; dismissing their importance is a grave error."

Characteristic among indigenous cultures of North America was the famous "vision quest," in which a young man (often an apprentice shaman) would go into the wilderness to pray and fast, fast and pray. After several days, he would be visited by visions, often in the form of an animal that would, in the words of the great Inuit shaman Igjugarjuk, "open the mind of a man to all that is hidden to others." As a result of this vision quest, the boy often ended up with a totemic spirit, an animal that served as his personal symbol or protector. The shaman may conclude the process with "animal familiars" or "power animals"—an animal or animals that help him learn and heal. So close is the identification with the animal that the shaman may be perceived as part animal, an essential component of sacred tribal dances around the world and the ancient cave paintings from Europe. In some cultures, the shamans believe that they actually become the animals, as do the Tirio shamans in the northeast Amazon, who claim the ability to turn into jaguars and roam the jungle at night. Among many tribes, the shaman becomes a bird, omniscient by virtue of his or her ability to look down from above and see things invisible to all others. In the case of the Navajo, as we saw in the last chapter, the bear is the medicinal plant master who taught the Indians about *Ligusticum* and all other healing plants.

The realization that much of shamanic knowledge is based on animals' use of plants is relatively new to Western scientific thought. As we saw in the previous chapter, many healing plants employed by tribes people have probably been learned from local animals. The legends of these cultures often feature sagas explaining how people first learned of useful plants (agricultural and medicinal) from forest creatures. In these cases, animals are, perhaps both metaphorically and literally, the bringers of wisdom.

Joseph Campbell suggested that true shamanism is the religion of the original hunting societies; with the advent of agriculture, cultures became more communally oriented and their religious beliefs changed. While this argument is somewhat hypothetical, what is more certain is that the manifestations of shamanistic religion have been seen as a threat by other organized religions, particularly Christianity, which saw itself in direct competition with belief systems that offered extraordinary experiences to the adherents: "The white goes into his church and talks about Jesus; the Indian walks into his teepee and talks to Jesus," wrote one anthropologist, describing peyote rituals among Native American peoples. But consider this passage from the Book of Job: "But ask now the beasts, and they shall teach thee; and the fowls of the air, and they shall teach thee."

The supreme irony of our suppression of, or disregard for, shamanic religions or other medical practices that rely on natural products is not only the extraordinary therapeutic gifts they have already provided us, but our undeniable need for more of these healing potions to treat "incurable" diseases. The witches of medieval Europe, burned at the stake for their heretical beliefs, were the shamans and/or herbalists of their day. It was their ethnopharmacopeia that gave us aspirin and digitalis. And if we had paid closer attention to their custom of applying moldy bread to wounds, we might have" discovered" penicillin several centuries earlier than Alexander Fleming's research in the 1920s.

A similar situation transpired in our own country. We have all heard about how Squanto and his fellow Indians taught the Pilgrims how to farm the land, but what did the settlers use for medicine? Native American medicinal plants cured the Pilgrims' ailments just as Native American crops filled the European bellies. And prior to the arrival of these Europeans, some of the original Americans had learned that mold could hasten the healing of wounds and local foxglove could treat certain heart problems. Native American healers independently invented syringes and enemas, developed a local anesthetic, and conducted head surgery. Every medicinal plant valued by the settlers was taught to them by local tribespeople. Some of these species entered into commercial, over-the-counter drugs: the yellow color of Murine eyedrops was until recently due to alkaloids extracted from the goldenseal herb. Others, like cascara sagrada (a common ingredient in many laxatives), are sold in many pharmacies. And new medicines are still being developed from plants originally employed by Native Americans: extracts of American bloodroot now serve as an antiplaque agent in toothpastes.

Even some of the most troublesome medical problems are being treated by ancient Indian medicines. Benign prostate enlargement (BPH) afflicts tens of thousands of American men. The fruits of the saw palmetto, a scrubby palm from the southeastern United States, have proven extremely effective at reducing the symptoms: as effective, it has been claimed, as a medicine marketed by Merck. Neither nature nor the shaman has all the answers to the ills that plague us, but both have some—I would say many—of these answers. Urgently needed is an approach that is more humble, more spiritual, more environmental, and more open-minded. The great anthropologist Weston LaBarre, who collaborated with R. E. Schultes on his early peyote research, wrote of the South American Indian:

> As scientists we cannot afford the luxury of an ethnocentric snobbery which assumes *a priori* that primitive cultures have nothing whatsoever to contribute to civilization. Our civilization is, in fact, a compendium of such borrowings, and it is a demonstrable error to be-

lieve that contacts of "higher" and "lower" cultures show benefits flowing exclusively in one direction. Indeed, a good case could probably be made that in the long run it is the "higher" culture which benefits the more through being enriched, while the "lower" culture not uncommonly disappears entirely as a result of the contact.

Twenty years ago, I stumbled across the most moving account of this ongoing tragedy that I have ever seen—and it was all because of an earache.

A common and painful ailment suffered by researchers working in the rain forest is fungal infection of the ear. The hot and wet environment of the tropics turns eardrums into petri dishes ripe for the cultivation of fungal invaders. When I began working in the Amazon in the late 1970s, I developed these infections on such a regular basis that before departing I would schedule appointments to have my ears examined at the university clinic upon my return to the States. I quickly learned that if I mentioned my occupation to the physician on duty, she or he would often tell me at great length that ethnobotany was what they really wanted to do with their careers but that they had student loans, a mortgage, a family, and so on, which was why they had been unable to pursue this dream.

I vividly remember going into the clinic with a terrible earache after an expedition to the jungles of southern Venezuela. After examining my ear, attending physician Dr. Jonathan Strongin asked if I had any idea where I might have picked up such a peculiar fungus. "Sure," I replied, "I've just returned from South America."

He asked what I had been doing south of the border, and I gave a distinctly noncommittal reply. He said, "You know, I lived with Indians in the Peruvian Amazon for several years while I was doing my Ph.D. in anthropology, which is how I became interested in healing."

Intrigued, I made a mental note of his name, looked up his dissertation, and found one of the most poignant statements ever recorded on the inextricable interrelationship between people, plants, healing, and belief:

> Since the time of their initial contact, the missionaries have openly discouraged the [shamans], viewing them as AntiChrists.... [Another anthropologist reported] that in the Shimaa region there was a powerful [shaman] who had to abandon his craft because he felt he no longer had the support of the Machiguenga people in his area. This shaman used ayahuasca to take the form of a bird to travel far and wide at a great height to discern the cause of illness. However, he felt that because the missionaries had so successfully eroded the traditional faith of his people, he could no longer continue to cure. For without the faith of the population, while in the avian form he would not be able to return to his body and [would] crash in the forest far from home ...

# Drug Culture:
# Everybody Uses Something

DANNY MONROE WILCOX

A common scene in America today is the politician in a loud, critical panic about the "rise of the drug culture." When mentioned, a lot of us automatically assume that the use and trade of illicit drugs is the primary focus. Yet most Americans have only a vague awareness of the traditional and historical uses of medicinal plants. Nor is much attention given to the use of psychoactive substances to achieve spiritually significant, ecstatic visions since prehistoric times. No connection is made with drugs such as alcohol and tobacco, which are permitted by social and legal convention. Absolutely no account is taken of the over-the-counter drug industry or the business of prescription medicine. Most Americans are totally oblivious to the origin and development of these practices, but still manage to distinguish between the good drugs and bad drugs. The term *drug* has been too narrowly defined for popular understanding. Americans tend to perceive drugs as substances that are illegal, used despite legal and social prohibitions. This restricted description is not the result of any informed research, but a concept generated and accepted through the active process of culture. The term *drug* should be employed to refer to any non-food substance that is used for medicinal, spiritual, or even recreational purposes. The concept of culture also is quite misunderstood by most Americans, used to mean something exotic or even alien. Therefore, the popular interpretation of *drug culture* generates a narrow, restricted image of people unlike ourselves who engage in illegal and immoral activity. This image reflects beliefs that are magically conjured to the surface upon hearing the phrase.

An adequate description of drug culture depends on an awareness of the early human use of medicinal and psychoactive substances. It must be based on the fact that virtually every culture has its own complex system of substance utilization. The most basic interaction between substance, culture, and the individual is best understood in a pan-human context. The most fundamental meaning of drugs among human beings must be appreciated to correctly apply the concept of *drug culture* to our current social problem. In addition to understanding such broad similarities, particular groups make specific adaptations to natural and social environments. It is important to consider the distinctive drug culture groups in America. Various scenarios can demonstrate the wide variation in competing beliefs and behaviors that are culturally patterned. We also must look at the aspects of specific drug cultures that profoundly affect people beyond the boundaries of the American nation-state. It is important to know how various substances have meaning within the cultural context, how these meanings are conceived in the idealized value system of the culture, and how they actually are operationalized in the reality of daily existence. Through such an approach, the specific category of *drug culture* in American diversity could be examined using factual, rather than cultural knowledge.

## The Rise of Drug Culture

Human beings have used pharmacologically active substances from prehistoric times to the present. The healing properties of specific plants have been known for millennia. Ethnobotanical and archaeological work have clearly shown the great extent and antiquity of such knowledge (Furst 1972). Substance use in all cultures has meaning. The most basic reason people have used, and continue to use, medicines is for healing. Both physical maladies and mental conditions can be treated by various agents. Many effective pharmacological substances are used, but whether or not the medicines achieve the desired result is frequently of secondary importance. The culturally patterned belief that certain drugs actually work can be just as meaningful. The most fundamental meaning of drugs to the user is that they can affect health and well being. Mental, emotional, or spiritual states are directly related to the well being of the individual. Such problems also may be treated with certain substances. The psychological benefits of being administered a drug that the user believes will be effective can be substantial. In traditional societies where most substances must be prepared and utilized according to social, ceremonial, and ritual prescriptions, this is particularly true. The ritual and ceremonial contexts for healing ensure that what people believe has a significant impact on behaviors associated with the particular medicines. The ritual basis for much healing is as important as the pharmacological efficacy of the medicine (Radcliffe-Brown 1952).

The medicinal use of substances is an important part of the adaptive process of culture. Over thousands of years, people have learned that certain plants prepared in specific ways have a predictable effect on people's health. They believe these things heal them. At the same time, they may believe the use of substances that are ritually, ceremonially, and socially prohibited may lead to illness, madness, or death. While these beliefs often may be correct, cultural knowledge frequently can be at odds with the facts. Psychoactive substances are used because people believe these drugs are endowed with specific properties that can affect a person's physical health or spiritual well being. Such experiences, mediated through altered states of consciousness, have important meanings. Traditionally, this type of experience is sought as an integral part of the spiritual essence of life. The ecstatic visionary has the ability to "see" what explains the world more thoroughly, what makes it comprehensible, and how to manipulate unseen forces for the adaptive benefit of all members of the group. Substances with psychoactive properties have been used for the purpose of achieving spiritually significant, altered states of consciousness for thousands of years (Furst 1972). Shamans are ritual specialists who often are associated with specific knowledge about healing and visionary experience. These medicine men and/or women have specialized information concerning the ritual preparation and administration of different substances. Healing, in many traditional societies, is properly sought through the shaman's direction, as are vision quests. Shamans were probably the first real specialists to appear in foraging societies. The particular roles of physicians and priests in the modern world have developed from shamanistic origins. But early peoples did not distinguish between the two roles. Healer and spiritual advisor could not be separated. This double role continued in most cultures until relatively recent times. At present, scientific medicine and religious prescriptions generally are considered mutually exclusive. Although some religious traditions stress the healing power of the spiritual life and some doctors advocate "holistic" medicine, our rational, scientific approach to health and religion is noticeably dualistic. People in traditional cultures usually do not make such hard distinctions between material reality and the spirit life.

Just as the curing of physical ailments is adaptive, the use of psychoactive plants also can be considered adaptive. If the realm of human life cannot be separated from that of various spirits, visions that are catalyzed by psychoactive substances can be made an integral part of the overall decision-making process. Social and subsistence behavior can be affected by this type of substance use. It would seem obvious that the meanings of various medicinal and psychoactive substances are probably different for members of traditional cultures as opposed to the meanings ascribed to recreational drugs commonly used in American society. However, the primary importance of the medicine or drug is not only associated with the specific cultural meaning attached, but with the pan-human fact that substances have meaning and are useful in relation to the health and welfare of the individual user and the group.

Generally speaking, we can say with confidence that human beings have been using various substances for medicinal, spiritual, and recreational purposes for thousands of years. We also can be fairly certain that, although the cultural meaning of various substances may differ greatly between specific cultures, the one common fact is that these substances always have meaning. Drugs are sometimes sacred, sometimes profane, but always meaningful. The individual's view of the particular meaning of a given substance is culturally determined. Through the belief and world view of the group, the individual will be fairly certain of the truth regarding the use of drugs. Whether comparing traditional cultures in different parts of the world, traditional cultures to modern nation states, or different cultural groups within modern American society, this seems to be the case. Although the meaning of drug use will vary according to the cultural membership of the individual user or abstainer, drug use will always have a meaning attached. The specific group will believe their own interpretation is the correct view.

No matter the interpretation, the one general fact is that there are very few, if any, human groups that have not used drugs in meaningful ways. This includes psychoactive substances. The very old and near worldwide, native production and use of alcohol (Marshall 1979) and the pervasive use of hallucinogens clearly show that just about everyone uses drugs. Whether medicinal, spiritual, or recreational, everybody uses. The most essential meaning of drug use is to affect the health and welfare of the user. The ceremonial context of use contributes to this basic meaning and gives it ritual and social importance. The only real difference between them lies in the complex of substances and beliefs about the proper way to use them. The "rise of drug culture" has definable roots and patterns in ancient human experience and has occurred a very long time ago. For millennia, traditional human cultures mediated the meaningful use of drugs through ritual, ceremony, and belief. This continued to be the case in contemporary life and is not likely to change anytime in the near future.

## Development of Drug Culture

The humble, indigenous beginnings of drug culture gave rise to a variety of drugs, and after the development of human civilizations it also gave rise to further specialization in religious institutions. The ritual and religious leaders maintained knowledge and the authority to sanction the use of various substances. As state-level organization developed, this authority was no longer based primarily on the ecstatic shaman's spiritual leadership, but became codified in law. Historically, religious specialists, such as priests in western Europe, became the official dispensers of medicines. Others who had some special knowledge of plants and potions were considered witches. During inquisitions, these illegal practitioners of medicine often were prosecuted as devil-worshipers. The penalty for such unsanctioned drug pushing was often death.

The period of Enlightenment and Age of Reason elevated scientific explanation to a prominent position and contributed to the dualistic separation of medical versus religious knowledge. Eventually, doctors became the sole legitimate authority in the use of drugs. Priests and preachers were restricted to spiritual healing without the benefit of medicines or other substances, but they still were recognized as the sole legitimate authority on spiritual knowledge. Those who practiced either one without the expressed consent of the established medical or religious institution were considered quacks and heretics and persecuted accordingly. Szasz (1987) clearly demonstrates this dynamic interaction. Ritual, ceremony, and social relations are important to the meaning of drugs in the context of cultural knowledge. A drug is considered positively and its use encouraged in some instances. Other drugs may be considered physically and spiritually harmful and culturally prohibited. Often in recent history it is possible to look at the major psychoactive substances and see the development of prohibition after a period in which use of the drug was tolerated, if not embraced, as some kind of wonder drug. By looking at the use, development, and eventual prohibition of most naturally occurring, traditionally used drugs for healing and recreation, we can see how cultural knowledge determines people's beliefs about drugs. The development of synthetic substances over the past century also impacts the cultural knowledge we have, which determines people's beliefs about drug control. A historical perspective illuminates the actual role of cultural knowledge in the decisions to permit or prohibit various substances and ultimately leads to a description of contemporary drug culture.

# The Use and Control of Drugs

The most basic psychoactive, pharmacopeia that traditionally has been available to various cultures in different regions of the world consists of alcoholic beverages, tobacco products, opium, coca, marijuana, and hallucinogenic plants. No culture utilizes all of these substances, but almost all cultures permit or encourage the use of at least one of them. These drugs have been used by a wide variety of cultures for thousands of years. For example, alcoholic beverages have an almost worldwide distribution. Indigenous North America is the major exception, but even though there are a few cultures that had no knowledge or prohibited the use of alcohol, most utilize some form of alcoholic beverage. Ethnohistorical work and modern ethnography demonstrate not only the widespread use of alcohol, but also the invariably ceremonial context of most drinking in traditional societies (Mandelbaum 1965; Heath 1981).

Anthropological studies of traditional cultures have caused many to conclude that "addiction" per se is not observed in these cultures (Heath 1983). Even in cultures where heavy drinking occurs, it appears that the ceremonial context of the drinking somehow mitigates against the debilitating, recreational, excessive use found in modern societies (Heath 1984). After the development of the distillation process and the introduction of hard liquor, problems with alcohol became more apparent. Benjamin Rush, one of the signers of the Declaration of Independence, wrote a paper called *The effects of ardent spirits on the human mind and body* in 1786. This early work outlined basic differences in acute and chronic drunkenness, and suggested that some drunks were a product of the environment and others simply inherited the problem (Levine 1978). The introduction of whiskey to the Native American populations caused well-known problems, and many concluded that the problem was genetic. But Leland (1976) thoroughly discredited "the

firewater myth," and MacAndrew and Edgerton (1969) demonstrated that Native Americans drank the way they did because they had learned it from hard drinking, hard living, and cutthroat European trappers and frontiersmen. These researchers also showed that even abnormal behavior under the influence of alcohol was not the result of the pharmacological effects of alcohol, but learned behavior. In other words, drunken comportment was determined by cultural rules just as normal behavior.

But drunkenness increasingly became perceived as a threat to society in the late nineteenth and early twentieth centuries. Various temperance groups and religious institutions agitated for the prohibition of alcoholic beverages in this country and drinking ultimately was outlawed. Most people are familiar with the results of the experiment to make drinking alcohol illegal, but most do not realize that, ironically, it probably contributed significantly to the development of increasingly serious alcohol and criminal problems in this country (Levine 1984). Since the failure of that experiment, alcohol has received the blessing of American culture as a legally approved, highly psychoactive, recreational drug. Most Americans drink some form of alcoholic beverage, and the ceremonial and social importance of participation can be observed at bars, restaurants, business meetings, and Super Bowl parties. The social context of most drinking is a reflection of the basic meaning of alcohol for Americans who drink (Douglas 1987). The acceptance of a drink on a dare by the adolescent serves as a rite of passage to adulthood. Workers gather after hours to ceremonially celebrate the end of the day. Business people share the ritual of a drink or a glass of fine wine in order to demonstrate that they are suitably refined. Embraced by cultural approval, alcohol is still legal despite its being the most extensive drug problem in the United States.

Opium was first grown in the Near East. People have utilized opium for at least 2,000 years as the greatest pain killer the world has ever known. Many people also smoked opium recreationally, but it is erroneous to assume that opium smoking is something pushed upon western civilization by indigenous cultures of the East. Most Americans are vaguely aware of the "Opium Wars" between Great Britain and China in the last century. However, many mistakenly think it was fought because the Chinese were trying to extend the opium trade to the west. Ironically, imperial Britain wanted to force them to accept the sale of opium to its people. It was a great, money-making product and considered worth the military costs. The subsequent immigration of Chinese to the United States in the nineteenth century ensured that Americans would be introduced to opium smoking. Most Chinese claimed that it was an important aid to the heavy labor in which they were employed. Numerous opium dens operated in San Francisco. These businesses were closed down as racist attacks on Chinese immigrants were intensified. At the beginning of the twentieth century, the attacks were so visceral and effective that the U.S. Congress prohibited further immigration by the Chinese. They also prohibited opium smoking, which had been effectively associated with the Chinese as a particularly bad habit in order to justify the racism (Inciardi 1990). In the West, opium smoking was recognized as a health problem. Morphine was refined from opium and hailed by all as the wonder drug that could effectively cure the habitual opium smoker. The product, while a great analgesic, did not live up to its billing with regard to opium smokers because a morphine habit was even harder to kick. Heroin was refined and hailed as the "wonder drug" to cure morphine addiction, but again, the same problem. Propagandists effectively associated all of these problems with racial minorities (particularly the Chinese), determined that they were dangerous to the individual's health and spirit, and outlawed their unprescribed use in the early twentieth century. Since the drugs are so effective as pain killers, their use under the care of a bona fide, licensed physician was and still is permitted. All other use is subject to criminal prosecution.

Coca leaves have been used by the Native Americans of the Andean highland regions for thousands of years. Chewed in combination with other substances, it is a stimulant and provides a mild increase in heart rate, oxygen exchange, and wards off fatigue. These are important adaptive effects for people living and working at extremely high altitudes. In the late 1800s cocaine was refined from coca and identified as the new wonder drug for the treatment of other addictions and even of some mental illnesses, including depression. Coca was an active ingredient in Coca Cola until the early 1900s when it was outlawed. Some of the physicians and others who had touted the potential benefits had discovered some of the debilitating effects of chronic use (Inciardi 1991), but this health hazard was not the overriding concern of those who agitated for its prohibition. The harmful effects of the drug were associated with a racial minority. This time African-Americans were the example of what could happen if the substance was not strictly controlled. Particularly in the South, people were presented propaganda that depicted drug-crazed, black males engaging in such violent acts as rape (usually of white women) and murder. The campaign was successful and the drug was prohibited by law (Park & Matveychuk 1986).

Marijuana is a euphoriant used by traditional people for ages. The Bantu peoples of Africa use it and claim that they get more energy for work. Americans use it and say that it slows them down. This is an excellent example of the different ways that cultural knowledge can mediate the negative effects of any substance. Perfectly legal in this country until the 1930s, marijuana was used by many people, but most frequently it has been associated with the Mexican migrant farm-workers in the Southwest. Again, the propaganda machine effectively associated the Mexican-Americans and African-Americans with reefer madness, and these ethnic minorities became the focus of arguments to prohibit its use. Violence and terminal laziness were said to be the most predictable side effects. These racist arguments succeeded once again, and the use or possession of marijuana was prohibited by law (Lyman & Potter 1991). Interestingly, with the rise of the counterculture and the conversion of a large majority of the white, middle-class, young people to the hippie, flower child movement, marijuana began to gain enormous popularity. Suddenly, the majority of white, middle-class kids were criminalized by their use of marijuana. Laws in most states called for stiff, felony prosecution. Almost overnight millions of members of the predominant cultural group in this country were at risk for being punished as criminals. Shortly thereafter,

most states relaxed their marijuana laws. But cultural resistance to the decriminalization of marijuana has kept it a prohibited and illegal drug.

The 1960s also introduced many Americans to the use of hallucinogenic substances. Mushrooms were the most frequently encountered, but others such as peyote had a brief, if somewhat limited, tenure. Along with the discovery of the development of LSD-25, a lot of young Americans were bombarded by suggestions to "turn on, tune in and drop out." This message was totally unacceptable to mainstream American culture. Federal and state governments moved quickly to outlaw these substances, and dirty looking, hippie dropouts were used as the characteristically other and alien examples of what would happen if one used such hallucinogens. Madness and self-induced death were the predicted outcome. People were mobilized to outlaw these drugs through a basic fear of alien cultures they did not understand.

Tobacco first was used by Native Americans as a hallucinogenic. This was not your regular filter smoke, but a powerful and extremely potent form of tobacco. It was smoked, chewed, and even administered as an enema for quick and efficient absorption into the bloodstream. It also was smoked or chewed chronically in some cultures. For Americans, tobacco use is a failed experiment. In the early part of the century, tobacco companies began to manufacture pre-rolled cigarettes in order to make it more convenient to smoke. Somewhat later, tobacco companies came up with the filter tip. This enabled a great many individuals who otherwise could not tolerate the strong smoke in their lungs to successfully smoke cigarettes. "Light" cigarettes increased the population of smokers. Advertising, such as Virginia Slims for the ladies, the Malboro Man, the freshness of menthol, and Charley Camel, has been enormously successful. The downside for the business is that they also have contributed to enormous health-care costs related to smoking. Still, there is no evidence that any of the sacred, spiritual species has ever passed into secular use. Tobacco use is perfectly legal and, although attitudes currently are changing in America, it is almost universally condoned by American culture. At the moment, tobacco companies are extremely nervous and upset about recent moves to have tobacco regulated by the Federal Drug Administration (FDA) as a habit-forming drug. Tobacco-related illnesses will be responsible for as many as one-half a million deaths this year in the United States. That is roughly four or five times the 100,000 deaths that will be attributed to alcohol, which is roughly four or five times the 25,000 deaths that can be demonstrated to be caused by all other illegal and legal drugs that are available in the country (Zimring & Hawkins 1992).

Obviously, our priorities are culturally conditioned rather than being based on whether or not a substance is good or bad, innocuous or dangerous. Our cultural knowledge actually leads us to permit the use of alcohol and tobacco despite tragic consequences. Our cultural assumptions lead us to prohibit the use of other psychoactive drugs despite the sometimes modest problems associated with their use. Our culturally determined beliefs assure us that we know the "truth" about drugs.

Synthetic drugs, such as barbiturates and depressants, amphetamines and other central nervous system stimulants, seem to have a similar history. Upon discovery they were hailed as new wonder drugs and later it became obvious that there were side effects, at which time the controls were reinforced. The more possible it is to use a drug recreationally, the more intense the pressure to control. These drugs can be prescribed only by a physician and are otherwise illegal to possess or consume. Despite the illegality of taking a prescription drug that has been specifically provided to someone else, almost all of the students in my drugs and culture class have taken someone else's prescription drug. It is often the parent who provides the drug to the child in order to affect health. Furthermore, a huge black market exists. The trade of prescription drugs, particularly sedatives and stimulants, is substantial. Even though our legal system does all it can to restrict these substances, success is only partial. We can observe the difference between the idealized value of the strict control of prescription medicine and daily reality. For example, the parents who give their child some tranquilizers to medicate the effect of some personal trauma are not considered deviants, but good and caring parents. If that same child takes a few of the pills to school and gives them to friends for the same reason, that child is breaking the law and can be prosecuted as a criminal, a drug pusher. The over-the-counter drug industry is one area that does not actually provide many drugs for recreational use. But in the day-to-day reality of the drug business, the over-the-country industry has an enormous impact on what we believe drugs are all about. While "take only as prescribed" is commonly written on packaging and even stated in some broadcast advertising, there can be little doubt that many individuals determine for themselves what might be the proper dosage. So there is some reason to think that there are inherent, potential dangers in some over-the-counter drugs, even though the FDA assures Americans that these minor drugs are harmless, "if taken as directed."

The most culturally pervasive aspect of the over-the-counter industry is the massive amount of advertising. No matter what the product, the most basic message to the potential customer is that a product means relief, is available, and can profoundly and positively affect the user. The healing can be expected to take place immediately, if not sooner. The user gets "safe, quick, and easy" relief from pain and suffering. The idealized cultural value concerning the over-the-counter and prescription medicines is one that is consistent with the most basic meaning of all drug use, namely, that these substances can heal us or improve our state of being. The reality of the legal drug business is that people increasingly believe that it is some substance or drug they need in order to feel better. Importantly, in this respect, they are readily available at the corner drugstore. The positive value of drugs as operationalized in our culture leads directly to experimentation and the use of illegal substances. If all of these advertised remedies work, and someone tells a friend about experience with an illegal drug, and they attest to the efficacy of that remedy for improving one's state of being, and thus it is not too far a leap to try it out. The ceremonial necessity of sharing a cure or mind-altering drug with a cohort extends to all aspects of drug culture, legal or illegal.

The basic and traditional human pattern of drug use was one in which medicinal and psychoactive substances generally were used in a ritual and ceremonial context. The shaman or witch usually was consulted as the legitimate healer within the culture. The recreational use of substances was likewise confined by social and ceremonial prescription. Certain drugs were prohibited and considered profane. Culturally determined drug use produced beliefs about drugs. The significance of belief with regard to healing and curing agents is not restricted to traditional cultures, but is also manifest in modern American society. Most Americans believe that their prescription for antidepressants, valium, or librium will help them to cope. They believe prescribed antibiotics will help heal their viral infections. They believe that the sinus, hemorrhoid, headache, or stomach medicines they buy over the counter will be effective in alleviating minor problems. Sometimes these beliefs are appropriate, and at other times they reflect the superstitious and magical thinking we are so quick to criticize. While the unmistakably deleterious effects of alcohol, tobacco, and some illegal drugs can be demonstrated, people often take these drugs in the belief that they positively affect their well being. Recreational drugs relax them and help them to deal with everyday life in a more pleasant context than otherwise would be possible. They believe that they need help and they believe that a drug helps.

## Major Constituent Drug Cultures in the United States

Virtually everyone in this country is a member of a drug culture. They may participate in more than one specific cultural group. In each culture, members use a range of drugs based on their cultural knowledge and belief. Each culture utilizes a particular set of substances according to these beliefs. Each discourages the use of drugs it believes are really harmful or dangerous. Each is in competition with the other: economically, politically, socially, and morally. It is necessary to separate the different drug cultures that are major constituents of what might be called the American drug culture. At present, two primary classes of drugs are used: legal and illegal. There are three categories that are legally permitted: alcohol products, tobacco products, and pharmaceutical products that are dispensed legitimately. These pharmaceuticals include prescription drugs and over-the-counter remedies, only some of which are psychoactive; the remainder are medicinal.

Almost all Americans are members of the over-the-counter and prescription drug culture. Doctors prescribe and most responsible people participate in order to positively affect their health and well being. They buy these drugs in the belief that they are ill, they need them, and they will be healed by them. None of these drugs is to be used recreationally, only medicinally. Economically, it is big bucks and politically, it is correct. The two-thirds of the adult American population who drink some form of alcoholic beverage constitute the drug culture of alcohol. While user behavior is widely variable, they generally claim that alcohol promotes a spirit of conviviality and togetherness, relieves anxiety and inhibitions, and positively affects their well being. They consume alcoholic beverages in the belief that these results actually will occur. The drug is used ceremonially, recreationally, and medicinally. Economically, it is big bucks. Politically, it is correct in most cases. Over one-half the adult population smokes or chews tobacco. This drug culture is a self-described group of drug "addicts." While their behavior may appear irrational, they seem to believe that they have to keep doing it, and are in constant competition with non-members for space and air. They believe that it calms their nerves, even though the drug stimulates the cardiovascular system. The drug is only used recreationally and not medicinally. Economically, it is big bucks. Politically, it is now incorrect, despite the fact that it used to be sexy and cool.

The other primary class of drug culture is the illegal drug culture. This includes the medically and legally unauthorized use of prescription drugs, as well as the use of substances that are prohibited by law. The common thread in this culture is the illicit nature of the use, but this group is also widely diverse. Marijuana smokers, pill poppers, cocaine snorters, heroin shooters, speed freaks, and vision seekers all believe that their state of well being will be meaningfully affected in some way as a result of their drug use. Members of this particular drug culture are in belligerent competition with nonmembers. This competition can result in disagreements over the meaning of drugs and the incarceration of hundreds of thousands of individuals. These drugs are used recreationally and also as self-prescribed medicines. Heroin junkies frequently may refer to the drug as "my medicine." Economically, it is big bucks. Politically, it is dangerous. Legally, it is prohibited. Socially, it's rejected. Morally, it's wrong. Criminally, it's a big boost. Practically, it is tough to study. Tragically, it is a mess.

One of the most instructive examples of the confusing relationship between meaning, drugs, culture and the individual is revealed by the problems associated with the use of crack cocaine. In the late 1970s and early 1980s, cocaine began to gain notoriety as a fashionable and trendy drug associated with fashionable, trendy, and wealthy people. At the time, the cost of the drug was prohibitive to potential middle-class consumers. A perusal of media coverage in the late 1970s and early 1980s demonstrates that cocaine was not initially seen as a broad-scale threat to American society. The cost of the drug seemed to preclude general use among the majority of the people in the country. The rich seemed to be the primary population at risk.

By the mid-1980s, the supply of cocaine was sufficient to reduce the price significantly. Though still expensive, many middle-class consumers were able to occasionally purchase cocaine for recreational purposes through the very same distribution system used to sell marijuana and other popular, illicit substances. The essential meaning of the drug was positive for most users. It was something to spice up a social occasion, and the cost seemed to mitigate against habitual use. For abstainers, cocaine meant another threat to the established standards of behavior. As the use of cocaine became more widespread and popular, the legal, medical and political authorities convincingly and accurately associated the cocaine trade with the Columbian drug cartels, potential medical problems faced by habitual and occasional users, and the personal, financial difficulties of obtaining a drug that a middle-class individual really cannot afford. The public death of college basketball player Len Bias occurred as a crescendo of panic that swept the country.

Not coincidentally, the introduction of smokeable crack was occurring at about the same time. Previously, smoking cocaine had involved free-basing. Richard Pryor had almost burned himself to death, and Ricky Nelson and his band had died as a result of a plane crash in which a fire had apparently started while the passengers had been free-basing. Again, this had been a problem of the rich. But cocaine in crack form succeeded in two important respects. First, smoking crack delivers the drug much more quickly and efficiently to the brain. This results in a much more dramatic effect, increases the depressive kickback after the drug wears off, and heightens the individual's desire for another dose. Second, and probably most important, it made a form of cocaine available to consumers at a much lower cost. Distribution of the drug now could be extended to the working and the lower class neighborhoods, to the inner city and the ghettos. After the crack trade had been established in the African-American community, predictable problems became evident. The criminal enterprise controlling the crack trade through intimidation and violence, among other methods, became associated with crack houses, children distributing the product, murder, gangs, and heinous crimes. The economic reality of the trade in communities mired in poverty meant that there was a new product that could be sold to make money. The social reality of crack use was that the population had a drug available that was strongly associated with rich, sports and entertainment heroes. Obviously, it was embraced by many individuals as a very trendy, exciting, and profitable thing to do.

It would be a grave error to suggest that all or even most crack use is African-American, nor would it be accurate to suggest that all or even most African-Americans use crack. But to read the daily newspaper or watch the TV, one would assume that the crack "problem" is exclusively African-American. Reams of TV footage have been presented, showing raids and busts on crack houses, videos of gangs, and drug busts, which the authorities assure us will put a big dent in the criminal enterprise. These raids appear to target African-American communities almost exclusively (Shoemaker 1989). In 1995, there is not a great deal of concern about powdered cocaine, but "crack in the inner city" (euphemism for black neighborhoods) is constantly purported to be "the number one drug problem facing the country today." Even though crack is a significant problem, it is absolutely ludicrous to suggest that it is a greater threat to the health and welfare of the people in this country than even alcohol or tobacco consumption. But people believe it. Most white, middle-class people only associate crack with the African-American community. Law enforcement and political institutions feed the media information that generates and reinforces the association. Although it is not, by far, the worst drug problem Americans face, it is apparently comforting to believe that the worst problem is not one in which the predominant cultural group has any active culpability. This is the same racist propaganda that has accompanied almost every effort to prohibit drugs by law. In the meantime, the meaningful relationships between drugs, cultures, individuals, and American society remains obscured.

# Conclusions and Suggestions

The "war on drugs" has been a miserable failure because it does not take into account the basic meaning of drugs to all users and abstainers. Nor do those who advocate such an approach understand that people use all drugs because they are meaningful. The ceremonial and ritual contexts of interaction within a drug culture do not just cause drug use, they generate beliefs and behaviors with respect to much more than just different drugs. Attempting to incarcerate just anyone who is a participating, cultural member of the wrong group is proving costly, ineffective, and counterproductive. Prison culture is also a reality, and those who spend time there generally learn and accept the predominant values. This fosters the continuing growth of an entire cultural group who most assuredly will become even more alienated from mainstream America and will not change any of their beliefs regarding drugs. As much as 40 percent of the prison population in this country are jailed because of drugs. Upon release, the problem is still there because the beliefs are still there (Wilcox 1994).

The prohibition of certain drug cultures also has had the unfortunate effect of supporting and maintaining a huge black market, criminal enterprise. The business is so lucrative that violent behavior is common in the United States and other countries. The worldwide production and distribution system is incredibly complex and efficient. Attempts to convince third-world countries to quit producing drugs never can be successful. Drug products have traditional meaning to poor, rural people, as well as the newer meaning of freedom from poverty, hunger, and disease. Sanctions to stop the distribution of illegal drugs in this country never will be any more successful than was Prohibition. The distribution system for illegal drugs is a grass roots operation. The demand and supply is there. Friends help each other acquire drugs. No neighborhood or community exists without connections.

The adoption of recreational marijuana use by a large majority of young people in the 1960s continued for at least a decade. During that time, the basic distribution system for nearly all illicit drugs was formidably developed by entrepreneurs who previously were restricted to very narrowly defined groups of customers. Marijuana use by such an overwhelming middle class population ensured that as new drugs were introduced, the economic system of distribution would be in place to sell them to a larger number and wider variety of people. It would be interesting to know what would have happened had the federal government legalized marijuana 25 years ago. Without the daily participation of middle class consumers in the distribution system, drugs such as speed, cocaine, crack, and heroin may have been much harder to acquire. Some of our fashionable drugs might not have caused as many problems as they have on such a broad scale in American society.

The conflict is not over the use of drugs as much as it is a conflict over the meaning of human life and the role of drugs in our lives. Fuzzy cultural beliefs must be replaced with facts. The meaning of drugs to the user and abstainer must be understood in a cultural context. The search for the culturally embedded meanings of drugs can lead researchers to examine reality rather than idealized illusions of the relationship between the individual, the culture, American society, and drugs. Based on such research we may be able to create rational domestic and foreign policies, and explain the desire, alienation, insecurity, cruelty, fear, and loathing that make so many of us believe we need chemically psychoactive assistance in our daily lives.

# References

Douglas M. 1987. *Constructive Drinking: Perspectives on Drink from Anthropology*. New York: Cambridge University Press.

Furst P. 1972. *Flesh of the Gods: The Ritual Use of Hallucinogens*. New York: Praeger.

——— 1976. *Hallucinogens and Culture*. Novato, CA: Chandler & Sharpe Publishers.

Heath D. B. 1981. *Alcohol Use and World Cultures: A Comprehensive Bibliography of Anthropological Sources*. Toronto: Addiction Research Foundation.

Heath D. B. 1983. "Sociocultural Perspectives on Addiction". In *Etiological Aspects of Alcohol and Drug Abuse*. E. Gottheil et al. (eds). Springfield, IL: Charles C. Thomas, pp. 223–237.

——— 1984. "Cross Cultural Studies of Alcoholism". *Recent Developments in Alcoholism*, Vol. 2. M. Galanter (ed). New York: Plenum Press, pp. 405–416.

Inciardi J. A. 1990. *Handbook of Drug Control in the United States*. Westport, CT: Greenwood Publishing.

——— 1991. *The Drug Legalization Debate*. New York: Sage Publications.

Levine H. G. 1978. "The Discovery of Addiction". *Journal of Studies on Alcohol* 39:143–174.

——— 1984. "The Alcohol Problem in America: From Temperance to Alcoholism". *British Journal of Addiction* 79:109–119.

Leland J. H. 1976. *Firewater Myths: North American Indian Drinking and Alcohol Addiction*. New Brunswick: Rutgers Center Alcohol Studies, Monograph 11.

Lyman M. D. & Potter G. W. 1991. *Drugs in Society: Causes, Concepts, and Control*. Cincinnati: Anderson Publishing Co.

MacAndrew C. & Edgerton R. B. 1969. *Drunken Comportment: A Social Explanation*. Chicago: Aldine Publishing.

Mandelbaum D. G. 1965. *Alcohol and Culture. Current Anthropology* 6:281–293.

Marshall M. 1979. *Beliefs, Behaviors, and Alcoholic Beverages: A Cross Cultural Survey*. Ann Arbor: University of Michigan Press.

Park P. & Matveychuk W. (eds). 1986. *Culture and Politics of Drugs*. Dubuque: Kendall/Hunt Publishing.

Radcliffe-Brown A. R. 1952. *Structure and Function in Primitive Society*. New York: Free Press.

Shoemaker P. (ed). 1989. *Communications Campaigns About Drugs: Government, Media and the Public*. Hillsdale, NJ: Lawrence Erlbaum & Associates.

Szasz T. 1987. *Ceremonial Chemistry: The Ritual Persecution of Drugs, Addicts and Pushers*. Revised edition. Holmes Beach, FL: Learning Publications, Inc.

Wilcox D. M. 1994. *Alcoholic Thinking: An Ethnographic Narrative of the Changing World View Among Recovering Urban Alcoholics in Alcoholics Anonymous*. Ann Arbor, MI: University Microfilms, Inc.

Zimring F. & Hawkins G. 1992. *The Search for Rational Drug Control*. New York: Cambridge University Press.

# The Secrets of Haiti's Living Dead

## A Harvard botanist investigates mystic potions, voodoo rites, and the making of zombies.

GINO DEL GUERCIO

Five years ago, a man walked into l'Estère, a village in central Haiti, approached a peasant woman named Angelina Narcisse, and identified himself as her brother Clairvius. If he had not introduced himself using a boyhood nickname and mentioned facts only intimate family members knew, she would not have believed him. Because, eighteen years earlier, Angelina had stood in a small cemetery north of her village and watched as her brother Clairvius was buried.

The man told Angelina he remembered that night well. He knew when he was lowered into his grave, because he was fully conscious, although he could not speak or move. As the earth was thrown over his coffin, he felt as if he were floating over the grave. The scar on his right cheek, he said, was caused by a nail driven through his casket.

The night he was buried, he told Angelina, a voodoo priest raised him from the grave. He was beaten with a sisal whip and carried off to a sugar plantation in northern Haiti where, with other zombies, he was forced to work as a slave. Only with the death of the zombie master were they able to escape, and Narcisse eventually returned home.

Legend has it that zombies are the living dead, raised from their graves and animated by malevolent voodoo sorcerers, usually for some evil purpose. Most Haitians believe in zombies, and Narcisse's claim is not unique. At about the time he reappeared, in 1980, two women turned up in other villages saying they were zombies. In the same year, in northern Haiti, the local peasants claimed to have found a group of zombies wandering aimlessly in the fields.

But Narcisse's case was different in one crucial respect; it was documented. His death had been recorded by doctors at the American-directed Schweitzer Hospital in Deschapelles. On April 30, 1962, hospital records show, Narcisse walked into the hospital's emergency room spitting up blood. He was feverish and full of aches. His doctors could not diagnose his illness, and his symptoms grew steadily worse. Three days after he entered the hospital, according to the records, he died. The attending physicians, an American among them, signed his death certificate. His body was placed in cold storage for twenty hours, and then he was buried. He said he remembered hearing his doctors pronounce him dead while his sister wept at his bedside.

At the Centre de Psychiatrie et Neurologie in Port-au-Prince, Dr. Lamarque Douyon, a Haitian-born, Canadian-trained psychiatrist, has been systematically investigating all reports of zombies since 1961. Though convinced zombies were real, he had been unable to find a scientific explanation for the phenomenon. He did not believe zombies were people raised from the dead, but that did not make them any less interesting. He speculated that victims were only made to *look* dead, probably by means of a drug that dramatically slowed metabolism. The victim was buried, dug up within a few hours, and somehow reawakened.

The Narcisse case provided Douyon with evidence strong enough to warrant a request for assistance from colleagues in New York. Douyon wanted to find an ethnobotanist, a traditional-medicines expert, who could track down the zombie potion he was sure existed. Aware of the medical potential of a drug that could dramatically lower metabolism, a group organized by the late Dr. Nathan Kline—a New York psychiatrist and pioneer in the field of psychopharmacology—raised the funds necessary to send someone to investigate.

The search for that someone led to the Harvard Botanical Museum, one of the world's foremost institutes of ethnobiology. Its director, Richard Evans Schultes, Jeffrey professor of biology, had spent thirteen years in the tropics studying native medicines. Some of his best-known work is the investigation of curare, the substance used by the nomadic people of the Amazon to poison their darts. Refined into a powerful muscle relaxant called D-tubocurarine, it is now an essential component of the anesthesia used during almost all surgery.

Schultes would have been a natural for the Haitian investigation, but he was too busy. He recommended another Harvard ethnobotanist for the assignment, Wade Davis, a 28-year-old Canadian pursuing a doctorate in biology.

Davis grew up in the tall pine forests of British Columbia and entered Harvard in 1971, influenced by a *Life* magazine story on the student strike of 1969. Before Harvard, the only Americans he had known were draft dodgers, who seemed very exotic. "I used to fight forest fires with them," Davis says. "Like everybody else, I thought America was where it was at. And I wanted to go to Harvard because of that Life article. When I got there, I realized it wasn't quite what I had in mind."

Davis took a course from Schultes, and when he decided to go to South America to study plants, he approached his professor for guidance. "He was an extraordinary figure," Davis remembers. "He was a man who had done it all. He had lived alone for years in the Amazon." Schultes sent Davis to the rain forest with two letters of introduction and two pieces of advice: wear a pith helmet and try ayahuasca, a powerful hallucinogenic vine. During that expedition and others, Davis proved himself an "outstanding field man," says his mentor. Now, in early 1982, Schultes called him into his office and asked if he had plans for spring break.

"I always took to Schultes's assignments like a plant takes to water," says Davis, tall and blond, with inquisitive blue eyes. "Whatever Schultes told me to do, I did. His letters of introduction opened up a whole world." This time the world was Haiti.

Davis knew nothing about the Caribbean island—and nothing about African traditions, which serve as Haiti's cultural basis. He certainly did not believe in zombies. "I thought it was a lark," he says now.

Davis landed in Haiti a week after his conversation with Schultes, armed with a hypothesis about how the zombie drug—if it existed—might be made. Setting out to explore, he discovered a country materially impoverished, but rich in culture and mystery. He was impressed by the cohesion of Haitian society; he found none of the crime, social disorder, and rampant drug and alcohol abuse so common in many of the other Caribbean islands. The cultural wealth and cohesion, he believes, spring from the country's turbulent history.

During the French occupation of the late eighteenth century, 370,000 African-born slaves were imported to Haiti between 1780 and 1790. In 1791, the black population launched one of the few successful slave revolts in history, forming secret societies and overcoming first the French plantation owners and then a detachment of troops from Napoleon's army, sent to quell the revolt. For the next hundred years Haiti was the only independent black republic in the Caribbean, populated by people who did not forget their African heritage. "You can almost argue that Haiti is more African than Africa," Davis says. "When the west coast of Africa was being disrupted by colonialism and the slave trade, Haiti was essentially left alone. The amalgam of beliefs in Haiti is unique, but it's very, very African."

Davis discovered that the vast majority of Haitian peasants practice voodoo, a sophisticated religion with African roots. Says Davis, "It was immediately obvious that the stereotypes of voodoo weren't true. Going around the countryside, I found clues to a whole complex social world." Vodounists believe they communicate directly with, indeed are often possessed by, the many spirits who populate the everyday world. Vodoun society is a system of education, law, and medicine; it embodies a code of ethics that regulates social behavior. In rural areas, secret vodoun societies, much like those found on the west coast of Africa, are as much or more in control of everyday life as the Haitian government.

Although most outsiders dismissed the zombie phenomenon as folklore, some early investigators, convinced of its reality, tried to find a scientific explanation. The few who sought a zombie drug failed. Nathan Kline, who helped finance Davis's

expedition, had searched unsuccessfully, as had Lamarque Douyon, the Haitian psychiatrist. Zora Neale Hurston, an American black woman, may have come closest. An anthropological pioneer, she went to Haiti in the Thirties, studied vodoun society, and wrote a book on the subject, *Tell My Horse*, first published in 1938. She knew about the secret societies and was convinced zombies were real, but if a power existed, she too failed to obtain it.

Davis obtained a sample in a few weeks.

He arrived in Haiti with the names of several contacts. A BBC reporter familiar with the Narcisse case had suggested he talk with Marcel Pierre. Pierre owned the Eagle Bar, a bordello in the city of Saint Marc. He was also a voodoo sorcerer and had supplied the BBC with a physiologically active powder of unknown ingredients. Davis found him willing to negotiate. He told Pierre he was a representative of "powerful but anonymous interests in New York," willing to pay generously for the priest's services, provided no questions were asked. Pierre agreed to be helpful for what Davis will only say was a "sizable sum." Davis spent a day watching Pierre gather the ingredients—including human bones—and grind them together with mortar and pestle. However, from his knowledge of poison, Davis knew immediately that nothing in the formula could produce the powerful effects of zombification.

Three weeks later, Davis went back to the Eagle Bar, where he found Pierre sitting with three associates. Davis challenged him. He called him a charlatan. Enraged, the priest gave him a second vial, claiming that this was the real poison. Davis pretended to pour the powder into his palm and rub it into his skin. "You're a dead man," Pierre told him, and he might have been, because this powder proved to be genuine. But, as the substance had not actually touched him, Davis was able to maintain his bravado, and Pierre was impressed. He agreed to make the poison and show Davis how it was done.

The powder, which Davis keeps in a small vial, looks like dry black dirt. It contains parts of toads, sea worms, lizards, tarantulas, and human bones. (To obtain the last ingredient, he and Pierre unearthed a child's grave on a nocturnal trip to the cemetery.) The poison is rubbed into the victim's skin. Within hours he begins to feel nauseated and has difficulty breathing. A pins-and-needles sensation afflicts his arms and legs, then progresses to the whole body. The subject becomes paralyzed; his lips turn blue for lack of oxygen. Quickly—sometimes within six hours—his metabolism is lowered to a level almost indistinguishable from death.

As Davis discovered, making the poison is an inexact science. Ingredients varied in the five samples he eventually acquired, although the active agents were always the same. And the poison came with no guarantee. Davis speculates that sometimes instead of merely paralyzing the victim, the compound kills him. Sometimes the victim suffocates in the coffin before he can be resurrected. But clearly the potion works well enough often enough to make zombies more than a figment of Haitian imagination.

Analysis of the powder produced another surprise. "When I went down to Haiti originally," says Davis, "my hypothesis was that the formula would contain *concombre zombi*, the 'zombie's cucumber,' which is a *Datura* plant. I thought somehow *Datura*

# Richard Schultes

*His students continue his tradition of pursuing botanical research in the likeliest of unlikely places.*

Richard Evans Schultes, Jeffrey professor of biology emeritus, has two homes, and they could not be more different. The first is Cambridge, where he served as director of the Harvard Botanical Museum from 1970 until last year, when he became director emeritus. During his tenure he interested generations of students in the exotic botany of the Amazon rain forest. His impact on the field through his own research is worldwide. The scholarly ethnobotanist with steel-rimmed glasses, bald head, and white lab coat is as much a part of the Botanical Museum as the thousands of plant specimens and botanical texts on the museum shelves.

In his austere office is a picture of a crew-cut, younger man stripped to the waist, his arms decorated with tribal paint. This is Schultes's other persona. Starting in 1941, he spent thirteen years in the rain forests of South America, living with the Indians and studying the plants they use for medicinal and spiritual purposes.

Schultes is concerned that many of the people he has studied are giving up traditional ways. "The people of so-called primitive societies are becoming civilized and losing all their forefathers' knowledge of plant lore," he says. "We'll be losing the tremendous amounts of knowledge they've gained over thousands of years. We've interested in the practical aspects with the hope that new medicines and other things can be developed for our own civilization."

Schultes's exploits are legendary in the biology department. Once, while gathering South American plant specimens hundreds of miles from civilization, he contracted beri-beri. For forty days he fought creeping paralysis and overwhelming fatigue as he paddled back to a doctor. "It was an extraordinary feat of endurance," says disciple Wade Davis. "He is really one of the last nineteenth-century naturalists."

Hallucinogenic plants are one of Schultes's primary interests. As a Harvard undergraduate in the Thirties, he lived with Oklahoma's Kiowa Indians to observe their use of plants. He participated in their peyote ceremonies and wrote his thesis on the hallucinogenic cactus. He has also studied other hallucinogens, such as morning glory seeds, sacred mushrooms, and ayahuasca, a South American vision vine. Schultes's work has led to the development of anesthetics made from curare and alternative sources of natural rubber.

Schultes's main concern these days is the scientific potential of plants in the rapidly disappearing Amazon jungle. "If chemists are going to get material on 80,000 species and then analyze them, they'll never finish the job before the jungle is gone," he says. "The short cut is to find out what the [native] people have learned about the plant properties during many years of living in the very rich flora."

—G.D.G

was used in putting people down." *Datura* is a powerful psychoactive plant, found in West Africa as well as other tropical areas and used there in ritual as well as criminal activities. Davis had found *Datura* growing in Haiti. Its popular name suggested the plant was used in creating zombies.

But, says Davis, "there were a lot of problems with the *Datura* hypothesis. Partly it was a question of how the drug was administered. *Datura* would create a stupor in huge doses, but it just wouldn't produce the kind of immobility that was key. These people had to appear dead, and there aren't many drugs that will do that."

One of the ingredients Pierre included in the second formula was a dried fish, a species of puffer or blowfish, common to most parts of the world. It gets its name from its ability to fill itself with water and swell to several times its normal size when threatened by predators. Many of these fish contain a powerful poison known as tetrodotoxin. One of the most powerful nonprotein poisons known to man, tetrodotoxin turned up in every sample of zombie powder that Davis acquired.

Numerous well-documented accounts of puffer fish poisoning exist, but the most famous accounts come from the Orient, where *fugu* fish, a species of puffer, is considered a delicacy. In Japan, special chefs are licensed to prepare *fugu*. The chef removes enough poison to make the fish nonlethal, yet enough remains to create exhilarating physiological effects—tingles up and down the spine, mild prickling of the tongue and lips, eu-

phoria. Several dozen Japanese die each year, having bitten off more than they should have.

"When I got hold of the formula and saw it was the *fugu* fish, that suddenly threw open the whole Japanese literature," says Davis. Case histories of *fugu* poisoning read like accounts of zombification. Victims remain conscious but unable to speak or move. A man who had "died" after eating *fugu* recovered seven days later in the morgue. Several summers ago, another Japanese poisoned by *fugu* revived after he was nailed into his coffin. "Almost all of Narcisse's symptoms correlated. Even strange things such as the fact that he said he was conscious and could hear himself pronounced dead. Stuff that I thought had to be magic, that seemed crazy. But, in fact, that is what people who get *fugu*-fish poisoning experience."

Davis was certain he had solved the mystery. But far from being the end of his investigation, identifying the poison was, in fact, its starting point. "The drug alone didn't make zombies," he explains. "Japanese victims of puffer-fish poisoning don't become zombies, they become poison victims. All the drug could do was set someone up for a whole series of psychological pressures that would be rooted in the culture. I wanted to know why zombification was going on," he says.

He sought a cultural answer, an explanation rooted in the structure and beliefs of Haitian society. Was zombification simply a random criminal activity? He thought not. He had discovered that Clairvius Narcisse and "Ti Femme," a second victim he interviewed, were village pariahs. Ti Femme was regarded as a thief. Narcisse had abandoned his children and deprived his brother of land that was rightfully his. Equally suggestive, Narcisse claimed that his aggrieved brother had sold him to a *bokor*, a voodoo priest who dealt in black magic; he made cryptic reference to having been tried and found guilty by the "masters of the land."

Gathering poisons from various parts of the country, Davis had come into direct contact with the vodoun secret societies. Returning to the anthropological literature on Haiti and pursuing his contacts with informants, Davis came to understand the social matrix within which zombies were created.

Davis's investigations uncovered the importance of the secret societies. These groups trace their origins to the bands of escaped slaves that organized the revolt against the French in the late eighteenth century. Open to both men and women, the societies control specific territories of the country. Their meetings take place at night, and in many rural parts of Haiti the drums and wild celebrations that characterize the gatherings can be heard for miles.

Davis believes the secret societies are responsible for policing their communities, and the threat of zombification is one way they maintain order. Says Davis, "Zombification has a material basis, but it also has a societal logic." To the uninitiated, the practice may appear a random criminal activity, but in rural vodoun society, it is exactly the opposite—a sanction imposed by recognized authorities, a form of capital punishment. For rural Haitians, zombification is an even more severe punishment than death, because it deprives the subject of his most valued possessions: his free will and independence.

The vodounists believe that when a person dies, his spirit splits into several different parts. If a priest is powerful enough, the spiritual aspect that controls a person's character and individuality, known as *ti bon ange*, the "good little angel," can be captured and the corporeal aspect, deprived of its will, held as a slave.

From studying the medical literature on tetrodotoxin poisoning, Davis discovered that if a victim survives the first few hours of the poisoning, he is likely to recover fully from the ordeal. The subject simply revives spontaneously. But zombies remain without will, in a trance-like state, a condition vodounists attribute to the power of the priest. Davis thinks it possible that the psychological trauma of zombification may be augmented by *Datura* or some other drug; he thinks zombies may be fed a *Datura* paste that accentuates their disorientation. Still, he puts the material basis of zombification in perspective: "Tetrodotoxin and *Datura* are only templates on which cultural forces and beliefs may be amplified a thousand times."

Davis has not been able to discover how prevalent zombification is in Haiti. "How many zombies there are is not the question," he says. He compares it to capital punishment in the United States: "It doesn't really matter how many people are electrocuted, as long as it's a possibility." As a sanction in Haiti, the fear is not of zombies, it's of becoming one.

Davis attributes his success in solving the zombie mystery to his approach. He went to Haiti with an open mind and immersed himself in the culture. "My intuition unhindered by biases served me well," he says. "I didn't make any judgments." He combined this attitude with what he had learned earlier from his experiences in the Amazon. "Schultes's lesson is to go and live with the Indians as an Indian." Davis was able to participate in the vodoun society to a surprising degree, eventually even penetrating one of the Bizango societies and dancing in their nocturnal rituals. His appreciation of Haitian culture is apparent. "Everybody asks me how did a white person get this information? To ask the question means you don't understand Haitians—they don't judge you by the color of your skin."

As a result of the exotic nature of his discoveries, Davis has gained a certain notoriety. He plans to complete his dissertation soon, but he has already finished writing a popular account of his adventures. To be published in January by Simon and Schuster, it is called *The Serpent and the Rainbow*, after the serpent that vodounists believe created the earth and the rainbow spirit it married. Film rights have already been optioned; in October Davis went back to Haiti with a screenwriter. But Davis takes the notoriety in stride. "All this attention is funny," he says. "For years, not just me, but all Schultes's students have had extraordinary adventures in the line of work. The adventure is not the end point, it's just along the way of getting the data. At the Botanical Museum, Schultes created a world unto itself. We didn't think we were doing anything above the ordinary. I still don't think we do. And you know," he adds, "the Haiti episode does not begin to compare to what others have accomplished—particularly Schultes himself."

**GINO DEL GUERCIO** is a national science writer for United Press International.

---

# Body Ritual Among the Nacirema

Horace Miner

The anthropologist has become so familiar with the diversity of ways in which different peoples behave in similar situations that he is not apt to be surprised by even the most exotic customs. In fact, if all of the logically possible combinations of behavior have not been found somewhere in the world, he is apt to suspect that they must be present in some yet undescribed tribe. This point has, in fact, been expressed with respect to clan organization by Murdock (1949: 71). In this light, the magical beliefs and practices of the Nacirema present such unusual aspects that it seems desirable to describe them as an example of the extremes to which human behavior can go.

Professor Linton first brought the ritual of the Nacirema to the attention of anthropologists twenty years ago (1936: 326), but the culture of this people is still very poorly understood. They are a North American group living in the territory between the Canadian Cree, the Yaqui and Tarahumare of Mexico, and the Carib and Arawak of the Antilles. Little is known of their origin, though tradition states that they came from the east. According to Nacirema mythology, their nation was originated by a culture hero, Notgnishaw, who is otherwise known for two great feats of strength—the throwing of a piece of wampum across the river Pa-To-Mac and the chopping down of a cherry tree in which the Spirit of Truth resided.

Nacirema culture is characterized by a highly developed market economy which has evolved in a rich natural habitat. While much of the people's time is devoted to economic pursuits, a large part of the fruits of these labors and a considerable portion of the day are spent in ritual activity. The focus of this activity is the human body, the appearance and health of which loom as a dominant concern in the ethos of the people. While such a concern is certainly not unusual, its ceremonial aspects and associated philosophy are unique.

The fundamental belief underlying the whole system appears to be that the human body is ugly and that its natural tendency is to debility and disease. Incarcerated in such a body, man's only hope is to avert these characteristics through the use of the powerful influences of ritual and ceremony. Every household has one or more shrines devoted to this purpose. The more powerful individuals in the society have several shrines in their houses and, in fact, the opulence of a house is often referred to in terms of the number of such ritual centers it possesses. Most houses are of wattle and daub construction, but the shrine rooms of the more wealthy are walled with stone. Poorer families imitate the rich by applying pottery plaques to their shrine walls.

While each family has at least one such shrine, the rituals associated with it are not family ceremonies but are private and secret. The rites are normally only discussed with children, and then only during the period when they are being initiated into these mysteries. I was able, however, to establish sufficient rapport with the natives to examine these shrines and to have the rituals described to me.

The focal point of the shrine is a box or chest which is built into the wall. In this chest are kept the many charms and magical potions without which no native believes he could live. These preparations are secured from a variety of specialized practitioners. The most powerful of these are the medicine men, whose assistance must be rewarded with substantial gifts. However, the medicine men do not provide the curative potions for their clients, but decide what the ingredients should be and then write them down in an ancient and secret language. This writing is understood only by the medicine men and by the herbalists who, for another gift, provide the required charm.

The charm is not disposed of after it has served its purpose, but is placed in the charm-box of the household shrine. As these magical materials are specific for certain ills, and the real or imagined maladies of the people are many, the charm-box is usually full to overflowing. The magical packets are so numerous that people forget what their purposes were and fear to use them again. While the natives are very vague on this point, we can only assume that the idea in retaining all the old magical materials is that their presence in the charm-box, before which the body rituals are conducted, will in some way protect the worshipper.

Beneath the charm-box is a small font. Each day every member of the family, in succession, enters the shrine room, bows his head before the charm-box, mingles different sorts of holy water in the font, and proceeds with a brief rite of ablution. The holy waters are secured from the Water Temple of the community, where the priests conduct elaborate ceremonies to make the liquid ritually pure.

In the hierarchy of magical practitioners, and below the medicine men in prestige, are specialists whose designation is best translated "holy-mouth-men." The Nacirema have an almost pathological horror and fascination with the mouth, the condition of which is believed to have a supernatural influence on all social relationships. Were it not for the rituals of the mouth, they believe that their teeth would fall out, their gums bleed, their jaws shrink, their friends desert them, and their lovers reject them. (They also believe that a strong relationship exists between oral and moral characteristics. For example, there is a ritual ablution of the mouth for children which is supposed to improve their moral fiber.)

The daily body ritual performed by everyone includes a mouth-rite. Despite the fact that these people are so punctilious about care of the mouth, this rite involves a practice which strikes the uninitiated stranger as revolting. It was reported to me that the ritual consists of inserting a small bundle of hog hairs into the mouth, along with certain magical powders, and then moving the bundle in a highly formalized series of gestures.

In addition to the private mouth-rite, the people seek out a holy-mouth-man once or twice a year. These practitioners have an impressive set of paraphernalia, consisting of a variety of augers, awls, probes, and prods. The use of these objects in the exorcism of the evils of the mouth involves almost unbelievable ritual torture of the client. The holy-mouth-man opens the client's mouth and, using the above mentioned tools, enlarges any holes which decay may have created in the teeth. Magical materials are put into these holes. If there are no naturally occurring holes in the teeth, large sections of one or more teeth are gouged out so that the supernatural substance can be applied. In the client's view, the purpose of these ministrations is to arrest decay and to draw friends. The extremely sacred and traditional character of the rite is evident in the fact that the natives return to the holy-mouth-men year after year, despite the fact that their teeth continue to decay.

It is to be hoped that, when a thorough study of the Nacirema is made, there will be a careful inquiry into the personality structure of these people. One has but to watch the gleam in the eye of a holy-mouth-man, as he jabs an awl into an exposed nerve, to suspect that a certain amount of sadism is involved. If this can be established, a very interesting pattern emerges, for most of the population shows definite masochistic tendencies. It was to these that Professor Linton referred in discussing a distinctive part of the daily body ritual which is performed only by men. This part of the rite involves scraping and lacerating the surface of the face with a sharp instrument. Special women's rites are performed only four times during each lunar month, but what they lack in frequency is made up in barbarity. As part of this ceremony, women bake their heads in small ovens for about an hour. The theoretically interesting point is that what seems to be a preponderantly masochistic people have developed sadistic specialists.

The medicine men have an imposing temple, or *latipso*, in every community of any size. The more elaborate ceremonies required to treat very sick patients can only be performed at this temple. These ceremonies involve not only the thaumaturge but a permanent group of vestal maidens who move sedately about the temple chambers in distinctive costume and headdress.

The *latipso* ceremonies are so harsh that it is phenomenal that a fair proportion of the really sick natives who enter the temple ever recover. Small children whose indoctrination is still incomplete have been known to resist attempts to take them to the temple because "that is where you go to die." Despite this fact, sick adults are not only willing but eager to undergo the protracted ritual purification, if they can afford to do so. No matter how ill the supplicant or how grave the emergency, the guardians of many temples will not admit a client if he cannot give a rich gift to the custodian. Even after one has gained admission and survived the ceremonies, the guardians will not permit the neophyte to leave until he makes still another gift.

The supplicant entering the temple is first stripped of all his or her clothes. In every-day life the Nacirema avoids exposure of his body and its natural functions. Bathing and excretory acts are performed only in the secrecy of the household shrine, where they are ritualized as part of the body-rites. Psychological shock results from the fact that body secrecy is suddenly lost upon entry into the *latipso*. A man, whose own wife has never seen him in an excretory act, suddenly finds himself naked and assisted by a vestal maiden while he performs his natural functions into a sacred vessel. This sort of ceremonial treatment is necessitated by the fact that the excreta are used by a diviner to ascertain the course and nature of the client's sickness. Female clients, on the other hand, find their naked bodies are subjected to the scrutiny, manipulation, and prodding of the medicine men.

Few supplicants in the temple are well enough to do anything but lie on their hard beds. The daily ceremonies, like the rites of the holy-mouth-men, involve discomfort and torture. With ritual precision, the vestals awaken their miserable charges each dawn and roll them about on their beds of pain while performing ablutions, in the formal movements of which the maidens are highly trained. At other times they insert magic wands in the supplicant's mouth or force him to eat substances which are supposed to be healing. From time to time the medicine men come to their clients and jab magically treated needles into their flesh. The fact that these temple ceremonies may not cure, and may even kill the neophyte, in no way decreases the people's faith in the medicine men.

There remains one other kind of practitioner, known as a "listener." This witch-doctor has the power to exorcise the devils that lodge in the heads of people who have been bewitched. The Nacirema believe that parents bewitch their own children. Mothers are particularly suspected of putting a curse on children while teaching them the secret body rituals. The counter-magic of the witch-doctor is unusual in its lack of ritual. The patient simply tells the "listener" all his troubles and fears, beginning with the earliest difficulties he can remember. The memory displayed by the Nacirema in these exorcism sessions is truly remarkable. It is not uncommon for the patient to bemoan the rejection he felt upon being weaned as a babe, and a few individuals even see their troubles going back to the traumatic effects of their own birth.

In conclusion, mention must be made of certain practices which have their base in native esthetics but which depend upon the pervasive aversion to the natural body and its functions. There are ritual fasts to make fat people thin and ceremonial feasts to make thin people fat. Still other rites are used to make women's breasts large if they are small, and smaller if they are large. General dissatisfaction with breast shape is symbolized in the fact that the ideal form is virtually outside the range of human variation. A few women afflicted with almost inhuman hypermammary development are so idolized that they make a handsome living by simply going from village to village and permitting the natives to stare at them for a fee.

Reference has already been made to the fact that excretory functions are ritualized, routinized, and relegated to secrecy. Natural reproductive functions are similarly distorted. Intercourse is taboo as a topic and scheduled as an act. Efforts are made to avoid pregnancy by the use of magical materials or by limiting intercourse to certain phases of the moon. Conception is actually very infrequent. When pregnant, women dress so as to hide their condition. Parturition takes place in secret, without friends or relatives to assist, and the majority of women do not nurse their infants.

Our review of the ritual life of the Nacirema has certainly shown them to be a magic-ridden people. It is hard to understand how they have managed to exist so long under the burdens which they have imposed upon themselves. But even such exotic customs as these take on real meaning when they are viewed with the insight provided by Malinowski when he wrote (1948:70):

> Looking from far and above, from our high places of safety in the developed civilization, it is easy to see all the crudity and irrelevance of magic. But without its power and guidance early man could not have mastered his practical difficulties as he has done, nor could man have advanced to the higher stages of civilization.

# REFERENCES

Linton, Ralph. 1936. *The Study of Man*. New York, D. Appleton-Century Co.

Malinowski, Bronislaw. 1948. *Magic, Science, and Religion*. Glencoe, The Free Press.

Murdock, George P. 1949. *Social Structure*. New York, The Macmillan Co.

From *American Anthropologist,* June 1956, pp. 503–507. Published by the American Anthropological Association.

# Baseball Magic

GEORGE GMELCH

On each pitching day for the first three months of a winning season, Dennis Grossini, a pitcher on a Detroit Tiger farm team, arose from bed at exactly 10:00 a.m. At 1:00 p.m. he went to the nearest restaurant for two glasses of iced tea and a tuna sandwich. Although the afternoon was free, he changed into the sweatshirt and supporter he wore during his last winning game, and, one hour before the game, he chewed a wad of Beech-Nut chewing tobacco. After each pitch during the game he touched the letters on his uniform and straightened his cap after each ball. Before the start of each inning he replaced the pitcher's resin bag next to the spot where it was the inning before. And after every inning in which he gave up a run, he washed his hands.

When asked which part of the ritual was most important, he said, "You can't really tell what's most important so it all becomes important. I'd be afraid to change anything. As long as I'm winning, I do everything the same."

Trobriand Islanders, according to anthropologist Bronislaw Malinowski, felt the same way about their fishing magic. Among the Trobrianders, fishing took two forms: in the *inner lagoon* where fish were plentiful and there was little danger, and on the *open sea* where fishing was dangerous and yields varied widely. Malinowski found that magic was not used in lagoon fishing, where men could rely solely on their knowledge and skill. But when fishing on the open sea, Trobrianders used a great deal of magical ritual to ensure safety and increase their catch.

Baseball, America's national pastime, is an arena in which players behave remarkably like Malinowski's Trobriand fishermen. To professional ballplayers, baseball is more than just a game. It is an occupation. Since their livelihoods depend on how well they perform, many use magic to try to control the chance that is built into baseball. There are three essential activities of the game—pitching, hitting, and fielding. In the first two, chance can play a surprisingly important role. The pitcher is the player least able to control the outcome of his own efforts. He may feel great and have good stuff warming up in the bullpen and then get into the game and not have it. He may make a bad pitch and see the batter miss it for a strike out or see it hit hard but right into the hands of a fielder for an out. His best pitch may be blooped for a base hit. He may limit the opposing team to just a few hits yet lose the game, or he may give up a dozen hits but still win. And the good and bad luck don't always average out over the course of a season. Some pitchers end the season with poor won-loss records but good earned run averages,

and vice versa. For instance, this past season Andy Benes gave up over one run per game more than his teammate Omar Daal but had a better won-loss record. Benes went 14–13, while Daal was only 8–12. Both pitched for the same team—the Arizona Diamondbacks—which meant they had the same fielders behind them. Regardless of how well a pitcher performs, on every outing he depends not only on his own skill, but also upon the proficiency of his teammates, the ineptitude of the opposition, and luck.

Hitting, which many observers call the single most difficult task in the world of sports, is also full of risk and uncertainty. Unless it's a home run, no matter how well the batter hits the ball, fate determines whether it will go into a waiting glove, whistle past a fielder's diving stab, or find a gap in the outfield. The uncertainty is compounded by the low success rate of hitting: the average hitter gets only one hit in every four trips to the plate, while the very best hitters average only one hit every three trips. Fielding, as we will return to later, is the one part of baseball where chance does not play much of a role.

How does the risk and uncertainty in pitching and hitting affect players? How do they try to exercise control over the outcomes of their performance? These are questions that I first became interested in many years ago as both a ballplayer and an anthropology student. I'd devoted much of my youth to baseball, and played professionally as first baseman in the Detroit Tigers organization in the 1960s. It was shortly after the end of one baseball season that I took an anthropology course called "Magic, Religion, and Witchcraft." As I listened to my professor describe the magical rituals of the Trobriand Islanders, it occurred to me that what these so-called "primitive" people did wasn't all that different from what my teammates and I did for luck and confidence at the ball park.

## Routines and Rituals

The most common way players attempt to reduce chance and their feelings of uncertainty is to develop and follow a daily routine, a course of action which is regularly followed. Talking about the routines ballplayers follow, Pirates coach Rich Donnelly said:

> They're like trained animals. They come out here [ballpark] and everything has to be the same, they don't like anything that knocks them off their routine.

Just look at the dugout and you'll see every guy sitting in the same spot every night. It's amazing, everybody in the same spot. And don't you dare take someone's seat. If a guy comes up from the minors and sits here, they'll say, 'Hey, Jim sits here, find another seat.' You watch the pitcher warm up and he'll do the same thing every time. And when you go on the road it's the same way. You've got a routine and you adhere to it and you don't want anybody knocking you off it.

Routines are comforting, they bring order into a world in which players have little control. And sometimes practical elements in routines produce tangible benefits, such as helping the player concentrate. But what players often do goes beyond mere routine. Their actions become what anthropologists define as *ritual*—prescribed behaviors in which there is no empirical connection between the means (e.g., tapping home plate three times) and the desired end (e.g., getting a base hit). Because there is no real connection between the two, rituals are not rational, and sometimes they are actually irrational. Similar to rituals are the nonrational beliefs that form the basis of taboos and fetishes, which players also use to reduce chance and bring luck to their side. But first let's look more closely at rituals.

Most rituals are personal, that is, they're performed by individuals rather than by a team or group. Most are done in an unemotional manner, in much the same way players apply pine tar to their bats to improve the grip or dab eye black on their upper cheeks to reduce the sun's glare. Baseball rituals are infinitely varied. A ballplayer may ritualize any activity—eating, dressing, driving to the ballpark—that he considers important or somehow linked to good performance. For example, Yankee pitcher Denny Neagle goes to a movie on days he is scheduled to start. Pitcher Jason Bere listens to the same song on his Walkman on the days he is to pitch. Jim Ohms puts another penny in the pouch of his supporter after each win. Clanging against the hard plastic genital cup, the pennies made a noise as he ran the bases toward the end of a winning season. Glenn Davis would chew the same gum every day during hitting streaks, saving it under his cap. Infielder Julio Gotay always played with a cheese sandwich in his back pocket (he had a big appetite, so there might also have been a measure of practicality here). Wade Boggs ate chicken before every game during his career, and that was just one of dozens of elements in his pre and post game routine, which also included leaving his house for the ballpark at precisely the same time each day (1:47 for a 7:05 game). Former Oriole pitcher Dennis Martinez would drink a small cup of water after each inning and then place it under the bench upside down, in a line. His teammates could always tell what inning it was by counting the cups.

Many hitters go through a series of preparatory rituals before stepping into the batter's box. These include tugging on their caps, touching their uniform letters or medallions, crossing themselves, tapping or bouncing the bat on the plate, or swinging the weighted warm-up bat a prescribed number of times. Consider Red Sox Nomar Garciaparra. After each pitch he steps out of the batters box, kicks the dirt with each toe, adjusts his right batting glove, adjusts his left batting glove, and touches his

helmet before getting back into the box. Mike Hargrove, former Cleveland Indian first baseman, had so many time consuming elements in his batting ritual that he was known as "the human rain delay." Both players believe their batting rituals helped them regain their concentration after each pitch. But others wonder if they have become prisoners of their own superstitions. Also, players who have too many or particularly bizarre rituals risk being labeled as "flakes," and not just by teammates but by fans and media as well. For example, pitcher Turk Wendell's eccentric rituals, which included wearing a necklace of teeth from animals he had killed, made him a cover story in the *New York Times Sunday Magazine*.

Some players, especially Latin Americans, draw upon rituals from their Roman Catholic religion. Some make the sign of the cross or bless themselves before every at bat, and a few like the Rangers' Pudge Rodriguez do so before every pitch. Others, like the Detroit Tiger Juan Gonzalez, also visibly wear religious medallions around their necks, while some tuck them discretely inside their undershirts.

One ritual associated with hitting is tagging a base when leaving and returning to the dugout between innings. Some players don't "feel right" unless they tag a specific base on each trip between the dugout and the field. One of my teammates added some complexity to his ritual by tagging third base on his way to the dugout only after the third, sixth, and ninth innings. Asked if he ever purposely failed to step on the bag, he replied, "Never! I wouldn't dare. It would destroy my confidence to hit." Baseball fans observe a lot of this ritual behavior, such as fielders tagging bases, pitchers tugging on their caps or touching the resin bag after each bad pitch, or smoothing the dirt on the mound before each new batter or inning, never realizing the importance of these actions to the player. The one ritual many fans do recognize, largely because it's a favorite of TV cameramen, is the "rally cap"—players in the dugout folding their caps and wearing them bill up in hopes of sparking a rally.

Most rituals grow out of exceptionally good performances. When a player does well, he seldom attributes his success to skill alone. He knows that his skills were essentially the same the night before. He asks himself, "What was different about today which explains my three hits?" He decides to repeat what he did today in an attempt to bring more good luck. And so he attributes his success, in part, to an object, a food he ate, not having shaved, a new shirt he bought that day, or just about any behavior out of the ordinary. By repeating that behavior, he seeks to gain control over his performance. Outfielder John White explained how one of his rituals started:

> I was jogging out to centerfield after the national anthem when I picked up a scrap of paper. I got some good hits that night and I guess I decided that the paper had something to do with it. The next night I picked up a gum wrapper and had another good night at the plate… I've been picking up paper every night since.

Outfielder Ron Wright of the Calgary Cannons shaves his arms once a week and plans to continue doing so until he has a bad year. It all began two years before when after an injury he shaved his arm so it could be taped, and proceeded to hit three homers over the next few games. Now he not only has one of the smoothest swings in the minor leagues, but two of the smoothest forearms. Wade Boggs' routine of eating chicken before every game began when he was a rookie in 1982. He noticed a correlation between multiple hit games and poultry plates (his wife has over 40 chicken recipes). One of Montreal Expos farmhand Mike Saccocio's rituals also concerned food, "I got three hits one night after eating at Long John Silver's. After that when we'd pull into town, my first question would be, "Do you have a Long John Silver's?"" Unlike Boggs, Saccocio abandoned his ritual and looked for a new one when he stopped hitting well.

When in a slump, most players make a deliberate effort to change their rituals and routines in an attempt to shake off their bad luck. One player tried taking different routes to the ballpark; several players reported trying different combinations of tagging and not tagging particular bases in an attempt to find a successful combination. I had one manager who would rattle the bat bin when the team was not hitting well, as if the bats were in a stupor and could be aroused by a good shaking. Similarly, I have seen hitters rub their hands along the handles of the bats protruding from the bin in hopes of picking up some power or luck from bats that are getting hits for their owners. Some players switch from wearing their contact lenses to glasses. Brett Mandel described his Pioneer League team, the Ogden Raptors, trying to break a losing streak by using a new formation for their pre-game stretching.[1]

## Taboo

Taboos are the opposite of rituals. The word taboo comes from a Polynesian term meaning prohibition. Breaking a taboo, players believe, leads to undesirable consequences or bad luck. Most players observe at least a few taboos, such as never stepping on the white foul lines. A few, like the Mets Turk Wendell and Red Sox Nomar Garciaparra, leap over the entire basepath. One teammate of mine would never watch a movie on a game day, despite the fact that we played nearly every day from April to September. Another teammate refused to read anything before a game because he believed it weakened his batting eye.

Many taboos take place off the field, out of public view. On the day a pitcher is scheduled to start, he is likely to avoid activities he believes will sap his strength and detract from his effectiveness. Some pitchers avoid eating certain foods, others will not shave on the day of a game, refusing to shave again as long as they are winning. Early in the 1989 season Oakland's Dave Stewart had six consecutive victories and a beard by the time he lost.

Taboos usually grow out of exceptionally poor performances, which players, in search of a reason, attribute to a particular behavior. During my first season of pro ball I ate pancakes before a game in which I struck out three times. A few weeks later I had another terrible game, again after eating pancakes. The result was a pancake taboo: I never again ate pancakes during the season. Pitcher Jason Bere has a taboo that makes more sense in dietary terms: after eating a meatball sandwich and not pitching well, he swore off them for the rest of the season.

While most taboos are idiosyncratic, there are a few that all ball players hold and that do not develop out of individual experience or misfortune. These form part of the culture of baseball, and are sometimes learned as early as Little League. Mentioning a no-hitter while one is in progress is a well-known example. It is believed that if a pitcher hears the words "no-hitter," the spell accounting for this hard to achieve feat will be broken and the no-hitter lost. This taboo is also observed by many sports broadcasters, who use various linguistic subterfuges to inform their listeners that the pitcher has not given up a hit, never saying "no-hitter."

## Fetishes

Fetishes or charms are material objects believed to embody "supernatural" power that can aid or protect the owner. Good luck charms are standard equipment for some ballplayers. These include a wide assortment of objects from coins, chains, and crucifixes to a favorite baseball hat. The fetishized object may be a new possession or something a player found that happens to coincide with the start of a streak and which he holds responsible for his good fortune. While playing in the Pacific Coast League, Alan Foster forgot his baseball shoes on a road trip and borrowed a pair from a teammate. That night he pitched a no-hitter, which he attributed to the shoes. Afterwards he bought them from his teammate and they became a fetish. Expo farmhand Mark LaRosa's rock has a different origin and use:

> I found it on the field in Elmira after I had gotten bombed. It's unusual, perfectly round, and it caught my attention. I keep it to remind me of how important it is to concentrate. When I am going well I look at the rock and remember to keep my focus, the rock reminds me of what can happen when I lose my concentration.

For one season Marge Schott, former owner of the Cincinnati Reds, insisted that her field manager rub her St. Bernard "Schotzie" for good luck before each game. When the Reds were on the road, Schott would sometimes send a bag of the dog's hair to the field manager's hotel room.

During World War II, American soldiers used fetishes in much the same way. Social psychologist Samuel Stouffer and his colleagues found that in the face of great danger and uncertainty, soldiers developed magical practices, particularly the use of protective amulets and good luck charms (crosses, Bibles, rabbits' feet, medals), and jealously guarded articles of clothing they associated with past experiences of escape from danger.[2] Stouffer also found that prebattle preparations were carried out in fixed ritual-like order, similar to ballplayers preparing for a game.

Uniform numbers have special significance for some players who request their lucky number. Since the choice is usually limited, they try to at least get a uniform that contains their lucky number, such as 14, 24, 34, or 44 for the player whose lucky number is four. When Ricky Henderson came to the Blue Jays in 1993 he paid outfielder Turner Ward $25,000 for the right to wear number 24. Oddly enough, there is no consensus about the effect of wearing number 13. Some players will not wear it, others will, and a few request it. Number preferences emerge in different ways. A young player may request the number of a former star, hoping that—through what anthropologists call *imitative* magic—it will bring him the same success. Or he may request a number he associates with good luck. While with the Oakland A's Vida Blue changed his uniform number from 35 to 14, the number he wore as a high-school quarterback. When 14 did not produce better pitching performance, he switched back to 35. Former San Diego Padre first baseman Jack Clark changed his number from 25 to 00, hoping to break out of a slump. That day he got four hits in a double header, but also hurt his back. Then, three days later, he was hit in the cheekbone by a ball thrown in batting practice.

Colorado Rockies Larry Walker's fixation with the number three has become well known to baseball fans. Besides wearing 33, he takes three practice swings before stepping into the box, he showers from the third nozzle, sets his alarm for three minutes past the hour and he was wed on November 3 at 3:33 p.m. Fans in ballparks all across America rise from their seats for the seventh inning stretch before the home club comes to bat because the number seven is lucky, although the origin of this tradition has been lost.

Clothing, both the choice and the order in which they are put on, combine elements of both ritual and fetish. Some players put on their uniform in a ritualized order. Expos farmhand Jim Austin always puts on his left sleeve, left pants leg, and left shoe before the right. Most players, however, single out one or two lucky articles or quirks of dress for ritual elaboration. After hitting two home runs in a game, for example, ex-Giant infielder Jim Davenport discovered that he had missed a buttonhole while dressing for the game. For the remainder of his career he left the same button undone. For outfielder Brian Hunter the focus is shoes, "I have a pair of high tops and a pair of low tops. Whichever shoes don't get a hit that game, I switch to the other pair." At the time of our interview, he was struggling at the plate and switching shoes almost every day. For Birmingham Baron pitcher Bo Kennedy the arrangement of the different pairs of baseball shoes in his locker is critical:

> I tell the clubies [clubhouse boys] when you hang stuff in my locker don't touch my shoes. If you bump them move them back. I want the Pony's in front, the turfs to the right, and I want them nice and neat with each pair touching each other.... Everyone on the team knows not to mess with my shoes when I pitch.

During streaks—hitting or winning—players may wear the same clothes day after day. Once I changed sweatshirts midway through the game for seven consecutive nights to keep a hitting streak going. Clothing rituals, however, can become impractical. Catcher Matt Allen was wearing a long sleeve turtle neck shirt on a cool evening in the New York-Penn League when he had a three-hit game. "I kept wearing the shirt and had a good week," he explained. "Then the weather got hot as hell, 85 degrees and muggy, but I would not take that shirt off. I wore it for another ten days—catching—and people thought I was crazy." Also taking a ritual to the extreme, Leo Durocher, managing the Brooklyn Dodgers to a pennant in 1941, is said to have spent three and a half weeks in the same gray slacks,

blue coat, and knitted blue tie. During a 16-game winning streak, the 1954 New York Giants wore the same clothes in each game and refused to let them be cleaned for fear that their good fortune might be washed away with the dirt. Losing often produces the opposite effect. Several Oakland A's players, for example, went out and bought new street clothes in an attempt to break a fourteen-game losing streak.

Baseball's superstitions, like most everything else, change over time. Many of the rituals and beliefs of early baseball are no longer observed. In the 1920s and 1930s sportswriters reported that a player who tripped en route to the field would often retrace his steps and carefully walk over the stumbling block for "insurance." A century ago players spent time on and off the field intently looking for items that would bring them luck. To find a hairpin on the street, for example, assured a batter of hitting safely in that day's game. Today few women wear hairpins—a good reason the belief has died out. To catch sight of a white horse or a wagon-load of barrels were also good omens. In 1904 the manager of the New York Giants, John McGraw, hired a driver with a team of white horses to drive past the Polo Grounds around the time his players were arriving at the ballpark. He knew that if his players saw white horses, they'd have more confidence and that could only help them during the game. Belief in the power of white horses survived in a few backwaters until the 1960s. A gray haired manager of a team I played for in Drummondville, Quebec, would drive around the countryside before important games and during the playoffs looking for a white horse. When he was successful, he would announce it to everyone in the clubhouse.

One belief that appears to have died out recently is a taboo about crossed bats. Some of my Latino teammates in the 1960s took it seriously. I can still recall one Dominican player becoming agitated when another player tossed a bat from the batting cage and it landed on top of his bat. He believed that the top bat might steal hits from the lower one. In his view, bats contained a finite number of hits, a sort of baseball "image of limited good." It was once commonly believed that when the hits in a bat were used up no amount of good hitting would produce any more. Hall of Famer Honus Wagner believed each bat contained only 100 hits. Regardless of the quality of the bat, he would discard it after its 100th hit. This belief would have little relevance today, in the era of light bats with thin handles—so thin that the typical modern bat is lucky to survive a dozen hits without being broken. Other superstitions about bats do survive, however. Position players on the Class A Asheville Tourists, for example, would not let pitchers touch or swing their bats, not even to warm up. Poor-hitting players, as most pitchers are, were said to pollute or weaken the bats.

## Uncertainty and Magic

The best evidence that players turn to rituals, taboos, and fetishes to control chance and uncertainty is found in their uneven application. They are associated mainly with pitching and hitting—the activities with the highest degree of chance—and not fielding. I met only one player who had any ritual in connection with fielding, and he was an error prone shortstop. Unlike hitting and pitching, a fielder has almost complete control over the outcome of his performance. Once a ball has been hit in his direction, no one can intervene and ruin his chances of catching it for an out (except in the unlikely event of two fielders colliding). Compared with the pitcher or the hitter, the fielder has little to worry about. He knows that, in better than 9.7 times out of 10, he will execute his task flawlessly. With odds like that there is little need for ritual.

Clearly, the rituals of American ballplayers are not unlike that of the Trobriand Islanders studied by Malinowski many years ago.[3] In professional baseball, fielding is the equivalent of the inner lagoon while hitting and pitching are like the open sea.

While Malinowski helps us understand how ballplayers respond to chance and uncertainty, behavioral psychologist B. F. Skinner sheds light on why personal rituals get established in the first place.[4] With a few grains of seed Skinner could get pigeons to do anything he wanted. He merely waited for the desired behavior (e.g. pecking) and then rewarded it with some food. Skinner then decided to see what would happen if pigeons were rewarded with food pellets regularly, every fifteen seconds, regardless of what they did. He found that the birds associate the arrival of the food with a particular action, such as tucking their head under a wing or walking in clockwise circles. About ten seconds after the arrival of the last pellet, a bird would begin doing whatever it associated with getting the food and keep doing it until the next pellet arrived. In short, the pigeons behaved as if their actions made the food appear. They learned to associate particular behaviors with the reward of being given seed.

Ballplayers also associate a reward—successful performance—with prior behavior. If a player touches his crucifix and then gets a hit, he may decide the gesture was responsible for his good fortune and touch his crucifix the next time he comes to the plate. If he gets another hit, the chances are good that he will touch his crucifix each time he bats. Unlike pigeons, however, most ballplayers are quicker to change their rituals once they no longer seem to work. Skinner found that once a pigeon associated one of its actions with

the arrival of food or water, only sporadic rewards were necessary to keep the ritual going. One pigeon, believing that hopping from side to side brought pellets into its feeding cup, hopped ten thousand times without a pellet before finally giving up. But, then, didn't Wade Boggs eat chicken before every game, through slumps and good times, for seventeen years?

Obviously the rituals and superstitions of baseball do not make a pitch travel faster or a batted ball find the gaps between the fielders, nor do the Trobriand rituals calm the seas or bring fish. What both do, however, is give their practitioners a sense of control, with that added confidence, at no cost. And we all know how important that is. If you really believe eating chicken or hopping over the foul lines will make you a better hitter, it probably will.

# Bibliography

Malinowski, B. *Magic, Science and Religion and Other Essays* (Glencoe, Ill., 1948).

Mandel, Brett. *Minor Players, Major Dreams*. Lincoln, Nebraska: University of Nebraska Press, 1997.

Skinner, B.F. *Behavior of Organisms: An Experimental Analysis* (D. Appleton-Century Co., 1938).

Skinner, B.F. *Science and Human Behavior* (New York: Macmillan, 1953).

Stouffer, Samuel. *The American Soldier*. New York: J. Wiley, 1965.

Torrez, Danielle Gagnon. *High Inside: Memoirs of a Baseball Wife*. New York: G.P. Putnam's Sons, 1983.

# Notes

1. Mandel, *Minor Players, Major Dreams,* 156.
2. Stouffer, *The American Soldier*
3. Malinowski, B. *Magic, Science and Religion and Other Essays*
4. Skinner, B.F. *Behavior of Organisms: An Experimental Analysis*

Department of Anthropology, Union College; e-mail gmelchg@union.edu

Revised version of "Superstition and Ritual in American Baseball" from *Elysian Fields Quarterly,* Vol. 11, No. 3, 1992, pp. 25-36. © September 2000, McGraw-Hill/Dushkin, with permission of the author, George Gmelch.

# UNIT 7

# Sociocultural Change: The Impact of the West

## Unit Selections

## Key Points to Consider

- What is a subsistence system? What have been the effects of colonialism on formerly subsistence-oriented socioeconomic systems?

- How do cash crops inevitably lead to class distinctions and poverty?

- What ethical obligations do you think industrial societies have toward respecting the human rights and cultural diversity of traditional communities?

- If the Aztecs did not think of the Spanish Conquistadores as gods, what did they really think of them?

- Are the disparities of wealth and power in the world fair?

- What should your nation's policy be towards genocidal practices in other countries?

- What have been the social, economic, and health consequences of the shift from the use of betel and kava to alcohol, tobacco, and marijuana in Oceania?

- Is global warming a fact? Are human activities responsible for it? What should we do about it?

## Student Website

www.mhcls.com/online

## Internet References

Further information regarding these websites may be found in this book's preface or online.

**Human Rights and Humanitarian Assistance**
   http://www.etown.edu/vl/humrts.html
**The Indigenous Rights Movement in the Pacific**
   http://www.inmotionmagazine.com/pacific.html
**RomNews Network—Online**
   http://www.romnews.com/community/index.php
**WWW Virtual Library: Indigenous Studies**
   http://www.cwis.org/wwwvl/indig-vl.html

The origins of academic anthropology lie in the colonial and imperial ventures of the past five hundred years. During this period, many people of the world were brought into a relationship with Europe and the United States that was usually exploitative and often socially and culturally disruptive. For over a century, anthropologists have witnessed this process and the transformations that have taken place in those social and cultural systems brought under the umbrella of a world economic order. Early anthropological studies—even those widely regarded as pure research—directly or indirectly served colonial interests. Many anthropologists certainly believed that they were extending the benefits of Western technology and society while preserving the cultural rights of those people whom they studied. But representatives of poor nations challenge this view and are far less generous in describing the past role of the anthropologist. Most contemporary anthropologists, however, have a deep moral commitment to defending the legal, political, and economic rights of the people with whom they work.

When anthropologists discuss social change, they usually mean change brought about in preindustrial societies through long-standing interaction with the nation-states of the industrialized world. In early anthropology, contact between the West and the remainder of the world was characterized by the terms "acculturation" and "culture contact." These terms were used to describe the diffusion of cultural traits between the developed and the less-developed countries. Often this was analyzed as a one-way process in which cultures of the less developed world were seen, for better or worse, as receptacles for Western cultural traits. Nowadays, many anthropologists believe that the diffusion of cultural traits across social, political, and economic boundaries was emphasized at the expense of the

real issues of dominance, subordinance, and dependence that characterized the colonial experience. Just as important, many anthropologists recognize that the present-day forms of cultural, economic, and political interaction between the developed and the so-called underdeveloped world are best characterized as neocolonial.

Most of the authors represented in this unit take the perspective that anthropology should be critical as well as descriptive. They raise questions about cultural contact and subsequent economic and social disruption.

In keeping with the notion that the negative impact of the West on traditional cultures began with colonial domination, this unit opens with "Why Can't People Feed Themselves?" and includes "The Arrow of Disease."

Even the widely disseminated narrative account of the Conquest of Mexico, says Camilla Townsend ("Burying the White Gods: New Perspectives on the Conquest of Mexico), was nothing more than a dehumanizing fabrication—a convenient explanation that ignored the facts.

Finally, "A Pacific Haze: Alcohol and Drugs in Oceania" deals with a specific aspect of culture affected by the impact of the West: the traditional uses of psychoactive drugs and their more recent harmful applications.

Of course, traditional peoples are not the only losers in the process of cultural destruction. All of humanity stands to suffer as a vast store of human knowledge—embodied in tribal subsistence practices, language, medicine, and folklore—is obliterated, in a manner not unlike the burning of the library of Alexandria 1,600 years ago. We can only hope that it is not too late to save what is left.

# Why Can't People Feed Themselves?

## Frances Moore Lappé and Joseph Collins

*Question:* You have said that the hunger problem is not the result of overpopulation. But you have not yet answered the most basic and simple question of all: Why can't people feed themselves? As Senator Daniel P. Moynihan put it bluntly, when addressing himself to the Third World, "Food growing is the first thing you do when you come down out of the trees. The question is, how come the United States can grow food and you can't?"

*Our Response:* In the very first speech I, Frances, ever gave after writing *Diet for a Small Planet*, I tried to take my audience along the path that I had taken in attempting to understand why so many are hungry in this world. Here is the gist of that talk that was, in truth, a turning point in my life:

When I started I saw a world divided into two parts: a *minority* of nations that had "taken off" through their agricultural and industrial revolutions to reach a level of unparalleled material abundance and a *majority* that remained behind in a primitive, traditional, undeveloped state. This lagging behind of the majority of the world's peoples must be due, I thought, to some internal deficiency or even to several of them. It seemed obvious that the underdeveloped countries must be deficient in natural resources—particularly good land and climate—and in cultural development, including modern attitudes conducive to work and progress.

But when looking for the historical roots of the predicament, I learned that my picture of these two separate worlds was quite false. My two separate worlds were really just different sides of the same coin. One side was on top largely because the other side was on the bottom. Could this be true? How were these separate worlds related?

Colonialism appeared to me to be the link. Colonialism destroyed the cultural patterns of production and exchange by which traditional societies in "underdeveloped" countries previously had met the needs of the people. Many precolonial social structures, while dominated by exploitative elites, had evolved a system of mutual obligations among the classes that helped to ensure at least a minimal diet for all. A friend of mine once said: "Precolonial village existence in subsistence agriculture was a limited life indeed, but it's certainly not Calcutta." The misery of starvation in the streets of Calcutta can only be understood as the end-point of a long historical process—one that has destroyed a traditional social system.

"Underdeveloped," instead of being an adjective that evokes the picture of a static society, became for me a verb (to "underdevelop") meaning the *process* by which the minority of the world has transformed—indeed often robbed and degraded—the majority.

That was in 1972. I clearly recall my thoughts on my return home. I had stated publicly for the first time a world view that had taken me years of study to grasp. The sense of relief was tremendous. For me the breakthrough lay in realizing that today's "hunger crisis" could not be described in static, descriptive terms. Hunger and underdevelopment must always be thought of as a *process*.

To answer the question "why hunger?" it is counterproductive to simply *describe* the conditions in an underdeveloped country today. For these conditions, whether they be the degree of malnutrition, the levels of agricultural production, or even the country's ecological endowment, are not static factors—they are not "givens." They are rather the *results* of an ongoing historical process. As we dug ever deeper into that historical process for the preparation of this book, we began to discover the existence of scarcity-creating mechanisms that we had only vaguely intuited before.

We have gotten great satisfaction from probing into the past since we recognized it is the only way to approach a solution to hunger today. We have come to see that it is the *force* creating the condition, not the condition itself, that must be the target of change. Otherwise we might change the condition today, only to find tomorrow that it has been recreated—with a vengeance.

Asking the question "Why can't people feed themselves?" carries a sense of bewilderment that there are so many people in the world not able to feed themselves adequately. What astonished us, however, is that there are not *more* people in the world who are hungry—considering the weight of the centuries of effort by the few to undermine the capacity of the majority to feed themselves. No, we are not crying "conspiracy!" If these forces were entirely conspiratorial, they would be easier to detect and many more people would by now have risen up to resist. We are talking about something more subtle and insidious; a heritage of a colonial order in which people with the advantage of considerable power sought their own self-interest, often arrogantly believing they were acting in the interest of the people whose lives they were destroying.

# The Colonial Mind

The colonizer viewed agriculture in the subjugated lands as primitive and backward. Yet such a view contrasts sharply with documents from the colonial period now coming to light. For example, A. J. Voelker, a British agricultural scientist assigned to India during the 1890s wrote:

> Nowhere would one find better instances of keeping land scrupulously clean from weeds, of ingenuity in device of water-raising appliances, of knowledge of soils and their capabilities, as well as of the exact time to sow and reap, as one would find in Indian agriculture. It is wonderful too, how much is known of rotation, the system of "mixed crops" and of fallowing.... I, at least, have never seen a more perfect picture of cultivation."[1]

None the less, viewing the agriculture of the vanquished as primitive and backward reinforced the colonizer's rationale for destroying it. To the colonizers of Africa, Asia, and Latin America, agriculture became merely a means to extract wealth—much as gold from a mine—on behalf of the colonizing power. Agriculture was no longer seen as a source of food for the local population, nor even as their livelihood. Indeed the English economist John Stuart Mill reasoned that colonies should not be thought of as civilizations or countries at all but as "agricultural establishments" whose sole purpose was to supply the "larger community to which they belong." The colonized society's agriculture was only a subdivision of the agricultural system of the metropolitan country. As Mill acknowledged, "Our West India colonies, for example, cannot be regarded as countries.... The West Indies are the place where England *finds it convenient* to carry on the production of sugar, coffee and a few other tropical commodities."[2]

Prior to European intervention, Africans practiced a diversified agriculture that included the introduction of new food plants of Asian or American origin. But colonial rule simplified this diversified production to single cash crops—often to the exclusion of staple foods —and in the process sowed the seeds of famine.[3] Rice farming once had been common in Gambia. But with colonial rule so much of the best land was taken over by peanuts (grown for the European market) that rice had to be imported to counter the mounting prospect of famine. Northern Ghana, once famous for its yams and other foodstuffs, was forced to concentrate solely on cocoa. Most of the Gold Coast thus became dependent on cocoa. Liberia was turned into a virtual plantation subsidiary of Firestone Tire and Rubber. Food production in Dahomey and southeast Nigeria was all but abandoned in favor of palm oil; Tanganyika (now Tanzania) was forced to focus on sisal and Uganda on cotton.

The same happened in Indochina. About the time of the American Civil War the French decided that the Mekong Delta in Vietnam would be ideal for producing rice for export. Through a production system based on enriching the large landowners, Vietnam became the world's third largest exporter of rice by the 1930s; yet many landless Vietnamese went hungry.[4]

Rather than helping the peasants, colonialism's public works programs only reinforced export crop production. British irrigation works built in nineteenth-century India did help increase production, but the expansion was for spring export crops at the expense of millets and legumes grown in the fall as the basic local food crops.

Because people living on the land do not easily go against their natural and adaptive drive to grow food for themselves, colonial powers had to force the production of cash crops. The first strategy was to use physical or economic force to get the local population to grow cash crops instead of food on their own plots and then turn them over to the colonizer for export. The second strategy was the direct takeover of the land by large-scale plantations growing crops for export.

# Forced Peasant Production

As Walter Rodney recounts in *How Europe Underdeveloped Africa*, cash crops were often grown literally under threat of guns and whips.[5] One visitor to the Sahel commented in 1928: "Cotton is an artificial crop and one the value of which is not entirely clear to the natives..." He wryly noted the "enforced enthusiasm with which the natives... have thrown themselves into... planting cotton."[6] The forced cultivation of cotton was a major grievance leading to the Maji Maji wars in Tanzania (then Tanganyika) and behind the nationalist revolt in Angola as late as 1960.[7]

Although raw force was used, taxation was the preferred colonial technique to force Africans to grow cash crops. The colonial administrations simply levied taxes on cattle, land, houses, and even the people themselves. Since the tax had to be paid in the coin of the realm, the peasants had either to grow crops to sell or to work on the plantations or in the mines of the Europeans.[8] Taxation was both an effective tool to "stimulate" cash cropping and a source of revenue that the colonial bureaucracy needed to enforce the system. To expand their production of export crops to pay the mounting taxes, peasant producers were forced to neglect the farming of food crops. In 1830, the Dutch administration in Java made the peasants an offer they could not refuse; if they would grow government-owned export crops on one fifth of their land, the Dutch would remit their land taxes.[9] If they refused and thus could not pay the taxes, they lost their land.

Marketing boards emerged in Africa in the 1930s as another technique for getting the profit from cash crop production by native producers into the hands of the colonial government and international firms. Purchases by the marketing boards were well below the world market price. Peanuts bought by the boards from peasant cultivators in West Africa were sold in Britain for more than *seven times* what the peasants received.[10]

The marketing board concept was born with the "cocoa hold-up" in the Gold Coast in 1937. Small cocoa farmers refused to sell to the large cocoa concerns like United Africa Company (a subsidiary of the Anglo-Dutch firm, Unilever—which we know as Lever Brothers) and Cadbury until they got a higher price. When the British government stepped in and agreed to buy the cocoa directly in place of the big business concerns, the smallholders must have thought they had scored at least a minor victory. But had they really? The following year the British formally set up the West African Cocoa Control Board. Theoretically, its purpose was to pay the peasants a reasonable price for their crops. In practice, however, the board, as sole purchaser, was able to hold down the prices paid the peasants for their crops when the world prices were rising. Rodney sums up the real "victory":

> None of the benefits went to Africans, but rather to the British government itself and to the private companies.... Big companies like the United African Company and John Holt were given... quotas to fulfill on behalf of the boards. As agents of the government, they were no longer exposed to direct attack, and their profits were secure.[11]

These marketing boards, set up for most export crops, were actually controlled by the companies. The chairman of the Cocoa Board was none other than John Cadbury of Cadbury Brothers (ever had a Cadbury chocolate bar?) who was part of a buying pool exploiting West African cocoa farmers.

The marketing boards funneled part of the profits from the exploitation of peasant producers indirectly into the royal treasury. While the Cocoa Board sold to the British Food Ministry at low prices, the ministry upped the price for British manufacturers, thus netting a profit as high as 11 million pounds in some years.[12]

These marketing boards of Africa were only the institutionalized rendition of what is the essence of colonialism—the extraction of wealth. While profits continued to accrue to foreign interests and local elites, prices received by those actually growing the commodities remained low.

# Plantations

A second approach was direct takeover of the land either by the colonizing government or by private foreign interests. Previously self-provisioning farmers were forced to cultivate the plantation fields through either enslavement or economic coercion.

After the conquest of the Kandyan Kingdom (in present day Sri Lanka), in 1815, the British designated all the vast central part of the island as crown land. When it was determined that coffee, a profitable export crop, could be grown there, the Kandyan lands were sold off to British investors and planters at a mere five shillings per acre, the government even defraying the cost of surveying and road building.[13]

Java is also a prime example of a colonial government seizing territory and then putting it into private foreign hands. In 1870, the Dutch declared all uncultivated land—called waste land—property of the state for lease to Dutch plantation enterprises. In addition, the Agrarian Land Law of 1870 authorized foreign companies to lease village-owned land. The peasants, in chronic need of ready cash for taxes and foreign consumer goods, were only too willing to lease their land to the foreign companies for very modest sums and under terms dictated by the firms. Where land was still held communally, the village headman was tempted by high cash commissions offered by plantation companies. He would lease the village land even

more cheaply than would the individual peasant or, as was frequently the case, sell out the entire village to the company.[14]

The introduction of the plantation meant the divorce of agriculture from nourishment, as the notion of food value was lost to the overriding claim of "market value" in international trade. Crops such as sugar, tobacco, and coffee were selected, not on the basis of how well they feed people, but for their high price value relative to their weight and bulk so that profit margins could be maintained even after the costs of shipping to Europe.

# Suppressing Peasant Farming

The stagnation and impoverishment of the peasant food-producing sector was not the mere by-product of benign neglect, that is, the unintended consequence of an overemphasis on export production. Plantations—just like modern "agro-industrial complexes"—needed an abundant and readily available supply of low-wage agricultural workers. Colonial administrations thus devised a variety of tactics, all to undercut self-provisioning agriculture and thus make rural populations dependent on plantation wages. Government services and even the most minimal infrastructure (access to water, roads, seeds, credit, pest and disease control information, and so on) were systematically denied. Plantations usurped most of the good land, either making much of the rural population landless or pushing them onto marginal soils. (Yet the plantations have often held much of their land idle simply to prevent the peasants from using it—even to this day. Del Monte owns 57,000 acres of Guatemala but plants only 9000. The rest lies idle except for a few thousand head of grazing cattle.)[15]

In some cases a colonial administration would go even further to guarantee itself a labor supply. In at least twelve countries in the eastern and southern parts of Africa the exploitation of mineral wealth (gold, diamonds, and copper) and the establishment of cash-crop plantations demanded a continuous supply of low-cost labor. To assure this labor supply, colonial administrations simply expropriated the land of the African communities by violence and drove the people into small reserves.[16] With neither adequate land for their traditional slash-and-burn methods nor access to the means—tools, water, and fertilizer—to make continuous farming of such limited areas viable, the indigenous population could scarcely meet subsistence needs, much less produce surplus to sell in order to cover the colonial taxes. Hundreds of thousands of Africans were forced to become the cheap labor source so "needed" by the colonial plantations. Only by laboring on plantations and in the mines could they hope to pay the colonial taxes.

The tax scheme to produce reserves of cheap plantation and mining labor was particularly effective when the Great Depression hit and the bottom dropped out of cash crop economies. In 1929 the cotton market collapsed, leaving peasant cotton producers, such as those in Upper Volta, unable to pay their colonial taxes. More and more young people, in some years as many as 80,000, were thus forced to migrate to the Gold Coast to compete with each other for low-wage jobs on cocoa plantations.[17]

The forced migration of Africa's most able-bodied workers—stripping village food farming of needed hands—was a recurring feature of colonialism. As late as 1973 the Portuguese "exported" 400,000 Mozambican peasants to work in South Africa in exchange for gold deposited in the Lisbon treasury.

The many techniques of colonialism to undercut self-provisioning agriculture in order to ensure a cheap labor supply are no better illustrated than by the story of how, in the mid-nineteenth century, sugar plantation owners in British Guiana coped with the double blow of the emancipation of slaves and the crash in the world sugar market. The story is graphically recounted by Alan Adamson in *Sugar without Slaves*.[18]

Would the ex-slaves be allowed to take over the plantation land and grow the food they needed? The planters, many ruined by the sugar slump, were determined they would not. The planter-dominated government devised several schemes for thwarting food self-sufficiency. The price of crown land was kept artificially high, and the purchase of land in parcels smaller than 100 acres was outlawed—two measures guaranteeing that newly organized ex-slave cooperatives could not hope to gain access to much land. The government also prohibited cultivation on as much as 400,000 acres—on the grounds of "uncertain property titles." Moreover, although many planters held part of their land out of sugar production due to the depressed world price, they would not allow any alternative production on them. They feared that once the ex-slaves started growing food it would be difficult to return them to sugar production when world market prices began to recover. In addition, the government taxed peasant production, then turned around and used the funds to subsidize the immigration of laborers from India and Malaysia to replace the freed slaves, thereby making sugar production again profitable for the planters. Finally, the government neglected the infrastructure for subsistence agriculture and denied credit for small farmers.

Perhaps the most insidious tactic to "lure" the peasant away from food production—and the one with profound historical consequences—was a policy of keeping the price of imported food low through the removal of tariffs and subsidies. The policy was double-edged: first, peasants were told they need not grow food because they could always buy it cheaply with their plantation wages; second, cheap food imports destroyed the market for domestic food and thereby impoverished local food producers.

Adamson relates how both the Governor of British Guiana and the Secretary for the Colonies Earl Grey favored low duties on imports in order to erode local food production and thereby release labor for the plantations. In 1851 the governor rushed through a reduction of the duty on cereals in order to "divert" labor to the sugar estates. As Adamson comments, "Without realizing it, he [the governor] had put his finger on the most mordant feature of monoculture:... its convulsive need to destroy any other sector of the economy which might compete for 'its' labor."[19]

Many colonial governments succeeded in establishing dependence on imported foodstuffs. In 1647 an observer in the West Indies wrote to Governor Winthrop of Massachusetts: "Men are so intent upon planting sugar that they had rather buy foode at very dear rates than produce it by labour, so infinite is the profitt of sugar workes...."[20] By 1770, the West Indies were importing most of the continental colonies' exports of dried fish, grain, beans, and vegetables. A dependence on imported food made the West Indian colonies vulnerable to any disruption in supply. This dependence on imported food stuffs spelled disaster when the thirteen continental colonies gained independence and food exports from the continent to the West Indies were interrupted. With no diversified food system to fall back on, 15,000 plantation workers died of famine between 1780 and 1787 in Jamaica alone.[21] The dependence of the West Indies on imported food persists to this day.

## Suppressing Peasant Competition

We have talked about the techniques by which indigenous populations were forced to cultivate cash crops. In some countries with large plantations, however, colonial governments found it necessary to *prevent* peasants from independently growing cash crops not out of concern for their welfare, but so that they would not compete with colonial interests growing the same crop. For peasant farmers, given a modicum of opportunity, proved themselves capable of outproducing the large plantations not only in terms of output per unit of land but, more important, in terms of capital cost per unit produced.

In the Dutch East Indies (Indonesia and Dutch New Guinea) colonial policy in the middle of the nineteenth century forbade the sugar refineries to buy sugar cane from indigenous growers and imposed a discriminatory tax on rubber produced by native smallholders.[22] A recent unpublished United Nations study of agricultural development in Africa concluded that large-scale agricultural operations owned and controlled by foreign commercial interests (such as the rubber plantations of Liberia, the sisal estates of Tanganyika [Tanzania], and the coffee estates of Angola) only survived the competition of peasant producers because "the authorities actively supported them by suppressing indigenous rural development."[23]

The suppression of indigenous agricultural development served the interests of the colonizing powers in two ways. Not only did it prevent direct competition from more efficient native producers of the same crops, but it also guaranteed a labor force to work on the foreign-owned estates. Planters and foreign investors were not unaware that peasants who could survive economically by their own production would be under less pressure to sell their labor cheaply to the large estates.

The answer to the question, then, "Why can't people feed themselves?" must begin with an understanding of how colonialism actively prevented people from doing just that.

## Colonialism

- forced peasants to replace food crops with cash crops that were then expropriated at very low rates;
- took over the best agricultural land for export crop plantations and then forced the most able-bodied workers to leave the village fields to work as slaves or for very low wages on plantations;
- encouraged a dependence on imported food;

- blocked native peasant cash crop production from competing with cash crops produced by settlers or foreign firms.

These are concrete examples of the development of underdevelopment that we should have perceived as such even as we read our history schoolbooks. Why didn't we? Somehow our schoolbooks always seemed to make the flow of history appear to have its own logic—as if it could not have been any other way. I, Frances, recall, in particular, a grade-school, social studies pamphlet on the idyllic life of Pedro, a nine-year-old boy on a coffee plantation in South America. The drawings of lush vegetation and "exotic" huts made his life seem romantic indeed. Wasn't it natural and proper that South America should have plantations to supply my mother and father with coffee? Isn't that the way it was *meant* to be?

# Notes

1. Radha Sinha, *Food and Poverty* (New York: Holmes and Meier, 1976), p. 26.
2. John Stuart Mill, *Political Economy*, Book 3, Chapter 25 (emphasis added).
3. Peter Feldman and David Lawrence, "Social and Economic Implications of the Large-Scale Introduction of New Varieties of Foodgrains," Africa Report, preliminary draft (Geneva: UNRISD, 1975), pp. 107–108.
4. Edgar Owens, *The Right Side of History*, unpublished manuscript, 1976.
5. Walter Rodney, *How Europe Underdeveloped Africa* (London: Bogle-L'Ouverture Publications, 1972), pp. 171–172.
6. Ferdinand Ossendowski, *Slaves of the Sun* (New York: Dutton, 1928), p. 276.
7. Rodney, *How Europe Underdeveloped Africa*, pp. 171–172.
8. Ibid., p. 181.
9. Clifford Geertz, *Agricultural Involution* (Berkeley and Los Angeles: University of California Press, 1963), pp. 52–53.
10. Rodney, *How Europe Underdeveloped Africa*, p. 185.
11. Ibid., p. 184.
12. Ibid., p. 186.
13. George L. Beckford, *Persistent Poverty: Underdevelopment in Plantation Economies of the Third World* (New York: Oxford University Press, 1972), p. 99.
14. Ibid., p. 99, quoting from Erich Jacoby, *Agrarian Unrest in Southeast Asia* (New York: Asia Publishing House, 1961), p. 66.
15. Pat Flynn and Roger Burbach, North American Congress on Latin America, Berkely, California, recent investigation.
16. Feldman and Lawrence, "Social and Economic Implications," p. 103.
17. Special Sahelian Office Report, Food and Agriculture Organization, March 28, 1974, pp. 88–89.
18. Alan Adamson, *Sugar Without Slaves: The Political Economy of British Guiana, 1838–1904* (New Haven and London: Yale University Press, 1972).
19. Ibid., p. 41.
20. Eric Williams, *Capitalism and Slavery* (New York: Putnam, 1966), p. 110.
21. Ibid., p. 121.
22. Gunnar Myrdal, *Asian Drama*, vol. 1 (New York: Pantheon, 1966), pp. 448–449.
23. Feldman and Lawrence, "Social and Economic Implications," p. 189.

**FRANCES MOORE LAPPÉ** and **DR. JOSEPH COLLINS** are founders and directors of the Institute for Food and Development Policy, located in San Francisco and New York.

From *Food First: Beyond the Myth of Scarcity* by Frances Moore Lappé and Joseph Collins, 1977, pp. 99–111. © 1977 by the Institute for Food & Development Policy. Reprinted by permission of Ballantine Books, a division of Random House, Inc.

# The Arrow of Disease

**When Columbus and his successors invaded the Americas, the most potent weapon they carried was their germs. But why didn't deadly disease flow in the other direction, from the New World to the Old?**

JARED DIAMOND

The three people talking in the hospital room were already stressed out from having to cope with a mysterious illness, and it didn't help at all that they were having trouble communicating. One of them was the patient, a small, timid man, sick with pneumonia caused by an unidentified microbe and with only a limited command of the English language. The second, acting as translator, was his wife, worried about her husband's condition and frightened by the hospital environment. The third person in the trio was an inexperienced young doctor, trying to figure out what might have brought on the strange illness. Under the stress, the doctor was forgetting everything he had been taught about patient confidentiality. He committed the awful blunder of requesting the woman to ask her husband whether he'd had any sexual experiences that might have caused the infection.

As the young doctor watched, the husband turned red, pulled himself together so that he seemed even smaller, tried to disappear under his bed sheets, and stammered in a barely audible voice. His wife suddenly screamed in rage and drew herself up to tower over him. Before the doctor could stop her, she grabbed a heavy metal bottle, slammed it onto her husband's head, and stormed out of the room. It took a while for the doctor to elicit, through the man's broken English, what he had said to so enrage his wife. The answer slowly emerged: he had admitted to repeated intercourse with sheep on a recent visit to the family farm; perhaps that was how he had contracted the mysterious microbe.

This episode, related to me by a physician friend involved in the case, sounds so bizarrely one of a kind as to be of no possible broader significance. But in fact it illustrates a subject of great importance: human diseases of animal origins. Very few of us may love sheep in the carnal sense. But most of us platonically love our pet animals, like our dogs and cats; and as a society, we certainly appear to have an inordinate fondness for sheep and other livestock, to judge from the vast numbers of them that we keep.

Some of us—most often our children —pick up infectious diseases from our pets. Usually these illnesses remain no more than a nuisance, but a few have evolved into far more. The major killers of humanity throughout our recent history—small-pox, flu, tuberculosis, malaria, plague, measles, and cholera—are all infectious diseases that arose from diseases of animals. Until World War II more victims of war died of microbes than of gunshot or sword wounds. All those military histories glorifying Alexander the Great and Napoleon ignore the ego-deflating truth: the winners of past wars were not necessarily those armies with the best generals and weapons, but those bearing the worst germs with which to smite their enemies.

The grimmest example of the role of germs in history is much on our minds this month, as we recall the European conquest of the Americas that began with Columbus's voyage of 1492. Numerous as the Indian victims of the murderous Spanish conquistadores were, they were dwarfed in number by the victims of murderous Spanish microbes. These formidable conquerors killed an estimated 95 percent of the New World's pre-Columbian Indian population.

Why was the exchange of nasty germs between the Americas and Europe so unequal? Why didn't the reverse happen instead, with Indian diseases decimating the Spanish invaders, spreading back across the Atlantic, and causing a 95 percent decline in *Europe's* human population?

Similar questions arise regarding the decimation of many other native peoples by European germs, and regarding the decimation of would-be European conquistadores in the tropics of Africa and Asia.

Naturally, we're disposed to think about diseases from our own point of view: What can we do to save ourselves and to kill the microbes? Let's stamp out the scoundrels, and never mind what *their* motives are!

In life, though, one has to understand the enemy to beat him. So for a moment, let's consider disease from the microbes' point of view. Let's look beyond our anger at their making us sick in bizarre ways, like giving us genital sores or diarrhea, and ask why it is that they do such things. After all, microbes are as much a product of natural selection as we are, and so their actions must have come about because they confer some evolutionary benefit.

Basically, of course, evolution selects those individuals that are most effective at producing babies and at helping those babies find suitable places to live. Microbes are marvels at this latter requirement. They have evolved diverse ways of spreading from one person to another, and from animals to people. Many of our symptoms of disease actually represent ways in which some clever bug modifies our bodies or our behavior such that we become enlisted to spread bugs.

The most effortless way a bug can spread is by just waiting to be transmitted passively to the next victim. That's the strategy practiced by microbes that wait for one host to be eaten by the next—salmonella bacteria, for example, which we contract by eating already-infected eggs or meat; or the worm responsible for trichinosis, which waits for us to kill a pig and eat it without properly cooking it.

As a slight modification of this strategy; some microbes don't wait for the old host to die but instead hitchhike in the saliva of an insect that bites the old host and then flies to a new one. The free ride may be provided by mosquitoes, fleas, lice, or tsetse flies, which spread malaria, plague, typhus, and sleeping sickness, respectively. The dirtiest of all passive-carriage tricks is perpetrated by microbes that pass from a woman to her fetus—microbes such as the ones responsible for syphilis, rubella (German measles), and AIDS. By their cunning these microbes can already be infecting an infant before the moment of its birth.

Other bugs take matters into their own hands, figuratively speaking. They actively modify the anatomy or habits of their host to accelerate their transmission. From our perspective, the open genital sores caused by venereal diseases such as syphilis are a vile indignity. From the microbes' point of view, however, they're just a useful device to enlist a host's help in inoculating the body cavity of another host with microbes. The skin lesions caused by smallpox similarly spread microbes by direct or indirect body contact (occasionally very indirect, as when U.S. and Australian whites bent on wiping out "belligerent" native peoples sent them gifts of blankets previously used by smallpox patients).

More vigorous yet is the strategy practiced by the influenza, common cold, and pertussis (whooping cough) microbes, which induce the victim to cough or sneeze, thereby broadcasting the bugs toward prospective new hosts. Similarly the cholera bacterium induces a massive diarrhea that spreads bacteria into the water supplies of potential new victims. For modification of a host's behavior, though, nothing matches the rabies virus, which not only gets into the saliva of an infected dog but drives the dog into a frenzy of biting and thereby infects many new victims.

Thus, from our viewpoint, genital sores, diarrhea, and coughing are "symptoms" of disease. From a bug's viewpoint, they're clever evolutionary strategies to broadcast the bug. That's why it's in the bug's interests to make us "sick." But what does it gain by killing us? That seems self-defeating, since a microbe that kills its host kills itself.

Though you may well think it's little consolation, our death is really just an unintended by-product of host symptoms that promote the efficient transmission of microbes. Yes, an untreated cholera patient may eventually die from producing diarrheal fluid at a rate of several gallons a day. While the patient lasts, though, the cholera bacterium profits from being massively disseminated into the water supplies of its next victims. As long as each victim thereby infects, on average, more than one new victim, the bacteria will spread, even though the first host happens to die.

So much for the dispassionate examination of the bug's interests. Now let's get back to considering our own selfish interests: to stay alive and healthy, best done by killing the damned bugs. One common response to infection is to develop a fever. Again, we consider fever a "symptom" of disease, as if it developed inevitably without serving any function. But regulation of body temperature is under our genetic control, and a fever doesn't just happen by accident. Because some microbes are more sensitive to heat than our own bodies are, by raising our body temperature we in effect try to bake the bugs to death before we get baked ourselves.

## We and our pathogens are now locked in an escalating evolutionary contest, with the death of one contestant the price of defeat, and with natural selection playing the role of umpire.

Another common response is to mobilize our immune system. White blood cells and other cells actively seek out and kill foreign microbes. The specific antibodies we gradually build up against a particular microbe make us less likely to get reinfected once we are cured. As we all know there are some illnesses, such as flu and the common cold, to which our resistance is only temporary; we can eventually contract the illness again. Against other illnesses, though—including measles, mumps, rubella, pertussis, and the now-defeated menace of smallpox—antibodies stimulated by one infection confer lifelong immunity. That's the principle behind vaccination—to stimulate our antibody production without our having to go through the actual experience of the disease.

Alas, some clever bugs don't just cave in to our immune defenses. Some have learned to trick us by changing their antigens, those molecular pieces of the microbe that our antibodies recognize. The constant evolution or recycling of new strains of flu, with differing antigens, explains why the flu you got two years ago didn't protect you against the different strain that arrived this year. Sleeping sickness is an even more slippery customer in its ability to change its antigens rapidly.

Among the slipperiest of all is the virus that causes AIDS, which evolves new antigens even as it sits within an individual patient, until it eventually overwhelms the immune system.

Our slowest defensive response is through natural selection, which changes the relative frequency with which a gene appears from generation to generation. For almost any disease some people prove to be genetically more resistant than others. In an epidemic, those people with genes for resistance to that particular microbe are more likely to survive than are people lacking such genes. As a result, over the course of history human populations repeatedly exposed to a particular pathogen tend to be made up of individuals with genes that resist the appropriate microbe just because unfortunate individuals without those genes were less likely to survive to pass their genes on to their children.

Fat consolation, you may be thinking. This evolutionary response is not one that does the genetically susceptible dying individual any good. It does mean, though, that a human population as a whole becomes better protected.

In short, many bugs have had to evolve tricks to let them spread among potential victims. We've evolved counter-tricks, to which the bugs have responded by evolving counter-counter-tricks. We and our pathogens are now locked in an escalating evolutionary contest, with the death of one contestant the price of defeat, and with natural selection playing the role of umpire.

The form that this deadly contest takes varies with the pathogens: for some it is like a guerrilla war, while for others it is a blitzkrieg. With certain diseases, like malaria or hookworm, there's a more or less steady trickle of new cases in an affected area, and they will appear in any month of any year. Epidemic diseases, though, are different: they produce no cases for a long time, then a whole wave of cases, then no more cases again for a while.

Among such epidemic diseases, influenza is the most familiar to Americans, this year having been a particularly bad one for us (but a great year for the influenza virus). Cholera epidemics come at longer intervals, the 1991 Peruvian epidemic being the first one to reach the New World during the twentieth century. Frightening as today's influenza and cholera epidemics are, through, they pale beside the far more terrifying epidemics of the past, before the rise of modern medicine. The greatest single epidemic in human history was the influenza wave that killed 21 million people at the end of the First World War. The black death, or bubonic plague, killed one-quarter of Europe's population between 1346 and 1352, with death tolls up to 70 percent in some cities.

The infectious diseases that visit us as epidemics share several characteristics. First, they spread quickly and efficiently from an infected person to nearby healthy people, with the result that the whole population gets exposed within a short time. Second, they're "acute" illnesses: within a short time, you either die or recover completely. Third, the fortunate ones of us who do recover develop antibodies that leave us immune against a recurrence of the disease for a long time, possibly our entire lives. Finally, these diseases tend to be restricted to humans; the bugs causing them tend not to live in the soil or in other animals. All four of these characteristics apply to what Americans think of as the once more-familiar acute epidemic diseases of childhood, including measles, rubella, mumps, pertussis, and smallpox.

It is easy to understand why the combination of those four characteristics tends to make a disease run in epidemics. The rapid spread of microbes and the rapid course of symptoms mean that everybody in a local human population is soon infected, and thereafter either dead or else recovered and immune. No one is left alive who could still be infected. But since the microbe can't survive except in the bodies of living people, the

disease dies out until a new crop of babies reaches the susceptible age—and until an infectious person arrives from the outside to start a new epidemic.

A classic illustration of the process is given by the history of measles on the isolated Faeroe Islands in the North Atlantic. A severe epidemic of the disease reached the Faeroes in 1781, then died out, leaving the islands measles-free until an infected carpenter arrived on a ship from Denmark in 1846. Within three months almost the whole Faeroes population—7,782 people—had gotten measles and then either died or recovered, leaving the measles virus to disappear once again until the next epidemic. Studies show that measles is likely to die out in any human population numbering less than half a million people. Only in larger populations can measles shift from one local area to another, thereby persisting until enough babies have been born in the originally infected area to permit the disease's return.

Rubella in Australia provides a similar example, on a much larger scale. As of 1917 Australia's population was still only 5 million, with most people living in scattered rural areas. The sea voyage to Britain took two months, and land transport within Australia itself was slow. In effect, Australia didn't even consist of a population of 5 million, but of hundreds of much smaller populations. As a result, rubella hit Australia only as occasional epidemics, when an infected person happened to arrive from overseas and stayed in a densely populated area. By 1938, though, the city of Sydney alone had a population of over one million, and people moved frequently and quickly by air between London, Sydney, and other Australian cities. Around then, rubella for the first time was able to establish itself permanently in Australia.

What's true for rubella in Australia is true for most familiar acute infectious diseases throughout the world. To sustain themselves, they need a human population that is sufficiently numerous and densely packed that a new crop of susceptible children is available for infection by the time the disease would otherwise be waning. Hence the measles and other such diseases are also known as "crowd diseases."

Crowd diseases could not sustain themselves in small bands of hunter-gatherers and slash-and-burn farmers. As tragic recent experience with Amazonian Indians and Pacific Islanders confirms, almost an entire tribelet may be wiped out by an epidemic brought by an outside visitor, because no one in the tribelet has any antibodies against the microbe. In addition, measles and some other "childhood" diseases are more likely to kill infected adults than children, and all adults in the tribelet are susceptible. Having killed most of the tribelet, the epidemic then disappears. The small population size explains why tribelets can't sustain epidemics introduced from the outside; at the same time it explains why they could never evolve epidemic diseases of their own to give back to the visitors.

That's not to say that small human populations are free from all infectious diseases. Some of their infections are caused by microbes capable of maintaining themselves in animals or in soil, so the disease remains constantly available to infect people. For example, the yellow fever virus is carried by African wild monkeys and is constantly available to infect rural human populations of Africa. It was also available to be carried to New World monkeys and people by the transAtlantic slave trade.

Other infections of small human populations are chronic diseases, such as leprosy and yaws, that may take a very long time to kill a victim. The victim thus remains alive as a reservoir of microbes to infect other members of the tribelet. Finally, small human populations are susceptible to nonfatal infections against which we don't develop immunity, with the result that the same person can become reinfected after recovering. That's the case with hookworm and many other parasites.

All these types of diseases, characteristic of small, isolated populations, must be the oldest diseases of humanity. They were the ones that we could evolve and sustain through the early millions of years of our evolutionary history, when the total human population was tiny and fragmented. They are also shared with, or are similar to the diseases of, our closest wild relatives, the African great apes. In contrast, the evolution of our crowd diseases could only have occurred with the buildup of large, dense human populations, first made possible by the rise of agriculture about 10,000 years ago, then by the rise of cities several thousand years ago. Indeed, the first attested dates for many familiar infectious diseases are surprisingly recent: around 1600 B.C. for smallpox (as deduced from pockmarks on an Egyptian mummy), 400 B.C. for mumps, 1840 for polio, and 1959 for AIDS.

Agriculture sustains much higher human population densities than does hunting and gathering—on average, 10 to 100 times higher. In addition, hunter-gatherers frequently shift camp, leaving behind their piles of feces with their accumulated microbes and worm larvae. But farmers are sedentary and live amid their own sewage, providing microbes with a quick path from one person's body into another person's drinking water. Farmers also become surrounded by disease-transmitting rodents attracted by stored food.

---

**The explosive increase in world travel by Americans, and in immigration to the United States, is turning us into another melting pot—this time of microbes that we'd dismissed as causing disease in far-off countries.**

---

Some human populations make it even easier for their own bacteria and worms to infect new victims, by intentionally gathering their feces and urine and spreading it as fertilizer on the fields where people work. Irrigation agriculture and fish farming provide ideal living conditions for the snails carrying schistosomes, and for other flukes that burrow through our skin as we wade through the feces-laden water.

If the rise of farming was a boon for our microbes, the rise of cities was a veritable bonanza, as still more densely packed human populations festered under even worse sanitation condi-

tions. (Not until the beginning of the twentieth century did urban populations finally become self-sustaining; until then, constant immigration of healthy peasants from the countryside was necessary to make good the constant deaths of city dwellers from crowd diseases.) Another bonanza was the development of world trade routes, which by late Roman times effectively joined the populations of Europe, Asia, and North Africa into one giant breeding ground for microbes. That's when smallpox finally reached Rome as the "plague of Antonius," which killed millions of Roman citizens between A.D. 165 and 180.

Similarly, bubonic plague first appeared in Europe as the plague of Justinian (A.D. 542–543). But plague didn't begin to hit Europe with full force, as the black death epidemics, until 1346, when new overland trading with China provided rapid transit for flea-infested furs from plague-ridden areas of Central Asia. Today our jet planes have made even the longest intercontinental flights briefer than the duration of any human infectious disease. That's how an Aerolíneas Argentinas airplane, stopping in Lima, Peru, earlier this year, managed to deliver dozens of cholera-infected people the same day to my city of Los Angeles, over 3,000 miles away. The explosive increase in world travel by Americans, and in immigration to the United States, is turning us into another melting pot—this time of microbes that we previously dismissed as just causing exotic diseases in far-off countries.

When the human population became sufficiently large and concentrated, we reached the stage in our history when we could at last sustain crowd diseases confined to our species. But that presents a paradox: such diseases could never have existed before. Instead they had to evolve as new diseases. Where did those new diseases come from?

Evidence emerges from studies of the disease-causing microbes themselves. In many cases molecular biologists have identified the microbe's closest relative. Those relatives also prove to be agents of infectious crowd diseases—but ones confined to various species of domestic animals and pets! Among animals too, epidemic diseases require dense populations, and they're mainly confined to social animals that provide the necessary large populations. Hence when we domesticated social animals such as cows and pigs, they were already afflicted by epidemic diseases just waiting to be transferred to us.

For example, the measles virus is most closely related to the virus causing rinderpest, a nasty epidemic disease of cattle and many wild cud-chewing mammals. Rinderpest doesn't affect humans. Measles, in turn, doesn't affect cattle. The close similarity of the measles and rinderpest viruses suggests that the rinderpest virus transferred from cattle to humans, then became the measles virus by changing its properties to adapt to us. That transfer isn't surprising, considering how closely many peasant farmers live and sleep next to cows and their accompanying feces, urine, breath, sores, and blood. Our intimacy with cattle has been going on for 8,000 years since we domesticated them—ample time for the rinderpest virus to discover us nearby. Other familiar infectious diseases can similarly be traced back to diseases of our animal friends.

Given our proximity to the animals we love, we must constantly be getting bombarded by animal microbes. Those invaders get winnowed by natural selection, and only a few succeed in establishing themselves as human diseases. A quick survey of current diseases lets us trace four stages in the evolution of a specialized human disease from an animal precursor.

In the first stage, we pick up animal-borne microbes that are still at an early stage in their evolution into specialized human pathogens. They don't get transmitted directly from one person to another, and even their transfer from animals to us remains uncommon. There are dozens of diseases like this that we get directly from pets and domestic animals. They include cat scratch fever from cats, leptospirosis from dogs, psittacosis from chickens and parrots, and brucellosis from cattle. We're similarly susceptible to picking up diseases from wild animals, such as the tularemia that hunters occasionally get from skinning wild rabbits.

In the second stage, a former animal pathogen evolves to the point where it does get transmitted directly between people and causes epidemics. However, the epidemic dies out for several reasons—being cured by modern medicine, stopping when everybody has been infected and died, or stopping when everybody has been infected and become immune. For example, a previously unknown disease termed *o'nyong-nyong* fever appeared in East Africa in 1959 and infected several million Africans. It probably arose from a virus of monkeys and was transmitted to humans by mosquitoes. The fact that patients recovered quickly and became immune to further attack helped cause the new disease to die out quickly.

The annals of medicine are full of diseases that sound like no known disease today but that once caused terrifying epidemics before disappearing as mysteriously as they had come. Who alive today remembers the "English sweating sickness" that swept and terrified Europe between 1485 and 1578, or the "Picardy sweats" of eighteenth- and nineteenth-century France?

A third stage in the evolution of our major diseases is represented by former animal pathogens that establish themselves in humans and that do not die out; until they do, the question of whether they will become major killers of humanity remains up for grabs. The future is still very uncertain for Lassa fever, first observed in 1969 in Nigeria and caused by a virus probably derived from rodents. Better established is Lyme disease, caused by a spirochete that we get from the bite of a tick. Although the first known human cases in the United States appeared only as recently as 1962, Lyme disease is already reaching epidemic proportions in the Northeast, on the West Coast, and in the upper Midwest. The future of AIDS, derived from monkey viruses, is even more secure, from the virus's perspective.

The final stage of this evolution is represented by the major, long-established epidemic diseases confined to humans. These diseases must have been the evolutionary survivors of far more pathogens that tried to make the jump to us from animals—and mostly failed.

Diseases represent evolution in progress, as microbes adapt by natural selection to new hosts. Compared with cows' bodies, though, our bodies offer different immune defenses and different chemistry. In that new environment, a microbe must evolve new ways to live and propagate itself.

The best-studied example of microbes evolving these new ways involves myxomatosis, which hit Australian rabbits in 1950. The myxoma virus, native to a wild species of Brazilian rabbit, was known to cause a lethal epidemic in European domestic rabbits, which are a different species. The virus was intentionally introduced to Australia in the hopes of ridding the continent of its plague of European rabbits, foolishly introduced in the nineteenth century. In the first year, myxoma produced a gratifying (to Australian farmers) 99.8 percent mortality in infected rabbits. Fortunately for the rabbits and unfortunately for the farmers, the death rate then dropped in the second year to 90 percent and eventually to 25 percent, frustrating hopes of eradicating rabbits completely from Australia. The problem was that the myxoma virus evolved to serve its own interest, which differed from the farmers' interests and those of the rabbits. The virus changed to kill fewer rabbits and to permit lethally infected ones to live longer before dying. The result was bad for Australian farmers but good for the virus: a less lethal myxoma virus spreads baby viruses to more rabbits than did the original, highly virulent myxoma.

For a similar example in humans, consider the surprising evolution of syphilis. Today we associate syphilis with genital sores and a very slowly developing disease, leading to the death of untreated victims only after many years. However, when syphilis was first definitely recorded in Europe in 1495, its pustules often covered the body from the head to the knees, caused flesh to fall off people's faces, and led to death within a few months. By 1546 syphilis had evolved into the disease with the symptoms known to us today. Apparently, just as with myxomatosis, those syphilis spirochetes evolved to keep their victims alive longer in order to transmit their spirochete offspring into more victims.

**H**ow, then, does all this explain the outcome of 1492—that Europeans conquered and depopulated the New World, instead of Native Americans conquering and depopulating Europe?

**In the century or two following Columbus's arrival in the New World, the Indian population declined by about 95 percent. The main killers were European germs, to which the Indians had never been exposed.**

Part of the answer, of course, goes back to the invaders' technological advantages. European guns and steel swords were more effective weapons than Native American stone axes and wooden clubs. Only Europeans had ships capable of crossing the ocean and horses that could provide a decisive advantage in battle. But that's not the whole answer. Far more Native Americans died in bed than on the battlefield—the victims of germs, not of guns and swords. Those germs undermined Indian resistance by killing most Indians and their leaders and by demoralizing the survivors.

The role of disease in the Spanish conquests of the Aztec and Inca empires is especially well documented. In 1519 Cortés landed on the coast of Mexico with 600 Spaniards to conquer the fiercely militaristic Aztec Empire, which at the time had a population of many millions. That Cortés reached the Aztec capital of Tenochtitlán, escaped with the loss of "only" two-thirds of his force, and managed to fight his way back to the coast demonstrates both Spanish military advantages and the initial naïveté of the Aztecs. But when Cortés's next onslaught came, in 1521, the Aztecs were no longer naïve; they fought street by street with the utmost tenacity.

What gave the Spaniards a decisive advantage this time was smallpox, which reached Mexico in 1520 with the arrival of one infected slave from Spanish Cuba. The resulting epidemic proceeded to kill nearly half the Aztecs. The survivors were demoralized by the mysterious illness that killed Indians and spared Spaniards, as if advertising the Spaniards' invincibility. By 1618 Mexico's initial population of 20 million had plummeted to about 1.6 million.

Pizarro had similarly grim luck when he landed on the coast of Peru in 1531 with about 200 men to conquer the Inca Empire. Fortunately for Pizarro, and unfortunately for the Incas, smallpox had arrived overland around 1524, killing much of the Inca population, including both Emperor Huayna Capac and his son and designated successor, Ninan Cuyoche. Because of the vacant throne, two other sons of Huayna Capac, Atahuallpa and Huáscar, became embroiled in a civil war that Pizarro exploited to conquer the divided Incas.

When we in the United States think of the most populous New World societies existing in 1492, only the Aztecs and Incas come to mind. We forget that North America also supported populous Indian societies in the Mississippi Valley. Sadly, these societies too would disappear. But in this case conquistadores contributed nothing directly to the societies' destruction; the conquistadores' germs, spreading in advance, did everything. When De Soto marched through the Southeast in 1540, he came across Indian towns abandoned two years previously because nearly all the inhabitants had died in epidemics. However, he was still able to see some of the densely populated towns lining the lower Mississippi. By a century and a half later, though, when French settlers returned to the lower Mississippi, almost all those towns had vanished. Their relics are the great mound sites of the Mississippi Valley. Only recently have we come to realize that the mound-building societies were still largely intact when Columbus arrived, and that they collapsed between 1492 and the systematic European exploration of the Mississippi.

When I was a child in school, we were taught that North America had originally been occupied by about one million Indians. That low number helped justify the white conquest of what could then be viewed as an almost empty continent. However, archeological excavations and descriptions left by the first European explorers on our coasts now suggest an initial number of around 20 million. In the century or two following Columbus's arrival in the New World, the Indian population is estimated to have declined by about 95 percent.

The main killers were European germs, to which the Indians had never been exposed and against which they therefore had neither immunologic nor genetic resistance. Smallpox, measles, influenza, and typhus competed for top rank among the killers. As if those were not enough, pertussis, plague, tuberculosis, diphtheria, mumps, malaria, and yellow fever came close behind. In countless cases Europeans were actually there to witness the decimation that occurred when the germs arrived. For example, in 1837 the Mandan Indian tribe, with one of the most elaborate cultures in the Great Plains, contracted smallpox thanks to a steamboat traveling up the Missouri River from St. Louis. The population of one Mandan village crashed from 2,000 to less than 40 within a few weeks.

The one-sided exchange of lethal germs between the Old and New worlds is among the most striking and consequence-laden facts of recent history. Whereas over a dozen major infectious diseases of Old World origins became established in the New World, not a single major killer reached Europe from the Americas. The sole possible exception is syphilis, whose area of origin still remains controversial.

That one-sidedness is more striking with the knowledge that large, dense human populations are a prerequisite for the evolution of crowd diseases. If recent reappraisals of the pre-Columbian New World population are correct, that population was not far below the contemporaneous population of Eurasia. Some New World cities, like Tenochtitlán, were among the world's most populous cities at the time. Yet Tenochtitlán didn't have awful germs waiting in store for the Spaniards. Why not?

One possible factor is the rise of dense human populations began somewhat later in the New World than in the Old. Another is that the three most populous American centers—the Andes, Mexico, and the Mississippi Valley—were never connected by regular fast trade into one gigantic breeding ground for microbes, in the way that Europe, North Africa, India, and China became connected in late Roman times.

The main reason becomes clear, however, if we ask a simple question: From what microbes could any crowd diseases of the Americas have evolved? We've seen that Eurasian crowd diseases evolved from diseases of domesticated herd animals. Significantly, there were many such animals in Eurasia. But there were only five animals that became domesticated in the Americas: the turkey in Mexico and parts of North America, the guinea pig and llama/alpaca (probably derived from the same original wild species) in the Andes, and Muscovy duck in tropical South America, and the dog throughout the Americas.

That extreme paucity of New World domestic animals reflects the paucity of wild starting material. About 80 percent of the big wild mammals of the Americas became extinct at the end of the last ice age, around 11,000 years ago, at approximately the same time that the first well-attested wave of Indian hunters spread over the Americas. Among the species that disappeared were ones that would have yielded useful domesticates, such as American horses and camels. Debate still rages as to whether those extinctions were due to climate changes or to the impact of Indian hunters on prey that had never seen humans. Whatever the reason, the extinctions removed most of the basis for Native American animal domestication—and for crowd diseases.

The few domesticates that remained were not likely sources of such diseases. Muscovy ducks and turkeys don't live in enormous flocks, and they're not naturally endearing species (like young lambs) with which we have much physical contact. Guinea pigs may have contributed a trypanosome infection like Chagas' disease or leishmaniasis to our catalog of woes, but that's uncertain.

Initially the most surprising absence is of any human disease derived from llamas (or alpacas), which are tempting to consider as the Andean equivalent of Eurasian livestock. However, llamas had three strikes against them as a source of human pathogens: their wild relatives don't occur in big herds as do wild sheep, goats, and pigs; their total numbers were never remotely as large as the Eurasian populations of domestic livestock, since llamas never spread beyond the Andes; and llamas aren't as cuddly as piglets and lambs and aren't kept in such close association with people. (You may not think of piglets as cuddly, but human mothers in the New Guinea highlands often nurse them, and they frequently live right in the huts of peasant farmers.)

The importance of animal-derived diseases for human history extends far beyond the Americas. Eurasian germs played a key role in decimating native peoples in many other parts of the world as well, including the Pacific islands, Australia, and southern Africa. Racist Europeans used to attribute those conquests to their supposedly better brains. But no evidence for such better brains has been forthcoming. Instead, the conquests were made possible by Europeans nastier germs, and by the technological advances and denser populations that Europeans ultimately acquired by means of their domesticated plants and animals.

So on this 500th anniversary of Columbus's discovery, let's try to regain our sense of perspective about his hotly debated achievements. There's no doubt that Columbus was a great visionary, seaman, and leader. There's also no doubt that he and his successors often behaved as bestial murderers. But those facts alone don't fully explain why it took so few European immigrants to initially conquer and ultimately supplant so much of the native population of the Americas. Without the germs Europeans brought with them—germs that were derived from their animals—such conquests might have been impossible.

---

**JARED DIAMOND** is a contributing editor of *Discover*, a professor of physiology at the UCLA School of Medicine, a recipient of a MacArthur genius award, and a research associate in ornithology at the American Museum of Natural History. Expanded versions of many of his *Discover* articles appear in his book *The Third Chimpanzee: The Evolution and Future of the Human Animal,* which won Britain's 1992 COPUS prize for best science book. Not least among his many accomplishments was his rediscovery in 1981 of the long-lost bowerbird of New Guinea. Diamond wrote about pseudo-hermaphrodites for *Discover's* special June issue on the science of sex.

---

Reprinted with permission of the author from *Discover* magazine, October 1992, pp. 64–73. © 1992 by Jared Diamond.

# Burying the White Gods: New Perspectives on the Conquest of Mexico

Camilla Townsend

I N 1552, Francisco López de Gómara, who had been chaplain and secretary to Hernando Cortés while he lived out his old age in Spain, published an account of the conquest of Mexico. López de Gómara himself had never been to the New World, but he could envision it nonetheless. "Many [Indians] came to gape at the strange men, now so famous, and at their attire, arms and horses, and they said, 'These men are gods!'"[1] The chaplain was one of the first to claim in print that the Mexicans had believed the conquistadors to be divine. Among the welter of statements made in the Old World about inhabitants of the New, this one found particular resonance. It was repeated with enthusiasm, and soon a specific version gained credence: the Mexicans had apparently believed in a god named Quetzalcoatl, who long ago had disappeared in the east, promising to return from that direction on a certain date. In an extraordinary coincidence, Cortés appeared off the coast in that very year and was mistaken for Quetzalcoatl by the devout Indians. Today, most educated persons in the United States, Europe, and Latin America are fully versed in this account, as readers of this piece can undoubtedly affirm. In fact, however, there is little evidence that the indigenous people ever seriously believed the newcomers were gods, and there is no meaningful evidence that any story about Quetzalcoatl's returning from the east ever existed before the conquest. A number of scholars of early Mexico are aware of this, but few others are. The cherished narrative is alive and well, and in urgent need of critical attention.[2]

In order to dismantle a construct with such a long history, it will be necessary first to explain the origins and durability of the myth and then to offer an alternate explanation of what happened in the period of conquest and what the indigenous were actually thinking. In proposing an alternative, I will make three primary assertions: first, that we must put technology in all its forms—beyond mere weaponry—front and center in our story of conquest; second, that we can safely do this because new evidence from scientists offers us explanations for divergent technological levels that have nothing to do with differences in intelligence; and third, that the Mexicans themselves immediately became aware of the technology gap and responded to it with intelligence and savvy rather than wide-eyed talk of gods. They knew before we did, it seems, that technology was the crux.

In the last twenty years, scholars have made room for alternative narratives in many arenas, demonstrating that power imbalances explain the way we tell our stories. Yet despite our consciousness of narrative as political intervention, the story of the white gods in the conquest of Mexico has remained largely untouched. It is essentially a pornographic vision of events, albeit in a political rather than asexual sense. What most males say they find so enticing about pornography is not violent imagery—which after all takes center stage relatively rarely—but rather the idea that the female is *not* concerned about any potential for violence or indeed any problematic social inequalities or personal disagreements but instead enthusiastically and unquestioningly adores—even worships—the male. Certainly, such a narrative may be understood to be pleasurable in the context of the strife-ridden relationships of the real world. Likewise, it perhaps comes as no surprise that the relatively powerful conquistadors and their cultural heirs should prefer to dwell on the Indians' adulation for them, rather than on their pain, rage, or attempted military defense. It is, however, surprising that this element has not been more transparent to recent scholars.

Perhaps this relatively dehumanizing narrative has survived among us—in an era when few such have—because we have lacked a satisfactory alternative explanation for the conquest. Without such a misunderstanding, how could a handful of Spaniards permanently defeat the great Aztec state?[3] It is a potentially frightening question—at least to those who do not want the answer to be that one group was more intelligent or more deserving than another. The notion that the Indians were too devout for their own good, and hence the victims of a calendric coincidence of tragic consequences, is highly appealing. We can argue that it was no one's fault if the Indians thought the Spanish were gods and responded to them as such. The belief was part and parcel of their cosmology and does not by any means indicate that they were lacking in intelligence or that their culture was "less developed." Thus even those participating in colonial semiosis with a sympathetic ear, who study Indian narratives alongside colonists' fantasies, often avoid or deny the Europeans' superior ability to conquer *in a technical sense*, making statements that simply are not believable. One has suggested that, "but for the cases of some spectacularly successful conquistadors," the indigenous might have killed off all approaching colonizers as successfully as the South Sea Islanders did away with Captain Cook, another that, if the last Aztec king, Cuauhtemoc, had met with better fortune, the Aztecs might have "embarked upon their own version of the Meiji era in Japan."[4]

The obvious explanation for conquest, many would argue, is technology. The Spanish had a technological advantage large enough to ensure their victory, especially if we acknowledge that their technology included not only blunderbusses and powder but also printing presses, steel blades and armor, crossbows, horses and riding equipment, ships, navigation tools—and indirectly, as a result of the latter three, an array of diseases.[5] But even here we are in dangerous waters, as some would thereby infer a difference in intelligence. Felipe Fernández-Armesto writes: "I hope to contribute to the explosion of what I call the *conquistador*-myth: the notion that Spaniards displaced incumbent elites in the early modern New World because they were in some sense better, or better-equipped, technically, morally or intellectually."[6] But why need we conflate the latter three? One group can be better equipped technically without being better equipped morally or intellectually. A people's technology is *not* necessarily a function of their intelligence. Even a superficial observer of the Aztecs must notice their accurate calendar, their extraordinary goldwork and poetry, their pictoglyph books: such an observer calls them intellectually deficient at his or her peril.

Science can now offer historians clear explanations for the greater advancement of technology among certain peoples without presupposing unequal intelligence. Biologist Jared Diamond presents this new knowledge coherently and powerfully in *Guns, Germs, and Steel: The Fates of Human Societies*, which has not received the attention it deserves from historians.[7] He sets out to provide a non-racist explanation for "Why the Inca Emperor Atahuallpa Did Not Capture King Charles I of Spain." After marshalling well-known evidence that turning from a hunter-gatherer lifestyle to sedentary farming leads to increasing population and the proliferation of technological advances—including guns, steel, and (indirectly) germs—he says that we must then ask ourselves why farming developed earlier and/or spread more rapidly in certain parts of the world. The answer lies in the constellation of suitable—that is, protein-rich—wild plants available in a particular environment at a particular time—which scientists can now reconstruct. It is a highly risky endeavor to turn from hunting and gathering to farming. It makes no sense to do so, except on a part-time basis, for sugar cane, bananas, or squash, for instance; it makes a great deal of sense to do it for the wheat and peas of the Fertile Crescent (and certain other species that spread easily on the wide and relatively ecologically constant east-west axis of Eurasia). In the case of the Americas, one rushes to ask, "What about corn?" Indeed, it turns out that after the millennia of part-time cultivation that it took to turn the nearly useless wild *teosinte* with its tiny bunches of seeds into something approaching today's ears of corn, Mesoamericans became very serious full-time agriculturalists. But by then, they had lost valuable time—or so we say if they were in a race with Eurasia. In 1519, it would turn out that, unbeknownst to either side, they *had* been in a something akin to a race. Establishing that the Mexicans had not had protein-rich crops available to them for as long as their conquerors, and

thus had not been sedentary as long, allows us to understand the technical disparities that existed without resorting to comparisons of intelligence or human worth. Diamond's work relieves us of an old burden. We may proceed more freely with our business as historians.

OUR FIRST TASK MUST BE TO ASK OURSELVES whence came the myths associated with the conquest. The simple truth is that, by the 1550s, some Indians were themselves saying that they (or rather, their parents) had presumed the white men to be gods. Their words became widely available to an international audience in 1962, when Miguel León-Portilla published *The Broken Spears: The Aztec Account of the Conquest of Mexico*, translated from his 1959 *Visión de los vencidos*. The work was perfectly timed to meet with the political sympathies of a generation growing suspicious of the conquistadors' version of events. The volume was printed in at least eleven other languages and has remained a common reference for a variety of scholars. It is an invaluable book, communicating the fear, pain, and anger experienced by the Mexica when their great city of Tenochtitlan crumbled.[8] Yet, ironically, the same text that lets sixteenth-century Nahuas speak "within hearing distance of the rest of the world"[9] also traps them in stereotype, quoting certain statements made at least a generation after the conquest as if they were transparent realities. "When Motecuhzoma heard that [the Spanish] were inquiring about his person, and when he learned that the 'gods' wished to see him face to face, his heart shrank within him and he was filled with anguish. He wanted to run away and hide."[10]

Numerous scholars have analyzed these words while ignoring their context. The best-known such work is Tzvetan Todorov's *Conquest of America: The Question of the Other*. Although quick to say there is no "natural inferiority" (indeed, he aptly points out that it is the Indians who rapidly learn the language of the Spanish, not the other way around), he insists that it is the Spaniards' greater adeptness in manipulating signs that gives them victory. While the Spanish believe in man-man communication ("What are we to do?"), the Indians only envision man-world communication ("How are we to know?"). Thus the Indians have a "paralyzing belief that the Spaniards are gods" and are "inadequate in a situation requiring improvisation."[11] Popular historians have been equally quick to accept this idea of indigenous reality, often with the best intentions. Hugh Thomas's recent monumental 800-page volume is a case in point. Thomas uses apocryphal accounts as if they had been tape-recorded conversations in his portrayal of the inner workings of Moctezuma's[12] court. "The Emperor considered flight. He thought of hiding ... He decided on ... a cave on the side of Chapultepec." Thomas does this, I believe, not out of naïveté but out of a genuine desire to incorporate the Indian perspective. He does not want to describe the intricate politics of the Spanish while leaving the Indian side vague, rendering it less real to his readers.[13]

With such friends, though, perhaps the indigenous and their cultural heirs do not need enemies. A different approach is definitely needed, or the white gods will continue to inhabit our narratives. In beginning anew, let us first ask what sources we have available. We in fact have only one set of documents that were undoubtedly written at the time of conquest by someone who was certainly there—the letters of Cortés. The *Cartas* are masterful constructions, loaded with political agendas, but we are at least certain of their origin, and Cortés never wrote that he was taken for a god. Andrés de Tapia, a Spanish noble who was a captain under Cortés, wrote an account predating López de Gómara's, and, in the 1560s, two aging conquistadors wrote their memoirs: Francisco de Aguilar, who by then had renounced worldly wealth and was living in a Dominican monastery, dictated a short narration, and Bernal Díaz del Castillo, then a landholder in Guatemala, wrote a long and spicy manuscript that has come to be beloved by many.[14]

Besides the testimony of these few conquistadors, we have the writings of priests who were on the scene early, and who were bent on making a careful study of indigenous beliefs, the better to convert the natives. In 1524, twelve Franciscan "Apostles" arrived in Mexico City and were warmly greeted by Cortés. One of them, Fray Toribio de Benavente (known to posterity by his Nahuatl name, "Motolinía" or "Poor One"), wrote extensively.[15] The efforts of the Franciscans led to the founding in 1536 of a formal school for Indian noblemen in Tlatelolco in Mexico City and culminated during the 1550s in the work of Bernardo de Sahagún, who spent years orchestrating a grand project in which students did extensive interviews with surviving notables of the *ancien régime*. The most complete extant version is the Florentine Codex.[16] The Dominican Fray Diego Durán, though not born until the 1530s, is also particularly valuable to us because he moved with his family from Seville to Mexico "before he lost his 'milk teeth,'" was raised by Nahuatl-speaking servants, and became fluent in the language.[17]

The last group of sources were produced by the indigenous themselves, but here is the heart of the problem: we have none that date from the years of conquest or even from the 1520s or 1530s. There are sixteen surviving pre-conquest codices (none from Mexico City itself, where the conquerors' book burning was most intense), and then, dating from the 1540s, statements written in Nahuatl using the Roman alphabet, which was then rapidly becoming accessible to educated indigenous through the school of Tlatelolco.[18] The most famous such document about the conquest is the lengthy Book Twelve of the Florentine Codex. Although it was organized by Sahagún, and the Spanish glosses were written by him, the Nahuatl is the work of his Indian aides.[19] At the end of the century, a few indigenous men wrote histories. Don Fernando de Alva Ixtlilxochitl, a descendant of the last king of Texcoco, near Tenochtitlan, was prolific.[20] Though removed in time, he is worth reading, having access to secretly preserved codices; he railed against Spaniards who had confused matters by making false assertions that were taken as truth.[21]

These, then, are the rather limited documents we have to work with. James Lockhart has used circumstantial evidence to argue that we must be mistaken in our notion that the Mexicans responded to the Spanish in the early years with fatalism and awe. Even though we have no indigenous records produced at contact, we have a corpus of materials from the 1550s, including not only explicit commentary on events but also the data preserved in litigation and church records:

> What we find ... is a picture dominated in so many aspects by patently untouched pre-conquest patterns that it does not take much imagination to reconstruct a great deal of the situation during the missing years. It would be a most unlikely scenario for a people to have spent twenty-five undocumented years in wide-mouthed amazement inspired by some incredible intruders, and then, the moment we can see them in the documents, to have relapsed into going about their business, seeking the advantage of their local entities, interpreting everything about the newcomers as some familiar aspect of their own culture.[22]

It is in this context that we must approach the later understanding that the Aztecs were convinced that their own omens had for years been predicting the coming of the cataclysm, and that Cortés was recognized as Quetzalcoatl and the Europeans as gods. The most important source for all of these legends is Book Twelve of the Florentine Codex. Lockhart notes that it reads very much as if it were two separate documents: the first part, covering the period from the sighting of the European sails to the Spaniards' violent attack on warrior-dancers participating in a religious festival, reads like an apocryphal fable (complete with comets as portents), while the second part, covering the period from the Aztec warriors' uprising against the Spaniards after the festival to their ultimate defeat over a year later, reads like a military archivist's record of events.[23] Indeed, this phenomenon makes sense: the old men being interviewed in the 1550s would likely have participated as young warriors in the battles against the Spanish, or at least have been well aware of what was transpiring. On the other hand, they would most certainly *not* have been privy to the debates within Moctezuma's inner circle when the Spaniards' arrival first became known: the king's closest advisers were killed in the conquest, and at any rate would have been older men even in 1520.

Still, the fact that the informants for the Florentine were not acquainted with the inner workings of Moctezuma's court only proves that they were unlikely to have the first part of the story straight; it tells us nothing about why they chose to say what they did. It seems likely that they retroactively sought to find particular auguries associated with the conquest. The Florentine's omens do not appear to have been commonly accepted, as they do not appear in other Nahuatl sources.[24] Interestingly, Fernández-Armesto notes that the listed omens fall almost exactly in line with certain Greek and Latin texts that are known to have been available to Sahagún's students.[25]

Why would Sahagún's assistants have been so eager to come up with a compelling narrative about omens? We must bear in mind that they were the sons and grandsons of Tenochtitlan's most elite citizens—descendants of priests and nobles. It was their own class, even their own family members, who might have been thought to be at fault if it were true that they had had no idea that the Spaniards existed prior to their arrival. Durán later recorded some of the accusations against seers as they had been reported to him:

Motecuhzoma, furious, cried, "It is your position, then, to be deceivers, tricksters, to pretend to be men of science and forecast that which will take place in the future, deceiving everyone by saying that you know what will happen in the world, that you see what is within the hills, in the center of the earth, underneath the waters, in the caves and in the earth's clefts, in the springs and water holes. You call yourselves 'children of the night' but everything is a lie, it is all pretense."[26]

Here Moctezuma himself is the speaker; whether any particular individual ever gave vent to such rage at the time is unknowable. What is clear is that the person speaking years later still felt deceived. It begins to seem not merely unsurprising, but indeed necessary, that Sahagún's elite youths should insist that their forebears *had* read the signs and had known what was to happen. In their version, the Truth was paralyzing and left their forebears vulnerable, perhaps even more so than they might have been.[27]

The idea that Cortés was understood to be the god Quetzalcoatl returning from the east is also presented as fact in Book Twelve. Moctezuma sends gifts for different gods, to see which are most welcome to the newcomers, and then decides it is Quetzalcoatl who has come. There are numerous obvious problems with the story. First, Quetzalcoatl was not a particularly prominent god in the pantheon worshiped in Mexico's great city. The one city in the empire where Quetzalcoatl was prominent, Cholula, was the only one to mount a concerted attack against Cortés as he made his way to the Aztec capital. Many aspects of the usual post-conquest description of Quetzalcoatl—that he was a peace-loving god who abhorred human sacrifice, for example— are obviously European mythological constructs, thus rendering the whole story somewhat suspect. Furthermore, in the Codex itself, when the earlier explorer Juan de Grijalva lands on the coast in 1518, *he* is taken to be Quetzalcoatl. So much for the explanation that Cortés happened to land in the right year, causing all the pieces to fall into place in the indigenous imagination.

Susan Gillespie has made a careful study of every sixteenth-century text (pre-and post-conquest) where Quetzalcoatl appears, and has proven that the story as we know it did not exist until Sahagún edited the Florentine Codex in the 1560s. Quetzalcoatl certainly was a deity in the Nahua tradition. If we take as our only sources the pre-conquest codices, archaeological remains of temples, and recitations of pre-conquest religious ceremonies recorded elsewhere, we are left with certain definite elements. Quetzalcoatl was, as his name indicates, a feathered serpent, a flying reptile (much like a dragon), who was a boundary maker (and transgressor) between earth and sky. Like most gods, he could take various forms and was envisioned differently in various villages and epochs: he could be the wind, for example. His name became a priestly title, an honorific for those liminal humans whose role it was to connect those on earth to those beyond. In myth, he was associated with the city of the Toltecs, an ancient state-building people who had preceded the Aztecs in the Central Valley of Mexico. As the invading Mexica often claimed legitimacy by insisting that they were the heirs of the Toltecs, the symbol of Quetzalcoatl often ap-

peared as an iconographic legitimator of a kingly line. In the Aztec ritual calendar, different deities were associated with each cyclically repeating date: Quetzalcoatl was tied to the year Ce Acatl (One Reed), which is correlated to the year 1519 (among others) in the Western calendar.[28]

There is no evidence of any ancient myths recounting the departure or return of such a god, but, in the early years after conquest, discrete elements of the story that has become so familiar to us do appear separately in various documents, with the main character being mortal rather than divine. The wandering hero is called Huemac or Topiltzin ("Our Lord" as in "Our Nobleman"); he is not given the name "Quetzalcoatl" until the 1540s, and then not in Nahuatl language texts. He is sometimes said to have ruled Tollan; the city is sometimes said to have fallen in connection with his exile; the prophecy of his return is occasionally made.[29] Motolinía rendered the story relevant to Cortés: Quetzalcoatl (in his version, a mortal apotheosized into a god, in good European tradition) was sent away to build up other lands, but people in Mexico awaited his return, and when they saw the sails of Cortés they said, "Their god was coming, and because of the white sails, they said he was bringing by sea his own temples." Then, remembering that all the Spaniards were supposed to have been gods, Motolinía quickly added, "When they disembarked, they said that it was not their god, but rather many gods."[30]

The elements did not all appear in the same narration until Sahagún's Codex drew them together in the 1560s—although references to the more traditional god Quetzalcoatl and a separate mortal hero named Huemac are also peppered throughout the Codex. By that time, Spanish priests had been interacting with the locals for years, and new European elements had been incorporated almost seamlessly: as they were wont to do elsewhere, the priests had theorized that a Christian saint had previously visited the New World, and such a man makes his appearance in these stories as the hero Quetzalcoatl, now a peace-loving man who is driven into exile because of the people's belief in the devil (the god Huitzilopochtli), and who foretells his own return.[31] In about 1570, the author of the "Anales de Cuauhtitlan" became the first Nahua to put all these elements together. To the generation of the 1570s, it seemed logical that their forebears had believed thus, for it provided a needed explanation why they had made such an ineffective defense.[32]

Even if it is untrue that anyone in 1519 thought Cortés was Quetzalcoatl, there remains the question of whether or not Cortés and his men were in general perceived to be gods. Cortés did not claim that he was accorded godly status. It is, however, apparently true that the Nahuas frequently referred to the Spanish as *teotl* or *teutl* (plural *teteo'* or *teteu'*), which the Spanish rendered in their own texts as *teul* (plural *teules*); they translated this word as "god." Sahagún's students in the 1550s clearly believed their parents had used *teotl* as a form of address in their dealings with the Spanish, and this was a matter less open to reinterpretation than some others.[33] Several conquistadors insisted on it. Perhaps the best question is not whether the Indians used the word *teotl* in their groping efforts to categorize the Spaniards before they had any political relation to them but rather why they did so, what it meant to them.

To turn an obvious point into a less obvious one, the indigenous had to call the Spaniards something, and it was not at all clear what that something should be. It is noteworthy that in Durán's history the issue first surfaces in the initial communication efforts of the Indian translator Malinche. "She responded, 'The leader of these men says he has come to greet your master Motecuhzoma, that his only intention is to go to the city of Mexico.'" But in the next interchange: "The Indian woman answered in the following way: 'These gods say that they kiss your hands and that they will eat.'"[34] In the Nahua universe as it had existed up until this point, a person was always labeled as being from a particular village or city-state, or, more specifically, as one who filled a given social role (a tribute collector, prince, servant). These new people fit nowhere; undoubtedly, they had a village or city-state somewhere, but it was not in the known world, and their relationship to it was not clear. Later, they were called "Caxtilteca" (people of Castile), but that came after closer acquaintance. There was no word for "Indian," of course, and the indigenous struggled in certain situations. How to describe the woman translator, for example, who came with the newcomers but was not one of them? She became "a woman, one of us people here."[35] If there were no "Indians," there were no "Spanish" in opposition to them. So what to call the new arrivals? One of them might be a *tecuhtli*, a dynastic lord ruling over his own people, but he was not so in relation to "us people here." The Nahuatl word for king was *tlatoani*, meaning "he who speaks." Tellingly, in Nahuatl texts where the Spaniards have previously been referred to as *teotl*, first Cortés and then the viceroy become *tlatoani* after the Europeans vanquish the Indians and are in a position of authority over them.[36]

In the Florentine Codex, the moment of political surrender is described by the warriors: "There goes the lord Cuauhtemoc going to give himself to the gods" (*teteu'*). Yet, in the preceding pages, the enemy has been described as execrable rather than divine: in fact, when the Spaniards are temporarily expelled, the warriors perform ceremonies "in gratitude to their gods (*teotl*) for having freed them from their enemies." Tellingly, in the negotiations *after* the surrender, when the Spaniards are demanding full restitution of all the gold and jewels they were ever given, they are termed "our lords" as in "our earthly overlords" (*totecuiovan*, from *tecuhtli*), but in a moment of rage, a leading priest whose tone indicates he does not yet feel he owes allegiance cries out, "Let the god (*teotl*), the Captain [Cortés] pay heed!" He then refuses to pay, until the defeated Cuauhtemoc calms him and uses the word *tecuhtli* again.[37]

Sixteenth-century dictionaries say that *teotl* meant simply *dios*, but they, we must remember, were written years later, after semantic shifts had occurred in the process of Indians and priests working together.[38] Bernal Díaz first says that *teotl* meant "god" (*dios*) or "demon" (*demonio*). We might assume he meant "demon" only in the sense that the Christians called the entire Nahua pantheon "devils," but an anecdote that he relates indicates otherwise. The Spaniards seem to have been given to understand—quite accurately—that the word could mean "devil" in the sense of a capricious immortal over whom mortals had no control, or a ceremonial human impersonator of

such a character. After the Spanish had gleaned the word's meaning, they thought to reinforce the notion as follows:

> [Cortés said], "I think we'll send Heredia against them." Heredia was an old Basque musketeer with a very ugly face covered with scars, a huge beard, and one blind eye. He was also lame in one leg ... So old Heredia shouldered his musket and went off with [the Indians] firing shots in the air as he went through the forest, so that the Indians should both hear and see him. And the *caciques* sent the news to the other towns that they were bringing along a *Teule* to kill the Mexicans [Aztecs] who were at Cingapacinga. I tell this story here merely as a joke and to show Cortés' guile.[39]

This story is barely comprehensible unless one accepts that the Spanish had been told the word *teotl* encompassed notions of "powerful one" and "deity impersonator." For the impression one is left with here is not that the locals thought the Spaniards were glorious and divine beings but rather that they envisioned them as bizarre sorcerers who owed allegiance to no one and whose powers could potentially be turned against the Aztec overlords and tax collectors. It is even conceivable that the indigenous were referring to "deity impersonators" as potential sacrifice victims for the Aztecs; certainly, *teotl* is used in that sense in descriptions of religious ceremonies elsewhere in the Florentine.

That the word had some ambiguity embedded within it is made clear in several texts. Durán's history—written in Spanish by a Spaniard who spoke Nahuatl and had Nahuatl sources—provides revealing examples. While the Spaniards are wending their way toward the city of Mexico, Moctezuma decides to send out medicine men to combat them. If the newcomers were really understood to be "gods" according to the term's definition in Spanish, then such an action makes no sense—since sorcerers fought human enemies, not gods. Durán's narrator deals with this inconsistency by having a close adviser to the king mention tactfully that such a step will probably be useless. Not long after, Moctezuma prepares to "receive the gods" in his city but then makes the following speech within the same paragraph: "Woe to us! ... In what way have we offended the gods? What has happened? Who are these men who have arrived? Whence have they come?"[40] Given the varied implications of the term *teotl*, it is not surprising that the Spaniards chose to understand it simply as "god" and to forget about the Heredia incident. Bernal Díaz himself, after his initial avowal, never mentions the second definition again. In other cases, it is clear that the Spanish chose translations of ambiguous passages most in keeping with the notion that they were perceived as divine.[41]

Motolinía was the only Spaniard present in the early 1520s who explicitly addressed this issue. He asserted that, in the first villages the Spaniards entered, the locals thought that the horse-and-man figures were single beings, like classical centaurs, one imagines. Within days, they learned of their error, saw that "the man was a man and the horse a beast," and so had to seek new words. They used *mazatl* (deer) to refer to the horses, and they used the Spanish corruption of their own initial label (*teotl*), or *teul*, to refer to the people, as the Spanish were now introducing themselves as such. They knew no other word for the newcomers until after the victory, when they were instructed to call them *cristianos*. Some Spaniards complained about that shift, Motolinía says scornfully, preferring to be called *Teules*.[42]

IN THE DEBATES ABOUT WHAT REALLY HAPPENED at the time of conquest, two facts stand out. Acknowledging them both simultaneously is perhaps counterintuitive, as they appear to be in opposition to each other; they are not. First, it was much more difficult than is commonly imagined for the Spanish to vanquish the Aztecs; the Europeans were in desperate straits on more than one occasion. Second, it was inevitable that Cortés and his men—or some other soon-to-follow expedition—would conquer the Aztecs. They had the technological advantage. The outcome was no coincidence. The Spanish conquest of the Mexicans against large numerical odds was replicated in innumerable other confrontations in the Americas—between Francisco Pizarro and the Incas, Hernando de Soto and the Alabama Indians, the English settlers and the Algonkians, etc.—and much later between Europeans and Africans. Yet the victory was never facile, for those less well equipped in a technological sense still did all they could to defend their own interests.

Cortés rapidly learned from his translators what he needed to know—that the Aztec army was the most powerful in the land, that the king offered city-states the alternative of joining the empire peacefully and paying an annual tribute or of fighting and facing brutal defeat, that the Spaniards' most effective strategy would be to turn people against the hated overlords. In July 1519, he scuttled his ships so his men would not be tempted to turn back, and struck inland to seek the Aztec capital of Tenochtitlan. First, however, he sent one ship to Spain with the news of his coastal explorations, the information he had received thus far about the Mexican empire, and his hopes of claiming that state on behalf of Carlos V. He did this partly because he was a traitor in a legal sense, having launched his expedition from Cuba without the governor's permission, and so needed to make a case in his own defense. Equally important, he knew he would need reinforcements and supplies. In order not to lose contact with the wider world, he left a number of men in the newly founded town of Vera Cruz who would be there to meet reinforcements (or enemies) when they arrived. That the Veracruzanos not starve or be killed, Cortés took several coastal Indian chiefs hostage.[43]

The story has been told many times of how Cortés and his men made their way to Tenochtitlan—fighting when necessary, turning the Indians against each other through clever ruses, detecting plots and putting them down, and finally coming face-to-face with the great Moctezuma on the causeway leading to the island city. There, according to Cortés, Moctezuma welcomed him, and shortly after agreed to become a vassal of the Spanish king. One week later, following an ancient European tactic of war, Cortés claimed to have seized Moctezuma's person and placed him under house arrest, so that he could rule through him, and Moctezuma agreed to remain in custody even when Cortés later offered to release him upon a promise of good behavior. Cortés ruled the empire successfully for over five months and then learned that an army from the Caribbean under Captain Narváez had landed at Vera Cruz in pursuit of him. Leaving a contingent in the city, Cortés made for the coast, and there he brought the hundreds of newcomers over to his side. Yet the temporary division in the Spanish ranks had become visible to the indigenous, and they rebelled, ejecting the Spaniards from their city in the famed Noche Triste.

Even though posterity has tended to accept it, the story is in fact more than a little difficult to believe. The idea that the Aztecs peacefully surrendered their kingdom fits well with the notion that the Mexica responded to the Europeans as gods. If we do not proceed on that assumption, however, the story flies in the face of common sense. The Spanish numbered only about five hundred, the city folk a quarter of a million. The Spanish had only one translator to tell them what was occurring; Moctezuma's people could watch every move that every Spaniard made. Simply to eat every day, the Spaniards were desperately dependent on those they dreamed of ruling. How vulnerable they were in this regard becomes painfully clear in the Codex Aubin, in which a resident of Tenochtitlan recalled that, when the people later stopped feeding the invaders, the horses began to eat the straw mats that lined the floors. Although it is certainly true that the Spanish maintained a "seize the king" policy both before and after Tenochtitlan, early in their dealings with the impressive Aztecs, the newly arrived Spanish were unlikely to have been arrogantly sure of their course. They certainly did not have the power to arrest the emperor without bringing on a state of chaos, as events proved.[44]

John Elliott and others have explained the content of Cortés's letter to the king, which subsequently formed the basis for the story as we have come to know it.[45] Besides justifying the actions he had taken without receiving royal permission, Cortés was using language to leap another legalistic hurdle: Carlos V could only annex territories that came to him voluntarily or through a just war. It was thus very important that Moctezuma swear fealty to the Spanish monarch early in the letter, *before* his people rebelled, when they technically became traitors. Placing Moctezuma under arrest without his protesting the Spaniards' right to do so was a crucial symbolic step.

Francis Brooks has argued that there is strong evidence against Cortés having immediately arrested Moctezuma. First, although he was supposedly in full control of the kingdom from November to May, Cortés made no effort to inform anyone else in the world of his successes, even though he had men perfectly capable of building ships, as they later proved. Second, Cortés's own story contradicts itself often, describing Moctezuma as a prisoner one moment and in control the next.[46] Cortés himself describes what he was doing during those months—continuing to become acquainted with Moctezuma and the city, consulting the mapmakers, sending representatives to visit surrounding towns, collecting gifts of gold, and waiting for his ship to return with an answer from Spain.[47] It is perfectly possible to believe that he was doing all these things as an honored visitor but not as the leader of a handful of coup-staging interlopers.

It is, however, equally certain that Moctezuma was put in irons before the end of the drama. There is real evidence that it occurred in April of 1520, coinciding with the sudden appearance of his rival Captain Narváez. At that point, Cortés had nothing left to lose. On the one hand, a Spanish army larger than his own had arrived on the coast with the intention of arresting him; on the other hand, the Aztecs were aware of this turn of events and planned to use it to their advantage. Only with a gun to Moctezuma's head could Cortés assure the newly arrived Spaniards that he was in control of the kingdom and gain their allegiance, as well as stave off an indigenous uprising. Numerous sworn witnesses in later court cases claimed that Spanish soldiers guarded Moctezuma around the clock in this period. Durán mentions eighty days of confinement, which would indeed place the arrest in April.[48] Cortés claimed that Moctezuma begged to be of service to the Spanish king in defending the land against these evil new arrivals, but that scenario is so preposterous as to be laughable, except when considered in the legalistic light discussed above. Indeed, no other Spaniard writing about these events described them thus: the others universally described Moctezuma's obvious hostility (or duplicity).[49] One is left thinking that Cortés did protest too much; it is quite likely that, rather than swearing eternal friendship, he chose this moment to have Moctezuma clapped in irons. Yet precisely because his situation was so precarious, it was particularly important that he portray his control of the region as long-term.[50]

The accounts of the other conquistadors are replete with inconsistencies concerning their purported power. "While I stayed ... I did not see a living creature killed or sacrificed," wrote Cortés. "The great Moctezuma continued to show his accustomed good will towards us, but never ceased his daily sacrifices of human beings. Cortés tried to dissuade him but met with no success," wrote Bernal Díaz.[51] In the midst of describing Moctezuma's palaces, Francisco de Aguilar seemed almost visibly to recall that he was supposed to be describing a prisoner: "They brought him ... fish of all kinds, besides ... fruits from the seacoast ... The plates and cups of his dinner service were very clean. He was not served on gold or silver because he was in captivity, but it is likely that he had a great table service of gold and silver."[52] Aguilar went on to say (as per Cortés) that the arrest had taken place because the Spanish had learned that Moctezuma had plotted against them and had ordered one of the men left in Vera Cruz to be killed. Aguilar and Andrés de Tapia and a third man had been sent to the coast to ascertain the truth of the matter. But de Tapia's own account says Indians were sent on that errand.[53] His description of the five-month period of supposed Spanish control seems odd: "In this manner we stayed on, the marques keeping us so close to our quarters that no one stepped a musket-shot away without permission."[54]

The friars who wrote about the events also undermined the notion of an immediate arrest,[55] and, although later indigenous sources accept it, the earliest known indigenous record does not. The Annals of Tlatelolco was probably written in the mid-1540s, possibly based on a story that had been memorized in the late 1520s. Here, Moctezuma is detained sometime after Cortés finds he must leave for the seashore and before the Spanish initiate a massacre at a religious festival, leading directly to their own expulsion. Until that point, the city's only relationship with the newcomers had been to provide them with food, water, and firewood, as they would have done for any honored guests.[56]

Just as we must refrain from imagining that the Spanish arrived with the power to arrest Moctezuma immediately, we must also avoid the equally wrong-headed assumption that they were able to defeat the Aztecs militarily with a few well-aimed shots. When Cortés struck inland from Vera Cruz, he had only fifteen horses with him. Later, when the Aztecs rebelled and ejected the Spanish from the city, between four and six hundred men were killed as they fled along the causeways leading out of the city, along with at least a thousand Tlaxcalan allies. Narrow passages rendered the Europeans vulnerable to attack: on at least two different occasions, over forty Spaniards were ambushed and killed while traveling through gorges.

Yet, in the end, it was no accident that the Europeans won. I have recounted the difficulties the Spanish faced, the impossibility of their having taken over immediately, in order to be more credible in saying that Europeans were bound to destroy the Mexicans eventually. Although it can be argued that diseases weakened both the Mexica and the Spaniards' Indian allies, and thus were not determinant, there remained a huge divide between the military capabilities of the two sides. Outside the city, on open ground, the Spanish were nearly invincible. After regrouping in the wake of their expulsion from the city, Cortés launched a campaign against Tenochtitlan. Several weeks and numerous battles later, one Spaniard died of his wounds, and Cortés mourned "the first of my company to be killed ... on this campaign."[57] What nearby village chief could say the same? The Spanish had learned how to use what they had to enable groups of two hundred men to withstand masses of enemies. Both their harquebus and crossbow firings were able to slice through the Indians' cotton armor, and, because of their weapons' range, they could attack lethally when the Indians were still distant; furthermore, mounted Europeans carrying long metal lances could forge a path through the throngs. The Indians could fire their arrows at six times the rate of a Spanish blunderbuss, but to no avail, because metal armor rendered the Europeans nearly impervious.[58]

The horses were of utmost importance. Three horses could turn a dire situation into a rout. They could even solve the problem of food supplies: clusters of armed horsemen could take a village or market by surprise and return with what the Spanish needed. The Europeans' own engineering experience was also crucial. As soon as they arrived in Tenochtitlan, Cortés put his master shipbuilder to work on four brigantines in case they should be needed to escape across the lake. They later came in handy in the final battles in the canals of the city: "The key to the war lay with them ... As the wind was good, we bore down through the middle of them, and although they fled as fast as they were able, we sank a huge number of canoes and killed or drowned many of the enemy, which was the most remarkable sight in the world."[59]

It is true as many have maintained that the Spanish would have been crushed by greater numbers in the long run or starved to death had they not worked with Indian allies ("special forces" style). A few hundred Spaniards became an unbeatable force only when combined with thousands of indigenous pouring in behind them. Cortés himself and several other chroniclers willingly attest to this. "When the inhabitants of the city saw ... the great multitude of our allies—although without us, they would have had no fear of them—they fled, and our allies pursued them."[60] What we must understand, though, is that the technological advantage was what, in the last analysis, made it possible for the Spanish to retain their indigenous allies. The indigenous learned quickly that they did not have the requisite technology: they saw that their civilian populations could not survive the onslaughts of the Spaniards even in the short term, and they recognized the undeniable long-range importance of the Europeans' maritime connections to distant lands.

Much ink has been spilt over the question of why the Tlaxcalans, for example, traditional enemies of the Mexica, briefly battled the Spaniards, then sided with them as their unwavering and most significant allies. The Tlaxcalans had little love for the Mexica and could not afford the luxury of acquiring another powerful enemy in the persons of the Spanish. Cortés, however, tells us what the clincher was. "I burnt more than ten villages, in one of which there were more than three thousand houses, where the inhabitants fought with us, although there was no one [no warriors] there to help them." He kept 'round the clock guard of their camp with their long-range weapons to make sure the Tlaxcalans did not retaliate in kind, "which would have been so disastrous." When they sued for peace, Cortés explained, "They would rather be Your Highness's vassals than see their houses destroyed and their women and children killed."[61] Likewise, when Cortés and the other survivors of the Noche Triste made it back to Tlaxcala, they made it their business within days to attack villages that were not friendly to them. Most sued for peace. "They see how those who do so are well received and favored by me," wrote Cortés, "whereas those who do not are destroyed daily."[62] Meanwhile, Moctezuma offered one year's tax relief to those who refrained from going over to the Spanish, but that was a distant carrot compared to the immediate threat constituted by mounted lancers riding through town. When a set of villages received emissaries from Tenochtitlan, the Spanish torched the towns. "On the following day three chieftains from those towns came begging my forgiveness for what had happened and asking me to destroy nothing more, for they promised that they would never again receive anyone from Tenochtitlan."[63]

More important than any weapons or horses the Spanish had with them, however, were Spanish ships, which had the potential to bring endless reinforcements. One of Cortés's first acts after fleeing from Tenochtitlan had been to send two expeditions loaded with treasure, which they were to use to purchase horses and weapons. Before they could return, in mid-1520, seven ships loaded with men and supplies appeared off the coast, for word had spread since Cortés had dispatched his initial messages in 1519.[64] Three more fully stocked vessels would arrive in early 1521. Even though we have since tended to overlook it, Europeans of the time understood how crucial this factor was. When Aguilar narrated his memory of the post–Noche Triste period, he said first that other ships had arrived and then that the Indian towns had chosen to "offer themselves peaceably."[65] Cortés recalled, "One of my lads, who knew that nothing in the world would give me such pleasure as to learn of the arrival of this [new] ship and the aid it brought, set out by

night [to bring me word], although the road was dangerous."[66] Indeed, Cortés was so well aware of the importance of his connection to the rest of the world that he made it his first order of business to build and staff forts along the road from Tenochtitlan to the sea, before proceeding with a campaign against Tenochtitlan.

At last he was ready: "When, on the twenty-eight of April ... I called all my men out on parade and reckoned eighty-six horsemen, 118 crossbowmen and harquebusiers, some 700 foot soldiers with swords and bucklers, three large iron guns, fifteen small bronze field guns and ten hundredweight of powder,... [t]hey knew well ... that God had helped us more than we had hoped, and ships had come with horses, men and arms."[67] After only a few days of battle, it was clear to many of the towns surrounding Tenochtitlan how well supplied the Spanish now were. "The natives of Xochimilco ... and certain of the Otomí,... came to offer themselves as Your Majesty's vassals, begging me to forgive them for having delayed so long." After a major defeat suffered by the Spanish, in which forty were captured and sacrificed, many of the Spaniards' allies withdrew again. It is commonly accepted that they returned only when the Nahua priests' predictions of a great victory to occur within the ensuing eight days did not come true. Cortés, though, outlines events as follows: first messengers arrived from Vera Cruz telling of the arrival of yet another ship and bringing powder and crossbows to prove it, and then, in the next sentence, "all the lands round about" demonstrated their good sense and came over to the Spaniards' side.[68] Perhaps, after all, the Indians' decisions were less spiritually than practically motivated.

We must now expand our list of relevant technological implements to include printing presses. The comparatively quick and widespread communication channels available to the Spanish gave them a geopolitical perspective throughout the events that the Aztecs, for all their intelligence, even brilliance, simply lacked. At the end of sixteenth century, Matteo Ricci, a Jesuit missionary to China, would make a comment about books that the Aztecs would have appreciated, although they themselves envisioned texts in other ways: "The whole point of writing things down ... is that your voice carries for thousands of miles."[69] Matteo Ricci read the Spanish, Portuguese, and Italian explorers, who themselves read Ibn Battutah and Marco Polo. As Todorov put it, "Did not Columbus himself set sail because he had read Marco Polo's narrative?"[70] In 1504, Amerigo Vespucci published his suggestion that what Columbus had found was not the tip of the Orient but a New World, and, by 1511, Peter Martyr's Latin compendium of reported observations on the New World was available to educated Europeans everywhere—within five years, it would even make its way into the best-read fiction of the day.[71] In 1509, the Spanish crown promulgated a law that no royal official was to do anything to impede the sending of any information about the Indies back to Spain.[72]

Albrecht Dürer is known for having spoken with awe of Aztec art that had been shipped back by Cortés and that he saw in an exhibit in the town hall in Brussels: "All the days of my life I have seen nothing that rejoiced my heart so much as these things, for I have seen among them wonderful works of art, and I marveled at the subtle intellects of men in foreign parts."[73] What is less well known is that Dürer saw these objects in July of 1520. Over a year before the conquest was complete, the Europeans were already putting on exhibits of their findings and spreading the word throughout their continent. Yet, on the other side of the sea, the Aztecs did not even know what to call the newcomers in their midst. The inequality of their positions is stunning, the subtle intellect of the Aztec artists notwithstanding.

WHAT, THEN, WERE THE INDIGENOUS THINKING? Available evidence indicates that the Aztecs responded to their situation with clear-sighted analysis of the technological differential, rather than by prostrating themselves before the "white gods."[74] As difficult as it is, let us first consider what we know of Moctezuma's thoughts. The version of the king's response that later became popular was the vision of Moctezuma sighing and lapsing into paralyzing depression, but the evidence that we have about the steps taken by Moctezuma indicates that he actually behaved like the experienced twenty-year sovereign he was. All sources agree that, after the first sighting of a Spanish ship in 1517, he had the sea watched from various vantage points. When Cortés and his men landed near today's Vera Cruz and began conversing with the locals, Moctezuma sent court painters to record the numbers of men, "deer," and boats.[75] Even though the Spaniards saw these paintings as quaint, we must keep in mind that Moctezuma moved within a world in which accurate counts concerning distant territories were kept as pictoglyphic records as a matter of course.[76] As the Spanish began their ascent toward Tenochtitlan, Moctezuma organized a veritable war room. "A report of everything that was happening was given and relayed to Moctezuma. Some of the messengers would be arriving as others were leaving ... There was no time when they weren't listening, when reports weren't being given."[77] Cortés also reported that Moctezuma's messengers were present in every town they visited, watching every step they took. Bernal Díaz said by the time the Spaniards got to the capital, the sermon they had given frequently along the way had been repeated so often to Moctezuma that he asked them not to give it again, as the arguments were by now familiar to him.[78] Despite his intelligence and his organizational apparatus, however, Moctezuma still had the problem that his frame of reference was not as wide as that of the Spaniards: Durán's informant said that he called for priests and sages from different parts of the kingdom to consult their libraries and traditions and tell him who these strangers were, but they could find nothing. Only one man said anything useful, describing the power of the Spaniards and mentioning that the first explorers were merely there to scout a route, that others would return.[79]

The words of Moctezuma's that we have come from Cortés, who claimed to quote a long speech of greeting in which Moctezuma turned over his kingdom to the Spaniard.[80] The elaborate statement may well have been loosely based on something that Moctezuma actually said—minus the immediate surrender of his entire kingdom—as it employs the classic courtly Nahuatl style, makes no reference to Cortés being Quetzalcoatl or any other god, and mentions facts that would otherwise have been

unknown to the Spanish at this early date—that the Aztecs themselves were migrants to the region and had a long history of banished kings—which Moctezuma found sufficient to explain the arrival of the newcomers. Later, Cortés actually has Moctezuma insist to his Spanish audience that he himself is *not* a god, and does not possess untold wealth: "I know that [my enemies] have told you the walls of my houses are made of gold, and that the floor mats in my rooms ... are likewise of gold, and that I was, and claimed to be, a god; ... The houses as you see are of stone and lime and clay ... Then he raised his clothes and showed me his body, saying, 'See that I am of flesh and blood like you and all other men.'" This may have been invented by Cortés.[81] But a Nahuatl speaker would have been very likely to use "floor mats" and "flesh and blood" as important metaphors; their poets did so frequently. Indeed, one is hard-pressed to think of a convincing political reason for Cortés to throw in this particular paragraph. On the other hand, Moctezuma had every reason to make the statement—to minimize the extent of his wealth and in order to work his way around in courtly and indirect speech in true Nahuatl style to his impolite punch line: he wanted it known that he did not believe the Spaniards to be gods. One is even more inclined to read the statement this way in that it is apparently how the Spanish read it then, judging from the style in which both López de Gómara and Bernal Díaz recounted the incident. Bernal Díaz embellished: "You must take the [stories] as a joke, as I take the story of your thunders and lightnings."[82]

If we cannot be certain of what Moctezuma said, we can at least analyze his actions as a text of sorts: indeed, his decision to allow the Spaniards and many hundreds of their Tlaxcalan allies to enter his city has been analyzed for many years as if it were a declaration of sentiment. In lieu of the traditional interpretation that he was a coward or a fool, scholars have proffered various motivations—caution, a desire for secrecy, a need to wait for the dry season.[83] There is a central explanation for Moctezuma's decision, however. Besides attempting to turn the potential conquerors back by offering them annual tribute, the emperor apparently did try to have the Spanish killed at least twice while they were still distant; somebody certainly gave the order to attack them. Yet, when the Spaniards were nearing the city, "Moctezuma did not give orders for anyone to meet them in battle."[84] He could not: he knew now that the Spaniards won battles in the open field. Even if he had had time to arm every warrior in his kingdom and then surround and destroy the Spanish with the sheer force of numbers, he would have been politically destroyed. The casualties would have been immense, beyond anything ever seen, and the people of the Central Valley accepted the arrogance of their Mexica neighbors in exchange for peace and the privilege of living close to power. If the Aztecs could not deliver a quick victory on the outskirts of their own capital, they were doomed; so if his army could not win quickly and easily here—and Moctezuma knew they could not—then they could not fight. At the time, Cortés and his followers did not understand the political situation well enough to grasp this fact; centuries later, posterity tends to lose sight of the realities of that world. Not so those who wrote a few decades later. Said López de Gómara: "It seemed unfitting and dishonorable for him to make war upon Cortés and fight a mere handful of strangers who said they were ambassadors. Another reason was that he did not wish to stir up trouble for himself (and this was the truest reason), for it was clear that he would immediately have to face an uprising among the Otomí, the Tlaxcalans, and many others." Said Bernal Díaz: "Moctezuma's captains and *papas* also advised him that if he tried to prevent our entry *we would fight him in his subject towns.*"[85]

It is reasonable to assume that, while Cortés and his men were in the city gathering information about the kingdom, Moctezuma was also attempting to gather information about them. It may have been his hope that they would eventually leave of their own accord. Almost all accounts except the letter by Cortés indicate that it was Moctezuma's messengers who first told of the arrival of Captain Narváez: it was the Mexican king who told the Spanish the news, not the other way around. Whether Moctezuma was initially behind it or not, his people did raise a rebellion against the Spanish as soon as Cortés returned from the coast. Moctezuma himself became known for the speeches he made from the rooftops in which he asked the warriors to lay down their arms. "Let the Mexica hear: we are not their match, may they be dissuaded [from further fighting]."[86] By then, he was in irons, and so has been seen as a coward doing his best to save his life. But it is possible that he, the warrior king who had led so many successful campaigns, preached peace in relation to the Spanish out of true conviction that his people would be destroyed if they pursued violence. In interpreting his actions, we would do well to remember that if so, *he was right*. Moctezuma, with his knowledge of the capabilities of both sides, was one of the few Mexica in a position to be able to see the *longue durée*.[87]

Inga Clendinnen has studied the reactions of the Mexica warriors to the Spanish. She finds evidence that, despite the great respect the Aztecs had for the horses, they held the Spanish men themselves in outright contempt. When the Spanish returned to retake the city, there is no evidence that the warriors operated according to sacred signs or astrology; instead, they put immediate practicality before all else. Contrary to popular opinion, they did not fight to take prisoners for sacrifice rather than to kill: they did not even want the Spanish for sacrifice, and, when they had a chance to destroy them, did so with a blow to the back of the head, as they did with criminals. In general, the only use the warriors made of sacrifice in this campaign was as a tool to instill terror in the hearts of the Spanish who were close enough to see what they were doing.[88]

We have significant evidence about the military men's attitude toward technology. The Aztecs cleverly used their own inventions against their enemies whenever they could. When the Spanish approached the city in what was to be the final campaign, the Indians secretly opened a dike in an effort to trap the opposing forces on an island that was connected to land by only one causeway.[89] More often, though, the indigenous were in the position of needing to decode Spanish tactics and technology as quickly as possible, rather than showing off their own. Through keen observation, they were able to make remarkable headway. First, there was the question of seizing some of the Spaniards' powerful weapons and learning to use them. They quickly put captured lances to use but recognized that the Spaniards' other

weapons were more powerful: "The crossbowman aimed the bolt well, he pointed it right at the person he was going to shoot, and when it went off, it went whining, hissing and humming. And the arrows missed nothing, they all hit someone, went all the way through someone. The guns were pointed and aimed right at people ... It came upon people unawares, giving no warning when it killed them. However many were fired at died, when some dangerous part was hit: the forehead, the nape of the neck, the heart, the chest, the stomach, or the abdomen."[90] These weapons, however, were more difficult to use: at one point, some captured crossbowmen were apparently either forced to shoot at their countrymen or to give lessons to Aztec soldiers; in either case, the arrows went astray. And the guns of course would not work without powder, even if the Aztecs could have learned to make bullets. When they captured a cannon, they recognized they had neither the expertise nor the ammunition to make it useful to themselves. The best they could do was make it impossible for the Spanish ever to regain it: they wisely sank it in the lake.[91] The second pressing concern was to thwart Spanish technology even if they could not harness it themselves. The natives made extra long spears and managed to take an occasional horseman by surprise, killing the beast and pulling down the rider. Canoe men learned to zigzag so rapidly that guns could not be trained on them, and, once, they were able to lure two Spanish boats into shallow water and capture them.[92] Yet what they could do in this regard was limited.

As frustrated as they were by their technological shortcomings in comparison to the Spanish, at no point do the warriors seem to have responded as if they were awestruck. In one case, the Spanish decided to build a catapult to turn against the city. Cortés wanted to believe that the Indian observers were petrified: "Even if it were to have had no other effect, which indeed it had not, the terror it caused was so great that we thought the enemy might surrender. But neither of our hopes was fulfilled, for the carpenters failed to operate their machine."[93] Little did he know that, in Indian memory, the incident would border on the humorous:

> And then those Spaniards installed a catapult on top of an altar platform with which to hurl stones at the people ... Then they wound it up, then the arm of the catapult rose up. But the stone did not land on the people, but fell [almost straight down] behind the marketplace at Xomolco. Because of that the Spaniards there argued among themselves. They looked as if they were jabbing their fingers in one another's faces, chattering a great deal. And [meanwhile] the catapult kept returning back and forth, going one way and then the other.[94]

Indeed, this relatively straightforward view of Spanish accomplishments is pervasive in Nahua accounts of the war. European technology is mentioned frequently—not as something mystifying in the hands of gods but as the clear and concrete explanation for indigenous military losses. As early as the Annals of Tlatelolco, writers mentioned at the key point in their narration that "the war leaders were dying from the guns and iron bolts." As late as the end of the century, Ixtlilxochitl mentions that a local king decides to heed his sister and not try to stop

Cortés: she warned of "a young man with a light in one hand that would exceed that of the sun, and in the other an *espada*, which was the weapon that this newly arrived nation used."[95] The Florentine Codex, in the middle of the century, is full of the "We are not their match" concept to which Moctezuma gives full voice before he dies; indeed, it is the messengers' comment upon their first return from seeing the newcomers.

Reading Book Twelve from start to finish, including the first part, which contains the obviously revisionist account of the facts, as well as the more faithful second section, one is left with two predominant images—which surely speak to the most profound impressions the Indians received and passed on to their children. Both images are direct reflections of the technological discrepancy between the peoples involved, of which the narrators are clearly very much aware. First, page by page, the mounted Spaniards in their clanking armor with their metallic weapons move ever closer to the great city. That the Spanish had passed through the Iron Age was certainly not lost on the Mexica. The word *tepoztli* (metal, or iron) appears more than any other. The initial report Moctezuma is given is presented in three sections. First come the Spaniards' weapons. "Their war gear was all iron. They clothed their bodies in iron, they put iron on their heads, their swords were iron, their bows were iron, and their shields and lances were iron." Next, the horses are described, and last the vicious dogs who accompany their masters. Later, when the Indians attempt to fight, they lose dramatically. "Not just a few but a huge number of them were destroyed." After killing yet more Indians in Cholula, the Spanish set out again: "Their iron lances and halberds seem to sparkle, and their iron swords were curved like a stream of water. Their cuirasses and iron helmets seemed to make a clattering sound." When they file into Tenochtitlan, their metal weapons and armor are described in even greater detail, filling whole pages.[96]

Secondly, throughout the narrative, although the Indians do not know who the newcomers were, the newcomers know enough about the world to search for Moctezuma; they will not rest until they find him. First, Cortés uses his knowledge to flatter. "I want to see and behold [your city], for word has gone out in Spain that you are very strong, great warriors." The Spaniards ask many questions. "When Moctezuma heard this, that many and persistent inquiries were being made about him, that the gods wanted to see his face, he was greatly anguished." Later: "When they saw [an Aztec general] they said, 'Is this one then Moctezuma?'" On the causeway, Cortés greets the king: "Is it not you? Is it not you then? Moctezuma?" and Moctezuma at last answers, "Yes, it is me."[97] This element makes the indigenous feel at least as vulnerable as do the metal weapons: the Spaniards have somehow used their knowledge to make their way to the heart of Aztec power, but the Aztecs could not begin to envision a similar expedition to the seat of Carlos V. They now knew about the ships, but only a few—probably Moctezuma, for example—had seen the compasses and printed books in the possession of the Spaniards. Ordinary people could only begin to piece together an explanation. What is remarkable is that they knew this is what needed to be explained.

This is a case in which the ending is only the beginning. In the first few years after the conquest was complete, the Aztecs exhibited few signs of believing that gods walked in their midst. Motolinía tells us that, for the first five years, no one paid any attention to the priests who were attempting to reach out to the people. In 1526, the Franciscans held a marriage ceremony for a prince, but when they tried to convince others to follow his example, the Indians said dismissively that Spanish men themselves had more than one woman. When the fathers opened a school and Cortés ordered the indigenous nobles to send their sons, the families sent servants as substitutes. They had no intention of turning their children over to such men and were confident that the newcomers were too stupid or ill informed to know the difference.[98] What would they have said if they could have known that posterity would insist they believed the Spaniards to be divine?

# Notes

I would like to thank the friends and colleagues who read, critiqued, and improved earlier versions of this work: Antonio Barrera, James Lockhart, Frederick Luciani, John Graham Nolan, David Robinson, Andrew Rotter, Kira Stevens, Gary Urton, and Anja Utgennant, as well as Michael Grossberg, Allyn Roberts, and the anonymous *AHR* reviewers.

1. Lesley Byrd Simpson, trans. and ed., *Cortés: The Life of the Conqueror by His Secretary* (Berkeley, Calif., 1965), excerpted from Francisco López de Gómara, *Historia de la conquista de México* (Zaragoza, 1552), 137. (Although all research was conducted in the Spanish originals, in the interest of communication I have here cited published English translations wherever there exists an edition that is generally considered definitive. Where there is none, I have provided translations myself.)

2. Several scholars have recently alluded to the unlikelihood of the commonly accepted scenario, among them Susan D. Gillespie, *The Aztec Kings: The Construction of Rulership in Mexica History* (Tucson, Ariz., 1989); James Lockhart, ed. and trans., *We People Here: Nahuatl Accounts of the Conquest of Mexico* (Berkeley, Calif., 1993); and Ross Hassig, *Time, History and Belief in Aztec and Colonial Mexico* (Austin, Tex., 2001). None have made it the focus of any work. This stands in contrast to South Pacific history, at least as written by anthropologists. Gananath Obeyesekere set out to challenge the "fact" that Captain Cook was received as the god Lono in Hawai'i in 1779 in *The Apotheosis of Captain Cook: European Mythmaking in the Pacific* (Princeton, N.J., 1992), thereby earning for himself several awards but also the anger of Marshall Sahlins in *How "Natives" Think: About Captain Cook, for Example* (Chicago, 1995). Prominent Mexicanists who have accepted the legends include David Carrasco, *Quetzalcoatl and the Irony of Empire: Myths and Prophecies in the Aztec Tradition* (Chicago, 1982); Jacques Lafaye, *Quetzalcóatl and Guadalupe: The Formation of Mexican National Consciousness, 1531–1813*, Benjamin Keen, trans. (Chicago, 1976); Miguel León-Portilla, ed., *The Broken Spears*, Lysander Kemp, trans. (Boston, 1962); and H. B. Nicholson, *Topiltzin Quetzalcoatl: The Once and Future Lord of the Toltecs* (Boulder, Colo., 2001). Similar ideas about the Indians having accepted the newly arrived whites as gods developed elsewhere in the New World as well, but space limitations prevent treatment of that subject here. For musings on the situation in the Andean world, see Olivia Harris,

"'The Coming of the White People': Reflections on the Mythologisation of History in Latin America," *Bulletin of Latin American Research* 14, no. 1 (1995): 9–24.

3. On the word "Aztec": this was a term introduced generations later by outsiders to talk about a political conglomeration. The ethnic group who held power called themselves the Mexica (pronounced me-SHEE-ka). They, and most of the people they governed, were Nahuas, or speakers of the Nahuatl language. For ease of communication, I will most often use the more generally known term. On the nature of the Aztec state: it is now understood by experts that the "empire" in fact consisted of profoundly divided ethnic groups residing in separate city-states, thus rendering it particularly vulnerable to the invading Europeans, as will be discussed. However, in conversations with colleagues from other fields, I have learned that it is essential to state unequivocally that the Aztecs did represent an advanced state—with a capital city larger than any in Europe, a regularized taxation system in which accounts of collections and expenditures were kept, and a profoundly imperialist tendency toward expansionism. For a discussion of the great differences between, for example, the Aztecs and the more nomadic groups familiar to most U.S. historians, see John E. Kicza, *Resilient Cultures: America's Native Peoples Confront European Colonization, 1500–1800* (Upper Saddle River, N.J., 2003).

4. Felipe Fernández-Armesto, "Aztec Auguries and Memories of the Conquest of Mexico," *Renaissance Studies* 6 (1992): 303; Hugh Thomas, *Conquest: Montezuma, Cortés and the Fall of Old Mexico* (London, 1993), 601.

5. Scholars have argued that the Europeans' advanced agricultural lifestyle, alongside animals and their use of ships, contributed to the spread of disease and hence the development of antibodies that the American indigenous did not have. The point may be moot in the case of the defeat of the Aztecs, for, although their soldiers were brought low by smallpox, the same was true of the Spaniards' allies, on whom they relied for their victory. See Ross Hassig, *Mexico and the Spanish Conquest* (London, 1994), 101–02.

6. Fernández-Armesto, "Aztec Auguries," 288.

7. Jared Diamond, *Guns, Germs, and Steel: The Fates of Human Societies* (New York, 1997). Gale Stokes included this Pulitzer Prize-winning book in a review essay, "The Fates of Human Societies: A Review of Recent Macrohistories," *AHR* 106 (April 2001): 508–25. He begins, "Not many historians would subtitle their book, 'The Fates of Human Societies,'" and goes on to say that it is biologist Jared Diamond who has had the nerve. Although Stokes's overall argument is that macrohistory when done well (and he implicitly includes Diamond's work in this category) certainly has its uses, Diamond's theme of "Eurasia-meets-the-rest-of-the-world [and wins]" is lost in the rest of the essay, which focuses instead on the equally interesting question of why Europe, as opposed to China, became the leader of the modern world. Almost nothing has been written about the book in Latin Americanist journals. To my knowledge, only one recent textbook on colonial America opens with an explicit consideration of Diamond's argument: Stanley N. Katz, John M. Murrin, and Douglas Greenberg, eds., *Colonial America: Essays in Politics and Social Development*, 5th edn. (New York, 2001).

8. León-Portilla has done important work beyond the ivory tower as well, bringing Nahuatl-speaking indigenous poets to work at Mexico's most prestigious universities and supporting *indigenista* movements in other ways. His political significance must not be underestimated.

9. Jorge Klor de Alva, "Foreword," to León-Portilla, *Broken Spears*, xi.

10. León-Portilla, *Broken Spears*, 35. Most of the book conveys similar images, coming from texts written in the 1550s and later. As of 2000, a new textbook became available that translates Nahuatl primary sources into English (*Victors and Vanquished: Spanish and Nahua Views of the Conquest of Mexico*, published by Bedford/St. Martin's). The book's editor, Stuart B. Schwartz, is well acquainted with the work of his colleague James Lockhart on early Mexico, and includes mention of some controversy over the existence of the Quetzalcoatl myth—but unfortunately only after recounting the story as if it were true. Books that promise to be helpful in teaching include Matthew Restall, *Seven Myths of the Spanish Conquest* (New York, 2003); Stephanie Wood, *Transcending Conquest: Nahua Views of Spanish Colonial Mexico* (Norman, Okla., forthcoming); and another by James Lockhart (see note 18 below).

11. Tzvetan Todorov, *The Conquest of America: The Question of the Other* (New York, 1984), 63, 69, 75, 87. See Inga Clendinnen's analysis of this text in "Cortés, Signs, and the Conquest of Mexico," in Anthony Grafton and Ann Blair, eds., *The Transmission of Culture in Early Modern Europe* (Philadelphia, 1990). See also Clendinnen, "Fierce and Unnatural Cruelty: Cortés and the Conquest of Mexico," *Representations* 33 (1991): 65–100.

12. On the spelling of the Mexican emperor's name: the English and Germans later used "Montezuma," but none of the players on the scene did. The correct spelling of the name in Nahuatl is debatable and, in any case, somewhat alienating to non-Nahuatl speakers. I am using the most common Spanish form ("Moctezuma") except where quoting someone who uses a different version.

13. Thomas, *Conquest*, 180. There are many such examples in the book. Nor is this argument limited only to Thomas. Viewers of Michael Wood's recent BBC series "Conquistadors" (2000) will not have failed to detect his interest in and sympathy for the Indians. Yet he, too, subscribes to the white gods theory and quotes the *Broken Spears* text verbatim—and without raising hackles. His reviewer in *The Chronicle Review* mentions that he might well be more critical of the "Black Legend" concerning Spain but argues that "his treatment of the natives is politically faultless" (Diana de Armas Wilson, "Killing for God and for Gold," May 4, 2001). There is a beautiful new trade book that likewise takes the old stories for granted: Neil Baldwin, *Legends of the Plumed Serpent: Biography of a Mexican God* (New York, 1998).

14. The most useful edition of Cortés is *Letters from Mexico*, J. H. Elliott, intro., and Anthony Pagden, trans. and ed. (New Haven, Conn., 1986). Bernal Díaz is valuable despite the fact that he takes the structure of his book, almost section by section, from López de Gómara, alternating between plagiarizing his words and arguing vociferously and explicitly with them. A few have even argued that he fantasized his own participation in the conquest, given that he situates himself at the heart of all the action and that his name fails to appear on one list of participants housed in the Archive of the Indies in Spain. But all the chroniclers plagiarized; all exaggerated their own role; and no extant list of men or equipment is complete. There is evidence that he was there (in 1540, both Cortés and the viceroy wrote to the emperor on his behalf), and the text includes many details that only a participant would have thought of or gotten right. The most careful positioning of Bernal Díaz in relation to his contemporaries has been accomplished by Rolena Adorno, "Discourses on Colonialism: Bernal Díaz, Las Casas, and the Twentieth Century Reader," *Modern Language Notes* 103 (1988): 239–58; and "The Discursive Encounter of Spain and America: The Authority of Eyewitness Testimony in the Writing of History," *William and Mary Quarterly* 49 (1992):

210–28. The edition of Bernal Díaz used here is *The Conquest of New Spain*, J. M. Cohen, ed. (London, 1963), trans. from *Historia verdadera de la conquista de la nueva España por Bernal Díaz del Castillo*, Joaquín Ramírez Cabañas, ed. (Mexico City, 1955). The chronicles of Andrés de Tapia and Francisco de Aguilar are found in Patricia de Fuentes, ed., *The Conquistadors: First-Person Accounts of the Conquest of Mexico* (Norman, Okla., 1993). Another supposedly firsthand account is now known as the chronicle of the "Anonymous Conquistador." It appears to have been written by someone who never actually saw Mexico City. Bernardino Vásquez de Tapia also left a brief military summary. Another conquistador named Ruy González later wrote a letter to the king, but, as the latter two do not help significantly with the issue under discussion, I will leave them aside. See Arthur P. Stabler and John E. Kicza, "Ruy González's 1553 Letter to Emperor Charles V: An Annotated Translation," *The Americas* 42 (1986).

15. He had some direct sources: in the earliest days, Motolinía worked with Malinche, the Indian woman translator who had worked with Cortés; later, he came to know well the young Indian nobles who studied Latin and other subjects with the fathers, even though communication was at first minimal. He noted with humor, "The first one who taught singing ... was an old friar who barely knew a single word of the Indians' language,... and he spoke as quickly as if he were speaking to students in Spain. Those of us who heard him could not help laughing ... It was a marvelous thing that even though at first they understood nothing ... in a short time they understood and learned the songs." Fray Toribio de Benavente Motolinía, *Historia de los indios de la Nueva España* (Madrid, 1988), 271.

16. The original is housed in the Laurenziana Medicean Library, Florence. A facsimile edition is *Códice florentino* (Florence, 1979). An English edition is Arthur J. O. Anderson and Charles Dibble, eds., *The Florentine Codex: General History of the Things of New Spain* (Salt Lake City, 1950–82). Sahagún's earliest version of the text is published as *The Primeros Memoriales*, Thelma Sullivan, H. B. Nicholson, Arthur J. O. Anderson, Charles Dibble, Eloise Quiñones, and Wayne Ruwet, eds. (Norman, Okla., 1997). On the Franciscan agenda in general, see John Leddy Phelan, *The Millennial Kingdom of the Franciscans in the New World*, 2d edn. rev. (Berkeley, Calif., 1970).

17. He interviewed extensively, often asking about codices he knew villagers still had, once venting his frustration at "Indian wordiness in telling fables—when anyone is willing to listen to them they go on forever," but generally providing a sympathetic ear and recording certain perspectives that are obviously indigenous. Of course, we must approach his work cautiously: he did, for example, insert statements clearly made by contemporaries into the mouths of historical figures. He has Moctezuma make this bitter speech before the Spaniards arrive: "They will reign and I shall be the last king of this land. Even though some of our descendants and relatives may remain, even though they may be made governors and given states, they will not be true lords and kings but subordinates, like tax collectors or gatherers of the tribute that my ancestors and I have won. Our descendants' only task will be to comply with the commands and orders of the strangers." Diego Durán, *The History of the Indies of New Spain*, Doris Heyden, ed. (Norman, Okla., 1994), 511–12.

18. James Lockhart in *We People Here* has gathered together the only six of these statements that describe the conquest and were written before 1560, after which date it is unlikely that people who had clear memories of the events still lived. This is an invaluable collection because it includes careful transcriptions of both the Nahuatl text and the Spanish summaries, and yet it is accessible to everyone because it includes translations of each. A "student-friendly" edition is in preparation at Stanford University Press.

19. On the methods of interviewing and the names and positions of those Indians who did the interviewing, see Lockhart, *We People Here*; and Alfredo López Austin, "The Research Method of Fray Bernardino de Sahagún," in Munro S. Edmonson, ed., *Sixteenth-Century Mexico: The Work of Sahagún* (Albuquerque, N. Mex., 1974).

20. There were a number of indigenous (or mestizo, but Indian-identified) writers in this period, including a grandson of Moctezuma named Don Fernando de Alvarado Tezozomac, Diego Muñoz Camargo from Tlaxcala, and Don Domingo de San Antón Muñón Chimalpahin from Chalco. None left work as extensive or as useful in the case of this particular project as Ixtlilxochitl, and so in the interest of space, I am leaving them aside. Chimalpahin, however, deserves special mention because he wrote for a Nahua audience. In his accounts, the Spaniards appear not as gods but as a set of foreign invaders. The year summaries for 1519–1522 resemble other year summaries. "The year Three House, 1521: At this time Quauhtemoctzin [Cuauhtemoc] was installed as ruler of Tenochtitlan in Izcalli in the ancient month count, and in February in the Christian month count, when the Spaniards still occupied Tlaxcala. He was a son of Ahuitzotzin." Arthur J. O. Anderson and Susan Schroeder, eds., *Codex Chimalpahin* (Norman, Okla., 1997), 167. See also Susan Schroeder, "Looking Back at the Conquest: Nahua Perceptions of Early Encounters from the Annals of Chimalpahin," in Eloise Quiñones Keber, ed., *Chipping Away on Earth* (Lancaster, Calif., 1994), 377–97.

21. For example: "No me he querido aprovechar de las historias que hartan de esta material, por la diversidad y confusión que tienen entre sí los autores que hartan de ellas, por las falsas relaciones y contrarias interpretaciones que se les dieron." Fernando de Alva Ixtlilxochitl, "Sumaria Relación de la Historia General de Esta Nueva España desde el origen del mundo hasta la Era de Ahora," in *Obras históricas*, Edmundo O'Gorman, ed., vol. 1 (Mexico City, 1975), 525. There is no question that Ixtlilxochitl is a problematic source if one is looking for a "pure" Indian voice: he sometimes relied, for example, on the "Codex Xolotl" (Charles Dibble, ed., *Códice Xolotl* [Mexico City, 1951]), which is clearly a post-conquest creation, and he was personally and politically embedded in elite Creole culture. For a discussion of the latter issue, see Jorge Cañizares-Esguerra, *How to Write the History of the New World: Historiographies, Epistemologies, and Identities in the Eighteenth-Century Atlantic World* (Stanford, Calif., 2001), esp. 221–25. I read him, however, as having a distinctly indigenous perspective in subtle ways. For example, he inserts "por lengua de Marina" (through the words of Malinche) frequently when summarizing communications made with the Spanish—even, in one case, when a local king was asking Cortés and his men to accept some local girls as sleeping partners. "Historia de la nación chichimeca," in *Obras históricas*, O'Gorman, ed., vol. 2 (Mexico City, 1977), 214.

22. Lockhart, *We People Here*, 5.

23. Lockhart, *We People Here*, 18. It is worth noting that other sources purportedly based on interviews with those involved reflect this same bipartite treatment—a history that reads like a recitation of myths suddenly becomes a detailed and realistic description of battle scenes. See Ixtlilxochitl, "Compendio Histórico del Reino de Texcoco," in *Obras históricas*, vol. 1. Ross Hassig also concludes after working extensively with the second part of Book Twelve, "The Aztecs did not lose their faith, they lost a war." *Mexico and the Spanish Conquest*, 149.

24. The one exception was the Tlaxcalan Diego Muñoz Camargo. Writing in 1580, he claimed that people in his city were also pre-occupied with the foretellings of the white gods, but as proof he offered the same set of omens that took the Aztec capital as their point of reference, "an unimaginable attribute of a source resting on authentic Tlaxcalan tradition" (Lockhart, *We People Here*, 17). The repetition of details shows that Muñoz Camargo clearly copied straight from the Florentine.

25. Fernández-Armesto, "Aztec Auguries."

26. Durán, *History of the Indies of New Spain*, 493. This is a motif in Durán's text.

27. In other versions, less famous to us today, the seers and sorcerers similarly speak the Truth, but to no effect because Moctezuma has grown proud and will not listen. See Stephen Colston, "'No Longer Will There Be a Mexico': Omens, Prophecies, and the Conquest of the Aztec Empire," *American Indian Quarterly* 9 (1985): 244. Ixtlilxochitl relies on this tradition in "Compendio Histórico del Reino de Texcoco," in *Obras históricas*, 1: 450–51. Additionally, Sahagún's young men were mostly from Tlatelolco, once a neighboring city-state, not Tenochtitlan proper, and although they were in many ways identified with the Aztecs, their ancestors had in fact been conquered; thus, as Kevin Terraciano has pointed out to me in a personal communication, they may have found it satisfying to represent the heart of the Aztec state as crumbling in panic.

28. Gillespie, *Aztec Kings*, esp. 197–98. For a detailed study of the feathered serpent motif throughout Mesoamerica, see Enrique Florescano, *The Myth of Quetzalcoatl* (Baltimore, 1999).

29. Following is a drastic oversimplification of the transformation of the narrative: I refer the reader to Gillespie's *Aztec Kings* for further details (185–95). In the 1530s, in the first three Spanish texts recounting Aztec history, supposedly as told to the writers by locals, two would-be kings fight, and one ends up leading his followers away (also a common trope in the pre-Hispanic codices); in one version, probably recorded by a well-known friar and linguist, Andres de Olmos, the important hero is named Ce Acatl (One Reed), which is as close as we come to the name "Quetzalcoatl." In the early 1540s, however, while the mortal hero is still "Huemac" in the Nahuatl text "Historia Tolteca Chichimeca" from the Puebla area, he is in Spanish texts explicitly named Quetzalcoatl, apparently in honor of the god in several cases, or as a man who was deified after his death (a common element of European mythology) in Motolinía's and Andrés de Tapia's works.

30. Motolinía, *Historia de los Indios*, 107–08.

31. For a full treatment of the church's intellectual wrestling with the Indian question, see Lafaye, *Quetzalcoatl and Guadalupe*. The most popular version among clerics held it that Quetzalcoatl had in fact been the apostle St. Thomas. It was not only the New World's Christian missionaries who looked for evidence that God had sent previous emissaries to the lands they hoped to convert. By the late sixteenth century, the Jesuits in China also believed they had found proof of an earlier presence. (Personal communication from David Robinson.)

32. At the end of the century, various authors continued to "mix and match" the contrasting elements. In the case of Ixtlilxochitl, his personal trajectory regarding the legend closely paralleled that of his century. As a very young man, while he is still according to his own testimony struggling simply to decipher certain codices or stories and summarize them, he describes the rise and fall of the hero Topiltzin, making no mention whatsoever of Quetzalcoatl or of anyone fleeing by sea or promising to return. There is a fragmentary document attached to a later work, apparently intended to be a commentary on an accompanying picture, now lost, in which he suddenly says that Topiltzin at last went east and died there and was burned to ashes along with all his treasure, but that he promised to return in the year One Reed, which was when the Spanish came. In a later work, Ixtlilxochitl introduces a section on the pre-Toltec period, which he had never mentioned before, and here he presents a sinless virgin hero "whom they called Quetzalcoatl, or by another name, Huemac" who had come from the east and would come again. The character does not appear anywhere else in the volume; the narrative continues in a more traditional vein. In the magnum opus he wrote before his death, Ixtlilxochitl begins with a full chapter on Quetzalcoatl, who by now is a fully delineated character, indeed, the first great historian of the Americas (implicitly a precursor to Ixtlilxochitl himself), who leaves records of his own great works for posterity to find, and who passes away by sea, promising that when he returned his children would become "the lords and possessors of the earth." Thus Ixtlilxochitl left Aztec history intact yet framed it between the by-now expected departure of the early saint and the arrival of the Spanish. Ixtlilxochitl, "Sumaria Relación de las cosas de la Nueva España" [c. 1600] (273, 387), and "Compendio Histórico del Reino de Texcoco" [c. 1608] (529), in *Obras históricas*, vol. 1; Ixtlilxochitl, "Historia de la Nación Chichimeca," in *Obras históricas*, 2: 7–9. Durán inserts the story even more awkwardly into his manuscript.

33. Lockhart, *We People Here*, 20.

34. Durán, *History of the Indies*, 499–500.

35. This phrase was used in writing a few more times in the sixteenth century, and Lockhart has taken it as the very apt title of his book.

36. "Annals of Tlaltelolco" and "Historia Tolteca-Chichimeca," both in Lockhart, *We People Here*, 271, 287.

37. "Book Twelve of the Florentine Codex," in Lockhart, *We People Here*, 244, 179, 252, respectively. The priest's resistance to using the term that binds him as a vassal is particularly noteworthy in that the Spanish tortured those Mexica leaders who did not participate in helping them locate missing gold and jewels.

38. Louise Burkhart has studied the Franciscans' early efforts to "translate" religion. Theirs was no easy task, as the Nahuas did not see the universe as a struggle between good and evil but rather between order and chaos. There was, for example, no word for "sin," and so the word for "damage" was made to suffice. By the 1530s, the word chosen for "devil" or "demon" was *tlacatecolotl*, or human-owl, a shape-changing sorcerer of legends, so that *teotl* could mean "God" in the Christian sense. In 1519, however, the Spanish were on their own in trying to understand and translate Nahuatl concepts. They seem to have come remarkably close in their initial comprehension of what they were being called. "A single divine principle—*teotl*—was responsible for the nature of the cosmos, negative aspects of it as well as positive ones ... *Teotl* could manifest itself in ritual objects, images, and human deity-impersonators—forms not necessarily consistent with the Western conception of deity." Burkhart, *The Slippery Earth: Nahua-Christian Moral Dialogue in Sixteenth-Century Mexico* (Tucson, Ariz., 1989), 36–42.

39. Bernal Díaz, *Conquest of New Spain*, 112, 117.

40. Durán, *History of the Indies*, 513, 524–25.

41. In the Florentine Codex, for example, Sahagún's students wrote that when Moctezuma was in hopes of establishing a tributary relationship with the Spanish by giving them annual gifts, he ordered his men, "Xicmotlatlauhtilican in totecuio in teotl." This translates best as "Address our political lord, the *teul*, in a courtly

manner," but it was given in the Spanish gloss done by Sahagún as "Worship the god in my name." Lockhart, *We People Here*, 68–69.

42. Motolinía, *Historia de los Indios*, 193–94. A similar corruption that became a permanent name, with no meaning attached, is "Malinche." After receiving her as a slave, the Spaniards christened her "Marina." As she was the all-important translator, the Indians added the honorific "-tzin" and called her "Malintzin." (They did not have the sound for "r" in their language.) The Spanish heard "Malinchi" or "Malinche," and that became her name, familiar to both groups, with few people knowing how it had come about.

43. Cortés, "Second Letter," in Elliott and Pagden, *Letters from Mexico*, 51. It is important to note that, in the earliest dealings with the Nahuas, it was the lord of Cempoala who took the initiative and made overtures to Cortés, not the other way around.

44. James Lockhart and Stuart Schwartz have noted in *Early Latin America* (Cambridge, 1983) both that a standard mode of operation was developed early on in the period of conquest and that the Aztecs more than any other group gave the Spaniards pause. I would argue that by the time Pizarro faced Atahualpa in Peru, he had reason to have greater confidence than Cortés could immediately have had that he could use the techniques even when facing a great empire.

45. J. H. Elliott, "Introduction," to Cortés, *Letters from Mexico*; Clendinnen, "Cortés, Signs, and the Conquest of Mexico." See also Eulalia Guzmán, *Relaciones de Hernán Cortés a Carlos V sobre la invasión de Anahuac* (Mexico City, 1958).

46. Francis Brooks, "Motecuzoma Xocoyotl, Hernán Cortés and Bernal Díaz del Castillo: The Construction of an Arrest," *Hispanic American Historical Review* 75 (1995): 164–65. López de Gómara did see the awkwardness of the communication issue, and wrote, "Now that Cortés saw himself rich and powerful, he formed three plans: One was to send to Santo Domingo and the other islands news of the country and his good fortune." He then implied that Cortés had never quite had the time to see to it before Captain Narváez and his men appeared. López de Gómara, *Cortés: The Life of the Conqueror*, 187.

47. Cortés, "Second Letter," in Elliott and Pagden, *Letters from Mexico*, 113.

48. Brooks, "Motecuzoma," 181; Durán, *History of the Indies*, 531.

49. This even includes López de Gómara, usually faithful to the Cortesian narrative, in *Cortés: The Life of the Conqueror*, 188–89.

50. The fact that no Spaniard ever publicly accused Cortés of lying about his ability to arrest the Mexican king within a week of his arrival is not as significant as it first appears. Even those many conquistadors who later came to hate him (and even testify against him on other matters, financial and personal) would have understood, consciously and unconsciously, the importance of maintaining a united voice regarding the Spanish legal right to govern the indigenous population. Juan Cano, married to Moctezuma's daughter Isabel, did later claim in a lawsuit over his wife's inheritance that it was untrue that the Mexica lords had gathered before the conquest to swear loyalty to the Spanish and cede their property, or that, if they had gathered together, they could not possibly have understood the purport of the proceedings. Significantly, he reversed himself in his next document and attempted to use other legal precedents to protect his wife's property: someone had apparently made it quite clear to him how quickly he would lose the judges' sympathy if he touched on the issue of the Spanish right to rule in the first place. For the latter,

see "Relaciones de la Nueva España" (Madrid, 1990), 153, cited in Thomas, *Conquest*, 325.

51. Cortés, "Second Letter," in Elliott and Pagden, *Letters from Mexico*, 107; Bernal Díaz, *Conquest of New Spain*, 276.

52. "The Chronicle of Fray Francisco de Aguilar," in Fuentes, *Conquistadors*, 148.

53. "The Chronicle of Andrés de Tapia," in Fuentes, *Conquistadors*, 39.

54. "Chronicle of Andrés de Tapia," in Fuentes, *Conquistadors*, 44.

55. Motolinía skipped from Moctezuma's welcoming speech on the causeway to the arrival of Narváez, without addressing who ruled in the interim (*Historia de los Indios*, 55). Durán writes in his own inimitable style: "According to traditions and to paintings kept by certain [indigenous] elders, it is said that Motecuhzoma left the sanctuary with his feet in chains [the day he welcomed the Spaniards]. And I saw this in a painting that belonged to an ancient chieftain from the province of Tezcoco. Motecuhzoma was depicted in irons, wrapped in a mantle and carried on the shoulders of his dignitaries. This seems difficult to believe, since I have never met a Spaniard who will concede this point to me. But as all of them deny other things that have always been obvious, and remain silent about them in their histories, writings and narrations, I am sure they would also deny and omit this, one of the worst and most atrocious acts committed by them. A conqueror, who is now a friar, told me that though the imprisonment of Motecuhzoma might be true, it was done with the idea of protecting the lives of the Spanish captain and his men" (*History of the Indies*, 530–31). Durán, anxious to demonstrate the ways in which the Indians were victimized, is willing to move the day of arrest forward to the day of arrival—even more impossible to believe. But his source is a native picture that would, if in the standard format, only have been meant to portray a significant episode, not necessarily to give it a date. It was apparently that same native source that told Durán Moctezuma had been imprisoned eighty days. Interestingly, the "conqueror who is now a friar" was probably Aguilar, who said in his statement for public consumption that Moctezuma had been arrested as a traitor to the Spanish king, not in a desperate power ploy intended to protect their own lives.

56. "Annals of Tlaltelolco," in Lockhart, *We People Here*, 257. There has been controversy surrounding the age of this manuscript, as it bears the date "1528" in the scribe's handwriting, but this would not have been possible, as Nahuatl speakers had not yet learned to write their language in the Latin alphabet. Lockhart convincingly dates it to the 1540s in *We People Here*, 39–42. This document's potentially very early date makes it essential that we consult it in the general matter under discussion in this article. Even though it makes no reference whatsoever to Cortés being taken for Quetzalcoatl, it does use the word *teotl* or "god" to designate the Spaniards, as we would expect, given the analysis of Book Twelve. What the speakers may have meant by this has been addressed by Anja Utgennant, University of Cologne, "Gods, Christians and Enemies: The Representation of the Conquerors in a Nahuatl Account," paper presented at "El Cambio Cultural en el México del siglo XVI," University of Vienna, June 6–13, 2002.

57. Cortés, "Third Letter," in Elliott and Pagden, *Letters from Mexico*, 176.

58. Hassig, *Mexico and the Spanish Conquest*, 52, 65–68. Hassig notes that a few did fall to slingstones, and others died when minor wounds became infected.

59. Cortés, "Third Letter," in Elliott and Pagden, *Letters from Mexico*, 212.

60. Cortés, "Second Letter" (131) and "Third Letter" (218), in Elliott and Pagden, *Letters from Mexico*. There are numerous additional examples.

61. Cortés, "Second Letter," in Elliott and Pagden, *Letters from Mexico*, 60, 62, 66. In case Cortés had some unfathomable reason for making this story up, confirmation is easily found in the words of a Tlaxcalan warrior as recounted to Durán: "If you wish to have my opinion I shall give it to you: have pity upon your children, brothers, the old men and women and orphans who are to die, all of them innocent, perishing only because we [noblemen] wish to make a defense." *History of the Indies*, 522. Some of the other conquistadors clearly felt squeamish about this, or wanted to defend themselves from the likes of Las Casas, for later accounts include strange stories of villages they could have plundered at this point but did not. (See Aguilar, Tapia, and Bernal Díaz.) Durán notes the inconsistency and says the Indians definitely remembered events the way Cortés did.

62. Cortés, "Second Letter," in Elliott and Pagden, *Letters from Mexico*, 156, 158.

63. Cortés, "The Third Letter," in Elliott and Pagden, *Letters from Mexico*, 181. The Florentine Codex, like Durán, confirms these stories, only telling them with a tragic rather than triumphant tone.

64. Two were sent to the aid of Narváez; four constituted an independently got-up exploratory venture from Jamaica, and one was sent by Cortés's father in Spain.

65. Aguilar, in Fuentes, *Conquistadors*, 157; Bernal Díaz, in *Conquest of New Spain*, 309, also comments on the affection and joy with which new arrivals were greeted.

66. Cortés, "Third Letter," in Elliott and Pagden, *Letters from Mexico*, 182. See also 147–48, 164–65, 191–92.

67. Cortés, "Third Letter," in Elliott and Pagden, *Letters from Mexico*, 207.

68. Cortés, "Third Letter," in Elliott and Pagden, *Letters from Mexico*, 221, 247.

69. Jonathan D. Spence, *The Memory Palace of Matteo Ricci* (New York, 1984), 22.

70. Todorov, *Conquest of America*, 13. Indeed, Columbus annotated his copy of Marco Polo's book.

71. One of the speakers created by Sir Thomas More in *Utopia* was supposed to have sailed with Vespucci: his utopia was thus a New World island. More drew explicitly from Vespucci's 1504 work as well as from Martyr's 1511 volume, seamlessly stirring in elements of ancient European tales of fantasy. It was a popular book: *Utopia* was published in Latin in 1516, 1517, 1518, and 1519, in German in 1524, and in English in 1551. Interestingly, the 1517 edition contained a map of "Utopia" drawn by Ambrosius Holbein (younger brother to Hans Holbein); it bears striking resemblances to a stylized map of Tenochtitlan that appeared in Nuremberg in 1524 in a Latin translation of Cortés's Second and Third Letters (supposedly based on a sketch sent back by Cortés).

72. Lewis Hanke, *The Spanish Struggle for Justice in the Conquest of America* (Philadelphia, 1949), 9. Jared Diamond in his previously cited chapter "Collision at Cajamarca: Why the Inca Emperor Atahualpa Did Not Capture King Charles I of Spain," in *Guns, Germs, and Steel*, shows in an interesting way that Spanish guns alone could not have accomplished Pizarro's purpose for him but that the total constellation of Spanish technology was of paramount importance.

73. Dürer's diary, quoted in Benjamin Keen, *The Aztec Image in Western Thought* (New Brunswick, N.J., 1971), 69.

74. We must sift our usual expectations. The Spanish, for example, imagined that the Nahuas were overawed by their first sight of European ships, and we have tended to repeat this. In fact, they seem to have recognized them for what they were—boats that were larger and more impressive than their own. Durán asserts that the native messenger found them "wondrous and terrifying" but then elaborates that the messenger "described how, while he had been walking next to the seashore, he had seen a round [water]hill [the same word used for "village" or "settlement"] or [water]house [same word used for "boat"] moving from one side to another until it had anchored next to some rocks on the beach." Durán, *History of the Indies*, 495. Durán's text gives the Spanish for "hill" and "house," contributing to the myth that the Indians perceived the boats as floating mountains or great houses, like temples. However, any Nahuatl speaker cannot help but wonder what his Nahuatl source originally said, as the word for "village" or "settlement" in Nahuatl is "water-hill," and the word for "boat" is "water-house." Thus it is quite likely that the speaker meant to say, "He saw some sort of settlement, a boat, moving from side to side," and his Spanish hearer or reader mistakenly removed the prefix meaning "water" from the two words, thinking it referred to the fact that the messenger had seen these things in the water. This view is supported by another messenger's comment a few pages later (505): "Before showing him the paintings he narrated that some men would come to this land in a great wooden hill. This wooden hill would be so big that it would lodge many men, serving them as a home. Within it they would eat and sleep." In the Florentine Codex, after the famous hyperbole, Moctezuma's emissaries reached the Spanish ship by canoe and reported matter-of-factly: "They [the newcomers] hitched the prow of the [Indians'] boat with an iron staff and hauled them in. Then they put down a ladder" (Lockhart, *We People Here*, 70).

75. Several conquistadors, Durán's source, and the Florentine Codex all refer to this event.

76. Cortés, "Second Letter," in Elliott and Pagden, *Letters from Mexico*, 94. Walter Mignolo, *The Darker Side of the Renaissance: Literacy, Territoriality and Colonization* (Ann Arbor, Mich., 1995), studies Spanish resistance to seeing the kinds of information conveyed in Aztec records and maps; see esp. 296–313. On the topic in general, start with Elizabeth Hill Boone, "Aztec Pictorial Histories: Records without Words," in Boone and Mignolo, eds., *Writing without Words: Alternative Literacies in Mesoamerica and the Andes* (Durham, N. C., 1994).

77. Florentine Codex, in Lockhart, *We People Here*, 94.

78. Bernal Díaz, *Conquest of New Spain*, 222.

79. Durán, *History of the Indies*, 503–06.

80. Some form of the speech Cortés attributes to Moctezuma appears in most of the later Spanish accounts, and a variation in the Florentine Codex. For several centuries, it was assumed that these sources were quoting the king verbatim; more recently, it has been assumed that the king said nothing of the kind. The truth probably lies in between. For examples of courtly Nahuatl speech, see Frances Karttunen and James Lockhart, eds., *The Art of Nahuatl Speech: The Bancroft Dialogues* (Los Angeles, 1987).

81. J. H. Elliott, "The Mental World of Hernán Cortés," *Transactions of the Royal Historical Society*, 5th ser., 17 (1967): 41–58.

82. López de Gómara, *Cortés: The Life of the Conqueror*, 140–42; Bernal Díaz, *Conquest of New Spain*, 223–24.

83. See esp. Clendinnen, "Cortés, Signs, and the Conquest of Mexico," 97–98; and Hassig, *Mexico and the Spanish Conquest*, 77.

84. Florentine Codex, in Lockhart, *We People Here*, 106.

85. López de Gómara, *Cortés: The Life of the Conqueror*, 134; Bernal Díaz, *Conquest of New Spain*, 205 (emphasis added).

86. Florentine Codex, in Lockhart, *We People Here*, 138. Almost all the sources mention such speeches on his part.

87. It is possible to get a sense of what the commoners thought about the Spanish during all this time. Nahua sources refer not only to the foreigners' insatiable demand for gold but also to the overwhelming quantities of food and water that they consumed—and that the city folk were asked by Moctezuma to provide. Not only food, added Sahagún's students, but also hundreds of bowls, pitchers, and pans. One presumes that there may also have been the usual tensions over women, but only a single particularly egregious incident regarding lewd glances at sacred women made its way into the oral tradition that was passed on to Sahagún. "[Before the ceremonies] the women who had fasted for a year ground up the amaranth ... in the temple courtyard. The Spaniards came out well adorned in battle equipment ... arrayed as warriors. They passed among the grinding women, circling around them, looking at each one, looking upon their faces. And when they were through looking at them, they went into the great palace." Far from regarding the Spanish as gods, the city dwellers apparently saw them as dish thieves and profaners of the sacred. Florentine Codex, in Lockhart, *We People Here*, 122, 128.

88. Clendinnen, "Cortés, Signs, and the Conquest of Mexico," esp. 107–14. She notes that there may have been one exception—a single incident in which the Indians seem to have come close to killing Cortés and apparently chose not to, perhaps hoping to take him alive so as to sacrifice his still-beating heart to the gods. Hassig, *Time, History and Belief*, echoes her incredulity that Aztec political and military leaders were making practical decisions based on religious tradition rather than realpolitik.

89. Cortés, "Third Letter," in Elliott and Pagden, *Letters from Mexico*, 175.

90. Florentine Codex, in Lockhart, *We People Here*, 146.

91. Clendinnen, "Cortés, Signs, and the Conquest of Mexico,"107; and Hassig, *Mexico and the Spanish Conquest*, 121, both working with the texts of Cortés, Bernal Díaz, Durán, and the Florentine Codex. It is possible that Indians were learning to make some of the Spanish goods, since Cortés mentions having nails, pitch, oars, and sails made locally, but he probably meant that Spaniards were manufacturing them. "Second Letter," in Elliott and Pagden, *Letters from Mexico*, 157.

92. The Spanish describe such memorable events as atrocities, but they are recounted with pride in the Florentine Codex; Lockhart, *We People Here*, 188, 192, 210, 232. For a thorough discussion, see Hassig, *Mexico and the Spanish Conquest*, 129–33.

93. Cortés, "Third Letter," in Elliott and Pagden, *Letters from Mexico*, 257.

94. Florentine Codex, in Lockhart, *We People Here*, 230. Lockhart also comments on this incident in the same volume (7).

95. Ixtlilxochitl, "Historia de la Nación Chichimeca," in *Obras históricas*, 2: 244.

96. Florentine Codex, in Lockhart, *We People Here*, 80, 90, 96, 110.

97. Florentine Codex, in Lockhart, *We People Here*, 74, 86, 98, 116.

98. Motolinía, *Historia de los Indios*, 147–48, 173, 276. If we believe that the 1540s write-up of the initial conversations between the Franciscan Apostles and the Aztec priests represents a close approximation of what was said, then we have a 1524 indigenous statement to the effect that not only are the Spaniards not divine but they do not even have the right to determine how the indigenous shall worship. The speech begins with exaggerated courtesy, "Our lords, leading personages of much esteem, you are very welcome to our lands and towns. We ourselves, being inferior and base, are unworthy of looking upon the faces of such valiant personages." In true courtly Nahuatl style, the speaker builds gradually to his point: "All of us together feel that it is enough to have lost, enough that the power and royal jurisdiction have been taken from us. As for our gods, we will die before giving up serving and worshiping them. This is our determination; do what you will ... We have no more to say, lords." "Chapter 7: In Which the Reply of the Principal Holy Men to the Twelve Is Found," *Coloquios y doctrina cristiana*, in Kenneth Mills and William B. Taylor, eds., *Colonial Spanish America: A Documentary History* (Wilmington, Del., 1998), 21–22. Jorge Klor de Alva has worked extensively with the *coloquios* on the question of their veracity. See, for example, "The Aztec-Spanish Dialogues of 1524," *Alcheringia/Ethnopoetics* 4 (1980): 52–193. While acknowledging that we have only a text based on notes made at the time, he asserts the probability that the notes reflect a genuine resistance to the Spanish priests, as other evidence suggests. The notion that the Aztecs simply accepted what the Christians had to say in a "spiritual conquest" has been abandoned by scholars. To begin, see Burkhart, *Slippery Earth*; and most recently, Viviana Díaz Balsera, "A Judeo-Christian Tlaloc or a Nahua Yahweh? Domination, Hybridity and Continuity in the Nahua Evangelization Theater," *Colonial Latin American Review* 10 (2001): 209–28.

**CAMILLA TOWNSEND** is an associate professor of history at Colgate University. She is a comparativist, whose book *Tales of Two Cities: Race and Economic Culture in Early Republican North and South America* (Austin, Tex., 2000) explores contrasting colonial legacies in the Chesapeake and the Andean region. Recently, she has concluded that New Spain is crucial to comparative colonial studies and has made the study of Nahuatl her focus. Her book *Malintzin: The Woman Who Went with Cortés* is forthcoming from the University of New Mexico Press, and a study of "The Chalcan Woman's Song" in the *Canares Mexicanos* is in process.

From *The American Historical Review*, Vol. 108, no. 3, June 2003, pp. 659–687. Copyright © 2003 by American Historical Association. Reprinted by permission of the American Historical Association and Camilla Townsend.

# The Price of Progress

JOHN BODLEY

*In aiming at progress... you must let no one suffer by too drastic a measure, nor pay too high a price in upheaval and devastation, for your innovation.*

Maunier, 1949: 725

UNTIL RECENTLY, GOVERNMENT planners have always considered economic development and progress beneficial goals that all societies should want to strive toward. The social advantage of progress—as defined in terms of increased incomes, higher standards of living, greater security, and better health—are thought to be positive, *universal* goods, to be obtained at any price. Although one may argue that tribal peoples must sacrifice their traditional cultures to obtain these benefits, government planners generally feel that this is a small price to pay for such obvious advantages.

In earlier chapters [in *Victims of Progress*, 3rd ed.], evidence was presented to demonstrate that autonomous tribal peoples have not *chosen* progress to enjoy its advantages, but that governments have *pushed* progress upon them to obtain tribal resources, not primarily to share with the tribal peoples the benefits of progress. It has also been shown that the price of forcing progress on unwilling recipients has involved the deaths of millions of tribal people, as well as their loss of land, political sovereignty, and the right to follow their own life style. This chapter does not attempt to further summarize that aspect of the cost of progress, but instead analyzes the specific effects of the participation of tribal peoples in the world-market economy. In direct opposition to the usual interpretation, it is argued here that the benefits of progress are often both illusory and detrimental to tribal peoples when they have not been allowed to control their own resources and define their relationship to the market economy.

## Progress and the Quality of Life

One of the primary difficulties in assessing the benefits of progress and economic development for any culture is that of establishing a meaningful measure of both benefit and detriment. It is widely recognized that *standard of living*, which is the most frequently used measure of progress, is an intrinsically ethnocentric concept relying heavily upon indicators that lack universal cultural relevance. Such factors as GNP, per capita income, capital formation, employment rates, literacy, formal education, consumption of manufactured goods, number of doctors and hospital beds per thousand persons, and the amount of money spent on government welfare and health programs may be irrelevant measures of actual *quality* of life for autonomous or even semiautonomous tribal cultures. In its 1954 report, the Trust Territory government indicated that since the Micronesian population was still largely satisfying its own needs within a cashless subsistence economy, "Money income is not a significant measure of living standards, production, or well-being in this area" (TTR, 1953: 44). Unfortunately, within a short time the government began to rely on an enumeration of certain imported consumer goods as indicators of a higher standard of living in the islands, even though many tradition-oriented islanders felt that these new goods symbolized a lowering of the quality of life.

A more useful measure of the benefits of progress might be based on a formula for evaluating cultures devised by Goldschmidt (1952: 135). According to these less ethnocentric criteria, the important question to ask is: Does progress or economic development increase or decrease a given culture's ability to satisfy the physical and psychological needs of its population, or its stability? This question is a far more direct measure of quality of life than are the standard economic correlates of development, and it is universally relevant. Specific indication of this *standard* of living could be found for any society in the nutritional status and general physical and mental health of its population, the incidence of crime and delinquency, the demographic structure, family stability, and the society's relationship to its natural resource base. A society with high rates of malnutrition and crime, and one degrading its natural environment to the extent of threatening its continued existence, might be described as at a lower standard of living than is another society where these problems did not exist.

Careful examination of the data, which compare, on these specific points, the former condition of self-sufficient tribal peoples with their condition following their incorporation into the world-market economy, leads to the conclusion that their standard of living is *lowered*, not raised, by economic progress—and often to a dramatic degree. This is perhaps the most outstanding and inescapable fact to emerge from the years of research that anthropologists have devoted to the study of culture change and modernization. Despite the best intentions of those who have promoted change and improvement, all too often the results have been poverty, longer working hours, and much greater physical exertion, poor health, social disorder, discontent, discrimination, overpopulation, and environmental deterioration—combined with the destruction of the traditional culture.

# Diseases of Development

*Perhaps it would be useful for public health specialists to start talking about a new category of diseases.... Such diseases could be called the "diseases of development" and would consist of those pathological conditions which are based on the usually unanticipated consequences of the implementation of developmental schemes.*

Hughes & Hunter, 1972: 93

Economic development increases the disease rate of affected peoples in at least three ways. First, to the extent that development is successful, it makes developed populations suddenly become vulnerable to all of the diseases suffered almost exclusively by "advanced" peoples. Among these are diabetes, obesity, hypertension, and a variety of circulatory problems. Second, development disturbs traditional environmental balances and may dramatically increase certain bacterial and parasite diseases. Finally, when development goals prove unattainable, an assortment of poverty diseases may appear in association with the crowded conditions of urban slums and the general breakdown in traditional socioeconomic systems.

Outstanding examples of the first situation can be seen in the Pacific, where some of the most successfully developed native peoples are found. In Micronesia, where development has progressed more rapidly than perhaps anywhere else, between 1958 and 1972 the population doubled, but the number of patients treated for heart disease in the local hospitals nearly tripled, mental disorder increased eightfold, and by 1972 hypertension and nutritional deficiencies began to make significant appearances for the first time (TTR, 1959, 1973, statistical tables).

Although some critics argue that the Micronesian figures simply represent better health monitoring due to economic progress, rigorously controlled data from Polynesia show a similar trend. The progressive acquisition of modern degenerative diseases was documented by an eight-member team of New Zealand medical specialists, anthropologists, and nutritionists, whose research was funded by the Medical Research Council of New Zealand and the World Health Organization. These researchers investigated the health status of a genetically related population at various points along a continuum of increasing cash income, modernizing diet, and urbanization. The extremes on this acculturation continuum were represented by the relatively traditional Pukapukans of the Cook Islands and the essentially Europeanized New Zealand Maori, while the busily developing Rarotongans, also of the Cook Islands, occupied the intermediate position. In 1971, after eight years of work, the team's preliminary findings were summarized by Dr. Ian Prior, cardiologist and leader of the research, as follows:

*We are beginning to observe that the more an islander takes on the ways of the West, the more prone he is to succumb to our degenerative diseases. In fact, it does not seem too much to say our evidence now shows that the farther the Pacific natives move from the quiet, care-free life of their ancestors, the closer they come to gout, diabetes, atherosclerosis, obesity, and hypertension.*

Prior, 1971: 2

In Pukapuka, where progress was limited by the island's small size and its isolated location some 480 kilometers from the nearest port, the annual per capita income was only about thirty-six dollars and the economy remained essentially at a subsistence level. Resources were limited and the area was visited by trading ships only three or four times a year; thus, there was little opportunity for intensive economic development. Predictably, the population of Pukapuka was characterized by relatively low levels of imported sugar and salt intake, and a presumably related low level of heart disease, high blood pressure, and diabetes. In Rarotonga, where economic success was introducing town life, imported food, and motorcycles, sugar and salt intakes nearly tripled, high blood pressure increased approximately ninefold, diabetes two- to threefold, and heart disease doubled for men and more than quadrupled for women, while the number of grossly obese women increased more than tenfold. Among the New Zealand Maori, sugar intake was nearly eight times that of the Pukapukans, gout in men was nearly double its rate on Pukapuka, and diabetes in men was more than fivefold higher, while heart disease in women had increased more than sixfold. The Maori were, in fact, dying of "European" diseases at a greater rate than was the average New Zealand European.

Government development policies designed to bring about changes in local hydrology, vegetation, and settlement patterns and to increase population mobility, and even programs aimed at reducing certain diseases, have frequently led to dramatic increases in disease rates because of the unforeseen effects of disturbing the preexisting order. Hughes and Hunter (1972) published an excellent survey of cases in which development led directly to increased disease rates in Africa. They concluded that hasty development intervention in relatively balanced local cultures and environments resulted in "a drastic deterioration in the social and economic conditions of life."

Traditional populations in general have presumably learned to live with the endemic pathogens of their environments, and in some cases they have evolved genetic adaptations to specific diseases, such as the sickle-cell trait, which provided an immunity to malaria. Unfortunately, however, outside intervention has entirely changed this picture. In the late 1960s, sleeping sickness suddenly increased in many areas of Africa and even spread to areas where it did not formerly occur, due to the building of new roads and migratory labor, both of which caused increased population movement. Large-scale relocation schemes, such as the Zande Scheme, had disastrous results when natives were moved from their traditional disease-free refuges into infected areas. Dams and irrigation developments inadvertently created ideal conditions for the rapid proliferation of snails carrying schistosomiasis (a liver fluke disease), and major epidemics suddenly occurred in areas where this disease had never before been a problem. DDT spraying programs have been temporarily successful in controlling malaria, but there is often a rebound effect that increases the problem when spraying is discontinued, and the malarial mosquitoes are continually evolving resistant strains.

Urbanization is one of the prime measures of development, but it is a mixed blessing for most former tribal peoples. Urban health standards are abysmally poor and generally worse than in rural areas for the detribalized individuals who have crowded into the towns and cities throughout Africa, Asia, and Latin America seeking wage employment out of new economic necessity. Infectious diseases related to crowding and poor sanitation are rampant in urban centers, while greatly increased stress and poor nutrition aggravate a variety of other health problems. Malnutrition and other diet-related conditions are, in fact, one of the characteristic hazards of progress faced by tribal peoples and are discussed in the following sections.

## The Hazards of Dietary Change

The traditional diets of tribal peoples are admirably adapted to their nutritional needs and available food resources. Even though these diets may seem bizarre, absurd, and unpalatable to outsiders, they are unlikely to be improved by drastic modifications. Given the delicate balances and complexities involved in any subsistence system, change always involves risks, but for tribal people the effects of dietary change have been catastrophic.

Under normal conditions, food habits are remarkably resistant to change, and indeed people are unlikely to abandon their traditional diets voluntarily in favor of dependence on difficult-to-obtain exotic imports. In some cases it is true that imported foods may be identified with powerful outsiders and are therefore sought as symbols of greater prestige. This may lead to such absurdities as Amazonian Indians choosing to consume imported canned tunafish when abundant high-quality fish is available in their own rivers. Another example of this situation occurs in tribes where mothers prefer to feed their infants expensive nutritionally inadequate canned milk from unsanitary, but *high status*, baby bottles. The high status of these items is often promoted by clever traders and clever advertising campaigns.

Aside from these apparently voluntary changes, it appears that more often dietary changes are forced upon unwilling tribal peoples by circumstances beyond their control. In some areas, new food crops have been introduced by government decree, or as a consequence of forced relocation or other policies designed to end hunting, pastoralism, or shifting cultivation. Food habits have also been modified by massive disruption of the natural environment by outsiders—as when sheepherders transformed the Australian Aborigines' foraging territory or when European invaders destroyed the bison herds that were the primary element in the Plains Indians' subsistence patterns. Perhaps the most frequent cause of diet change occurs when formerly self-sufficient peoples find that wage labor, cash cropping, and other economic development activities that feed tribal resources into the world-market economy must inevitably divert time and energy away from the production of subsistence foods. Many developing peoples suddenly discover that, like it or not, they are unable to secure traditional foods and must spend their newly

acquired cash on costly, and often nutritionally inferior, manufactured foods.

Overall, the available data seem to indicate that the dietary changes that are linked to involvement in the world-market economy have tended to *lower* rather than raise the nutritional levels of the affected tribal peoples. Specifically, the vitamin, mineral, and protein components of their diets are often drastically reduced and replaced by enormous increases in starch and carbohydrates, often in the form of white flour and refined sugar.

Any deterioration in the quality of a given population's diet is almost certain to be reflected in an increase in deficiency diseases and a general decline in health status. Indeed, as tribal peoples have shifted to a diet based on imported manufactured or processed foods, there has been a dramatic rise in malnutrition, a massive increase in dental problems, and a variety of other nutritional-related disorders. Nutritional physiology is so complex that even well-meaning dietary changes have had tragic consequences. In many areas of Southeast Asia, government-sponsored protein supplementation programs supplying milk to protein-deficient populations caused unexpected health problems and increased mortality. Officials failed to anticipate that in cultures where adults do not normally drink milk, the enzymes needed to digest it are no longer produced and milk *intolerance* results (Davis & Bolin, 1972). In Brazil, a similar milk distribution program caused an epidemic of permanent blindness by aggravating a preexisting vitamin A deficiency (Bunce, 1972).

## Teeth and Progress

*There is nothing new in the observation that savages, or peoples living under primitive conditions, have, in general, excellent teeth.... Nor is it news that most civilized populations possess wretched teeth which begin to decay almost before they have erupted completely, and that dental caries is likely to be accompanied by periodontal disease with further reaching complications.*

Hooton, 1945: xviii

Anthropologists have long recognized that undisturbed tribal peoples are often in excellent physical condition. And it has often been noted specifically that dental caries and the other dental abnormalities that plague industrialized societies are absent or rare among tribal peoples who have retained their traditional diets. The fact that tribal food habits may contribute to the development of sound teeth, whereas modernized diets may do just the opposite, was illustrated as long ago as 1894 in an article in the *Journal of the Royal Anthropological Institute* that described the results of a comparison between the teeth of ten Sioux Indians were examined when they came to London as members of Buffalo Bill's Wild West Show and were found to be completely free of caries and in possession of all their teeth, even though half of the group were over thirty-nine years of age. Londoners' teeth were conspicuous for both their caries and their steady reduction in number with advancing age. The difference was attributed primarily to the wear and polishing caused by the traditional Indian diet of coarse food and the fact that they chewed their food longer, encouraged by the absence of tableware.

One of the most remarkable studies of the dental conditions of tribal peoples and the impact of dietary change was conducted in the 1930s by Weston Price (1945), an American dentist who was interested in determining what caused normal, healthy teeth. Between 1931 and 1936, Price systematically explored tribal areas throughout the world to locate and examine the most isolated peoples who were still living on traditional foods. His fieldwork covered Alaska, the Canadian Yukon, Hudson Bay, Vancouver Island, Florida, the Andes, the Amazon, Samoa, Tahiti, New Zealand, Australia, New Caledonia, Fiji, the Torres Strait, East Africa, and the Nile. The study demonstrated both the superior quality of aboriginal dentition and the devastation that occurs as modern diets are adopted. In nearly every area where traditional foods were still being eaten, Price found perfect teeth with normal dental arches and virtually no decay, whereas caries and abnormalities increased steadily as new diets were adopted. In many cases the change was sudden and striking. Among Eskimo groups subsisting entirely on traditional food he found caries totally absent, whereas in groups eating a considerable quantity of store-bought food approximately 20 percent of their teeth were decayed. This figure rose to more than 30 percent with Eskimo groups subsisting almost exclusively on purchased or government-supplied food, and reached an incredible 48 percent among the Vancouver Island Indians. Unfortunately for many of these people, modern dental treatment did not accompany the new food, and their suffering was appalling. The loss of teeth was, of course, bad enough in itself, and it certainly undermined the population's resistance to many new diseases, including tuberculosis. But new foods were also accompanied by crowded, misplaced teeth, gum diseases, distortion of the face, and pinching of the nasal cavity. Abnormalities in the dental arch appeared in the new generation following the change in diet, while caries appeared almost immediately even in adults.

Price reported that in many areas the affected peoples were conscious of their own physical deterioration. At a mission school in Africa, the principal asked him to explain to the native schoolchildren why they were not physically as strong as children who had had no contact with schools. On an island in the Torres Strait the natives knew exactly what was causing their problems and resisted—almost to the point of bloodshed—government efforts to establish a store that would make imported food available. The government prevailed, however, and Price was able to establish a relationship between the length of time the government store had been established and the increasing incidence of caries among a population that showed an almost 100 percent immunity to them before the store had been opened.

In New Zealand, the Maori, who in their aboriginal state are often considered to have been among the healthiest, most perfectly developed of people, were found to have "advanced" the furthest. According to Price:

> *Their modernization was demonstrated not only by the high incidence of dental caries but also by the fact that 90 percent of the adults and 100 percent of the children had abnormalities of the dental arches.*

Price, 1945: 206

## Malnutrition

Malnutrition, particularly in the form of protein deficiency, has become a critical problem for tribal peoples who must adopt new economic patterns. Population pressures, cash cropping, and government programs all have tended to encourage the replacement of traditional crops and other food sources that were rich in protein with substitutes, high in calories but low in protein. In Africa, for example, protein-rich staples such as millet and sorghum are being replaced systematically by high-yielding manioc and plantains, which have insignificant amounts of protein. The problem is increased for cash croppers and wage laborers whose earnings are too low and unpredictable to allow purchase of adequate amounts of protein. In some rural areas, agricultural laborers have been forced systematically to deprive nonproductive members (principally children) of their households of their minimal nutritional requirements to satisfy the need of the productive members. This process has been documented in northeastern Brazil following the introduction of large-scale sisal plantations (Gross & Underwood, 1971). In urban centers the difficulties of obtaining nutritionally adequate diets are even more serious for tribal immigrants, because costs are higher and poor quality foods are more tempting.

One of the most tragic, and largely overlooked, aspects of chronic malnutrition is that it can lead to abnormally undersized brain development and apparently irreversible brain damage; it has been associated with various forms of mental impairment or retardation. Malnutrition has been linked clinically with mental retardation in both Africa and Latin America (see, for example, Mönckeberg, 1968), and this appears to be a worldwide phenomenon with serious implications (Montagu, 1972).

Optimistic supporters of progress will surely say that all of these new health problems are being overstressed and that the introduction of hospitals, clinics, and the other modern health institutions will overcome or at least compensate for all of these difficulties. However, it appears that uncontrolled population growth and economic impoverishment probably will keep most of these benefits out of reach for many tribal peoples, and the intervention of modern medicine has at least partly contributed to the problem in the first place.

The generalization that civilization frequently has a broad negative impact on tribal health has found broad empirical support (see especially Kroeger & Barbira-Freedman [1982] on Amazonia; Reinhard [1976] on the Arctic; and Wirsing [1985] globally), but these conclusions have not gone unchallenged. Some critics argue that tribal health was often poor before modernization, and they point specifically to tribals' low life expectancy and high infant mortality rates. Demographic statistics on tribal populations are often problematic because precise data are scarce, but they do show a less favorable profile than that enjoyed by many industrial societies. However, it should be remembered that our present life expectancy is a recent phenomenon that has been very costly in terms of medical research and technological advances. Furthermore, the benefits of our health system are not enjoyed equally by all members of our society. High infant mortality could be viewed as a relatively inexpensive and egalitarian tribal public health program that offered the reasonable expectation of a healthy and productive life for those surviving to age fifteen.

Some critics also suggest that certain tribal populations, such as the New Guinea highlanders, were "stunted" by nutritional deficiencies created by tribal culture and are "improved" by "acculturation" and cash cropping (Dennett & Connell, 1988). Although this argument does suggest that the health question requires careful evaluation, it does not invalidate the empirical generalizations already established. Nutritional deficiencies undoubtedly occurred in densely populated zones in the central New Guinea highlands. However, the specific case cited above may not be widely representative of other tribal groups even in New Guinea, and it does not address the facts of outside intrusion or the inequities inherent in the contemporary development process.

# Ecocide

*"How is it," asked a herdsman... "how is it that these hills can no longer give pasture to my cattle? In my father's day they were green and cattle thrived there; today there is no grass and my cattle starve." As one looked one saw that what had once been a green hill had become a raw red rock.*

Jones, 1934

Progress not only brings new threats to the health of tribal peoples, but it also imposes new strains on the ecosystems upon which they must depend for their ultimate survival. The introduction of new technology, increased consumption, lowered mortality, and the eradication of all traditional controls have combined to replace what for most tribal peoples was a relatively stable balance between population and natural resources, with a new system that is imbalanced. Economic development is forcing *ecocide* on peoples who were once careful stewards of their resources. There is already a trend toward widespread environmental deterioration in tribal areas, involving resource depletion, erosion, plant and animal extinction, and a disturbing series of other previously unforeseen changes.

After the initial depopulation suffered by most tribal peoples during their engulfment by frontiers of national expansion, most tribal populations began to experience rapid growth. Authorities generally attribute this growth to the introduction of modern medicine and new health measures and the termination of intertribal warfare, which lowered morality rates, as well as to new technology, which increased food production. Certainly all of these factors played a part, but merely lowering mortality rates would not have produced the rapid population growth that most tribal areas have experienced if traditional birth-spacing mechanisms had not been eliminated at the same time. Regardless of which factors were most important, it is clear that all of the natural and cultural checks on population growth have suddenly been pushed aside by culture change, while tribal lands have been steadily reduced and consumption levels have risen. In many tribal areas, environmental deterioration due to overuse of resources has set in, and in other areas such deterioration is imminent as resources continue to dwindle relative to the expanding population and increased use. Of course, population expansion by tribal peoples may have positive political consequences, because where tribals can retain or regain their status as local majorities they may be in a more favorable position to defend their resources against intruders.

Swidden systems and pastoralism, both highly successful economic systems under traditional conditions, have proved particularly vulnerable to increased population pressures and outside efforts to raise productivity beyond its natural limits. Research in Amazonia demonstrates that population pressures and related resource depletion can be created indirectly by official policies that restrict swidden peoples to smaller territories. Resource depletion itself can then become a powerful means of forcing tribal people into participating in the world-market economy—thus leading to further resource depletion. For example, Bodley and Benson (1979) showed how the Shipibo Indians in Peru were forced to further deplete their forest resources by cash cropping in the forest area to replace the resources that had been destroyed earlier by the intensive cash cropping necessitated by the narrow confines of their reserve. In this case, certain species of palm trees that had provided critical housing materials were destroyed by forest clearing and had to be replaced by costly purchased materials. Research by Gross (1979) and other showed similar processes at work among four tribal groups in central Brazil and demonstrated that the degree of market involvement increases directly with increases in resource depletion.

The settling of nomadic herders and the removal of prior controls on herd size have often led to serious overgrazing and erosion problems where these had not previously occurred. There are indications that the desertification problem in the Sahel region of Africa was aggravated by programs designed to settle nomads. The first sign of imbalance in a swidden system appears when the planting cycles are shortened to the point that garden plots are reused before sufficient forest regrowth can occur. If reclearing and planting continue in the same area, the natural patterns of forest succession may be disturbed irreversibly and the soil can be impaired permanently. An extensive tract of tropical rainforest in the lower Amazon of Brazil was reduced to a semiarid desert in just fifty years through such a process (Ackermann, 1964). The soils in the Azande area are also now seriously threatened with laterization and other problems as a result of the government-promoted cotton development scheme (McNeil, 1972).

The dangers of overdevelopment and the vulnerability of local resource systems have long been recognized by both anthropologists and tribal peoples themselves. But the pressures for change have been overwhelming. In 1948 the Maya villagers of Chan Kom complained to Redfield (1962) about the shortening of their swidden cycles, which they correctly attributed to increasing population pressures. Redfield told them, however, that they had no choice but to go "forward with technology" (Redfield, 1962: 178). In Assam, swidden cycles were shortened from an average of twelve years to only two or three within just twenty years, and anthropologists warned that the limits of swiddening would soon be reached (Burling, 1963: 311–312). In the Pacific, anthropologists warned of population pressures on limited resources as early as the 1930s (Keesing, 1941: 64–65). These warnings seemed fully justified, considering the fact that the crowded Tikopians were prompted by population pressures on their tiny island to suggest that infanticide be legalized. The warnings have been dramatically reinforced since then by the doubling of Micronesia's population in just the fourteen years between 1958 and 1972, from 70,600 to 114,645, while consumption levels have soared. By 1985 Micronesia's population had reached 162,321.

The environmental hazards of economic development and rapid population growth have become generally recognized only since worldwide concerns over environmental issues began in the early 1970s. Unfortunately, there is as yet little indication that the leaders of the new developing nations are sufficiently concerned with environmental limitations. On the contrary, governments are forcing tribal peoples into a self-reinforcing spiral of population growth and intensified resource exploitation, which may be stopped only by environmental disaster or the total impoverishment of the tribals.

The reality of ecocide certainly focuses attention on the fundamental contrasts between tribal and industrial systems in their use of natural resources, who controls them, and how they are managed. Tribal peoples are victimized because they control resources that outsiders demand. The resources exist because tribals managed them conservatively. However, as with the issue of the health consequences of detribalization, some anthropologists minimize the adaptive achievements of tribal groups and seem unwilling to concede that ecocide might be a consequence of cultural change. Critics attack an exaggerated "noble savage" image of tribals living in perfect harmony with nature and having no visible impact on their surroundings. They then show that tribals do in fact modify the environment, and they conclude that there is no significant difference between how tribals and industrial societies treat their environments. For example, Charles Wagley declared that Brazilian Indians such as the Tapirape

> are not "natural men." They have human vices just as we do.... They do not live "in tune" with nature any more than I do; in fact, they can often be as destructive of their environment, within their limitations, as some civilized men. The Tapirape are not innocent or childlike in any way.
>
> Wagley, 1977: 302

Anthropologist Terry Rambo demonstrated that the Semang of the Malaysian rain forests have a measurable impact on their environment. In his monograph *Primitive Polluters*, Rambo (1985) reported that the Semang live in smoke-filled houses. They sneeze and spread germs, breathe, and thus emit carbon dioxide. They clear small gardens, contributing "particulate matter" to the air and disturbing the local climate because cleared areas proved measurably warmer and drier than the shady forest. Rambo concluded that his research "demonstrates the essential functional similarity of the environmental interactions of primitive and civilized societies" (1985: 78) in contrast to a "noble savage" view (Bodley, 1983) which, according to Rambo (1985: 2), mistakenly "claims that traditional peoples almost always live in essential harmony with their environment."

This is surely a false issue. To stress, as I do, that tribals tend to manage their resources for sustained yield within relatively self-sufficient subsistence economies is not to make them either innocent children or natural men. Nor is it to deny that tribals "disrupt" their environment and may never be in absolute "balance" with nature.

The ecocide issue is perhaps most dramatically illustrated by two sets of satellite photos taken over the Brazilian rain forests of Rôndonia (Allard & McIntyre, 1988: 780–781). Photos taken in 1973, when Rôndonia was still a tribal domain, show virtually unbroken rain forest. The 1987 satellite photos, taken after just fifteen years of highway construction and "development" by outsiders, show more than 20 percent of the forest destroyed. The surviving Indians were being concentrated by FUNAI (Brazil's national Indian foundation) into what would soon become mere islands of forest in a ravaged landscape. It is irrelevant to quibble about whether tribals are noble, childlike, or innocent, or about the precise meaning of balance with nature, carrying capacity, or adaptation, to recognize that for the past 200 years rapid environmental deterioration on an unprecedented global scale has followed the wresting of control of vast areas of the world from tribal groups by resource-hungry industrial societies.

## Deprivation and Discrimination

*Contact with European culture has given them a knowledge of great wealth, opportunity and privilege, but only very limited avenues by which to acquire these things.*

Crocombe, 1968

Unwittingly, tribal peoples have had the burden of perpetual relative deprivation thrust upon them by acceptance—either by themselves or by the governments administering them—of the standards of socioeconomic progress set for them by industrial civilizations. By comparison with the material wealth of industrial societies, tribal societies become, by definition, impoverished. They are then forced to transform their cultures and work to achieve what many economists now acknowledge to be unattainable goals. Even though in many cases the modest GNP goals set by development planners for the developing nations during the "development decade" of the 1960s were often met, the results were hardly noticeable for most of the tribal people involved. Population growth, environmental limitations, inequitable distribution of wealth, and the continued rapid growth of the industrialized nations have all meant that both the absolute and the relative gap between the rich and poor in the world is steadily widening. The prospect that tribal peoples will actually be able to attain the levels of resource consumption to which they are being encouraged to aspire is remote indeed except for those few groups who have retained effective control over strategic mineral resources.

Tribal peoples feel deprivation not only when the economic goals they have been encouraged to seek fail to materialize, but also when they discover that they are powerless, second-class citizens who are discriminated against and exploited by the dominant society. At the same time, they are denied the satisfactions of their traditional cultures, because these have been sacrificed in the process of modernization. Under the impact of major economic change family life is disrupted, traditional social controls are often lost, and many indicators of social anomie such as alcoholism, crime, delinquency, suicide, emotional disorders, and despair may increase. The inevitable frustration resulting from this continual deprivation finds expression in the cargo cults, revitalization movements, and a variety of other political and religious movements that have been widespread among tribal peoples following their disruption by industrial civilization.

## Bibliography

Ackermann, F. L. 1964. *Geologia e Fisiografia da Região Bragantina, Estado do Pará.* Manaus, Brazil: Conselho Nacional de Pesquisas, Instituto Nacional de Pesquisas da Amazonia.

Allard, William Albert, and Loren McIntyre. 1988. Rondônia's settlers invade Brazil's imperiled rain forest. *National Geographic* 174(6):772–799.

Bodley, John H. 1970. *Campa Socio-Economic Adaptation.* Ann Arbor: University Microfilms.

_____. 1983. *Der Weg der Zerstörung: Stammesvölker und die industrielle Zivilization.* Munich: Trickster-Verlag. (Translation of *Victims of Progress.*)

Bodley, John H., and Foley C. Benson. 1979. Cultural ecology of Amazonian palms. *Reports of Investigations,* no. 56. Pullman: Laboratory of Anthropology, Washington State University.

Bunce, George E. 1972. Aggravation of vitamin A deficiency following distribution of non-fortified skim milk: An example of nutrient interaction. In *The Careless Technology: Ecology and International Development,* ed. M. T. Farvar and John P. Milton, pp. 53–60. Garden City, N.Y.: Natural History Press.

Burling, Robbins. 1963. *Rengsanggri: Family and Kinship in a Garo Village.* Philadelphia: University of Pennsylvania Press.

Davis, A. E., and T. D. Bolin. 1972. Lactose intolerance in Southeast Asia. In *The Careless Technology: Ecology and International Development,* ed. M. T. Farvar and John P. Milton, pp. 61–68. Garden City, N.Y.: Natural History Press.

Dennett, Glenn, and John Connell. 1988. Acculturation and health in the highlands of Papua New Guinea. *Current Anthropology* 29(2):273–299.

Goldschmidt, Walter R. 1972. The interrelations between cultural factors and the acquisition of new technical skills. In *The Progress of Underdeveloped Areas,* ed. Bert F. Hoselitz, pp. 135–151. Chicago: University of Chicago Press.

Gross, Daniel R., et al. 1979. Ecology and acculturation among native peoples of Central Brazil. *Science* 206(4422): 1043–1050.

Hughes, Charles C., and John M. Hunter. 1972. The role of technological development in promoting disease in Africa. In *The*

*Careless Technology: Ecology and International Development,* ed. M. T. Farvar and John P. Milton, pp. 69–101. Garden City, N.Y.: Natural History Press.

Keesing, Felix M. 1941. *The South Seas in the Modern World.* Institute of Pacific Relations International Research Series. New York: John Day.

Kroeger, Axel, and François Barbira-Freedman. 1982. *Culture Change and Health: The Case of South American Rainforest Indians.* Frankfurt am Main: Verlag Peter Lang. (Reprinted in Bodley, 1988a:221–236.)

McNeil, Mary. 1972. Lateritic soils in distinct tropical environments: Southern Sudan and Brazil. In *The Careless Technology: Ecology an International Development,* ed. M. T. Farvar and John P. Milton, pp. 591–608. Garden City, N.Y.: Natural History Press.

Mönckeberg, F. 1968. Mental retardation from malnutrition. *Journal of the American Medical Association* 206:30–31.

Montagu, Ashley. 1972. Sociogenic brain damage. *American Anthropologist* 74(5):1045–1061.

Rambo, A. Terry. 1985. *Primitive Polluters: Semang Impact on the Malaysian Tropical Rain Forest Ecosystem.* Anthropological Papers no. 76, Museum of Anthropology, University of Michigan.

Redfield, Robert. 1953. *The Primitive World and Its Transformations.* Ithaca, N.Y.: Cornell University Press.

_____. 1962. *A Village That Chose Progress: Chan Kom Revisited.* Chicago: University of Chicago Press, Phoenix Books.

Smith, Wilberforce. 1894. The teeth of ten Sioux Indians. *Journal of the Royal Anthropological Institute* 24:109–116.

TTR: *See under* United States.

United States, Department of the Interior, Office of Territories. 1953. *Report on the Administration of the Trust Territory of the Pacific Islands* (by the United States to the United Nations) for the Period July 1, 1951, to June 30, 1952.

_____. 1954. *Annual Report, High Commissioner of the Trust Territory of the Pacific Islands to the Secretary of the Interior* (for 1953).

United States, Department of State. 1955. *Seventh Annual Report to the United Nations on the Administration of the Trust Territory of the Pacific Islands* (July 1, 1953, to June 30, 1954).

_____. 1959. *Eleventh Annual Report to the United Nations on the Administration of the Trust Territory of the Pacific Islands* (July 1, 1957, to June 30, 1958).

_____. 1964. *Sixteenth Annual Report to the United Nations on the Administration of the Trust Territory of the Pacific Islands* (July 1, 1962 to June 30, 1963).

_____. 1973. *Twenty-Fifth Annual Report to the United Nations on the Administration of the Trust Territory of the Pacific Islands* (July 1, 1971, to June 30, 1972).

# A Pacific Haze:
# Alcohol and Drugs in Oceania

MAC MARSHALL

A ll over the world people eat, drink, smoke, or blow substances up their noses in the perennial quest to alter and expand human consciousness. Most of these substances come from psychoactive plants native to different regions—coca, tobacco, and peyote, in the New World; khat, coffee, and marijuana in North Africa and the Middle East; betel and opium in Asia. Some people use hallucinogens from mushrooms or tree bark; others consume more exotic drugs. Produced by fermentation, brewing, or distillation of a remarkable variety of raw materials—ranging from fruits and grains to milk and honey—traditional alcoholic beverages were found almost everywhere before the Age of Exploration.

As European explorers trekked and sailed about the globe between 1500 and 1900, they carried many of these traditional drugs back to their homelands. Different exotic drugs became popular at different times in Europe as the explorers shared their experiences. In this manner, tea, tobacco, coffee, marijuana, and opium gained avid followers in European countries. Today, this worldwide process of drug diffusion continues at a rapid pace, with changes in attitudes toward different drugs and the introduction of new laws governing their use varying accordingly.

Oceanic peoples were no exception to the widespread quest to expand the human mind. From ancient times they used drugs to defuse tense interpersonal or intergroup relations, relax socially, and commune with the spirit world. Betel and kava were far and away the most common traditional drugs used in the Pacific Islands. The geographical distribution of these two drugs was uneven across the islands, and, in a few places (for example, Chuuk [Truk]), no drugs were used at all before the arrival of foreigners. Kava and betel were not only differentially distributed geographically, but they were also differently distributed socially. Every society had rules governing who might take them (and under what circumstances) that limited their consumption, often only to adult men.

In the four-and-a-half centuries since foreign exploration of the Pacific world began, the islanders have been introduced to several new drugs, most notably alcoholic beverages, tobacco, and marijuana. This chapter discusses substance use in the contemporary Pacific Islands by examining the history and patterns of use of the five major drugs found in the islands today: alcohol, betel, kava, marijuana, and tobacco. To the extent that reliable information exists, such recently introduced drugs as cocaine and heroin are also discussed. The primary concern of the chapter is with the negative social, economic, and health consequences that result from consumption of alcohol, tobacco, and marijuana in the contemporary Pacific Islands.

## Betel and Kava

"Betel" is a convenient linguistic gloss for a preparation consisting of at least three distinct substances, two of which are pharmacologically active: the nut of the *Areca catechu* palm, the leaves, stems, or catkins of the *Piper betle* vine, and slaked lime from ground seashells or coral. These substances usually are combined into a quid and chewed. In some societies, people swallow the resultant profuse saliva, while in others they spit out the blood red juice. Kava is drunk as a water-based infusion made from the pounded, grated, or chewed root of a shrub, *Piper methysticum*. Whereas betel ingredients can easily be carried on the person and quickly prepared, kava makings are not as portable, and its preparation calls for a more involved procedure. Betel is often chewed individually with little or no ceremony; kava is usually drunk communally, and frequently accompanied by elaborate ceremonial procedures.

Betel chewing appears to have originated long ago in Island Southeast Asia and to have spread into the islands of the Western Pacific from there. While betel use is widespread in Melanesia (including the New Guinea Highlands where it has recently been introduced), it is absent from the Polynesian Triangle, and it is found only on the westernmost Micronesian islands of Palau, Yap, and the Marianas (Marshall 1987a).

In most parts of the Pacific Islands where betel is chewed, its use occupies a social position akin to coffee or tea drinking in Western societies. For example, Iamo (1987) writes that betel is chewed to stimulate social activity, suppress boredom, enhance work, and increase personal enjoyment among the Keakalo people of the south coast of Papua New Guinea. Similarly, Lepowsky (1982) comments that for the people of Vanatinai Island in Papua New Guinea, shared betel symbolizes friendly and peaceful social relations. Iamo notes that betel consumption "is rampant among children, young people, and adults" in Keakalo; that is, it has few social constraints on its use, except in times of scarcity (1987:146). Similarly, "Vanatinai people chew betel many times a day," and they also begin chewing betel early in childhood: "By the age of eight to ten, boys and girls chew whenever they can find the ingredients" (Lepowsky 1982:335).

In those parts of Papua New Guinea where the betel ingredients can be produced in abundance, such as Keakalo and Vanatinai, they figure importantly as items of exchange or for sale as "exports" to surrounding peoples. The enterprising Biwat of East Sepik Province are remarkable in this regard. They trade *Areca* nut, *Piper betle*, and locally grown tobacco with other peoples in the vicinity, carry these products by canoe to the regional market town of Angoram (98 miles away), and occasionally even charter a small airplane to sell as far away as Mount Hagen in the Western Highlands Province (Watson 1987).

Traditionally, kava was drunk only in Oceania, the world region to which the plant appears native. Kava drinking occurred throughout the high islands of Polynesia (except Easter Island, New Zealand, and Rapa), on the two easternmost high islands of Micronesia (Pohnpei and Kosrae), and in various parts of Melanesia, particularly Fiji, Vanuatu, and New Guinea proper. Kava and betel were often in complementary distribution, although there were some societies where both were routinely consumed.

Whereas betel is chewed by males and females, old and young, kava is different. In most Pacific Islands societies, at least traditionally, kava drinking was restricted to men, and often to "fully adult" or high-status men. Although its consumption was thus restricted, young, uninitiated or untitled men, or young women, usually prepared it. These distinctions were notably marked in the elaborate kava ceremonies of Fiji, Tonga, and Samoa. Wherever it was used, however, kava played important parts in pre-Christian religion, political deliberations, ethnomedical systems, and general quiet social interaction among a community's adult men.

On the island of Tanna, Vanuatu, for example, Lindstrom (1987) argues that getting drunk on and exchanging kava links man to man, separates man from woman, establishes a contextual interpersonal equality among men, and determines and maintains relations of inequality between men and women. Kava is drunk every evening on Tanna at a special kava-drinking ground, separated from the village, and from which women and girls are excluded. Lindstrom argues that kava (which is grown by women) is both itself an important exchange item and symbolically represents male appropriation and control over women and their productive and reproductive capacities. Tannese men fear that women intoxicated on kava would become "crazed" and usurp men's control over them, become sexually wanton, and cease to cook. Lindstrom concludes, "Gender asymmetry in Tannese drunken practice maintains and reproduces social relations of production and exchange" (1987:116).

Among the Gebusi of Papua New Guinea's Western Province, the men of a longhouse community force their male visitors to drink several bowls of kava in rapid succession, usually to the point of nausea. This is done to prevent the chief antagonists at ritual fights or funeral feasts "from disputing or taking retaliatory action against their hosts during a particularly tense moment in the proceedings" (Knauft 1987:85). Forced smoking of home-grown tobacco is used in an analogous manner "to forestall escalation of hostilities" among a people for whom homicide tied to sorcery accusations is a leading cause of male mortality. As on Tanna, Gebusi women never drink kava. Both

peoples link kava to sexuality: Lindstrom (1987:112–113) describes a Tannese-origin myth of kava that he calls "kava as dildo"; Knauft (1987:85–88) notes that kava often serves as a metaphor for semen in jokes about heterosexual relations or the ritual homosexuality practiced by the Gebusi.

As is typically the case in human affairs, these long-known and highly valued drug substances were deeply rooted in cultural traditions and patterns of social interaction. Pacific Islands peoples had developed culturally controlled ways of using betel and kava that usually precluded abuse.[1] Users also were unlikely to develop problems because of the relatively benign physiological effects of these two substances and because neither drug by itself seems to produce serious harmful disease states when consumed in a traditional manner.

Kava drinking leads to a variety of physical effects, perhaps the most pronounced of which are analgesia, muscle relaxation, and a sense of quiet well-being. In addition to its ceremonial and recreational uses, kava is a common drug in Oceanic ethnomedicine, and kava extracts also are employed in Western biomedicine. Of the various drugs discovered by human beings around the world, kava seems to be one of the least problematic. Its physiological effects induce a state of peaceful contemplation and euphoria, with the mental faculties left clear, and it produces no serious pathology unless taken (as by some Australian Aborigines since 1980) at doses far in excess of those consumed by Pacific Islanders. The most prominent effects of prolonged heavy kava consumption among Oceanic peoples are a dry scaly skin, bloodshot eyes, possible constipation and intestinal obstruction, and occasional weight loss (Lemert 1967). Even excessive kava use does not produce withdrawal symptoms, and all of the above conditions are reversible if drinking is discontinued.

The situation with betel is somewhat more complex. The main physical effect obtained by betel chewers is central nervous system stimulation and arousal producing a sense of general well-being (Burton-Bradley 1980). Arecoline, the primary active ingredient in betel, also stimulates various glands, leading to profuse sweating and salivation, among other things. Beginners typically experience such unpleasant symptoms as nausea, diarrhea, and dizziness, and prolonged use leads to physiological addiction. There is some preliminary experimental evidence that arecoline enhances memory and learning, and it is being explored as a possible medicine for patients suffering from Alzheimer's disease (Gilbert 1986).

Considerable controversy surrounds the health risks of betel chewing, particularly as regards its possible role in the development of oral cancer (MacLennan et al. 1985). This debate has been confounded by the fact that many betel chewers in Southeast and South Asia (where most of the clinical data have been collected) add other ingredients to the betel chew, most commonly, and notably, tobacco. A summary of the epidemiological evidence available to date leads to the conclusion that chewing betel using traditional ingredients without the addition of tobacco probably does not carry any significant risk for oral cancer (Gupta et al. 1982).[2] Occasionally, a betel chewer develops what Burton-Bradley (1966) calls "betel nut psychosis," following a period of abstinence and in response to a heavy dose of the drug. This acute reversible toxic psychosis is characterized by delusions and hallucinations in predisposed individuals, but it must be emphasized that its occurrence is rare. There is thus no conclusive evidence that regular betel chewing without the addition of tobacco results in physical or mental health problems for most people. Like kava, betel appears to produce a relatively harmless "high."

As usually taken in Oceania, not only do kava and betel consumption pose few—if any—health risks, but neither drug leads to intoxicated behavior that is socially disruptive (indeed, quite the contrary). The plants from which these substances are derived are locally grown and quite readily available, and the processes for making and taking these two traditional drugs do not require commercial manufacture. In the past twenty years, some cash marketing of both drugs has developed, but this is primarily by smallholders or local concerns, and neither substance is handled by multinational corporations. Thus, kava and betel do not have negative social and economic consequences for the Pacific Islands societies where they are used.

# Alcoholic Beverages

Pacific Islanders, like most North American Indians, had no alcoholic beverages until Europeans brought them early in the contact period. Initially, most islanders found alcohol distasteful and spat it out, but eventually they acquired a fondness for what sometimes was called "white man's kava." During the late eighteenth and first half of the nineteenth century, whalers, beachcombers, missionaries, and traders arrived in the islands in growing numbers. Many of them were drinkers and provided models of drunken behavior for the islanders to copy. Some of them established saloons in the port towns, and alcohol was widely used as an item of trade with the islanders. By at least the 1840s, missionaries to the islands, reflecting temperance politics in the United States and Great Britain, began to speak out forcefully against "the evils of drink" (Marshall and Marshall 1976).

As the European and American powers of the day consolidated colonial control over Oceania in the nineteenth century, they passed laws prohibiting islanders from consuming beverage alcohol. While such laws usually had strong missionary backing, they were also intended to maintain order, protect colonists from the possible "drunken depredations of savages," and serve what were deemed to be the islanders' own best interests. Despite prohibition, production of home brews continued in some areas, theft provided an occasional source of liquor, and the drinking of methylated spirits offered a potentially deadly alcohol alternative in some parts of the Pacific (Marshall 1988:579–582).

Colonially imposed prohibition laws remained in place until the 1950s and 1960s, when they were set aside one after another in the era of decolonization. Since then, the establishment of new Pacific nations has fostered a maze of legal regulations surrounding alcohol use, and it has also led to the encouragement of alcohol production and marketing. In many different parts of the Pacific Islands, problems have accompanied the relaxation of controls and the expansion of availability.

It is generally true around the world that more men drink alcoholic beverages than women, and that men drink greater quantities than women, but these gender differences are particularly pronounced in most of Oceania. In many of the islands,

there are strong social pressures against women drinking, reinforced by church teachings, that effectively keep most women from even tasting alcoholic beverages. With a few exceptions, it is usually only Westernized women in the towns who drink on any sort of a regular basis. Boys below age fourteen or fifteen seldom, if ever, drink, but by the time they are in their late teens or early twenties, nearly all of them partake of alcohol. So much is this the case that in Chuuk (Truk) drinking and drunkenness is called "young men's work" (Marshall 1987b).

These gender differences have resulted in profoundly different attitudes toward alcohol by men and women that sometimes have resulted in outspoken social opposition by women to men's drinking and its attendant social problems (see Marshall and Marshall 1990). Weekend binge drinking by groups of young men—especially in towns—frequently leads to social disruption and confrontations that have been labeled "weekend warfare" in one Micronesian society (Marshall 1979).

For many Pacific Islanders, alcoholic beverages have come to symbolize "the good life" and active participation in a modern, sophisticated lifestyle. Beer is usually the beverage of choice in Oceania, and, in some places, it has been incorporated into ceremonial exchanges surrounding such events as bride price payments, weddings, and funerals. In the Papua New Guinea Highlands' Chuave area, beer is treated as an item of wealth and "has assumed a central role in inter- and intraclan prestations" (Warry 1982:84). Cartons of beer have been endowed with a number of social and symbolic qualities in common with pork, the most highly esteemed traditional valuable. For example, the success of a ceremony is judged, increasingly, by the amount of beer, as well as pork, available for display and distribution; beer in cartons has a known value and the twenty-four bottles are easily divisible; like pigs, the stacked cartons of beer (sometimes as many as 240!) are appropriate items for display; alcohol is a social facilitator in these sometimes tense feast situations; beer—like pork and other foodstuffs—is consumable; and, like pork, beer is used at feasts both as a tool to create relationships and as a weapon to slight rivals (Warry 1982).

The chief problems associated with alcohol use in Oceania are social ones, although it is difficult to divorce these from the interrelated public health and economic costs. Among the more prominent and widespread social problems are domestic strife, particularly wife beating; community fighting and disruption, often with attendant trauma and occasional fatalities; crime, and drunk-driving accidents.

In the post–World War II era, these alcohol-related problems have been a continuing concern of community-based and government agencies in Pacific Islands countries. For example, a seminar was held in 1977 on "Alcohol Problems with the Young People of Fiji" (Fiji National Youth Council 1977), and, in 1986, Catholic youth in the Highlands of Papua New Guinea rallied to oppose alcohol abuse (*The Times of Papua New Guinea 1986a*). Other examples of community-based concerns are church women's groups who championed a legal prohibition against alcohol on Weno, Chuuk (Moen Island, Truk) (Marshall and Marshall 1990), and an ecumenical Christian training center in Papua New Guinea (the Melanesian Institute) that has given voice to village peoples' concerns over abuse of alcohol for many years. Within a decade after it became legal for Papua New Guineans to drink, the government felt it necessary to sponsor an official Commission of Inquiry in 1971 to assess the widely perceived problems that had ensued. Less than ten years later, another investigation of alcohol use and abuse under national government auspices was launched in Papua New Guinea through its Institute for Applied Social and Economic Research (IASER). Such government commissions and groups of concerned citizens usually produce recommendations for action; however, serious and effective alcohol control policies are rarely forthcoming.

Although they have received less attention in the literature, primarily because of the absence of adequate hospital records and autopsy reports for Pacific Islands countries, the physical and mental illnesses linked to either prolonged heavy ethanol intake or binge drinking appear to be considerable. Among these are alcoholic cirrhosis, cancers of the upper respiratory and upper digestive tracts, death from ethanol overdose, alcoholic psychoses, and suicide while under the influence of alcohol.

In recent years, researchers have focused on non-insulin-dependent diabetes mellitus (NIDDM), which has increased in urbanized and migrant Pacific Islands populations (for example, Baker et al. 1986; King et al. 1984). With changes from traditional diets to "modern" diets of refined foods and higher intakes of fats, sugar, sodium, and alcoholic beverages, some Micronesian and Polynesian populations have shown what is thought to be a hereditary susceptibility to NIDDM, which apparently is only expressed with a change from the traditional rural lifestyle. Urban and migrant islanders typically engage in less physical activity and have higher levels of obesity than their rural nonmigrant counterparts. Given that individuals with diabetes are more vulnerable to the hypoglycemic effects of alcohol because alcohol interferes with hepatic gluconeogenesis (Franz 1983:149; see also Madsen 1974:52–53), heavy drinking that may produce complications for diabetics poses an added health risk.

# Tobacco

Although the Spanish and Portuguese introduced tobacco into the East Indies from the New World in the late sixteenth and early seventeenth centuries, and although this new drug spread rather quickly to the island of New Guinea via traditional trade routes, *Nicotiana tabacum* did not reach most Pacific Islands until the nineteenth century. It became a basic item of trade and even served as a kind of currency during the heyday of European exploration and colonization of Oceania. The first German plantations on the north coast of New Guinea near Madang were tobacco plantations, and the crop continues to be grown commercially in Fiji and Papua New Guinea. In the 1800s, pipe and homemade cigar smoking were quite popular; today manufactured cigarettes dominate the market in most parts of the Pacific Islands. The prevalence of tobacco smoking by both men and women in Pacific Islands populations is much higher than in the developed countries of Australia, New Zealand, and the United States, and higher than in most developing nations elsewhere in the world (Marshall 1991). In some isolated rural parts of Oceania, nearly everyone in a community smokes—including children as young as eight or ten years of age.

With the decline in tobacco use in the developed nations of the West, the multinational corporations that control global production and marketing of this drug have shifted their emphasis to the huge and rapidly growing market in the Third World. Developing countries offer few restrictions to tobacco companies: most such countries have no maximum tar and nicotine levels, no laws restricting sales to minors, no advertising limits, no required health warnings, and no general public awareness of the serious health risks associated with smoking (Stebbins 1990). As a result, tobacco consumption has grown steadily in Third World countries, leading public health experts to predict and document the beginning of a major epidemic of diseases known to be linked to chronic tobacco use. During the 1980s, numerous studies have been published by health care professionals and other concerned individuals noting these alarming trends and calling for action. Studies documenting these problems exist for Africa, Latin America, and Asia, and researchers have begun to chronicle the same sad story for Oceania (Marshall 1991).

As with the upsurge in alcohol use and its aggressive marketing by multinational corporations in Pacific Islands countries, so it is, too, with the production and sale of commercial tobacco products, particularly cigarettes. Almost any store one enters in Oceania today displays tobacco advertisements prominently inside and out, and has numerous tobacco products readily available for sale. Among the many ploys used to push their brands, the tobacco companies sponsor sweepstakes contests with large cash prizes which can be entered by writing one's name and address on an empty cigarette pack and dropping it into a special box for a drawing. Tobacco firms also routinely sponsor sporting events, with trophies and prizes in cash and in kind. In other promotions, those who present fifteen empty packs of the pertinent brands are given "free" T-shirts emblazoned with the cigarette brand name.

The association of tobacco smoking with serious cardiovascular and respiratory diseases—lung cancer, chronic bronchitis, and emphysema—is by now well known. These diseases are particularly linked to the smoking of flue-cured commercial cigarettes, which now have been readily available in Oceania for about thirty years. As the Pacific Islanders who have smoked such cigarettes for many years develop health problems, more suffer from these smoking-related illnesses (Marshall 1991). One New Zealand study shows that those Maori women who smoke heavily during pregnancy produce infants of a lower average birth weight than those of Europeans or other Pacific Islanders in New Zealand (Hay and Foster 1981). Another study shows Maori women to have a lung cancer rate that is among the world's highest (Stanhope and Prior 1982).

As yet, there have been few efforts to gain control over the smoking epidemic in Pacific Islands countries. In one, the Fiji Medical Association announced a campaign to ban cigarette advertising following a directive from the Fiji Ministry of Health to stop smoking in all patient areas in government hospitals (*Pacific Islands Monthly* 1986). But the most encouraging program has been mounted in Papua New Guinea. In the early 1980s, an antismoking council was established there by members of the medical profession (Smith 1983), and, following several years of public debate, Parliament passed the Tobacco Products (Health Control) Act in November 1987. This law mandates various controls on tobacco advertising, requires health warning labels on cigarette packs and cigarette advertisements, and provides the authority to declare various public places as nonsmoking areas. As of March 1990, these included all national and provincial government offices, the offices and buildings of all educational institutions (other than staff quarters), all hospitals, health centers, clinics and aid posts, cinemas and theatres, public motor vehicles (PMVs), and all domestic flights on scheduled airlines. While there are some enforcement problems, the Department of Health has mounted an aggressive antismoking campaign (tied to the anti-betel-chewing campaign), and this is likely to have a positive impact over the next few years.

Despite the encouraging signs in Papua New Guinea, public-health-oriented antismoking campaigns have met with relatively small success to date in the face of the large sums of money devoted to advertising by the tobacco multinationals. Much more effort is needed in community and public health education if this preventable epidemic is to be brought under control in Oceania.

## Marijuana

Unlike the use of alcohol, betel, kava, and tobacco, marijuana smoking is uniformly illegal in Oceania. Nonetheless, the plant is now grown quite widely in the islands and has a substantial number of devotees. In part because its cultivation and use is against the law, fewer data are available on marijuana smoking than on the other four common Pacific drugs.

Native to central Asia, marijuana diffused to Oceania much more recently than alcohol or tobacco. While it doubtless was present in such places as Hawaii and New Zealand well before World War II, in other island areas like Micronesia or the New Guinea highlands, it appears to have been introduced only during the 1960s and 1970s.

While considerable controversy surrounds the long-term health effects of marijuana smoking, certain things are by now well known and give cause for concern. Marijuana induces an increased cardiovascular work load, thus posing a potential threat to individuals with hypertension and coronary atherosclerosis. Both of these health problems have been on the rise in Pacific Islands populations, especially in urban areas (Baker et al. 1986; Patrick et al. 1983; Salmond et al. 1985), and both can only be worsened by marijuana use.

Marijuana smoke is unfiltered and contains about 50 percent more cancer-causing hydrocarbons than tobacco smoke (Maugh 1982). Recent research has shown that "marijuana delivers more particulate matter to the smoker than tobacco cigarettes and with a net four-times greater burden on the respiratory system" (Addiction Research Foundation 1989:3). This same work revealed significant structural changes in the lungs of marijuana smokers, with a higher rate among those who also smoked tobacco. These changes are associated with chronic obstructive lung disease and with lung cancer. Another study has found significant short-term memory impairment in cannabis-dependent individuals that lingers for at least six weeks after use of the drug is stopped (Schwartz et al. 1989). As was discussed above for tobacco, the limited amount of research that has been done shows respiratory illnesses to be major serious diseases in Oceania. Clearly, smoking marijuana will simply raise the inci-

dence of health problems that were already significant in the Pacific Islands even before marijuana gained popularity.

In the Pacific Islands, as in the United States, marijuana growing is attractive because it yields a higher cash return per unit of time per unit of land than other agricultural crops. Even though marijuana is grown as a cash crop and often sold by the "joint," the plant is easy to grow, requires little attention, and thrives in most island environments. As a result, most marijuana consumed in the Pacific Islands, like betel and kava, is locally grown and not imported by drug cartels or multinationals. Even so, marijuana grown in the islands is sometimes exported to larger and more lucrative markets (Nero 1985). This has become the subject of major police concern in Papua New Guinea, where there are some indications that organized crime may be involved in the purchase of marijuana grown in the highlands to be sent overseas (for example, *Niugini Nius* 1990). It will be well nigh impossible to uproot marijuana from Oceania today, but much more could be done to educate islanders about the health risks associated with its use.

## Other Drugs

As of 1989, hard drugs such as cocaine and heroin have made little headway in Pacific Islands communities. The most dramatic example of a place where such penetration has begun is Palau, where heroin first showed up in the early 1970s (Nero 1985:20–23). By 1985, cocaine was being used in Palau as well, and, by then, a number of Palauan heroin addicts had been sent to Honolulu for detoxification and treatment (Polloi 1985).

Although the Palauan case is somewhat unusual for the Pacific Islands at present, there are increased reports of hard drugs being shipped *through* the islands from Asia for metropolitan markets in Australia, New Zealand, and North America. Clearly, given the ease of air travel and relatively lax security and customs checks, more hard drugs will appear in the islands in the coming years.

## Conclusions

Oceania's traditional drugs—betel and kava—create few if any social problems and pose minimal health risks to users. Moreover, these drugs are locally produced, and even when they are sold in the market the profits remain in islanders' hands and enrich the local economy. From an economic perspective, the cropping and selling of marijuana in most of the Pacific Islands operates in much the same way: small growers cultivate the plant for their own use or to sell in local markets. The major differences between marijuana and betel and kava are that marijuana is illegal and that smoking marijuana poses significant health risks. Oceania's other two major drug substances are produced and distributed in a very different manner and pose much more serious social and public health problems.

Over the past decade, an accumulation of studies has shown that alcoholic beverage and tobacco multinational corporations have increasingly targeted developing countries as prime markets for their products (for example, Cavanaugh and Clairmonte 1985; Muller 1978; Stebbins 1990; Wickström 1979). This marketing involves aggressive advertising, often aimed especially at young people and women. Frequently, it takes the form of joint ventures with host governments, on the grounds that large profits can be shared (which ignores the significant health and social costs involved). The multinationals also have become infamous for inducing governments (for example, the United States) to threaten trade embargoes against countries that balk at the unrestrained marketing of alcohol and tobacco products within their borders (*The Nation's Health* 1989).

The developing countries of Oceania have been subject to this "legal pushing" of harmful substances, even though their populations are small and transport poses certain logistical problems. Breweries, ultimately owned by huge overseas corporations, operate in French Polynesia, Western Samoa, Tonga, Fiji, Vanuatu, and Papua New Guinea, and there are distilled beverage producers in Fiji and Papua New Guinea.

For example, domestic production of hard liquor began in Papua New Guinea in 1985 by Fairdeal Liquors Pty. Ltd. Fairdeal imports raw materials (concentrates and ethanol) from its parent corporation based in Malaysia and from other overseas sources. The company then mixes and bottles both its own brands and selected internationally known brands on franchise (for example, Gilbey's gin, Jim Beam whiskey) in its factory in the Port Moresby suburb of Gordons. Initially, Fairdeal was able to market its own product ("Gold Cup") in small, clear plastic sachets for around 35 cents (U.S.) each. These were a marketing success but a social disaster because irresponsible storekeepers sold them to children as well as adults, and because many men drank them to excess. The ensuing public outcry led the Prime Minister to ask the company to withdraw the sachets from the market two months after they were introduced. Following the outcry from concerned citizens, especially in the highlands (*The Times of Papua New Guinea* 1986), Fairdeal briefly closed its Port Moresby factory in December 1986 because the national government also imposed a 1,200 percent increase in the import tax on the concentrate used to produce liquor (*The Times of Papua New Guinea* 1986). But even with this momentary setback, Fairdeal continues to market its own brands in bottles for half the price of comparable imports. This is possible because by bottling locally the company still avoids paying as much excise duty as that paid by importers of alcoholic beverages that are bottled abroad.

It was announced in mid-1989 that new breweries would be built in Papua New Guinea and Western Samoa (*Pacific Islands Monthly* 1989). The Papua New Guinea venture, which since has fallen through, was to be constructed at Kerowagi in Simbu Province, and represented a proposed joint venture among Danbrew Consult of Denmark and the five highlands provincial governments. At least two highlands provincial premiers had to be cajoled into committing their provinces to participation in this scheme, and the highly controversial project was opposed by women's organizations and church groups. Papua New Guinea's major brewery—South Pacific—itself a subsidiary of the Heineken Group, bought out its sole competitor (San Miguel, PNG) early in 1983. San Miguel (PNG) was a subsidiary of "the most successful conglom-

erate group in the Philippines," a group that held overseas interests in mining, brewing, fishing, finance, and development in nine different countries in Asia and Europe (Krinks 1987).

In 1978, War on Want published a slender volume entitled, *Tobacco and the Third World: Tomorrow's Epidemic?* Just over a decade later, the *question* in that book's title has been answered—a smoking epidemic has swept the Third World, and the Pacific Islands have not been immune to this global trend. While cigarettes and stick tobacco are locally produced in Papua New Guinea and Fiji by subsidiaries of the giant British Tobacco Company, the overwhelming majority of tobacco products sold in Oceania today are commercial cigarettes imported from the developed countries, principally Australia, New Zealand, and the United States. Promotional campaigns continue to have few, if any, restrictions placed upon them, and the costs of sweepstakes and raffle giveaways is small compared to the substantial profits to be earned once new consumers are "hooked."

A haze hangs over the Pacific Islands today, a result of widespread alcohol and tobacco abuse and of the smokescreens put up by multinationals to buy off politicians under the guise that production and marketing of these legal drugs contributes to economic development. In fact, the public health costs of alcohol and tobacco use and the social disruption surrounding alcohol abuse *undermine* economic and social development over the long run. If Pacific Islands governments do not develop more effective systems to prevent and control the aggressive marketing of alcohol and tobacco by multinationals, then the haze in the air and the glazed looks on the faces of island citizens will increase. The resultant social and health costs can only weaken Oceanic communities and make more difficult their dream of building prosperous, healthy, modern societies.

*Acknowledgment*: I am grateful to Linda A. Bennett for useful comments on an earlier version of this chapter.

# Notes

1. This statement remains true for Pacific Islanders; however, Australian Aborigines, to whom kava was introduced in the 1980s, and who consume it in quantities far in excess of those taken by Pacific Islanders, have developed such clinical side effects as weight loss, liver and kidney dysfunction, blood abnormalities, and possible pulmonary hypertension (Mathews et al. 1988; Riley and Mathews 1989).

2. Recently, in Papua New Guinea, and possibly elsewhere in the Pacific Islands, lime manufactured by commercial chemical firms has been substituted for lime produced in the traditional manner from ground seashells or coral. There is some evidence to suggest that the industrially manufactured lime is much more caustic than that traditionally used by Pacific betel chewers, and that this may increase the risk of oral cancer. Although controlled studies to demonstrate this have yet to be done, the Papua New Guinea Department of Health has mounted an active public health campaign advising people that if they chew betel, they run a risk of developing oral cancer.

# From Baffin Island to New Orleans

BRUCE E. JOHANSEN

Several yellow jacket wasps were sighted in Arctic Bay, a community of 700 people on the northern tip of Baffin Island at more than 73 degrees North latitude, during the summer of 2004. Noire Ikalukjuaq, the mayor of Arctic Bay, said he knew no word in the Inuit language for the insect.

In Kaktovik, Alaska, a village on the Arctic Ocean, a robin built a nest during the summer of 2003—not an unusual event in more temperate latitudes but quite a departure where, in the Inupiat language, no name exists for robins.

During the summer of 2004, hunters found half a dozen polar bears that had drowned about 200 miles north of Barrow, on Alaska's northern coast. They had tried to swim for shore after the ice had receded 400 miles. A polar bear can swim 100 miles—but not 400.

Global warming is leaving its evidentiary trail in melting ice as well as in the heating of the seas. The wrath of intensifying hurricanes and typhoons stoked by warming oceans has already devastated parts of the subtropics. The yellow jacket, the robin, the drowned polar bears, and the hurricane triplets—Katrina, Rita, and Wilma—are harbingers of an ominous future.

The Inuit can empathize with the people of New Orleans. You probably haven't seen Inuits on the evening news, but some hunters have died after falling through unseasonably thin ice. Sheila Watt-Cloutier, president of the Inuit Circumpolar Conference, testified before the Senate Commerce Committee hearing on global warming on August 15, 2004. She said the Inuits' ancient connection to their hunting culture may disappear within her grandson's lifetime, as the melting ice makes it difficult for them to get to their traditional hunting and harvesting areas.

"My Arctic homeland is now the health barometer for the planet," she said. "We are an endangered species."

When I first met Watt-Cloutier in Iqaluit during the summer of 2001, she was just beginning to tackle global warming. Now she takes her case to international diplomatic and scientific forums. Equally at home in ornate conference halls and in a small boat hunting seals with other Inuit near Baffin Island, Watt-Cloutier leads about 155,000 Inuit who are struggling to maintain some semblance of tradition in a swiftly changing, melting, and often polluted Arctic homeland. She has the delicacy of a diplomat, the precision of a scientist, and the verve of a social activist.

In her spacious house overlooking Frobisher Bay, she serves visitors some of the best Arctic char sushi on the planet, along with an urgent message: "Protect the Arctic and you will save the planet. Use us as your early-warning system. Use the Inuit story as a vehicle to reconnect us all so that we can understand the people and the planet are one."

Climate change in the Arctic is accelerating year by year. During the summer of 2004, compared to the previous year, enough Arctic ice to blanket an area twice the size of Texas melted. The same trend continued this summer. In the past, weak-ice years often were followed by years in which ice was restored. This kind of balancing hasn't been occurring recently.

"If you look at these last few years, the loss of ice we've seen ... is rather remarkable," says Mark Serreze of the National Snow and Ice Data Center at the University of Colorado. Scientists now talk seriously of an ice-free Arctic in the summer. The main point of debate is how soon this will happen.

In January 2004, Watt-Cloutier sent me an e-mail from Baffin Island: Frobisher Bay had just frozen over for the season at a record late date. "We are finally into very 'brrrrrr' seasonal weather, and the bay is finally freezing straight across," she wrote. "At Christmastime, the bay was still open and as a result of the floe edge being so close we had a family of polar bears come to visit the town a couple of times." The previous Christmas, rain had fallen in Iqaluit, an unprecedented event.

Two weeks before writing me, Watt-Cloutier was representing the Inuit at a U.N. conference on climate change in Milan, Italy. "Talk to hunters across the North and they will tell you the same story—the weather is increasingly unpredictable," she told the gathering. "The look and feel of the land is different. The sea-ice is changing. Hunters are having difficulty navigating and traveling safely. We have even lost experienced hunters through the ice in areas that, traditionally, were safe! ... Our elders, who instruct the young on the ways of the winter and what to expect, are at a loss."

It's about 4,000 miles from Baffin Island to New Orleans. But the same phenomenon that is threatening the Inuits' way of life may have wreaked havoc on the Gulf Coast.

Hurricanes are heat engines. They live and die according to the warmth of the water over which they move. Although other factors were involved, one important reason why Katrina, Rita, and Wilma blew up so quickly into three of the six most intense hurricanes in U.S. history was the temperature of the Gulf of Mexico and surrounding seas, 88 to 90 degrees at summer's peak, 2 to 4 degrees above recent averages.

Water temperatures vary for reasons other than global warming. Atlantic hurricanes intensify in twenty to thirty year cycles, following changes in water temperature. We are presently in the active phase of such a cycle, aided by generally rising air and water temperatures. Thus, the number and intensity of hurricanes over Florida and the other Gulf Coast states have been unusually high during the past several years. Hurricanes also intensify under calm high pressure in the upper atmosphere, which reduces wind shear that tears them apart.

Shortly after Katrina pounded the Gulf Coast, P. J. Webster and colleagues, writing in *Science*, linked rising water temperatures directly to the number, duration, and intensity of tropical cyclones. The researchers found that the number of storms in the two most powerful categories, 4 and 5, had risen to an average of eighteen a year worldwide since 1990, up from eleven in the 1970s. Other studies assert that Webster and colleagues, by going back only to the 1970s, missed a cyclical peak in numbers of hurricanes during the 1960s. The argument about an increase in intensity, however, has stood up to scrutiny.

In addition to cycles in hurricane activity and warming temperatures, the coastline marshes of the Mississippi Delta that once afforded the coast some protection have been subsiding for decades, mainly because water and oil have been pumped out of the ground. The Mississippi Delta also has been laced with oil companies' transport canals, further weakening the coastline.

Each severe hurricane compounds these long-term trends. Most of Katrina's damage resulted from storm surge and flooding, rather than wind. Hurricane Camille's winds were stronger than Katrina's, but thirty-six years ago the storm surge did not reach many areas that were wrecked this year. This may be because as ice melts around the world, sea levels are slowly rising. Warmer water also expands and occupies more space.

Since 1900, sea levels have risen 12.3 inches in New York City, 8.3 inches in Baltimore, 7.3 inches in Key West, 22.6 inches in Galveston, and six inches in San Francisco. The rate of increase has been accelerating over time. (The wide range results from the rising or falling of the land itself. San Francisco is rising; the East and Gulf coasts are subsiding.)

Many scientific studies have forecast that the sea level may rise between eight and twenty inches during the twenty-first century, making life on the East and Gulf coasts of the United States precarious.

All of these factors are cumulative. In coming decades, temperatures will be higher, on average, than today. Hurricanes, when they occur, will be more severe, and the land will have subsided substantially. We can expect intensifying climate calamities, as millions of environmental refugees flee their low-lying homes with the approach of each season's storms.

Among scientists who follow the pace of global warming, anxiety has been rising that the Earth is reaching (or may even have passed) a "tipping point," with the effects of greenhouse warming surpassing any foreseeable human ability to contain or reverse it.

Sir John Houghton, one of the world's leading experts on global warming, told the London *Independent*: "We are getting almost to the point of irreversible meltdown, and will pass it soon if we are not careful."

"The climate is changing much more quickly than scientists had projected only a few years ago," says Ross Gelbspan, author of *The Heat Is On* and *Boiling Point*. "We are seeing impacts—accelerating migrations of species, the thawing of the Siberian and Canadian tundra, the drying of the Amazon rainforest—that researchers did not expect to see until near the end of the twenty-first century. As a result, scientists are concerned about natural systems crossing invisible thresholds and taking on their own irreversible momentum."

As Arctic ice melts, darker-colored water absorbs more heat. Thawing permafrost adds greenhouse gases to the atmosphere, as do the increasing numbers of wildfires (especially those which burn underground stores of peat).

Carbon dioxide levels in the atmosphere also are rising, fed by, among other things, the increasing fossil-fuel use in the United States and other countries, slash-and-burn agriculture in places like Indonesia and Brazil, increasing wildfires, as well as rapid industrialization using dirty coal in China and India. Rising levels of carbon dioxide in the oceans will be making them more acidic, causing the calcium-carbonate shells of marine animals (such as corals and plankton) to dissolve.

In August 2005, climate researchers reported that a large area of western Siberia was undergoing an unprecedented thaw that could dramatically increase the rate of global warming, as melting permafrost injects additional carbon dioxide and methane into the atmosphere. Permafrost across a million square kilometers, an area as large as France and Germany combined, has already started to melt, reported Sergei Kirpotin at Tomsk State University in western Siberia and Judith Marquand of England's Oxford University. What was until recently a barren expanse of frozen peat had turned, during the summer, into a broken landscape of mud and lakes, some more than a kilometer across. Kirpotin told the *Manchester Guardian Weekly* that the situation was an "ecological landslide that is probably irreversible and is undoubtedly connected to climatic warming."

By the end of this century, temperatures may reach a level that may melt solid methane in the oceans. During past periods of rapid warming, tens of millions of years ago, methane in gaseous form (called "clathrate") has been released from sea floors in intense eruptions, following an increase in temperatures of up to 8 degrees Celsius, which is within the range projected by many climate models for the end of this century. Scientists call these explosions the "clathrate gun" or "methane burp." Once such reactions begin, they feed themselves, dramatically accelerating the rate of warming in the atmosphere.

Will humankind be able to dodge this bullet? If so, how? The short answer, according to many scientists, is to cut fossil fuel consumption by about 70 percent within the next fifteen to twenty years. That's what would be required to stabilize greenhouse-gas levels in the atmosphere before natural feedbacks begin to accelerate warming beyond control.

Such swift action is not likely. Evidence of warming reveals itself to us in a forty-to-fifty-year feedback loop. We are feeling warming now in response to the fossil fuels that were burned in about 1960. Since then, world consumption has risen several times over.

Increasingly efficient use of energy and diplomatic action are beginning to slow the rate of increase in greenhouse gases worldwide, however. "The growth rate … peaked near 1980," according to James Hansen, director of the Goddard Institute for Space Studies, writing with Makiko Sato in the *Proceedings of the National Academy of Sciences.*

In Denmark, for example, most families now own a share of a wind turbine. Some areas of Germany derive a substantial proportion of their energy from wind and solar power. In Spain, building codes have been amended to require use of passive solar power. Hansen and many other experts warn, though, that these changes are not sufficient and that the window of opportunity is narrowing with each passing day.

The Inuit are not waiting. Watt-Coultier and the Inuit Circumpolar Conference have assembled a human rights case against the United States. They have invited the Washington-based Inter-American Commission on Human Rights to visit the Arctic to witness the devastation being caused by global warming.

While the commission is not a tribunal that can issue binding verdicts, a finding in favor of the Inuit against the United States could become useful evidence in future attempts to successfully sue the United States on climate-change grounds in international legal forums.

"We want to show that we are not powerless victims," says Watt-Coultier. "These are drastic times for our people and require drastic measures. The Earth is literally melting. If we can reverse the emissions of greenhouse gases in time to save the Arctic, then we can spare untold suffering."

---

**BRUCE E. JOHANSEN,** Frederick W. Kayser Professor of Communication at the University of Nebraska at Omaha, is author of the forthcoming "Global Warming in the 21st Century." He wrote "Arctic Heat Wave" for *The Progressive*'s October 2001 issue.

# What Native Peoples Deserve

ROGER SANDALL

THE ROOSEVELT Indian Reservation in the Amazon rain forest is not a happy place. Last year, the Cinta Larga Indians slaughtered 29 miners there, and in October the Brazilian who was trying to mediate the conflict was murdered at a cash machine. Neither of these events represented anything new. The reserve, located 2,100 miles northwest of Rio de Janeiro, and named for Theodore Roosevelt when he visited Brazil in 1913, is also where a notorious massacre of Cinta Larga by rubber tappers took place in 1963; only one child in the village survived.

The immediate cause of the recent violence is not rubber but diamonds. The Roosevelt Indian Reservation may be sitting on one of the world's largest deposits, and no one wants to leave it in the ground—neither the Indians, nor the itinerant diggers (*garimpeiros*), nor the government. But, under present Brazilian law, no one is free to begin digging, either. And this brings us to the deeper cause of murder and mayhem in the region.

Under Brazil's constitution, the country's Indians are not full citizens. Instead, they are legal minors, with the status of a protected species. This has one singular benefit for the Indians: the twelve Cinta Larga responsible for last year's killing of 29 wildcat prospectors may enjoy immunity from prosecution and never face jail. But there is also a downside. As wards of the state, the Indians are denied the right to mine their own land.

As for outsiders, they must apply for permits to dig, and face endless bureaucratic delays that more often than not lead nowhere. The outcome is predictable: frustrated in their own wishes, and hard-pressed by the impatient diggers, Indians make private deals, which then go sour—and the shooting starts.

At issue here is not just the law; the law is itself the product of an idea, or a set of ideas, concerning certain underlying questions. What should be done about endangered enclave societies in the midst of a modern nation? Can they, or their land, or their minerals be cut off and preserved, frozen in time, pristine and inviolate, forever? Should they be?

THE MASSACRE of the Cinta Larga in 1963 gave rise to a Brazilian state inquiry that became known as the Figueiredo Report (after the official in charge of the investigation). The inquiry was meant to find out about the shockingly grave deficiencies and abuses that were then being tolerated by the Indian Protection Service, including the use of individual Indians as slaves. Once it was completed, the old agency was closed down, and a new one created to replace it.

There the matter might have rested had not the London *Sunday Times* caught a whiff of scandal. The paper dispatched the travel writer Norman Lewis to Brazil; though he did not meet any Indians, he found all he needed in the Figueiredo Report. "By the descriptions of all who had seen them," Lewis reported, "there were no more inoffensive and charming human beings on the planet than the forest Indians of Brazil."

Having established a scene of primal innocence, Lewis proceeded to tell of the atrocities against the Cinta Larga, warning that they were being pushed to the brink of extinction and that there might not be a single Indian left by 1980. He concluded: "What a tragedy, what a reproach it will be for the human race if this is allowed to happen!" Reprinted all over the globe, his sensational article had profound and lasting effects.

The first of these effects was to enshrine a form of extreme protectionism, not only as a temporary means to an end—the human and cultural survival of the indigenous peoples of Brazil—but as an end in itself. Soon, all those working for Indian interests were of a single opinion: the only way to protect these tribal peoples was to create inviolable sanctuaries where they would "live their own lives preserving their own culture on their own land."

The second effect was to galvanize a number of English explorers, writers, and anthropologists into setting up a permanent international lobby. The name of this flourishing body is Survival, self-described as "the world's leading organization supporting tribal peoples." Two men who have been associated with it from the outset are John Hemming and Robin Hanbury-Tenison.

Hemming, who served for two decades as the director of the Royal Geographical Society, has written a number of books about South America, among them an indispensable three-volume history of the impact of civilization on Brazil's indigenous peoples—*Red Gold, Amazon Frontier*, and *Die If You Must*, the last of which appeared in 2003.* Hanbury-Tenison, Hemming's long-time friend, was also a founder of Survival and is today its

*Macmillan, 887 pp.,$28.50 (paper)

president. Less well-known but also important is the documentary filmmaker Adrian Cowell, who has spoken up on behalf of the Amazonian Indians for nearly 50 years.

According to a recent article by Hemming in the British monthly *Prospect*, the campaign to ensure the survival of the Amazonian peoples appears to have succeeded. This is also the gist of the final chapter of *Die If You Must*, where he wrote:

> The Indians will survive physically. Their populations have grown steadily since a nadir of near-extinction in the mid-20th century. Having fallen to little more than 100,000 in the 1950's, they have more than tripled to some 350,000 and are generally rising fast.

The health of the Indians is basically good, Hemming reported in *Die If You Must*. The killers of yesteryear—measles, TB, pneumonia, cholera, and smallpox—are rare. Their land is also secure: "a remarkable 11 percent of the land-mass of Brazil is now reserved for Indians. The 587 indigenous areas total almost 260 million acres—an area greater than France, Germany, and Benelux combined." Environmentalist ideals and indigenous interests have been reconciled: "From the air, [one reservation] now stands out as an immense rectangle of verdant vegetation framed by the dismal brown of arid ranch-lands."

I T WAS in the 1950's and 60's that Hemming, Hanbury-Tenison, and Cowell, three young men from Oxford and Cambridge, launched themselves on the world. They were talented and energetic, they had good connections, and above all they shared a boyish taste for adventure. At Eton they probably read about Lawrence of Arabia; at Oxford, where Hemming and Hanbury-Tenison roomed together, they already knew that "exploring" was what they wanted to do most. They regarded the rain forests of Brazil as a natural field for their endeavors, and in no time they were paddling up the Amazon in canoes.

Adrian Cowell was a Cambridge man, and his precocity as an explorer makes an impressive tale in itself. As a student in 1954 he joined a university Trans-Africa Expedition. The following year he was in Asia. Then, as he relates in *The Heart of the Forest* (1961), "the Oxford and Cambridge Expedition to South America ... brought me to the Amazon forest." Thereafter he joined the Brazilian Centro Expedition, an enterprise associated with the creation of the new national capital of Brasilia. Its purpose was "to canoe down the Xingu River and burn an airstrip at the exact geographical center of Brazil."

It was all tremendous fun and very romantic—a word that occurs spontaneously in the books of Hanbury-Tenison, who has written voluminously about his explorations and today runs a booking agency for exotic locations. Here, from his website, is a typical passage about an early adventure in Afghanistan:

> A sound like distant thunder made me look up at the rich blue cloudless sky before I turned to see twenty wild horsemen in turbans and flowing robes bearing down on me. They carried long-barreled rifles and had daggers in their belts. Beside their spirited horses

loped large, hairy hounds. With their Genghis Khan moustaches and fine, aquiline noses they were almost caricatures of the bandits we had been warned about. I should have been frightened, but all I could think was that if I had to go I could not have found a more romantic end.

This tells us quite a bit about the attitude of all three men toward indigenous peoples. In light of that attitude, Hanbury-Tenison must have been taken aback when, in 1971, he called on the anthropologist Margaret Mead at the Museum of Natural History in New York to tell her about Survival International (as Survival was then called), and she gave him a piece of her mind. Mead at the age of seventy was a very different person from the idealistic young woman who had visited Samoa in 1926. By 1971, she was fiercely *un*romantic, and the spectacle of yet another young Oxford "explorer" embarking on yet another expedition up the Amazon must have set her teeth on edge. With sturdy good sense she tried to talk him out of his fantasies.

In his 1973 book, *A Question of Survival*, Hanbury-Tenison describes this "small, beady-eyed dumpling of a lady who sailed into the attack as I came through the door":

> The main point that annoyed [Mead] was the concept, unstated by me, that primitive peoples were any better off as they were. She said she was "maddened by antibiotic-ridden idealists who wouldn't stand three weeks in the jungle" ... and the whole "noble savage" concept almost made her foam at the mouth. "All primitive peoples," she said, "lead miserable, unhappy, cruel lives, most of which are spent trying to kill each other." The reason they lived in the unpleasant places they did, like the middle of the Brazilian jungle, was that nobody else would.

There was much talk in those days about the pharmaceutical benefits of rain forests, and Hanbury-Tenison and his friends were sure that the Amazon was about to make a huge contribution to the world's health. (This was a little before the discovery of the supposed wonders of jojoba oil.) But Mead was having none of it:

> She said that to protect [the Indians] on the grounds that they could be useful to us or contribute anything was nonsense. "No primitive person has *ever* contributed *anything*, or ever will," she said. She had no time for suggestions of medical knowledge or the value of jungle lore.

The only grounds on which Mead relented were broadly humanitarian. For one thing, the Indians' "art, culture, dancing, music, etc. was pleasant and attractive and their grandchildren might thank us for trying to preserve or at best record it now that we have the proper technical means [i.e., tape and film] for doing so." For another thing, "it was bad for the world to let these people die, and the effort to prevent their extermination was good for mankind even if it failed."

For the rest, however, Mead vehemently denied that the Indians had any special reasons for being protected, as she denied any advantage of one race over another. She also claimed emphatically that they all wanted one thing only, and that was to have as many material possessions and comforts as possible. Those still running away in the jungle were the ones who had encountered the most unpleasant savagery from Europeans, and even though they might be having no contact now, if they could possibly get hold of any aluminum pots they would use them.

ALTHOUGH FAITHFULLY recorded by Hanbury-Tenison, Mead's argument was as lost on him in 1971 as it is lost today on legions of like-minded people who teach or mouth the slogans of multiculturalism. What Mead herself failed to grasp was that, naive though he may have sounded, Hanbury-Tenison and his friends had been radicalized, and they were never going to accept her bleak view of the tribal world. It was not that they had been reading Marx; instead, they had been reading Norman Lewis's digest of the worst parts of the Figueiredo Report, including Figueiredo's judgment that "the Indians [had] suffered tortures similar to those of Treblinka and Dachau."

Torture, indeed, was too tame a word for what had taken place. In 1963, there had been massacres of the Cinta Larga tribe in Rondonia. One gunman's taped testimony describes how an employee of a rubber company named Chico Luis

> gave the chief a burst with his tommy gun to make sure, and after that he let the rest of them have it.... [A]ll the other guys had to do was finish off anyone still showing signs of life.... [T]here was a young Indian girl they didn't shoot, with a kid of about five in one hand, yelling his head off.... Chico shot the kid through the head with his .45 and then grabbed hold of the woman—who by the way was very pretty. "Be reasonable," I said, "why do you have to kill her?" In my view it was a waste. "What's wrong with giving her to the boys? They haven't set eyes on a woman for six weeks. Or we could give her as a present to [their boss] de Brito."

But Chico would not listen:

> He tied the Indian girl up and hung her head downward from a tree, legs apart, and chopped her in half right down the middle with his machete. Almost with a single chop I'd say. The village was like a slaughterhouse. He calmed down after he'd cut the woman up, and told us to burn down all the huts and throw the bodies into the river.

This is unbearable: but it is not essentially different from what had happened to many Indians in Latin America after 1492. The lawless frontier was for centuries a refuge for loners, criminals, and violent psychopaths who had nothing to lose and could act with impunity. Those who went searching for El Dorado in the 1540's behaved like packs of marauding wolves, seizing food from the same Indian villagers whom they then en-

slaved as porters, and who were tortured or killed when they failed to cooperate. As one learns from Hemming's three-volume work, this sort of thing has had a very long history indeed.

Colonial nations fashion their heroes from the timber at hand, much of which is twisted and full of knots. Australia, for example, invites its citizens to admire an unappealing Irish bandit named Ned Kelly. But the Kellys smell sweet alongside Brazil's much romanticized *bandeirantes*. What are often referred to as expeditions of "pathfinders" from São Paulo into the interior in the first half of the 17th century were mostly slave raids aimed at catching, chaining, and marching back to the coast as many Indians as a group of well-armed and ruthless men could seize.

To be sure, there was sometimes a genuinely exploratory aspect to such forays. In *Red Gold*, Hemming offers a balanced account of this phase of Brazilian expansion inland, and fairly describes the ordeals of the *bandeirantes* themselves. Since slave-raiding was a central feature of traditional Indian culture, too, the journeys engaged whites, Indians, and those of mixed ancestry (*mamelucos*) in a common enterprise:

> The Indians contributed their forest skills and geographical knowledge. They soon grasped the purpose of the mission and became expert enslavers of other natives. Although brutalized and worked hard by the captains of the *bandeiras*, the Indians probably enjoyed service on them. It was quite normal for Tupi warriors to make long marches through the forests to attack enemy tribes.

IN THE course of his own periodic visits to Brazil, Adrian Cowell appears to have come rather closer to the realities of Amazonian Indian life than either Hanbury-Tenison or Hemming. As a result, although aware of the horrors long endured by Indians at the hands of slavers, settlers, and frontier psychopaths, he was also more prepared to face up to the grimmer aspects of the native cultures themselves, and of the horrors Indians had long inflicted on each other.

In *The Heart of the Forest* (1961), Cowell writes in idyllic prose of the partnership he formed with an Indian hunter, carrying his friend's gun and studying his craft, teaching himself to decoy wildfowl by imitating their calls. But he also reports how, in 1958 on the Xingu River, there were continual killings of itinerant Brazilian rubber tappers (*seringueiros*) by Indians, and of Indians by *seringueiros*. A Juruna Indian told him how

> first we lived lower down the Xingu and worked for the *seringueiros*, but they killed many [Indians] with rifles. So we came up here past the great rapids and lived till the *seringueiros* say they are friends and gave us rifles. So we went downriver again and worked for the *seringueiros* till they killed more Juruna. Then we killed many *seringueiros* and came back here and killed Trumai and Kamayura Indians. Then the Txukahamae tribe came and killed almost all of us so that we are only twelve now.

That is the way things were and always had been. And this, too, was a seemingly ineradicable aspect of the culture that Cowell thought worthy of being saved. Back in 1967, he had joined the brothers Claudio and Orlando Villas-Boas in an attempt to contact and "pacify" the elusive Kreen-Akrore. But violence in the camp was making it hard to manage a community where different tribal groups had been brought together for their own safety. The captions on a page of photographs in Cowell's 1973 book, *The Tribe that Hides from Man*, read like the list of casualties on some exotic war memorial: "*Above*: Javaritu, a Trumai killed by Tapiokap. *Above*: Pionim, a Kayabi, killed Tapiokap to avenge his brother-in-law." And so on.

Much has been written about the endeavor of the Villas-Boas brothers to establish the Xingu Indian refuge and entice the tribal remnants of the Kayabi or Txikao or Suya to join it. A passage from *The Tribe that Hides from Man* offers a glimpse into the thought processes of Claudio, a "Marxist philosopher" in the Latin American manner:

> Look around this camp and you will see Indians are more loving than we are. But the expression of their love is confined to the limits of this society. They cut a hole in the wilderness to contain their family, but outside this camp is the jungle where they kill meat for food, bamboo for arrows, leaves for their beds. Killing is the essence of forest existence, and if you stopped it, the forest and the Indian would die. Within the Indian mind there is a complete division between the duties within the group and the absence of duty in the land of killing outside.

At one time, Claudio suggested that Indians should feel free to kill white *seringueiros* or any other uninvited marauders who came into the Xingu Park. While warning them of the inevitable costs of this practice as a permanent way of life, he understood that, according to the tribal code, revenge killing was natural, habitual, and inevitable. Nor was this the only aspect of Amazonian Indian culture that was hard to reconcile with modern life. Strict rules of seclusion were found among all the upper-Xingu tribes. Women were subjected to draconian punishments for violations of taboo. In a British television documentary from the 1970's, a young Mehinacu woman was asked what would happen if she were to glimpse, even accidentally, the sacred flutes played by the men. She would be gang-raped, she replied, smiling sadly as if in recognition that in the genteel world of her white interviewer, such sexual punishments—culturally authorized, approved, indeed mandatory—were unthinkable.

H EMMING'S ACCOUNT of Amazonian life is hard on the efforts of Christian missionaries, and especially hard on Jesuits ("fanatical missionaries intent on replacing native society and beliefs with their own Christian model"). One line of grudging appreciation will be followed by the word "but" and ten lines of disparagement. As his impressive study proceeds from volume to volume, he is consistently severe, his language becomes more tendentious, and an austere secularism dictates his judgment of religious matters. In his recent article in *Prospect*, he seems to approve wholeheartedly only of the politically radical priests who began to appear in the 1960's—

"trained anthropologists who did not try to undermine indigenous beliefs and ceased to be aggressive proselytizers." Before that point, his view of Catholic missionary activity is mainly negative.

But what exactly were the religious authorities to do when they first arrived from Portugal and had to deal, for example, with the Tupinamba? Did they not have a clear obligation both to undermine and to prohibit certain indigenous beliefs? In modern times, we have seen the rise of whole political cultures gripped by pathology, with hideous consequences; so, too, sick ethnic cultures evolved historically in the tribal world. Few quite so sick as the Tupinamba have been recorded before or since.

They loved human flesh. Prestige and power centered on the ritual slaughtering of prisoners. In an account prepared by Alfred Métraux for the Smithsonian's *Handbook of South American Indians* (1948), we read that the killing and eating of these prisoners (who were fattened for the purpose) "were joyful events which provided these Indians with the opportunity for merrymaking, aesthetic displays, and other emotional outlets." Métraux then describes what took place at a cannibal feast after the victim's skull was shattered:

> Old women rushed to drink the warm blood, and children were invited to dip their hands in it. Mothers would smear their nipples with blood so that even babies could have a taste of it. The body, cut into quarters, was roasted on a barbecue, and the old women, who were the most eager for human flesh, licked the grease running along the sticks. Some portions, reputed to be delicacies or sacred, such as the fingers or the grease around the liver or heart, were allotted to distinguished guests.

That Portuguese settlers in the 16th century did not cope very well with this aspect of the Indian tribal world is probably true. That the missionaries who came after them did not handle the situation as they might have done is also likely. But if they had been around at the time, would John Hemming, or Robin Hanbury-Tenison, or Adrian Cowell, or the entire staff of Survival have done much better? Would any of us?

"All primitive peoples," Margaret Mead had said to her young Oxford visitor, "lead miserable, unhappy, cruel lives, most of which are spent trying to kill each other." She was overdoing it, but she had a point—a point largely lost sight of in today's systematic sentimentalizing of the Stone Age.

O F COURSE, as we have seen, Mead also acknowledged that certain aspects of Indian culture—"their art, culture, dancing, music, etc."—deserved to survive, for the enjoyment of the people themselves and for the admiration of humanity as a whole. That, indeed, is more or less what has happened today in the Xingu Park and places like it elsewhere. On display in such places is a pacified, deranged, and somewhat feminized version of Amazonian culture, of the kind that middle-class travelers from the West like to see: a theatrical world where dressing-up in feathered regalia, ritual ceremonies, and communal dancing never stop.

Hemming, who welcomes the prospect of self-determination, claims that "modern indigenous policy seeks to empower tribes to manage their own affairs." Yet both self-determination and empowerment imply literacy and modern education; and here the picture is less clear. Officially, the children are learning to read and write, and in the last chapter of *Die If You Must*—a chapter with the title "Present and Future" Hemming makes three rather perfunctory references to schooling. But at the same time, he strongly implies that in his vision of the future it does not matter whether the children learn to read and write or not, because others will be there to do things for them.

Who are these others? According to Hemming, the external political affairs of the Indians on the Xingu reserve are "supported by a remarkable contingent of 33 non-government organizations, a fireless band of missionaries, anthropologists, well-wishers, journalists, doctors, and lawyers, both in Brazil and abroad." As for their internal welfare, that is served by a "resident tribe of whites, composed of social scientists, doctors, teachers, nurses, biologists, and agronomists from all parts of Brazil." With friends like these, who needs self-determination?

What Hemming is describing is the fruit of the inviolable-sanctuary approach to cultural survival. This rests on what might be called fortress theory, and has two cardinal principles: that "culture" and "people" and "land" should be seen as indivisible, and that they can be kept this way forever in a suitably constructed territorial redoubt. Whatever is happening in the world around them, ethnic cultures should, insofar as possible, be preserved unchanged. With the help of an army of administrative personnel, custodially responsible for seeing to it that they go on wanting only the same things they have always wanted, their heritage will be kept alive. Social change—at least as it affects these picturesque tribal peoples—is bad, and should be stopped.

Among the Xingu Park Indians, it is in fact safe to say that the older generation remains strongly attached to its remote lands, and intends to go on living there, hunting animals and gathering fruits. But what do younger Indians want to do with their lives? If there is one thing we have learned from modern history, it is that individuals often outgrow their ethnic cultures, find life in a fortress claustrophobic, and choose to move on. In contrast to museum exhibits, real human beings have a way of developing ideas and ambitions and desires—including for aluminum pots—beyond the ken of conservators. Fortress theory, multicultural "essentialism," and the enduring cult of the noble savage are the enemies of those ambitions and human desires.

In the final paragraph of *Die If You Must*, Hemming wonders uneasily whether the pessimists might have the last laugh after all—whether the Amazon's "beautiful, ancient, and intricate cultures will be maintained only artificially as curiosities for tourists, researchers, or politically correct enthusiasts." That is quite possible. But it is hardly the only undesirable possibility. Preserving ancient cultural patterns is laudable, but it is not enough. No society in history has ever stood still, and however beautiful, and ancient, and intricate traditional cultures may be, it is wrong to lock people up inside them and throw away the key. Uprooting the dishonest and patronizing Western cult of the noble savage will be the work of generations; but as far as today's Amazonian Indians are concerned, the main priority must surely be to ensure that those among them who do not want to play the obliging role of historical curiosities, endlessly dressing up for visitors whose expectations they feel bound to fulfill, are able to find something else to do in the modern world—on the reservation or off it. In that quest we can only wish them well.

**ROGER SANDALL** taught anthropology for many years at the University of Sydney in Australia and is the author most recently of *The Culture Cult*. His essay, "Can Sudan Be Saved?," appeared in the December 2004 COMMENTARY.

# Index

# Index

fattening room, 129–130
Fediuk, Karen, 82
female genital mutilation (FGM), 30; 129
fertility, replacement, 100–101
fetishers, 140
fetishes, 142, 180
Figueiredo Report, 230
Fillmore, Millard, 85, 86, 87
Finde-siecle America, 35
"Fish Camp," 37
Florentine Codex, Book Twelve, 199, 200, 201
force, use of, 36
fraternal polyandry, 95–97
*fugu,* 173

## G

Gallo, Robert, 55, 57
"gaman," 115
genetic variation, natural versus engineered, 148
Geneva Conventions, 38
gift giving: Hopi culture of, 85–88; Indian marriages and, 110
global warming, 84: effects in Artic, 227–229; sea levels and, 228
gluconeogenesis, 82–83
Gomara, Francisco Lopez de, 197
Gossart, John E., Jr., 30, 31
Great Depression, 132
*Guns, Germs, and Steel: The Fates of Human Societies* (Diamond), 198
Gusii, child-rearing in, 103, 106

## H

hallucinogenic substances, use in America, 167
*Hamlet,* interpreted by tribal elders in Africa, 71–75
Hanbury–Tenison, Robin, 230–234
Hemmings, John, 230, 232, 233, 234
hermaphrodites, 120, 121
HIV/AIDS, 23, 24, 28, 55, 147, 159, 191
Hmong, 146, 149–150
Hodel, Donald, 31
Holocaust, 30; denial, 54–55
Hopi: cycle of religious ceremonies of, 86; division of labor among, 85–86; gift culture of, 85–88
human diseases of animal origin, 190–196
Hume, David, 31
hunger, Third World, 185–190; cash crops and, 186; suppressing peasant farming, 187
hurricanes, 228

## I

Incas, 195
indigenous knowledge, 146, 147, 150; of ecosystem, 148–149
infant development, cross cultural studies and, 103–108; feeding and, 106; sleep and, 107
infant mortality, Third World: Catholic church and, 101; maternal grief and, 101
infant/caregiver dyad, 105
infanticide, passive, 99
insurgency: defined, 38; fighting, 39–40
International Council for Science, 146

Inupiaq Eskimos, understanding of nature by, 78–80
Inupiat diet, 81–84
Irons, William, 152
Ituri Pygmies, 3
Iwu, Maurice, 147

## J

Jacobson, Cecil B., 37
Japan, marriage in, 114–117
Jennings, Caleen Sinnette, 53
joint family, 110

## K

Kaaindja, Fauziya, 29, 30
kabaka, 36
kachina, 120
Kaczynski, Theodore, 29, 35
Katrina, 228
kava, 221–223
Keller, Evelyn Fox, 56
kibbutzim, secular vs. religious, 153, 154
king, divinity of, 35
King, Steven, 147
kinship relationships, 2, 4, 8
kinship society, 86
ko'lhamana, 120
Koyuon Indians, 78, 80

## L

Lakota, 121
language: metaphors and, 55–57; different registers of, 46–50
Layde, Peter, 35
Levinson, Richard, 149
Lewis, Norman, 230
lexicon vocabulary, 46
"liberation theology," 101
Lipstadt, Deborah, 54–55
literal meaning, 66–67
loneliness, 37
"love match," 109

## M

Maffi, Luisa, 149
Manifest Destiny, 87
malaria, sickle-cell trait and, 215
Malinowski, Bronislaw, 152
malnutrition, tribal adaptation to new economic patterns and, 217–218
marabouts, 140, 141
marijuana, 167; in Oceania, 225
marketing boards, Third World agriculture and, 186–187
marriage: arranged, in India, 109–113; dowry and, 113; types of in Tibet, 95
Mbuti, 139
Mead, Margaret, 231–232
measles, 192; rinderpest and, 193
menstrual cycle, 126; in industrial cultures, 127; lactation and, 127–128; in natural-fertility populations, 127; women's health and, 128
menstrual huts, 125,. 126
menstrual taboos, 125–128

Mesoamericans, agriculture and, 198
Mesopotamia, 36
Message: defined, 63; metamessages and, 62–70
metacommunicating, 63, 64
metamessage: defined, 63; implication of incompetence and, 69
Mexico, conquest of, 195–213; technology and, 203;
microbes: human responses to, 191–192; nature of described, 191; passive-carriage strategies, 191
Micronesia, development in, 214–220
Miller, Tim, 35
Mills, C. Wright, 132
"mismatch theory," 35
Moctezuma, 199–207
Mohave, 121, 122
moral code, universal, cultural diversity and, 32
mortal selective neglect, 99
myxomatosis, 194

## N

n–3 fatty acids, 83
*nadle,* 120
Narcisse, Clairvius, 171, 173–174
National Center for Complementary and Alternative Medicine, 147
National-security establishment, anthropology and, 38–41; ethnocentrism and, 39
"nationbuilding," 39–40
"natural aspirin," 83–84
natural selection: handicaps, religion and, 152
"naturalistic fallacy," 31
Navajo origin tale, 120
Nazi, 30
Nejelsky, Paul, 30
"nervos," 31
New World, absence of disease, 195–196
Ngando, 139–145: illnesses of God and, 142; illnesses of man and, 142; interdependence with Aka Pygmy, 139; medical therapy options for, 141
*ngangas,* 139–145; apprenticeship and, 140; diagnostic practices, 140–141; powers of, 143–144; six attributes of, 140; vaccination and, 140
NIH International Cooperative Biodiversity Groups (ICBG), 146, 147
Nile Valley, 36
Noche Triste, 202
non–human primates, weaning and, 107
nutrients, essential, 82; Eskimos and, 81–84

## O

o'nyong-nyong, 194
omega–3 fatty acids, 83–84
opium, 166; use in America. 166–167
optimal foraging theory, 151
over-the-counter drug industry, 168
oxyticin, 35

## P

parenting models, 105

# Test Your Knowledge Form

We encourage you to photocopy and use this page as a tool to assess how the articles in *Annual Editions* expand on the information in your textbook. By reflecting on the articles you will gain enhanced text information. You can also access this useful form on a product's book support Web site at *http://www.mhcls.com/online/*.

NAME: _____     DATE: _____

TITLE AND NUMBER OF ARTICLE: _____

BRIEFLY STATE THE MAIN IDEA OF THIS ARTICLE:

_____

LIST THREE IMPORTANT FACTS THAT THE AUTHOR USES TO SUPPORT THE MAIN IDEA:

_____

WHAT INFORMATION OR IDEAS DISCUSSED IN THIS ARTICLE ARE ALSO DISCUSSED IN YOUR TEXTBOOK OR OTHER READINGS THAT YOU HAVE DONE? LIST THE TEXTBOOK CHAPTERS AND PAGE NUMBERS:

_____

LIST ANY EXAMPLES OF BIAS OR FAULTY REASONING THAT YOU FOUND IN THE ARTICLE:

_____

LIST ANY NEW TERMS/CONCEPTS THAT WERE DISCUSSED IN THE ARTICLE, AND WRITE A SHORT DEFINITION: